P9-BYW-413

ALSO BY LETITIA BALDRIGE

Letitia Baldrige's Complete Guide to a Great Social Life

Letitia Baldrige's New Complete Guide to Executive Manners

Letitia Baldrige's More Than Manners!:
Raising Today's Kids to Have Kind Manners and Good Hearts

In the Kennedy Style:
Magical Evenings in the Kennedy White House

Legendary Brides: From the Most Romantic Weddings Ever,
Inspired Ideas for Today's Brides

A Lady, First: My Life in the Kennedy White House
and the American Embassies of Paris and Rome

LETITIA BALDRIGE'S
New Manners for New Times

A Complete Guide to Etiquette

LETITIA BALDRIGE

SCRIBNER

New York   London   Toronto   Sydney   Singapore

SCRIBNER
1230 Avenue of the Americas
New York, NY 10020

For information about special discounts for bulk purchases,
please contact Simon & Schuster Special Sales:
1-800-456-6798 or business@simonandschuster.com

DESIGNED BY ERICH HOBBING

Text set in New Caledonia

Manufactured in the United States of America

1 3 5 7 9 10 8 6 4 2

Library of Congress Cataloging-in-Publication Data is available.

ISBN 0-7432-1062-X

An earlier edition was published as
Letitia Baldrige's Complete Guide to the New Manners for the 90s

To my husband,
BOB HOLLENSTEINER—
a wonderful man and the perfect antidote
to a hyperactive writer. He is calm, quiet, and restrained—
and the first to admit it's not easy living with
a book-writer spouse. He also has a perfect defense mechanism:
He doesn't read what I write!

CONTENTS

PART 2

ANSWERS TO QUESTIONS ABOUT MANNERS
YOU THOUGHT THAT NO ONE HAD TO
ASK ANYMORE 219

PART 3
THE RITES OF PASSAGE   245

PART 4:
THE ART OF ENTERTAINING   403

PART 5:
DIFFICULT TIMES: HEALING YOURSELF AND OTHERS WHEN TROUBLE STRIKES   563

ACKNOWLEDGMENTS

I am greatly in debt to Scribner's indomitable Susan Moldow, vice president and publisher, who was kind enough to ask for another book from me, and perceptive enough to realize that in spite of all the other etiquette books "out there," there was still a rather urgent need in the marketplace for a revision reflecting human behavior *today*, with no holds barred. There is a whole new generation in place since my early works on good behavior. Too many young people are just plain needy on the subject of what to do in the workplace and in social situations. Perhaps it's the duty of their elders to teach them in such a way that they don't even know they are being taught. When they learn to be at ease, hopefully they will influence, even reach their young peers to do the same ("trickle-down manners," if you will).

If we can even just cool down some of the boiling negatives in our society, such as disrespecting, cheating, hurling insults, and committing road rage, we will have made strong steps forward in teaching the young that this is the way to behave, and not the way they see the actors behaving on their favorite TV programs, action videos, and film.

Of course, I am indebted to a true legend in her time in the publishing world, Eleanor Rawson (of Rawson Associates, a private imprint of Scribner), who had faith in me and published seven of these books on behavior with me, starting in the early 1980s. Eleanor and I "glowed" through (ladies don't "sweat," of course) the hard work of meeting head-on every kind of social behavioral problem, never finding any one of them too intimidating, embarrassing, or unanswerable. Eleanor's team was wonderful, including Grace Shaw, the essence of cool and kind.

Today, for this book, I have a new young editor at Scribner, Brant Rumble, whose patience has been formidable, and who has said "Do it!" every time I questioned the wisdom of some new tactics on behavioral matters. He is the kind of editorial boss every writer wants to have.

I must admit that everyone at Scribner has been marvelous for me and to me, including Nan Graham, Roz Lippel, Pat Eisenmann, Erich Hobbing, and copy editor Estelle Laurence.

This book never would have been written without the calm, encouraging assistance of someone who has always been in my corner—Sandi Gelles-Cole.

For the second time, she has come to my aid as a freelance editorial consult-ant, weaving all the diverse parts into an understandable whole—a Herculean task. And my hat's off to my part-time secretary and dear old friend, Helen Brown, who smiles through all my tears of rage and keeps me from capsizing the boat. Thanks also to the always bubbling Dede Dunn, who does invaluable book research for me on the computer and takes me to the 1 P.M. movies once in a while for brain therapy. And to Jeanne Flynn, the massage therapist of all therapists, who talks about her dogs while I talk about our dogs all through the massage. And to Lisa Dubloug, a treasure who comes once a week to make me take deep breaths properly. And, of course, my friend Derrick Ford—who is a computer genius for the government on any day except Sunday, when he's a preacher! I call him every time I'm ready to blow up when I'm on-line. He saves my computer for me, and helps me regain composure, but I keep beg-ging him to shorten his endlessly long voice mail messages, during which he recites a prayer or two and exhorts the Lord to give us all a happy day with all His blessings.

I must also say a word about my partner in etiquette crimes—fellow author, Mary Mitchell of Philadelphia. A stalwart supporter, she has plotted and planned many a course of manners with me, and our philosophical travels through the maze of today's society have helped me reach important conclu-sions on just what is happening to our runaway national behavior patterns.

Manners from the Heart

This book is nothing if not a personal statement. You can hear my own voice clearly all the way through it—sometimes full of enthusiasm and sounding like a cheerleader, sometimes showing complete disapproval (*Don't go there, don't do that!*) and at other times evincing a mixture of shock and acceptance of reality. (*It doesn't mean you have to like it, it simply means you have to live with it, and then, for heaven's sake, move on!*) In the present, we don't have time to challenge everything in behavior that seems to have gone wrong in the last half century, so we should pick our battles wisely and well. I first began to write about manners in my American embassy days in Paris and Rome, only as a sideline to my business. Then I took over Amy Vanderbilt's work in the 1970s after her death, and since then I have written a dozen books on etiquette and entertaining under my own name. In the decade since I wrote my *Complete Guide to the New Manners,* there have been manifold changes in people's lifestyles, marriage rituals, eating habits, language, entertaining concepts, work habits, child-raising, and sexual behavior.

I have combined advice and information for a person's private and business lives under the covers of this one book, because the two worlds so overlap today, it's difficult to separate them anymore. Even volunteer work today often requires management expertise with big budgets and regulatory issues. Today in books "less is more" from where I sit. At times it seems people in business do not have the time to read anything longer than a cartoon. What could easily be four books on the subject of etiquette must now be shrink-wrapped into one. Moses was lucky. His rules were written in stone. Our modern ones are more like skywriting. In my writing I have been obliged to rewrite some of the rules of manners that I had thought were inextricably woven into the fabric of our society, destined to lie there calmly and gracefully forever. I marvel at the way girls my age grew up, decades ago, accepting without contention our mothers' decisions on how to dress, how to wear our hair, and at times, it seemed, how to breathe. When my mother saw me dressed in a cotton dress, with bare legs and sandals on a ninety-nine-degree day, she would make me change and put on stockings, whether I was on my way to play in a piano recital or do an errand for her at the neighborhood grocery store. In public one was *always* properly dressed, or else one did not emerge.

1

And then there is the major revolution in how we communicate with one another, using the in-your-face products handed to us by the world leaders of technology. These products in turn spawn the need for other sets of rules governing the way people use their little gadgets that ring, buzz, and throb like agitated beehives, completely upsetting the peace and serenity of anyone within hearing distance. If Thomas Edison were alive today, he would be appalled at what has happened to his telephone—and to the manners of the customers who use them.

Compassion is a wonderful thing, and the more I study the field of behavior from a sociological point of view, the more I realize that a society without compassion, even with all the right rules of behavior, is a dead one. It's very hard to live without structure, and manners are the best vehicle there is to provide us with it. They give us security, a feeling that if we do the right thing and avoid the wrong thing, everything will be all right. The trick is to know in advance what *is* the right thing, so you can avoid the other. Your heart will usually tell you which way to go, because remember, good manners (keep remembering there are *bad* manners, too) are soft and full of heart, not hardened with selfishness.

In *New Manners* my editor has allowed me to use my own way of talking as I write—at times rather breezy and slangy. There are many new subjects introduced that have never before been treated in etiquette books, but the old traditional ones are given their proper place too, including advice on how to get married. (The traditionalists alas are being run over and squashed in the marketplace by a thundering herd of product sellers and so-called "wedding planners," who wouldn't recognize respect for the ritual and traditions if they saw them!)

But disapproval of another's choices is not allowable. People can get married any way they please. We are a great, vigorous, ambitious country, formed by people from every nation in the world, and untrammeled by our past. We are a miraculous mixture of many colors, races, religions, and values. Let's hope that our new young leaders will simply wander to the etiquette section of libraries and bookstores once in a while and take a good long, hard look. Of course, I must admit it's difficult to be wrestling with the subtleties of marriage customs, when at the same time there is a rising number of people proudly advocating for cohabitation *without marriage*. Our times are—well—screwy.

My book is new in that advice and information for a person's private and working lives are cojoined instead of being separated into two books. The two worlds overlap so thoroughly, it is sometimes difficult to distinguish between them these days, what with stay-at-home fathers, single mothers taking care of the children and bringing in the bread, more and more people working from their homes, and children growing up sometimes forced to cope with three or four sets of parents. Therefore, take your pick of the advice, anything from instructions on how to use a fork and knife (carefully, please) to suggestions for a nice way to celebrate a baby's birth or to respectfully mourn someone's passing. It's all about getting through *life* in the best and happiest way.

It's important to understand the difference between manners and etiquette: Etiquette is protocol, a set of behavior rules you can memorize like a map, which will guide you safely through life. Manners are much more, since they are an expression from the heart on how to treat others whether you care about them or not. Manners teach you how to value another's self-esteem and to protect that person's feelings. Etiquette consists of firm rules made by others who have come before, telling you to do this and do that on specific occasions. Etiquette means acting with grace and efficiency, very laudable in itself, but your manners are *yours,* yours to use in making order out of chaos, making people feel comfortable, and giving pleasure to others. Etiquette is at times stiff and starchy (watch an official receiving line if you want to see an example of it). Manners are taking aside a guest standing in that line who obviously is bewildered and doesn't know what to do, and whispering to that person how to proceed. "No, don't embrace the host. Shake her hand, state your name clearly with a big smile on your face, and tell her how delighted you are to meet her."

The primary purpose of any book on manners is to provide guidelines about the *how, what, where, when,* and *why* in the social graces. In arming yourself with this knowledge, you develop a sense of security. You're reassured that the way you're behaving is the right way. This is also a book about *being happy,* which is not a contradiction in terms, because when you're nice to someone else (even just a stranger on the telephone), that someone else is nice back to you, and suddenly two people feel good about themselves and each other, and spread their good feelings. And that's what happiness is.

Times are tough. And yet, there's great energy out there—a great capacity for good everywhere that human beings are. It's in the air. We just have to act positively, seize the initiative, and hold on tight. If we open our eyes wide and remove their fixation on a screen so we can see reality, not images around us, if we remove our cell phones so we can hear the world around us, and if we look and talk to one another, we'll find that energy. We'll be able to channel it toward the solution of human problems. We'll be nice to one another, even when we don't feel like it. We'll start getting along well, even with strangers, even when we're being given the runaround in a crowded store or even when someone who doesn't like the way we drive is honking and hurling strong epithets at us. (Instead of giving that person the finger in return, we just might concentrate on being a better driver and hope that the other driver's obviously traumatized life eases up, and that he hasn't sprained that overused finger.)

If we channel the energy that's in the air, negatives can be willed into positives, and we can all move toward a solution of today's common problems. My definition of a really admired person—someone who has real class—is a person who has only one kind of manners: the caring kind. I remember hearing the late Ambassador Clare Boothe Luce (at that time my boss at our embassy in Rome, but at all times my role model and mentor) answer a reporter who had asked for a definition of "a really classy person." The reporter's notebook and pen were poised for a typically long Luce dissertation. "A person with class is someone you want to be around—all the time," she answered simply.

The reporter paused and finally asked, "That's it?"

"There's no need for anything more," she replied.

Today's real manners, the kind that describe someone others want to be around, are those that:

- Make you pick up a piece of litter someone left on your neighbor's sidewalk—or on anyone's sidewalk, for that matter.
- Cause you to rush to a friend's house to see what you can do when you hear a member of that person's family is in trouble.
- Inspire you to go up to the hired waitress at your dinner party who has just dropped a large platter of sliced veal all over the floor in front of your guests, to help her clean up the mess, and then to pat her arm and tell her to forget about it—" It doesn't matter at all."
- Make you realize that it's not worthwhile wondering who should go through the revolving door first, but it is worthwhile rushing to help an elderly or disabled stranger through the revolving door.
- Help you notice some tiny garnet roses in a shop window, so you buy a small bouquet of them to bring home to your spouse or your significant other or maybe to a child.
- Motivate you to jump into a conversational lull when someone has just said something embarrassing, thus restarting everyone's conversation so that the one who made the gaffe can pull himself together again.
- Cause you to discover, when your longtime laundryman delivers the shirts, that it's the man's twenty-fifth wedding anniversary, so you give him the bottle of champagne you were saving in the fridge for your own special occasion.
- Have you bring an entire supper over to a family on their moving day.
- Remind you that a friend's car is being repaired, and the person desperately needs it today, so you lend yours.
- Make you rip an article out of one of your magazines, to send to a friend or colleague who would be greatly interested in it.
- Motivate you to leave a big bunch of balloons in the office of a friend who has something to cheer about.
- Cause you to buy a special-interest self-help book for a young person who is just starting a job in that field.
- Remind you to buy some concert tickets as a gift and arrange transportation for a lonely elderly friend whose great love is music.

Today that person who's so nice to be around, as Clare Luce put it, is not the Mr. Billionaire-Business-Whiz kid who yells obscenities at his driver when he makes a mistake, or the Mrs. Nouveau-Riche who screams at her maid when she can't find her pantyhose.

That person who's so nice to be around:
- Is a consummate host.
- Is a consummate guest.
- Has good table manners.
- Has a pleasant, well-modulated voice, uses good grammar, and has a graceful vocabulary.
- Is someone who returns others' hospitality, gifts, dinner invitations, and kindnesses in a grateful, generous manner.
- Is a good communicator—someone who makes telephone calls, sends e-mails, and writes letters, who is in touch with people, instead of expecting everyone else to communicate with her.
- Seeks out the wallflower at a social event and brings that person into the group.
- Is a person who rises to defend anyone who is being unfairly criticized.
- Is a conveyor of good, not bad, news.
- Is adept at making introductions and being introduced, saying hello or good-bye—and makes everyone feel good while it's happening.

The crux of everything said above, and of everything in this book, of course, is the *home*. Home is where it *all* starts—manners, good character, values, ethics, social conscience. Home is where a child witnesses and can absorb the good example of caring parents or relatives. Home is where comfort and support can be found, where one person automatically makes an effort to help other members of the family and, in turn, is helped himself. Talk about success—a happy home is what real success is about, the proof positive of thinking about other people, of having their comfort and their happiness in mind. Home is where the discipline is, too—that wonderful magical chisel that sculpts the child into a beautiful work of art—a nice, in-control human being. Home is where the small child learns not just from parents but from grandparents, too, so that the child will be a shining mirror image of the best of both generations.

But wait a minute. Isn't this picture unrealistically rosy for these times? Where are all the homes today in which the small child grows up in the constant company of both parents and grandparents? Isn't Mom off working? Are the parents divorced? Is there a confusion of stepparents and stepchildren around? Is the television going all the time so that no one has to talk—either about her own problems or someone else's? Are the family teenagers off on their own, out of the home, doing their own thing most of the time? Isn't anyone who happens to be home likely to be standing around the fridge or the microwave, eating with his fingers, while the nurturing dining table—the seat of conversation, manners, and the learning of human skills—stands there empty, unused, except as a storage surface?

And how about the delicious interchange of generations that used to be grouped around the dining table? Is the surviving grandparent in a retirement home? Is everyone too tired at night to sit down and just talk to one another? Where is the humanity in all this?

I believe in fighting. Since the development and polishing of manners is not a one-shot operation but a continuous process that begins no place else but home, I think we can fight to put the home back in all of us again. And if we don't have children, then we can spend a lot of time with someone else's, who are perhaps neglected in this early training of manners, morals, ethics, and values. How about inviting a niece, nephew, grandchild, or godchild over for dinner? Every time you throw in a little lesson on how to act, making it fun and following it up with a favorite food, that child is going to love you and learn from you.

First the youngster may learn what not to do. ("Don't scream while at the table, and for heaven's sake, take your fingers out of the salad plate!") Next, the child learns how to do the nice thing—a big step up, by the way, from simply knowing not to do something wrong. (Suddenly you'll hear your child say, "Can I bring this present to Suzy's house, Mommy? I think she'd like it. Teacher says she's sick and feels really bad.") Then you'll see the proof that your child has a heart, and you can pat yourself on the back. This is how manners are gradually built into a young person's character. This is how a beautiful human being is formed—one who will walk through life automatically reacting in a "you-they" way, instead of an "I-me" way.

Growing children aren't the only ones who need others to care about them. We all do. In a fast-moving, high-pressure age, the need to be *happy* is universal. Late in the 1970s, I completely revised *The Amy Vanderbilt Complete Book of Etiquette*, the first of a series of books on manners. It addressed problems created by the social confusion of the sixties, a decade in which we survived the antiestablishment youth rebellion, the shock of women leaving home and going to work, and the blurring in definition of men's and women's roles. In the 1980s, I wrote my *New Complete Guide to Executive Manners*, to help that increasing population of families who spend most of their time at work to feel more secure in their relationships in that environment. I followed that book with my *New Complete Guide to a Great Social Life*, because so many young people in the workplace—and other singles, too—complained to me that they really didn't *have* a social life in this busy world. Then came *More Than Manners!* on the subject of instilling character in children. With each book addressing these human concerns, I have found people increasingly thirsty for knowledge about what to do and when to do it, and for information on how to show *their awareness* of other people's feelings.

In 1923, Emily Post wrote the first really comprehensive book telling Americans how to behave. Her readers—middle- and upper-middle-class people—listened and learned, eager to move up another notch in their own social stratum. This was long before such terms as "diversity," "multicultural," "tolerance," and a "celebration of differences" were integrated into our vocabulary.

Some of us are still trying to rise to the next social level, enabled by a goodly supply of money and natural good manners. Many more of us are curious about the meaning of all this society-protocol-etiquette business. What does "the right thing" mean in any given situation, and just what is "proper behavior" in trying situations that no one has ever had to face before? We are a charge-ahead democratic society, perplexed by the new challenges. We'll get there. We just need to self-educate ourselves more. And observe. And listen. And read. And while we're doing all that, *we will have learned how to cope*.

Probably most of us would like to be thought of by others as moving through the world with grace and ease—no simple skill. There is no one-week, easy cram course for it. One of the great things about growing older—into your forties, fifties, sixties, and onward—is that the longer you live, the more you know about how to handle yourself, what to do and when to do it. Unfortunately, you can't call up answers to social problems with a flick of a key and a glance at the monitor screen. They're never that simple.

It's a question of learning and using the proper mix of information and consideration—whether you're tipping someone, coping with your grandmother when she comes to live with you or with an adult child who won't leave the nest, dealing with the plumber or a member of the board of directors, or talking to your boss as you're waiting together in an airport for three hours. By the time you have an instinctive feel for what to do in all these situations, you could write this book—and I'd be the first to read it!

If you believe that the definition of happiness is having good relationships, and if you believe that good manners are essential to that feeling, then you must also believe that one natural result of a person's good manners is that individual's state of happiness.

Good relationships don't just happen in the everyday course of events. They are the result of someone's hard work and caring. They are constantly, dynamically changing, being refined and fine-tuned. We can't escape a constant interaction with people (unless we choose to live as hermits). We interact all day long with family members, friends, and just plain people—the people at our place of work, in the gas station, on the bus, at our house of worship. We react to the toll-road ticket taker, the doctor, barber, manicurist, and to the people who deliver our packages, collect our garbage, and read our utility meters. They are, each and every one, individuals worthy of respect and consideration; when they behave as if they are not and are beastly to us, we must find a way to control our anger, so that we do not take it out on another human being. (When I am unjustly treated in a nasty manner, I immediately imagine myself sticking many pins into a pin cushion, and in my mind that takes care of the person who did me wrong. I recommend you find your own avenue of harmless revenge.)

When we graduate from the self-obsessed "I-I-Me-Me" school of philosophy into a life of caring about other people, we begin to react automatically to those other people, whether they are close friends or not. We react in a uniform, decent, and considerate manner. It's not something we stop to think about. We just do it.

PART 1

EVERYDAY RELATIONSHIPS
FOR OUR TIMES

CHAPTER 1

Family Manners

THE FAMILY, IDEALISTICALLY SPEAKING

I feel that one of a writer's tasks is to remind the reader of the importance of his own role in the family, the community, even the world. Understanding our own importance in affecting the lives of those close to us should make us accept the responsibilities attached. We should be able to recognize the details of the whole picture—the ones that make others look upon us with admiration or with no respect whatsoever. Of course, being part of that picture requires us to be born into a family in the first place, and hopefully, grow up in one feeling loved, learning how to behave, and eventually discovering an important truth—that knowing what the rules are, and then following them, is the easiest way to make our way through this life. We adults are responsible for making that miraculous thing called a *conscience* grow within the children of our family. It's up to us to make sure that, along with maintaining a child's proper growth patterns and intellectual maturation, we also make sure that our children will go to school armed with a clear understanding of what is right and what is wrong, in other words, with a conscience *intact*. Children can then carry this great gift into adult life: into the workplace, the community, and their own families.

That is an ideal portrait of a nuclear family, reproducing itself and handing down its values to each successive generation. But it's not really the picture of society today, is it? Over 78 million Americans are growing up in single-parent households. We have made many long voyages sailing away from the concept of family in the last fifty years. It's difficult to brag about something as affirmative as family values in a climate of unspeakable crime and abuse, one in which our big cities seem to be incapable of defending the average citizen. Even the bucolic countryside with its peaceful little towns can be infected with an epidemic of sleaze.

Each one of us can contribute to the cause of helping families in trouble, whether or not we have a viable family of our own. If values aren't being passed down within a family, because no one seems to know what they are, then we can help teach them—in a gentle and nondictatorial fashion, including by our own example—to the people who cross regularly in and out of our lives (baby-sitter, executive assistant, hairdresser, physical trainer, music teacher, housekeeper, gardener, saleswoman, garage mechanic, clinic technician, who-ever!). When a great friend of yours gets a divorce, that does not mean that you must divorce that person's children, to whom you have been close. Keep up those precious relationships. The death of someone's spouse should mold all the members of that family, living near and far, into a more cohesive unit, so that the incantation "We're here for you" really means something. Siblings can answer even an unspoken SOS within a family, and come together to form a wall of protection and healing for the one who needs help. Anyone who sees something broken in a family she loves can often fix it, but don't do as I have all through my life, try to fix up something "when it ain't broke" in the first place!

MANNERS WITH THOSE CLOSE TO YOU

It's only common sense. The people closest to you warrant an extra measure of consideration, including a baby, someone's new spouse, or someone who has just been feeling depressed. After all, they're part of your daily life, and noth-ing can sour the atmosphere quite so much as friction among family members and others sharing a common living space. If it takes a great deal of work and resolve to keep that set of relationships warm and smooth, so what? What is of greater importance?

When I hear someone refer to "the Nuclear Family" I immediately picture a house, with the top floor occupied by the recipients of great affection and respect—the parents or grandparents of either person. My spouse and I are on the floor below, so we can keep tabs on all the floors, above and below. Our children are on the floor below us. (Perhaps dogs also live on all three floors of bedrooms.) Somehow a new spouse, or a significant other, and any stepchil-dren from past marriages can always manage to fit into this house. So can chil-dren who have left the nest after school and then returned for one reason or another. Every single occupant of this house should share the load of support, responsibility, encouragement, and fulfillment of certain duties. (A baby has only the duty to smile once in a while and keep its noise down to a bearable decibel.) Above all, each occupant must learn sensitivity toward every other member of this family. The cement holding this complex set of relationships together is simply good manners and thinking about someone other than oneself all the time. The basis of this strong building material is, of course, something called *love*.

Courtesies That Hold
Your Nuclear Family Together

If you're fortunate enough to be one of those in a traditional nuclear family, look around you. You're in a key position. Look at that symbolic house. There may be family on the top floor (your parents and grandparents); you and your spouse or significant other occupy the center of the house, and the ground floor is occupied by your children, your mate's children, their children to come. What you do, what you teach, the example you give, the kindness you show, has a major effect on the happiness of the people on the floors above and below.

Consideration and good manners cement many different family relationships, but it's the relationships that evolve out of marriage or partnerships that particularly benefit from kindness and we-ness.

For example, family members can do many things to be nice:

• When a family member is in the hospital, visit often, but also call every day to inquire "How are things going?" and ask "What can I do for you?" Also, most important of all, be a fountain of happy news, good stories, and events of human interest. An upbeat voice on the telephone can do more for a patient's morale than anything else, except, perhaps, bringing the patient's favorite ice cream or a roast beef dinner from a good restaurant!

Organize the family members to take turns visiting and checking up on the care of this person. Do not abandon a family member—ever.

• Faithfully remember every anniversary of note, birthday, and any event worth celebrating in that person's life. Take, for example, when a little nephew receives his First Communion. Send him a card and add a message by hand: "This is a big event in your life, Ricky. It's a very special day and we'll all be there with you, when you receive the sacrament." You just might add as an afterthought to the card a check for $10 or any amount you care to send.

• Take note of any achievement in your family:
  • When a grandson makes the rowing team at college, send him a congratulations card, saying how proud everyone is of him.
  • When you hear that a niece played the piano in a concert at school, send her a card saying you hear she played like a Paderewski, and you are so proud of her!
  • When you hear that your brother, living in another city, has won a tennis tournament, send him a teasing congratulatory e-mail, saying something like, "It's plain to see all of the tennis instruction I gave you in past years is bearing fruit."
  • When you happen to know that the recipe of your aged, ailing grandmother for angel food cake was used at a family birthday

party, send her a note about it, including a snapshot of family members at the party.

• Notice when someone seems to be having a hard time, physically, mentally, emotionally, or financially, and take action to help. When the family doesn't seem to be aware of—or care about—the sufferings of one of their members, it is a lamentable situation that needs correcting. When family members move to help, it makes the whole world seem bright with promise and good tomorrows.

• Initiate all kinds of reasons why the family should get together. It takes only one person to galvanize the whole group. Help organize family reunions on holidays, wedding anniversaries, second and third weddings, whatever! With e-mail, there is no excuse for anyone to say, "I didn't know about it . . ."

• Make sure that someone is doing the family history. You may be of the opinion that "someone else should do it." Realistically, it is a lot of work, but only one person should be delegated to do it. Otherwise, it won't get done. Get Great-Uncle Harry a little tape recorder, teach him how to use it if he doesn't know how, and have him talk into it whenever he is feeling clear-headed and anxious to reminisce. Gather family papers and photos, copying the important ones and sending everything back eventually. When there are family reunions, you can be the one with the tape recorder, catching people's memories of past holiday gatherings, anniversary celebrations, children's graduations, or any occasion when funny or endearing incidents may have occurred. Train family members to send you an e-mail when they suddenly remember something of note. Be the family archivist. Your family is precious. Save it, for handing down to future generations, for everyone—cousins, stepsisters, ex-parents-in-law. Family pets, going way back into the generations, are also very worthy of inclusion in the family history.

With Your Mate

A prime cause for unhappiness in marriage (when I use the word "marriage" in this book I mean a long-term committed relationship) is when one begins to take the other for granted. Some commonsense suggestions to remember:

• There must be compromise, on matters large and small.

• A spouse or significant other deserves building up every so often, never putting down, in front of family members.

• When one of the pair suffers a major disappointment it is a signal for the other one to drop everything and help.

• Even if you don't like your partner's parents, be a good actor.

• Be equally nice to all of your mate's friends so you will have the right to demand the same.

• Be punctual for the engagements your significant other deems important.

- Give in once in a while on major decisions, if it means your marriage will be saved.
- Compliment your partner often. Every time there's a social event, for example, make a fuss over your mate. "How handsome (or beautiful) you look tonight!"
- Don't make fun of your partner's failures or faux pas. Then maybe your partner will do the same for you. Brag about your mate's successes to everyone. Then maybe your mate will do the same for you.
- An unexpected little gift every now and then for which there is no reason is a genius idea.
- Keep in constant touch with one another, no matter where you are or what you're doing. (Remember, however, always to keep the rules of good cell phone etiquette in mind.)
- Learn about what your partner does all day. Be able to discuss your partner's job or profession intelligently and proudly.
- Consult one another as equal partners on everything major concerning the children, and never let them feel anything but equal love or concern from both parents.

WITH YOUR MOTHER- AND FATHER-IN-LAW

When you marry, your mate's parents become part of your inner family and should be treated as such. Give them love and respect from the outset, and you'll not only win their reciprocated love and respect—you'll strengthen your relationship with your own spouse.

- Make them feel their visits to your home are welcome, not an imposition.
- Arrange to have your children see them as often as possible.
- Don't take their baby-sitting help for granted; remember how pressured they may be by their own problems, so don't abuse their kindness.
- Never criticize them within earshot of your children; always refer to them with affection and respect.
- If they live in another town, telephone them regularly, and always observe their birthdays and anniversary.
- If one of them becomes widowed, give much more of yourself than before to the remaining one.
- If one of them grossly oversteps the bounds of acceptable behavior, either in advising or criticizing you or your children, explain what that person has done wrong with tact and kindness. Keep your voice calm and show you are in control of your emotions. Cool down; the situation will get better if you take the lead. (And no matter how poor your relationship may be at any given moment, never cut anyone off from a grandchild.)

• Have your children write thank-you notes to their grandparents within a week of receiving any gifts from them.

• Welcome instead of resent it when grandparents give your children some needed lessons in table manners when they take them out for a meal or quiet them in public.

• Welcome their moments of reminiscing, and tape those conversations whenever possible for your family history. Make them feel a part of your generation, too. (That means comments like this are never heard in your house: "You wouldn't understand, because you're too old.")

• Never make fun of their forgetfulness or other signs of aging. Never allow your children to tease their grandparents, but rather treat them *always* with respect. Remember, someday you will be there, too.

With Your Son and Daughter-in-Law or Daughter and Son-in-Law

When you are the parents-in-law, be the best there are. The most important basis of a happy relationship with your children and their spouses is to accept that they must lead their own lives and raise their children their way, not yours.

• Learn to sit on any criticism you might have of how they live or how they are raising your grandchildren—because, realistically, they will not be interested in your views.

• When your advice *is* sought, give it freely and lovingly, then drop the subject and don't expect to receive such a request very often.

• If you can't say something nice about their house and its decor, don't say anything at all. Walk into their house with smiles, not criticisms.

• Don't push too aggressively for invitations; appreciate the fact that they may be very busy—too busy to entertain you.

• Ask them out to dinner more often than they ask you to their house. Be very sensitive to their reaction when you suggest coming over—it may be the wrong time, in which case, back off.

• If you sense marital discord, don't question anyone about it. Wait until one of them speaks to you—and never ever question the children about it.

Remember your son- or daughter-in-law's birthday with the same enthusiasm you remember your child's.

• Offer to baby-sit, but don't act as though this puts them in your debt.

• If you're feeling neglected, call them, but just to check in, never to complain. A surefire way to cheer yourself up is to talk to your grandchildren on the telephone.

• Always pick up after yourself in their house; offer to help them clean up, too. If they say no, don't argue!

• Help them out if you can when they're going through a tough time financially. This may result in giving them a loan at no interest, in forgiving a debt, or in devising some creative way out of their problem. (As a daughter who had her hand in her father's pocket her entire life, I can say with conviction that it takes a wonderful parent to remain generous for so many years!)

• Apologize when you've irked your son- or daughter-in-law, even if you feel innocent. Always take the first step to ask forgiveness, and keep those lines of communication open. In-laws become greatly upset with each other for the most insignificant of reasons. Deal with anything negative at once, so that a small sore does not become a festering wound.

ROOMMATE ETIQUETTE

If you share an apartment or house as an adult with a roommate or roommates of the same sex (and we are not talking here about a homosexual arrangement), trampling on one another's nerves is almost inevitable. There are times when another person's habits or lack of courtesy will seem insufferable, but if roommates are well intentioned and prepared to share equal responsibilities, the relationship can and should become successful.

• Be up front with one another. Don't allow some unspoken resentment to magnify itself in importance. Don't sulk. Roommates who communicate well and speak frankly to each other have a successful household. Unaired problems are never solved—they just expand to the point of a possible implosion.

• Share the work involving the household equally. Discuss the division of responsibilities if one of you feels they are not fairly balanced. And if you have a chore, do it in good time and without complaint. Sloppiness and procrastination on the part of one person can make the best sort of relationships grow sour.

• One roommate should help out the other when one of them has a guest—either by getting out of the apartment, or by helping to clean it and prepare for the visitor.

• Learn to entertain in tandem, to get along with each other's friends, and to mix the two sets equally when you jointly entertain. It goes without saying that a primary rule in any shared housing is: Steal not thy roommate's boyfriend (or girlfriend).

• Rigorously record expenses—everything from long distance calls to a shared bottle of wine, room cleaning supplies to newspaper subscriptions. Settle and pay up accounts quickly at the end or beginning of each month.

• Take accurate telephone messages for your housemates, and make sure you leave them where the one to whom they are directed can see them the minute that person comes home.

• Be neat. Nothing gets on a person's nerves more than living with a slob, or worse, two slobs.

• Don't dominate the guest list of every party, expecting that your friends be the only ones regularly invited to have dinner at your house. Ask your roommates if they wouldn't like to invite their friends to the next one. Your housemates should help with the cleanup and offer to contribute toward the cost of the food if they are guests at your dinner party, and vice versa.

• Do not bring a third party into the apartment for purposes of sex. This is important for people of the opposite as well as the same sex who are living together. It is unfair to usher in someone and then close the door to engage in sex while your roommates are there. "It's no different from what it was like in our coed dorm. We live together like brothers and sisters, exactly as we did in college," said one recent graduate.

Comments from apartment mates of both sexes:

Young woman: "I feel safer with a man in the house. This is not a good neighborhood, and I'd be scared if it weren't for Joe."

Young woman: "You have no idea how useful George is to Betsy and me. He is a really handy man—does a hundred things a month to keep this place going. George is an important part of our lives!"

Young man: "We like having Jenny living with us. Yes, she's one heck of a good cook. We do all the cleaning up, but she does the cooking, and we have such incredible gourmet meals! Besides, she's our friend. We confide in each other, help one other with emotional problems."

I think it's a good idea to accept a young person's explanation that the living arrangement is free from sexual innuendo. After all, if there was going to be any hanky-panky between two people, they would not have to rent a special house in which to do it.

However, a young person who chooses to live with one or more members of the opposite sex should realize that flying in the face of convention engenders certain problems. For example:

• Others are going to think of you as having sexual relations with one or more of your roommates of the opposite sex, even when you are not. It is just a natural jump to such a conclusion. Don't be defensive about it. If you are not sexually involved with your roommates, deny it matter-of-factly to anyone who insinuates it and then drop the subject: "We are living together as friends, not as lovers. It's a very ordinary, nonsexual relationship."

If you *are* having a sexual relationship with a roommate, my advice is to drop the pretext that you are just friends sharing the rent together. Two people who are sexually involved have a difficult time concealing that from anyone else. (Three people involved in sex together have a 300 percent more difficult time!)

If sex is part of the monthly rent arrangement, it might be a good idea for the two of you to make plans to file a joint income tax return next year. (In other words, get married!)

• When you have a social life that is more successful than that of your roommates, there is likely to be jealousy and resentment on their part. If that is the case, it's wise to learn to be cool—in other words, keep quiet—about the parties you attend, the dates you go on, and the amusing and exciting experiences you have that your roommates do not share. There is no point in engendering more jealousy than necessary.

• On the other hand, your roommate does not have the right to expect to be invited everywhere you go. It's important to establish your independence the minute you begin your cohabitation arrangement. Make it clear to everyone that you will lead your own life at night and on weekends, that you will be a good citizen of the house, but that you do not expect to be cross-examined on a continuing basis about what you're doing and whom you're seeing.

• Say nice things, rather than snide and critical things, about the dates your roommate brings to a meal or a party in your house. Part of getting along in life is to build people up, rather than cut them down, which is what criticizing a roommate's date or friend would amount to.

THE NEW FAMILY FORMATION: ADULTS (HOPEFULLY) LIVING TOGETHER HARMONIOUSLY

AN ADULT CHILD RETURNS TO THE NEST

"I can't believe it," one of my college classmates said at our reunion, "in our one small block alone, we have five families with their children living home again—ages twenty-five to thirty-five! I thought we were unusual with both an adult son and a daughter camping with us again, but I feel so sorry for our neighbors next door. Their daughter, son-in-law, and two children have moved in on them. My husband and I are home free in comparison!"

Another classmate added in a tone that was meant to be funny but really wasn't, beneath the surface, "Our daughter has moved back, too. We think she is taking the tack that if she irritates us seriously long enough, we'll die from exasperation and then she'll have the house to herself!"

The skyrocketing costs of home purchases and apartment rentals have made it impossible for many young people who are in the early stages of their careers or studying for advanced degrees to live in their own homes. Usually the parents are initially delighted to have their young back in the nest again, but often that euphoria does not last for long. The occupants of the household begin to get on each other's nerves. Parents begin to find their privacy and their routines invaded; the adult children begin to wonder why their parents don't have the capacity, much less the desire, to understand their need for freedom and independence.

In the best of all worlds, when an adult child moves back into the parents' home, both generations will sit down at the bargaining table and lay out all the ifs, ands, and buts of the new living arrangements, so there will be no secrets or unpleasant surprises. The contract can always be renegotiated if one party feels unduly put upon! It's important that both generations understand every rule, responsibility, and financial obligation of the new living arrangement, and that each respects the lifestyle of the other—even though the parents rightly consider that their home is their home and not "the home of these unfeeling monsters we've raised," as one parent phrased it to me one day.

Details to Be Worked Out Beforehand

• What compensation or reimbursement is to be made to the parents for room and/or board?

• What work is to be done for the parents in the home (such as cleaning, marketing, cooking, driving) in addition to or in place of financial compensation for room and/or board?

• What kitchen privileges and responsibilities will your offspring have (including replacing popular fridge items when the adult child uses them up)?

• The rules of privacy ("You don't go into my room, and I won't go into your room" . . . "You don't touch my mail, and I won't touch your mail").

• The entertaining privileges the child will have, and the rules on vacating the house to be respected by the parents when this entertaining occurs.

Ordinary noise limitations in the household with respect to things like television, radio, and stereo systems.

• What the rules are concerning guests in the offspring's room.

• The extent of the redecoration allowed (or perhaps urged by the parents) of the adult child's living quarters at the child's expense.

• Rules on the garaging and parking of the offspring's automobile, motorcycle, or bicycle. Keeping "stuff" in storage or the garage calls for neatness and rules.

• Rules of orderliness to be carefully observed in the household (examples: kitchen to be left in apple-pie condition before leaving it for one second; no dirty running shoes on the living room carpet; no dirty laundry piled on top of the washing machine and just left there).

• Rules governing the use of the washer and dryer, the hours in which the vacuum may be run, and who will answer the doorbells and telephones. (In some houses, even though the adult child has a cell phone, part of the deal is that when he is home, he answers every call on the family telephone and takes messages for his parents when they are out.)

I have seen a returned-home child make his parents furious and then watched his parents turn to mush when the reprobate returned with a dozen roses and a sentimental note of apology for "Mom." I witnessed a returned-home daughter make retribution to her father for taking his car unannounced and causing him to miss an important business appointment. (She had his car washed, greased, and filled with gas; she put a bagful of his favorite home-baked brownies on the car seat and left a note telling him that he was "the greatest father in the whole wide world and how could I have done such a terrible thing to such a wonderful person?")

In a reestablished adult family home there will be moments of wonderful family togetherness, love, and support; there will probably also be moments of anguish and extreme irritation, but if each member of the household tries to make the living arrangements function smoothly, the reestablished unit can be one of the greatest and happiest lifetime experiences of any of its members.

When a Parent Lives with You

Until the middle part of the last century, grandparents lived with the families of the next two generations until they died. It was the accepted thing. Houses were bigger then, but also, it was the only humane thing to do—there was no alternative. In spite of the occasional bickering and sometimes strong disagreements, families grew closer and children greatly benefited from the extra measure of love and wisdom afforded by the different generations surrounding them. In those days you "put up with your parents until they died," because you loved them and they had loved you for a lot longer than you could remember.

After World War II, following the baby boom, living space was at a premium and people became increasingly jealous of their privacy and their rights. Rest homes, retirement communities, and housing for the elderly became part of our social environment.

Now, just as there are many more postgraduate children who have returned to the nest, there are also more widowed grandparents once again living with an adult child and that child's spouse. It is often much less costly to the older people's children to have them at home than to pay for their independent housing and health care. It is generally much more compassionate to have them live with their children, but usually no one feels it to be the perfect solution for the aged parent or that person's family.

If an aged parent has come to live with you, look upon the strongly positive side of it. A grandparent (often the grandmother is the survivor, as women tend to outlive their husbands) may have an incredible potential for contributing to the development and education of her grandchildren. The new living arrangement tends to work if all generations exert self-control, give an extra measure, learn to cooperate and sacrifice, and celebrate, rather than resent, their differences.

What the Children Should Be Taught

The children should be taught to show respect and deference to their grandfather or grandmother. For example:

- Food should be offered first to any older person at table.
- Grandmother's visitors should be treated politely as honored guests in the house.
- The noise from a tape cassette, VCR, or "boom box" should be held down to a normal level when Grandmother is home.
- Her rest hour should be respected.
- Her telephone messages should be carefully taken, and her mail given to her unopened.
- Her room should not be entered, except with her permission.
- Children should be encouraged to seek her advice and opinion on matters. To ask Grandmother's opinion is important, not only as an act of kindness to make her feel an important member of the family but also to gain her insight and wisdom on a particular subject.
- Children should be encouraged to confide in her without turning her into an adversary against one of the parents or another sibling. A grandparent often has experience and skills in handling troubling family disputes and can offer helpful advice to a young child in coping with problems. However, she should not allow herself to be lobbied by a child to favor him or her over the siblings.

What You Might Do

- Give a grandparent his or her own space. Grandmother really needs her own room—hers to keep clean, but also hers in which to maintain her privacy. A son or daughter or son- or daughter-in-law really doesn't have the right to go through the older person's mail, personal effects, drawers, and closet—unless that person is incompetent. If there is some information that must be solicited for reasons of health, legal, or economic matters, ask Grandmother; don't go behind her back. Mutual trust is paramount to the success—even the survival—of a cross-generational living arrangement.
- Remember not to take advantage of her presence by laying too much housework or too many baby-sitting responsibilities on her. She is not, after all, a paid domestic employee, and although most likely she will want to work to repay your hospitality (and help out financially), she should not be treated like a domestic in terms of work responsibility, hours worked, and the like.

If she is strong and in good health, she will watch the children while you are on vacation or out socially or at work, but hopefully you will not abuse this convenient presence in your house. Whether her financial contributions are helping pay household expenses, or whether she is unable to contribute anything toward household expenses, she should not be judged or treated according to her fiscal liabilities or assets. She should be treated as a parent deserving of your love and respect, without whom you or your spouse would not have been born. (If your aging parent has an unfortunate disposition and is entirely selfish and uncooperative, hopefully you will have made alternate arrangements so she won't be living with you anyway!)

• Make her living quarters as pleasant as possible, with a personal television set and radio, if possible. Her room should be attractive, freshly painted, and cheerful when she comes to live with you. Put in her room some cherished mementos, photographs, and perhaps a favorite piece or two of furniture from her former house. This will ease the difficult adjustment from a life of independence to one she will consider to be dependent on you. Having her own little space will give her a much-needed sense of dignity.

One couple I know invited their widowed grandmother to live with them. She had become increasingly crippled with arthritis and couldn't manage alone anymore. They added on a small room and bath to their modest house, paid for by the grandmother from her savings. It was on the first floor, so that she would not have to manage stairs. The daughter had asked her mother several months before she came to live with them what her very favorite bedroom had looked like. When the mother walked into her new room in her daughter's home, she found it decorated with those same colors and fabric ideas (even a new carpet in the exact shade of green of a favorite old rug the mother had described to her daughter and her daughter had remembered). What could have been a traumatic experience for the mother became a happy one. She immediately felt comfortable in the new living arrangement.

• Preserve feelings of independence. It is important that a grandparent have control of his own money—as long as he is capable of managing it. He should have his own bank account, checks, and deposit slips; if he cannot get to the bank alone, someone should take him regularly, so that he can maintain a semblance of financial independence. If he is a person of means, he should have his own lawyer and financial adviser, so that you can never be accused of trying to manipulate him. If he is expected to (and, of course, is able to) contribute monthly to household and other expenses, those costs should be written down and carefully understood by all parties in advance, so that he will know his responsibilities and not feel his money is being taken for granted or wrested from him capriciously.

• Allow a grandparent to receive her own friends. On occasion, if she is up to it, the resident grandparent should be able to entertain without feeling she is upsetting anyone. She should know well beforehand what morning or afternoon—or evening—the living room, kitchen, and dining room are hers for entertaining.

• Make sure that the older member of the family gets taken to church, to the doctor, and takes medication at the proper times. You should be the eyes and ears of your senior resident, all the more so as the person grows older and becomes forgetful on occasion.

• Refrain from criticizing the grandparent for occasional forgetfulness and other signs of growing older. You and your children should keep reminding yourselves that someday you will be in the same situation. Therefore, never make fun of a grandparent or her friends. As the person living in the household ages, tolerance and patience will be required by everyone living there. (All you have to do is to keep remembering the Golden Rule: "Do unto others as you would have others do unto you"—because one day you will be old yourself!)

What the Grandparent-in-Residence Should Remember

• Always respect the privacy of the younger generations in the house. Do not enter their rooms uninvited, go through their drawers, or listen in on their telephone calls.

• Refrain from "horning in" on the younger generations' social activities at home, unless specifically invited. You should remain in your own room when your children or grandchildren are entertaining their friends. You might offer to help prepare the food or clean up, but do not be present when the guests arrive, tempting though it is to take a peek at what the younger generation is up to. (Perhaps it's just as well not to know.)

• Refer to everyone's possessions as belonging to their specific owners, not to you. For example, you should refer to the family automobile as "John and Barbara's car" not "our car." If the house belongs to your children and is not owned by you, refer to it as "my daughter and son's house," not "my house." In other words, as grandparent-in-residence, remember "to each his own."

• Do not complain about the food that is served (unless, of course, it is insufficient, and then it's time to have a frank discussion with your children). Perhaps they need more money for the food budget; perhaps your daughter needs more help with the cooking. It is not for you to criticize the condition of your daughter's or daughter-in-law's house, however. If you find it untidy in comparison with the house you used to keep, you can always ask if she would like you to help take care of it. If she refuses, then accept it the way it is.

• Keep your own room wonderfully clean and neat, regardless of how the rest of the house looks. This will influence your grandchildren. They will be able to discern the difference between a well-kept and a slovenly house.

• Offer to help with housework, cooking, and baby-sitting chores as much as you are able to. If you give more than is expected of you, you will probably find that the others give back more to you in return.

• Handle your own financial affairs as long as you can. Sometimes it's a question of consciously concentrating hard and thinking carefully when money matters are discussed, so that you will remain as independent as possible.

• Provide surprises and treats once in a while, when you are financially able to or if you have made a gift with your hands. I know a grandmother who always bakes a specially decorated cake for the birthday of each member of the family; she outdoes herself year after year in her creativity. I know a creative grandfather, too, who lives with one of his sons and his family and is full of surprises. One spring the garden suddenly burst forth into bloom with five new azalea bushes that no one had seen him plant the year before. In front of each bush was the name of a family member (painted on a small wooden stick). Even the family dog had a beautiful new bush named after him.

• Avoid taking sides with your children in a marital dispute or in arguments over the grandchildren. Be known as someone who offers wise counsel, even mediation services *when requested,* and as someone who is scrupulously fair, unprejudiced, and noninterfering. Become a master of the disappearing act when family fights are in progress. Never challenge the parents over their discipline decisions.

THE FAMILY FORUM

I used to marvel at a friend who had her father-in-law living with her family from the age of seventy-two to ninety-two. She and her husband built shelves on the walls of his room to house his many golf trophies. His room contained furniture from his old home, including the antique bed that he and his wife had shared until she was killed in an automobile accident. I remember how much we all loved "Grandpa," as everyone called him, including his five grandchildren and all their friends. Family arguments and complaints were all handled in a "Family Forum" meeting, which was called when necessity warranted it. Matters were fully discussed, with all generations present, and remedial action to be taken was written in chalk on a blackboard hanging on the kitchen wall. Here is what was written on the blackboard one week.

Family Forum

Grandpa: Promises to stop clicking his loosened false teeth, because it drives
everyone, repeat everyone, crazy.

Will make not one but two batches of his famous fudge, in repentance
for not keeping his promise to Sarah to greet her slumber party friends.

Father: Will get the car washed, as he promised to before Christmas, because his wife is furious.

Will fix the window in Jim's room, as he promised to last September, because Jim is furious.

Decrees that one night a week there will be NO rock music played in the house, and he wins that one.

Mother: Will let Sarah wear makeup once a month, to all-girl parties.

Will get off Joey's back about his socks.

Won't let it happen again that there's no soda in the fridge.

Jim: Will keep, not cancel, his appointment with the skin doctor next week.

Will remember to leave his boots in the mud room, and not ruin the carpets.

Will put his jeans in the wash when they are dirty.

Will pick the rock music three nights a week without interference.

Sarah: Won't swipe Mom's makeup, and won't clean it off on a face towel.

Will pick the rock music three night a week without interference.

Will not talk on her cell phone longer than fifteen minutes on any one call, an hour apart.

Joey: Will tie his socks together before they go in the wash.

Will not be allowed to pick the music—until Jim goes away to school, and then he inherits Jim's rights to music selection.

Will quit wiping his runny nose on his sleeve.

Annie: Will go quickly to the bathroom if she thinks she's going to throw up, instead of aiming for the rug.

Will not leave her dolls on the living room floor when Mom and Dad have guests.

Will be nice to the sitter.

Georgie: Knows he will not be smiled at in his high chair any longer if he puts the palm of his hand in the boiled egg and then puts his hand on the wall.

Promises he won't pull again so hard on Mom's pearl necklace that he breaks it. (Three times is enough, Georgie!)

This was one Family Forum that really brought results!

Good relationships are the result of an affirmative attitude toward life. They are the result of someone stepping forward, making an effort—even making a sacrifice—and saying:

"I like what I see."

"I'll give him [or her] the benefit of the doubt, if I don't like what I see."

"This person could be important to me—now or in the future."

"This is a person I could help in some way."

"This is a member of my family—to be loved and supported, in spite of some bad chemistry between us."

We are like the dancers in an ancient French square dance—the *quadrille*—as we step in and out of each other's lives, back and forth, making fascinating patterns with family members, friends, coworkers, and others who cross our paths in the course of a day. When we are the first to reach out with a smile, friendly bantering, and an emanation of warmth and good cheer, our relationships with others cannot help but be good. A flower tilts toward the sun; a human being turns toward another warm and kind human being. The similarity between good relationships and good manners is not only obvious—the two are one and the same!

YOU ARE SINGLE BUT STILL PART OF A FAMILY

FIGHTING THE GOOD FIGHT
AGAINST LONELINESS

Loneliness is a desolate, negative state. It means being out of the tribe. Most people who have achieved a certain success say that they don't care if it's lonely at the top, but once they begin to recognize the "clan's" power in society, they begin to care very much.

We should talk in terms of the positive. If your ultimate goal as a single person is to find a great mate, or to have many wonderful friends, or both, there are definite ways in which you can polish your facets to attract the right people:

- Be nice to other people all the time, not just part of the time.
- Be mindful of the important personal details of the lives of those around you, such as:

    the anniversary of the death of his loved one
    the birth of her child
    his birthday
    the date of her wedding anniversary
    their child's First Communion
    a young person's senior prom, graduation, and other major events
    that mark that person's reach for maturity
    a friend's first day on a new job
    a major event in a person's life, such as a swearing-in ceremony to
    become a citizen of the United States

As a friend, you should mark these events at least with a telephone call or an e-mail. You don't have to mark all of these occasions with a gift, but at least acknowledge the event and congratulate the parties involved. If you can't remember dates and special occasions, record them in your calendar or diary, have an office associate remind you, or put Post-its all over the place to move you to action. Too often single people think they have a permanent excuse for ignoring special occasions in their friends' lives. ("If I were married, my wife would be taking care of these things.") Lame excuses are worse than none at all.

• Become known as a wonderful host and a delightful guest as well. This means you are seldom a "taker" but always a "giver."

• Your brain is well exercised, which means you're current on world events, the cultural and educational scene, the business world, and the political one as well. You are interesting and fun to be with.

• You have made yourself as physically attractive as possible, which means staying in shape, eating right, paying attention to your hair, adopting meticulous grooming habits, dressing well and, if you're a woman, using makeup artfully. (All of this takes time, but it's worth it.) Our world is not equal and just, and in the opinion of most, a sloppy woman looks worse than a sloppy man.

• You have learned how to maintain a happy frame of mind, which can be willed, no matter what good or bad circumstances surround you.

• You spend a good amount of quality time and effort not only in the pursuit of money but also in the act of giving it away intelligently.

• You have learned that you are the secret to your own success with friends. You always take the first steps, you do the inviting, you think up the amusing thing to do that will please the entire group, you keep everyone connected and informed as plans become more complicated, whether it's for a trip, an excursion, or a party. Don't complain about how you "always have to do everything." Just do it. There always has to be a total giver in every joint undertaking. The fact that you are always there, ready and able to assume the leadership in the group time after time, is a gift, not a chore!

• You never have a moment's hesitation over one question: whether or not the world is a better place for your having been in it. The answer must always be "Yes."

MAKING FRIENDS OF YOUR FAMILY

The smart live-aloner doesn't complain about the state of singleness, and scoffs at any suggestion of needing sympathy. Quite the contrary. Independence is considered a great gift by the happy live-aloner, whose sense of purpose, and often, sense of humor, affects everyone around in a most positive way.

"I live alone" is a statement that should be made with pride, not embarrassment. It means you are self-sufficient, which requires a variety of talents. *Even though you may live alone, the world around you is your family.* Start counting all those friends—in your neighborhood alone—in your house of worship, in the stores you patronize, your workplace, and the places where you study and exercise.

The people who inhabit these spaces alongside you are all potential friends. You can measure the validity of each friendship by analyzing how often you talk to one another, how much you look forward to seeing them each time, how interested you are in their lives and they in yours. You have really succeeded in your personal relationships when, in answer to the question, "Who are your friends here?" you can reply without thinking, "Everyone here is my friend." If the supermarket butcher has a bright smile on his face when he sees you, if the garage repairman has a new story to tell you while he's inspecting the engine of your car, if the people waiting to catch the 7:50 A.M. bus at your corner smile and nod with recognition when they see you, and are always ready with some mundane comment on the weather in an effort to make conversation, then consider yourself "a person with friends." A broad definition of a "friend" is someone of either sex and any age, who recognizes you, is glad to see you, is happy to have you hang out with him even for a few minutes while waiting for a train, and is ready to give you small bits of information on "how things are going" in his life, just as you are ready to return the favor.

Being single is not a deprived state of loneliness. I had a single friend who was constantly seeking sympathy from everyone she knew. If you asked her how she was, she would answer with a litany of how bad things were. People began to cross the street to avoid having to greet her. She resembled a depressionlike germ, which she would have been happy to spread around to everyone else. Underneath it all, she was a smart, attractive woman with a lot to offer, but it was thoroughly disguised when glazed over with depression. One day I passed a doughnut shop and saw a "special" on Krispy Kremes advertised in their windows—three each of four kinds. I knew she loved this product, and I knew she was the kind of person who never received any presents, so I bought a box for her as a gift. In the middle of the frankly tantalizing array of doughnutery, I placed a little piece of paper, on which I had typed on my computer:

> *Some people see the gooey, luscious, creamy confection of the doughnut.*
> *Some people see only its hole.*

She got the message and took it well, because it came from a friend, not from someone wishing her harm. She also consumed every single one of those Krispy Kremes . . . and didn't let me have one of them!

Another friend of mine, who was single until she was fifty-two, had a famous "Singles Wall" in her apartment. When she met an eligible bachelor, or a special single woman friend, she would have that person sign her wall. It became a great status symbol to be able to say, "Yes, I've signed Anne's wall. I'm a Single Signer." The wall also became a great conversation piece all over the city. Everyone who went to her apartment for a drink wanted to see the wall right away and was very offended if they were not asked to sign. At times single friends would have to stand on her bed to reach high near the ceiling, in order to find room on the wall for a witty saying or drawing to go with their signatures. If any of the signers subsequently got married, she would run a fine line through their names, which made the wall even more interesting. No matter how dirty and dingy-looking it became, people were still signing on it when she moved away to get married. She had one last emotional wall party the night before she moved out, which some people equated to the jubilant tearing down of the Berlin Wall. Many of her guests suggested she cut down a segment of the wall and install it in her new home, an idea that was knocked down by her fiancé because of its logistical impossibility, as well as his feeling of discomfort to have to live with the names of all those single men she had known!

Reasons to Be Glad You Are Single

1. Make a list of all your everyday friends, including the many at work. It should be a large, impressive list that will surprise you when you see it. If it's not, you need to start working on attracting more everyday friends.
2. Consult your list of names and add to it every time you start feeling sorry for yourself. Count yourself lucky to have the gift of extra time that family-involved people do not have. The single life affords you more time to develop your full potential, so look at it in those terms.
3. When you're single, you have more time for stimulating pursuits—educational, cultural, travel, and sports-related.
4. You have the luxury of all the bathroom time you need. You can take a leisurely shower without an impatient line waiting outside, making loud, sarcastic comments.
5. You have only yourself to blame for a misplaced wireless gadget or any piece of precious electronic equipment. Within a family, hours of angry searching might result when someone misplaces something that causes a computer, TV, or any piece of electronic equipment to cease functioning.
6. You can sleep when you want (note that I am omitting "with whomever you want"), eat when you want, and run your life on your very own schedule.
7. You can enjoy the alternating rhythms of life—the noise and bustle of working around people and the refreshing solitude of life at home.
8. You will have the time to become inspired to help your community. Involve yourself in volunteer work. Put your heart, mind, and energy

into the giving of yourself, because by doing anything to help others— i.e., reading to the blind, driving the elderly to their medical appointments, teaching children how to read, helping out in a hospital, sending e-mail messages for the incapacitated—enormous satisfaction will be derived from your efforts. Being needed is a universal need in itself!

9. You may have time to serve on a nonprofit board, so work toward that end.

10. You may have time to help someone with his or her political campaign. Volunteer!

11. You can run for office yourself. (Why not?)

12. When you're feeling "down," take a walk by yourself, for the sole purpose of noticing the beauty around you, anything from a pot of geraniums on a terrace to a city fountain spouting water in the sun and making rainbows, or from a group of small children playing hopscotch in the park to a beautifully carved stone balustrade on the balcony of the building across the street.

13. Treat yourself to a trip—either a well-organized group tour of people who are as interested as you are in Scottish castles, European golf courses, or skin diving in the Aegean Sea, or making a solo trip, where you will see and experience three times as much as if you were traveling with others.

14. Get yourself a public library card, and go on a reading binge, alternating great books with your favorite trash. Remind yourself that a wonderful book is a never-fail companion in your leisure hours.

15. If you haven't been much exposed to great music, borrow albums of classical music and the music of other countries from the library. It will only add spice if you throw into the mix, from time to time, some old favorites of rock-and-roll, rap, Cole Porter, Gershwin, soul, hip-hop, jazz, and Latin rhythms.

16. Practice your pen! Write wonderful letters, to all the people of whom you have sadly lost track. There's one phrase that brings so much happiness to people—"I've often thought of you through these past months [or years]." A good letter takes time to compose, to make what you have to say sound fascinating, and to rekindle the bonds of great old friendships. Tie up those communication lines once again, and don't let them loosen.

17. Repaint and refurbish your apartment to the extent that your finances will allow it. With new colors around you, a change of textures, art on the walls, you will become reenergized into doing more things and enjoying them more than you could possibly have imagined.

18. Try some new activities, such as:
    - learning a new sport or taking up yoga

- exploring aromatherapy
- acquiring a new pet, and thus a new love in your life
- finding a totally new mental stimulation, such as learning a foreign language, taking flying lessons, studying painting, writing a children's book, or becoming a dessert chef for your friends.

If you're wondering why bother doing all this, the answer is simple. You will find that you're much better company in others' opinion, and there is no way now that you could be designated as that most loathsome of creatures—a *bore*. You will have used your "alone time" wisely and well.

IF YOU WANT TO STOP BEING SINGLE

Advice Number One: Take off your blinders and really look around you. There may be someone close by who is eligible, but whom you have just never considered in that light. Don't take for granted friendships with people of the opposite sex who share some of your interests, and who are single and "fairly" attractive. Some of these casual friendships might be worthy of cultivating into something else. (There are many degrees of attractiveness, and it is usually in the eye of the beholder.)

Advice Number Two: Let your friends know you're in the market. The more people are aware of your search, the better the chance for successful encounters.

Caveats:
- Don't put your friends on the spot and demand reports on how and what they are doing.
- Don't nag them and keep suggesting things they can do to help you.
- Go cheerfully on any date they have arranged for you. If it was a disaster, don't tell them why. Just say it was mutually disappointing, but you are hopeful for the next one. Always thank them enthusiastically, and never cast aspersions on their taste in men (or women) for you. They might hit a bull's-eye with the next candidate.
- Your message to your friends should remain: I'm so grateful for your efforts, and please keep trying!

Advice Number Three: Attend every social gathering you can work into your schedule. If you're invited to four Christmas parties on the same night, which can often happen among young working people, accept all four. You never, never know. Schedule your travel time and how much time you must spend at each party place. (It can be done!)

If you hate cocktail parties, go to them anyway, with a smile on your face and an optimistic attitude.

Advice Number Four: Initiate your own intelligence-gathering network. Ask friends in other divisions of your company to let you know immediately who of the opposite sex in their division has just lost a spouse or gotten divorced; in other words, someone who is newly single. (One friend of mine, divorced at fifty, sent a pair of binoculars to a couple of married fellow executives. The card sent with the binoculars urged them to "look long and hard for me." They did, with eventual success in their mission, even though they did not have to use binoculars!)

Caveats:
- Try not to sound desperate. This can be accomplished by always keeping your sense of humor and asking friends to help you without pressuring them. (One woman I know demanded that a good friend in another office give her a written report on monthly sightings of eligible men in her business area, which ultimately caused the end of their longtime friendship.)

Advice Number Five: Regularly check your local neighborhood newspapers for the activities open to the public. Some of these will be free, some will be at a minimum cost. These are also often listed in the weekend edition of your major local newspaper and are great "people finders."

Advice Number Six: Be Meetable. When you're out in public, ask yourself: "What's my face doing right now? When your face is in repose, do you look like someone armed with a dangerous weapon? Do you look worried, upset, frightened, or just plain mean, even if you're not? Most of us do not know what kind of expression is on our faces when we're not thinking about it—or, to put it another way, when we're not thinking about others, just about ourselves. You can scare off people who would have made interesting friends if they had not contemplated your face in repose. Make a small smile, relaxing your facial muscles and turning up your mouth just a little. Look in a mirror and notice the pleasing effect this has on your eyes and your whole facial expression. The effect is warm and attractive. Try looking that way (adopting this "face set") all the time. Think about it when you're driving or walking down the street. It will become a habit.

When you attend a business or social affair, *present yourself as someone who is pleasant and approachable.* (I will always remember what a senior manager, an eligible bachelor, said about a supposedly good-looking woman he had just met: "No, I did not find her attractive. She was in great shape and all that, but her face in repose was that of a dog—a dog that seemed to be barking at me.")

When you accidentally catch a glimpse of yourself in a mirror, what kind of face do you see? A pleasant one? A half smile? A scowl and a frown or a bark? What you see accidentally in a mirror is what other people see when they're looking at you. Your expression should say:

"I'm a very nice person, nice-looking, too. I'm glad to be here, and yes, please talk to me. I would be happy to talk to you."

THE OPPORTUNITIES FOR MEETING PEOPLE ARE ENDLESS

It's up to you, your energy, and your determination. There is no excuse for loneliness—if you're not physically, mentally, or financially handicapped, and even then, loneliness can be avoided. Look at your life as though it were a box, full of good experiences you have already had, but with room for many more to be placed inside. Enjoy thinking about the experiences already in that box—your life—but resolve to add many new ones. There is no excuse for wasting time. Get going! And, by the way, in this book do not expect to find singles bars as a suggested method for meeting people—or finding romance *on-line*. If you have the slightest premonition of danger when you're out in the single "jungle," just get out of there quickly.

Options for Finding and Meeting People

• Volunteer your heart, hands, and expertise in your community. Nice people you would enjoy knowing are doing likewise. It's the most natural way to make conversation and to find out necessary information.

• PTA and school organization meetings—for a single parent, these meetings are fertile ground for you to make new friends and jump-start your social life.

• Sports—in which to participate or spectate. The surest way of making many new sports-minded friends is to show off your skills, and most important, your good sportsmanship.

• Join a house of worship. The people you meet will make pleasant friends in regular circumstances, but could become essential in times of sadness or trouble. Check into the programs available for singles.

• Attend live performances (plays, ballet, opera, concerts). Get a comprehensive taste of activities you've never tried before, and substitute them for some of the mind-numbing hours previously spent in front of the television or movie screens.

• On the beach—seaside or lakeside. Bring with you a picnic bigger than what you need, as well as your children or your dog. The extra food might come in handy when you start a good conversation with someone new.

• Playground sports. There are activities like softball in which you can invite yourself to join, and you will be usually welcomed, if you know how to play. It also helps if you have a charming, gracious manner, so that they will want you to join them, not just tolerate your presence. You can have a good time even if you don't know how to play. "I'm new here. I'm really anxious to join in. Maybe there's something useful I could do for the game."

• Activities related to your children. These are fun—like city- and park-sponsored Easter egg hunts, playground picnics, and Halloween costume judgings. It is also a great way to meet parents of children the ages of yours. I know one young mother who, on the first weekend in a new city, volunteered her services as a face painter at a park party for kids, and by the end of the day, she had five invitations from parents on the playground to come visit them and their children.

• Don't forget dog walks. When you see the same people every day or night walking their dogs, it is easy to strike up friendly conversations, and then, eventually, "Maybe you and your spouse would come over for a drink some night. Oh, and yes, your dog is invited, too." (If the person does not have a spouse, so much the better!)

• Amateur theatrical and singing groups. If you enjoy being a ham, it's very pleasant to find others with an equal inclination. Every ham needs an audience, too, so that might be your role, at first, to appreciate the talents of the others.

• Book clubs. These can be for intellectuals, historians, or gossip hounds. Find your level, and go to the meetings, which are sometimes in private homes, or in coffeehouses or restaurants. If there isn't one available, start one. Your local bookstore will help you get names of people who might be prospective members.

• Poetry societies. If there aren't any weekend poetry reading café hangouts in your community, start one, perhaps even in your home.

• Bird-watching. Some of the most charming people in the world are avid bird-watchers. Find this out for yourself, but first, find out where these groups are located. In order to be prepared, you'll need:

　　a good pair of binoculars

　　an illustrated book of birds (You'll have to know the difference
　　　　between a robin and a hawk!)

　　comfortable walking shoes

• Movie clubs. Best when combined with dinner for singles. This is a sure-fire way to enjoy yourself, because the following elements are possibly present:

　　new people to meet

　　good food

　　a good movie

Any one of these should make it worthwhile for you.

• Marinas. Hanging out around the boats, asking intelligent questions, and showing enthusiasm for them can often result in an invitation to "come aboard." People who sail and who know how to crew are often invited right on the spot to join a group.

• Gardening clubs. Precious friendships and great romances have begun with trowels in hand, digging in the dirt. Local and city gardens usually have projects desperately in need of volunteers. Many good things can flower while you're digging in the dirt with interesting people!

• Car race concourses and rallies. A sport for passionate people. Check it out if that's your style. You can become a car-race groupie without having to endanger yourself or your wallet, but be sure you have the right clothes. Copy what others wear to begin with until you find your own style.

• Dances. Sometimes finding people who like and know how (the two are synonymous) to dance seems like a daunting task. Take some lessons yourself. You'll meet people who like to dance at the classes. Be creative and organize not only waltz and foxtrot evenings in someone's home or in a restaurant, but also have the newest dance fads staged, whatever they are. At a restaurant or bar, for example, arrange an evening of "Bhangra" dance music (Indian hip-hop based on the centuries-old Punjabi folk music). You can get teachers, musicians, and local flavor wherever there is a South Asian community. Maybe you would prefer to see what the restaurants and bars have to offer in the Latin dance rhythms. A local dance studio can probably arrange an evening of teaching the latest Latin dances. You should ask everyone to chip in on the expenses.

• Health clubs. These are a mecca for those who like to meet other people interested in fitness, or for those who are just interested in enlarging their roster of contacts. Often the busiest, most interesting and gainfully employed people work out very early in the morning before work, which can make it difficult to spark witty conversation! Still, I suggest every young person check out the fitness set.

• Shopping, particularly for food. You may have noticed an attractive person two or three times a week shopping for food at your local market at the same hour. Unobtrusively make note of what is in that person's basket. Is he obviously shopping for one or two persons? He may act helpless about choosing a ripe melon, so help him out. You may solicit his opinion on which brand of hearty soup to buy. After a few "serious conversations" like this one, you can ask, "Are you the cook in your house, or does your wife [husband] take care of that department?" You'll find out rather quickly this way if he is married. If the answer is "separated," or "getting a divorce," it is best to start shopping at another supermarket quickly.

• Adult extension classes. When you improve your brain, you find nice people doing exactly the same thing in your class. There are endless opportunities in this field to make new friends; it is very natural to ask a "classmate" to join you for coffee, either before or after class. Then in casual conversation, you can find out if that person is married. (By the way, a wedding ring—either on the finger or absent from the finger—is never a foolproof sign.)

• Bridge groups. There are bridge clubs in big cities—ask around. There are bridge "groups" also in small towns everywhere. Ask at your church or synagogue, for starters. Do not get turned off by the way the person who might be the object of your affection plays the game. Some people are not meant to be at the same bridge table. (My husband and I, for example. The last time we played bridge together, also our first, was on our honeymoon—forty years ago.) Inquire about neighborhood poker games. This is a great way for a newcomer to make friends. But a caution here: Frequent only the games with minuscule stakes.

• Train and subway platforms, bus stops. Conversation is inevitable if you see the same people at the same place every morning. One of my good friends, a woman in her forties, met her husband on a Grand Central Station platform, commuting from White Plains into New York every morning at eight-thirty. They saw one another thirty-nine mornings before bothering to smile or acknowledge one another. Then they started to talk, and were married seven months after their first conversation.

• Computer clubs. This is a great place to socialize, and for all the great minds who congregate at these sessions, there are many lonely, socially insecure ones. It's a great way for a single person to become the most popular person in the group, just by showing up with a batch of brownies one day, or by bringing invitations to "come to my house for a plate of pasta next week."

• Flying lessons and festivals. The environment at these events where private flying lessons are given is romantic. Ask anyone who has fallen in love with a pilot. Look around you and check out the other people as carefully as you check out the airplanes.

• Wilderness clubs, hunting and fishing enthusiasts—preservation groups, too. People passionate about the environment, who are also interested in these sports, are meticulous about the preservation of the wild, and always ready to meet like-minded people. Get out your hiking boots, and pack some irresistible sandwiches in your backpack. (I remember one young woman fell in love with a fellow hiker because of the picnic he brought for everyone to share. "Recipes from *Gourmet* magazine sure made him my kind of sportsman!")

• Foreign language clubs. If you are faced with having to learn a language for your career on a trip, you will find many others in the same boat. The grind of studying another language can become a delightful source of social interaction. Perhaps your company has expanded business activities to China and you must learn Chinese. Dinner at a Chinese restaurant, tickets to a Chinese play or movie with fellow students, can be a pleasant aftermath of a class. If you just like the sound of another language, go for it! Take lessons and immerse yourself in that culture.

• Your alumni association's social activities. A good alumni group in every major city is a constant provider of good opportunities to socialize. If your school's alumni association is laggard in performing this function, get a few friends to join you and change the situation.

• Art classes. Art classes form the perfect bonding situation, with students politely praising one another's work and eventually finding it easy to invite someone to "come over for soup and salad Sunday night." And you don't have to worry about what to wear since people "dress down" when they're painting or handling clay.

• Investment clubs. Many of these are gender-specific. Find out where they are in your neighborhood or business community and you will find them convivial and fun, as well as perhaps rewarding financially.

• Political campaign headquarters. Volunteer your services with the candidate who seems to have the greatest number of volunteers in your age group. (It helps if you believe in the candidate!) There's a lot of energy and action in these places, and many new friendships to be forged while pursuing an important cause.

• Historical societies. These are fun because history is educational and amusing and young in spirit. Attend meetings, volunteer to raise money, help with the research and the grunt work in mounting exhibits, and you'll make a multitude of intelligent new friends.

• Singles clubs. These can be fabulous but duds, too. Check them out carefully beforehand by talking to present and past members.

• Wine tastings. These make for chatty evenings with an assemblage of wine connoisseurs, as well as those who pretend to be connoisseurs, and people who just want to be around people who are experts, or even phony experts. Read up on wines, and check out the subject on the Net so that you are armed with a smattering of knowledge.

• Travel groups. Check the classified ads and do research on the local university and museum groups that have organized interesting trips. You will return either loving or loathing your fellow travelers (see chapter 5), you will have learned a lot, and everything will have been planned for you. It also gives you something to talk about in the year ahead.

• Chess club. If you know how to play, join a local chess club, or find out where the games are being played in your city, turn on the charm, and invite yourself into the group. If you don't know how to play, and you have the time and inclination, take lessons and learn, because it will give you a lifetime of pleasure and intellectual stimulation. If you are lonely, and the only player you know lives in another city, learn how to play the game with that person on the Net.

• Meeting people on the Net and in singles bars. This, in my opinion, is no way to meet a future spouse or even a future date. The process is too full of peril, and I have heard too many bad stories. I'd pull down the shade on these two, because there are so many other ways to meet people and make friends, ways that are safer.

COMPLETE TURNOFF QUESTIONS
NEVER TO ASK A SINGLE PERSON

Now that there are so many single people, no one need be self-conscious about it any longer. It's unkind to tease single people, to draw attention to their singleness, to make jokes about pairing them up with so-and-so, when that other person is totally unsuitable. Single people really resent questions like the examples below, so don't ask them, whether seriously or in jest:

- Bet you're desperate to get married, aren't you?
- Just why *aren't* you married, anyway?
- Is sexual incompatibility the reason?
- What's the matter—afraid of any responsibility?
- Do you think your age is a problem?
- Are you gay—is that why you're not married?
- Do you think you don't make enough to support a mate?
- You're accused of being too particular. Do you think you can afford to be?
- Are you afraid of having children—is that why you're single?
- Been burned before—is that it?
- What's your definition of an attractive person of the opposite sex?
- If you could have anyone in town to marry, who would it be?

IF YOU WANT TO PLAY MATCHMAKER

1. What kinds of questions do you ask of a single person before offering suggestions to fix up that person? Answer: very general ones—mostly, "Where do you live, where do you work, have you ever been married before? How long have you been divorced? Do you have any children?" Any effort to arrange a romance between two people requires having some necessary information first.

2. For how long do you maintain a leadership role in this "fix-up" activity? Answer: If you feel sorry for a friend, or that friend has asked you to help, two attempts at fixing up someone with a member of the opposite sex is enough for you to do. A third attempt would be a *very* generous gesture on your part, and you do not have to try again after that, unless you are fully committed to the project. After all, it requires a lot of time and work to arrange these introductions. (An example of a couple being fully committed to finding a husband for a female friend is the pair who were skiing in the Italian Alps. They were confined to a *rifugio* while seeking shelter from a blizzard, and in talking through the night with another skier, an attractive stranger, everyone trying to

keep from freezing, they talked about their shy maiden lady friend. The couple introduced the single woman to the Italian back in the States. They were married a year after. In his wedding toast to his bride, the groom said, "Pure mountain air makes you think straight." If she had been a guest at a crowded cocktail party, he might never have given her a second thought.

GAY AND LESBIAN COUPLES—THEY ARE FAMILIES, TOO

In the best of all worlds, heterosexuals and homosexuals work well together in their jobs and share a mutual dignity and respect for one another in their social lives. The homosexual communities are a growing minority, increasing in political and purchasing power, and in demanding their rights. Some people are uncomfortable around gays and lesbians and don't know how to make conversation with them. These groups live increasingly in and around the major cities of the world, so people who feel shy and uptight with them are just going to have to get over it.

Good manners dictate that in social interactions, straights and gays avoid discussing sexual topics, which generally grow negative and can even become inflammatory. Anti-gays who use slang terms such as "fag," "fruit," "pansy," "queer," or "dyke" (referring to a woman), or terms far more disgusting, are showing bias and a lack of intelligence. Such terms should be rigorously avoided around children, who all too easily pick up the habits of their parents and repeat them at school, thus assuring another generation of unfair discrimination against gays and lesbians.

Yes, there are homosexuals with objectionable behavior, just as there are straight people with objectionable behavior. You don't have to agree with their quest for a legal right to marry. You don't have to think it is amusing when a man dresses as a woman or a woman as a man, as happens in transsexual communities. The graceful integration of homosexuals into our society is often hindered by conscious or unconscious biases on the part of the straight community, but at the same time, that bias is accentuated by a minority of homosexuals flaunting their sexual activities in full public view. Straights or gays making out in public is distasteful, immoral, and an offensive way of drawing attention to themselves. In a polite society, prejudice arises inevitably, but it should be controlled and not allowed by any separate group to become intrusive, confrontational, and unjust.

When you encounter a gay person in the normal course of events, don't fixate on the person's sexual preference; focus on that individual's accomplishments and aspects of personality that mark that person's humanity.

GOOD MANNERS TOWARD GAYS AND LESBIANS

Much of the following advice is unnecessary in cities with a large homosexual population, because there is intermixing at school and at work:

• It's rude to ask a person boldly outright if he or she is homosexual. In fact, sexual topics in general should be avoided, unless the conversation takes place in complete privacy.

• It's meaningless to assume that any definition of "the homosexual community" reflects the views of all homosexuals, any more than a definition of "the heterosexual community" reflects the views of all heterosexuals.

• People who refer to gays even at home in slang terms such as "fag," "fruit," "pansy," "queer," and "dyke" (a term for women), are going to turn their children into bigoted, prejudiced adults just like themselves. When you hear anyone else gay-bashing, step in to stop it. "Hey, that's not fair to make fun of him in that nasty way. Let's change the conversation, okay?"

• If you invite a homosexual couple to your home overnight or for a weekend, it is appropriate to put them in the same bedroom. If you feel squeamish about this, because homosexuality is frowned on in your religion or by you or someone else in your family, then don't invite them, or else put them up in a hotel. Your guests should be sensitive to this situation. When I was growing up, my parents would never stand for unmarried guests of the opposite sex staying in the same room of our house. Now that I'm much older, I realize that sex will occur, if the protagonists wish it to, in a Kentucky barnyard or in a suite at the Peninsula Hotel in Hong Kong, at three in the morning or three in the afternoon. (That still didn't make it moral in my late mother's eyes!)

• A lesbian's parents may be the victims of probing, mean questions from their friends. Hopefully, they will answer unequivocally that they stand by their child and accept her decision. I remember overhearing a loud, pushy woman asking a good friend how she could support her son's decision to come out as a gay, and the good friend made the perfect answer: *"It was easy. My husband and I love him."*

• A person's friend should not "out" him before the person decides to do so. After all, it is a major decision, and the person should be allowed to do it when and how he wishes, not shamefully and defensively—particularly in respect to the family.

• Do not invite a gay or lesbian to a social event in the evening or on a weekend without that person's partner (if there is a partner at that time). Put both partners' names on the envelope address and in any salutation. "Dear Andy and Pete," or "Dear Mr. Cates and Mr. Donnell." You do not have to invite the partner if the meal is just business-oriented and not social.

• Don't invite a gay man who is by himself or a woman by herself to be the date of a single man or woman at your party.

• Just as I say repeatedly that husbands do not have to be seated next to their wives at a formally seated meal, so a gay or lesbian couple do not have to be seated next to one another at a meal. Every guest, regardless of sex, is supposed to be a "giver" in a social situation, to keep conversation lively, and to help out the host. (As with married couples, an exception should be made to this seating rule if one of the pair is extremely shy and insecure.)

• Ask the couple how they wish to be introduced at large family gatherings, so there won't be a great deal of fumbling and mumbling of names when they're being presented to other guests.

• If a same-sex couple is partnered in their own eyes, even if not in the eyes of the state or the church, they should be introduced and referred to as partnered, in the same way as a married heterosexual couple. This is particularly important at large family gatherings, such as a wedding or a funeral. (Family acceptance is a number-one priority for their happiness.)

• When introducing a gay or lesbian couple, you could say, "This is Mark Whitberg and his partner, Jerry Sanfide."

• Send only one formal invitation, not two, to a homosexual couple. Put both their names on the envelope, listed alphabetically (one on top of the other), and with their mutual address on the lines beneath:

Ms. Gretchen Bushnell
Ms. Hillary Fortnum
765 Fifth Avenue, etc.

(A thank-you note to the host by either one of the partners is appropriate.)

• Some people who are unaccustomed to being with gays or lesbians may be tongue-tied at small parties. When they don't know what to say and just look down, everyone present is uncomfortable. If you make an effort to talk to these guests and get everyone involved in a general conversation, the party mood will be revived, and your hosts will be forever grateful to you.

I heard one young man telling about how he decided he was going to befriend the one lesbian ever hired by his firm. He bragged about his quest, and felt very hip because he asked questions about sexual relationships among her friends. They were stupid, overly personal questions, until she finally appealed to a supervisor to deal with him. The young manager had received all the wrong signals and handled their working relationship in all the wrong ways. Fortunately, he was later educated on the subject of "human relations" by someone in human resources.

As is true with well-mannered straights, well-mannered gays and lesbians do not talk openly about their sex lives in social situations. They do not enjoy being questioned about their lifestyle or habits, as though they were being interviewed on a gossipy TV talk show. Once this is generally understood, people of civility move on to any other conversational subject, and everything turns out just fine, thank you.

WHEN A GAY COUPLE ADOPTS A CHILD

When a homosexual couple adopts a child or one of the partners has a child, thanks to a previous marriage, in-vitro fertilization, or perhaps a surrogate mother, it is absolutely unconscionable to do anything other than support the child as she grows up. Regardless of how you personally feel about this manner of producing a child, your language and actions should always be supportive and kind. Realize that the more your children come to learn about the lifestyle of gay or lesbian parents, or gay single parents, the more your children should learn never to gossip about those children, or leave them out of parties and play-dates, or tease or make fun of them. How you, a straight person, may personally feel about it, does not matter. Theirs *is* a family, to be treated with the same respect afforded to anyone else in class or on the playground, and you must never take out your prejudices on those children.

THE KEEPERS OF YOUR HOUSE— THEY ARE FAMILY, TOO

When I was growing up, a house wasn't a home unless it was endlessly scrubbed, washed, and polished with an almost fanatical devotion. If you had so much as a smudge on one of the lace curtains in the window, neighbors sniffed with disdain at your laxity in matters that count. We are certainly in another era now. Women have gone to work, sometimes men undertake the domestic duties while their wives earn salaries, and as for the house, families are lucky if occasionally things are freshened up and sprayed with different products to give an appearance of cleanliness and polish. Forget the scrubbing and intensive work.

If you have a career today, you thank your lucky stars for finding "good help," but finding the individuals is not enough. They must be trained, be treated nicely, and led to understand the scope of their duties. The goal is to keep them loyal to your household and not ready to defect at the first rustle of more paper bills headed their way from "domestic kidnappers." People who "steal" other people's household helpers, in search of cooks, butlers, maids, gardeners, and the number-one object of envy—a good baby nurse-governess-sitter—constitute one of the newer, more loathsome types of criminals, because the perpetrator is usually someone you know, someone who has seen how well your staff works for you, and perhaps has even been entertained by you.

There is nothing more luxurious, pleasant, and gracious than a well-trained staff taking care of you, your lovely, polite children, your magnificent house, your cars, and your award-winning gardens. What a beautiful painting that would make! The trouble with this picture is that you may be fairly new to the universally recommended state of "being rich," and might therefore be ill at ease in giving direction to a household staff. Another aspect of keeping this perfect painting from being finished enough to hang in a museum is that the only people you can find for domestic service may be untrained, and you may not know how to train them, or they may not wish to accept training in this profession anyway! Sometimes the staff feels grander than their grand employers. Sometimes, they do not speak English and you do not speak their language, and good communication is impossible.

Working with Non-English-Speaking Employees

You should send a non-English-speaking employee to school to learn English, but have someone tutor you, as well, in the other person's language. This effort on your part will do more to cement this person to your family than any other gesture you could make. Often people who work in someone else's home feel that their job is demeaning. If you can change the mind-set of your employees on this matter, you will have a successful, smooth-running house. Getting over all these hurdles in the training process is no easy matter. It's important that you show this individual that his or her job has great dignity and merit in your eyes.

Before You Employ Someone in Your Home

• Check out their references carefully, if they are to live in your home, particularly if they will be involved with your children. Character is going to be as important as skills in this respect.

• Pay for a thorough physical examination, if they are to live or work regularly in your home.

• Have them undergo special drivers' training, even if they claim to be excellent drivers. Oversee the checkups on the vehicle used for driving your children.

• Make life pleasant for live-in help in your house, including: a nice bedroom, with a TV, good closet space, and a comfortable chair, lamp, writing table, and her own little fridge in her room, if possible. If your employee must do a lot of errands for you, and ferry your children around, the car should be in excellent shape.

• Obey the law, and have an accountant figure out federal withholding on the employee's salary, your responsibilities in paying their Social Security, as well as Workers Compensation and liability insurance for property damage caused by an employee. Paying them "off the books" is simply not an option. The legality of any non-American employees is a priority. If you like this employee, pay for all her legal fees involved in the acquisition of an alien registration card.

- The law tells you how much time off you must give those who work every day, as well as annual vacations, in accordance with federal regulations. It is nice to be flexible in the direction of giving them more rather than less time off.
- Compensate them well, instead of trying to get away with saving a buck here and there. A housekeeper who works even only once or twice a week deserves a paid vacation, paid sick days, a birthday present, and a year-end bonus.
- Train them, or have someone else train them. They should have pride in their jobs as well as in their own abilities. Let them know you consider their jobs to be highly responsible ones, requiring special skills.
- Compliment them *every time* they do a nice job for you.
- Lay out their duties clearly, with every responsibility carefully spelled out on paper. If they are new arrivals from another country, have the description of their duties translated into their language, and printed out in both languages, so there will be no misunderstandings.

Special Recommendations
for Your Sitter and Child Caregiver

- Rigorously obey the rules about children four and under using seat belts in a vehicle. Leave an extra car seat at home in case your sitter has to take your child somewhere in an emergency (and you are away from home in the family car with its car seat).
- Make certain that their living accommodations are comfortable, if they "live in," with the proper amount of privacy, and if they come only for the day, there should be a comfortable place in your home for them to sit and relax when not on duty.
- Make it absolutely clear when your caregiver is out with your children, they are not to be socializing with other sitters, such as in the park or at a coffeehouse. The caregiver is supposed to be giving full attention to the child!
- Give your caregiver a cell phone while she's on duty, so that you can get her at any hour, wherever she is with your child, and so that she can use it for an emergency. Impress upon her that she is *not* to use it for personal calls while she is on duty.
- Have a neighbor check on your sitter if she is not playing with the child

out of doors, as she is supposed to do. You do not want a sitter who simply parks the child near a TV set while she watches her favorite programs all day.

• When your child is under the age of four, the sitter should stay with him, even if your child is playing with someone else and the caretaker of that "someone else" is present. This is no time for the sitter to take a break herself. Your child is her primary responsibility.

• Make sure your sitter is not burdened on the playground or anywhere else with the responsibility of someone else's child. Emphasize that she is to take care of your child, not other children whose sitters are her friends.

• Make sure you tell your sitter how you manage your "time-outs" with your child. You don't want your hard work in training your child in good manners to vanish because the sitter is reluctant to enforce rules or doesn't even know what they are. Explain where and how your little one is accustomed to a time-out.

• Emphasize again and again that she has great influence on the character of your child, that she must impress on your child the concepts of fair play and the difference between right and wrong. At the same time, insist that your children treat her with respect, and not invade her privacy.

• If a maid or caregiver lives with you, insist that the children not burst in on her room but respect her privacy. "No, Patty, you may not go through Maria's purse. Put those things back immediately." "No, Josh, you may not burst in on Maria like that in her room. Never go in her room unless she asks you to."

SPECIAL TRAINING FOR WORKERS IN GRAND HOUSES

Cheerful, clean, attractive people to work in your house are a treasure if you find them, but they usually need training. *Be creative about finding the people who can train your new staff.*

Housekeeper

Make an appointment with the head housekeeper of a first-class hotel in your city to come to you on her day off to discuss the possibility of her training your own housekeeper and maids on her time off, for which she will be handsomely compensated by you. It's better to square your arrangement with the hotel management, so that they don't find out by accident and suspect the head housekeeper of taking advantage of her hotel job. You can always promise, in addition, to send a lot of business to that hotel, to make them happier about doing this favor for you.

The housekeeper can train the maids in:
- Making the perfect bed.
- Keeping the bathrooms in pristine order.
- Caring for the floor coverings—wall-to-wall carpeting, area rugs, wood floors, and hard surfaces.
- Removing dirt from every part of the house, and sprucing up, whether it's plumping all the pillows, washing the mud left in bad weather on the front hallway floors, coping with dog accidents on the rugs, removing dog hairs from the upholstery, removing dead flowers from the vases, keeping silver bibelots polished, aligning window shades and draperies properly, and removing dust from the lampshades as well as bits of "flotsam and jetsam" found down beneath the sofa cushions!

The "Upstairs Maid"

She should be knowledgeable about fine linens—which should be hand-washed and which should be sent to the dry cleaners. She should brush the coats and suits in the closet, polish the shoes and brush the suede ones, know how to launder Madame's fine lingerie, and know and care for the "look" of her employers and their living abode, little details that you and your spouse may never have thought you would need to know!

Butler

If you have a full-time butler (which you probably don't), he generally drives for you, does errands, helps with the housecleaning, serves your meals, and tends bar. Again, arrange with the best hotel or restaurant in town to let you hire their prized maître d'hôtel, on one of his days off, to train your butler in the proper service of food and drink. He should learn:
- how to serve a seated meal properly.
- how to open a bottle of wine or champagne as though he's been doing it all his life.
- how to make and serve the cocktail du jour drinks, pass the nuts and hors d'oeuvres, and know when to replenish a guest's drink.
- how to maintain a proper inventory of the locked-up liquor supply, with special attention to the wines needed for any particular party.
- how to coordinate with the housekeeper so that the silver is properly polished in time for the big parties, the glasses shiny and spot-free, the fancy cocktail napkins and table linens laundered and in place, and the proper coat

checking facilities set up (coat racks either stored in the house or rented from the caterer).

• how to coordinate with the valet parking service to keep the guest parking running smoothly.

• how to instruct the extra staff called in for your big, important parties. He should know how to work with any caterer's staff, to show them how things are to be done "your way," the right way.

Making Your Household Staff Function Efficiently

Be sure to:
1. Make a daily list of their duties and responsibilities.
2. Arrange for their own food—to make sure there is enough delivered for their needs, including when you are out of town. They should not expect to eat the filet mignon and veal chops being served at your party, but they should have good food like their choice of fish, beef, green vegetables, and pasta.
3. Make sure they dress properly. Uniforms are practical and save on a person's wardrobe. In a "grand house," you have the right to request that your domestic staff wear uniforms that you purchase for them.

   If they refuse to wear them, considering them demeaning, don't argue. Let them wear their own clothes, but you can demand that they have a neat, professional appearance.

   Butler: White jacket, white shirt, black bow tie, black pants, black hose and shoes in spring and summer . . . Black jacket and pants in winter, although a white jacket may be worn informally during the day in any season.

   Chauffeur: A black suit, winter or summer weight, with white shirt, black necktie, leather gloves, and black chauffeur's cap. Works around the house by day in khakis and white cotton shirt or polo shirt.

   Maids: Today's uniforms are usually short-sleeved, and come in black, pale gray, and all other pastel colors. (My favorite: pastel-striped dress with white collar and cuffs.)

What Should Your Domestic Staff Call You and What Should You Call Them?

• Call them what they wish to be called ("Jim" for the butler or "Mrs. Graybar" for an older, conservative housekeeper, if that is what she prefers).

• If your staff is of the old school (over fifty), have them address you by "Mr. or Mrs." with your last name. Many young people today will only use first names, no matter to whom they are speaking. Some mistakenly consider addressing someone by a last name as demeaning to the young person. This is wrong but not worth fighting a war over. Let it ride.

• The person in your kitchen who prepares regular meals would be referred to as "Cook," but if yours is a "grand house" with someone in the kitchen with impressive experience and a well-established reputation, call him or her "Chef."

THE "CHARACTER FACTOR"

(Namely, your good character and your treatment of the staff brings out their good character!)

1. No matter how much you pay your staff, how many days off they have, or how fancy their living quarters are, if you do not treat them with respect, it will be an unhappy, disastrously run household. You will kill their morale and remove any motivation they might have had to serve you well. If you treat them unkindly or as anything other than as human beings just like yourself, *you* will be the real loser.

2. Know the names of their children. Know what is going on of import in their private lives. In other words, treat them like human beings. When a daughter graduates from high school, get her a present, and try to help her win a scholarship to college. When a member of their family is ill, make sure that person receives the proper medical treatment.

3. Thank them and praise them for a job well done—after a party, for example. As soon as dinner is over, while the guests are drinking after-dinner coffee, go into the kitchen and say "Well done!" to the cook/chef and the wait staff.

4. Criticize them without raising your voice, so that others cannot hear you, saving them from embarrassment.

5. Remember their birthdays with cards, perhaps some money or a present, or a birthday cake.

6. Make sure, if they're religious, that they get to services every week.

7. Give them credit for having brains. Give them the daily newspaper and weekly newsmagazines when you're finished with them.

8. Lend them books, if they're interested. Lend them a computer, so they can improve their computer skills while living with you.

9. Encourage their mental development and job aspirations, even if the last thing you want to see happen is that they move up and on, out of domestic service. You will prove what a great person you are, and no doubt they will prove what grateful people they are in many ways.

10. Include any caregiver, maid, or wait staff in your holiday family celebrations. If they live with you, they are members of the family, and
you should treat them as such.

IF YOU'RE USING A CATERER FOR YOUR PARTY

- Don't keep changing the menu or number of guests.
- Be sure to have everything clearly understood well before the party, even
details such as will there be regular coffee and decaf, too? Who is supplying the
cocktail napkins? Will sugar and sweetener be passed with the after-dinner coffee? At what time is dinner to be served? At what exact hour is the bar to be
closed at the end of the evening?
- Specify how the wait staff is to be dressed. Generally, black trousers, white
shirts, and black ties for the men, black skirts or slacks for the women, with
white shirts and perhaps even black ties. No athletic shoes or jeans!
- Have a place for the catering staff to change and leave their personal
effects.
- Be sure to arrange for them to be fed at some point.

CHAPTER 2

The Manners
That Make Children Great

Teaching your children manners is also teaching them values, ethics, and morals. The child's character develops and is shaped through his life experiences, but also in a major way through the influence and teaching of the people to whom he is close and whom he loves. In the best of all worlds, parents and children are politer to one another than to anyone else.

Since our children are our greatest national resource, and since in the opinion of many the moral fabric of this country is unraveling, a parent's responsibility in raising children today is monumental!

It's a heavy enough burden when there are two parents, but in today's society, with both parents working or with so many single, divorced, or remarried parents, the problems bearing down on the child seem to reproduce themselves like quickly dividing cells. Among current problem situations:

- Hostile stepparents and stepsiblings
- Hostile in-laws in a new marriage situation
- Latchkey children left on their own too much
- Victims of drug and alcohol abuse by parents in the home
- Children with undiagnosed learning difficulties
- The bad influence of peer pressure
- Fear of what is happening in the world

That's a pretty heavy sackful of problems, but it does not take into account the resilience of children, particularly their native intelligence and their durability. Regardless of the problems both children and parents face in today's society, single parents can take heart. It takes only *one caring parent* (or relative or any loving adult close to the child) to shape and mold the child's character *for the good.*

Manners, together with ethics, values, and morals, are the basis of character, and these forces for good really cannot be separated. They are a homogenous unit. In the final analysis, we must do all we can to show children the right way—and then trust them. They are the leaders of tomorrow and will have to deal with the mess today's adults are leaving them. They are our nation's hope and will most likely do far better than the present generation of adults, who have been watching rather helplessly the unraveling of the moral fiber of our country in an era of drugs, crime, and sexual excess.

Children need us to teach them *discipline,* for one thing, as well as *a firm sense of right and wrong.* If you are not a parent, you can be a terrific aunt or uncle, godparent, grandparent, cousin, stepfather, stepmother, stepbrother or -sister, nurse, baby-sitter, day-care center director, teacher, pastor, youth center director, coach, community volunteer, Big Brother, Big Sister, and office role model or mentor. Collectively and individually, we have enormous influence on a child with whom we spend time.

The ability to choose between the assistance offered by good people versus that offered by bad people is the moment of truth for a young person. The selection of peers and choice of leaders to follow means the success or failure of a young life.

HOW A CHILD LEARNS TO DISTINGUISH BETWEEN RIGHT AND WRONG

THE EXAMPLE OF HER PARENTS

Children learn from their parents' behavior. If parents do something a child feels is basically wrong, or if they accept behavior on the child's part that is basically wrong, "wrong" soon turns to "right." For example:

• A child who hears his parents talking to each other about new ways in which they can cheat on their income tax will conclude that it's all right to cheat the government.

• A child who watches a parent trying to get out of a ticket by lying to a police officer will conclude that disrespect for the law and lying to a policeman are acceptable.

• When a child grabs a package of candy from the supermarket rack one day and a small packet of cookies the next, and her mother sees that but doesn't pay for the item, the child will conclude that it's all right to steal from the supermarket.

• When a child's mother puts coins in a slot to get a newspaper from a rack on the street and then takes three papers (one for herself and two for her neighbors) but pays for only one, the child will conclude that it's all right to pay for one thing but to help yourself to more if you can get away with it.

• When a child returns from a birthday party with a prize won in a game and tells his parents that he cheated in order to win it and then they don't take proper action, that is, make the child confess and then apologize to the birthday child's parents, he will conclude that it's all right to cheat. Since his parents don't insist that he return the prize, he believes that it's all right to cheat if you're not caught.

• When a parent regularly returns from the office with a briefcase full of office supplies for personal use at home, the child will conclude that it's all right to steal things from the office.

• A child might hear her mother say, upon receipt of a duplicate order of something that already arrived from a mail order house, "How nice! They sent a second set of glasses by mistake. I'll keep it to give to Mary Ellen for a wedding gift." The child then concludes that if the catalogue retailer makes a mistake, it's perfectly all right to take advantage of that.

When children see parents accept situations that are morally wrong, it inspires them to grow up to become liars, cheats, and thieves—or perhaps extortionists, inside traders, and stock manipulators. If we parents do not teach our children ethics, how else will they learn?

MORAL LESSONS A SMALL CHILD GLEANS FROM PARENTS THROUGH READING AND CONVERSATION

A child learns to understand right from wrong at a very early age—with the help of his parents—through words spoken in a conversation and words read in a book. For example, when reading aloud a bedtime story—a fairy tale—with his little girl at night, a father might comment as he reads along, "Now, that's a bad person who would do a thing like that, isn't it?"

His daughter would say, "Yes, a very naughty person."

The father might add, "You'd *never* do a thing like that, now, would you, Suzy? It's wrong to do something like that. Even if the other kids in your class think it is okay, you know it isn't, right?"

A lesson would hopefully have been learned, and father and daughter could continue happily along in their story.

As they go through all the stories, week after week, with her father emphasizing the *bad* things people do and the *good* things people do, with punishment meted out for the bad things, the little girl will develop a growing sense of right and wrong, identifying herself always with the right.

Her father might explain to her once in a while how mean it is to be cruel to someone—in other words, "You don't do a bad thing only because you'll be caught and punished, but more important, you don't do a bad thing because it hurts someone else." The little girl will begin to imitate her father when they come to a certain part of the story, reacting with sympathy for the victim of an injustice. Even at age three or four, she will be developing a social conscience.

A child sitting at the dinner table can absorb any number of little moral lessons from the way his parents talk about what has happened in the world today—in their city, in their small social circle, or in their respective work environments. A child can pick up the parents' reactions to someone who has been dealt an injustice, to someone who has done a bad thing and is being punished for it, or to someone who is suffering because of another person's bad deed. When a parent answers a child's questions with patience, the child will come to see through the parents' eyes the drama of good and evil and the need for one person to help another. A child might, for example:

- Hear her parents discussing how to help a friend of theirs who is in financial need.
- Hear about a person who stole money from someone else but was caught and will pay for that crime.
- Listen to his parents' creative ideas of ways to extend a helping hand to a friend of theirs who is ill.
- Learn about heroism in the description of a fireman's or policeman's rescue of someone.
- Overhear the parents' plans to help a family in which there has been a death.
- Learn to take action personally when something sad happens to a friend.

Learning how to take action is particularly important. Take the example of a young boy who has learned that his friend's puppy recently died.

"Bobby," his mother might say, "Jimmy must feel very sad that his puppy died yesterday."

"He feels awful bad."

"Well, let's do something about that, don't you think?"

"What do you mean?"

"Well, how about doing something to make Jimmy feel better?"

"Let's do that. But . . . how?"

"Well, maybe you could bring him a present to cheer him up."

"Yes, a present! What will you get him as a present?"

"I thought I'd let you figure that out, Bobby."

"I don't know."

"What would you like to receive if your puppy had just died?"

"Well, maybe I'd like a new car to race."

"Do you want to go with me to the store this afternoon to see if there's a little car you think Jimmy would like?"

"Yes, let's go, Mommy. I'll make Jimmy feel better. I'll get him a nice car to race around and around—or maybe a puppy from the toy store that looks like his."

These are important lessons to be learned.

WHEN YOUR CHILD IS CURIOUS
ABOUT A DISABLED PERSON HE SEES IN PUBLIC

When a child encounters a person on crutches, an unusually small person, someone with a bizarre feature, or perhaps someone who is all bandaged up, often he will stare and then ask you in a loud voice, "What's wrong with that man?" or say, "Look at that funny-looking woman's face." You should, of course, tell your child to be quiet, not to stare, and that you will explain about that "very nice man" (or woman) when you both get home. A child might become frightened by seeing someone who is "different" in any way, so if necessary calm him in a low voice. If you are close by the person your child has asked about, whisper an apology as you leave—something like, "I'm very sorry my child said what he did. He just doesn't understand, and I apologize for any discomfort his remarks have given you."

THE HELP THAT RELIGIOUS FAITH CAN GIVE

In my opinion—and as a result of observing the behavior of people through many decades—if you believe in God, one of the greatest gifts you can give to your children is a religious faith. Even if you don't have a faith yourself or attend church, temple, or mosque services regularly, get your children to a service once a week. You might try different churches until they find one they like. By getting them to a house of worship regularly, you may be giving them the strongest and most effective help and support they will ever have in their lives, and you will certainly be giving them the opportunity to learn about right and wrong.

Parents who read Bible and other religious stories every night to their children, explaining the moral lessons contained in those pages, instill a respect not only for God (and Allah) but for other human beings in the hearts of their children. A respect for the Supreme Being and for other humans is, after all, the foundation of manners, morals, ethics, and values.

BASIC BEHAVIOR RULES YOUR CHILD
OF TEN OR OLDER SHOULD KNOW

By the time a boy and girl reach the age of ten, they should be reasonably well-socialized human beings, with good manners. In other words, they should be aware of almost all of the important tenets of good manners, lacking only the adult polish and the behavior nuances still to come—hopefully, by the end of their high school years.

• As your children grow, from preschool age and onward, ask your public librarian about books on children's manners that you can read with them. More come into the marketplace every year, including comic books featuring beloved cartoon figures and fairy tale characters. They make the learning of manners fun instead of a chore.

• Help your child make a game out of manners. For example, you can devise a multiple choice quiz for your eight-year-old, as a friend of mine did. She and her daughter worked on their quiz together, and once it was put into good English, it was run off on a photocopying machine. The third grader had great fun giving the quiz to her classmates at school. Here are some of their twenty-five questions:

You spill spaghetti sauce on the tablecloth at your friend's house. You:
  a. Wipe it up with your fingers and then clean your fingers on your dress.
  b. Run out to the kitchen to get more sauce, because your friend's mom wants you to enjoy your dinner.
  c. Apologize to your friend's mom, and then ask your friend's mom if you may get some wet paper towels from the kitchen to do a better job of cleaning it up.

You receive duplicate presents from guests at your birthday party. You:
  a. Give one back to the friend you like least and ask her to exchange it for something else.
  b. Thank both friends and tell them you will really have fun with the gift, and that you will exchange the other one yourself for something you would also like, and you will then be able to thank them for two wonderful presents instead of just one.
  c. Tell them you are going to take both back and get a much bigger, nicer present in exchange.

A boy hits you during recess. You:
  a. Go up to him during the next recess and hit him back—only harder.
  b. Tell him that you are going to forget it this time, because he obviously didn't mean to do what he did, but if he does it again, you will make him very sorry that he did.
  c. Go screaming to the school principal to get him punished.

Correct answers: c, b, b

The Basics

By the time your child has reached the age of ten, he or she should have established a pattern of behavior that reflects a developing sense of manners.

The well-behaved child should:

• Stand whenever an adult from the outside enters the room—even if it is just your friend from next door popping in to borrow something, and even if the child is doing her own thing (listening to music, talking to pals, watching TV, or reading). Whenever an adult comes into the room, the child should rise automatically and say something in greeting, even if it is as brief as, "Hello, Mrs. Smith." The child doesn't need to keep popping up and down every time Mrs. Smith comes through the room on her visit. Once is enough. If a parent introduces someone the child has never met before, a handshake should go along with the child's greeting of "Hello."

• Stand by his or her chair at the dining table until all adults are seated. (A boy pulling the chair back for an older woman guest is, alas, an anachronism.)

• Pass the food first to the guests and her parents before helping herself; wait to begin eating until an adult has begun to do so.

• Defer to adults in conversation (which means simply that the child doesn't interrupt conversation in progress but waits until there is a pause to say what she wants to say).

• Be kind to and protective of younger brothers and sisters.

• Have good table manners (see chapter 9, "Table Manners That Take You Anywhere").

• Know how to talk to an adult and help act as a parent's cohost. For example, when the daughter of the household meets a visitor in the hallway of her house, who has come to see her father, she should shake his hand and say with a smile, "Hello, Mr. Gray. I'm Amalia, nice to see *you* again. Here, I'll put your coat in the closet."

"Thank you, Amalia, nice to see you again."

"My father will be down right away. Would you like to sit down in the living room?" She then shows him into the living room and turns on some more lights in the room to make it more cheerful.

With this Amalia has done her duty and made the guest comfortable, so she may now leave, unless she can make an even greater effort to stay and chat until her father arrives for his meeting with Mr. Gray.

Other marks of well-mannered children:

• A child should realize that in public places it is rude to make a lot of noise with friends that upsets other people (on public transportation, at the beach, in a movie, on the street, or wherever).

- He should refrain from yelling to others in the house. (Hopefully, the parents don't yell, either!)

- She should show respect for elders at all times. That means no sassing, acting fresh, or defying authority. (Respect for parents, grandparents, teachers, the pastor, policemen, and anyone else *in a position of authority* should be instinctive.)

- He should answer when spoken to and not just maintain a sullen silence.

- The well-mannered child doesn't interrupt anyone else who is speaking.

- She respects the family home—and those of friends, too—which means not tracking in mud onto the floors, not putting feet up on a table or on the arms of the sofa, not eating on the floor and getting food on the carpet (particularly hard-to-clean items like greasy popcorn, pizza, soda, and melted ice-cream bars).

- The child should follow the house rules as to when and how the telephone is used and be able to take careful telephone messages for everyone else in the house.

- Children should keep their own rooms straightened on a routine basis.

- They should have good bathroom manners, including not staying in the bathroom so long that others don't have their allotted time. They should routinely pick up after themselves so that the bathroom remains tidy.

- A child should do any assigned household chores cheerfully, punctually, and efficiently—without wearing a long face.

- The child plays music at a low decibel level so as to allow others in the house to go about their tasks in relative peace.

- He is mindful of the privacy of everyone else in the house, including that of siblings.

- She refrains from upsetting others with a loud cracking of chewing gum or an explosion of bubble gum.

- They do not push in ahead of anyone: they wait their proper turn in line, to go through a door, into an elevator, or onto an escalator or bus. They do not jostle others while walking down a crowded passageway, and they do not walk down the street four or five abreast, forcing everyone to move aside.

- They always say "Thank you" after anyone steps back to allow them through or holds a door for them.

- The well-mannered child is a good host and does what his guest wants to do, not what he wants to do. He does not desert a guest to go off to follow a personal agenda but offers a guest what the guest would like to eat, and lets the guest select the TV programs.

- She says "Excuse me" when inadvertently brushing against anyone or when hurrying by and obliging someone to make way for her.

- The well-mannered child has been taught to write a thank-you note for every gift (including any from grandparents, aunts, uncles, or friends of any age) or after every meal at a friend's house or as a friend's guest in a restaurant.

- He is punctual and doesn't hold up the family when they are going somewhere.
- He is respectful of the driver of a car and does not bother that person, knowing that is dangerous.
- The child is respectful of any laws governing the environment—discards litter properly and is careful of trees, lawns, flowers, and bushes when playing.
- He has learned—and scrupulously follows—the rules of safety (and good manners), whether crossing the street (with a green light), rowing a boat on the lake (and observing the safety rules in the water), riding a bike (and following traffic rules), ice-skating (and being careful not to run into people), and the like.
- The well-mannered child is kind to animals and never mistreats them.

TEENAGERS NEED A FEW MORE RULES

Above and beyond the general rules that all children from ages ten to twenty should know, there are a few special ones that particularly apply to teenagers.

Even if their friends have no rules, your teenage children should be mindful of the following:

- Their noise level in the house (from the radio, tapes, VCR, TV, digital systems, or even a musical instrument they're learning to play—drums, for example).
- Their handling of your car or their own. They should be clear about the unacceptability of using up your gas and not informing you, borrowing your car without your permission, eating with friends in your car without a thorough cleanup of the resulting mess, blocking the driveway with their own car, and the like.
- Not picking up after their parties in your house. Make it clear you object to their leaving the sink full of dishes, ashtrays full of broken potato chips, illegally consumed empty beer cans stashed beneath your slipcovered sofa and easy chairs, and the like.
- Drinking up all the cold sodas in the fridge and not replacing them with fresh bottles. Leaving half-empty cans of soda around to tip over and stain your floors is even more irritating.
- Getting telephone calls from their friends late at night, and tying up the house telephone all the time.
- Strewing athletic equipment and clothes all over the house—such as a smelly basketball sneaker in the entrance foyer, a jockstrap on a radiator, a pair of running shorts draped on the back of the sofa, a sweaty sweatshirt and pair of athletic socks drying out over the big lampshade. The young future Olympic contenders of America often make their home resemble a run-down gymnasium!
- Their behavior regarding drugs and alcohol. They should not only know

that they may not use them but that their friends may not use them in your house.

But with all of that, we should remember that the teenagers in this country are still the sweetest kids in the world!

TWENTY-TWO COMMON TEENAGE EXAMPLES
OF A FAMILY'S BAD MANNERS AND OVERSIGHTS

1. To ignore a request from the parents, or even to "pass the buck" to another sibling, when there's a chore to be done, an errand to be run, a favor to be granted.
2. To be someone who cannot keep a secret, who is the family "snitch."
3. To go through a family member's mail or listen to telephone calls, read e-mails, or commit any other sin against the privacy of someone else in the family.
4. To borrow a car, a piece of clothing, or anything without the owner's express permission, and once given, failing to return it in a timely fashion and in perfect condition.
5. To refuse to lend a possession desperately needed by a sibling, whether it's a car, a piece of clothing, or an electronic device needed for work.
6. To make fun of someone in the family who may have erred or shown poor judgment, thus humiliating that person even more.
7. To criticize a family member's friends, including the parents'.
8. To refuse to help make the house presentable when company is coming.
9. To mistreat or not give proper care to a sibling's pet.
10. To taunt a sibling about a boyfriend or girlfriend.
11. To be cavalier about immediately transmitting a message for a family member.
12. To point out a sibling's inadequacies to the person's peers at school.
13. To make fun of a family member's handicap or affliction.
14. To react without sympathy when a sibling is in crisis, whether it's depression over a boyfriend or girlfriend, humiliation over an athletic failure, or anguish over not being admitted to the college of choice.
15. To be unhelpful or even rude to a parent's or grandparent's visitor.
16. To feel one is above helping a sibling in need of advice about physical appearance, yet feel free to criticize that sibling on matters that are termed "unwelcome interference."
17. To be a bad influence on younger siblings because of the child's own behavior in the home.

18. For the child to think it's "cool" to show disrespect to a parent; or for parents to feel they can show lack of respect for a child.

19. For any member of the family to be too busy to lend a sympathetic ear to anyone else.

20. To remain angry at any family member, regardless of who's right and who's wrong. "The family" is too precious to allow anything to seriously rupture its cohesiveness.

21. To allow the younger members of "the tribe" to abrogate their duty to take care of their elders, when they need compassionate care.

22. To try to cause further divisions in the family between step-relatives, half brothers and sisters, with all generations trying to outmaneuver one another.

HOUSEHOLD TELEPHONE RULES

1. Whoever answers the phone does it promptly, efficiently, and politely, taking messages, even soliciting helpful information (like cell phone numbers and hotel names), and doesn't forget to relay them.

2. Whoever answers has been trained to answer by the second or third ring, and that goes for whoever is in the house, from the caregiver to Grandma. There is no yelling about whose responsibility it is to answer. Whoever is the closest gets it. No one is allowed to say, "I know it's not for me, so *you* get it."

3. Whoever answers understands the importance of the quality and volume of the voice. The voice answering should proudly represent this family in its best possible light and not sound like a whining, illiterate animal. If you are feeling out of sorts, don't take it out on the person at the other end of the line, because then the caller will feel that yours is a nasty house. Force a cheerful note into your voice, and in doing that, you will feel better yourself, and you will certainly make life easier for the person who has called.

4. Cold callers are treated with respect, not yelled at abusively. If the child tells his mother, "It's a lady from the XYZ Insurance Company wanting to talk to you about a new something or other," his mother should say, "Tell her we have full coverage and are not interested in anything. *But be sure you thank her for calling us.*" Explain to your child that one must be polite to the unwelcome solicitor.

5. Tell your children that "phone hogs" are not tolerated in the house. Whether they have their own cell phones or use the family line, it's all the same. The spending of hours on the phone is wasted time and energy, creates noise pollution in the house, and keeps young people away from their studies or from any number of more worthwhile pursuits.

6. Teach your children that the world is not sweet and kind, and that people will be rude to them, hang up on them, and will speak to them in unpleasant ways on the telephone. Your children will, however, sound resolutely upbeat on the instrument, and will do a great acting job. If a child says to you, "But why do I have to be nice on the telephone with someone who isn't nice?" your answer might be, "Because that person doesn't know any better, and guess what, you *do* know better!"

A Few Dating Manners

Whether it's a boy asking a girl for a date or vice versa, rejection is always feared, and when it comes, it's always worse than one ever imagined it could be!

When a boy asks a girl on a date:
 • He should ask her far enough ahead so that she has time to prepare, and so that she doesn't think she was the fifth and last person he called (even if it's true).
 • He should square with her as to all the details—where they are going, what they are going to do, who is going to do it with them. This gives her the chance to coordinate her wardrobe with any other girl who will be along (important for a girl's sense of security).
 • He should be punctual. Every minute he is late is stressful for her. As the minutes tick by, she probably is wondering if she is being stood up.
 • At the end of the date, he should see her to her door, not leave her fumbling for her key outside her house. It is no longer just good manners to see her safely inside, it is a question of security.

When a girl asks a boy on a date, unless she is a beauty, she often has to sell him on the idea of going out with her far more aggressively than he would have to sell her if he were doing the asking. Unless he's a total disaster, a boy can say, "Wanna do somethin' Saturday night?" and chances are the girl will quickly say "Cool." This unfair situation is just one of the sad facts of life in a society that still clings to the outdated notion of gallantry—that a man is always supposed to ask a woman for a date (even if it doesn't work that way).

A girl can successfully ask a boy for a date if she takes these steps in preparation. (These suggestions will help a boy asking a girl for a date.)
 • She gives him plenty of lead time, so he knows he isn't a last-minute substitute for someone else.
 • She gets (or arranges to purchase) tickets to a really marvelous event in keeping with the boy's interests, whether it's a game, movie, concert, or seats in the audience for the *David Letterman Show.*

• The shy one extends the invitation by writing everything in a note, showing how well organized she is—including that she is providing transportation and paying for the tickets, dinner, and parking. If she were to invite him face to face, her nerves might get the better of her—she could botch the job of selling this beautifully planned evening. If she were to invite him to his face, she might also scare him into a quick regret to her invitation. A note gives a shy young man time to savor the proposal for all its plus attributes. It also gives him time to wiggle out of the invitation by finding the perfect excuse.

The girl should keep the date quiet in advance and not go talking all over about it so that they are both teased by their friends before the date even takes place.

Out on the date, both should remember:

• To be appropriately and nicely dressed for each other. When they meet for the date, he shouldn't look as though he's just finished a shift in a coal mine and she shouldn't look as though she just finished cleaning the garage. Young people should make an effort to look clean and in fashion on a date—whether it's a dressy occasion or an informal get-together with just a bunch of friends. The theory is that the bigger the effort you make for a date, the more fun it will turn out to be (an old wives' tale that is mostly true!).

• To have it completely understood by both who pays for what on the date, so that there are no embarrassing moments. They should be prepared to offer to help each other out with money if things cost more than the person who originally asked for the date estimated. They can agree to "go dutch," if that is the best way to handle financial matters.

• To let their respective parents know where they will be, and to follow the rules of the more stringent of the two sets of parents on the time the date is to end.

• To give each other proper attention during the date and not flirt with other people present.

• To be agreeable to the plans made, whatever they may be, and not to try to change everything around—and particularly not to complain and whine in disapproval as the date continues.

• Never to speak pejoratively of the other—before, during, or after the date. The boy who moans to his friends, "I'm stuck with a real dog as a date tomorrow night," and the girl who describes her date to her friends as "a complete nerd—it shows you how desperate I must be to get out the door," do not sound cool to their friends; they sound mean and untrustworthy.

• To thank the other person at the end of the date, and within a week to write a thank-you note to the date—or the date's parents if a family meal or a weekend visit was involved.

Making the Rules Easier to Take

• When you give children the rules of citizenship for your household, make sure they adhere to them, but also that they understand the reason and logic behind them. ("Johnny, one of your chores is to rinse the dishes, load the dishwasher, and clean up. You didn't do it—again. Each one of us has our own chores. Would you prefer to do your own job, or to force me to do it and miss preparing the next meal before I leave for work? I think I would be very angry and you would be very hungry if that happened.")

• Instead of ordering them to act in a certain way, give them the humanity behind the rules of good manners toward others. ("Jane, the reason I ask you to stand up when Mrs. Johnson comes into our house is because she is an older friend of mine, a member of the mayor's staff, and she deserves respect from a young person. Someday, you'll be her age and you will be very pleased when a young person gets up to shake your hand and gives you a cheery Hello when you enter her house.")

• Criticize your child's friends only in private, and only fairly. ("I know he's a good friend of yours, so I'm telling this to you without the others hearing me. He is disrespectful of this house. He puts his dirty boots up on the coffee table and mars the wood, he leaves his coat lying on the floor instead of hanging it up, and he uses bad language all the time. I think you ought to tell him quietly that he should respect this house—and us—more than he does when he comes here.")

• Listen to your child when he feels passionate about something. Check to see if you have laid down unfair rules in comparison to all the other parents whom you admire. ("I hate to bother you, Sue, but I'm just trying to find out if Jim and I are being unfair to Jim, Jr. We have always ordered him home on Saturday nights by eleven P.M., and he claims all the other kids don't have to be in until one A.M. What's the rule in your household, and do you know what it is in other classmates' families?")

• Don't, however, go against your basic religious and philosophical convictions, just to please your children. ("I don't care if the other kids are allowed to miss church this Sunday to go to the circus. In this family we go to church every Sunday. It's one of the things that makes us strong. We thank God for our blessings, and we don't abandon something so important just because something else conflicts that would be a lot more fun.")

• Don't remove their last particle of self-esteem if your children fail at something. Instead, fire them up with self-confidence to be able to face the next challenge. ("Hey, everyone has to lose at times. Not making the team does not mean you're a failure. You're a wonderful child, and you'll have other opportunities. You'll do better the next time. You're no less a person in this family's eyes, so buck up and forget it.")

• Give your kids the opportunity to be present at dinner with your adult friends; teach them to benefit from and to look forward to these experiences. ("Mr. and Mrs. Wellington are joining us for dinner tonight. He was a great tight end in his college football days and is now a lawyer who does a lot of volunteer work for our community. He's an inspiration. And his wife is very nice—she works in retailing and can tell you all about the fashion world. You're lucky to have these two here and to be able to ask them anything you want.")

• Make it possible for them to spend ample time with their grandparents on both sides, whether you are married or divorced. Grandparents provide an important cross-generational influence, and a child's bonding with her grandparents will be one of the greatest affirmative influences on her life. Even if your feelings toward your ex-mate are bitter, never take it out on your ex-in-laws. Instead, keep them close to your children. They can play an important supporting role as long as they live.

• When a child has a major role (playing in a piano concert, appearing in a class play, playing with the team in an important game), be there. No matter how important the business deal, you can take enough time off at least to appear, even if you have to leave early. No matter how demanding your employer is, you can always explain and work double compensatory time to repay your employer for your absences on these occasions. If you positively cannot attend an important occasion relating to your child, ask a favorite relative or friend of yours to stand in for you and make a full report afterward. (That is better than being a complete no-show.)

• Make a game out of anything from a family physical fitness project to an intellectual exercise, such as reading the daily newspaper thoroughly and then answering an informal quiz on its contents. When the family does things together, when conviviality and affection set the mood, children learn and grow in emotional stability. They receive love, and they learn how to give it back to others. Someday they will raise their own children in the same fashion.

• Ask them at the end of each day how their day went, so you can detect anything from a little problem to a real hurt. "All right, now it's Billy's turn. What happened today?" If Billy says something "just terrible" happened at school today, his parents and siblings can all contribute advice on how to handle it. As his parents, you can remind him again of the best of those problem-solving ideas when he says good night.

• Describe your own day, too, to your children in the evening hour. They should understand what you do, be able to describe it accurately to others, and feel proud of you. It helps them to know grown-ups have problems, too, which they also have to work to solve. ("I had a really bad day. The monthly figures came in, down again, and the boss told me to let three more people go in our department—at once. I had to tell them there were no more jobs for them, and it hurt. But, in answer to your question of what else I did, I sat them down and began calling other companies that might be able to use them. I wrote them enthusiastic letters of reference. I told them this job change might be a great opportunity for them. I'm spending this whole week helping them clear their desks, go through the Help Wanted ads, and write good résumés. I'm doing everything I can to help them.") Children feel more secure when they hear their parents talk about helping out other people; it teaches them to be unselfish and helpful to others. It shows them how problem solvers work.

• When you buy young children clothing, they have no choice but to wear it. When they develop a sense of fashion, which can occur early in grade school, allow them as much freedom as possible in making their own selections. From junior high school on, students want to be dressed according to the latest trends in their school, to which parents a generation away can't possibly be attuned. Within the limits of budget and propriety, let your children select what they want to wear.

WHAT'S A PIECE OF FURNITURE?

If the tradition of teaching manners and values around the family dining table no longer exists in your home, like so many others, then a substitute can and should be found. You can be sitting around a coffee table, or perched on a stool in the kitchen. You can be hanging around the fireplace, or sitting uncomfortably on juvenile furniture in some child's nursery while you make believe there's a party going on with the dolls and bears. An adult can affect a child whether in the act of driving him to school, watching that child skateboard (and applying the Band-Aids after), waiting in a movie line, or walking to church. Conversational targets of opportunity will always present themselves. An adult can make one point understood today, and another two days from now. The child will be listening even if he pretends not to be. The dining room isn't the only room in the house, the dining table the only piece of furniture.

An uncle can do a terrific job working on his nephew's manners at a McDonald's. You don't need great furniture for that. You need someone with a heart who cares about someone else. Ketchup is ketchup, whether you're spilling it all over a plastic table, with a paper carton holding your burger, or whether your burger is on a porcelain plate on a Chippendale mahogany table purchased from a Christie's auction estate sale.

You could easily spend your entire lifetime worrying over the sad state of our society, but action is far better than worry. It takes a lot of energy and time to worry; it takes the same amount of energy and time to turn in another direction, to rediscover the importance of family in our lives, and to help other people find their own substitute families. We can be and even should be a member of more than one family today. There are people needing us wherever we look, wherever we go. Under the heading of "rights and privileges," it is my contention that it is a right and a privilege for everyone to serve as a family member for someone who does not have one. We have no idea of the power of our own example. When we intercede in an argument, for example, and soothe both sides, we are not only stopping the fight but making both sides feel better. We have done a "There, there, it will be all right" kind of act that a parent should have done for his child. When you see a child stop, unprompted, to pick up something for an elderly or disabled stranger, and you say, "What a nice person you are to have done that!" you are reinforcing that child's niceness. Your smile and tone of voice are high praise to him. You are playing the role of a parent when that child might not have a parent around, or perhaps has a parent who does not care about such matters.

Family *is* all around us. People are all around us. We can turn one into the other. We ourselves should become family to anyone who needs us and whom we choose to help. Within the family good behavior is taught, rewarded, and passed down to posterity. We can do that with our own relatives, the children of friends, and our children's classmates. We can do that to a stranger with a smile and a compliment for something that person does. We need to show good behavior, reward it, and reinforce it.

A group of children return from your daughter's dance recital rehearsal and troop into your kitchen for a soda, cookies, and carrot sticks.

"Your mom's really nice," you hear them telling your daughter. A high compliment. Sweet golden words for your daughter to hear. "Your mom always lets us come to your house," they continue explaining to your child. You've got a bunch of little girls in pink tutus in your kitchen who think you're great. Later you hear two of your daughter's guests not being nice to one another, having a word fight, and there are even tears.

"Hey, hey." You decide to interrupt them in a softly chiding voice. "We don't do that, we don't make people unhappy in our house." (You have now equated manners with happiness, a smart move.)

"But she—" One is protesting loudly, and the other one, too. You interrupt them. "I don't care who's at fault or who started it. I want both of you to shake hands right now, look each other in the eye, smile, and say, 'Sorry.' Have you got that? okay, do it now!"

They do it, very sheepishly, you tell them how wonderful they are, and their smiles start to become genuine. The storm has blown over, and the little girls in pink tutus have learned something that might possibly stick. They will also be more anxious than ever to come to your house again, and each time they do, you can give them another lesson or two in how to get along in this world. They can feel the spirit of compromise and cooperation in your house. You make them into virtual members of your family. Your own daughter has learned something important, too—to try mediation instead of accusation when two people are disagreeing. You've just passed something down to her. You've taught her the responsibility of being a hostess, a hostess who makes sure everyone gets her own cookies and her own chance to be heard.

Perhaps you are a father who has raised two sons who are grown up and out of the nest. You coach the baseball games of the league in your neighborhood, just because you know:

- they desperately need a coach
- you know a thing or two about coaching
- these are nice kids who deserve the chance to play ball

So you give up a lot of free time and activities you would much rather be doing. You become a volunteer, when you have very little free time as it is. You find the boys and girls you coach do not have the same attitude toward good sportsmanship with which you were raised—i.e., that it is *everything*. Some of the children try to get away with whatever they can. They don't show respect for the coach, and they tease the players who aren't all that good. They belittle the opposing team and even their own team when they "mess up." You discover, by asking around, that they are bullies who very possibly don't have any fathers, only stressed-out mothers.

You work privately, first with the awkward, unathletic boys, and you get the word out to the bullies that these are the boys who show great promise and potential, and you will work to bring that out in them. You tout them as "really good player material." The bullies begin to want some of the same attention. You invite them to watch one of the great baseball movies made in the last twenty years on a VCR in your house. You discuss the good guys and the bad guys at the end of the film, while you're having sodas. The movie is full of lessons about good sportsmanship, and you talk about it a little. As the boys file out, you say, "Hey, guys, what are you supposed to do now? Aren't you forgetting something?"

They now remember to say thank you, and one of the toughest of the boys, whose father is dead, whispers how much he really liked the film. Then you whisper back, "You know, if your dad were around, he would have taken you to see this movie—you know that, don't you?"

The tough kid replies, "Yes, I guess—yeah, he probably would have taken me to see it." His eyes will be showing a sense of pride, just thinking about his late father doing something like that for him even if it never would have happened. There are some values being passed down during all of this.

YOUR ROLE IN YOUR CHILDREN'S RELATIONSHIPS

WITH SIBLINGS

The forging of a closeness among brothers and sisters as they grow up is one of the greatest assets you can help them bank for their future happiness. Rivalry among siblings usually lessens by the time they go to college, but it is how the parents teach respect for one another in the early years that really helps solidify the sibling bonds that are so important in adult life. For example, when your children are small, it's the time to teach them:

- A respect for the other person's possessions. ("You leave my things alone and I won't touch yours.")
- A polite way of borrowing. (The child asks nicely, and returns the item when it was promised and in perfect condition.)
- A respect for the sibling's friends, whether referring to that friend in conversation or welcoming that friend to the family home.
- The importance of acting as a support system for each other—to stand up for each other, to rise to the other's defense if one of them is maligned at school, and to be loyal to each other inside and outside the home.

The Sibling with a Physical or Mental Handicap

It is truly inspirational to observe large families in which there is a handicapped child who is consequently the most loved and the most loving member of the family. Such a fortunate child will be watched over by his siblings all through life—long after the parents have died.

A child who is special deserves to be supported constantly within the family, but sometimes that child is teased or resented by siblings because she embarrasses them. This is yet another tough problem for the parents. There comes a time when they must help a sibling understand his responsibility toward the special child in the family.

Explain that although the brother or sister takes more of the parents' time, that does not mean that the others are loved any less. Resolve to make it up to the other children in other ways.

When there is only one sibling of a special child, parents naturally worry about what will happen to the child after their death. The parents should instill in their son or daughter that "You have been given an extra measure of strength and goodness from God to enable you to take care of your brother [or sister] after we have gone."

Addressing Adults

What do your children call your friends or the adult members of your family?

- Traditionally, children address adult family members with a name or title indicative of their position in the family.
  - Parents are called "Mommy" or "Daddy," "Mama" or "Papa"—"Mom" or "Dad," or "Mother" and "Father" when the children are older—or other nicknames derived from those names.

- Grandparents are called "Grandpa" and "Grandma," "Grandfather" and "Grandmother," or any number of nicknames, like "Gammy," "Gamma," "Gampops," "Grandaddy." When there are two sets of grandparents around, it sometimes confuses small children. One solution is for the children to use the grandparent title with the grandparent's given name, such as "Gamma Joan," "Grandpa George," "Grandma Cynthia," and "Grandpa Jim."

- Relatives are called by their title and given names: "Aunt Ginny," "Uncle Charlie," and so forth.

- In a break with tradition, some people insist that their children call all their friends and their relatives by their first names. I find this awkward, and it must be very difficult for a child to call his parents' friends by their first names and all other adults (such as teachers, the doctor, the minister, and the dance instructor) by their last names.

Some parents go to the extent of having their young children call them by their first names—all in the desire to show independence, perhaps hoping to be perceived as nonconformists. It is a free country. Parents can teach their children whatever they wish, but I believe that by encouraging nonconformist usage, the parents may be making it just that much more difficult for their children to learn deference and respect for older people.

- Your college-age children, if they are mature young people, might be urged by friends who feel they are young enough to be your children's peers to stop calling them "Mr. Brown" and "Mrs. Wentworth." If your friends specifically ask the children to address them by their first names, tell your children to do so—if they feel comfortable. It's always uncomfortable at first, but with time it becomes more automatic. However, if they feel it is improper at the age of twenty suddenly to address someone who is fifty by a first name, they should not be forced to.

- By the time children reach college age, if they are close to their aunts and uncles—and by mutual consent—they often drop the "Aunt" and "Uncle" and just use older adults' given names. It is a compliment to the aunt and uncle when it happens.

PARENTS SPEAK TO THEIR CHILDREN ABOUT SEX

A MOTHER SPEAKS TO HER DAUGHTER

Mothers and young daughters should have a special, private, and trusting relationship when it comes to matters concerning sex. In this era of sexually transmitted diseases, learning how to say no to a boy who wants sex is one of the most important things a mother can teach her daughter. First, a mother should explain *why "no" has to be said*—whether the mother's reasons are based on morality and religious conviction or on concern for her daughter's health and safety. Second, there is a well-mannered way of saying no to a man—without making him feel he repulses the woman, or making him think she is cold and frigid, or making him feel badly rejected for even having made the suggestion. (If he tries to use force, of course, there is no reason to be nice or to think of his feelings; the only importance in this situation is to escape or to get help—and fast.)

This advice is offered as one possibility in helping a mother put into words the caution that is so necessary today in approaching the concept of sex among young people. The advice is obvious, but the obvious is often difficult for a mother to articulate to a young daughter.

I think that a mother today should bring back a caution that meant a lot to the women of my day and before me: the question of a young woman's *reputation*. We referred to "it" all the time. To lose it meant social banishment. To say a girl was "easy" was tantamount to branding her with a scarlet letter forever. After 1965, concern for one's reputation went out of style, and moral standards came to be regarded as archaic and irrelevant. However, the more the words "ethics" and "morality" float through the air today, the more caution will be practiced in sexual activity. The danger of AIDS and other sexually transmitted diseases has lessened the pressure on everyone to be held in their peers' esteem as sexual athletes. There are strong reasons for not engaging in sex these days; the logical result is that the word "reputation" may once again become something of importance to a young woman.

A mother talking to her young daughter might explain, after pointing out the reasons why a girl should say no to sex, that a turndown should be made in a pleasant way, not an abrupt or even mean way. For example: "If a man makes a move on you, don't react with great disdain—'What? Sex with *you?* You must be kidding!'—which guarantees that you will never see that man again. Remember, men who have been turned down in a nice way often become great friends and beaux—and have even turned into great husband material at a later date. Therefore, say no firmly, if that's the way you feel, but couch the rejection with some kind words—for example, 'I'm sorry, I can't do that. I'm not ready for that kind of relationship, even though I think you're a really great person.' Or, 'We hardly know each other. I would like to continue seeing you very much, but you will have to understand that I'm not ready to sleep with you.'"

The mother might continue, "If he says, 'But why?'—which he might say very persistently—be prepared with your answers. Don't be afraid to come out with any of these reasons:

"'Because I have strong moral and religious feelings about this subject. You can laugh all you want, but I am saving myself for the man I marry.'" (Most young men are stopped cold with that one. It's an old-fashioned argument that a modern macho type has difficulty handling.)

"'Because of AIDS, herpes—all of that. And don't give me that condom jazz either, because I know there are a lot of mistakes made, even with condoms. I don't know you well enough. I'm not ready for a sexual relationship at this point in our friendship. If that is all you want from me, I guess this is good-bye.'

"*Flattery helps soothe a rejected soul.* For example, you might sugarcoat your rejection with something like this: "'I have a *really* good time with you, and I think you're a terrific guy. But I don't know you well enough to make our relationship sexual at this point. If you can't have an equally good time with me without the sex, then I guess we had better not see each other again. I guess the real truth is that I like to be with you more than you like to be with me.'

"His response will be, 'Then show how much you like me.' Your next move is to repeat what you said, that you are not going to have sex with him, that you are not ready, and that you had better not see each other again."

The majority of today's young men respect a young woman of moral integrity—call it virtue, self-control and self-discipline, or anything you want. A man who has been rejected in his quest for sex, if he has character and is really attracted to the woman, will keep coming back. And a long period of getting to know each other and having fun together, without the pressures of sleeping together, can logically lead to love, marriage, and all the sex that goes with it.

I have put this discussion of a mother's advice to her daughter in my own words. Hopefully, other women will use their own words. It is time to talk about sex when a daughter becomes sexually active, which could be in her lower teens. In the "old days," it was just before her wedding, a thought that elicits great laughter from the young today. Sometimes mothers never talk to their daughters about sex, which is too bad, but as one woman remarked sadly the other day, "My daughter knows far more than I do about these matters." That loss of innocence is not to be applauded but deeply regretted.

A FATHER SPEAKS TO HIS SON

Much that I have said in the preceding section about advice from a mother to her daughter holds true also for a father speaking to his son. Values are not something that are popped like bubble gum out of a teenager's mouth. The groundwork for a set of values is laid in childhood. If a boy grows up hearing his father constantly "talk macho," jokingly referring to girls as "broads," sharing laughs with his son as to which woman on TV has the sexiest body, and in general making a joke out of sexual stereotypes of women, there is no way that his boy, upon entering his teens, will understand the meaning of respect for women. There is no way under those circumstances that a father will be able to advise his son on self-control and good manners when he is on a date.

A father first teaches his son to respect women by respecting his own wife, and by referring to women in dignified terms in the presence of his children. It is his example that instills the attitude that women are to be treated as equal human beings, emotional and intellectual partners, not as objects created for pleasure.

In the matter of sex, a father would be wise to help his son understand his own sexual appetite and how important self-control is in his relationships with girls. Hopefully, they have discussed just how you get sexually transmitted diseases, and if the father knows that his son is sexually active, he has carefully explained when and how to use condoms.

THE E-MAILING KIDS' GENERATION

When parents are in the process of turning a child into a decent, social human being, the use of e-mail can be an important part of that training.

The Adult Watches Out for Foul Language in E-Mails

Some people use foul language to draw attention to themselves and to those whom they don't like.

Adults: *en garde* for your kids' engaging in this "cool" behavior.

Young people sending lewd messages to their classmates are engaging in sexual harassment. If older people are sending these messages, it can be very serious stuff. There are perverts out there, sexually stalking innocent people via e-mail, particularly young people.

Adults: *en garde*

Chat rooms: As someone said, "For children to have to make friends by bonding with strangers on-line in chat rooms is pathetic." Kids need to forge relationships face to face in a healthy environment around normal people.

Adults: *en garde*

Parents should block out the computer's undesirable locations where children's e-mail activities are being fostered. They need to eradicate messages from unwanted visitors from their children's on-line viewing with their friends. They should teach the kids that any individual's request to meet them or one of their friends, or engage in sex talk, or post-pornographic photographs and sexual information on-line, is forbidden and dangerous. If it takes frightening your children to make them aware, *do it*.

Adults: *en garde*

Safety measures to take:

Know what your child is doing on-line.

Establish rules and keep to them.

Limit your child's time on-line.

Edit outgoing e-mails for as long as you can. "I bought this new computer because you promised to let me see your e-mails, to see how you're coming along with grammar and spelling. I'm asking you to deliver on your promise. That includes your conversations in chat rooms."

Invest in software that allows you to block out unwanted sites.

GUARDING YOUR CHILD AGAINST THE PERILS OF DRUGS AND ALCOHOL

"Socially acceptable drugs" has to be one of the most ironic phrases ever coined in modern-day use. *There really is no socially acceptable nonmedicinal drug.* All are abused for the most part, even though people may start out using small amounts. Every second or third glass of liquor or beer begins to be dangerous, not socially acceptable. Every puff of a marijuana cigarette is against the law and potentially harmful—it's like lighting matches in a dry forest. It's a quick step up from a drag on a marijuana cigarette to speed, crack, cocaine, heroin, PCP, opium—through the entire spectrum of mind-altering drugs.

• Attack the subject of drug use as early in a child's development as you can make her understand it. Teach your son and daughter to like and respect their minds, so they won't feel the need for altering them, and to love and respect their bodies, so they won't willfully harm them. Five-year-olds watching violence on television that is associated with drugs quickly come to know the lingo. They don't really understand drug use, but they know it's there and that it's dark and dangerous and very "grown-up." Often they find it fascinating—another glamorous vestige of being grown-up, in the same category as getting a driver's license in order to have wheels and hang out with one's friends.

Make drug taking *un*fascinating to your small children. Make it *un*glamourous. Please don't claim your child never sees "bad" things on television. This may be true in a few rare cases, but most children, even if TV is regulated in their own homes, find it is not regulated in their friends' homes. Show me a five-year-old with older brothers and sisters who doesn't watch violence and gore on television right along with them—and I'll show you an unusual (but amazingly caring and wonderful) family.

When you see people selling drugs on the street, point them out to your child. Let the child see the seediness of that scene. Point out people reeling around high on drugs, which you can see in any large city. Maybe the pathetic and sordid effects of drug and alcohol abuse will sink in. Do not protect your child by keeping him ignorant on this subject. Educate your child forthrightly when you see the horror of it around you.

• The most important weapon of all in teaching a child to refuse drugs is the example set by you, the parents! You cannot teach a child to renounce addictive drugs (including tobacco) if you, a parent, indulge in them. You cannot say to a child, "Do as I say, not as I do."

• Comment on the day's news about drug dealers being apprehended. When children eat their meals, their ears are usually innocently wide open, even if you don't think they are paying any attention to what you're saying about the news in today's papers or on the evening telecast. As adults talk to one another, the children usually take it all in, particularly if the subject is something as dangerous as drugs, which most parents discuss in alarmed tones. Children can detect the importance of the subject in their parents' tone of voice and emphatic way of speaking. Let your children eavesdrop on your discussion of this subject. Speak in simple terms that they can understand.

When you mention "the bad, terrible men and women who sell those drugs," and how drugs ruin people's lives, and how people must be punished for selling, buying, or using the stuff, a child begins to look at the subject as a real-life example of evil and the need to punish those forces of evil. A child may or may not question you further at the dinner table after you switch to another subject. But then again, she might open up and tell you something you had no idea of—about drug selling going on close to or in a school, for example.

• Every so often reinforce in the mind even of a kindergarten child the evil connotation of drugs—that they are like a wicked witch or a bad dragon. Don't overkill the subject, just give them a gentle reminder that they have the power to refuse taking something that will always hurt them in the end. (If your teenager is in fast company, it isn't a bad idea to arrange with the school for a class tour of a rehab facility. It's a very sobering experience.)

One night a friend of mine, a young father, wrote in his journal, word for word as well as he could remember it, the conversation he had just had with his six-year-old son while the latter was getting ready for bed. He later showed it to me.

His son told him something that had greatly impressed him and his class— that two fourteen-year-olds in the upper school had been arrested on the school grounds at noon that day for selling drugs to other students. The father said he hoped his little boy would never touch the stuff.

Billie, the son, asked him, "What do drugs taste like? Yummy, like candy or soda?"

"No, sometimes they don't taste at all. People swallow them or take them by sticking a needle into a vein in their arm." The little boy grabbed his arm as if in pain at this thought. "Or they smoke drugs like in a pipe or a cigarette."

"Sounds dumb. And it hurts. Why?" asked Billie.

"Because it makes them feel good for a very little while."

"Well, what's bad about that?"

"Because then later they feel awful, and they get weak and sick and can't play games or do their homework."

"It's easy. The bad will go away when they just stop."

"No, they can't stop."

"Why can't they?"

"Because when they keep doing it, they can't stop. They're trapped, like an animal caught in a hunter's trap. They just keep taking it and wanting more and taking it—and poisoning themselves more each time."

"Sounds stupid. Just how bad do the drugs make them feel after a while, Daddy?" The little boy continued to pepper his father with questions, wanting to know about how bad drugs make you feel and, if they did, why people took them.

"Well," his father said, "remember when you had that really bad sore throat last month?" The little boy nodded his head affirmatively. "And how you felt when you had that last bad cold at Christmas and were all stuffed up, feverish, and hot?"

Billie nodded yes again.

"And how you felt when you had your appendix out?"

Billie said, "Yeah. It really hurt."

"Well, that's how people who take illegal drugs eventually feel. The medicine the doctor tells you to take when you're sick doesn't make you feel bad. That kind of drug makes you feel well. We're talking about *illegal drugs*—bad stuff, the kind those boys were selling near your school."

"I'll never do that!" Billie said very firmly.

"I hope you don't, son."

Billie received an excellent lesson that night. Three years later, I asked his father if Billie had ever again mentioned the "Don't take drugs" lesson his father once taught him. "Yes." Bill Senior smiled. "It took, like a vaccination. He brought home his class paper from school last week, with an 'A' on it. His paper was titled 'Drugs Are Bad. Don't Take Them.'"

DRUGS AND THE VULNERABLE TEENAGER

When your child enters the teens, the lure of drugs, alcohol, and tobacco is much more intense, particularly when the cool kids in school are experimenting with these dangerous substances. Now is the time to watch your child's friends, to help her entertain often in your home rather than in someone else's, where you don't know the parents or even know if they are home. (It is also imperative that your child does not go to someone's home where parents are present but are doing drugs or drinking to excess.)

One way to keep children off drugs is to know what they are doing in their free time, where and with whom they are spending free time. If you urge your children to hold their parties in your house and get college students (who are "clean and sober" obviously) to serve as paid chaperones, then you, the parents, can be out of the house, but the children will be under the watchful eyes of those "really grown-up college guys" (of either sex).

It's the parents who don't care, who are too busy with their own lives and don't know what's going on in their children's lives, who let these young people slip away from them. It's a selfish, unthinking parent who won't go to the effort of helping a child have friends over rather than forcing him to seek entertainment elsewhere, and possibly under dangerous circumstances.

When you hold a newborn in your arms, you promise to do everything in the world for that child, to love and protect him forever. I guess it's a promise we all make, but it's more important to keep it than to make it. And the teen years are when it's particularly important to be alert to your child's development.

THE KINDS OF DRUGS AROUND US

If a child is curious about drugs, be ready to answer the questions as to what they are and what they are called.

- Alcohol and tobacco, the gateway drugs, can become addictive and introduce a person to the drug culture.

- Inhalants can be poisonous and dangerous, and young children often fall prey to them. Inhaling anything, from hair spray and gasoline to airplane glue, can give a person—particularly a child—a dizzy kind of high. One of the most popular inhalants is butyl nitrite, which causes blood vessels to expand and can have serious consequences.

- Marijuana and hashish. Smoking the chopped-up leaves or the dark brown resin from the tops of the *Cannabis sativa* plant may give the smokers pleasure, but it also impairs their performance in anything from driving a car to working on a machine. The smoker may suffer disorientation, but most important of all, it's an easy jump from marijuana or hashish up to another illegal, more powerfully addictive drug.

- Depressants (or "downers") are drugs that calm the central nervous system. People take these when they're feeling hyper, nervous, or agitated. The sedative Quaalude (the brand name for methaqualone), also known as "ludes" or "sopors," is one of the very hazardous drugs young people are attracted to because of its reputation for enhancing sexual experience. It is also sold in counterfeit tablets containing other substances that can produce unexpected, dangerous reactions.

- Stimulants do the opposite of what a depressant does to you. They wake you up, and fight drowsiness. The most popular stimulant is caffeine (found in coffee, tea, and cola). Taken often and for a long time, it becomes addictive. Amphetamines (speed), methamphetamines, crack, and cocaine (coke) are in this category. The drug world has its own terminology for the terrible pursuit of pleasure through stimulants. "Chasing the dragon," for example, is smoking cocaine and heroin at the same time.

• Narcotics. The painkillers in medicine derived from opium or made synthetically, such as codeine, morphine, and Demerol, are all narcotics and very addictive. Heroine is a narcotic as well and is becoming more and more affordable—in some places less expensive than marijuana. Parents beware.

• Dilavdin, oxycontin, vicodin. These are available by prescription and "on the street."

• Hallucinogens. These are called perceptual drugs because a person who takes them changes his perception of the reality of the world around him. PCP ("angel dust") and LSD are the best known. There are also botanical hallucinogens growing in nature—for example, the psilocybin ("magic mushrooms") of Mexico and mescaline.

• Designer drugs. Ecstasy (or "x") is a relatively new entry to the drug scene. It's a pill that is in the perceptual drug category. Some powerful drugs used in anesthesia are also hitting the drug scene.

TEACHING YOUR YOUNG CHILD
ABOUT ALCOHOL

Across the country, there are children, some as young as sixth graders, who gain access to alcohol and drugs. Some children drink or take drugs before going to school. It's no longer a worry to face when the kids are in high school. It's a worry to face in grade school!

When you first smell alcohol on your child's breath—or when she first tells you about classmates drinking in school—it's time to teach the child about the dangers and addictiveness of alcohol. (If you have a drink in your hand when you start this talk, forget it, let someone else teach your child about alcohol.)

If you smell alcohol on your young child more than once, don't just punish him. Work on him quickly, as a family unit (almost as though you were doing a family intervention with a confirmed adult alcoholic to force that person into treatment). You want to save this child from becoming an alcoholic. The danger signals are flashing all over the place. Talk to your family doctor. Get older brothers, sisters, aunts, and uncles to sit down in a group and explain the seriousness of the child's actions and the almost certain outcome of his becoming an alcoholic if he continues. Contact Alcoholics Anonymous and find out about its excellent children's programs. Talk to the local alcoholic rehabilitation clinic to collect some ammunition and advice. In other words, get ready to scare the pants off the child in your family who is drinking.

He probably regards drinking as macho or sophisticated, glamorous, big-time movie-hero stuff. Dispel those notions, even if in the great old movies chic heroes are always drinking and smoking.

Teenage Drinking

If your child is in high school and tells you there is lots of drinking among classmates:

• Tell your child that if she just has to try a drink or a special cocktail, you will let her try it home *with you.*

• Show your child how drinkers, all of whom started out taking just an occasional drink but then became hooked on alcohol, ruin their bodies, get bloated and red in the face, become nutritionally starved, have liver problems, and seriously damage their hearts. Most serious of all, alcohol abuse results in brain damage, and you have only to point out a homeless alcoholic lying in the street in any large city to make that point to your child. Alcohol is debilitating to the system, yes, but it also damages a young person's looks and, ultimately, her ability to stay alive.

• Agree with your child that, yes, a drink might make a shy young person less shy and more at ease at a party, but it's a temporary, phony kind of comfort. The life of the party, high on alcohol, very quickly becomes the bore of the party. The only real party high is one you make yourself, with your own wonderful contribution to the group—giving of yourself and making an effort to make others feel good.

• Impress upon your child that even mild social drinking will dull his reflexes. Tell your child about the thousands of fatal automobile accidents every year in which merely social drinking is involved. Make him understand the devastating penalties underaged youths pay who are involved in an accident and found to be drinking.

• Your child can't really know how quickly alcohol will take effect in his system. It hits some people faster than others. The effect depends upon a person's weight—and on other factors, such as heredity and how much food a person has eaten recently. Don't let your child get away with bragging about being able to drink anyone "under the table," or about having an amazing capacity for alcohol—no one does.

• If your daughter's peers are all drinking in college and you know she will, too, warn her to sip a drink slowly and to eat as often as possible along with it to provide a kind of blotter for the alcohol.

• If your young daughter is a drinker, share an occasional article with her on what alcohol does to babies in the womb. The evidence is compelling, and it is enough to stop many young women from ever taking a drink during their childbearing years.

WHERE TO GET HELP

The National Clearing House for Alcohol and Drug Information publishes a free *National Directory of Drug Abuse and Alcoholism Treatment and Prevention Programs,* which lists alphabetically all of the many resources available by state and then by city. In order to obtain a copy of this directory, write to:

> National Clearing House for Alcohol and Drug Information
> P.O. Box 2345
> Rockville, MD 20852

In all middle-size to large cities, ask Directory Assistance for the telephone number of the local chapter of these national support groups:
- Alcoholics Anonymous
- Narcotics Anonymous

The local chapter will refer you to the local:
- Adult Children of Alcoholics (ACOA)
- Alanon (Family Members of Alcoholics)
- Alateen (Children of Alcoholics)

You may also call the National Institute on Drug Abuse (NIDA) hot line, 1-800-662-HELP, to ask for the names of free drug treatment centers in your area. Call this hot line weekdays between 9 A.M. and 3 A.M.; on weekends, call between noon and 3 A.M.

WHEN YOUR CHILDREN BECOME ADULTS:
KEEP YOUR FAMILY TOGETHER

- Arrange family reunions as often as possible. Check ahead with the children on all their schedules, so that no one is left out.
- Urge your offspring to support a sibling's choice of mate; have everyone contribute to a warm welcoming of the new member of the family.
- Help them all keep in touch with one another. (One of my favorite ideas for helping children stay in touch is the mother who has always paid for all the long distance telephone calls her five adult children make to each other. She claims that although the reimbursements are extensive, she has never enjoyed paying for anything so much.)
- When someone needs help, subtly suggest to the other siblings the ways in which they can help—whether it's to buck up a failing marriage or to lend

a little money to someone who has a sudden financial need. Encourage them to act as surrogate parents for their brothers and sisters in times of family distress (for example, standing in for the bride's mother or father if either is seriously ill at the time of a daughter's wedding).

• Keep them all aware of their various successes, too, even if it means sending a regular family newsletter to the younger generation, bearing only happy news of each sibling and his family.

NICE WAYS TO TREAT OTHER FAMILY MEMBERS

Remember, it's generous and wonderful to take care of your friends, but your family deserves even more attention. A family should be the most effective support mechanism there is for each member, and if your family is not, what a wonderful project for you to undertake—to help turn them into being more helpful family members!

- When a family member is in the hospital:
  - Call every day to cheer up that family member and organize other family members to make visits.
  - Ask if there is anything you can do.
  - Leave messages for the patient with a nurse at the floor nursing station, if you cannot get through on the telephone.
  - If the patient has a laptop with her, have family and friends send short, happy, upbeat e-mails.
  - Get the office staff to send recorded messages giving news, nothing sad or worrisome.
  - If the doctor says it's okay, send some of the patient's favorite ice cream, well marked with her name, that will be put in the hospital freezer on her floor. Send an entire cooked roast beef or lobster dinner to the patient, if she is allowed to have it.
- Mark faithfully in some small way an anniversary of note in a family member's life—birthday, wedding anniversary, and the like.
- Recognize anything of importance in the family, such as when a nephew makes the college rowing team, a niece comes in second in the city's spelling bee, a brother gets a job promotion. When you know that your aged, ailing grandmother's recipe for angel food cake was used at a family party, send her a note about it, including a snapshot of the party in progress. When a nephew receives his First Communion, send him a card—"This is a big event in your life, Ricky. It's a very special day, and we'll all be there to celebrate, even in spirit, including people like me, who live in another city." You might include a check with the card, to make it extra special. If your stepdaughter is to be bat mitzvahed, and you can't be present, send her a wonderful letter and gift. In other words, *act*.

- Do errands, household chores, and desk work for any friend or family member who's incapacitated.
- Notify friends of the family member when there is particularly good—or bad—news to report. In other words, if a person—or the family—is too busy or incapacitated to communicate with close friends, offer to do it for him. It could be the greatest gift you could give.
- Check on a family member's health options, insurance coverage, etc., when she is incapable of doing it alone.
- Notice when someone in the family seems to be having a hard time, physically, mentally, emotionally, or financially. Don't just notice it, offer your help.
- Diplomatically, bring a physical problem to a family member's attention, which, if left unattended, might hurt his popularity and career. ("Grandpa, let me take you to the hearing aid specialist. You don't seem to be able to hear us these days, and it makes us feel we're far away from you.")
- Urge a family member to seek needed help—therapy, counseling, and the like—when she has difficulty expressing herself or she is unable to relate to friends.
- Investigate the financial dilemma of a family member and obtain professional advice and even the loan of money for this person.
- Become surrogate parents as much as possible for children in the family who have lost their parent(s) through a death or divorce. Show up at their school games and class performances, and cheer them on as any loving parents would. Grandparents, uncles, aunts, and cousins are very important at a time like this.
- Send e-mails and greeting cards to relatives to mark major holidays and special festivities. I buy many seasonal and special occasion greeting cards at one time, stamp them, and have them at the ready to address, to write a personal note inside, and to send. This way there is something appropriate always available, from the birth of a baby to sympathy for a bad case of poison ivy. It becomes second nature to mark someone's misfortune with a cheery studio card, and it is an effective act of kindness toward people ages two through a hundred and two.
- Include a widow or widower family member in your dinner parties once in a while. No one would be able to measure the gratitude you will receive from that guest in return.
- Initiate reasons why the family should get together. It takes only one person to galvanize an entire group into jointly celebrating family holidays, anniversaries, second and third weddings, and the like. With the existence of e-mail, there is no excuse for anyone to say, "I didn't know anything about it."
- Make certain that someone is doing a written and recorded family history to be handed down to all future generations. It's hard work, and one person should be put in charge (because a committee of family members will do noth-

ing). Volunteer if no one else does. Include all the stepsisters and brothers, the stepparents and everyone who passed in and out of your family via marriages and remarriages. Give Great-Uncle Harry a tape recorder, and Cousin Susan, too, to record reminiscences regularly. Catch family members' memories of past reunions, and wonderful stories of everyone, still alive or gone. Train family members to send you e-mails whenever they suddenly remember something of import. Save every family photograph you can find, and caption them with a date, place, and people's names. Your family is precious, so undertake the task of family archivist with enthusiasm. And don't forget all the family pets. They deserve inclusion in the family history!

Keeping a family together is a job. There isn't a more important one in this world. The more a child is helped to grow up by siblings, parents, grandparents, and other adults, the more likely he is to do the very same thing as an adult with the generations to come. Once you're a parent, you remain one, no matter how grown up your children are. And since you were once a child, there's always a little of that in you, too.

That's what families are all about.

Everyday Manners Out in the World

A person who is loved and popular—a person with naturally good relationships—does not turn her behavior on and off like a spigot, according to the person she is with at any given time. The person who had a smile and a good word for a member of the family also has it for the postman, the man who brings her car up from the lower levels of a garage, the receptionist in the executive's office where she has an appointment, and the person who sells her the morning paper.

Our relationships with *everyone* are important. I remember asking a question of a simply wonderful woman who was greatly loved by everyone who came to know her: "Don't you get tired being nice to *everyone*?"

Her answer: "It's much more exhausting going back and forth—being nice to some people and not nice to others." In thinking over her words, I had to agree. It is a lot easier, for example, to thank a salesperson for her help and not complain about her inefficiency than it is to pick a fight with her and not carry the resulting bad feelings into the rest of the day. It's a negative reason for being nice perhaps, but come to think of it, any reason for being nice has value in this world of ours!

With good manners, attitude is as important as the act. You might give the world's biggest tip to the waiter but do it in a way that insults the person who earned it; on the other hand, you might make the slightest of thoughtful gestures that means so *much* to the recipient. The ultimate success of anything you do depends on how nicely you do it.

CHAPTER 3

Making Friends in a Busy World

Anyone who wants to get ahead in life, to be happy, and to attract others knows that friends are an absolutely necessary ingredient in the recipe. Friends help make it all worthwhile.

The smart way to look upon increasing your circle of friends is to realize that everyone is potentially a good one. I know from experience how easy it is to make the wrong snap judgment of a person. Many times I have met a person for the first time and found him to be anything—from an unintelligent, colorless dilettante to a mean and nasty individual—only to find out on the next occasion that this person is fascinating, articulate, and amusing.

THE FIRST STEP: MEETING PEOPLE
WHO MAY BECOME FRIENDS

In order to have good friends, you have to meet them first. But even before worrying about meeting people, you must be "meetable" yourself, or it just won't happen. Being "meetable" means that you:

- Walk down the street with a deliberately pleasant expression on your face (not a suffering frown, such as many of us have when we're trying to remember, "What were those six things I set out to buy that were so desperately needed?")
- Look as if you're having a great time at every party you attend, even if you're miserable. A smiling face, symptomatic of an upbeat personality, is like the flame that fascinates and draws the moths.
- Don't complain to others, even if your feet are hurting or if you are exhausted from a hard day. Whether people know you well or have just met you, they do not wish to hear how awful you feel. (That may only motivate them to convince you that they feel a lot worse.)
- Act fascinated by the new people you meet, even if they look very boring indeed. You never know until you have really had time to know someone whether or not a real pearl might be lying hidden in that unopened oyster shell.

BECOME CREATIVE
ABOUT HOW YOU USE YOUR LEISURE TIME

You will meet people only by getting out of your home, away from your hum-drum schedule, and into a new routine of extracurricular activities.

• Maybe you will meet the person of your dreams at the next cocktail party you attend. You should never turn down an invitation to a party. Go! You can never be sure that something delightful will *not* happen on any given evening—how are you going to know unless you go out? Don't turn down a blind date, either. He may be a dud but may have knockout friends. How will you know unless you go out with that person and meet those friends?

• Maybe you were destined to meet a special friend by joining a new association—for example, a miniature sailboat racing club. I know a divorced woman who found a new husband—a divorced man—as he was sailing boats with his little boy on a Saturday in the park. She and her little girl were sailing enthusiasts, too, so it was quite natural that the two single parents began chatting. Now this couple and their children can stage their own private regattas!

My daughter Clare and her husband, Jim, found each other poking around on a Saturday in an Irish bookstore in lower Manhattan. Since they were the only customers in the bookstore, they had plenty of time to talk. A shared interest in books on Ireland led to their engagement just a few months later. (Clare's unmarried women friends have been spending more time in book-stores on Saturdays ever since.)

• Perhaps you were meant to make friends working on a nonprofit project. There is a powerful need for volunteers in all cities today. And it's quite apparent that some of the nicest people in any community are those who give of themselves to help others and to make this a better world. A newcomer any-where can volunteer for a worthy cause and make close new friends through sharing worthwhile activities undertaken in a spirit of concern.

I know a senior citizen who pushes the book and magazine cart around one of New York's biggest hospitals. She is always smiling and cheering up patients and is much loved by them. Many of them remain her good friends when they leave the hospital. "I have such a busy social life," she told us. "I have a very dif-ficult time fitting it all in!" She added that she "is the happiest septuagenarian you'll probably ever see—between my volunteer work and the friends it brings me."

• Perhaps in sampling your city's cultural activities, you will meet a person who shares your interests. If you are a season ticket holder at the theater, con-cert hall, or ballet, for example, inevitably you will begin to make friends with others who hold tickets to the same performances. During the intermission, you will find yourself talking to other subscribers whom you see each time. You can discuss the performance, chat about other things, and then suggest going to have a cup of coffee or tea after the show.

• Look for the nearest place where you can engage in a sport in which you excel. If you are a passably good tennis player, skier, softball player, ice-skater, or croquet player, don't be shy. Start playing *better*. Pick up games; ask someone to be your partner or opponent—anything to let the world see how good you are. Others will want to play with you, and having "a bite to eat" afterward is a natural outcome of playing a good game. The friendship solidifies if, after you play a game, you break bread together.

• It may be helpful to join a church or temple group. So many activities are sponsored by houses of worship that a person participating in these activities inevitably meets a wide variety of people.

• Perhaps you should become active in your child's school. If you work hard to make the school better, you'll meet a sizable group of parents who will appreciate your ideas, time, and effort and will want to support you in your projects.

• You might try to learn a new skill. While you are working hard at it, you'll meet and make friends with others who have the same goals. Whether it's learning a foreign language, Japanese flower arranging, sculpting, belly dancing, the history of art, ice-boating, in-line skating, or Thai cooking, you will enjoy the company of others doing the same thing.

• Maybe, if you love the outdoors, you would enjoy joining groups that take overnight hikes on weekends. Sometimes these expeditions are for singles, sometimes they are for entire families, and other times they are for single parents with children. The newspapers generally list these outings (the listings may be more complete in suburban papers). By the time you have spent forty-eight hours huddled together in a cave for shelter during an endless rainstorm, there is no question but that you will emerge from it as good friends—or ardent enemies, but hopefully the former!

• Whatever you do, keep your eyes open. Pay attention to the people around you in your neighborhood—whether you're looking for a friend or a lover. She might be standing right next to you in the checkout line at the supermarket! People who are cynical and pessimistic in a city like New York might think that the person standing next to them in a checkout line could be dangerous, but there's another point of view: That person might be your next date!

It's a question of philosophy. There are those who look out the window and say, "There's sunshine with just a few clouds out there." Others say, "It's all cloudy out there, with just a bit of sunshine." Take your pick.

SOLIDIFYING A NEW FRIENDSHIP

Once you've made a real friend, nurture the relationship. An established friendship should be treasured, requiring not only loyalty but also time and attention.

- The best way to solidify that friendship is to invite that person to a meal. Once you meet someone who is simpatico and with whom you share good chemistry, don't let him (or her or them) evaporate into thin air just because everyone is too busy. Take the initiative. Use that person's telephone number. Invite him (or her or that couple) out to dinner—or to a Saturday or Sunday lunch. When you ask someone to share a meal, it is the ultimate compliment.

If you think your new friend or friends would feel more comfortable with others present, invite one or two other people as well. If you don't know one or two other people to ask, don't worry about it.

Either make reservations at a restaurant or plan a short cocktail hour and a delicious meal at home. Make it look as attractive as possible. Put some flowers around, have good music playing softly in the background, and show what a relaxed, caring host you are. The art of entertaining well is one of the greatest people assets there is, and it should be used as part of your repertoire for making friends.

- You should also be on the giving not the receiving end. This means that you repay your friends' hospitality and kindnesses. Sometimes repayment takes a different form, but it's a repayment nevertheless. For example, John and Agnes may invite the Masons to dinner quite often, but if the Masons work hard to get John and Agnes's children into a college where the Masons have a lot of clout, John and Agnes are not going to count the number of times the Masons come to dinner without a return dinner invitation.

- You should rise in defense of good friends when they are criticized. When you hear a mutual friend criticizing your friend, intervene. You don't have to mince any words: "That's an untrue accusation; I know it is. And even if it were true, it's disloyal to talk about him that way."

- Check in with a real friend on a regular basis, no matter how busy you may be and how unbusy she may be. Friends are to be enjoyed when it suits your schedule, but their needs also should be respected when it doesn't suit your schedule. You may be exhausted after working particularly hard at your office all week, but when a close friend who complains she never sees you anymore calls to ask your help with a project on your one free Saturday afternoon, extend yourself.

- Be ready to help in an emergency—short- or long-term. If a single-parent friend suddenly has to go to the hospital for a few days, offer to take care of his children in your own home during that time, or find another good solution. If a friend is moving, do everything from helping him pack to bringing him dinner and a bottle of wine on the evening of the move. If a friend's car is in the shop for a week, lend him your extra car, or pick him up and take him home every day on your way home from work.

- Be sensitive to a friend's emotions. When you sense that a married friend feels down, for example, be ready to help. Perhaps what she needs is just an invitation to dinner and a pep talk; perhaps what he needs is just a sympathetic ear; perhaps what they both need is the name of a good marriage counselor!

Remember that good friends:

- Never ask too much of each other. They never step over the bounds of good taste into excess. They never take one another for granted.
- Compromise on what they do together; one person's wish is not the only deciding factor. ("Look, since you're nice about going to Shakespeare this Saturday with me, I'll be glad to go to the baseball game with you next Saturday, okay?")
- Remember what's important to the other person and respect it, whether it's a birthday celebration, free time to concentrate on a hobby, or simply lending shopping expertise (to keep the other one from making any more wardrobe mistakes).
- Enjoy surprising one another with creative acts of kindness—for example, with:
  - An unexpected telephone call. ("I just called, because I happened to hear some Scottish music and it reminded me of our trip to Scotland.")
  - A timely unexpected visit. ("I know I'm not expected, but you didn't sound too chipper the last time I talked to you with that cold of yours, so I brought you some hot homemade soup.")
  - An unexpected gift (with a card that reads: "With love, from Aggie, just because it feels like spring outside today, and I wanted you to have some of the first daffodils to brighten up your office desk!").
  - Helping out when some assistance would really be needed (anything from taking over a friend's car-pooling duties when she isn't feeling well to lending a couple your lakeside cabin when they can obviously use a weekend of quiet and rest).

MANNERS AND FRIENDSHIP
IN THE GREAT OUTDOORS

SPORTS

Sports are as big an obsession today as they were in ancient Greece, where they symbolized skill, good health, lofty character, and leadership ideals. Today's great athletes still epitomize great skill and, when they are not abusing substances, good health. But so far as ideals of character are concerned, the modern-day athlete often has other goals. Our athletes concentrate on the millions of dollars earned through corporate sponsorships and commercial tie-ins.

The growth of logoed equipment—athletic shoes, workout clothes, sweatbands (and don't forget the underwear!)—has eroded the original ideals of sport.

The Goals of Sports

To win
To provide valuable exercise
To entertain while others watch

Three Grave Responsibilities in the Sports World Today

Safety for oneself, the team, and the spectators
Concern for the environment
The demonstration of good sportsmanship

The Player: Good Sportsmanship Is Really Kindness

A good sport:
- Never belittles anyone's skill.
- Lets the "little kids" play for a few minutes when they are dying to. "Let your sister play—it's her turn!"
- Doesn't make a novice skier accompany her down a difficult run, just because she's bored with the simpler runs.
- If he's a big man, doesn't smash the tennis ball at a woman up at the net, because he knows that's unfair, not because he's worried about a lawsuit.
- Is the one who puts away all the equipment at the end of the day, where it's supposed to be, from Ping-Pong balls to hockey pucks, from baseball bats to footballs, and from a lacrosse goal tender's mask to a skier's ski wax and a skater's blade sharpener.
- Insists on safety for any group for which he has responsibility. He knows when the ice is too risky for skating, when the ski run is too icy for safe runs, that certain high winds make it unsafe for sailing, that the fields are too slippery today for young riders, and that everyone should get out of the water because there's been a sighting of sharks.

The Importance of the Manners Involved in Sports:
The behavior of the players; the behavior of the spectators

The Player

Reasons why you may have trouble finding games and partners:
- You haven't learned the basic skills of the game (get some coaching, take some lessons, study videos, and practice, practice, practice).
- You don't know the rules of the game, which infuriates the other players, particularly your partner or the members of your team. Bluffing doesn't work.
- You have exaggerated your skills and made yourself out to be a first-rate player, when you're not. This can ruin everyone's enjoyment of the game. The smart player underplays his skills, leaving everyone pleasantly surprised.
- Sometimes you cheat. You lie about the number of strokes in your golf game. You call an opponent's ball "out" on the tennis court when it is not. This makes you about as popular as a road rager, and it's a serious black mark against character.
- You embarrass your colleagues by dressing inappropriately for the sport. You're the man who wears shorts that are too short or a getup that looks like a fireworks display or the woman wearing a thong at the pool party, or a guest coming aboard a boat not wearing rubber-soled shoes. If you are a novice, always ask what the dress requirements are before appearing ready to play.
- You don't take your game appointments seriously. You call to cancel at the last minute, or you just don't show up. As one amateur athlete remarked, "The no-show at a match is as despicable as the one missing at the altar when the wedding begins."
- You're very casual about being properly equipped. You're convinced you can always borrow a racket, a club, or balls from someone or else "It's not all that important anyway" . . . You ignore your host's request to bring your own life jacket on the fishing trip . . . You promised to bring the ice chest for the boat, but you forget . . .
- You don't offer to pay your own green fees or court rental at a club. Since you weren't the one to suggest drinks after the game, you feel you don't have to contribute a round.
- If you're really angry at your poor performance or bad luck, you let it all out in front of everyone. Complain, swear, throw your racket—anything you wish, to demonstrate your displeasure.
- You argue with the umpire or referee.
- You don't worry about things like allowing another golf foursome to play through if yours is slow, or for the tennis players on the court next to you to finish their point before asking that they return your ball, which has rolled onto their court.

- You forget about the high volume of your voice. Go ahead, yell a greeting to a player two courts away, and keep the loud laughter coming. People playing near you are usually bored and need to know that you are in good spirits.
- You are dramatic with your excuses for your bad playing. There's always "The sun's in my eyes" routine, or "The blister on my heel is just agonizing," or "I threw my knee out last week, and I'm afraid I've seriously injured it."
- If you have cut up the greens with your club, you don't worry about replacing the divots. Let the next players who arrive do it. If you've wrecked the surface of the tennis court, you don't bother to smooth it over or use the heavy roller. Let the next players do it. Let them fix the net, too, which loosened up and sagged during your game. If you've been using the practice court, you leave the balls scattered all around. It's too much of a bother to gather them up and put them back in the big basket provided for that purpose by the pro shop.
- You always blame your partners for your bad shots. Just call out to them, after your series of bad shots, "Gee, guys, we've got to shape up. Come on, let's get going!"
- If you think your doubles tennis partner is too weak a player, you jump in front of that person and try to take every shot. You wonder why people are applauding when you lose the point.
- You don't bother to shake hands with your partner or opponents after a game or to congratulate the winners, or to praise anyone for their exceptionally fine playing.
- You have decided to play a game of croquet, even if you think it is a silly game meant for nineteenth-century snobs, so you ham it up, make fun of the rules, and are too much of a cutup to try to win. The other players will remember your performance forever.
- You don't know how to ride, so you belittle the people in your group of friends who love the equestrian sport. You double over with laughter if they've taken a spill or when you see them in their jodhpurs and velvet hard hats. It's all a big joke to you, and it shows the great manners of the riders that they don't run right over you.

The Spectator

You can be sure to be loathed by the people around you if:
- You arrive late and crawl mindlessly over all the people sitting in your row several times during the game. Everyone stands up to allow you to pass by; when others come through, you just sit there and make them perform gymnastics to pass you.
- You pay no attention to the national anthem that starts the game, to the point of acting disrespectfully while it is played.

• Even if you know family and friends of a player are sitting nearby, you shout obscenities at the player during the game and defame the team.

• You disagree loudly and vociferously with every decision of the referee or umpire. Your creativity builds as you berate the players. There is now a unified spirit among the people sitting near you: they wish you would leave—quickly.

• You are not careful with the food and drink you purchase from the vendors. Mustard and soda are spilled on your neighbors with abandonment. They are also spilled all over the ground area in front of your seat, assuring that anyone passing through that row will get her shoes ruined in a sea of ketchup and nachos. You, of course, have prepared well for this game. You have worn an old pair of athletic shoes you were going to discard anyway.

• You throw as many bottles, cans, paper bags, and can openers as you wish on the ice or on the field if you are displeased with anything whatsoever during a game or match.

Note: Please, please do not take my negative advice literally.

MAKING FRIENDS AT WORK

The best way to make friends at work is to be a bright, sunny person, so that you lift up the spirits of others. Coworkers will want to be around you because you're the one with the sunny disposition.

• Be a good citizen around the office. Don't welch on your responsibilities (including getting coffee on a certain day, turning off the lights before going home, returning everything you borrowed from a colleague—on time and in good shape). Lend a helping hand, even when it's not your responsibility. If someone is stuck late on an emergency job, stay late once in a while to help out. That's what friends are for.

• Stick up for a friend who is being wrongfully criticized at the office, praise a friend who is doing a good job, and pass on helpful advice and information when that friend would find it useful.

• When you're new, take people to lunch! Invite your peers, even those higher up the corporate ladder, to a nice (not luxurious, just nice) restaurant for lunch. It's an investment. These lunches will help you learn office procedures and politics—and allow you to show how personable, intelligent, and attractive you are in a relaxed situation. They allow you and the other person to get to know one another. You spend so many hours at work, it really is important to have friends there. They are a necessary support system in helping you get through the day. However, don't come on too strong with these invitations. Don't look overeager and aggressive. Be subtle and discreet about those lunch invitations. Don't talk around the office about any of your lunch appointments with the higher-ups, or people will begin to think you're apple-polishing.

WIDENING YOUR HORIZONS
THROUGH VOLUNTEER WORK

The nonprofit world has always involved charity, generosity, love, and caring for others. But in today's mobile world it may also serve as the most efficient vehicle for newcomers in a community to form friendships and establish new business contacts. Volunteer service also provides people who serve on the boards of nonprofit institutions—women, in particular—invaluable management training for the business world.

The most important part of serving the nonprofit community is that whether you give your time or your money or both, you will receive enormous personal satisfaction. Knowing you have helped is one of the pleasantest of all experiences life has to offer.

CHOOSING A VOLUNTEER ACTIVITY

The best philanthropic work for you may be one in which you have a personal interest. You may be faced with a bewildering array of organizations needing your free time, your ideas, your hands, your present or future clout, and your money (however little that may be). If you have a personal reason for working for a nonprofit institution, you have the best kind of inbuilt motivation there is. Princess Yasmin Khan, for example, the daughter of the late film star Rita Hayworth, devotes her efforts to raising money to fight Alzheimer's— the disease that afflicted her mother through much of her later life. In fact, if it were not for Rita Hayworth, many Americans would not have been aware of the nature of this disease or of the need for research in fighting it. Betty Ford, wife of former President Gerald Ford, a victim of cross addiction to alcohol and drugs, works tirelessly to combat such addictions, and the successful Betty Ford Clinic in California is a testimonial to her efforts. A well-known businessman whose daughter is blind works nonstop to raise money for training the dogs that help the blind. Famous people who have had cancer always seem ready to make appearances and write articles to help the fight against this dreaded disease.

But for every celebrity out in front, there are hundreds of thousands of noncelebrities who have personally suffered with a disease or seen it touch a member of their family or a friend. That is motivation enough.

The health field is by no means the only one in serious need of volunteer time and money. Feeding and clothing the poor and the homeless . . . working with churches and temples to assist the very young or the very old . . . acting as surrogate parents to underprivileged children to keep them from becoming dropouts . . . women serving as role models to help economically deprived women work and support their families, particularly women newly released from prison . . . couples laboring to solve the disastrous financial problems of the arts and to stimulate their growth in small communities . . . parents going far beyond their usual responsibilities to help make their children's schools better—these are just a sampling of what is out there that needs doing.

Former First Lady Barbara Bush, who comes from a family of readers, has long been a leader in the literacy movement, well before her White House days. Her daughter-in-law First Lady Laura Bush has been a very effective advocate for our nation's libraries. First Lady Nancy Reagan brought dramatic attention to the treatment of drug problems. Jimmy and Rosalynn Carter have worked long and hard for better housing for the poor. Jacqueline Onassis was a leader in the fight for historic preservation in our cities. However, you don't need to be a member of a president's family to be effective in helping a cause.

You don't have to look far for suggestions on what you personally can do and where you can do it. You may only have to look around your neighborhood, listen to and read the local news. There is always enough time in a week to wring out a few more hours of service dedicated to others, even if you work hard at a job. The rewards are tremendous in terms of personal satisfaction. A New York woman made famous by the gossip columnists because of her lavish parties, French designer clothes, and incredible jewels works secretly in one of the toughest sections of New York in a special program for gifted black students. She goes there three times a week in a cab (not in her chauffeured Jaguar), dressed in the simplest clothes. When I saw her recently, we discussed her volunteer work. Her reputation around town is mainly that of a vapid, spoiled woman. Yet she looked at me with eyes full of pure joy as she confided, "You know, I have really made a difference there. I've been working with three kids in particular who are deep into the sciences, and I've found someone to pay for scholarships for them to the top colleges of their choice. Now the others want to excel in their own things and have me help them find scholarships, too. It's making a difference!"

• If you are fortunate enough to be able to donate a sizable amount of money to something, make it a quiet, anonymous gift. Word of your generosity will get around anyway, and you have no idea in this world of self-promotion how much people will admire you for your discretion and self-effacement in making your gift quietly, without fanfare. In other words, let others publicize and praise you. They will do it far more effectively than you could.

THE WAY TO GET ON
A NONPROFIT AGENCY BOARD

There are two ways to get on this kind of a board—through very generous donations that look as though they will never stop or through hard work and energy. Most people have to use the second route.

If you are new in town, decide on the field in which you wish to work, then go right to the main office at that organization and volunteer. If you know someone who is already there as a volunteer, then you can be introduced to the director of the organization, and the contacts are easily made. If you know no one within the organization, just go and present yourself. The question "What can I do to help?" is beautiful music to almost every pair of ears in the volunteer management world. It's the quality of your volunteer work that is going to make you a star. When you do the dirty jobs cheerfully, when you show an ability to follow someone's direction, and when you also show your own creativity and initiative, you will rise very naturally to important new positions of responsibility within the volunteer structure.

Here are the characteristics of what a director of volunteers at a hospital told me makes an outstanding volunteer, who then may become a candidate for an advisory board position. The volunteer:

- Takes direction with intelligence, obedience, and loyalty.
- Is punctilious about arrival time.
- Will remain longer than the required hours in case of an emergency.
- Doesn't accept a job and then announce that he is going on vacation for two months.
- When other obligations intrude so that volunteer hours must be temporarily curtailed, she reports it far enough in advance to allow time for a qualified substitute to be located.
- Dresses appropriately for the job—not flashily or ostentatiously, but professionally.
- Keeps meticulously accurate records when they are called for, such as in fund-raising.
- Respects the confidentiality of the institution and does not spread gossip about the people served there or the other volunteers; acts as a source of good public relations for the institution when talking about it in his family, work, or social milieu.
- Does not make personal telephone calls during volunteer hours.
- If her primary work is interaction with the people served by the institution, learns to polish his interpersonal skills, becomes even more sensitive to others' problems, and practices kindness and self-control, even when the people she is serving do not.

• Remains in a creative mode, so that he can suggest to management ways of doing things better and at less cost.

If Your Volunteer Motives Are Partly Social

Some people, men and women both, are primarily interested in helping organize benefits to widen their social lives. The way to work your way up in the social strata of a benefit committee is to offer to do any dirty work that needs to be done (such as helping to hand-address two thousand invitations). One woman I know did just that. She sat and wrote for days, listening to what her fellow addressers were saying about the people on the master list. "I learned more about the local scene while doing those invitations than I could have in fifty years under any other circumstances," she told me. She said it was the best orientation to the social scene in that community she could have received as a newcomer in that town.

A person who is a tireless worker in helping organize a benefit becomes admired and befriended by the other members of an organization. It is one of the best ways to widen the circle of friends who share your interests.

But the best motivation of all is to become involved in an organization that *truly* interests you and needs your help, whether it is in the area of fund-raising, giving volunteer hours, lending administrative expertise, or doing whatever you do well.

"I have a good volunteer job" means that you're useful, you enjoy what you're doing, you're in the mainstream, you give the gift of yourself, and you make good friends while you're doing it. Any one of those benefits makes volunteer effort well worth it.

Like anything of value, friends require loving care, whatever their age, sex, or socioeconomic level, and that attention should be consistent. No matter how busy you may be, you can always check in with a quick telephone call or note. You can't quantify your relationship with friends. The pleasure they give you in return for your acts of kindness toward them is immeasurable.

Making friends really does take a great deal of effort, and it seems you are always required to give more to them than they give to you. What is ironic is that your friends are probably saying the very same thing about you!

WORDS TO USE AT DIFFICULT TIMES

There are times when it's difficult to find the right thing to say or write to people who are going through a very tough time. Just the fact that you are trying to find a way to comfort them is a great gift to the other person. For example:

1. *When a friend has just lost her husband,* Eddie, in a tragic accident, it is usually easier to write words of comfort than to say them face to face.

   The first part of the letter would show that you know how terrible the loss is for your friend: "I know there's nothing I can say that's going to help. I know you must feel so awful, so filled with despair, that life seems like an ugly, inescapable black cloud. But Eddie wouldn't want you to be hurting this much. He would hate it. He would want you to miss him terribly, but at the same time to be strong and vow to get on with your life and make him proud. I know that's what you'll do. You're made of good stuff. You have always known how to tough it out, and you are certainly going to do that now."

   The second part of the letter would be a remembrance of the fun times you have all had together. Recall some amusing incidents, with her husband as the starring figure.

   The third part should contain compliments about the deceased person's life, and what made him so special and memorable: "There was never anyone who had a greater ability to put people immediately at ease. Eddie would make the shyest, angriest, most disturbed person relax and immediately feel at home when that person crossed your threshold. I've never seen anyone with such a gift. . . ."

   The fourth paragraph, the signoff, would include the fact that Eddie's friends will be there to comfort his widow: "Have courage, for his sake, but also for ours."

2. *When someone keeps trying to be your friend but just doesn't get it—* that you do not want his attention—nor do you want to hurt this person's feelings:

   "George, thanks again for the invitation, but I want to tell you something. You're a smart, intelligent guy. I wish we could be 'great friends,' as you described it. But I'm so busy with my job and home schedules, there just isn't time to add one more friend to my life. I don't even see my family and my closest friends enough, so I hope you'll understand why I've had to turn down all your nice invitations."

3. *When someone is courting you, wanting you to go on the board of a prestigious charity,* and you know a big donation would be expected from you—which you're not prepared to give:

   Write this person (and certainly don't just leave a message declining the "honor" by telephone or e-mail!). By writing, you can avoid talking personally to the charity executive who could apply pressure and talk you into it. (I know this too well from personal experience.) In your typed or handwritten letter (which should be hand-delivered or sent express):

   • Begin by saying how greatly honored you are to have received this board invitation, but you must decline.

- Mention how impressed you are by the invaluable work done for the community by this particular organization.
- In your final paragraph, add, "I regret that I am unable to take on additional activities at this time. I wish you, the Board, the officers and employees of the XYZ organization every good wish for a successful year ahead."

If you want to be *really graceful* about it, send a nice donation check along with your refusal letter.

4. *When you must let go an elderly, longtime employee* who reports to you. You doubly dread it because everyone loves this person.

This is a moment in which you must speak personally to her, and don't delay with that bad news. Lay it out in front right away, and spend the rest of the time telling her how sorry you are to have to let her go:

"You can't imagine, Aggie, how hard this is for me to tell you. Everyone in this company holds you in such high regard. Because we have been forced to make cuts right and left, every person remaining will be required to do two jobs simultaneously, until we pull up and out of this negative economic environment for our business. I want you to know that you have earned the respect—the love, too—of everyone here. You have been a role model for all the women employees during these past decades, and I can say the same thing for the men."

Explain that the Personnel Office will give her a severance package as generous as is possible, and review all of the perks she will still enjoy for the next year, such as medical, if that's the case. Give her some comfort: "Aggie, this is not the end of the road. You have so much talent—you'll find something, perhaps even in another field. We'll help you in achieving that, I promise."

5. *When a friend's marriage breaks up,* tell him or her:
   - How sorry you are (as is everyone) to hear the news.
   - How you realize how much this person must be hurting, "because it is devastating," and the readjustment will take some time.
   - How you would like to help in some way—any way—if only he would ask you.
   - How you are in the process of compiling a list of things you would like your friend to join you in doing on coming weekends, to keep busy and moving toward a new life. (By the way, don't forget to send your friend that list, after promising it as a healing device.)
   - Make sure that he has Thanksgiving, Christmas, Easter, and Fourth of July invitations, or invitations for the Jewish Holy Days.

6. *When someone goes bankrupt and loses everything:*
   Tell this person that you will always stand up for her as a friend, that her reputation will not be permanently damaged. Add, "I know you have lawyers working on your business, but remember, you have so

many loyal friends, people who may not be able to help you financially in these tough times, but who are here for you" with:

- shoulders to lean on
- bits of legal and financial advice that might prove helpful
- encouraging words about how she will get through this, emerge stronger than ever, and be able to put this entire experience behind her.

7. *When a good friend has a miscarriage:*

Make your friend realize that you know this is a moment of true, intense grief. Don't say things like, "Oh, you'll get pregnant right away again," or "Obviously something was wrong with the fetus, so you're lucky not to have to go through those problems later." Assure her that there is nothing that can assuage her pain, "but when the time is right, I am ready to join you in any project you feel strong enough to undertake." Add that, "When you're ready, I want to help you plan a memorial of some kind to honor your child." (That's what friends are for.)

8. *When a friend enters a long-term substance abuse program:*

- Reassure him that the decision is absolutely the right one, the constructive one, and the *courageous* one.

- Assure him that people look upon him as a person with a tremendous future, waiting to be realized, that was being compromised by the substance problem. Now he will be conquering that problem and *going forward* to an exciting realization of the promises his life now presents. In other words, use encouraging words to reiterate that he's going to be a winner (relating to conquering the abuse, and to his new, productive life).

- Sympathize with how difficult the program will be, but how all of his many, many friends are pulling for him and waiting for him to come back to them again.

9. *When someone is dying from sickness or injury:*

- Hold her hand or touch her in some way, showing you are not frightened or shocked by her appearance.

- Mention her religious faith, whatever it is, as the strong support system to help her in these last days.

- Tell her what a good life she has led, what a good person she has been, and how many people love her and will miss her.

- Remind her that you and others will help the family members she is leaving behind live through their grief, how you will help her spouse and children readjust and will keep watch over them.

- Remind her that she is someone who has made a difference in this life.

- Remind her that there is such joy ahead for her in *the next life,* including a release from all pain, as well as a peace and joy that is impossible for us to comprehend. If you have a religious faith, as the greatest gift of all at a time like this, you might say to her, "How wonderful to look forward to being with God!" (This is something I once said to a dying atheist, and he grinned at me and said, "Thank you.")

- Kiss her good-bye on the cheek or forehead, saying, "I'll be around, I'll be here," even if you have to leave the premises. This is telling the person that you are with her constantly in spirit.

10. *When you hear one of your "friends" has been bad-mouthing you* in your social circle.

It's definitely easier to put pen to paper (not in an e-mail) and to write a letter in which you can be much more civil, even gracious, than you really feel:

Dear Pam:

I have heard from several sources that you have been saying unpleasant things about me among our friends, and I felt it was only fair to ask you why this has happened to two people who have known one another for fifteen years, who have gone through happy and hard times together, but have always emerged with the bonds of friendship wound tighter than ever.

At least, that was how I felt. Something is obviously bothering you greatly. Please tell me what it is. It is ridiculous for two old friends to behave this way! If I have wronged you, I want to know how, and I want "to fix it, since it's broken."

I hope that a face-to-face meeting will occur sooner, rather than later.

GROWING OLDER WITH GRACE

Most people have their own interpretation of what constitutes the "middle-aged years." Even old age, or senior years, or whatever you want to call them (please omit that phrase "over the hill"), is difficult to define today, even visually. Plastic surgeons grow richer by the minute in our botoxed, decellulited, and face-lifted culture, as we continue to hide our ages. ("Hide" is a nicer word than "lie about.")

Many of us, men included, have obviously forgotten how to age with grace. Look at a woman with a face pulled beyond taut by surgery, and look at her vein-removed, surgically improved legs, now teetering in notoriously high sandals meant for someone under thirty-five, her mini-skirt riding high on an obviously mature thigh. If only the emptiness in many of those faces could be hidden, along with the sags and creases. I remember the Duchess of Windsor in her last decade of life, her face a marble mask, unable to open her mouth and chew because of the surgeries, and finally receiving her nourishment through a straw. Compare her to the "Queen Mum," mother of Queen Elizabeth II, whose untouched face, in her late nineties, was compared by a journalist to "the verdant serenity of a beautiful, natural English garden."

THE MIDDLE-AGED YEARS
SHOULD BE AND CAN BE THE BEST OF TIMES

• You are still fit and strong—or, if you have shirked exercise, you can become fit and strong with a little power named after "Will." With *will*power you can command yourself to do certain things, discipline your mind, body, and, yes, character. It is a true power surge.

• You now command a modicum, or perhaps a lot, of respect. You know "things." You have experienced "stuff," as the kids would describe it. Young people will look at you in admiration, because you've been there, and definitely done that. Even "the lads," as the British refer to young men of seventeen or a bit older, need to learn from you, and most of them know it.

• Because you are "wise," you can be a source of great comfort to the young. You can pass along the knowledge that no matter how dismal the picture seems, or how much a person has messed up, that young person can eventually emerge afloat, even victorious.

• You don't have to change babies' diapers anymore, unless your children are close by and you want to help. You get to hold the baby and give it back when it starts screaming or spitting up.

• You have some great stories to tell to those younger than you on subjects such as family, job, travel, creative successes, and victories over serious obstacles. You can bask in your earned admiration, because you have "filled the tank," so to speak, with the fuel of knowledge and awareness.

• You hopefully have more time during these years to improve your mind—get the kinks out of it, de-rust it. You're also wiser, so that you can make better choices resulting from those mind workouts.

SOME OPTIONS FOR IMPROVING THE MIND

1. *Be smart in choosing new hobbies.* Don't take up bridge, for example, if you live in a community where it is impossible to get four people together on a regular basis, or even four people who love the game with a passion.

2. *Get a library card.* Whether you're retired or not, saturate your brain with books, periodicals, lectures, on-line research, even a night course or an on-line course for credit. The more you read and study, the more brilliant a conversationalist you become, the happier you become

with new interests. You will be looked up to at your place of work. If you're on a retirement track, no one will think of you as a colleague whose time has come to slow down with age; you'll be seen as a colleague who is more vital and aware of the world than ever. What a great feeling it is to be sought out for your advice.

SOME OPTIONS FOR IMPROVING THE BODY

In the pursuit of a healthy, well-exercised body to maintain your youthful freshness and enthusiasm, make good friends of your fellow exercisers. They will remain important to you. For example:

1. *Get a gym membership* and use it faithfully.
2. *Hire a personal trainer* to get you started on the daily exercises you can do in the gym—but also at home. Don't get trapped by the constant advertising pitches of home gym equipment.
3. *Investigate what yoga classes can do for you.* You can find one in which people of your age, with the same aches and pains, are finding great relief as well as a more positive attitude.
4. *Take up aquatic aerobics.* You will find relaxation and become more limber, without harming those painful joints. You'll also find people your own age, feeling equally as silly as you may feel exercising in water. Your local YMCA might offer a gym membership that includes a pool.
5. If you're healthy, middle age is the perfect time to *become part of a team if you haven't been before*—volleyball, softball, bowling, boating competitions, even "croquet, anyone?" A healthy team spirit is good for your business, morale, and lineup of good friends.
6. *Investigate the calming exercises from the Far East,* like the Chinese T'ai Chi Ch'uan (calisthenics of very slow, controlled movements).
7. *Take a course of therapeutic massages,* which relieve tension in the head, neck, and entire body, and help free up swollen, stiff joints.

SOME OPTIONS FOR IMPROVING THE HEART

The heart's strings should be exercised, like everything else.

If you have missed these options earlier in your life, you can start now. Make up with family members with whom the tie has been broken. Regardless of who was at fault or what grievous offense was committed against you, take the initiative. Even if you know you were the innocent, aggrieved party, go to any family enemies and say, "I'm sorry, I am really sorry, and I want to have you in my life again." If they do nothing to reciprocate this selfless act, just wait. They will. As one grows older, every family member becomes triply important. If you are the one who always has to apply the glue to get the family talking to and supporting one another again, be glad you are there. *They* will be glad you are there, even if they can't express it.

Who said middle-aged people lead a depressing life, as they march toward an even more depressing one, old age? If you want to feel good about where you are, at this particular senior moment in life, make a few careful lists that will explain who you are, and what about you is being left to your descendants. These lists might reveal a great deal more about you to them than anything else:

> List 1: The greatest things I've witnessed through my entire life.
> List 2: My greatest accomplishments of which I'm most proud.
> List 3: The most wonderful people I have known—and why.
> List 4: What is still left for me to do.

> Conclusion: Some people are old before they reach adulthood. Some people don't have the time to grow old.

LEAVE YOUR REAL LEGACY BEHIND YOU

I wish I had known many of my ancestors. The only one I really ever knew was my uncle Rob Connell, who died a young balloon officer in World War I in France, because he left behind a leather-bound diary. He wrote amazing descriptions of what he was doing, and what he was thinking about—the guns of war, *les Boches* (as the Germans were called), and girls. He thought about girls a lot, but in the most courtly, gallant way.

Write your own memoirs. Or get some thoughts down, using a tape recorder. Put captions on the photographs you've taken, don't just stuff them in the drawer. All kinds of new technologies are coming along to help you record your thoughts and feelings while you are multitasking. In other words, *leave yourself behind* for future generations to come.

I get enormous pleasure fantasizing that many years from now someone might be reading one of my autobiographies, found in the Sociology or American History sections of the library, and think to themselves, "What a crazy lady! But, man, did she ever have a life!"

CHAPTER 4

Working Smart

It's quite logical to trace the growth of this country with the parallel trends in business. George Washington made a business out of farming at Mount Vernon, and was renowned for keeping an eye on the profit ledger, long before his roles in the American Revolution and the writing of the Declaration of Independence. Most important, ethics governed his entire life. Everyone looked up to him and was inspired by the way he handled every aspect of his challenges.

Compare this to our business leaders today. America has been shaken like a rag doll in its reputation and its ethics, with the revelation of each scandal that hits a major corporation and its senior management. Security today means constant awareness of the military threats to our country, terrorists, and urban snipers, but it also means we must accept new measures of security in business dealings. We can talk all we want about ethics and safety in business, but that all starts in the home—the conduct adults instill into children by talking to them and acting as role models for the way young people lead their own lives.

Nothing is more important than our behavior, because it defines how people judge us. Everything starts with manners, whether it's the social manners discussed throughout this book, or working manners, discussed in this chapter. Whether it's a question of being aware of other human beings, making them feel comfortable, or just meriting their trust, manners make society function and motivate people to work with one another.

Men and women in business today are now scrutinized for the old-fashioned precepts of loyalty, honesty, and integrity, as much as they are for their professional skills. Call these "people skills" if you wish, or "good manners," but they all go to shape a good, healthy business climate in which people respect one another.

Good manners do not change according to the time of day or the locale, or if a person is busy making a killing on the stock market or a big splash at a dinner party. They're built into the structure of our characters, and they can't be turned off and on at will, like a water faucet. They're instinctive and sincere. Otherwise, they are simply acts of hypocrisy, as much despised in business as in society.

Business etiquette requires that you know that business files and papers may not be taken out of your briefcase, discussed, or signed in a private club's dining room. Nor do you plunk a briefcase or tote bag down on someone's dining room table. Social manners require that you know enough to dance first with your host or hostess, as well as make some other "duty dances," before concentrating on the attractive person with whom you ardently wish to dance every dance. Having the self-control to think ahead and to be a keen observer of what's going on around you will enable you to navigate with ease the tricky seas of manners—whether you're networking at a business reception or coordinating the speakers in a conference panel or wondering if it's gauche to pour both chocolate and butterscotch sauce on your dessert at dinner.

It's been my experience that the most powerful tool in the world of business is a well-toned sense of humor. If you can laugh at yourself and own up to any errors you have made (and believe me, I know this, because I've spent a lifetime making them), you will be able to survive.

COMMONSENSE POLITE BUSINESS BEHAVIOR: GOOD TO KNOW!

Knowing how to be a good team member, as well as winning the respect and loyalty of your fellow workers, requires a major effort. Not only is it a lot of work, but once you've done it, you must keep on doing it. The only reason to make such an effort is because it is of great value to you.

Whatever your position in business—whether you're an executive or someone who's just stepped onto the bottom rung of the corporate ladder—simple commonsense consideration for others wins respect and marks you as a team player who is a real asset to the company.

• Be as nice to the people on the bottom of the job scale in your office as you are to the boss. Quite apart from the factors of kindness and respect involved, these people will become your friends and valuable supporters, which will probably prove to be the greatest asset of your career.

• Be loyal to and defend the boss inside or out of the office.

• Don't "rat" on anyone, unless that person is committing a serious offense (drug dealing, stealing, or the like).

• Unless you are a person's supervisor, don't criticize him directly, and especially not behind his back. After all, that person could be your boss one day.

• Help out the newcomers. Show them around, make them feel welcome and part of the team. Give them a feel for the politics of the office. In other words, follow the Golden Rule, because you would certainly want someone to do the same for you if you were the newcomer.

• Always keep your promises. Establish—and keep—your reputation as a person of good faith.

• Pay back your lunch obligations. Don't become known as the person who never picks up the check.

• Put things in their proper perspective by using your sense of humor. If you don't have one, work on it. This should be a top priority.

WHEN YOU'RE NEW IN THE OFFICE

• You need information—on how things work, on what everyone does, on the politics of the office. You find out the answers to all those questions by:

  - Asking intelligent questions of intelligent people when they have the time to talk to you. Timing is everything in the business world, and you must learn to be sensitive to it. Never try to take up someone's time when she is obviously late, on a deadline, or overloaded with work.

  - Going through the files, which reveals how the people in the company write their letters, talk to their customers or clients, and communicate among themselves.

  - Most important of all, *listening!* What you hear all around you is the best education of all. Some people when they are new in an office are so entranced with their efforts to impress people, they hear nothing else. They are not listeners and thereby often lose the forest just to save a couple of trees.

• Be nice to absolutely everyone, from the messenger to the CEO. If you want to look at it clinically, each person in that office environment may be key to the advancement of your career. But more important, when you are genuinely kind to everyone, you greatly improve the atmosphere and the general office morale. I learned long ago, by the way, that my best friends and supporters in *any* office are the clerical staff and receptionists.

• Ask your peers to lunch, one by one, so that you will get to know each one on a personal, relaxed basis (as well as obtain valuable information about the company or firm from each one).

• Be very modest about your past jobs and your qualifications for this one. People are immediately attracted to someone who downplays his importance. They usually conclude that person is more important than he actually is.

What to Say When You Are Belittled at Work

a. *In an office meeting* (take a firm stance with your reply):

"George, you are making some very unfair and inaccurate statements about me. I'm not going to take up everyone's time to deal with this now, but I certainly will, right after this meeting." (Don't forget to do it, and don't lose your courage, because in settling the matter away from others you're doing the right thing.)

b. *At a conference attended by representatives of several companies:*

"I'm sorry to interrupt these proceedings, but I thought we had an agenda to complete. These unfair innuendos against me leave me determined to remain a gentleman, hold my temper, and not retaliate against the unbusinesslike, destructive behavior of the earlier speaker."

c. *At a business-social event:*

"Mary, that's pretty strong stuff to toss out at a cocktail party. Why don't we limit those kinds of remarks to an office discussion, with just you and me in the room, and not before a cast of thousands?"

d. *When your boss makes disparaging comments about you in public, talk to her privately afterward:*

"Jennifer, that commentary on my work at the Monday staff meeting really hit me hard. I'm obviously disappointing you in a serious way, and I don't know exactly why, which is the hardest part. I promise I'll correct the situation if you will just square with me. I happen to love this company, and my job as well. I admire you and want you to consider me a good team member. Please give me a chance to improve. Give it to me straight."

e. *When someone tells you your executive assistant is "dissing" you openly around the office:*

"Aggie, I've heard from more than one source you've been criticizing me in public. That's not only disloyal, it's disruptive and harmful to the success of our projects. I think you owe me an explanation as to why you've taken this path. If you think it will help you get my job, you are badly mistaken. It works like that only in the movies. Now, come on. I've always trusted you before. Tell me what's going on here."

TO BE A WELL-LIKED, SUCCESSFUL EXECUTIVE

• Do not gossip. Senior management views the office gossip as a mean-spirited person who thinks she has more time to spend on nonwork-related conversation than she actually has!

• Do not put down anyone in front of others. The person who puts someone else down may think he looks clever and witty, but the perception of others is just the opposite. And put-downs can do real damage to the victim. In one of my jobs everyone called the office tightwad "Mr. Stingy." Forty years later I heard this nickname had followed him through the years. What an unfortunate way to be remembered.

- Always give credit where credit is due, which means not trying to collect praise for something not really of your doing.
- Always make reference to the team effort—i.e., "We did this" or "We did that," not "I then did this, and then I did that." This also implies taking the rap for the team when something goes wrong. The person who whines to senior management, "Of course, this wasn't my doing; it was John's and Mary's idea—I had nothing to do with it," shows a total lack of leadership, even if she did have nothing to do with it. How much better for her to say, "*We* can't let this happen again. I think *we* can solve the problem."
- Keep your promises—for example, when promising to stay late and help put a project to bed, making promised telephone calls or e-mails, or putting in a good word for someone as promised.
- Return telephone calls within twenty-four hours, or at least have someone else handle the matter for you. It is good manners and also good business to do this.
- Answer important letters within the week, unimportant mail within two weeks. If you delay longer, your reply loses validity and importance.
- Be punctual for all appointments—again, the nice thing to do, but also essential to the efficiency of operations. I'll never forget waiting in a CEO's office one day for the son of one of that company's directors to appear. He was thirty minutes late, which caused the CEO miss his train. When the CEO asked him what the purpose of his visit was, the young man replied that he wanted help in finding a job. The CEO, by now absolutely furious, told him, "There is definitely one company where you will never find a job, and that's this one." The young man's father later called the CEO and thanked him for teaching his overly casual son a good lesson.
- Keep everyone involved in a project informed. In other words, don't hold a project "close to the vest."
- If you are a senior manager, make sure your employees have a proper working environment, such as efficient desks, comfortable chairs, proper air circulation, and good lighting.
- Help the younger staff members with their training—by giving suggestions, answering their questions patiently, and in general serving as a friendly guiding hand while they learn the ropes. A thirty-year-old person can serve as a mentor for a twenty-five-year-old. All that is required of the tutor is more experience and a good amount of patience, and it really helps if he has a sense of humor.
- Answer all invitations within a week's time, and attend the event if you

accepted the invitation. The well-mannered executive respects an RSVP on an invitation and is never an unexplained no-show. When an executive is a no-show or shows up with an uninvited guest at a corporate or private social affair, it reflects badly on him or her and the company.

• Promptly return anything borrowed from a colleague, in perfect condition, and with a spoken or written word of thanks. I recently lent my personal computer for an entire afternoon to someone who claimed she desperately needed it. Once it was gone I became irritated and resentful until I went back to my computer, found it with its cover neatly on (which I always forgot), the keyboard cleaned with a special solution (it badly needed it), and a lovely note expressing how my loan of the computer had saved her from a fate worse than death. A good bottle of wine, tied with a ribbon, accompanied the note. All of a sudden, I didn't mind at all that she had tied up my PC.

• Be rigorous about repaying hospitality and acknowledging favors. You may be a dazzler at any party, but no host in the world is going to want to continue to invite you to functions at which you can shine and show your stuff if you never reciprocate or are never properly grateful.

• Be quick to drop a line (and go on record) to congratulate someone who has performed well. It's those words on a piece of paper that the recipient can read, reread, and show around to friends and family that make him feel proud and love the job.

• Enthusiastically defend at any level of management a colleague who has been wronged. It might be something as major as telling the big boss that the person in the office next to you was not the last person to leave the other night, and therefore could not have been the one who committed the security violation of leaving the safe open. It might be something as minor as defending the way a colleague who is being blamed for being a sloppy manager explained to the messenger where to take a certain envelope, which was brought to the wrong address.

• Know how to dress on business or social occasions, so that the company or firm is proud, not embarrassed, to have you representing them. (The executive who shows up for dinner without a jacket and tie in the dining room of a fancy resort like the Greenbriar, in West Virginia, makes others think that he and his company are a bunch of hicks.)

• Show deference to people who are senior, rather than treating them with the same "first-name, slap-on-the-back, we're-all-equal" attitude. I have seen many a senior executive in his sixties wince upon meeting a young executive from another company who immediately calls him by his first name or a nickname.

• Don't boast about your past—or present, for that matter. Someone who, because of family connections, is friendly with the CEO doesn't talk about it in the presence of colleagues. Nor does that person talk about parties she has been invited to and opportunities enjoyed that the others have not shared.

- Show compassion to a colleague who has had bad news. This means taking the person aside, perhaps with an arm around his shoulders, to say how sorry you are, and to ask if you may be of assistance in any way.

- Don't treat hot new information as your personal property, not to be shared with others. Someone who finds out something and then keeps it a secret until it can be presented to senior management is no team player. She should share it with colleagues—because she can still get the credit for discovering it.

- Don't waste company time with idle chitchat or personal telephone calls. Never bother someone by insisting on talking when that person is obviously trying to concentrate and finish a project.

- Talk lovingly about your spouse and children, but only minimally, so as not to distract the work of others.

- Write a personal letter to thank someone for a meal, gift, or favor. There is no question but that a person who writes personal notes is remembered fondly and gets ahead in life!

- Buck up a colleague who is feeling discouraged. Sometimes it takes as little as sticking your head in someone's office door and saying, "Hey, cheer up! This mess will be over soon, the sun will shine again, and you'll be on top of the world. A little patience! A little courage!" Sometimes it takes several meetings to persuade a friend who needs help to seek psychological counseling. No matter how hard you are working at the office, think about your colleagues, and help them when they need it. You might need help of this kind yourself some day.

- Organize a continuing show of office support for someone who is hospitalized, injured, or seriously ill. This means not just one bunch of flowers or one card signed by everyone in the office, but a message of affection—and office news—going out once or twice a week to that person.

- Introduce people so as to make each person sound—and feel—important and wonderful. At lunch in the executive dining room you can introduce a guest as "Elmer Snowden from Watkins and Meloy," or you can introduce him with praise and/or humor: "This is Elmer Snowden, one of the best accountants Watkins and Meloy has ever had in their firm since it was founded. Elmer is absolutely top drawer—and a nice guy in spite of it!" The second kind of introduction brings smiles all around and warms up the room.

- Remember to thank the little people who do all the work on a major event—such as the special events managers who arrange the travel, make the audiovisuals for presentations, copy necessary materials, organize conferences or corporate parties, and the like. This kind of recognition should be on the record—via personal letters to the people involved, in a verbal salute in front of the group, or in a tribute published in the company magazine. Meeting planners rarely receive the recognition they deserve, in the opinion of many.

• Work the entire time at a company party, instead of standing in a corner, chatting with office pals, enjoying the food and drinks. Every person in the host company should be out there, introducing guests, making sure that everyone has a drink and someone to talk to—and that everyone has met the corporate hosts. Members of the staff should remember they are hosts, not guests!

SOME ABCs OF EXECUTIVE ETIQUETTE

• Cultivate beautiful telephone manners:
  • Place your own calls.
  • Do not put people on endless hold.
  • Do not take telephone calls when someone with an appointment is sitting in your office.
  • When you have called a busy person, be sensitive about that person's time pressures.
  • Do not have your calls screened, or blow your stack when someone else does.
  • Apologize for dialing a wrong number.
• Rise and stand every time someone from the outside—a peer or someone more senior—enters the room. Men and women alike, of any age, should rise at their desks and step forward to greet their callers, just as you should rise and step forward to greet a new guest when he arrives at your or anyone else's party.
• Know how to introduce people properly—a younger person to a more senior one, a nonofficial person to a person with rank or a title, and so forth.
• Use a firm, practiced, but not bone-crushing handshake, and shake hands outside the office every time you meet someone or tell a person good-bye.
• Know how to make small talk with people senior to you or those who are strangers. The art of making good business conversation includes the ability to pass the time of day in agreeable conversation, talking about unimportant subjects while waiting for more substantial discussions to begin.
• Never expect anyone who answers to you to follow a rule you do not yourself obey.

TRAVELING WITH THE BOSS

When traveling with the boss, a young executive should always:
• Give the boss the best seat—in a restaurant or an airplane, in a taxi or limo (never let the boss sit in the back of the van!), on a bus or train.
• Unless instructed not to, take care of all baggage matters, checking into hotels, ordering cars, tipping, and paying the bills for lodging, meals, and transportation.

• Carry all of the heavy paraphernalia when you and the boss are in transit.

• Remain silent when the boss opens her briefcase or files and is studying them.

• Speak frankly if the boss asks direct questions, such as, "How are things coming along in your section?" or "Any particular complaints in your division?" (This is an opportunity to score some points for your section; it should not be looked upon as a chance to derail the career of someone you personally dislike.)

• Make it a top priority to make life easy and comfortable for the boss en route to any destination.

The number of today's very successful chief executive officers who began their careers as young assistants to other CEOs is legion. An MBA graduate commented wistfully, "Think of the contacts I'd make if I were the right arm and the aide-de-camp of the big boss. What an opportunity it would be for me to spend my time with the top brass!"

I reminded him that he wouldn't get the job of a CEO's right arm unless he had the skills and the polish necessary. "What kind of polish?" he asked quizzically.

"Manners," I replied.

"Oh, those," he said disdainfully. "I can learn those overnight."

"No, you can't," I replied.

"Well, how long does it take?"

"As long as it takes you to start thinking about someone other than yourself." End of conversation!

Meeting Manners

As the senior manager and chairman of the meeting, it's your job to:

• Decide on the goals of the meeting (that is, if it's necessary to hold it in the first place!).

• Make sure the appropriate people are invited, so that no one who should be there feels snubbed by not being part of it.

• Make sure those invited know what the purpose is.

• Select the right date and time, when most people can attend.

• Two days ahead, send the minutes of the previous meeting and any material the attendees should read beforehand.

• Make sure the venue is cleaned and is equipped with good lighting, proper ventilation, comfortable chairs, pads and pencils, water pitcher(s) and glasses.

• Assure that the audiovisual equipment will be in place (overhead screens, projectors, film equipment, recording devices, easels to hold large charts, and the like).

- Introduce to the group any newcomer or person from outside the company in a flattering manner.
- Start the meeting on time, and end it exactly on time, without allowing anyone to hog the discussions or distract everyone from the job at hand.
- Keep one eye on the agenda and the other on the clock.
- Call for a short break after an hour and a half, if the meeting is not yet finished.
- At the end, thank everyone for their presentations, particularly those who prepared the audiovisuals.
- Make sure everyone understands his or her future responsibilities as a result of this meeting.
- Set the date for the next meeting on this project or problem.
- Summarize the results of the meeting.
- End the meeting on an up tone, with a burst of energy, so that attendees will feel that whatever is to be accomplished will be accomplished.

As an attendee at an important meeting, it's your job to:

- Arrive on time, even a few minutes before.
- Introduce yourself to anyone new before the meeting starts.
- Take good notes.
- Turn off your cell phone completely.
- Bring all the proper materials connected with the subject to the meeting. This presumes you have done all your homework.
- Do not interrupt—ever. Wait your turn.
- Raise your hand, informally, when you want to say something, wait to catch the chairman's eye, and wait for the signal to begin.
- Watch your posture. Sit upright and act attentive. Showing signs of restlessness or boredom signifies a very negative attitude and will work, against you. No doodling, and for heaven's sake, no dozing. Arrange beforehand to have your neighbor rouse you if you start to nod off!
- Do not belittle the speaker, either in what you say or in what your expression and posture convey when someone is speaking.
- Don't be afraid to ask for a clarification of something you don't understand. (Just don't do it too often!)
- Thank the chairman, say a friendly good-bye to the newcomers at the meeting, enter the date for the next meeting in your day planner, and mark down what you are supposed to do for the next meeting.
- Remember to congratulate a coworker who made a specially fine presentation to the group. A four-word e-mail will do it: "Nice job today, Roger!"

RECEIVING A VISITOR TO YOUR OFFICE

Your manners really show when someone from the outside comes to see you. Your visitor may find your office is sloppy and disheveled-looking, or your assistant or the receptionist are inept and uncaring, or your way of receiving him is cold and unwelcoming.

1. When someone has an appointment *with you,* she has it with you, not with other staff members. Train whoever greets the visitors with appointments to smile broadly and repeat the person's name. "Good morning, Ms. Swenson." Have this staff aide show her where to hang her coat and where the rest room facilities are located. The question should also be asked, "May I do anything for you while you're waiting?"

2. Don't make your important visitor wait interminably, because it is insulting. If you're tied up with something you absolutely can't inter- rupt, greet her in the outer office, explain about the unforeseen crisis, apologize, and ask if she would like to reschedule the appointment or rather wait. Send a staffer every fifteen minutes to report on how much longer you will be. Make sure she has good reading materials while waiting, including the company's annual report, but also something more exciting than that.

3. Go out to the reception area yourself to escort any visitor into your office. Place her in a comfortable chair close to you, not across the room. If you are going to have your conversation in another part of your office, in a grouping of a sofa, two chairs, and a coffee table, gesture where she is to be seated, before you sit down yourself.

4. Know ahead of time why this person is coming to see you, so you won't waste time wandering all over on subject matter. There are a few things you might say at the very start, to show you are not a robot, even if you're dying to get on with this appointment and be finished. "How's Sara doing?" and "How's your golf game? Are you making any bogeys these days, or is the ball still ending up in the water?"

5. If the agenda for the visit is a lengthy one, offer your visitor water or coffee. I remember one executive in New York who used to keep me and everyone else waiting for interminable periods. Finally, he asked me one day, "Tish, since I'm always infuriatingly late for my appoint- ments, what can I do to soften everyone's anger?"

   I had an answer for him. "Put a basket of different kinds of very fresh gourmet cookies and some coffee where your visitors are wait- ing." He did, and not only that, the cookies proved to be so successful, he had some plastic bags placed next to the cookies, so that those waiting could slip a few extra cookies in their briefcases, and take them away. (Comfort food never fails to soothe.)

6. Hold your calls while a visitor is present, and be sure your cell phone is turned off. There is no greater nor more rude intrusion than the ringing of a cell phone when you are deep in a discussion.

7. Do *not* place any business calls yourself that have nothing to do with the visit, because it's the height of rudeness.

8. When someone from the outside comes to see you, you should always rise from behind your desk, shake hands with your caller, and motion him into a chair. (Logically, this is not necessary when someone from your own company comes in to talk to you, but it's smart to rise from your chair when your visitor is someone in senior management making a rare appearance.)

    At the end of the appointment, it is exceptionally gracious to "see that person out," i.e., accompany him to the outer reception area, in view of the elevators, and say good-bye there.

9. *Practice making introductions.* Try it out on your family, your friends, and office associates. *Become familiar with the protocol attached to it.*

    a. You introduce junior people *to* senior people: "George, this is a former classmate of mine passing through town, Amory Williams. Amory, this is George O'Rourke, our chief financial officer."

    b. You introduce a nonranked person *to* someone of rank: "Mr. Ambassador, may I present Janet Grayson, the chairman of this benefit. Janet, this is Ambassador Renwick, the American ambassador to Finland."

    Older people outrank young ones of equal importance. People who formerly held officially elected or appointed positions of rank outrank those with no rank, even if the latter are heads of important companies. If you are required to put "The Honorable" in front of a person's name on an invitation or place card, that person has rank.

CORPORATE JET ETIQUETTE

If someone is allowing you to fly on her corporate jet, there is a code of good manners to follow, including:

1. It's important not only to be on time at the airport, but to be there well in advance of takeoff. Allow for traffic accidents and fire trucks on your way to the airport. If you are responsible for the pilot missing his previously reserved place in line for takeoff, he will have to wait a long time for the next takeoff slot, and you will win the title of the most unpopular executive in the boardroom!

2. Carry your own baggage to the plane; don't give that responsibility to one of the crew members, who may be busy with more important duties before takeoff.

3. Wait to board until after your host has boarded. He, or perhaps the attendant on board, will "suggest" where you should sit. There will be business meetings of which you may or may not be a part, but you should be seated accordingly.

4. Don't fill the cabin space with your bulky packages—particularly at holiday time, when everyone has the same problem.

5. When served refreshments, don't ask for something different. The normal galley is equipped only for light food service. I traveled once with some directors and their wives on their corporate plane. One spouse endeared herself to everyone by loudly complaining that her favorite mustard was not available and that there were no french fries. Her ten-year-old son fairly bellowed complaints that there was no chocolate sauce for the ice cream. I heard one director on board say softly, "If he were my kid, I'd smack him." Another of the company officers whispered in my ear, "If I were the CEO, I'd get that director off the board just because of his wife's and son's behavior. Who can go through this scene again?"

6. Before leaving the plane, be sure to thank the crew and congratulate the pilot and copilot for a smooth, delightful flight. Write a note to the CEO, thanking her for allowing you to take the flight, and complimenting the pilot and crew for making the trip "so safe and comfortable." When you compliment a corporate officer on her jet, it's like praising her on the design of her office, even her home!

IF A MEMBER OF SENIOR MANAGEMENT DIES

In the event of the death of a senior VIP executive, because of illness or an accident, someone on a senior level within the company must immediately take charge of the funeral arrangements. Among the duties this company coordinator might undertake (working in conjunction with a family member, of course) are these:

- Immediately notify the lawyer of the deceased.
- Help the survivor make quick decisions with the funeral home and gravesite director.
- Notify every member of the extended family, including the business "family," such as the board of directors, and provide them with the date, time, and place of the funeral services as well as of any memorial services to be held at a later date.
- Assign a company person to:

- Assist the surviving spouse in the home.
- Arrange for the meals of those staying in the house during this period.
- Coordinate the plans for the funeral and memorial services.
- Help the surviving spouse with the choice of and instructions to anyone speaking at the service.
- Arrange for the honorary pallbearers at the service (distinguished business and social members of the community who were friends of the deceased).
- Assign a company person to handle the telephone calls and e-mail traffic.
- Assign a company person to make the necessary hotel reservations for family members coming to the services, have them met at the airport or train station, and supply their transportation needs while they are in town for the activities.
- Arrange for a catered or private club luncheon or late afternoon cocktail reception following the service for the attendees.
- Set up the payment of fees to the mortuary, the church or temple expenses, the postservices reception costs.
- Notify all company employees of the fund or charity to which the family wishes donations to be made.
- Oversee the preparation of the optional pamphlet (such a nice reminder!) given to every attendee at the service, printed with:
    - The name and dates of the life and death of the deceased.
    - The name of the house of worship.
    - Names and titles of the officiating clergy.
    - Sequence of hymns and prayers to be said by the congregation.
    - Names of soloists and musicians.
    - Names of any friends or family who will be making remarks.
    - An informal photograph of the deceased, shown smiling, on the cover or back page of the pamphlet.
- Disseminate the news of the death immediately (and funeral information when it becomes available) to all of the employees of the company worldwide, as well as to the various consultants, lawyers, and ad agencies with whom this executive worked. Notify all of the professional and nonprofit organizations with whom the deceased was connected as well as the alumni magazine of schools attended.
- Consult with the spouse on the wording of the paid death notice in the newspapers, which should be done at once.
- Compose a press release with accompanying photograph for the local (or perhaps national) media if the deceased is well known in the community.

Corporate Responsibility
When Serving Alcohol

Thankfully, one doesn't hear the bullying, insistent command by a host to his guest "Have another drink" anymore. Nor is anyone embarrassed by asking for "A glass of soda water, please."

Alcoholism and drug addiction are steadily increasing problems, and always have been, though it seems those kids who steal liquor from their parents and show up drunk are younger and younger—many still in grade school.

Corporations become surrogate parents in this situation, hopefully noticing when employees have an alcohol or drug abuse problem, and providing immediate counseling for the individual. It's important for every company, if they do not have a substance abuse counselor on staff, to have the information readily available for anyone who needs help.

Companies can be sued when drunken guests leaving their parties cause accidents. Therefore, company hosts should be cautious and alert about the problem. This means:

- Short cocktail receptions (one and a half hours maximum).
- A twenty-five- to thirty-minute drinking period before a luncheon, with only wines and fruit juices served.
- A maximum forty-five-minute drinking period before dinner.
- Instructing waiters to refill guests' wineglasses only once or twice during the meal, and never a full glass.
- Removing the car keys of any departing guest who is obviously inebriated.

When there are guests who are against the service of alcohol for religious reasons:

- The best way to entertain them is a breakfast, a lunch, or a tea.
- Certain Muslims enjoy a drink away from their own country, so offer them alcohol along with the tray of fruit juices and soft drinks.

I will never forget when, during my Foreign Service career at the American embassy in Rome, as an assistant to Ambassador Clare Boothe Luce and her husband, publisher Henry Luce, we staged a large diplomatic dinner at the embassy for the Secretary of Agriculture, Ezra Taft Benson, and his wife. The Bensons did not touch one morsel of the lavish food that night. I had ordered from the chef, Rocco, sherry in the consommé, white wine in the fish course, red wine in the meat sauce, and Cognac in the crème brûlée dessert. When the Luces noticed their guests of honor were not eating, the Bensons explained that as Mormons (he later became the Senior Elder of the church), they did not touch alcohol. My menu planning was one of my lower moments as Social Secretary to the embassy.

WHEN YOU HAVE TO LET SOMEONE GO
FOR ECONOMIC REASONS

When you have to let someone go for just cause, such as stealing, selling drugs, and/or blatant nonperformance of duties, it is an unpleasant, difficult task. But when you let go someone who has become a colleague and friend because of downsizing and economic conditions, it can be heartwrenching.

Be prepared when you give him the news. Do some research and have at your fingertips all of the policies governing separation from the company, such as:
- Number of weeks' notice that must be given
- Possible severance pay
- Access to an outplacement service
- The use of a desk, phone, and receptionist for a period of so many weeks, or at least an answering machine to take calls
- The continuation of medical coverage for a specified length of time, etc.

Do the firing when you know his spouse will be at home when the executive returns there from your discussion. Experts constantly argue over whether the bad news should be given on a Monday or a Friday. What matters a great deal more is that when you give the bad news, you devote sufficient time to it, to help the employee recover from the initial shock. Be prepared to comfort and console him in an appropriate manner (again, this is a responsibility of leadership).

WHEN YOU ARE THE ONE LET GO

- Tell your office friends the bad news, separately and in private, as soon as you hear it. You will want them to have the facts straight, so they will have the proper information to dispel rumors that you were let go for "just cause." You will want them to know how much you have appreciated working with them. At this point in your life, you need every friend you have. It is no time to stand back and be shy.
- Because unemployment is so widespread, people will not automatically discriminate against you or think you are inept. Avoid the "Oh, poor me" syndrome. It's important to show the world (and yourself) how resilient you are.
- Do everything you can to help an assistant who has been let go. Speak to

Human Resources about finding him another good job within the organization, be enthusiastic about his talents, and write a wonderful letter of recommendation to be kept in his file but which can also be used by him to look for a job outside the company.

• If you are a casualty of company downsizing, write a letter to your CEO, with a copy to Human Resources, putting on the record how highly you regard the company, and how much you enjoyed being a member of the team. Even if that is not true, you will want to leave behind you the sweet smell of success instead of the odor of rancor and bitterness. You can always point out the positive things you learned, the good experiences you had, and then highlight in detail the major contributions you made to the company. Show what a professional you are, instead of telling off the CEO, which may be your inclination.

• Go on record with a handwritten note of appreciation to every important colleague and associate inside or outside your office who was nice to you over the past few years. For example:

Dear Mort,

Although being caught in the downsizing of the company is very painful, I want you to know that one of the nicest aspects of my years with Aristel was having known and worked with you, a real professional. I'll miss our joint efforts on making projects like Equi an unqualified success, but I'll also miss our arguments over the NBA championships. Perhaps in the future, wisdom will come to you and you'll realize the Knicks are really superior to the Lakers.

I hope our paths will cross and crisscross often. You've been a real pal. I never thought I would tell a Lakers fan that I'd miss him, but I will miss you. And, of course, if any career ideas for me should come to you in the middle of the night, this is one time I give you permission to call me at that hour.

My very best to Margie and the kids.

• Never let up on accuracy and neatness in your letters, no matter how tired or bored you may be writing them. Never send out anything sloppy that pertains to you, even if you feel a certain mailing is just a longshot.

• Consult the latest list of management recruiting firms that work on retainers or on a contingency basis. You will wish to contact some of them.

• Take someone to lunch who will introduce you to her good friend, a leading executive recruiter. Your goal is to end up in that firm's computerized data bank.

• Think positively about going into an entirely different line of work, including an entrepreneurship. A complete change could be the most energizing step you could make.

• Call up the branch heads of your professional organizations in other parts of the country that are not hit as hard by the economy as your area. Ask them if they think you should visit their city: "I'm just testing the waters out your way, since I have a great deal of experience correlating to (that area's main industry) and would enjoy coming out there." Fax your résumé to each person you talk to, complete with a note of "thanks for any suggestions you might have."

• Contact your alma mater's placement service bureau, and keep them supplied with all of your various market-targeted résumés, not just one.

• If you were an overpressured, hyperactive executive in your last position, take some time to smell the roses, and use your precious free time to better yourself or make yourself happy. (Learn gourmet cooking? Study French? Take drawing lessons? Read the collected works of Shakespeare?)

• Eat healthy food and follow an energetic exercise regimen. Now is the time to get in shape. You have the time, and if you look better, you'll feel better and present a more affirmative picture to a prospective employer.

• Telephone or e-mail your old pals and former contacts all over the country to touch base and see if they know of any job activity in their part of the world. The sound of the human voice is very compelling to many people, and a follow-up letter or fax, containing excellent information on yourself, is a good reinforcement of that telephone call.

• Write a letter of thanks *immediately* after someone has done you a favor in your job search. When you write at once, your mind is fresher with details of what transpired and your language will therefore be more vivid.

• Don't sound "down"—or drag others down with you. No one wants to have a depressed "moper" around. Keep up your energy and keep that sparkling personality polished brightly; retain your sense of humor, so that people will want you around and be eager to help you.

• Accept every dinner invitation for yourself (and your partner, if you have one). You need cheering up, but you also need the exchange of ideas with other people. The sound of energy being expended on your behalf around someone's dinner table should be music to your ears.

• Don't stop entertaining. Even if you have to cut out all the frills of entertaining because of a reduced standard of living, invite people to your home, treat them well with hospitality and the warmth of caring, and you will *all* benefit. (Consider lunch or cocktails at your house instead of an elaborate dinner, or a bite after a film or tennis game or an outing at a local event.)

• Look upon your frustrating time of job hunting as a blessing in disguise as far as your family is concerned. You can be of immeasurable help to your spouse and get to know your children during real quality time that you never had before. It's important not to depress them with any negative feelings you may have yourself. Your family is your most precious asset.

• Realize that this may be a golden opportunity to go after that advanced degree you always wanted and knew you should have for your career's sake.

Perhaps you can get a temporary job (of lesser importance and with lower compensation than you would wish) that will tide you over while you attend night school. Besides, you may learn many new things on that job, even if it's just a polishing of your people skills.

• Realize that this may be the opportunity you've always wanted to learn a musical instrument. If you wanted to learn the guitar, for example, you might swap services with a guitar teacher (perhaps handle her children's car pool or take care of her lawn in exchange for weekly lessons).

• Realize, too, that you may never really have appreciated your city's architecture, museums, and parks. Often the things in a city that are free are its most exceptional assets. It's a brain wake-up to do something like taking out a couple of books on Greek and Roman sculpture from the public library and then spending time in the museum in the Greek and Roman sculpture wing. The interplay of new cultural knowledge, of reading and seeing, can be a real pleasure in your life.

• When you and that new position you worked so hard to land finally mesh, notify every person whose help you sought. It's not only polite, it's efficient. Even something like your university placement service should know the good news and stop giving your name to interested employers, and your college alumni magazine should carry the news of your new job in your class notes.

• Be proud of yourself that you have not only survived a long and grueling unemployment period, but perhaps have become a more important member of your own family, grown professionally, learned new skills, added to your résumé, and increased your self-worth. In the future you will probably show much more compassion and understanding of others who have just gone through what you have, and who have successfully survived.

FINDING A JOB IN AN UNSYMPATHETIC ENVIRONMENT

It can be tough in a time of prosperity, but finding a job in a time of downsizing and layoffs isn't just tough, it can be devastating.

1. *Get prepared. Make all the boring but necessary preparations.* Have the "perfect résumé" made for yourself. Pass it around among friends for a critique. They will probably suggest changes. Listen to them. Rewrite and edit it ten times. Then it ought to be good enough. You may need two or even three résumés, pitched to different businesses for which you feel qualified. If you have a special skill, you can probably describe it in five ways. For heaven's sake, make sure there's not a smudge or a misplaced comma, or a misspelled word anywhere in the résumé.

   Always bring several copies of your résumé to leave with an interviewer, who might pass them around to others.

2. *Research all the companies in which you're interested.* Compile a neat list of them—including addresses, telephone numbers, names of top officers with whom you will be communicating, their e-mail addresses, and fax numbers. Never call them on their private lines, or use their private fax or e-mail addresses, because it just might irritate them enough to kill your chances.

3. *Send for the company's annual report before you see anyone.* Memorize it, so you will never ask stupid questions.

4. *So, you've landed an interview date.* Congratulations! Have business friends help you with the posing of the right kinds of questions to ask at the interview—questions that will show you know a lot about the business and that you have faith in the company's future.

The Interview

• Don't just be punctual for your interview, arrive ten minutes early. This will give you time to pull yourself together and be calm. Make a friend of the receptionist. She might be able to help you out later and just happen to mention to the right people how nice you are, and how intelligent-sounding.

• When you meet the person interviewing you for the first time, put out your hand and say his name. (Even if you know the corporate culture to be a very informal one, if you haven't met the interviewer, say, "Mr. Mathews, it is very good of you to see me," *not* "Hello, Tom, you're nice to see me.")

• Don't take a seat until the interviewer motions you to sit down.

• Listen, first and foremost. What do they need? Why did they grant you an interview? Is there a job extant, or are they merely thinking about staffing possibilities for the future? It is more important to know *what the interviewer is saying* than to articulate what you want to say.

• Whatever you do, don't tell the interviewer you don't know what you want to do with your life and suggest that he could tell you about his company! He doesn't have time to brief you on the company nor the inclination to talk someone into wanting the job. He *expects* you to know about the company and to want the job—passionately.

• Find out if there are other qualified candidates being considered for the job for which you are being interviewed. This is intelligence that might be useful in competing for the position.

• Don't sound disappointed if the job in question is not the one you hoped it would be. Give it your best shot. It might turn out to be more interesting for you than the one you heard about. Besides, every experience is valuable, and you, in the meantime, are becoming "well rounded."

• Be ready to relocate if that's what they want. If you need the job and they will pay the moving expenses, it may mean a great step up for you. If you're not ready to relocate, and it's the only job opening they have, listen very politely to the description of the job. It might well be worth your taking the risk, so don't pass up the interview. Ask for a little time to think about it—but not too much—if they make an offer and you have any doubts.

• If you left a company for a negative reason, mention it simply, as a statement of fact, and briefly, but don't try to get the interviewer's sympathy. Don't be a whiner; there is nothing that will turn off the other person faster than to have you complain unendingly about how unfairly you were treated.

• In fact, don't make any negative comments whatsoever about your previous place of employment. Talk only of its positive aspects. Rather than saying, "Company X is run by a bunch of jerks who don't know what they're doing," say, "Company X is a leader in their field of technology, and I was privileged to be in a great spot to learn their operation from the inside."

• Tell the person interviewing you that you:
  • Have the greatest respect for this company and would be very proud to join their team.
  • Are a very hard worker.
  • Are enthusiastic about the company's future
  • Really want the job. Don't waffle about it or act indecisive.

• The wrap-up should always be nice letter, written or typed on good-quality stationery:
  • If you get the job, write a long, earnest letter of thanks to your contact, with the promise that you'll fulfill the company's expectations and more.
  • If you were merely interviewed and never really had a chance, write a short, grateful letter thanking the interviewer for her having seen and even considered you. Leave an outstanding impression with her. It may be important later.
  • If you are told you lost out at the end to someone else, write a careful letter of thanks to the interviewer, and add something like, "Whoever succeeded in dazzling you so much that he got the job is one lucky person." You never know: At the last moment, the winner might not be able to take the job, and if your nice, friendly, grateful letter is sitting in the Human Resources pending file on the official's desk, the next telephone call may be to you.

HUNTING FOR A NEW JOB
WHILE YOU ARE STILL EMPLOYED

You might (or should) feel a certain amount of guilt when you decide to search for a job elsewhere while you are still employed. It's probably important to feel this guilt, because then you will cause your present company the least amount of harm. (Remember, your company is still paying you; you should deal with the situation in the best possible way.) Two suggestions:

• Make calls concerning your job move on your cell phone or a pay phone on your lunch hour, away from your office. Don't use company time for your search.

• Make appointments only on your lunch hour, after hours, or on weekends. If an appointment starts to take much longer than you anticipated and you are supposed to be back at your office, be frank with the person interviewing you: "I feel very bad about this, but I'm overdue at my job. I hope you will let me return to finish this conversation. I'm needed back at my office." The interviewer will respect you rather than drop you for consideration for the new job. (If he doesn't, you should not want to work there anyway.)

As You Take Your Leave

When you are offered the new job, be frank with the person in the new company about your responsibilities to your present employer, assuming you feel a sense of obligation to him. You might say to your hoped-for new employer at this point: "When my boss hears that I am leaving and going to the competition, he will probably throw me out right then and there. He may ask me to empty my desk and leave. I hope that doesn't happen. I want to leave in an orderly, responsible way. I want to be able to say to my boss, 'I will find and then train a good person to take over this job. If it takes three or four weeks to accomplish this, my new company will wait for me.' I don't want to leave them in the lurch."

That would be the best of situations. If your present boss becomes furious when you tell him you're leaving and accuses you of disloyalty and makes other accusations, say calmly to him, "I'm really sorry you feel this way. I have loved this job. I admire this company and the people who work for it. I have been offered a much better opportunity, and for my own good, I must take it, but I will always be grateful for what I've learned here, for the opportunities you have given me, and for the friendships made here."

If you know you are going to leave, copy your Rolodex and any of your own personal, important files after hours. Do this before you inform your boss of your impending departure. He may want you to leave at once, which would not give you the time to take your own personal files.

Be prepared for some very uncomfortable moments, but if you keep your cool everything will turn out all right.

INFANT FEEDING AND BREAST-FEEDING IN THE OFFICE

Certain companies allow women employees to feed their babies at work. In fact, some even encourage it to the point of providing a special room with baby-changing tables, comfortable chairs for nursing mothers, plus a formula-heating device and refrigerator for storing bottles of formula.

Some offices do not have the space or financial resources to permit this service. A nursing mother should not breast-feed her baby in public in the office. It upsets many men, though they are embarrassed to admit it. Men look upon the female breast as a sex organ, and a certain amount of voyeurism comes into play if they catch a glimpse, even a quick one, of a colleague's bare breast. I think company policy has the right to insist that a woman breast-feed her baby out of sight—in the ladies' room, in an empty office, or wherever.

A company also has the right *not* to allow a woman to bring her baby to work. Some do allow it, most don't. A woman can find a company that will give her more leeway for her motherhood needs if she can't accept the policy of the company where she works. I have seen companies with two or more babies in baskets by their mothers' desks, all of whom were howling in unison while their mothers unsuccessfully tried to shush them. Such a scene is not businesslike; it is very unprofessional, and unless the company is all-female and the boss brings her babies to work, or unless there is a baby-care facility on the premises or nearby, a working mother should find someone to care for her child while she is at work. Some women successfully use the barter system and exchange services with another person. In a poor economy, companies have to cut costs rather than increase them, and mothers should become creative in solving their child-care problems themselves, until that wonderful day when companies have all found—or will have been forced by law to find—happy solutions for the problem of child care for working mothers.

TASTY TIDBITS OF ETIQUETTE (FOR YOUR BUSINESS OR SOCIAL LIFE)

Q. What do you do when you have brought your host a present, without a gift enclosure, and you're sure it's been lost in the shuffle.

A. You apologize to your host for having been dumb enough to leave behind a present without a card. Then identify the gift which, when it is eventually found, will have lost some of its allure.

Q. What kind of gift is appropriate for someone to whom you are indebted in a business sense, but you don't have the slightest idea of what to give her?

A. First, make certain her company policy permits her to accept gifts. Then do some research. Call her executive assistant or husband or grown daughter to find out what she passionately likes. That could be anything from a bottle of a favorite fragrance to another hippopotamus figurine to add to her collection.
- If she's a "leftie," get her a new pair of left-handed scissors.
- If she plays golf, give her a big box of the best kind of golf balls.
- If she has moved into a new house or apartment, give her a gift certificate to an art gallery that specializes in framed prints and small pieces of original art.

Q. As a young woman executive, one of three in our company, I was invited by a new member of our staff—a bachelor—to accompany him to a high-level buffet dinner reception given by our most important client. From the moment we arrived at the club where it was held, he absolutely ignored me. He did not check my coat, he simply barged into the ballroom and began circulating around, introducing himself to the most important guests and ignoring me so completely, I did not know what to do. I'm a strong independent woman, but he was so rude, it threw me, and I just sat in a corner like a waif. He didn't even sit with me at dinner.

A. I know what to do about him. He's an oaf and possessed of such pathetically bad manners, I fear for your company because of what he might do next to clients and potential business prospects. Buy him and have beautifully gift-wrapped a book on manners (mine, for example!). Write on the flyleaf, "I have never enjoyed giving anyone a gift more than this one." You don't even have to sign it, because he should know from whom it came.

Q. In this economy, the junior members of the firm are no longer given any entertaining allowance. Therefore, when we take any customers to dinner, it comes out of our own pockets. I want to invite a very successful man and his wife to join my wife and me for dinner. We are indebted to them and are wondering how to handle the type of place we take them. I can't possibly afford to take them to a restaurant like Le Cirque here in New York, but they probably consider it's a fait accompli that we're on a big fat expense account.

A. This is when you become creative. Research all the restaurants you've heard people talking about that are modestly priced, yet with delightful food. Pick one that is midpriced, but with charm and atmosphere. Your guests should know in advance that you are *not* on an expense account, and that fact will impress them greatly. They will realize you really wanted to take them to dinner. Tell your guests when extending the dinner invitation that you and your wife have found the company's new policy of no-expense-account entertaining to be a blessing in disguise, because you have uncovered the best little bistros in town, full of enthusiastic patrons and serving good food. Call the restaurant beforehand and explain that this older couple is very important to you businesswise and friendshipwise. I have never known a restaurant that didn't immediately accept that challenge and perform magic with the treatment of your table.

Q. I realize I have come down too hard on my staff in this economic emergency. They feel that each one is doing the job of three. I'm such a workhorse myself, I've been unaware of their feelings. I can't change the weight of their workload, but is there anything I should do personally to let them know how much I appreciate them?

A. It's time to give them a party—that has nothing to do with the holiday season or the company's anniversary. Hold the party in your home or in a restaurant. Invite their partners. Tell them to get dressed up (the men should wear coats and ties, for example). Write out and carefully practice beforehand a warm, clever toast to make to them.

Today's young executives and professionals are totally at ease working with technology, no matter how quickly new modes of communicating, researching, and storing data come on the market. But they are often ill at ease in social situations. At a reception held at the Wharton School of Business, one young woman remarked to me, "I'm embarrassed about being so embarrassed!" This after admitting in private that she had been nervous all week thinking about the party.

Many parents assumed that they know everything about appropriate and proper ways of relating to others and that their children would learn by osmosis. But they can know very little about what constitutes good manners, either in the home or on the job. Their children, now beginning to move up in today's workplace, often confess to me in my training courses that they know very little and want to learn much more. They feel a lack of certain personal skills. That makes one feel great hope for the future!

CHAPTER 5

The Manners
That Make Travel Easier

The opportunity to travel is precious. Yes, there are inconveniences and moments of great discomfort, but even people such as I, who must travel constantly and complain about it constantly, know that we would really feel deprived without it.

To go *somewhere else*—to see what *other* people are doing, to find out how they are feeling, to see how they look and dress, to eavesdrop on their conversations, and to be exposed to their culture, sports, and politics—is a fantastic plus. This stimulus holds true for travel to Smalltown America as well as to a great cosmopolitan city. For both the traveler and the people who live in the destination city or country, manners are the key to successful interaction. The well-mannered traveler is the best kind there is.

ENSURING A PLEASURABLE TRIP

HAVING A GOOD TIME WITH A TRAVELING COMPANION

Two people may be very good friends to begin with, but it's amazing how much better they will know each other after having traveled together. Being together day in and day out; many times having to share the same hotel, motel, or bed-and-breakfast room and bathroom; being forced to adjust to each other's preferences in restaurants; agreeing on activities according to separate likes and dislikes; being able to cope either with contracting stomach flu in a foreign city or taking care of the traveling companion who has it—these are all part of the pleasures and challenges of traveling together. The way you and your traveling companion share whatever experiences you have will make the trip a great success or an unmitigated failure. Willpower, compromise, and selflessness are the keys to a favorable outcome.

Any trip can be a success—if the people taking it will its success. That old cliché of having a positive attitude really works when you're traveling. If you arrive hot, tired, and dirty in a little Austrian hotel (with less than comfortable appointments in your room), you might look out the window and say to your traveling companion, "Isn't this a beautiful little town? Isn't it charming and quaint? Listen to the bells in the old bell tower. Come here and look!" Or you might look out the window and say to your traveling companion, "Come here and look at this dirty old place. What a dump this town is!" Needless to say, the first reaction will help make your traveling companion glad he or she accompanied you and eager to put on the same pair of rosy glasses you did when you looked out that window. One person in a group can pull all the others down, but one person can also pull all the others up.

If you insist on having a great time on your travels, you *will*. It's that old "positive attitude" again.

Actions That Will Ensure Your Trip's Success

- Have every aspect of the financial arrangements worked out well ahead of time. Make sure that each pays an equal share during the trip. (One way of organizing this is to have a cash kitty, from which each day's expenses are paid and accounted for and into which each person puts an equal amount of money each day.)
- In the preplanning stages, an agreement should be reached on:
  - The selection of the person who will handle the trip arrangements, payouts, dealing with the travel agent or making the reservations directly (on-line perhaps).
  - The budget to be followed (for example, what kind of hotels you will book—luxury, middle-priced, or modest).
  - The major tours to be taken in each country. Some people are beach-sitters, others café-sitters, others inveterate sightseers. A compromise should be reached before taking off on the trip.
  - The method of transport you will use—bus, train, airplane, boat, rented car, or car with driver.
  - The sports you wish to play or watch, including those games for which you will purchase tickets.
- It is advisable for each individual to keep a daily log of his own expenses as well, with his personal expenses carefully recorded (pressing and laundry, room service, long distance calls, faxes sent, wine ordered with meals), so that each person will be paying a fair share of the total expenses.
- Every evening, reach a consensus on the next day's plans. Alternate carrying out the wishes of each person, so that everyone has a turn deciding what the pair or group will do that day. If an agreement is impossible to reach, each should go off and do his or her own thing, which is healthy and often rewarding if you have been suffering from too much togetherness.
- If one of your companions falls ill, the best thing to do for him is to call

a doctor immediately, make sure he receives the proper medication and has been declared capable of being left alone at the hotel, and then take off to have an interesting day by yourself. Bring a small gift back to your friend, for he probably will be feeling very depressed at missing the day's planned activities.

• Always pack a couple of good books in your suitcase—an excellent antidote to boredom, insomnia, or a disagreement with your traveling companions. Don't repack those books. They make great gifts for the locals no matter where you are.

• If one of you is unduly irritated with the other, have an open discussion of what caused the irritation. Travelers in close quarters often become temporarily out of sorts, for one reason or another. The hostility can be defused by a frank and calm talk—and a little time spent apart (maybe only two or three hours), to regain some perspective on the friendship. I remember a talk I had on one trip after a friend and I had begun to get seriously on one another's nerves. She finally revealed that my constant chatting on the telephone with old school friends wherever we went was getting her down; I confessed that her hanging her underwear to dry out the window of whatever hotel we were staying in was getting to me. We laughed, shook hands, and avoided those annoying habits—and others we'd discussed—for the rest of our summer trip.

• Avoid bringing too much baggage, which slows down the entire trip and merits the wrath of any companions. Carry one large, expandable bag that you check on each flight and a tote containing your medications and basic cosmetics and toiletries that can fit under an airplane seat or in an overhead bin—both of which you can carry yourself if you have to (and you probably will have to).

• You should not resent it when your traveling companion receives an invitation from a personal friend that does not include you. Never take it for granted that you will be included in everything that your friend(s) may be invited to.

I remember traveling through Europe as a college student with a very glamorous friend who kept running into American male students, who immediately asked her out to dinner. I felt pretty left out and resentful until I took hold of myself and went off alone to concerts and the theater. Each time I did, during intermission I met people from that country in the lobby. They were perplexed to see a young American girl alone, and each night a couple or a family would invite me to dinner in a wonderfully characteristic local place. Then when my friend returned to the hotel after her date with an American boy, I frankly enjoyed making her jealous by recounting my own local-color experiences. They were usually more interesting than hers—to me, that is!

• When someone invites you to a social event on your trip, *write the host a thank-you note* within twenty-four hours. If your traveling companion is also invited, that person should write one, too. If you were the guest of honor at the party, you would send flowers or a present (with a note) to the host the next day.

• The holidays provide the perfect opportunity to renew the acquaintances you made during your foreign travels. Send each person a chatty Christmas or New Year's card, in which you mention how much you enjoyed seeing them. Give your address, and say how much you hope they will let you know when they come to the United States. If you became friends with your hotel manager or concierge, send them cards, too. A holiday greeting card is much more appreciated than an e-mail.

You will find that these new friends will last a lifetime if you are thoughtful enough to remember them during the holidays.

WHEN YOU'RE TAKING A PLANE

- Dress comfortably but nicely. Many well-heeled Americans dress down when they fly today. A person in a beat-up T-shirt, sawed-off jeans, and flip-flops hardly makes a great impression when emerging from the plane, dirty toenails and all, in another country. The well-dressed American, on the other hand, makes an instant, favorable impression on foreigners.
- It also helps your image (and makes everyone who has to look at you feel much better, too) if you carry your personal effects in suitcases, rather than in a series of plastic bags that look as if they were preused at the supermarket.
- Check your large piece of baggage, instead of carrying it on board. If you do carry it with you, be careful not to hit passengers in aisle seats as you walk through the cabin. Serious bruising may result.
- If you are seated next to a chatterer and you not only don't like chattering but you have work to do or a good book to read, say very politely, "I'm so sorry. I would really like to talk some more, but by the time we land I must have this work finished," or "I must return this book to the person meeting me, so I had better finish it," or some other logical excuse. When the meal is served, it is impossible to work or read your book, so that is the time to show a little kindness and converse with your undoubtedly chastened seatmate.
- If you are a parent with a small child, keep that child from running up and down the aisle. Not only is it very hard on the flight attendants, who have many duties to perform in a short space of time and are then obliged to keep stepping over and around the child in the aisle, but it is hard on the nerves of fellow passengers. In addition, it is also dangerous and against the FAA safety rules. (Many parents think letting their small children run up and down the aisle, getting everyone's attention, is just too cute for words, but it is not.) A wise parent traveling with small children brings a small tote bag for each, containing favorite toys and games, to keep a child busy and happy in his seat. Snacks and a drink are also packed, because the food service, if it exists at all, may be almost delusional.
- If you are traveling with a baby, change your infant's diapers in the privacy of a lavatory and *not* in the empty seat next to you!

• If you are sitting next to someone who is flying for the first time and is frightened, or who is an old hand at flying but still is very frightened, lend a helping hand. If you just talk in a calm, reassuring voice, you can do wonders to help soothe a frightened human being. The fear of flying is very real. If you explain what the sudden noises are, you will be a hero to your seatmate. ("That grinding noise you just heard is the sound of the landing gear being lowered.") If the person holds her ears and complains that they hurt, say something like, "The pressure really can hurt your ears a lot. I sympathize. Hold your nose and blow gently. Try swallowing again and again. Sipping water helps, as does chewing gum or using nasal spray."

When someone is in any obvious physical distress, ask if there's something you can do and push the flight attendant's call button.

• When the flight attendant comes by with the drinks cart, give him exact change for the beer or wine you order. Many people look upon the flight attendant as a convenient bank from whom they can get $20 or $50 bills changed into much-needed smaller money. The attendants have a tough enough time as it is getting their regular serving chores done without having to run up and down the aisle getting change each time someone buys a drink.

• Help keep the lavatory presentable. Everyone appreciates it when whoever uses the rest room last flushes the toilet, drains the water from the washbowl, stows away used paper towels, and in general leaves it looking as neat as possible. It requires everyone's cooperation to keep the rest rooms decent, particularly on those endless overseas flights.

• Leave your litter in a neat pile on your seat (newspapers, magazines, pieces of paper, candy and gum wrappers, and the like) when you leave the plane, in consideration of the cleaning crew, who may have just a few moments to do their job before the next group of passengers board.

• As you disembark, always thank the lined-up flight attendants. They are rarely thanked, and they usually try very hard to please the passengers. If the captain or cocaptain is standing in the doorway to the cockpit, thank him for "a good flight," a "job very well done," or a "great landing, Captain." Many passengers ignore the pilot and crew, so even a few paltry words of praise mean a lot.

YOUR HOTEL MANNERS

Hotel behavior says a lot about a person, such as whether she is a class act. It is readily apparent from the time of the check-in process at a hotel. If the line is too long, if the air-conditioning isn't working, if the promised accommodations aren't what was requested, if the room is too close to the elevator, if there's construction going on in that side of the hotel, if the room is next to the vending machines in the hall, if a no-smoking room was reserved (but the only one left is a smoking room, replete with excessive tobacco odors), the traveler checking in has no choice but to *sit on her frustrations.* Voicing them loudly doesn't help. (I've been known, in a state of total exhaustion, unable to check into my room and a victim of endlessly bad airplane delays, to go over to a lobby corner and mutter my displeasure in a low tone aimed at the wall— sending myself, in other words, to the corner for my own self-inflicted time-out.) This is my way of maintaining my sanity, even if others close by think I have lost it!

If you have been a victim of a series of hotel misdemeanors, make a clear list of everything that went wrong, and make sure the general manager of the hotel receives it. It is unfair to take out your justifiable rage on hotel employees who have no responsibility for the screw-ups. A well-written letter of complaint, devoid of emotion and sarcasm, with events described in detail, will get some action, the least of which might be an offer to put you up free on your next visit to that city.

One often hears a long symphony of complaints near the lodging's check-in desk. I watched a justifiably enraged businessman after learning his room wasn't ready yet, when Housekeeping had promised it would be ready by two-thirty. He had been waiting for three and a half frustrating hours, being told repetitively, "Sir, just a few more minutes." He now looked at his watch, grimaced, and in a gesture of desperation, opened his suitcase on the lobby floor, and immediately began to change from his gray business suit into a tuxedo for his next black tie event. He explained to anyone nearby who would listen that he was the master of ceremonies at an important event, starting now, and there was no time to do anything but get dressed and leave. The public got a five-second glance at his undershirt and white boxer shorts as he changed from his striped shirt with French cuffs into a white dress shirt and the rest of the tuxedo outfit. He deftly transferred the cuff links to the white shirt. With great modesty he quickly put on his black trousers with the black satin stripe down the sides, and attached a pair of brocaded braces to his pants. We were all simply spellbound watching him. It was deathly quiet in the lobby. It would have made a great commercial for a men's clothing company. No security person came near him, probably because he moved so fast they didn't even see him, and he was certainly not a streaker. Sitting down on a chair by one of the lobby columns, he removed his brown tasseled oxfords and changed his socks from brown patterned ones to black silk hose. Then he donned a pair of black patent pumps.

A stranger answered his call for help with his bow tie. "There's no mirror. I can't possibly tie this tie," he said to no one in particular. "Does anyone know how? Can someone help me?" Someone did, and tied it fast and well. Then the businessman gave his suitcase to the bellman with his hotel key, thanked again the man who had tied his bow tie, smiled at everyone around who had witnessed his astonishing performance, and dashed off to a taxi just as the spectators were orchestrating a round of applause for him there in the lobby of that Washington hotel.

Great Hotel Service

Extraordinarily good hotel service deserves to be saluted, every bit as much as inferior service deserves to be criticized. When you write a letter of warm praise for the management of any lodging where you stay, it has a great affirmative impact. (So many demands these days, so few thank-yous!) Include in your note the name of any of the employees who did a great job for you. Praise the concierge for having performed miracles. Describe a masterpiece of culinary perfection the chef served you, even if it was just a great bacon and eggs breakfast. Service employees today get so much criticism, they deserve every compliment thrown their way, particularly in a written note. The general manager will show it to the employee and others, and will keep a copy of it in the file. This recognition almost makes up for the fact an employee generally feels underpaid. The letter might also be responsible for his keeping his job or earning a promotion.

Don't forget to go on the record complimenting the general manager, when it's deserved. Most people forget the major role she plays in the comfort of a traveler.

I remember asking the manager of a hotel what he considered to be the most important aspect of a guest's behavior. His reply: "Not to steal our towels, blankets, glasses, rugs, hair dryers, and lamps."

"Really? I asked, both sceptical and horrified.

"Really," he answered.

YOUR B&B MANNERS

The small inns—the bed-and-breakfasts—are one of the delights of travel today in the United States. Generally they are managed by a husband and wife or same-sex partner team or an adventurous single person who loves people. (You have to love people to survive in the B&B business.)

Every such house in which I have stayed has had a fascinating history, such as in Lenox, Massachusetts, where I went to give a lecture to raise funds for "The Mount," the nearby mansion Edith Wharton designed and built for her home at the turn of the twentieth century. I spent the weekend in a lovely white nineteenth-century house, "The Gables," which made me feel that happy ghosts were wandering around it. Later I discovered this was Teddy Wharton's (Edith's husband) family home. I am Edith Wharton's biggest fan, and to discover I was sleeping in the childhood abode of the husband of one of the most gifted women of the nineteenth and twentieth centuries, made my lecture much more inspired.

Of course, I remember years ago in Cheyenne, Wyoming, when I stayed in a B&B with exactly the opposite kind of ambience. It was the clapboard house birthplace of a famous cowboy in American history. My late brother, Mac Baldrige, who was a rodeo performer on weekends all through his life, even when he was Secretary of Commerce in the Reagan administration, wanted to know all of the details of that home. He questioned me closely. What Old West artifacts were around? Was there hanging somewhere a Charles Russell painting of cowboys and Indians as only he could paint them? (There was—a copy—which did not matter at all.) Was there perhaps a historic saddle on display? (Yes, there was, right in the living room, displayed with the same pride as though it were a Rodin sculpture.)

One can obviously take children to historic places in every corner of the United States and teach them American history the easy way, whether the B&B is located on the prairies of Nebraska, next to a maritime center in Mystic, Connecticut, an inn near the southern plantations on the James River, an Amish settlement in Pennsylvania, an Indian reservation in Minnesota, or the lacy wrought-iron facades of New Orleans's French Quarter.

Manners in a B&B

- Treat the owners with great respect. You are not staying in a lavish hotel, so don't try to make the B&B measure up. There is no room service, so arrange your food necessities yourself.
- Ask the innkeepers the history of the town. They usually love to tell it, and it is almost always fascinating.
- You will receive a breakfast, usually in the dining room, and it may be either a basic Continental breakfast (coffee or tea, a glass of juice, perhaps some fruit, and an assortment of breads). Or it could be a gourmet breakfast of waffles, pancakes, or omelets. (The best breakfasts I ever had were at a restaurant/town-gathering spot in Marshfield, Missouri, a wonderful place of approximately six thousand people.
- Even if your breakfast was terrible, don't say so to the owners. They are usually very sensitive. The way the customers regard their inn means everything. It's their whole life. Write them a nice letter after you have left, telling them the things they might improve and fix, as well as what they handled particularly well.
- If any of your traveling companions feel at liberty to pocket a souvenir of the house, discourage it immediately. That sweet little china porcelain basket may be from Great-Aunt Susan's collection. It may be a sentimental favorite of the owner's. Quite apart from that, it's called stealing.

GOING ON A CRUISE?

Lucky you! There are long cruises and short ones, huge boats and smaller ones, and most of them are a lot of fun. Get ready to be disappointed by certain elements beyond your control—bad weather, too many old people, and perhaps a really boring table to which you've been assigned for dinner. (Remember, you can change your table easily.) Many travelers prefer the smaller boats, because they are quieter, there is more personal service, not too much noise or too many activities, and there are fewer people trying to impress other people. Also, the fashion code is more casual, a thought very appealing to many.

This section, however, will deal mainly with long luxury cruises, because they are the most fun for me to write about. Of course, I can't avoid remembering crossing the Atlantic back and forth in the late forties, fifties, and early sixties for my vacations. The government sent me first class, which made up—almost—for my low salary. It was total luxury with everyone dressing to the nines for dinner every night, with champagne and caviar matching the sparkling jewels, and with men who really knew how to dance twirling you around the dance floor to the music of really great orchestras. Everyone was beautifully turned out and the passenger list was filled with Rockefellers, Vanderbilts, and movie stars like Sophia Loren, Marlene Dietrich, the Gary Coopers, and the Jimmy Stewarts. I was very young, but I quickly learned, when my jaw dropped too much and too fast because of what I was seeing, to close it up again fast.

How to Have a Happy Cruise

• Book your cruise through a good travel agent. Essential. Particularly if the agent recently took that very same cruise. Read all the information brochures you're given—every word. You will have to make a deposit in order to hold your reservation. Choose a cruise, if you can, with some three-day stops in port, and significant side trips, so there won't be too many long uninterrupted days at sea, which for some people can become boring or claustrophobic, or both.

• Sign up for your choices of onshore excursions before even going on the cruise, or at the latest, before you unpack when you're aboard. The lists for the desirable excursions fill up quickly.

• Mark your bags with something like a ribbon, to be able to find them easily in the mountains of lookalike luggage. I have always written my initials in large letters with bright red nail polish on each piece. It's tacky looking but effective. I've never lost my luggage because of this, and no one wants to steal it, either, because of the less than cultured appearance of the suitcases!

• Remember, don't bring any towels (plenty on board), and whatever you forget can usually be easily replaced in one of the many shops on board.

• Remember, too, that if you bring your own liquor on board, trying to save money, you will have to pay a considerable corkage charge in the dining room and bars, so it is really not worth it.

• You will choose your stateroom immediately upon booking the cruise. They come in different sizes, locations, and prices. The expensive outside cabins on the upper deck are the most sought after, because the open portholes admit fresh air. Considering the price differential, an inside air-conditioned stateroom without a porthole is still luxury personified, and much less expensive. (Enjoy your scenery on deck during non-sleeping hours.)

• Once you have boarded, immediately prebook with the purser your dining hour choice (first or second seating). You may also call the line before departure to take care of this. The first seating, often at 6 P.M., is children-oriented, but many adults prefer it because the service is much faster, and they want to see a movie and retire early. If you are young and alone, or if you are a young couple, tell the purser you want the second seating and don't want to be put at a table with "old fogies." (Pursers can be magicians and they have big hearts.)

To many, a cruise with open seating in the dining room is preferable to being stuck at a table night after night with boring people. After I changed my table on the *Queen Elizabeth* one night, I remember a woman coming across the dining salon in a steaming rage. She literally hissed at me: "Why didn't you come back to our table? Weren't we good enough for you?" (Ouch!)

I wanted to say that she and her husband were such tough going, I would have preferred to miss dinner rather than sit through another meal with them, but I answered, "Oh, I was terribly involved in a business conversation with a certain group, and we haven't completed our discussions, so I must sit at their table. It could be a good business opportunity." (It was a white lie, yes, but at least I spared her feelings.)

• In open seating, you sit where you please at any meal, wherever there is a free place. You meet a lot of people this way. Simply approach the table and ask "May I join you?" Put out your hand to shake every hand at the table, with a big smile, meantime saying your name distinctly each time. Your tablemates will answer you with their names, and you can start asking them questions, and they in turn will ask you questions. By dessert time, you will be as comfortable with each other as old friends. If you would rather sit there glumly, saying nothing and feeling superior to your tablemates, you may certainly do so, but if you're agreeable, pleasant, and smiling, at that table you'll uncover every light that is hidden under any bushel.

• For social strivers, a seat at the captain's table at the second seating for at least one dinner, is obligatory. It is supposed to be a special treat, because frequent travelers on this line are seated there, as are any celebrities on board. I personally have found it to be a big bore, a table full of pretentious people, and not very high on the celebrity or society score either. I have always been eager to return the next night to my regular table, which is much more fun. The captain, of course, is always charming and attractive. He must regard this nightly duty of social management of his table as one of the least pleasant aspects of his lofty position in the maritime world.

• Well-behaved children are a welcome blessing on a cruise. Badly behaved ones make you feel happy to be either too young or too old to bear children! Buy "soda cards" for your own children, so they won't have to keep running to you all day for cash to pay for their sodas. There is a plethora of choices for kids of any age during the day—sports activities such as supervised swimming in the pool, games, reading sessions, art projects, age-appropriate movies, and the like. Don't take your children with you on a cruise if they have not learned to obey, to be quiet, and to be beautifully behaved—for which you will be appreciated by all on board.

• If you have more than one child with you, equip yourself and each of them with a walkie-talkie, so that they will be able to tell you where they are at any given time, and so that you can tell them in what part of the ship they should report to you for meals or whatever reason.

• Sign up for your deck chair after discussing it with the deck steward. Do you prefer the sunny side of the ship? The non-windy side? If you wish to be left alone in your deck chair, the steward will try to keep noisy chatterers away from you.

REMEMBER YOUR MANNERS

1. The walls of your stateroom do not easily protect you and the public from noise. Carry your noisy arguments to the stern of the ship, down into the noisy wake of the water.
2. Treat the ship's personnel with dignity, not contempt. They deserve to be thanked when they wait on you, particularly when they go far beyond their mandate to assist you with something.
3. Keep your children in control at all times, and teach them to be appreciative of everything done for them.
4. Don't sponge drinks off fellow passengers. Pay your share of bar bills.
5. Be pleasant to people. If strangers speak to you, don't treat them like intruders. It takes more time to be nice than rude to people, but look at your watch. You have the time to be nice!
6. Don't let someone ruin the pleasure of your fellow passengers by complaining all the time. You can handle this. For every negative point made by the complainer, answer that person, point for point, with some positive praise for the cruise. You'll be the hero.

7. Remember all the fun you had and the goals in making this trip. Did you want to lose weight and work on *la ligne*? Or did you want to gorge on food night and day? Did you want to play cards day and night? Did you need a rest badly? Did you need to patch up a relationship with your spouse or partner? Or did you just want to forget your worries for a precious few days? A good cruise can accomplish this, if you do *your* part.

Cruise Attire

If the passengers all dress well and are well-groomed, the entire cruise has a wonderful atmosphere and is guaranteed to be a success. Some people mistakenly dress in workout clothes (sweats, T-shirts, and the like) all day, even for informal dinners. (These are usually the people who don't exercise at all but want to give the impression that they're in great shape.) Usually, dinner is the one meal at which everyone should pay attention to how they look. On less luxurious cruises, some justify their sloppy appearance because there are no laws compelling them to look nice for the benefit of others. But if they would open their eyes and look carefully at the tastefully attired people around them, they just might be motivated to follow suit.

• For a man, a coat and tie is usually the dress for dinner (unless he is on a small ship).

• For a black tie evening, a man may rent a full tuxedo outfit on board. On smaller ships, black tie evenings are usually optional.

• Women should remember that evenings can be chilly on deck, and therefore bring sweaters and scarves.

• Women need bring only one evening dress that can be modified and worn for a second black tie event simply by changing the top and the costume jewelry. (For example, a long black crepe skirt is worn with a floral silk top, the flowers re-embroidered in paillettes, for one evening, and the same black skirt worn with a white crepe off-the-shoulder top and turquoise costume jewelry for the next.)

• If you are in great shape, you will have plenty of opportunities to show it off, with "poolside sittings," promenading on the deck, and sunbathing in your deck chair. If you can remember to follow commonsense rules of modesty, your fellow passengers will remember you with admiration rather than disgust. (Nix on g-string suits, thongs, postage stamp bikinis, and one-piecers that stretch—barely—to cover body parts better left unseen.)

• The main thing to remember is to bring far fewer clothes than you think you will need. The fewer suitcases the better, and there is very small closet space.

CRUISE TIPPING

If you are on the kind of cruise on which generous tips are included in the price, you won't have to agonize over what to give to whom, but if you are on one requiring you to tip everyone on the last night aboard, be prepared for what you are going to do. It's going to be one "big piece of change," as they say, so factor it into your cruise budget. Tipping customs vary according to the type of boat, your accommodations, the length of your cruise, and the efficiency, personality, and service of the crew. Of course, if you are with a special tour group, you will be told exactly what the tipping system is, and you will pay a lump sum to the tour director, but if you don't have a clue what to do:

• Ask your travel agent.

• Ask good friends who recently took the same cruise as yours what they gave and to whom.

• When you are booking your cruise, ask an official of the line what she recommends.

• Ask the ship's purser when you are on board what is acceptable, and you will get a frank answer!

• On embarking, establish good relations by dispensing some cash tips. For example, give $5 or $10 when you first board to your cabin steward when she does some small favor for you; slip $5 into the hand of your dining steward at the first meal, and tell him how glad you are to be in his care. This generosity will mean additional pampering while you're on board, and there is nothing wrong with that!

• At the end of a short cruise, tip your cabin steward and your dining room steward $3 per day minimum.

• Keep some dollars in your pocket to give out on an impromptu basis— for example, to the pool attendant or the tea steward, if you see them only occasionally and if you do not expect to give them a tip envelope when the voyage is over.

• It's wise to pay for and include the tip (15 to 20 percent of the total bill) for your drinks in the bar as you go along. Of course, if you prefer, you may run up a tab that you pay on the last day (paying as you go makes it less of a shock to settle up when you disembark for good).

• Give the wine steward 10 percent of the total wine bill, although some regulars tip 15 percent.

• Tip the service people (like hairdressers and masseurs) as you would on land—15 to 20 percent of the total bill each time.

• On a long cruise, tip some people once a week. For example:
  • Chief dining room steward $20 a week.
  • Assistant dining room steward $10 a week.

- Your dining room steward $25 a week.
- Your deck steward $20 a week.
- Your cabin steward $25 a week.
- Remember, if you are a couple or a family, you should tip three-fourths more per person in your family than you would tip if you were alone.
- Remember, too, if you are a famous, rich person, you should be generous with your tips. (Your public image begins to drop perceptibly if you're known around the ship as a "skinflint.")
- When your cruise is over, put all your tips—cash or checks—into separately addressed envelopes the last day at sea, and hand them personally to each person. It's very nice to put a little note inside each envelope, expressing your thanks—"You took extraordinarily good care of us . . ."; "I will miss all those wonderful meals you served me so well . . ."; "You made the entire trip such a pleasure for my wife and me."

Yes, tipping is a complicated question on a cruise. If anyone on board was nasty to you (very unlikely), you should greatly reduce the tip—but remember, it does represent a large part of the income of the employees of the ship.

There are now cruises in operation that build a hefty service charge into the cost of the cruise, and in this case there is no tipping. That may be the wave of the future, thank heavens!

WOMEN AND TRAVEL

MEN AND WOMEN TRAVELING TOGETHER ON BUSINESS

- An employer ultimately assumes her staff member's expenses on the road, because that person may be handling all of the fiscal chores, including checking in and out of the hotel, paying the bills, tipping the bellmen, and the like.
- When men and women executives are traveling together, it is important that the woman pay her own way exactly as a male colleague would do. That includes items such as her share of the taxi to the airport and the tip for the bellmen who handle their luggage and effects. It's wrong for a woman to allow her colleagues to pay for everything (or for her male companion to try to pay for everything) as though they were a couple (even though he will be reimbursed for her share of the expenses back at the home office). They should settle their accounts on a daily basis, or at the end of the trip.
- Women should carry their own bags and packages and help carry the load of business paraphernalia the team has brought with it.
- Men should not only invite their women traveling companions to have dinner with them on the road (Dutch treat, of course), but also to join them in

swimming, jogging, or using the hotel's health club. A lone woman executive does not have to say yes (and they may be hoping she won't say yes), but the only polite thing to do is to ask her to join them. It is particularly important if there are two or more men and only one woman on the trip, because then it is easy for the men to make the woman feel shut out.

Once when I accompanied some young executives on a business trip I observed their behavior (there were two other women and two men in this peer group). We arrived at our destination with two hours to kill. The men said in an unnecessarily sarcastic tone, "Well, you ladies are obviously going shopping, shopping, shopping!" Then they went off to take a sauna and a nap. At dinner in the conference center later, the squash pro at the health complex came by our table and said to the men, "Well, I don't know what you did this afternoon, but these two"—and he put a hand on each of the young women's shoulders—"took on the two top men players in this city, for two tough hours, and beat 'em!" I loved it. Later I asked the young women if they would have told the men about their great athletic accomplishment if the pro hadn't.

"Heavens, no," laughed one of them. "We would have much preferred to have them think we were shopping on the mall for two hours. It would have put them in a better mood than they will be now."

Coed Business Travelers Should Be Careful!

There should be no sexual pressures on a business trip, provided male and female travelers from the very beginning make it plain to each other that they are making a no-nonsense, "no fooling around" trip. The pair should not book not a hotel suite (two bedrooms and a living room), but rather two separate bedrooms. If, however, their company's travel people book them into a multi-bedroom company-owned suite in some hotel, that is a different story. In order to protect their privacy, a locked bedroom door is all that is necessary. (The male executive may feel the need of the locked door as much as the woman does.)

If the two are occupying the corporate suite together, quite logically they will be wise not to traipse around the living room and kitchenette in their night clothes. That might be done innocently by one person but could be taken by the other as a sexual signal.

If they have their own separate rooms and meet in one of the bedrooms during the day to confer on business matters (because they have confidential material they don't wish to display in the hotel restaurant or lobby or because they need a lot of space in which to spread out papers—all over the bed, tables, and floor), they should both be dressed in their work clothes. If one of them is wearing nightclothes, the other one should say, "Look, I know you didn't have time to get dressed, so I'll be outside in the hall, waiting, until you do get dressed." (That kind of statement is enough to discourage anyone with possible intentions of adding a little romance to the workload.)

Some women are very reputation-conscious (and I am glad they are). They become very nervous about what other people are thinking when they are seen traveling with male colleagues on business, particularly when their companions are married men. A woman should erase such a worry from her thoughts, however. In the first place, her own and her colleague's behavior are all that matter, not what other people are thinking. In the second place, the woman should realize that if she and her male traveling companion had wanted to have an affair, they certainly would not have had to go to the trouble of taking a business trip to another city in order to indulge in it. It is illogical for anyone to accuse an unattached pair on a business trip in another city of being romantically involved. (Most of them are too tired to fool around anyway.)

A woman's nervousness may heighten when a male companion takes one drink too many in the evening and he makes a serious or half-serious pass. (The possibility of a charge of sexual harassment begins to rear its ugly head.) The woman should keep her sense of humor at this moment but tell her colleague in no uncertain terms to lay off, that she is going to her room—by herself—and that she will have forgotten this episode by the next day. If he has grabbed her in a hallway, all she has to do is threaten to scream for the hotel security if he doesn't let her go. She, of course, has had enough sense not to go to his room with him after dinner (doing that with a man who has drunk too much during the evening is total stupidity), nor has she invited him into her room for any reason, including hearing that old canard, "I have some papers you really should see before tomorrow's meeting."

If a colleague of either sex drinks too much on the road, the one who is sober should be protective of the other, get that person to his or her room, and urge that person not to exit again before the next day. You really can't lock the person into the room—because that would be a fire hazard, for one thing—but be firm. One inebriated executive at a resort convention remarked angrily to me as I pushed him into his room, closing the door behind him, "Just who do ya think you are, my mother?" My answer was short. "Yes." That did it. He didn't emerge until the next morning, in time for breakfast but looking abashed. I whispered in his ear, "Forget it," and by the second cup of coffee, he had, because I obviously had. It is really a bad idea to tease a colleague about his or her behavior. (He called me "Mother" only two more times.)

A Woman Traveling Alone

Whether a woman is on business or on vacation, she should not feel intimidated about going alone into the bar in her hotel or out for an early dinner in any established restaurant in the city.

• If you are traveling alone and want a drink in your hotel's bar, just for a change of pace from your hotel room, bring your briefcase or some files with you, take a seat at a table, pretend to go through a couple of business papers, order your drink, and then relax. Your little performance at the beginning of your bar appearance has established you as a bona fide businesswoman and demonstrated your professional seriousness to the others in the bar. You have shown you are in town on business and are not to be suspected for one minute of being a hooker.

• If a man starts talking to you and you like his conversation and he then offers to buy you a drink, accept with ease. If he offers to buy you another, change the contract: You buy *him* a drink. If he offers you another, tell him two are enough. If he asks you to join him for dinner, tell him you would love to—in the hotel dining room, not outside. Then charge your dinner to your room, so he won't feel he has a right to accompany you to and through your hotel room door. Keep the relationship on an easy plane, but don't go out with a man you know nothing about, nor put yourself in the vulnerable position of having him in your hotel room—not even for a second. (A great old ploy of a man who is not staying at your hotel but wants to be with you in your room is, "Do you mind if I come up to use your bathroom?")

• A woman traveling alone may certainly go to the theater, ballet, concert, or a play unescorted, but she is vulnerable if she leaves her hotel to go to a bar or a nightclub alone. Particularly in a foreign country, this kind of independence could be dangerous.

• If you want to find a nice restaurant where you may go safely by yourself, ask your hotel concierge, the maître d'hôtel of the hotel dining room, or even the hotel management. Find out about taxi transportation back, or if it is very close, ask if it is safe for a woman to walk alone back to the hotel at night.

Never feel obliged, because you are alone and staying in a hotel, to stay in your room, staring at the four walls and ordering from room service. Get out and see things, do things, but move with wisdom, always following the suggestions of someone in the hotel who knows the area.

A word of caution: Don't let yourself be picked up by a man you don't know in this or any other country. Don't accept an invitation for the evening. Keep meeting him for lunch or tea, until you can find out something about him. If he asks you out in the evening, accept only with the proviso that another friend or another couple you know accompanies you.

SOME PRACTICAL ADVICE

DEALING WITH A TRAVEL AGENT

Your dealings with a travel agent will be successful if you communicate well with him—spell out exactly where you want to go, how you like to travel, what price accommodations you can afford, and what lifestyle you prefer.

- If you have trouble sleeping with the slightest noise, tell your agent, who will book you a room in the back of the hotel on a quiet street, instead of on the noisy, bustling front side of the hotel.

- If you are too tall to fit comfortably into an airplane coach seat, mention it and the agent will book you on an aisle, if possible—where there's a little more leg room. Or, providing you have no disabilities, you might ask for a seat on an exit row, the roomiest of all.

- If the agent knows you sleep in a big bed, she will make sure that is what awaits you in your hotel.

- If the agent knows you like picturesque, small hotels full of the local flavor, he will book you accordingly; if you let the agent know you prefer the flash of a big, modern, Las Vegas–type hotel, he will put you in one of those.

In other words, to be effective, talk to your agent and let that person know what you like. These preferences will then be entered into your personal file.

If you're like me, you regard a good travel agent not just as a necessity but as a hero. There is no trip too complicated, no change of reservations too frequent, no cancellation too onerous for this person to handle. A good travel agent always has a smile in her voice, even if she would like to throttle you at that particular moment. These agents must be diplomats, culture mavens, historians, experts on gourmet restaurants, geographers who are not allowed a margin for error, travel guides, shopping savants, and psychiatrists, ready to listen sympathetically to every traveler's lament or dream fantasy. They must know as much about ocean cruises as they do about the air shuttles that fly between Washington, New York, and Boston. They must juggle airline schedules and be knowledgeable about everything from the dates of opera performances in Rome's Baths of Caracalla to those of the British Open Golf Tournament. You should also insist that your agent be as shrewd as the most successful used-car dealer in getting you the best deal on the complicated and ever-changing prices of air tickets, car rentals, and the like.

Your travel agent works on a small commission, which you do not pay—it is paid by the people who fly you to your destination or feed and house you once you're there. So the agent does not cost you a cent. Respect for the agent means that along with all the short trips you ask her to use time to book for you, you also ask for her service on long hotel stays and big trips—such as an ocean cruise—on which she can make some money. It also means that you wait until you're sure of your plans. Don't ask an agent to work on an endless series of reservations, only to cancel them time and again.

A travel agent who has taken good care of you on a complicated trip deserves a letter of thanks from you when you return home, as well as recommendations of her services to your friends (and perhaps one of those many small gifts you brought home).

A WISE MOVE FOR THE OVERSEAS TRAVELER

The United States government provides great services free for those who travel abroad. If you are traveling to a country where you are worried about disease or where there has been military action, civil unrest, or a natural disaster, or even if you simply wish foreign visa information, dial the Citizens Emergency Center in the State Department in Washington (202-647-5225). If you are using a touch-tone phone, the recorded operator's voice will take you through a number of questions. You may select three countries in one region per telephone call, to listen to their travel advisories. You would not call the Citizens Emergency Center for a travel advisory on Switzerland, where nothing bad seems to happen and where even the trains run on time, but you would call for the latest travel advisory on the People's Republic of China.

Those using a touch-tone phone may call anytime for the recordings, but those using a rotary phone must call weekdays between 8:15 A.M. and 10 P.M. or on Saturdays from 9 A.M. to 3 P.M. (Eastern Standard Time), when the center itself is open for individual questions and problems. If you know how to skip around the Internet for this information, bravo to you!

The information on which the recorded travel advisories are based comes from State Department officials living in those areas. When you call, first you will hear a general summary of the travel advisory for that region, then a detailed one, including the very useful telephone numbers of United States consulates in those areas. If you wish, you may also ask that a copy of a particular travel advisory be mailed to you.

This service may also be used to find out about Americans who are in distress abroad—including their arrests, deaths, or medical emergencies. Again, the menu will guide you via touch-tone phone to the exact office in the State Department or to the exact number to call to obtain the information you need. If you must have information on an American in trouble abroad when the Citizens Emergency Center is closed (after hours or on Sundays and holidays), call the government operator in Washington, D.C., at 202-634-3600, and ask for instructions on how to reach the Citizens Emergency Duty Officer.

*   *   *

It's difficult to be a smiling, relaxed traveler these days, what with incidences of terrorism, canceled or oversold flights, hot trains on which the air-conditioning has broken down, jammed highways on which your car sits for hours without moving, and buses that fill up and leave without you. Just keep telling yourself what I have to keep repeating to myself day in and day out as I fly all over this great country of ours: "Relax. Worry is not going to make your schedule any easier; fretting is not going to change weather conditions. If the planes aren't flying and you can't get a seat on the train, you will have to travel tomorrow. There's nothing you can do about any of it, so breathe deeply and relax!"

If only all of us who must travel constantly could psych ourselves into a state of acceptance of whatever happens, we would be happier, healthier people. I keep telling myself, too, that even when the clerk behind the desk is being insolent, there really isn't anything she could do about the situation. She could be pleasanter, yes, but she is helpless. So keep your cool. You are helpless, too, when the planes aren't flying and you have to make an important speech on the other end. Look at the people remaining calm around you. They have important engagements, too. They are under pressure, too, but they're not taking it out on anyone, including themselves. Be *like them, almost stress-free.*

I think I've almost talked myself into it! Well, almost.

CHAPTER 6

The Art of Tipping

Questions of tipping bedevil people particularly because the custom seems to spread like a liquid spill and the proper amount changes constantly. For example, when should you tip? When should you not? How much is proper? Is it humiliating to undertip? Is it crass to overtip? When should you withhold a tip, and if you do, should you spell out exactly why you are withholding it, or should you just say nothing?

GENERAL GUIDELINES ON TIPPING

Tipping in America has become more of a habit than a reward for special service. Most of the tips I describe below are not absolutely necessary, but in my opinion, life should not consist merely of attempts to fulfill the necessaries. A tip shows your appreciation for a job well done in your behalf, and it does help supplement an income, raise morale, and *make a person like his job more.* The latter point is the most important justification of a tip.

Most people feel that their moral obligation to tip ceases entirely when the service is rendered in an irritable, sloppy, or inefficient manner. My philosophy is that you tip a great deal less when service is rendered in a negative way, but you still tip. Many people rely on their tips for the major part of their income, and to deprive them of what you had planned to give could be a real hardship. I always rationalize myself into giving an unpleasant person at least a small tip, because I feel (without any supporting evidence) that each time I encounter an obnoxious person, he has probably just lost a spouse or found out that his bank account is hopelessly overdrawn or that the children are in trouble at school—and that is why I am being treated so badly.

You most certainly should not give a tip when:
- A person is *overtly* very hostile and rude.
- A cabdriver deliberately takes you the long way to reach a destination, thus running up the meter far beyond what it should read.

If you feel the service should have been better:
- Tip a little less than you would have normally.
- When you leave, explain in a nice, calm way why you have tipped less.

Be ready for a possible explosion, because some people can't take criticism and will always blame you, not themselves. Others will learn by your just criticism and will perform better in the future because of it.

AT RESTAURANTS

When you are dining in a fast-food place, you tip:
- $1 for the server or table cleaner.

When you are dining in a modest restaurant, you tip:
- 15 percent of the bill.

When you are dining in a fine restaurant, you tip:
- 20 percent of the bill, minus wine and taxes, to the waiter (75 percent of this tip goes to the waiter and 25 percent to the captain).
- 8 percent of the cost of the wines to the sommelier (wine steward), with a minimum of $5.
- $2 to the ladies' room attendant ($3 if she does something special for you like lending you a sewing kit, finding you safety pins, brushing you off, and the like).
- $10 to the maître d'hôtel, if he gave you a particularly good table or tried hard to please you.
- $1 per coat to the coat check person ($2 additional if you have left tote bags, briefcase, dripping umbrella, and the like, in addition to a coat).
- $2 to $5 to the doorman for getting you a taxi (depending on how difficult it was to get).
- $3 to the valet parker for bringing your car around.

If you become mathematically confused by having to split the bill into different percentages, call the captain and tell him you wish to split the 20 percent of the bill tip between him and the waiter, with the waiter receiving three-quarters of it. Then explain you want them to add to your total service charge a tip of 8 percent of the wine cost. Let them do the figuring. They will be only too glad to oblige, but be sure to take a copy of the credit card voucher with you to check for accuracy. Don't, however, make paying your bill a cause célèbre. You certainly do not want to ruin a splendid restaurant meal by taking an unduly long amount of time to check the bill and pay the tip. That can quickly ruin the atmosphere of any successful dining experience.

VALET PARKING AND LIMOUSINE SERVICE

• When you are a guest at a large private party, usually the only person who needs tipping is the valet parker who finds and brings your car for you at departure time. Inquire first if the hostess has taken care of tips, and if she has, then do not add another one. If the hostess has not, give the valet $3 in a large city, $1 in a smaller one.

• If you are riding in a commercial limousine in a large city and the tip has not already been billed, tip 20 percent of the bill. In a smaller city, tip 15 percent.

The easiest way to handle it is to tell the limo service (when you contract for the driver) to put the proper percentage tip on your bill. You can always give the driver more when he leaves you if he has shown heroic behavior, such as outwitting a thief or a driver full of road rage.

WHEN YOU'RE TAKING A TAXI

In a place like New York, you pay a minimum 50-cent tip for a ride. For a $5.00 ride, tip $1.00. For a $10.00 ride, tip $1.50 to $2.00. For a long ride, such as out to the airports from mid-Manhattan, you would pay 15 to 20 percent of the total in tips. (If the driver really helps you with your baggage, other than just putting it in and out of his trunk—this is in the category of a small miracle—you would tip him more, once you have recovered from the shock.)

In a place like Washington, D.C., where drivers are paid on a confusing zone system, you usually tip the shorter rides up to the next dollar. For example, if your bill is $3.60, you would give him $4.00; if your bill is $4.50, you would give him $5.00. When your bill goes a lot higher, you would tip him up to 20 percent of the total bill.

If you are caught in a horrendous traffic jam with a zone taxi driver, forget what you should pay according to zone. Pay him up to $5.00 or $10.00 more for his time and the trauma of the traffic jam. The same goes for a meter taxi driver. Even though he is paid a small amount while waiting in traffic, tip him nicely when you have been caught in traffic, because he loses money during the waiting period. (If my New York taxi driver doesn't complain loudly all the way to the airport during slow traffic, grousing and grumping all the time, I give him an extra $2.00 or $3.00 over the regular tip; if he does gripe the entire way, I wait until I'm out of the cab, then I give him $1.00 extra and tell him his bad humor at my expense has cost him $2.00.)

WHEN YOU ARE STAYING IN A HOTEL

If it is a fancy, expensive place in a big city, give:
- $2 to the doorman, just for opening the door of your car.
- $5 to the bellman just for bringing one small suitcase to your room or, if a lot of luggage is involved, $10 to $20. In a first-class hotel, you do not tip the executive from the manager's office who may show you the way to your room as a courtesy.
- 20 percent of the room service bill (with a minimum of $2) to the room waiter each time food and drinks are brought, unless the room service charge and gratuities are already on the bill (either give cash, or write it on the bill).
- $2 per person per day to the maid. Leave the cash on your pillow or bathroom console so she will know it is for her, and not just some cash you forgot.
- $2 every time a bellman brings something to the room, such as the complimentary basket of fruit or a special newspaper you have requested.
- $5 to $10 for the bellman who does something special for you, like going to the drugstore to make a purchase or locating a strap for your broken suitcase.
- $1 to $5 for the valet service when your cleaning and pressing is brought to you ($1 when it is one or two items, $5 when a raft of clothes has been laundered and pressed). Of course, if you are not in the room when it is delivered, there is no tip. That is why the valet service usually waits until you are in the room before they bring you your things.
- $5 for the hotel employee who gets your car brought from the parking area.
- $1 to $2 to the doorman for getting you into a cab that is already in the hotel driveway.
- $5 to $10 for a doorman who searches in the rain or snow for a long time to find you a cab.
- $10 to a concierge who has made a real effort for you (such as getting good seats for you at a sold-out performance, handling your air tickets, and the like); $20 if the service was extraordinary.

A bellman who is not pressed into service to answer your needs logically does not receive a tip.

If you are in a less expensive hostelry or one in a small town, give:
- $1 to the doorman when you arrive or leave, if there happens to be one.
- $2 to the bellman—or, if a lot of luggage is involved, $5 to $10.

- 10 to 15 percent of the room service bill is usually put on the bill as a gratuity for the room waiter.
- $1 per night to the maid ($2 if two people are in the room).
- $1 every time a bellman brings something to your room (not, however, for room service, which is figured differently).
- $3 for the bellman who does something special for you.
- $1 for the employee who gets your car brought from the parking area.

If you wish to forgo most of the service and carry your one small bag, you are perfectly at liberty to do so, but:
- If you're in a posh hotel, you should not carry even one suitcase—that is the bellman's job and he will resent your doing it.
- If you have a very large suitcase or are struggling with several packages, you really should use the bellman standing by. If you don't, it looks as though you're too cheap to tip one.
- You are justified in carrying your own bag if you are very late leaving for your train or airplane and feel the bellman is late in appearing.

When you are in a luxury resort hotel where the service is included, everyone is taken care of in a plan—from the maids to the waiters, from the captains to the pool attendants. However, after a weekend of being cared for by an excellent maître d'hôtel in the dining room, you would give him—and him alone—a tip ($10 to $15 for a weekend for a family of four; $20 to $30 for a large family or a group weekend).

IF YOU'RE A WEEKEND GUEST IN A HOME
WITH A DOMESTIC STAFF

If you are fortunate enough to spend a long weekend or even a week as a guest of someone who has a domestic staff in the house, it's nice to demonstrate your gratitude for good service with a tip, even if you never lay eyes on some of the individuals who served you (as, for example, the cook).

- Give the maid (cash in an envelope) from $10 to $15 if she performed personal services for you, such as:
  - Unpacking your bags.
  - Bringing you tea.
  - Washing personal lingerie.
  - Pressing some of your things at the end of the weekend.
- Give the cook (or leave for her with the mistress of the house) $10. If you spend a whole week there, double the tip.

- If you're a houseguest in a home with a butler—a really rare creature—you would give him $20 for the weekend or for a house party.
- One friend of mine who lives in a beautiful house with a lovely garden—and has a large staff—reported that the staff member who gets the biggest tips in her house is the gardener. Each guest finds specially made bouquets of flowers from the garden placed in his bedroom each day—a kind of pampering that has all but disappeared.
- If someone's private chauffeur drives you for more than a half hour—such as out to the airport or from the country into the city—you might give him $5 to $10, depending on the length of the trip.
- You can always leave a lump sum with your hostess and have her distribute it equally among the staff.

WHEN YOU'RE AT THE HAIRDRESSER

This subject used to be divided into a man's barber and a woman's hairdresser, but the two have become unisex. Many men are having their hair washed and set, blow-dried, colored, permed, and given conditioning treatments as often as women—and in women's hair salons, too—even if there are still men who would not be caught dead in such a place and who still go to a plain and simple men's barbershop.

At an expensive, posh place, you would tip:
- 20 percent of the total bill to your hairdresser if you're having a cut or color or a perm or a blow-dry.
- $2 to the shampoo person.
- $2 minimum or 15 percent of the cost of the manicure to the manicurist.

At a modest establishment, you would tip:
- 10 percent of the bill to the hairdresser.
- $1 to the shampoo person (if your hairdresser and shampoo person are one and the same, $1 more for the shampoo).
- $1 to $2 to the manicurist.

There is much confusion over whether the owner of the shop is tipped or not. Many small shop owners charge more for their services and do not take tips, as a result. Some shop owners do not take tips but do not charge more, because they mistakenly think it is not dignified.

The only way you can discover what the practice is when you approach a new hair salon is to ask when you are making your appointment. Just come right out with the question, "Does the owner, with whom I have an appointment, accept tips?" That is the only way you'll know, because everyone has her own way of managing the question.

WHEN YOU ARE IN A RAILROAD CLUB CAR

When you have a first-class reserved seat in club car, you may be served a meal (part of the price of the ticket), which includes service. However, as you leave the train, if the porter has given you good service and helped you with your baggage, give him a $2 to $5 tip for a short trip.

For overnight and lengthy train trips, you would give your porter a $10 per night tip when you leave the train. If he does extra special service for you, you might make it $10.

TIP THE FAST-FOOD DELIVERER

Again, you are not obligated to tip the young person who brings something like a Domino's pizza to your home, but it's nice to do it. Give $1 for one or two regular-size pizza boxes, but if you have a large quantity or a group of oversized pizzas delivered for a party, tip $5. Large quantities are difficult to handle, and a tip helps make a tough job easier.

HOLIDAY TIPPING

This is a vast and complicated subject, but here's a general rule of thumb: You give a holiday tip or present, based on:
   • The kind of place (whether it's an expensive hair salon or restaurant, for example, or a modest one).
   • Your own personal resources and ability to give at holiday time.
   • Your personal relationship with the person being tipped.
   • The section of the country in which you live (you are obliged generally to expend more in tipping in a city like New York, Chicago, Dallas, or San Francisco, than you are in smaller cities).
   • How long you have used the service (how long your car has been in that garage, how many years you have been going to that masseuse, how many years your housecleaner has been in your employ).

A holiday present or gift of money can be a very personal thing. I know one woman whose entire life is wrapped up in her dog and her cats. She gives lavish presents each and every year only to her vet, her vet's receptionist, and the three people who operate the pet grooming salon her animals frequent.

I know another woman who spends all day working on fitness, sometimes with a trainer who comes to her home. During the holidays she tips the trainer $50, the equivalent of the cost of one session. She also works out at her health club (and has the muscles to prove it). Since everyone around there is so slim and in shape, she ironically presents the staff each Christmas with boxes of chocolates or homemade cookies!

I also know a man who last Christmas gave $100 as a holiday tip to his French teacher. He explained to me, "After a year's hard work, she accomplished the impossible. I manage to speak the language passably."

Many people have detailed lists of their Christmas gifts and tips carefully filed in their computers, so each year they simply look at what they did last year and update it.

The amount of money that Christmas costs individuals varies widely, according to their lifestyles and their ability to spend. The following is a comparison of the financial outlay for the holidays of a rich New York divorcée in her sixties and a twenty-eight-year-old woman living in New York on a $30,000 salary. This is not a comparison of what they spent on presents for relatives and friends; this is what they spent on the people who work for or serve them during the year.

What an Affluent New York Divorcée Recently Gave in Holiday Tips

Beauty salon
- Hairdresser: $100 check and $225 ski sweater (she sees him twice a week) $325
- Manicurist: $25 check and $50 silk scarf (she sees her once a week) $75
- Shampoo person: $20 check $20
- $20 boxes of chocolates to ten other staffers in that hair salon who do little things for her during the year $200
- $50 check to the receptionist/manager $50
  Note: She also, of course, regularly tips these people when they work for her during the week.

Health club
- Trainer: $100 check (she sees him two or three times a week) $100
- Four other staff members (such as the locker room attendants): $25 each $100

Apartment staff
- Superintendent of the building $200
- Eighteen service employees—doormen, back elevator
  men, relief men: $100 each $1,800

Garage staff
- Boss: $200; Seven men under him: $100 each $900

Personal Staff
- Private secretary (with her for fifteen years): $1,000
  plus a gold pin ($750) $1,750
- Personal maid (with her for twenty years): $1,000 and
  new winter coat ($250) $1,250
- Cook (with her for ten years): $500 and new winter
  coat ($250) $750
- Driver (with her for three years): $200 and a sweater
  ($150) $350
- Three regular deliverymen from the grocer: $25 each $75

*Donations to employees' Christmas fund of three
private clubs*
- $300 to each club $900

- Tips to maître d'hôtel of her three main restaurants: $100
  each $300
                                                      Total: $9,145

What a Young New York Career Woman Recently Gave in Holiday Tips

- Contribution toward present for her shared secretary
  at the office $20.00

Beauty salon (occasional visits)
- Hairdresser: tin of imported cookies $10.00
- Three others at the salon: a Christmas card (50 cents)
  with a chocolate Santa ($5.00 each) $16.50

- Superintendent (who "does *everything*" for her) $35.00
- Once-a-week cleaning lady: $10.00 and $5.00 bottle of wine $15.00
- Deliveryman from her grocery: $5.00 in a 50-cent
  Christmas card $5.50
- Her laundry deliveryman: $5.00 in a 50-cent Christmas
  card $5.50

- Newspaper deliveryman: $10.00 in a 50-cent Christmas
  card   <u>$10.50</u>
                                                   Total: $71.50

TIPPING THE PEOPLE WHO SERVE YOU IN YOUR HOME

Many people have baby-sitters, others cleaning ladies. Some have full-time cooks. Whatever you have, if that employee is an integral part of your life and helps in making your life easier, he or she should be well remembered at Christmas. Anyone who is part of your personal household, even on a part-time basis, deserves a personal present, not only a gift of money. Here are some suggested gifts and tips for the holidays—just to get you thinking creatively for yourself.

If this person has been working for you part-time and for only one or two years or less:
- Cleaning lady: $25 sweater and $50 check.
- Child-care person (several hours weekly): $50 sweater and $50 check.
- Laundress: $30 blouse and $20 check.
- Cook: $50 nightgown (or pajamas) and $50 check.
- Gardener: Book on gardens and $25 check.

Note: If these staff members have been part of your family for years, *double* or even *quadruple* their cash gifts!

If You Are Very Rich and Live in a Grand House

A live-in "au pair" girl (who will be with you a year only):
- $50 check and something personal (like costume jewelry earrings).
- A small gift to her (which costs about $20) from the children (for example, a book, pocket agenda, some of her favorite brand of makeup).

For the nanny:
- One month's salary equivalent (which might be as much as $2,500)
- A TV, VCR, or credit at a nearby video rental store.
- A personal gift from the children, such as a sweater.

For a live-in housekeeper and/or cook:
- One month's salary equivalent (which could be anything from $1,800 to $3,000)
- A gift from the employers, such as a warm bathrobe and slippers

For the butler:
- One month's salary equivalent (around $4,000)

- A gift from the employers for his room (new TV, computer, easy chair, radio for his car, etc.)

Part-time live-out secretary:
- $500 check.
- $200 good-quality handbag.

Holiday Tipping
in Your Staffed Apartment House

People who live in luxury apartment houses in big cities have a major expense at holiday time giving cash tips to every single person who works for the building. The bigger and the more luxurious the apartment house, the more generous the tenants are expected to be. In some apartment houses, tenants tip all through the year—every time the doorman gets them a taxi ($1), for example, or the electrician, handyman, or plumber comes to fix something ($5, $10, or $20—according to the number of hours worked on the problem). In these buildings, the men are tipped modestly at Christmas—from $10 to $50, according to how long they have worked in the building.

In the older cooperative apartment buildings, the tenants tip generously at Christmastime, because they tip only rarely for service during the year. As December approaches, the service in the building always seems to sparkle, as the doormen, elevator attendants, and service men rush to please and serve you. It's Christmas-tip time!

You tip the people in your building according to:
- How long you have lived there.
- How long each employee has been working there (the old-timers, regardless of their jobs, are tipped more).
- How luxurious the building is.
- How much the employee does for you.

When you are single and have lived in a modest walkup, without any staff other than a super, you would tip him:
- Perhaps $50 if he takes care of your mail and packages for you, helps you carry heavy things, and fixes your plumbing and stove problems.
- Only $20 if you hardly ever see him and he is not living on the premises, ready to help you.

When you are single and have been in a luxury co-op for only a year, for example, you might give:
- $25 to the superintendent (after the second year, it would be $50)

• $10 or $15 to each of the service employees (and there may be fifteen of them).

If one of the men has been there for twenty-five years, you would give him $5 more than the others; if one is new that year, you would give him $5 less than the others.

The more years you stay in that co-op, the higher you tip everyone. Your donation increases every year, bit by bit—perhaps $2 to $5 more, and perhaps $25 more one year to someone who has been of service.

When you have a family, particularly with small children who are demanding of the doormen and back service people, you would tip the staff more each year, according to the rambunctiousness of your kids and the size of your family. For example, a lawyer with a wife and three small children, living in a nice co-op on Riverside Drive in New York, tipped the super $75 and the service employees $25 each. A banker in a more lavish apartment on Fifth Avenue, who had lived there for eight years with a wife and three small children, tipped the super $150 and the other service employees $50 to $75 each.

Apartment house personnel tipping is a very personal thing; no one tells you that you have to do this or that. You simply adjust what most people do in your building to your own financial abilities and to how much work the staff does for you. This includes such things as:

• Delivering your newspaper to your door each day.
• Getting you and your guests taxis.
• Taking your letters to the mailbox.
• Distributing your delivered mail to you.
• Signing for and delivering your packages.
• Fixing your toilet when it leaks.
• Putting new batteries in your smoke detectors.
• Keeping your dog for you while you run back to the store to fetch what you forgot.

I know an elderly couple who have been living in the same splendid building on Fifth Avenue for fifty years and are barely surviving financially. The staff do not expect grandiose tips from them, nor do they even want them, because this couple is gracious and good to all of them all year long.

When You Have Your Car in a Private Garage

Many people in large cities are forced to keep their cars in expensive public garages, where they pay monthly. Some people tip the men in the garage monthly.

Unless you are a monthly tipper, remember that at holiday time the men expect a tip from you for their tender loving care of your car. Some customers of a small garage personally distribute envelopes to the men because they know them all well. It is easier, however, to give a lump sum to the boss and have him distribute it equitably. (A new hire would not get the same as a longtime worker would.) You can either donate a generous sum like $200 to a four-man garage, or the equivalent of one month's garage rent (which in New York goes easily as high as $500). In other parts of the country, the costs of garage space are not so high, so your Christmas tip to a hypothetical five-man garage might be $100.

Some big-city garage owners post the names of their customers and the amounts they give at Christmas on a large poster on the wall. It's not an attractive thing to do, but it sure works! No one wants to be thought of as cheap.

Needless to say, the owner of a Rolls-Royce should give twice as bountiful a garage tip at Christmas as the owner of a Toyota, and the owner of several cars housed in the garage should look upon his cars as spoiled children being lovingly tended by the garagemen. His tip should be very generous—commensurate with the attention that is lavished on his fleet.

WHEN YOU ARE IN A FOREIGN COUNTRY

It would require an entire book to cover the subject of tipping abroad. The practice is varied and custom-tailored to each culture. You must be very discreet and secretive about your tipping in the Far East—if you do it at all—and yet you should be flamboyant about it in countries like Egypt.

You tip the usher at plays and movies in Paris each time you're shown to your seat, but not at the Comédie Française, because it's a government theater. You leave a small tip at a French café for your *café filtre,* sometimes not at an Italian espresso bar. The rules on tipping taxi drivers and gas station attendants differ from country to country. In many countries the service at hotels and meals is included *("le service est compris"),* and in Switzerland, they take the "service included" seriously. In many other countries, it is customary to leave an additional tip on the table for the waiter even with the *service compris.*

Consult a reputable guidebook before you go to any foreign country. Chat with an American who has lived in that country, or question someone on the plane on the way over who knows the country's customs well. Write it all down—what percentage you tip the taxi driver, the waiter, the coat-check person, the bellman, the hairdresser. Make a detailed list, get your answers, and then you'll feel secure in what you're doing. Or ask a sophisticated travel agent ahead of time.

✿   ✿   ✿

Having spelled out the proprieties of tipping, I must emphasize that a tip is not the ultimate reward. How you treat those who serve you is far more important than the size of your tip.

I have seen big spenders throwing around $100 tips in the same casual way that children stuff pennies into their piggy banks. I have also seen lavish tippers treat people as though they were chattel, ordering them around in loud, arrogant tones.

When you show dignity and respect for a person's job, and when you express your thanks and a compliment, it means much more to that individual than a handful of dollars condescendingly proffered by a rude, mean person. Anyone in a service industry—anyone who waits on you and helps you function more comfortably as you move through your day—deserves nothing less than your recognition and sincere appreciation.

Remember, too, something else that is more powerful than a tip—a letter sent to management when you wish to commend the performance of an employee or group of employees. That kind of commendation entered into their personnel files helps them get faster promotions in the future.

CHAPTER 7

Dressing Appropriately

This is not a fashion book, so this short chapter will contain only a few basic guidelines and a fashion philosophy—my own.

It is impossible to talk about the right kind of business attire without mentioning that the way you look depends not only on how you dress but also on:

- Your posture and bearing—the way you move, stand, and sit in your clothes.
- Your grooming (without good grooming, *nothing* is fashionable or right).
- The way you think you look (self-confidence has no price tag).

It is also better to invest in a few quality things than in a rash of lesser-quality wardrobe items. Clothing made of good fabric and with a good cut lasts for years. For example, if you amortize the cost of what a good man's or woman's suit costs, over a period of three to four years' wear, you have bought a real bargain!

PROPRIETY AND APPROPRIATENESS

Of course, you can ruin your entire fashionable image if you break the laws of propriety. If you are a woman attending a concert after the office at which everyone else in the audience is dressed in business and daytime attire while you are in a sexy black dress with a sheer black chiffon top, you are inappropriately dressed. Music lovers don't care that you paid $6,000 to buy a leading American designer's dress, which you first spotted in a fashion magazine. In their eyes, you are inappropriately dressed for the occasion because people will be staring at you, to the detriment of concentration on the music. If you are ever in a quandary as to whether a certain invitation or a certain activity requires you to dress modestly, stop wondering. Unless you aspire to being a *bimba,* dress modestly and you will always be right!

At Church or Temple

We may be living in a very relaxed, informal time, but that still does not excuse our attending services in a house of worship dressed as though we have been cleaning out the garage! Summertime is the season that sees the worst apparel offenses. You see a landscape of men in sleeveless underwear shirts, bare hairy chests, and women parading on the street in short shorts with bare midriffs. Fortunately, we don't often see the worst cases of these in church or temple, but inappropriate informality is still all too common.

Shorts are really not proper at religious services (except at resorts and in places like Bermuda, where long, well-tailored shorts are a summer uniform for many men, but are properly worn with high knee socks and brightly polished leather shoes). Shorts are overly casual in the house of God, and just because so many do it doesn't make it right. A woman can easily throw on a cover-up for church. A man can easily don a pair of slacks over his shorts for the services. It is little enough to ask us to be respectful in our appearance.

THE RIGHT THING TO WEAR—WOMEN

- Remember that fashion should fit your lifestyle, age, figure, and job. If something is new and bizarre, don't chance it. Leave it for the models and young people in the creative businesses. Wait until three months after some strange new fashion trend bursts across the scene. It either will fizzle out like a spent firecracker or it will be tempered into a style that will look good on you.
- If you have a figure problem, ask your friends which outfits look best on you. In this way you will learn the kinds of styles and cuts that should guide your choices in the future.
- Always check yourself moving around in a three-way mirror in the store and always sit on a chair in front of that mirror before you buy any dress or pants. A frank appraisal is a good exercise before handing over your credit card. After all, you're bound to spend time sitting in a chair, and the sight of a woman seated with her chubby legs not held together can be a real "downer."
- Know when and where to wear pants and slacks:
  - It's fine to wear them for sports, physical work, and relaxation.
  - Don't wear them on formal occasions, such as to a wedding, unless the pantsuit fabric is formal (such as satin, chiffon, or velvet).
  - Don't wear tight pants if you have big thighs and a wide behind and care about how people perceive you from the rear!
- Your hemlines should reach to the best point on your leg:
  - As fashion dictates that season.
  - As the shape of your legs dictates.

- As your age dictates.
- As your seniority in your office and your job allows.

In other words, if you're young and have great legs, wear your skirts short, but *only if that is the fashion that season.* If you're over forty, you're wise not to raise your hems far above the knees, regardless of how proud you are of your legs and even if ten-inch-long skirts are the current hot fashion. By the time you're forty, decorum should become a qualifying factor in your appearance.

WHAT YOU WEAR TO A COCKTAIL PARTY

- In winter, a dressy suit—sometimes called a cocktail or theater suit—is always right; for example, a black wool or crepe suit with rhinestone buttons or a satin or velvet suit.
- A woman with a great figure is appropriately dressed for a cocktail party in a dressy well-cut pants suit.
- A short dressy dress of crepe, silk, brocade, chiffon, even cotton in hot weather, either covered up or décolleté, can be worn with dressy sandals or pumps. A small "cocktail bag" of silk, velvet, brocade, satin, or peau de soie is carried with this costume.
- Accessories might be:
  A satin bow or ornament in the hair.
  Sparkly earrings and bracelet.
  Simple button earrings and a very simple gold or silver necklace.

Never wear all these accessories at the same time. You'll look like a Christmas tree.

WHAT YOU WEAR TO A BLACK TIE AFFAIR

- Floor-length, short, or three-quarter-length evening gown; evening sandals or pumps; and an evening bag of silk, satin, peau de soie, velvet, or brocade material.
- Jewelry—same as for cocktail party, only slightly more of it.
- A fur, if you have one and the antifur demonstrators are not around.

WHAT YOU WEAR TO A WHITE TIE AFFAIR

- A full-skirted grand ballgown.
- Lots of jewelry but never too much.
- Fur wrap.
- Long white gloves.

What you don't own, you can borrow—or rent—but the possibility of your ever having to prepare for a white tie occasion is probably remote!

WHAT YOU WEAR TO SOMEONE'S PRIVATE CLUB

- Daytime dress or suit for lunch.
- Cocktail attire for drinks late in the afternoon.
- Formal attire if it's an evening party, such as a dinner dance.

If there are going to be sports activities, ask your hosts what to wear, because some clubs won't permit you in the dining room for lunch in your playing clothes, and some clubs require whites for the tennis courts. The only way you can be sure of there being no dress rules is to ask questions beforehand.

WOMEN AT THEIR OFFICES

- Don't wear glitter—in jewelry or fabrics. Those are for evening only.
- Wear quiet jewelry only. That means no clanking earrings, noisy bracelets, or dangling necklaces that jingle. Remember, "less is more."
- A minimum of makeup is also wise. That means no false eyelashes, heavy mascara, or overly thick eye shadow, or a bizarre-colored eyeliner. (No surprisingly colored nail polish, either, or nails decorated with flowers!)
- Never wear sexy, slinky dresses at the office. You might get a free dinner and then some out of it, but you might also lose your job.
- Don't dress like "Miss Prim" at the office, either.
- Never try to look like a man—or Little Orphan Annie, either.
- Do buy some bright-colored or interestingly patterned blouses, perhaps a great scarf, or put a smashing clip on your lapel.
- Your feet are important. You don't want to look like a hooker, but neither like a hospital nurse on duty! A woman manager staggering around in the latest stiletto heels usually looks more like a "wrong decision" than a smart executive.

You want to look with-it, not mousy-drab, and you want to look *right for you*, not for a size-0 fashion model.

THE RIGHT THING TO WEAR—MEN

To begin with, let me note that I am being very personal here in my likes and dislikes.

- If you work for a conservative firm, dress as the other men do—conservatively. Save your avant-garde Italian styles for your weekends.
- If you have a weight problem, dark-colored, single-breasted suits are best for you.
- Wear a lightweight suit in hot summer weather. A winter-weight fabric makes others hot looking at it, not to mention what the wearer must be feeling.
- Brown suits are only for the very fashion-secure. They are basically conspicuous, and if you choose a loud, brown-patterned fabric, it could look like a rusted shipwreck.
- Three-piece suits are the most conservative look of all. They wax and wane in popularity. They require masterful tailoring and quality fabric to make a man look trim.
- If you're worried about what to wear to an informal weekend gathering, you can't go wrong with a dark blue blazer or handsome sport coat, colored dress shirt or a polo shirt, and gray wool slacks. Check with your host to see if the men will be wearing ties; if you are a very junior executive, forget about wearing a foulard scarf around your neck. That's only for a senior executive or a Brad Pitt lookalike.
- In summer, khakis and white pants may be worn everywhere except at the most conservative city business event. Jeans with a great sports jacket looks wonderful, but better on a man than on a woman.
- A polo shirt or sweater looks great with slacks for a casual-dress event.
- A showing of a man's underwear shirt under his open collar is not a classy look, nor is a shirt unbuttoned at the neck to allow a glimpse of a gold chain and medallion in a forest of chest hair.
- Braces of any design or fabric are always in fashion and are a wonderful gift for a man who wears suits.
- Remember, you can buy a $2,000 suit but it won't help you at all sartorially if you are a tonsorial disaster. In other words, hair and beard must be neat.
- Never pair the jacket of a business suit with a pair of casual slacks. It doesn't work. Only a blazer, sports jacket, or sweater does the job for a casual look.
- White athletic socks are fine when worn with loafers, sneakers, or running shoes and shorts for leisure or vacation wear. Avoid them at all other times.

SANDAL ETIQUETTE

Sandals became such a hot fashion fad as the twentieth century slid into the twenty-first, they have become a commonplace uniform for many women. What is surprising is the number of men who now wear them, too. If the wearers lived in the jungle, no one would even notice, but the sight of open sandals on men in cities is still a changing traffic light.

The etiquette of when to wear sandals depends on:

- The weather (they look pretty silly in cold weather, and wool socks not only don't rescue but make worse their inappropriateness).
- The lifestyle of your locale (sandals look better on the streets of Santa Fe than they do in Minneapolis).
- The nature of your job (if you're in the financial world, chances are your clients would prefer to see you in dress shoes).
- The condition of your feet and toenails (anything from a corn or a bunion to a fungus disease of the nail can be pretty disgusting when revealed in sandals).
- Alas, your age (young bare feet are much better looking than aged ones). People generally agree that bare legs, tropical climates, and sandals go well together, especially at a beachside resort or at any kind of sports arena or athletic center. Although many people wear sandals with shorts and sundresses to work, even in major cities, the fact that they seem to be worn by just "everybody" does not make them totally acceptable from the viewpoint of aesthetics or suitability. A young executive, sockless, wearing big leather sandals with wide straps may look very much out of place in a conservative office.

I had written a newspaper column on this subject when two young people accosted me in a not-too-friendly manner at a meeting. "What's so wrong about our wearing our sandals in business? Why do you say it's wrong?"

"I didn't say it was 'wrong,' just that it's wise to be nicely dressed, particularly when you're young and in the corporate world, or even when you are in business for yourself."

The young man looked down at his feet. "So what's wrong with this look in a corporate headquarters?"

"It would help if you cleaned your toenails," I replied quickly, "and perhaps took the long hair off your toes. You look like you're growing a beard on those toes."

The stiletto-heeled sandals for women are another matter. They are very sexy, yes, but if a woman is focused on success in her career, she does not need to be held back by broken bones caused by those heels, whether the trip to the orthopedic surgeon occurs after wearing evening sandals at a black tie business affair, or wearing "dangerous" sandals while giving a lecture at an important seminar. You don't have to be unfashionably shod at work. There are many styles of shoes that are chic, modern, comfortable, and give support. I hate to think what the feet of today's supermodels will look like after a few more years of wearing skyscraper heels.

MEN'S FASHION DISASTERS

- Watch your socks when you sit down. If there's a section of hairy leg showing between the top of your socks and the bottom of your trousers, you know it's time for action. Quick, to the store for some over-the-calf-length socks (and you may need garters)!

- Holes in your socks are another downer. Combine the holey socks with scuffed-up shoes, and you're in real trouble.
- Short-sleeved business shirts worn without a jacket in the office look terrible, in most people's opinion, even if they don't have the courage to admit it. When it's hot and you're jacketless, you can always roll up the sleeves to the elbows of your long-sleeved dress shirt.
- White dress socks are:
  - Fine with an all-white summer suit.
  - Simply terrible with black or brown street shoes and a suit.
  - Even *worse* when worn with black street shoes and *shorts* at a resort.
- Another real downer is a shirt that's too small, with pillows of fat bursting out between the buttons.
- Watch those loud plaids. Fred Astaire wore them beautifully; so do horses in their blankets.

YOUR TIES

If people are always teasing you about your ties, let a colleague who is an accomplished dresser pick out your next ones for you.

- A tall man needs an extra-long tie; a heavyset man needs a wide one.
- Remember: if you wear a dark gray, shiny shirt with a dark suit and dark solid tie, you may be taken for a gangster.
- Wear your most conservative ties when your suits have a strong pattern or color; wear your bright or interestingly patterned ones with your most conservative dark suits.
- Pick up a color from your shirt for your tie, or vice versa, so there is at least a trace of color coordination.

YOUR JEWELRY

Less is more. A wristwatch or gold bracelet, a gold signet ring on your right hand, and a wedding ring on your left are enough. More than one bracelet begins to be too conspicuous, and gold neck chains on display are something most of us can live without viewing.

What You Wear to a Black Tie Affair

The classic black dinner suit (tuxedo) is always best. For resort wear, a man in a white dinner jacket with black evening trousers looks wonderful, but an all-black tuxedo looks trimmer, slimmer, patently more handsome. Black is *always* right.

- A white or colored (or patterned silk foulard) handkerchief may be tucked into a dinner jacket's upper left pocket to add a touch of panache.
- Never, never wear a brocaded, satin, or patterned dinner jacket. (I also recently saw a jacket with sequin detailing and mistook its wearer for a member of the band, not a guest.)

Winter Black Tie Variation

A jacket of a very dark jewel color or black velvet with black trousers (sometimes worn with velvet embroidered slippers in addition) would be worn only to a dinner party in someone's home, not in a public place.

- The shirt:
  - White, off-white, or very pale pastel.
  - Pleated, never ruffled.
  - Worn with a black tie of grosgrain, satin, or velvet (sometimes red or brocaded, for the holidays).

Some people like evening shirts with wing collars and small black bow ties. I am definitely not of that group, although I think such shirts look great on waiters.

- The trousers have black satin stripes down the sides. You may choose trousers with self-belted waists or trousers held up by suspenders (braces) that are buttoned or clipped onto the waistband.
- An evening vest (of black silk, velvet, or satin) *or a cummerbund* (usually matching the bow tie) is optional.
- The shoes and socks: Black patent dress pumps or dress oxfords are best. Black patent loafers are often worn, too, but are not as elegant. Long black silk hosiery worn with garters is appropriate.
- Jewelry. Wear small cuff links and studs of gold or pearl, or with stones, small enough to look real.
- A gray or black topcoat or overcoat with gloves. If you have a gray fedora, wear it! Forget the black top hat in today's world. Someone might take you for the doorman.

For a Summer Black Tie Event

For summer or resort wear, men often break out in plaids, stripes, or bright-colored dinner jackets, worn with black trousers; sometimes the trousers are very colorful, even in a wild print, so a black jacket looks best with them. A dress white shirt and a black tie complete the costume, although in summer there are often colorful matching cummerbunds or braces and bow ties to brighten up a black tuxedo. Summer is the time for creativity, color, and pattern to take hold.

WHAT YOU WEAR TO A WHITE TIE AFFAIR

Until 1960, white ties were often in evidence for grand soirées. Even if the chances are slight that you will ever have to wear this kind of formal wear—unless you get married in white tie and tails—it's fun to know what it's all about.
- Tailcoat of black wool and silk.
- White piqué tie with a stiff wing collar.
- Starched white shirtfront.
- White suspenders (braces).
- White waistcoat.
- Black patent pumps or dress oxfords with black silk hose.
- Pearl, diamond, or onyx studs and cuff links.
- White kid gloves.
- Black silk top hat if you want to be fully costumed.

A FINAL WORD OF ADVICE

Men should heed the same advice women are given: "Take someone with you whose taste you *know* is good before investing in a major purchase."

In summary, one might describe well-dressed people as those who dress properly for their job and their social life; who buy clothes according to fashion but also according to their figure and age; who have good powers of observation so that they can learn good taste from others who have it; who know how to look at themselves mercilessly in a mirror before making a purchase; and who would never ruin a terrific outfit by a lapse in good posture or grooming.

You may find all this difficult at first, but with practice it becomes instinctive, and then you'll hear yourself described as someone who really knows how to dress.

CHAPTER 8

Common Courtesies

It is reassuring to realize that the basis of contemporary manners is not a group of rules concocted by unknown people from yesterday. These rules are rooted in long-established principles of decent behavior toward others (even though their outer forms may have changed with the times).

We can see this well exemplified in a little book that George Washington copied and edited (as a school exercise) when he was only fifteen. It is titled *Rules of Civility & Decent Behavior in Company and Conversation.* I was privileged to be asked to write the introduction to the new edition. George Washington's exhortations on behalf of common courtesies are still relevant. He writes in his own style, as shown here, making spelling, punctuation, and grammatical errors. However, his advice is plain, simple common sense—and timely. For example, he:

- Warns us not to be party crashers. ("Go not thither, where you know not, whether you Shall be Welcome or not.")

- Tells us not to be critical. ("Reprehend not the imperfections of others for that belongs to parents Masters and Superiours.")

- Teaches us deference, something young executives would do well to heed in regard to senior management. ("When you meet with one of Greater Quality than yourself, Stop, and retire expecially if it be at a Door or Any Straight place to give way for him to Pass.") I would add "give way for him or her."

- Promotes kindness. ("Shew not yourself glad at the Misfortune of another though he were your enemy.")

- Calls for discreet behavior in public. ("Do not laugh too loud or too much at any Publick Spectacle.")

- Advocates the proper form of address in writing business letters and in making introductions. ("In writing or Speaking, give to every Person his due Title According to his Degree & the Custom of the Place.")

- Warns against bad company. ("Associate yourself with Men of good Quality if you Esteem your own Reputation; for 'tis better to be alone than in bad Company.")

- And cautions against becoming a bore. ("Be not Tedious in Discourse or in reading unless you find the Company pleased therewith.")

George Washington's boyish *Rules of Civility* brought him to the attention of the powerful English landowner Lord Fairfax of Virginia, who made him a surveyor and included him along with the British nobility in the estate's important social activities. It was here that Washington learned polished manners and social dexterity, assets that helped him gain the leadership of the army and eventually of his country. His rules prove that good manners, morals, ethics, and honest values are one and the same. Today's writers on this subject can only reinforce his wisdom in modern terms. If Washington were alive today, he might be addressing some of these subjects.

COMMON COURTESIES APPROPRIATE WHEN YOU ARE OUT AND ABOUT

ON THE STREET AS PEDESTRIAN OR DRIVER

• Jaywalking and crossing against the traffic light are illegal and could result in death. They are also rude. A defiance of the law by a pedestrian makes drivers slam on the brakes, shortens tempers, and at times causes the driver to desire another meeting with that lawbreaker, this time to run him down, not save his life! Washington would have written, with several errors in spelling and capitalization of words: "A person wishing to cross the street should wait patiently at the corner or crosswalk for the green light, and look carefully both ways before proceeding—even when the light turns green."

• On the other hand, a driver who swings relentlessly into a crowd of pedestrians while making a turn can incite the emotions of a lynch mob in the hearts of those pedestrians. A driver should calm down when trying to turn, will patience into herself, and wait until after the pedestrians have crossed with the green light. This requires incredible self-control when the thoughtless, exasperated drivers behind, who are also trying to make the turn, are blasting away on their horns to show how they feel about the slowness of the proceedings.

• Be a considerate car parker. A sloppy car parker makes life difficult for everyone. When you park, give yourself enough room to be able to get out of the spot, but don't park in such a way as to prohibit parking for two other cars that could otherwise fit into the space.

• Except in cases of emergency, forget you have a horn. An ear-shattering blast of your automobile horn just because you are irritated about something ruins the peace of hundreds of people around you, not just the person who made you angry. When you are in a traffic jam and unable to move, blaring away on your horn, you are doing everyone a great disservice.

• Drive with your lights at low beam at night when cars are coming at you from the opposite direction. It is really rude—and dangerous—to permit your brights to blind the drivers proceeding from the other direction.

- If you are a slow driver (and there's nothing wrong with that unless you drive the way a turtle moves), stay in the right-hand lane. Otherwise, you can cause havoc with drivers who want to go faster, forcing them to do a lot of lane-switching.

ON PUBLIC TRANSPORTATION

- Say a cheery hello to the driver when you board the bus, and say thank you when you leave. The driver certainly deserves your recognition—and gratitude, too—because he has, after all, had your life in his hands for a short while.
- As you board, if you see someone running hard to catch the bus, notify the driver and ask her to wait. (This same philosophy should motivate you to hold open the door of an elevator when you see someone running to make it before the door closes.)
- Male or female, you should get up and give your seat to any older person who looks frail, to anyone who is blind or disabled or on crutches, or to a very pregnant woman. Until the mid-1960s, this kind of rule did not have to be included in a book on manners. It was something everyone took for granted. Not any more!
- Silence is golden on a bus, train, or subway, which means that your well-behaved children do not play their own radios, and that they pipe down rather than become loud and boisterous, with good spirits.

AT MOVIES AND IN THE THEATER

- Silence is golden during a performance. Don't crack gum, rattle candy wrappers, or whisper.
- Arrive on time, so that when taking your seats you are not disrupting the view and the ambience on stage.
- Stay until the end of the performance. It's very disconcerting for a performer to see and hear people getting up and leaving the theater, whatever the reason. If you have to leave early, you can always stand at the back of the theater for the last act or the last part of the program, so that your departure will not be distracting.
- When you enter a filled row to take your seat, proceed facing the people in your row, not the stage. In this way the people you are disturbing can look at your face, not at your rear end, as you apologize for crawling over them.
- Pick up your candy wrappers, empty boxes of popcorn, and soda cans after the performance, and deposit them in the trash receptacle in the lobby. Everyone will love you for it—just as they despise the person who leaves all the aforementioned litter squishing around on the floor, soiling their shoes.

IN THE SUPERMARKET

- Restrain your child from grabbing merchandise off the shelves as you push your cart down narrow aisles. Don't allow your child to throw items on the floor somewhere or to open packages and eat from them without your paying for every item at the checkout counter.
- When something has been knocked off into the aisle, whether it was an act of God or a selfish human being who did it, pick it up and put it back. This will make it easier for other shoppers to go about their business without having to run a giant slalom race with their carts.
- Maneuver your shopping cart with grace and concern for others. Park the cart considerately, so that other shoppers can pass you easily with their carts as you stand looking at shelf offerings.
- When you're in the checkout line with a cart full of many purchases and the person behind you has only two or three items, wave him ahead of you. It's a "do unto others as you would have others do unto you" act of kindness.
- When you are finished unloading the groceries into your car, bring your shopping cart from the parking area to the cart storage area in the store. Customers who leave carts out in the parking lot, instead of returning them, make it difficult for others to park their cars. The store employees then have to interrupt their regular jobs to cope with the mess.

AT THE BEACH OR CAMPING

The wilderness—whether it's a beach, a forest campsite, a mountain trail, or a lakeside panorama—is precious and should be carefully protected by all of us, so that our descendants will also have it to enjoy one day. We should also be respectful of the people around us, who have come for vacation, just some hours of peace, to fish, or to have a chance to meditate, dream, and watch for birds. Courtesies to the wilderness are courtesies to other human beings to come at the same time. For example:

- Every proof of your having been in any area should disappear by the time you leave it. Every piece of litter should be disposed of in plastic bags that you take away with you and deposit in a proper receptacle (perhaps in your own garbage can at home). Not even a paper tissue should be visible.
- Hold down the sound if there are other people within earshot, and that includes your favorite radio program or tapes.
- If you made a fire, follow the safety rules for extinguishing it. Don't just cover the coals or embers with sand. Throw water on them and thoroughly douse them first. (Have you ever walked over what you thought was sand but proved to be just a light covering on top of still-hot coals?)

• If you're swimming in the ocean with an air mattress or surfboard, or if you're wind-surfing or in any kind of a boat, watch where you're going and what you're doing. It is not only rude but hazardous, while merrily riding the waves on your mattress, to run into a person who's peacefully swimming nearby. You could cause a serious accident that way.

It's important to teach your children that young daredevils who do outrageous things on something like a surfboard or any kind of boat, endangering the public around them, are immature show-offs and not worthy of being worshiped and adored by their coterie of girls and the young boys dying to become just like them.

AT A POOL

• The first rule concerning a friend's swimming pool is not to be forward in asking to use it. Wait until the friend invites you. People with pools complain that their friendships with others are tested to extreme limits by "friends" who expect to be able to use the pool all the time, who want to bring along their noisy children and houseguests, and then even friends of friends. There are times when the owners of a pool want no one but themselves using it, and it is their right to demand some peace and quiet for themselves.

• If you are fortunate enough to be invited, don't take the pool invitation as one to use the house, too. Pool owners complain that the people they have invited "for a swim" often wander through their house at will, using their telephones, kitchen, and bathrooms (even though there is a bathroom at the pool house). One friend told me she really resents people washing their towels in her washing machine while watching TV soaps without ever having asked permission!

• Remember, never use a friend's pool without knowing exactly the hours for which it is convenient for your host to have you, or without your hosts' having given permission for everyone you bring with you (including your children). One pool owner told me that if one more person brings along a noisy, pesky uninvited dog, he is going to call the police.

• Always shower before entering the pool. Many pool owners die a thousand deaths as they see their friends lather themselves with sun oil, mix it well with sweat from hours spent sunbathing, and then enter their pools. If there is no pool shower, use a garden hose.

• Don't use your host's towels. Always offer to bring your own. Some people will tell you not to bother; others will think you're the nicest guest they have ever had.

• Be sensitive to whether the people lying around the pool want to talk, read, or go to sleep. Play it by ear. Keep your ebullient personality to yourself if the prostrate bodies around you seem to be intent on remaining quiet or if they have their heads buried in books.

- At the end of the season, give your pool host a gift, as well as writing a grateful letter of thanks. It might be a useful gift that you noticed would be nice for the pool—for example, a new ice bucket to replace the old one, some lanterns to illuminate the area at night, some guest hand towels of paper, soap holders for the dressing room bathroom(s), a shower caddy for soap, and shampoo to hang on a wall of the stall shower.

- Keep your children in your view at all times—not only to keep them quiet but also to keep them safe. Teach them the importance of never crying "Wolf!" pretending they are in danger—a major lesson to learn in life.

THE MAGICAL GAME CALLED GOLF

Golf has undoubtedly become one of America's favorite pastimes. Whether it was the inspiration of a young minority golfer, Tiger Woods, and his amazing athletic and financial success, or whether it's the fact that a lot of strong business connections are made on the golf course, the sport has seen a rapid rise in interest in this country. When women are "allowed" to join an important mixed foursome, they may have a rare opportunity to impress a VIP in the business world. (I heard an avid, skilled tennis player, who has never played golf, bemoaning his fate: "I could kill for the opportunity those golfers have in that ridiculous game for making themselves look good to future customers!")

You've finally gotten away from the office, so business should not be transacted during a game. The sport provides the opportunity for *building good relationships, not for making sales.* A well-known business celebrity has an excellent strategy for stopping people who try to take advantage of him during a game. "Look," he says, before turning away, "the telephone number of my assistant is 000-000-0000." End of conversation between the "pushy one" and his VIP victim.

Dean W. Wharton, who writes the column "Golfer's Corner," for the West Shore Country Club in Camp Hill, Pennsylvania, maintains that knowing proper etiquette is paramount in making a good personal impression. If your guests are lacking in golf etiquette savvy, either don't invite them or help them out. Give them some of Dean Wharton's golf etiquette advice in advance about:

- Where they should meet you upon arrival at the club.
- Information they should have on the "Bag Drop" and parking.
- Whether soft spike shoes are required.
- Any other dress code restrictions.
- If your guest players don't know one another, give them some advance bio information, so that conversation will be effortless, but also held to the minimum during a game.

The consummate golf host:
- Arrives forty-five minutes early to pay the bill at the Pro Shop. (The putting green is a good place to meet, so that whoever arrives early can practice putting.)
- Lets the pro know who will be cart-partnering with whom, so that the proper golf bag will be put on the proper carts.
- Checks the golf carts for towels, drinks, and extra score cards.
- Makes sure that the guests have secured their valuables, cell phones, pagers, palm pilots, and any other gadgets in the locker provided for them. If they take them around the course, in operational mode, you, their unfortunate host, will be forever chided for allowing them to enter the club grounds.

The Commonest Breach
of Etiquette During Play

Standing in the wrong place while another golfer is hitting or putting. Avoid placing yourself in another player's peripheral vision, because it can be a serious distraction.

As a sophisticated golfer:
- You don't start playing the game without knowing it. You take some lessons, read a book or two, practice on a putting green, memorize the rules, and ask your twelve-year-old neighbor, who has been playing golf since he was nine, to take you around a course a few times, so that you won't be a total greenhorn.
- You never pretend to be a hot-shot golfer. Be modest and play with others at your level, otherwise be prepared to have people refuse to play with you. (Word gets around fast.)
- You take the commitment of a game seriously, and if, at the last minute, you must drop out of a foursome, you find someone else to fill it.
- You arrive not only on time but thirty minutes early to prepare to play.
- Since people greatly value their time, you do everything possible to speed up play.
- You practice your strokes while others are taking their practice swings or completing their shots.
- You follow your ball and mentally mark its position relative to a stationary object on the course.
- You take along several clubs while walking away from the cart toward your ball.
- Once at the green, you park the cart in line with the next tee.

- Allow any golfers closer to the pin (but off the green) to play first.
- If you have the "honor" to play first, get ready to hit as soon as you arrive at the tee.
- Approach your putt from the other side first, rather than taking the time to look at the putting line and then walking around your putt.
- If you are keeping score, don't delay the game by recording scores while the others are waiting for you to hit.
- If your foursome is falling behind, let faster groups play through.
- After making your shot, use your first step to replace your *divot* before returning your club to the bag.
- Upon reaching the green, fix your *ball mark* before you start to putt.
- If your ball is in a *bunker*, take a rake to repair the sand at once.
- Never make excuses for your poor playing. No one cares if you are hung over or have a sty in your eye or golf shoes that don't fit. And never react to your poor playing by throwing a tantrum on the course. Witnesses will crown you with the "Jerk of the Year Award."
- Any talking during play, particularly in a normal or loud tone, is totally unacceptable.
- Bring your own balls. In fact, bring some extra new ones to present to your coplayers if they need them. That will make your popularity ratio rise quickly.
- Be sure to thank everyone enthusiastically at the end of the game and send a very gracious thank-you note to your host, thanking him for everything from the drinks at the club to the greens fees he paid. Don't forget to say nice things about the other members of your foursome, and how much you enjoyed playing with them. (It doesn't matter if you didn't.)

I know nothing about golf, so I had to ask a very humble question of a crack woman golfer when we were watching a tournament at the Onwentsia Club in Lake Forest.

"In your opinion, what is the nicest thing that could be said of a woman golfer, I mean the highest compliment she could receive?"

"That's easy," she replied. "If I said, 'Oh, I had no idea Martha was even playing today,' that would be the highest praise. It means she is the quietest, politest, best behaved golfer at the club. She doesn't intrude on anyone's time, space, or game."

Many of us should be more Marthalike.

Note: Dean Wharton is a financial planner and has been an avid golfer from the age of twelve. He and his wife, Marcia, are accomplished speakers and writers on the subject of professionalism and manners in the business world (telephone: 717-697-0826).

COURTESIES TO OBSERVE WITH THOSE
YOU ENCOUNTER DURING YOUR DAY

YOUR MANNERS WITH THE EXPERT PROFESSIONALS
WHO SERVE YOU

When you engage a professional for his or her services, naturally you want the best service for the money you will spend. But don't forget, that professional is a fellow human being, too, who looks for and appreciates signs of respect from clients. You can be sure that the client who establishes a friendly, courteous relationship will get the best service.

• Respect the professional (whether your lawyer, doctor, or banker) for that person's education and experience.

• When a professional has performed a service exceptionally well for you, let that person know it. You show you are a person of class when, even though you may have paid for the services rendered, you also express public appreciation for the fine effort made for you. (This holds true whether an interior designer has made your house look wonderful, your investment counselor has made money for you, or your dentist did a great job capping your teeth.)

• Keep your appointments punctually. Time is money for a professional. That also means that random chitchat is inappropriate during an appointment with someone like a lawyer or surgeon.

• Don't take for granted anyone you consider to be a personal friend. And most certainly do not try to get free advice in social situations (such as asking a lawyer a personal legal question in the middle of a golf game or cornering a doctor at a cocktail party to ask him about a health problem). Make an appointment—and pay for that advice.

YOUR MANNERS WITH WAITERS

• Don't encourage the wait staff to tell the table their whole life story.

• Give him your attention when he comes to tell you the specialties and take your order. Don't expect that to be done properly if everyone is joking, talking, and paying no attention to the person trying to do his job.

• If you keep changing your mind, don't lose your temper over subsequent errors. (It's not the waiter's fault.)

• Call him "Waiter" (or "Waitress"); don't snap your fingers at him to get his attention.

• When something goes wrong with the order, do not voice criticisms at the waiter that everyone can hear. There are other factors—the kitchen help, for example—that could be responsible for what went wrong. When something is incorrect, inform the waiter in a quiet voice that cannot be heard by others.

• When things go well, praise, thank, and tip him generously. Tell the owner or manager, "Your waiter did a good job for us tonight." That's like giving him another big tip!

YOUR MANNERS WITH TRADESPEOPLE AND SALESPEOPLE

Tradespeople wish to be—and deserve to be—treated with respect and friendliness. When they are, they serve you more efficiently—and like their jobs a lot better, too.

• Don't just bark a command at a salesperson. First say hello and smile, then state what you want. Some people are so intent on having their own request satisfied that they fail to hear the clerk's nice "Good morning." Even if the clerk says nothing to you, toss a warm hello in her direction. It will make that person feel good, as well as ready to please you with good service.

• If you know the person's name or see his name tag, use it. When you remember the name of someone who serves you, it shows you respect that person.

• Communicate what you want in a clear and thorough manner. Don't expect the hair colorist in the beauty salon to be a psychic and know without being told explicitly that you wanted a golden blond instead of an ash blond tint today. Don't expect the salesclerk to know that you only buy support hose, not the regular kind. Don't expect the barber to automatically know the exact cut you want. Too often we think that people see the whole picture when we throw them just a detail. Explain everything carefully and slowly, so that those who serve you will do well by you.

• Keep any patronizing tone out of your voice. The person on the other side of the counter or the plumber working under your kitchen sink feels (and is) no less important than you.

• Make a few friendly remarks in the beginning to whoever is serving you. A stony silence throws a barrier between you. A friendly chat about anything from the weather to how the Cubs are doing this season will put you on comfortable, equal ground.

• Thank the other person for every service rendered, however small, and don't forget your smile (whether it's a smile of approval or of camaraderie is irrelevant).

• When someone has been particularly helpful to you on a big job, write a letter to that person's superior. It will be kept in her personnel file and could result in a promotion.

Your Manners with Strangers
Encountered Along the Way

Whether you go to school, have a job, or are running a household, almost every day of your life you encounter people whose names you do not know and may never learn, people who just happen to be in the same place at the same time as you.

Your method of interacting with these people is very telling about your basic character. You can avert your eyes and refuse to be aware of any stranger you see. Or you can do just a little something nice every once in a while to bring a little happiness into someone else's life. For example:

- If you give a person a warm smile for no reason, it might give a lift to the spirits of someone who is depressed.
- If someone is having difficulty getting through a revolving door and you slow it down so that she will be able to get through, you just might be giving that person the one nice moment in her day.
- If on the bus you see someone older, looking very tired and frail, and you get up to give that person your seat, the other person may not thank you properly, but he will be grateful to you.
- If the person ahead of you is about to drop packages or is laden with suitcases and bundles and you step up to flag the taxi for her, then open the taxi door and help her inside, you will make that person far happier than you can realize.
- When you emerge from a taxi and see someone running to hail it, if you leave the door open and tell the driver to wait, you are going to be loved by that running figure for having done such a kindness, even though you may not be around by the time he reaches the taxi.
- When you see someone running down the hallway to catch your elevator and you hold it, you will be awarded a mental Scout badge for a good deed.
- When you are emerging from the crowded subway stairway and apologize sincerely to the woman you inadvertently bumped in your haste, she will go to her office feeling a great deal better than before.
- When you see a short person trying to reach something on the top supermarket shelf and you say, "Here, let me get it," you demonstrate stature of character as well as of body.
- When you suggest that someone with only two items get ahead of you in the supermarket checkout line, you ease the stress of that person's day.

It doesn't matter if it's only a momentary friendly gesture. When you say a warm thank-you to everyone who holds a door for you or "I'm sorry" to anyone you have incommoded in the slightest, and when you spring to help anyone who needs assistance, anywhere, regardless of the person's sex, age, or appearance, you epitomize a person of good character and beautiful manners, and everyone else is going to want to be around you all the time!

What a lovely world it would be if all of us would make a little effort to be thoughtful and considerate of those around us, whether we know them or not. That modicum of consideration puts smiles on other people's faces (or at least, keeps the scowls away).

CHAPTER 9

Table Manners
That Take You Anywhere

The Right Thing to Do at Every Kind of Meal—
Or, How to Avoid Being a Klutz

When you stop to reflect, you can see the logic in the importance to others of your own table manners. Whenever people sitting at your table or even near you glance in your direction, they can't help but notice how you are handling yourself during the course of a meal. If your table manners are graceful, their perception of you will be very favorable.

You—no one else—will teach your children. It is you who sets the example to your children for table manners. They copy you, mimic you, and you should help, guide, and remind them of the right way to get through a meal. Like everything else in life, practice makes perfect.

I will always remember a friend of mine who despaired of her teenage son's table manners. Like his coterie of friends in high school—all jocks—he ate, as his mother described it, "exactly like a gorilla." She set an eleven by fourteen-inch mirror on an easelback in front of his place setting on the family table for a period of two weeks, and she privately warned the rest of the family not to make any comment, no matter how weird they thought it was to have a mirror sitting on the dining room table. Her son could not help but notice how unattractive it was when he ate certain foods with his fingers that were meant to be eaten with a fork—such as his salad and beans. He caught his reflection, whether he wanted to or not, when he took huge mouthfuls that distorted his face while he chewed. His mother caught him frowning when he saw himself in the mirror talking with his mouth full. No matter how hard he may have tried to escape his self-image, it was there, right in front of his plate. As a result of the temporary presence of that hated mirror, he learned to eat gracefully. (I might add that the promise of a nice reward from his parents also contributed to his changed eating habits.)

TABLE MANNERS BASICS

Since a person's behavior at table really signals a certain sensitivity to other people, it's very important that parents spend enough time at table with their children, right up through the teen years, to make sure that they are well grounded in the basic precepts of good table behavior. The environment today is not conducive to teaching manners, with all of us rushing all the time in the pursuit of our own agendas. After a tough day of work or school, it's so easy for each member of the family to heat up a frozen food choice in the microwave or pick up a pizza or "some Chinese" to consume in front of the television—or perhaps to the accompaniment of music tapes or a movie. Many of us seem to spend more time in front of screens, eating à la McDonald's, than we do at a table, eating with table implements.

There's nothing wrong with doing things the easy way in the twenty-first century. It's just that by the time our children are in high school, they should at least know how to sit at the table and eat their way nicely through a served meal. (That kind of savoir faire will help their careers later in the workplace.) By the end of college an adult should be completely at ease at table. For a young person beginning a career, awkwardness at the table can be the kiss of death to placing her in a really favorable entry-level position.

BODY LANGUAGE AT TABLE

If you are a parent, here are some pointers you might wish to communicate to your children:

• Maintain good posture at table. Observe to your child, "How nice you look at the table when your body is straight in the chair, with your feet together on the floor." This doesn't mean he has to sit ramrod-stiff like a West Point plebe at the table, but it does mean that he doesn't sit collapsed like a rag doll.

• You have options on what to do with your hands when not actually eating. You may prefer simply to rest them on the table (with the bottom of your wrists balanced on the table's edge), or you may prefer to leave your hands under the table in your lap. (Quiet hands look a lot better to others at the table than hands playing with utensils, with food on the plate, or with strands of hair!)

• It's certainly all right to rest an elbow or two on the table between courses, because that's a gesture that comes naturally to people engaged in animated conversation. While you are eating, though, it's best to keep elbows off the table.

• Sometimes (maybe often) it's boring just to sit there waiting for people to finish their plates and their endless conversations, but keep those fingers from drumming nervously on the table or from turning eating implements into drumsticks. You may not notice the rat-a-tat-tat sound, but it will grate on the nerves of anyone who hears it.

• When cutting something, keep your elbows as close to your body as possible, so your neighbor won't have your elbow in her ribs. (If possible, a leftie in the family should have a regular seat on the left end of the table—to make it as comfortable as possible for him and for everyone else.)

GENERAL RULES ON CONDUCT AT TABLE

• Food is passed or served at a family meal by a parent at the head of the table, most often in a counterclockwise movement around the table, starting with the person on the mother's or father's right—the honor guest. Take what you wish from the bowl or platter when it reaches you, then pass it on to the person to your right.

• "Please" and "Thank you" are basic to good manners at table. Rather than reach across the table to grab something you'd like, ask the person nearest to the item "Please" to pass it to you, and when you receive it, say a pleasant "Thank you." You may be proud of your long reach in basketball, but if you use it at the dinner table to fetch something way across the table, you might knock something over.

• When serving yourself, take modest portions of food—even of the things you love most, like french fries, taco chips, and hot fudge sauce to ooze over your ice cream.

• Adding an overdose of sauces and spices is ill-mannered. When you are in a fine restaurant or in someone's home, it is very rude to ask for a bottled sauce to pour all over your meat. It is an insult to the chef and to the quality of cooking. (Teach your children the difference in the nuances of dining at a hamburger chain or at a fine restaurant!) It is very gauche to pour salt and pepper all over the food before you have even tasted it. Have trust in your host's or the restaurant chef's culinary talents. You're supposed to be able to taste what lies beneath the sauce and spices.

• Cut your meat one piece at a time. When you were a child, someone probably cut up your entire piece of meat for you into small bites. As an adult, you're not supposed to do that for yourself. Cut one small piece, then eat it before cutting another.

• The only way to eat is quietly. It's important to chew only small bites of food—and to swallow them with the mouth closed. It's peaceful and quiet that way for everyone else around you.

• Don't eat too fast. Swallow each mouthful before shoveling in the next. How can anyone understand the fascinating things you have to say at the table if your mouth is full of food and words at the same time?

• Wipe your fingers and mouth often with your napkin. That's what it's for. You look much nicer without greasy fingers or a crumb or a dribble of something around your mouth!

• If you want a second helping in your own home, ask for it. If you are a guest in someone else's home, don't ask, because if there is more, it will be offered to you. If there is no more of what you have just requested, everyone becomes embarrassed, most of all you.

• Yes, you may mop up that delicious last bit of sauce remaining on your plate, provided you spear a small piece of roll or bread on your fork, squish it around in the sauce, and then put it in your mouth—taking care not to let it drip all over you as you do that. Don't take a piece of bread in your fingers and do the mopping up, because that can be very messy. Using the bread on the fork is much neater.

• If you are served a certain food in someone's home that you really dislike—like beets or liver, for example—rather than making a formal protest, just leave it on your plate. Push it around a little bit with your fork, and your abstinence from that food will probably go unnoticed. If someone says outright, "Jennifer, you haven't touched your fish," you might say, "I'm just not hungry, thank you," instead of "I hate fish!" or even worse, "I *never* touch fish because the water is so dirty these days."

Soup Has Its Own Rules of Etiquette

1. Tip your soup bowl or plate slightly away from you, and spoon a portion of the soup *away from you* (a less messy way to eat).
2. If you want to pick up your soup cup or bowl, do it only after anything floating around in it (bits of meat, cheese, mushrooms, etc.) has already been consumed. Then and only then can you pick it up and drink it down to the last sip.
3. Never blow on it to cool it down. Just wait. *Pazienza!*
4. Be careful to consume it noiselessly, which means "without a slurp."
5. If you have picked up your cup of soup to finish drinking it, chances are you will need to use your napkin to wipe off your mouth. Men with mustaches, take special care.
6. Never dunk a piece of bread or roll in the soup, as I have seen many people do. If you're offered a spoon and a small bowl of croutons, serve yourself some on top of the soup, if you desire, but only a very few.

DILEMMAS AT MEALTIME

Catching Food in Your Teeth

Never use a toothpick at table, even if you feel you have a gravel pit in your mouth. Try drinking some water to help the situation, and if you feel your teeth are really decorated with food, excuse yourself for a second to go to the restaurant rest room or to a bathroom in your host's home. There you can vigorously rinse your mouth—or even use your toothpick if you absolutely have to.

As far as sticking a knife blade or a fingernail into your teeth to remove food at the table, don't do it anywhere near anyone you've ever been in love with. (It will make them sick!)

When a Bug Appears

If a little bug crawls out of your salad, pick it up quickly with your napkin, without saying a word, and dispatch it (dead) under the table. Don't point it out with great glee (or revulsion) to anyone else sitting with you, because you might ruin the rest of the entire dinner for most of the people sitting at your table.

Coping with Garlic or Onion Breath

You may feel your presence at home, in the office, or at a party will be less than well received, given the amount of garlic you have just consumed at a particular meal. Any one of the following actions might help you deal with the problem, to everyone's relief:
- Chew and swallow some fresh parsley.
- Rub a piece of lemon over your tongue and the insides of your mouth.
- Chew a few coffee beans.
- Take some antacid.
- Use some mints.

MEALTIME DECORUM

SAYING GRACE

When you are a guest in someone's home, and grace will be said before the meal (which does not happen at dinner parties), follow your host's lead. He will either remain standing for the blessing of the food, in which case you do, too, or the host will sit and announce that grace will be said. Don't eat or drink anything before grace has been said. Remain silent with your head bowed until the end of the prayer, then put your napkin in your lap, and the meal will begin.

WHEN DO YOU START EATING?

The last person to be served is usually the father or mother at a family dinner or the host or hostess at a dinner party. Everyone else at the table should wait to eat until the last person is served or has served himself. An exception to this rule is when the food on the table is hot. Then it is the responsibility of the host to urge the guests to begin eating at once, as soon as they are served: "Please do start. Your soup will become cold, and it tastes so much better hot!"

If there is no hostess, then the woman guest of honor on the host's right should be the first one to begin eating at the table. Everyone else will follow her, so it's her responsibility to start. If the food in front of her is cold, she should wait until everyone at her table has been served and then begin. Her male host should not start before she does. I have attended many dinners at which the hostess or the female guest of honor has been engaged in animated chatter for what seems an eternity without picking up a knife and fork, leaving the rest of the guests at the table longing to begin to eat but feeling they must not "jump the gun."

SERVING YOURSELF FROM A PLATTER

All food bowls and platters should be passed to you from the left. If you are being served something like mashed potatoes, it is easy: You simply take a glob of it with the serving spoon, put it on your plate, and put the spoon back in the bowl. (If you make the handle of a serving spoon or fork messy, wipe it with your napkin before replacing it on the platter or bowl.) Serving yourself from a platter of meat slices or a small bird with a surrounding garniture is more complicated. Take the serving fork in your left hand and the spoon in your right, and scoop up the bird or slices of meat in order to transfer them to your plate. Help yourself to a bit of everything else on that platter that may appeal to you— some small potatoes, for example, or a stuffed mushroom, or a broiled tomato filled with peas, or whatever. Try not to eat something that is on the platter for decoration only. I remember the look of horror on my host's face the night I cut into a Styrofoam beehive in the center of the dessert platter. It was covered with chocolate designs, and I thought it was part of the dessert. I managed to wrestle a piece free from the beehive, but it upset the entire arrangement on the rest of the platter. Our pained host whispered to me, "If I were you, I wouldn't eat that; even chocolate sauce doesn't make Styrofoam taste good."

The main thing to remember about serving yourself from a platter is that you should leave the clean-handled serving utensils lying neatly side by side in a manner that makes it easy for the next person to serve himself.

Taking Modest Portions

As a guest, serve yourself modest portions of whatever is passed or whatever is on the buffet. You should always be thinking of how many others are still to be served and how much food there is. If the food supply is plentiful, you can always go back for more, which makes any host proud.

When a platter abounding in tiny lamb chops is passed to you, take two. If the lamb chops are medium or larger in size, take one. It is far better for you to serve yourself another the second time around than to watch your hostess's face freeze in horror because there is only enough for one jumbo lamb chop per person, and you have taken two.

When a platter with numerous small thin slices of a roast meat is passed, take two slices. If the slices are large and rather thick, take one slice. You can always take more when the platter is repassed.

Even if there is a gigantic bowl of your favorite pasta on the serving table, serve yourself a moderate portion. You can "pig out" the next time you go back—when you know everyone has food on his plate. You certainly don't want someone watching you go through the buffet line for the first time looking like a prize-winning glutton!

Tasting Other People's Food

When you are with friends in a restaurant famous for its cuisine, it may be proper to exchange small samplings of the different dishes brought to the table, but I and many other people find it a messy, ungraceful thing to do.

If your friends insist on sampling one another's food, ask for two or three small, clean plates, and transfer samples onto those plates with clean forks and spoons. Don't exchange food samples after everyone has begun eating; apportion any tasting samples *before* people have begun eating (a question of hygiene, not manners).

DIETS, DIETS, DIETS

If you're on a diet, you should stick to it, and good for you, but if you're someone's dinner guest, it's better not to make a grandstand play of it. If you have a medical problem that makes eating normal dinner party fare almost impossible, talk it over with your host prior to the event. Offer to eat your own meal at home beforehand and to join the group right after dinner, or to be present during cocktails and then to leave as the meal is about to be served. Or you can pretend to eat and just push the food around on your plate. The one option you don't have is to force your host to prepare a special meal for you.

If you're on a weight-loss diet, say nothing about it during dinner (since there is no more boring topic of conversation nor more hostile subject for another guest who is about to dive into a large piece of double fudge cake). Serve yourself generous portions of the foods that you may eat, and skip the rest. If you're served a fattening dessert your diet says you should not touch, take your fork and push it around a bit on the plate. Your hostess will probably be unaware you are faking it. A vegetarian can often serve himself a variety of non-meat dishes (and sometimes non-dairy products) such as salad, rice, vegetables, and fruit, without anyone's even realizing his vegetarian preferences. A vegan is something else again. I invite a vegan to tea, not to a meal.

IF YOU SPILL AT TABLE

The entire question of spilling at the table is an anxious one, both for the spiller and for the hostess in her home. The spiller would just as soon have the earth open up into a great hole into which he could disappear so as not to have to face the embarrassment. The hostess, in the meantime, usually tries to keep her cool and not show emotion—but inevitably wonders with despair just how ruined the table surface or the linens are as a result of the spill. It is a trying time for everyone.

• When you spill (or a waiter spills on you) some hot liquid such as tea, coffee, or soup, blot it with your napkin, so that you won't continue to spot all around you every time you pick up your dripping soup container.

• If you make just a very minor stain at your place, like some drops of gravy or sauce, dab at it unobtrusively and clean it as well as possible with three or four pats of your napkin, taking care to return the napkin to your lap folded in such a way so as not to transfer the stain from the napkin to your clothes.

• For a significant spill, what happens next depends on the circumstances. In a restaurant, your host should call over the waiter to cope with the cleanup of your mess. If there is a waiter or caterer serving the meal to you in someone's home, that person will attend to the cleanup of your spill. If the spill occurs in a home without serving help, you simply go to the kitchen and fetch whatever you need to clean it up. Perhaps a water-dampened cloth is all you need. Perhaps it is a minor stain that you can simply cover with another clean napkin. I always rub salt and club soda on a major stain. (My definition of a major stain is something like red wine, raspberry sauce, or a large blob of chocolate sauce.) Blot any stain with a clean napkin or towel, making sure first to clean off and cover the table surface beneath the table linens to protect the surface from the wine or club soda seeping down to it.

• If you spill badly in someone else's home, it can become a drama, particularly if a glass is broken or a delicate tablecloth is possibly ruined. A sincere apology to your host after you spill is important, but so is quick action. Ask your host if you may go into the kitchen to take care of the mess. Your host will either go with you to help gather the damp paper towels and whatever else is needed, or your host will firmly urge you to remain seated, because "It's nothing at all, and I will take care of it." In the latter case, keep your seat.

If there's a major ugly stain *all around* your place setting, ask your hostess for a large, clean napkin to cover the offending area. Otherwise, anyone at the table who looks in your direction will be mesmerized by the spots.

Without making a large production out if it, it's nice to apologize to the other guests or to your family for having spilled—simply because you *have* upset the harmony and relaxation of the meal. (If you can laugh at yourself and make a quick joke about being a classic mess-maker, so much the better, because everyone else will then laugh, relax, and cease feeling sorry for you.) Start a new topic of conversation, if one of the other guests hasn't thoughtfully already started one. The sooner the party gets back on track, with the accident forgotten, the better for everyone.

If you were responsible for serious stains on your host's linens, offer to send the host's linens to an excellent dry cleaner the next day. The same rule applies if you or a member of your family is responsible for damaging any of your hosts' possessions (such as when your child throws up on their prized rug or your dog makes a mess on it). Arrange to pay for and have the damaged goods picked up, and then cleaned or repaired and brought back to the host.

I remember so well when as a nineteen-year-old student and the only American at a dinner party in a splendid Parisian home, I upset a full glass of red wine all over the tablecloth. In one grand gesture I shattered one of the hostess's twelve prized eighteenth-century goblets and permanently ruined her prized early nineteenth-century Venetian lace tablecloth. The duchess taught me a lesson that night that I will never forget. The guests in that dining room were frozen with horror over what the *jeune Américaine* had just done. The duchess, obviously dying inside, smiled at me and said cheerfully, "It's nothing, Mademoiselle, absolutely *nothing*." Then she called to her maître d'hôtel to

"Bring Mademoiselle another glass of wine," and while a footman mopped up the mess, she quickly introduced another sprightly topic of conversation to spare me any further agony. When I arrived at her door the next morning, to see if I could take the cloth to the leading dry cleaner in Paris and the shattered glass to a well-known restorer, the butler told me they had already checked. "Nothing can be done, but Madame la Duchesse wishes Mademoiselle Baldrige to know that it is perfectly all right, and she has already forgotten it ever happened." I will never forget that woman and what "real class" she showed us all that night. Through the years, whenever my children or their friends broke our antique porcelains and our good stemware (which has happened frequently), I have remembered "Madame la Duchesse," drawn myself up tall, and said to the perpetrator of the accident, "It's all right. Don't let it worry you. It doesn't matter at all." (I admit, sometimes that is very difficult to say!)

USING YOUR FLATWARE PROPERLY

• Hold the knife, fork, and spoon deftly. Most Americans eat with the fork held in the right hand. You should grasp the fork with your thumb and forefinger, about three-quarters of the way up the handle. The thumb pushes against the back of the forefinger on top of the handle, and the other three fingers fit beneath the handle in ascending order. The middle finger buttresses the handle from beneath. *Hold your spoon the same way.* (Note: For left-handed people, the procedures described here should be reversed.)

The thumb and forefinger work together, the thumb applying pressure from the bottom. The forefinger, applying pressure from the top, stays a little

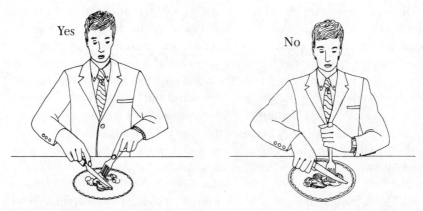

The proper way to cut your meat, when eating either American or Continental style, is shown here at left. Note the hand positions. Never grasp either knife or fork in a sort of clenched fist, as shown on the right.

closer to the fork tines than the thumb does. In this way you can wield the fork to the left and to the right, still maintaining a firm grip on it and making the implement do what you want it to.

The knife is held in the right hand with the thumb and middle finger grasping it halfway down the handle, and with the forefinger pressing down firmly on the top of the blade at the point where it joins the handle. The joint operation of knife and fork working properly is shown on page 194:

In my travels around the United States, observing young people on college campuses and in the workplace, I find many of them holding their forks in their left hands, making pugnacious fists while they draw their knives inefficiently across the meat, as if drawing a bow across a cello, and then clanking them down on the plate in order to change the fork and knife to the opposite hand.

The Continental Style of Eating

Since we are the only country in the world whose inhabitants shift the fork, after cutting, from the left hand to the right, perhaps we should take a look at other cultures. (Where our American custom began—of putting the knife down after cutting and before eating and shifting the fork back to the right hand—is still an enigma; many people in addition to me have researched the subject, including at the Library of Congress, without discovering the origin of this custom.)

In the Continental style of eating, the fork is held in the left hand and the knife in the right all through the meal. It is a logical, easy way of eating, and much quieter than the American system. (There isn't the clattering that occurs as one shifts the fork from the cutting position in the left hand to the eating position in the right, meanwhile laying the knife down on the plate each time.)

If you wish to eat in the Continental style, keep your fork always in your left

In the American style of eating, after cutting your meat you put your knife down on the plate, switch the fork to your right hand from the left, spear a piece of meat, and then eat it. (It's a lot of work, doing it that way, but that's the way we eat in this country.)

In the Continental style of eating, you keep your fork in your left hand and convey the food to your mouth after cutting each piece. The knife stays in your right hand and may subtly help get the meat or any food onto your fork. This is a much quieter, more graceful, and more efficient way of eating!

hand, usually with its tines down, and hold the knife always in your right hand—to cut food or to serve as a helper in pushing bits of food onto your fork. Even recalcitrant peas or corn kernels can be successfully captured with a fork and knife working together.

• Dessert is eaten more easily Continental style, too. You will find that when you become comfortable with eating Continental style, it is easier to eat almost any dessert by using two implements, a fork and a spoon. Eat the dessert with the spoon in your right hand and use the fork as a buttress on the left—or you may do the opposite, spoon in your left hand and fork in your right, whichever is more comfortable for you.

When eating dessert Continental style:

- Pie or cake à la mode is eaten with a fork and spoon—fork in the right hand, spoon in the left or vice versa if you prefer.
- Berries or any cut-up fruit is eaten with a fork and spoon—spoon in the right hand, fork in the left.
- Ice cream, puddings, and custards are eaten with a spoon only.

When I returned to this country eating Continental style after almost a decade abroad as a student and as a member of our Foreign Service, I was

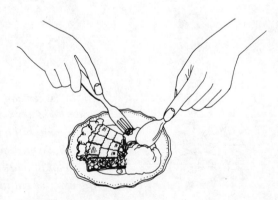

The proper way to eat pie à la mode is with a fork and spoon.

chastised by certain relatives and friends for being "un-American." Since then, so many Americans have traveled, lived abroad, and adopted the Continental style of eating that it is no longer conspicuous. In my opinion, parents should very seriously consider adopting the Continental style of eating when teaching their children to dine, simply because it is easier, quieter, and more efficient. The parents, of course, would first have to learn how to eat in this manner themselves in order to make it seem natural for the children to copy them.

Position of Implements When Pausing or When Finished Eating

When you pause in eating your food, American style, your knife (with its sharp blade turned inward) is already resting on the right side of your plate. Rest your fork, tines up or down, next to it on its left. This is also the position of your implements when you have finished the contents of your plate, and are ready to have it removed.

For the rest position, Continental style (shown on page 198), the fork is laid on the left side of the plate, tines down, and the knife on the right, angled from the lower outside of the plate toward the top center. When the diner has finished completely, she places her fork and knife next to each other on the right side of the plate, as Americans do, although often with the fork tines down.

• What do you do with your spoon? A spoon is meant to be laid to rest on the undersaucer and not left sticking up in any kind of cup or compote. (The soup spoon does, however, rest in the soup plate.) If you are served a tall glass of iced tea with a tall spoon or stirrer, balance this implement on the undersaucer when not in use. If there is no undersaucer, then the stirrer will have to remain upright in your glass. Be sure to grasp it between your index and

When you leave your fork and knife on the side of the plate in this position (fork tines may be up or down), it signals the waiter that you are through eating and that your plate may be removed.

This is the position to let the waiter know you have finished the course.

middle fingers while you drink your iced tea so that it does not fall out of the glass!

NAPKIN ETIQUETTE

As soon as you sit down at the table, spread your napkin across your lap. A luncheon-sized napkin (for example, sixteen inches square) should be unfolded the entire way, whereas a large dinner napkin (for example, twenty-three by twenty-three inches) should be unfolded only in half before placing it on your lap.

The most important thing to remember about a napkin is that it should stay on your lap until you have risen to leave the table. If you must leave the table during the meal for any reason, put your napkin on the seat of your chair, *not* on the table. When people are eating, the sight of someone's soiled napkin tossed on the table is very unappetizing!

When it comes time for everyone to leave the table, fold your napkin (not necessarily neatly) and leave it on the table to the left of the plate.

Using Your Napkin as a Bib

When you order a broiled lobster in a restaurant, the waiter might provide you with a bib to protect your clothing, but if you're not eating lobster, it looks pretty tacky to tie a large napkin bib style around your neck—unless, of course, you are a child. If you are eating a food that tends to spot your clothing (soup, for example, or spaghetti or certain salads dripping in dressing), it's possible to protect yourself in a graceful way. Pull your chair in close and lean over the table when you eat this splashy kind of food. Take a corner of your napkin with the fingers of your left hand and hold it up to your throat, spreading the napkin loosely over your chest. Still holding the napkin against you with your left hand, eat the food with the fork in your right hand. If anything splatters, it will land on your napkin, not on your clothes—and other people will hardly notice that you are holding your napkin up to your neck.

A woman should not blot her lipstick on her napkin. It just looks unattractive. During a trip to the ladies' room *before the meal,* a woman can blot her lipstick with paper tissue—a much better idea—and much easier on the host's or the restaurant's laundry operations!

If your family uses napkin rings (an old-fashioned custom, since most families use paper napkins these days instead of cloth ones that are laundered once or twice a week), teach your children to fold their napkins carefully and slip them into their rings before leaving the table.

FINGER BOWLS

The finger bowl—almost an anachronism today—is usually seen at a formally served dinner. The waiter brings you the finger bowl usually just before dessert is served (although in some houses the finger bowl is brought at the end of dessert, as a final ablution). This is a small bowl, often made of glass, and is three-quarters filled with cold or lukewarm water. A small flower or glass ornament is often floated in it. the waiter will place your finger bowl on a dainty doily (often made of linen or organdy and trimmed with lace) in the center of your dessert plate. From there on, it is up to you. Dip the fingers of each hand separately into the water and then dry them on your napkin—without making a large show of it. (You don't even have to rinse your fingers if they are perfectly clean.) Now lift the doily together with the finger bowl and place them at the upper left of your place setting (in the place where your butter plate would have been earlier).

For a formal dessert service, a waiter brings each guest a finger bowl filled with water, setting it on a little lace or organdy doily (optional), which in turn sits on the dessert plate. The dessert fork and spoon would be balanced on the plate in this case (instead of sitting at the top of the place setting throughout the meal, as is shown in most cases in this book). It's a nice touch to float a small fresh flower blossom in each finger bowl.

The arrival of finger bowls at the table perplexes many people. At a formal dinner last year I saw the chairman of one of America's largest corporations become puzzled by a finger bowl. He noticed others removing their bowls from their plates, so he followed suit, but he forgot to remove the doily with it. As a result, he served himself a generous portion of vanilla ice cream with raspberry sauce right on top of the doily (which was primarily stained by swimming in raspberry juice all during dessert). Many years ago, our eight-year-old daughter, during dinner in the posh Williamsburg Inn in Virginia, having never before seen a finger bowl, picked it up and took a hearty drink from it, delighting in the "funny-looking drinking glass." (The entire dining room wondered why the very dignified musicians playing chamber music close to our table were suddenly convulsed.) Recently I saw a young woman executive pick up the porcelain flower floating in her finger bowl and try to eat it. Fortunately, she did not succeed. (She explained to me afterward that she thought it was a candied flower—part of our dessert.)

In spite of such vicissitudes, finger bowls are very useful when supplied to your guests after eating certain messy foods: snails, for example, or lobster or steamed clams, or fresh corn on the cob. In this case, immediately following the course that would have made fingers messy, bring your guests finger bowls filled with warm water (and perhaps a thin slice of lemon floating in each bowl).

Don't rush out to buy finger bowls. Use your own pretty dessert or cereal bowls. And, of course, if you are serving oriental food, it is very nice to offer your guests *small hand towels that have been dipped into hot water scented with your favorite cologne.* The most important thing to remember about serving hot towels is for the host to have them picked up again immediately. The sight of guests forlornly holding used damp towels, not knowing what to do with them, hardly makes for a smooth dinner party.

The guest should dip fingertips in the finger bowl, wipe them on the napkin, then place the doily and finger bowl to the upper left of the place setting. The guest now moves the fork and spoon from the plate to the left and right sides of the plate, respectively. The empty plate is now ready to receive its helping of dessert.

HOW TO HANDLE DIFFERENT—
AND SOMETIMES DIFFICULT—FOODS

HORS D'OEUVRES

Keeping Hands Clean

It is difficult to consume hors d'oeuvres gracefully while you're holding a cocktail glass in your hands. During the cocktail hour you are constantly meeting people and shaking hands. If you shake hands with fingers dappled with mayonnaise or cheese dip, no one will be delighted to meet you! It's common sense to keep a paper cocktail napkin handy, so that you can wipe off your fingers whenever they pick up residue from the hors d'oeuvre you just ate. Even a cheese stick or a pretzel leaves your fingers in need of a napkin. I also advise everyone at cocktail parties to hold their iced drinks in their left hands, so that at least one hand is warm, dry, and ready to shake another's hands.

Disposing of Toothpicks

At cocktail parties toothpicks don't just stow themselves away, although guests wish they would. When you take a shrimp on a toothpick and dip it into a sauce, don't put the used toothpick back on the platter, because it certainly isn't appetizing for someone else who wants a shrimp. The wise hostess who insists on using toothpicks (and many of us refuse to serve hors d'oeuvres requiring them because of the hassle they create) provides containers throughout the cocktail area, so that people can easily dispense with them. If there isn't an ashtray or a dish or a wastebasket nearby, put your own used toothpicks in your cocktail napkin and then leave them in the kitchen or in the guest bathroom wastebasket before you leave. I have seen people stow their used toothpicks in plants, flower vases, under sofa cushions, in the aquarium, in the cuffs of men's trousers, in women's handbags, and in other people's pockets when they weren't looking.

Handling Difficult-to-Eat Hors d'Oeuvres

• When an hors d'oeuvre is hot, test it carefully and inconspicuously with your tongue before placing the entire thing in your mouth. Many inveterate cocktail party attendees have badly burned and scarred the insides of their mouths after failing to observe this precaution.

• When you select a hot puff pastry hors d'oeuvre, it might splash on you when you first bite into it. Wait until it cools, then try to swallow it whole. If you try to cut it in half with your teeth, you run the risk of having the soft hot contents give you—and maybe someone standing near you—an unwelcome shower.

• When you take a raw vegetable from a platter of crudités and then dip it into a sauce, hold your cocktail napkin beneath the vegetable until it reaches your mouth. Of course, the healthiest and the safest way, from the point of view of your cholesterol and dry cleaning bills respectively, is to consume the crudités without the dip.

• If the canapé you have put into your mouth tastes terrible, transfer it from your mouth into a cocktail napkin, and then search for a wastebasket. Turn your back to the guests while you take the hors d'oeuvre out of your mouth.

BREADS AND PASTRIES

A Roll and Its Crumbs

When you find a basket of rolls, bread, and breadsticks adjacent to your place setting at the table, pass it first to the person sitting next to you, then help yourself, and pass it to the person on your other side, who will then pass it on.

A roll should be pulled apart with the fingers into two or more parts; it should not be cut with a knife. Don't "butter ahead"; rather, butter each piece and then eat it.

If you have a butter plate, put your roll there. If you have no butter plate, keep the roll at the left side of whatever plate is in front of you.

Don't worry about sending a flight of crumbs in all directions as you break up the roll. Pick up as many crumbs as you can with your fingers, and put them on your plate. You can do it so naturally, as you talk, that no one will even realize you're doing it.

If someone is serving your table, the waiter will come by your place setting before the dessert course and remove the crumbs from all around the table—pushing them with a clean napkin onto a small plate or brushing them with a silver brush into a silver or metal container (a "crumber").

Handling Popular Breads and Pastries

• A muffin or a piece of toast should be cut in half, each half buttered separately and then eaten, perhaps spread with some jam.

• A hot popover should be opened, then buttered and eaten in small pieces immediately, because once it deflates and cools, it loses its charm.

• A sticky bun or a Danish should be cut in half with a knife—or in quarters, if it is very large—and then optionally buttered. (The term "buttered" means using butter, whipped butter, or margarine.)

- English muffins are already halved and toasted when they are served to you. Sometimes they are prebuttered. If you wish to put honey on the halves, take a large spoonful from the honey server, put it on your plate, and then spread it on the muffin half with your knife. This is true with jams and jellies, too. Spoon the desired quantity from the jar onto your plate, and then spread it onto your bread or roll with a knife (not a spoon).

- A baguette of French bread (a long thin loaf) is sometimes hard to tear apart with your fingers because the crust is so hard. A considerate host precuts it with a sharp knife into sections in the kitchen before it is brought to the table. Sometimes the baguette is preheated, sometimes even lightly prebuttered.

- Tiny hot biscuits are barely slit open, with a small amount of butter dropped inside. (If you take more than four of them, you have become a biscuit addict!)

THE RELISH TRAY

Sometimes, or rather, rarely today, you will find a relish tray—containing such things as small slices of celery and carrots, radishes, olives, and pickles—on the table when you sit down. If it is directly in front of you, pick it up, pass it first to the person on your left or right, then help yourself, and then pass it to the person on your other side, who will then continue it on its way around the table. If you have a butter plate, put your choices on it. If not, put your choices on the side of whatever plate is in front of you. Items from the relish tray are picked up with the fingers, put on the plate, and then eaten one by one. (In other words, don't put food offerings directly into your mouth from the relish tray.)

- If cottage cheese is part of the relish tray, and if you have a butter plate, spoon the desired amount onto that plate. Use your outside small fork, and, when finished, balance that fork on the butter plate until you need it again for the main meal.

- When eating olives, chew the olive, and then transfer the pit from your mouth onto your fork (your tongue will do this job for you) and then down onto your butter plate (or if there is no butter plate, then the one in front of you). If you absolutely cannot handle such a delicate operation, take the pit quickly from your mouth with your thumb and forefinger, and put it down onto the plate as inconspicuously as possible. (Do not follow the example of my brothers, who, when we were little and my parents were not present, spat the olive pits across the table at their adversary, namely, their sister.)

APPETIZERS

Soup

Soup is a very audible food. In the Japanese culture, slurping soup is normal and natural; in ours it is not. Sip your soup quietly, and if you are blowing on a spoonful to cool it down before swallowing it, do that quietly, too.

- When you are served soup in a soup plate, spoon it away from you.
- When you are dealing with soup *in a cup,* with bits of food floating in it (such as croutons, shredded carrot, or egg yolk), eat the soup until all of the solids have been consumed. Then you are free to pick up the cooled-down broth and sip it directly from the cup or bowl. (Never, however, pick up your soup *plate* to drink from directly or you'll go to the bottom of the etiquette class!)

You may pick up your cup of consommé and sip it, instead of spooning it, provided it is not scalding hot.

Caviar

There's great romance attached to the supreme status-symbol food called caviar (also served at the cocktail hour). It is one of the most expensive luxuries in the world. To be served a great caviar as the first course at a dinner party is to be outrageously pampered.

The famous Petrossian caviar importing company explains that the best caviar imported into this country today comes from the Caspian Sea area of the Soviet Union. The very fine Iranian caviar, because of the political unrest in recent years, is no longer available in sure quantities.

It takes an incredibly long time for the female sturgeon to yield the prized tiny eggs, hence the exorbitant price of the following caviar varieties:

The most luxurious food of all—caviar—is best served chilled over ice in a small bowl. Put a couple of spoonfuls onto your plate, then squirt some lemon juice on it. With your butter knife, spread the caviar on small pieces of toast or dark bread.

• Beluga: The eggs are light to dark gray in color. The female takes twenty years to yield eggs.

• Osetra: The eggs are light brown to golden. The female takes thirteen to fourteen years to yield eggs.

• Sevruga: The eggs are light to dark gray. The female takes four years to yield eggs (hence this is the most affordable of all).

Caviar should be kept in a cold part of the refrigerator (never in the freezer). Once opened, it should be consumed within twenty-four hours. (For many of us caviar lovers, it is quite impossible to imagine that there could be any left over.)

• The classic way to serve caviar is in a beautiful crystal bowl on a bed of cracked ice—to keep its temperature properly cold. When caviar is passed to you at the table, or when you approach it at a buffet table, put a heaping teaspoon on your plate. You will also find small squares of brown bread or toast, which you may butter or not. Spread the caviar on a small toast, and if you wish, add a touch of lemon juice. Some people also add minced hard-boiled egg yolk, minced onions, or sometimes even sour cream. Let's face it, by the time you pile all of that on top of the caviar, you will not even be able to taste it. Sirio Maccioni—owner of the famous New York restaurant Le Cirque—never brings all those caviar accompaniments to the table unless the diner specifically asks for them. The real caviar lover spreads it on plain toast, period.

If you are serving your guests caviar, give them glasses of cold champagne or chilled small glasses (shot glasses or liqueur glasses, for example) of ice-cold vodka.

There are many lesser caviars on the market, too, including red caviar, black caviar paste, and several new kinds of American caviar.

Snails

When a metal plate containing piping hot snails is put down in front of you as an appetizer course, you are in for a very special treat. You are also probably going to get garlic-butter sauce all over your fingers, as well as have garlic-flavored breath for at least the rest of the evening. Anyone planning a love tryst after dinner should either refrain from eating snails, or be certain that the other person orders them, too.

In some restaurants you will be provided with a metal pincerlike "snail grip-per," with which you hold the snail steady while you extract its insides with a tiny fork or nut pick. If no gripper is provided, hold each hot shell in your napkin in one hand (so as not to burn your fingers) while you extract the body with the other hand.

When the shells have cooled, it is proper to pick them up one by one and suck the delicious juice from inside. Or, if that is too adventurous for you, turn the shell upside down on the metal plate, and then sop up the buttery, garlicky sauce with small pieces of bread you have speared on your fork.

Shrimp or Crabmeat Cocktail

Shrimp and crabmeat cocktail are eaten with the smallest fork at your place setting (usually found on the outside left, but sometimes placed on the outside right). If there is a piece of lemon on your plate, spear it with your fork and then squeeze it carefully over the seafood. If a small container of sauce is provided with this appetizer, you may also spoon some over the shrimp or crabmeat, or you may take a forkful of the seafood and then dip it into the sauce before eating it.

If you are confronted with gigantic shrimp in a compote, you will have difficulty swallowing them whole. They may be tough, too, which means that your fork can't cut them into smaller pieces in the compote. Don't despair. Spear a jumbo peeled shrimp with your little fork, put it down on the saucer, and then take your knife and cut it into two or three pieces. If you are feeling adventurous, you may also take a large shrimp on your fork and bite it off into small pieces.

Steamed Clams

Hopefully, your thoughtful host has provided you with a couple of large napkins and perhaps even a bib to protect your clothing during a feast of steamed clams. (Steamed clams are the appetizer mainstay of a clambake, a lobster dinner, or a "shore dinner.") You should also be provided with your own empty bowl (or have easy access to a large communal bowl nearby) in which to toss your emptied shells. In addition, you should be provided with a tiny pot of melted butter and a consommé cup containing hot clam broth (made from the water in which the clams are steamed).

Your steamed clams should be open at least halfway. (If a clam stubbornly refuses to open, throw it away—it probably is bad.) Open your clam shell fully, hold it between the thumb and forefinger of your left hand, and then, with the fingers of your right hand, pull out the slippery clam body by its narrow neck. Slip the skin off the neck sheath with your fingers, discard it, and then dip the whole clam body either in the melted butter or in the cup of clam broth; then swallow it and delight in its deliciousness. It's very messy, but fun to eat. After consuming a whole plateful of steamed clams, you should be ready to rinse the fingers of both hands in water. (Guests should be provided with finger bowls of warm water for this part of the ritual. It's such a messy ritual; a bath after eating clams is more appropriate than just rinsing the fingers.)

Real clam lovers always consume their cup of broth before leaving this part of the meal. Bits of sand from the clams usually collect in the bottom of the cup, but an aficionado somehow manages to drink the broth without consuming a grain of sand.

Raw Oysters and Clams on the Half Shell

Raw oysters or clams nestled into a bed of ice on the plate are an expensive culinary treat. Hold the shell steady with the fingers of your left hand, and with your right hand, use the small oyster fork to lift the oyster or clam whole from its shell. (If any part of it sticks to the shell, use the fork to break it loose.) Then dip it into the small container of sauce in the middle of the plate. Some diners prefer just to squirt lemon juice on their oysters or clams, since they maintain a piquant sauce destroys the real flavor of the seafood.

You may pick up the empty shell and drain its juices into your mouth. This makes a slurpy sound and is not very pretty to witness, but in this case a purist does not care about appearances.

If you wish, drop some small oyster crackers into the container of sauce, and then fish them out and eat them with your oyster fork.

Mussels

Smoked or pickled mussels are sometimes served on toothpicks as hors d'oeuvres. Most often they are served as an appetizer in a garlicky broth in a soup plate—a dish called Moules Marinières. You may either extract the mussel from its open shell with a small oyster fork or nut pick, or you may pick up the shell, put the edge between your lips, and suck out the mussel and its juice in the shell. (Discard the empty shells on another plate.) While eating the mussels, spoon up the broth, too, because it is delicious.

This is another time to hold a napkin spread across your chest while eating with the other hand, and you will certainly need a finger bowl and a clean napkin after finishing your moules!

Meat

Always use a knife and fork to cut your meat, unless it is served in small, tender pieces, such as in a stew.

Cut and eat a piece at a time—don't cut ahead.

If you are served a steak or chop with a great deal of fat around it, it is preferable to cut off all the fat before you eat the meat.

Chops (Lamb, Veal, and Pork)

When others are present, you should cut off pieces of the meat with your knife and fork, rather than pick up the chop and eat directly from it. (Of course, what you do at home alone is your own business!) At a meal with friends, you can always ask the host, when you have cut the meat as close to the bone as you can, if he would mind if you finished off the last succulent bit of chop by holding it in your fingers. The host should urge all the guests to do the same (it is a compliment to the chops). Hold the chop with one hand only, and be sure to clean off your fingers and your mouth with your napkin as you go along. (Hopefully, you won't attempt this if the chop is covered in sauce.)

Chicken

The same principle applies to picking up a piece of chicken, turkey, or any other kind of fowl. Of course, if you are at a picnic, a barbecue, or any informal function out-of-doors, it's proper to eat chicken while holding it in your hands. Indoors, seated at a table, you should cut it down to the bone with your knife and fork, then ask your host if you may finish it off by holding it in your fingers. (It looks better not to, of course, and hopefully you won't try this at a White House state dinner, at lunch with your boss, or at your future mother-in-law's the first time you meet her!)

Small Birds

When you are served a small bird such as quail, eat it with a knife and fork for as long as you can (which won't be for very long). Then pick up the bird in one hand and eat off it until there is no more tender, flavorful meat left. Your host and everyone else at the table will be doing the same.

Barbecued Spareribs

I personally feel that spareribs, which must be eaten with the fingers, are so messy to eat that they do not belong at a party indoors. If you serve them in your house, be sure to provide your guests with extra napkins and finger bowls of warm water. (A friend serves them all the time, supplying his guests with bath towels for napkins!)

Fish

If you are served a fillet, eat it with a fish fork and knife (fish knives are rarely seen these days, except in good restaurants, so you may use any kind of knife given you).

In a restaurant, if you are served a fish that is not filleted, and if you are not adept at filleting yourself, ask the waiter to do it. He will either do it expertly himself right at the table, or, if he is not feeling self-confident, will take it out to the kitchen and have the chef do it. To do it yourself, insert the tip of your knife under the backbone, slide the knife under the entire skeleton, and then gently lift the skeleton with the knife. Put it on the side of your plate. If any tiny bones have been dislodged by this action and you find them later in a mouthful of fish, push them forward with your tongue onto your fork, then transfer them with the fork down onto your plate.

If you are served a fish with its head, and you're like me and would never eat the head, cut it off first before you fillet the fish. You can always ask the waitress for a small plate upon which to put the skeleton and the head—to be removed from the table—so that you can enjoy your fish without having its eyes staring at you. (A real fisherman would be appalled at this faintheartedness.)

• To squeeze lemon juice on your fish before eating it, use your fork to spear the piece of lemon that should be on your plate, and squeeze with the lemon still impaled on the fork tines. Cover the squeezing action with your fingers, so as to deflect any juice from squirting on your neighbor. Some restaurants solve the juice-squirting problem by covering a half lemon with a layer of gauze, so that one may squeeze it worry-free.

Lobster

Lobster is a rich, succulent delicacy, and the travail of getting the meat extracted from its shell is part of the enjoyment. No matter where you are, don't be afraid to don a bib before you attack a lobster. (Better a bib than a dry cleaning bill.)

Some people prefer to dip their pieces of lobster into a small container of melted butter before eating them; others dip them into a small container of mayonnaise. Still others prefer to put only lemon juice on their lobster meat.

If your lobster has not been thoroughly precracked for you in the kitchen (which is cheating, in my opinion), you will probably find a nutcracker and a tiny oyster fork or nut pick at your place. The nutcracker is used to crack the shell and the tiny fork to extract lobster meat from small, difficult-to-reach places. (Use a regular fork to eat the meat that comes from the larger part of the lobster.)

To eat lobster, you twist off a part of the lobster's body, hold the part in one hand, and use a nutcracker to break the shell with the other. Don't worry if it requires two or three tries.

With your left hand, hold the lobster steady on the plate, and with your right, twist off the big claws and place them on the side of the plate. Then, still steadying the lobster, lift up the tail meat with your fork, and cut it into small enough pieces so as to be able to dip and eat them. Then break off the small claws with your fingers and suck out—from the open end, of course—the sweet meat and its juice.

Now crack open the big claws on the side of your plate. Use your fork to extract the meat, cut it into small pieces, and dip them in the sauce of your choice.

Now it's time for the good meat in the stomach cavity—the green liver (called the "tomalley") and the coral (or "roe"), which is found in the female and is a great delicacy. Spear this meat with a fork, cut it into smaller portions, and dip it as desired. (Some people don't like the taste of this stomach cavity meat.)

Your host or restaurant should provide large bowls or platters into which the guests can throw the lobster shells as the contents are consumed. Some kind of finger bowl is also a necessity after finishing this course.

PASTA

The easiest way to eat noodles or stringy pasta is with a fork in your right hand and a large (dessert-size) spoon in your left. It requires practice to twirl the strands of pasta properly around the fork. Pile a small amount of pasta on your fork, and support it by pushing the spoon against it to keep it intact. Then bring the fork to your mouth. Some people use a piece of bread held in their left hand as a "pusher," to act like a spoon in keeping the noodles on the fork.

Keep your napkin spread in front of you as you eat, and lean close into the table to prevent pasta spills.

If you are a purist about eating spaghetti, linguine, or any other long, thin noodles, you will not use a spoon as a support. You will go it alone with the fork. The secret is in twining just a small number of strands around your fork (four or five). Keep turning your fork around slowly until all the strands are rolled compactly around it and you're ready to put it into your mouth.

If you're not a "purist" about eating spaghetti, use a large (dessert size) spoon to help you twist the strands of spaghetti around the fork.

When you first try this, you probably will have trails of spaghetti falling down from the fork, and you will lose as many strands as you manage to get wound around the fork. It's also common for the most professional of spaghetti eaters to err occasionally and to be obliged to slurp errant strands of spaghetti or angel hair up into their mouths. As with anything, however, practice makes almost perfect, and you will feel a great sense of achievement once you master the fork-only method of eating spaghetti.

If you find the sauce and the grated cheese sitting on top of your pasta, it is good form to mix it all up, like a chef's salad, before eating it. It is also good form to mop up the last bit of pasta sauce with a piece of bread speared on your fork.

What is not good form is to cut your strands of pasta into small, manageable pieces with your fork—unless you are a child!

VEGETABLES THAT ARE DIFFICULT TO EAT

The four vegetables most difficult to eat are:
- Peas (because they keep escaping from the fork)
- Artichokes (because they are complicated)
- Corn on the cob (because eating it results in grease all over your face and kernels stuck in your teeth)
- Asparagus

Peas

If you are eating Continental style, it is fairly easy to shove peas onto your fork, held in the left hand, while your knife in the right hand serves as a flying buttress. If you are eating American style, it helps to use a small piece of bread or roll to shove the recalcitrant peas onto your fork. (Of course, you still have to face the problem of getting the peas from the plate into your mouth. That requires a delicate balancing act on the fork.)

Artichokes

Served usually as an appetizer, the artichoke is consumed leaf by leaf. When you pull off a leaf, dip the rounded, soft, meaty end of it into the melted butter, vinaigrette, mayonnaise, or whatever has been provided in the small container at your place. Eat the leaf up to the part of it that is hard and inedible, and then discard it neatly in a pile of "used leaves" you arrange around the artichokes on your plate.

When you have eaten your way down to the central, gray, fuzzy part (the "choke"), spear it with your fork (or steady it with your fingers), hold it firmly, and then cut off the gray feathery part around and under it. You should now have a "bald" round-on-top gray heart devoid of any little leaves. Cut it out from its bed of larger leaves, and dip it. (Cut it into smaller pieces on your plate before eating it, if it is a large heart.) The artichoke heart is tender and flavorful—the best part of this formidable vegetable.

Corn on the Cob

Once again, fresh corn on the cob is great for family dinners and for parties held outdoors. For dinner in your home, however, it is far easier on your guests if you cut off the kernels from the cob in the kitchen and serve the corn buttered and seasoned in a bowl.

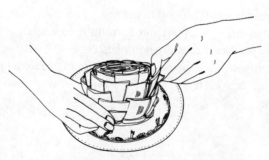

When you confront an artichoke, grasp it with one hand near the base to steady it, and with the other hand pull off the leaves one by one. Dip each leaf into the melted butter or mayonnaise container and then eat up to the part of it that is hard. Pile used leaves neatly in a ring around the artichoke on the plate or in the small container at your place.

If you are eating corn at a picnic, hopefully your host has already preseasoned and prebuttered the cobs. If not, and you have to butter the cob yourself, butter and season a few rows at a time and eat them, instead of having to hold an entire cob full of grease, which will then drip all over you.

Asparagus

Fresh asparagus may be eaten in one of two ways, depending upon how long it has been cooked and how much of it is buried in sauce: either with the fingers or with a knife and fork.

If the stalks are firm and the vegetable has been steamed for only a short time, hopefully the sauce has been put on the asparagus tips only. This is the moment for you to pick it up with your fingers, stalk by stalk, eating it down to the tough, inedible part, and then placing the "used" asparagus stalks back on the plate in a neat pile.

If the asparagus is overcooked and the stalk is entirely flexible, and if sauce has been poured all over, you can't use your fingers. Cut the vegetable into small manageable portions with your knife and fork as you eat it.

SALAD

Salad is a versatile food. It may be served as:
- A first course (such as chicken salad in half an avocado, or hearts of palm with lettuce and dressing).
- A side dish (such as a salad of mixed greens served with the main entrée).
- A separate course, between the entrée and dessert, provided it is accompanied by an assortment of cheeses and crackers.

Nutritionists say that salad should not be torn into small, manageable pieces until just before it is served, because otherwise some of the vitamin content escapes. However, the host should remember to have the leaves torn into small pieces instead of forcing his guests to cope with large leaves on their salad plates.

Cut unwieldy pieces of lettuce with a fork; if they can't be cut with a fork only, use your knife, too.

If salad is served as a vegetable on your entrée plate, use your entrée fork to eat it. If it is served on a separate side plate, you may—or may not—have been provided with a special salad fork in your place setting. (If there is none, use your entrée fork.)

If you are being served a separate course of salad and cheese, between the entrée and dessert, a separate plate will be put down before you. You should have as your utensils both a salad fork and a luncheon knife. Take small portions of one or two cheeses from the cheese tray, and two or three crackers. This is no time to exaggerate what you serve yourself (everyone is watching you at the table).

Be very careful if your salad is overdressed, because the dressing will splash on your clothes. If lettuce leaves fall off your overburdened salad plate, just pick them up and put them back on the plate. (It happens to me all the time.) If the fallen lettuce leaves behind it a big stain of dressing, dab at it with your napkin, and then forget about it.

FRESH FRUIT SERVED AT THE END OF A MEAL

In many countries, a bowl of fresh fruit is passed to guests, either as dessert or as a prologue to dessert. The following are some tips on eating fresh fruit when you are a guest:

• Apples. If you eat only peeled apples, then peel your apple with the fruit knife provided you. The easiest way to handle this is first to quarter the apple. Then use the knife to peel and remove the core from each quarter. Europeans often cut the entire apple into tiny pieces with their fork and knife as they go along, but if you wish to pick up an apple quarter and eat it in your fingers, that's all right, too.

• Bananas. If you are at the beach or on a picnic, you simply remove the peel and eat the banana whole. If you've chosen a banana to eat at someone's dinner table, remove the skin, leave it on the side of your plate, and cut the banana into small pieces with your fruit knife and fork. Then eat the pieces with your fork.

• Grapes. Usually you will find a pair of grape scissors passed with the bowl of grapes. Cut a nice cluster of grapes from the main branch, and put it on your plate. If there are no scissors, tear it off carefully with your fingers. Deposit the grape seeds into your fingers, and then transfer them to the plate as unobtrusively as possible. (Actually, it is much better if your host serves seedless grapes.)

If someone should ask you how to peel a grape, my answer is that you don't.

• Peaches and pears. Some people eat pears and peaches skin and all; some prefer to peel them. Peel first, if you must, then core the pear or remove the stone from the peach and quarter it. It is best to eat these fruits small piece by small piece, since they are full of juice and are more difficult to eat by hand than an apple.

Sliced peaches, of course, are served with milk or cream (and optionally sugar), and pears are often poached whole in a syrup sauce. It's only when you approach the whole, fresh fruit that some manual dexterity is required to eat them properly.

• Grapefruit. Your host (or the restaurant) should have removed almost all the seeds before it is presented to you. Hopefully, he will have already precut each little section, too, so that all you have to do is slide out each section with a spoon. If the grapefruit sections have not been precut, use a small knife or the serrated-edged grapefruit spoon to do the job.

It is proper when you have finished eating the grapefruit to pick it up and squeeze its juice onto your spoon, and then drink it.

• Oranges and tangerines. Use your fruit knife first to remove the peel. (If the peel is thick and loose, you can pull it off with your fingers.) Then pull the fruit apart into small, manageable sections before eating it. If your piece of fruit is covered with a network of white pulpy skin, remove that as well with your fingers. Spit any seeds into the palm of your hand, and then transfer them to the plate.

• Plums, cherries, apricots, kumquats. A small piece of fruit with a stone in its center is put whole in the mouth with the fingers. The fruit is chewed off the stone in the mouth; the pit is then pushed onto a fork or spoon with tongue action and then brought down onto the plate.

• Kiwis. The kiwi is peeled and then sliced like a tomato, and the thin slices are used in fruit cups and as decoration for salads and desserts.

• Melons, papayas, and pomegranates. These fruits are served ice-cold and are halved or quartered, depending on their original size. A fruit like papaya, with seeds in its center, is served to you with the seeds already removed. Scoop out the fruit from its shell with a spoon.

• Fresh pineapple. After the ends and the outer spiny skin of the pineapple have been removed with a sharp knife, the pineapple is sliced into thin round pieces. When served on a plate (either as is, or with some liqueur like Kirschwasser poured over it), it is eaten with a dessert fork and spoon.

• Watermelon. This is too informal and messy to include on a dinner party menu (unless it is cut up, with its seeds removed, as part of a fruit cup). The problem with serving a piece of watermelon at the table is the quantity of seeds, which requires a constant spitting of seeds into the palm of the hand and then down onto the plate. This fruit is greatly enjoyed when served at an informal outdoor party—at which seed spitting is tolerated in everyone, not just the children.

• Stewed fruit. If you are eating something like stewed prunes, eat around the pit by cutting away the fruit from the center. If the prune pit ends up in your mouth, remove it by fork (or spoon, if you are using a dessert spoon without a knife).

Informal Foods

- Triple-decker sandwiches. If you have a big mouth and are eating alone, you might as well put one end of the entire sandwich in your mouth and start to eat. If anyone else is present, cut each half of this giant sandwich into yet another half. If a quarter of the sandwich is absolutely too wide for your mouth, cut it up as you go along into smaller, manageable bites.

- Heroes. A hero is a sharing food, a group activity. The secret to the polite consumption of a foot-long or longer hero is to cut off an appropriate-size piece for yourself, judging by the number of people who will be sharing it with you, how much you like it, and how large it is. It is better to err on the side of a small portion and to return for more than to cut off too big a piece and cause a mutiny in the ranks because you took an overly generous amount. If you are the host of a gathering, precut the pieces in equal amounts. Then no one can complain about anyone else.

- Hamburgers and hot dogs. These are easy-to-eat finger foods. The problems that arise stem from an oversupply of sauce topping, not to mention sliced onions and pickled relish. Eat small portions of your hamburger or hot dog, because otherwise, your cheeks will be bulging with food (unattractive). Use napkins to hold the object, so that any sauce oozing out will hit the napkin and not your hands and clothing. If you're really worried about your clothes, stand holding the burger or dog well out from your body and lean over to eat it. (In this case, however, watch out for the shoes of everyone standing near you!)

  A smart burger or dog consumer always holds it in a napkin in one hand, and has a napkin or two at the ready in the other hand.

- Pizza. Pizza is an informal food, not served at dinner parties, so eat it as it is meant to be eaten—each pie-shaped wedge held in your hand. As you hold it, turn up the outside edges toward the center, to prohibit the filling from sliding off and out. Lots of napkins should be on hand.

- Tortillas. Tortillas are also meant to be eaten while held in your hand. The flat tortilla is lightly filled with a mixture such as frijoles (pinto beans); then it is rolled up and eaten like a sandwich, from end to end.

- French fries, shoestring potatoes, and potato chips. These are all meant to be eaten with the fingers. If the fries are greasy or covered with ketchup, you logically eat them with your fork—unless you are at an outside sporting event, in which case you use your fingers anyway. (Several napkins will also be required to repair the damage to your fingers—and possibly your clothes!)

  Potato chips are in the category of "noisy foods." Be careful, when eating them at a party, to take small bites and keep your mouth as closed as possible.

- Popcorn. Another noisy food. The easiest and healthiest kind to eat is salt- and butter-free popcorn. When a woman takes a handful of popcorn from the bowl and puts it in her mouth, swallowing as many kernels as she can, there goes her lipstick—all over her face. (Therefore a woman who is going to indulge in popcorn would be smart to blot her lipstick first!) No one looks very attractive with cheeks completely stuffed with popcorn; it's also easy to choke on.

I think we should all mind our manners and be concerned about the environment in our movie theaters, as that relates to popcorn! Moviegoers who do not spill their popcorn all over the floor, but instead carefully put their empty boxes in the trash cans after the film, are real heroes in today's society.

I learned another lesson about eating popcorn in my college days. I was introduced to a Supreme Court justice in his home in Washington by his daughter, a friend of mine. I had been consuming popcorn enthusiastically before being introduced, and I gave him a hearty handshake with my well-buttered, salty hand. He grimaced as if in pain, drew a large white handkerchief from his pocket, and proceeded to clean off his hand with a flourish. "Sir," I asked in an awed voice, "was I responsible for that?"

"Oh, no," he answered sarcastically, "it was Peter Pan."

Many parents have no idea that their children have less than passable table manners. When families do break bread together, both generations often are whizzing by each other at breakfast, or at dinnertime are consuming their meal, using their fingers, at a fast-food place. I watched as my college-age son pushed his hamburger aside one day, clutched a fresh batch of french fries with his fingers, and then dipped them into a pond of ketchup before plopping them into his mouth. His fingers and mouth dripping in grease and tomato sauce, he asked, "Mom, what would the manners experts say about my style of eating these fries?"

"Pretty gross, Malcolm," I replied.

He laughed and responded, "Have you ever watched yourself eating a pizza? Pretty gross, too, Mom." And that about sums up the state of America's table manners today! I guess we have to work a lot harder when we are using our knives and forks to compensate for those times when we aren't.

PART 2

Answers to Questions About Manners You Thought That No One Had to Ask Anymore

CHAPTER 10

New Manners
for an Ever-Changing Society

DATING TODAY

A real date is two people getting together at a specified time on a certain day (with advance notice and advance planning) for the purpose of doing something special. It's a date when someone asks you "to come over to my house for chili next Wednesday night," or announces, "I've two good seats for the soccer game Friday night. How about it?" It's a date when you're invited "to go to the new mall opening, and then we can get something to eat." It's a date when someone of the opposite sex asks, "How about going rollerblading with me next Saturday evening, and we can get some burgers after?" It's a date when someone invites you to a testimonial business dinner in a hotel ballroom, and it's a date when you're asked for a "walk in the woods to look at the autumn foliage."

A date may be just a pleasant coming together, or a payoff for a favor done, or it may be a delicate step in a courtship and mating dance. A date is good. It's an antidote to being alone.

Going Out on a Date
Is an Opportunity to Shine

The wonderful thing about this era in which we live is that women no longer have to sit at home passively and wait for the telephone to ring. A woman can properly pick up the telephone and ask a man out as easily as he can call to ask her out. It's an easy adjustment for the young, but a lot more difficult for women who are beyond college age. Asking a man out on a date may be a painful exercise for a woman, but she should take heart in the fact that asking a woman out on a date is just as painful for many a man! Maybe you're one of the vast world of shy people and you feel you don't stand out in a group. Maybe you're a little overweight or underweight, maybe you're not a great beauty or a handsome hunk of man. Maybe you feel uncomfortable at big parties in competition with others who appear to you to be better-looking, more successful, and popular. A person of the opposite sex who has caught your eye in the group may not be particularly attracted to you at that moment, so your strategy should be to get that person alone at some future time, away from the party crowd, so that she can get to know you—and in the process, get to like you.

Going out as a couple or in a foursome with a person who attracts you is the easiest way to show yourself at your best (with the exception, of course, of entertaining with zest in your own home, which provides your greatest showcase of all). Going out on a date allows the two of you to get to know each other in a relaxed, quiet milieu—which a party is not. The great thing about being with someone on a date is that it provides a chance to show your generous supply of intelligence, charm, and personality. You can demonstrate the kind of creative fun you know how to generate. You can display your strong points (and everyone has some of those).

But first there's this problem to resolve: How can you get someone to go out on a date with you when he may have no inclination to do so?

Asking the Person for the Date

Some people are so shy, they would rather live permanently in a cave than submit to the agony of asking someone out and then suffer being rejected. Here is some advice:

• It's smart to steel yourself for a rejection to your invitation, because the first person you ask may very well be busy, may be in a relationship with someone else, or may be working so hard that he or she literally does not have time to go out on a date. Or that person simply may not want to go out with you. That is not a serious kind of rejection. It happens to everyone, not just to you. Your goal in life should be to find the person who *does* want to and who *will* go out with you. That person is out there, but only you can find him. If you keep scanning the entire sea with your eyes, you can appreciate all the fish swimming by, so don't set your sights and hopes on just one of them.

• Get organized, but be creative, too. Make plans—fascinating plans—so that the person you want to have accompany you will really be excited at the prospect of what you have devised. Make it sound so exciting that it will be impossible to resist. Maybe you can get tickets for something that is extremely difficult to get tickets for; maybe you have an invitation to a glamorous occasion—anything from the grand opening of a restaurant to a special performance of the Bolshoi Ballet. Maybe you know a "wonderful fortune-teller we can go to," and with "dinner in my favorite Thai restaurant afterward." Maybe you live in a small town that will never see the Bolshoi or a Thai restaurant—there are still different things to do and organize in your community. You simply have to be alert, as though you have eyes in the back of your head and antennae in both ears, so that you know about the new, exciting things to do or places to go in your town before everyone else does.

• Ask the person for a date in a letter, carefully wording your invitation to sound enticing, which is often difficult to do in a telephone call. If you were to call, asking for a date, you might sound awkward, and it would be very easy for the other person to quickly turn you down. He or she might be in a hurry and might not even try to listen to you.

Try sending a handsome piece of handwritten stationery through the mail, describing the enticing evening or weekend activity you have arranged and asking the targeted person to join you. Your amusing letter might very well persuade that person to accept, whereas that same person might have turned you down flat at a party or on the telephone.

For example, try a note like this, which is breezy yet warm and holds out the promise of an entertaining evening.

Dear Jerry,

Someone told me that you are a contemporary classical music fan. Well, so am I—and I have two tickets to an extraordinary concert at Avery Fisher Hall on May 23 at eight o'clock. The American Composers Orchestra will play a program of all-new works.

Along with having a modern musical ear, I am also a passable cook, so I'd like to invite you for some preconcert chicken curry at my apartment at six o'clock.

Give me a call at my office, 000-0000, and I hope you can make it!

• Once you have that date arranged, it's up to you to be yourself—natural and considerate—so that the other person will be very glad to have accepted your invitation. As the nineties progress, there will be more and more reciprocation between the sexes; especially if both work, they will reciprocate in the areas of money, time, and effort expended in organizing a real date.

Dating Manners

• Give advance notice when making the date—at least three days before, so that there is time to prepare (to make a hair appointment, get a suit cleaned, or whatever). Anyone who calls up two hours beforehand to ask for a date is hardly paying a compliment to the other person.

• Consider the other person's interests when making the plans (for example, don't force a baseball-only fan to go to a ballet or vice versa).

• Try not to change the plans at the last minute.

• Have original, creative ideas about things to do and places to go.

• Be on time.

- Dress appropriately, so as not to embarrass the other person. (It is normal for a person to want to be proud of the way his date looks and is dressed.)
- Don't make a scene in public.
- Be sensitive to the other person's financial situation when the other person is paying.
- Be philosophical when things go wrong, without knocking the other person's ideas or planning expertise—in fact, to try to find something nice to say about the place, the food, the game, the show, or the other people at the party. (With a positive attitude, you can *always* find something good, even if you consider the situation pretty disastrous!)
- Don't keep complaining (a real killjoy action) if you don't feel well or are tired.
- Thank the other person at the end of the date, whether it's to show gratitude for the money spent or praise for the planning done or just to show pleasure for the pleasant companionship during the evening.
- Write a thank-you note after a special evening. ("You made me feel so good with that toast" . . . "I love the flowers you brought me" . . . "You were nice to fill up my car with a tank of gas when I wasn't looking" . . . "I hope someday in our lives we'll see another movie as great as that one" . . . "What a treat to have crab cakes like that" . . . "I really appreciated the way you took care of that guy in the stands who squirted mustard all over my dress!")
- The best way to make a good impression on a first date is to keep your sense of humor. People who are trying too hard to be charming can become very uptight when things go wrong. And things do go wrong. One of my goddaughters recounted the disasters on a recent date that she had initiated: The restaurant did not honor the table reservation she had made; the theater tickets weren't waiting for them at the ticket window of the theater; her date's coat got stolen from the coatroom in a nightclub where they had stopped to have a nightcap. When I insinuated that she probably would never see that young man again, she grinned and said, "I see him all the time. We just laughed all night long. I kept asking him, 'Now what will go wrong?' And something always did. He finally said that I was the kind of girl who would laugh if I lost my winning lottery ticket receipt, and he liked that."

Who Pays for What

Traditionally, on a date the man was supposed to pay for everything, but like many traditions, the custom has changed and molded itself into the new society to allow for common sense. Today, with women's equality and with women earning their own money, the cost of a date is often split. What doesn't change is that when someone asks another on a first date, the one who asks should pay for that date. If a woman asks a man for the first date, she should pay for everything from the garage parking charge to the coat check tip. On future dates, the two can compromise and split the costs according to their whims and resources. A rich man will always pay for his date; a rich woman who asks out a man who is not rich will always pay for him, too—but if she is smart, she will protect his ego and pay for the date without anyone else but him knowing it.

The important thing here is that both parties understand who is going to pay for what on the date *before* it ever takes place. There should never be any unpleasant surprises or embarrassing moments of "May I borrow some money?" Nothing ruins a great dinner in a restaurant faster than bickering over who gets the bill, whether someone is trying to push the bill off on someone else or grabbing the check to pay when the other person is already preparing to pay it.

People who have to watch their wallets should be honest and up-front when making the date. For example:

• A young man in school might say to his prospective date, "I can get two tickets to the game Friday night. I'd really like to have you go with me, but things are a little tight. Can you pay for your own ticket?"

• A woman who has been taken out on a date three times by a man might say, "It's certainly time for some reciprocity! Why don't I make my famous lasagne dinner for you Saturday night, and take you to the movies?"

• A young male executive on a starting salary might say to a female colleague, "I'd like to have dinner with you Friday night. I can either buy you a pizza dinner at Joe's, or we can have a fancy dinner at Le Manoir and go Dutch. Which would you like to do?" Chances are, she would prefer to go to a nice place and pay her own way.

Since men are sensitive about women paying for them in public, a woman should be equally sensitive about it. She can slip money to her date in an inconspicuous gesture under the table. She can give him money beforehand. She can discreetly slip her credit card to the waiter when he brings the check.

Women in their late sixties and onward, schooled in the old tradition of a man always paying, have difficulty with the perceived embarrassment of paying for a male escort's meals and tickets. They would be better off making an arrangement beforehand with the restaurant to send them a bill for the lunch or dinner to which they have invited a male companion. They can purchase tickets to plays and concerts beforehand. It's a question of getting organized in advance.

Some rich older women, of course, solve their escort-in-the-evening problem by keeping a young gigolo. This kind of date seems to have no reluctance at all being perceived as a man who never has to pick up the check!

IF YOU'RE MISERABLE ON THE DATE

If you're having a physically nasty time on a date (he is drunk and abusive or making sexual innuendos or strong-arming you), make a quick departure. You do not have to remain out of politeness and submit to that kind of behavior just because someone is paying for your dinner. Take whatever steps are available to escape from the situation, whether that means calling a cab, asking the restaurant manager to help you, summoning the police if the situation is really out of hand, or running into the street to find a public place that is open and will serve as a momentary refuge.

However, the chances of this kind of danger-ridden evening are minimal in comparison to your chances of having a completely boring evening. You might be fed up, disappointed, restless, embarrassed to be seen with your date, or bothered by her smoking. Don't escape. Just get through the evening. It won't last forever. Be a good sport, because it's great training in self-discipline, and you can never tell when this kind of training will serve you well in the future!

• Except, of course, when dealing with someone who is abusive, *always thank your date at the end of the evening.* You don't have to be hypocritical and gush your gratitude. Just say something like, "Thank you for all the trouble you went to," or "The dessert at that restaurant was really delicious," if that was the best part of the meal. Maybe the only thing good about the meal was the bread. (I remember a friend who was miserable on a blind date and praised the only thing she found worthy of mention at the restaurant—"They have the best ice water at that place!" she said, thanking her date for an evening that in her eyes had been totally terrible.) You can always find *something* to praise during the evening. It's polite to mention that one affirmative thing and then to shut up about all of the negative rest of it. Your justifiable frankness could really hurt the other person, and the pleasure in voicing that justifiable criticism isn't worth hurting someone else's feelings.

When the evening is finally over, your date may well say something like, "Well, I'll call you again soon" or "We must do this again very quickly." At that point you should control your panic, take a deep breath, and say something kind like, "No, I don't really think so." You might add, "I think you should ask out someone who's more on your wavelength. You see, I'm not. It's no fault of yours. It's nothing you've done. It's just that you and I don't share the same interests and attitudes. I'm sorry. Thank you for tonight." Then close the door. End of bad date. End of other person's expectations, and you have not committed the unpardonable—leading someone on.

Give Blind Dates a Chance!

Should you go out on blind dates? The answer is yes—even if you have been out on eighteen of them in the past year and all eighteen were frightful disasters. For all you know, the twenty-first will be the one.

Following are some tips on how to approach blind dates with an open mind, if not enthusiasm:

• Your friends are wonderful and loyal to arrange the blind date, even though you think they have no taste and have obviously no idea in the world what it is that attracts you in the opposite sex. Be grateful to them for trying. It would be a lot worse if they never tried.

• Remember the statistics. An incredibly large number of people around the world are happily married to spouses they met on blind dates. There is always a small chance you could become one of those statistics.

• Remember that the blind date, if he or she is not totally hopeless, has friends. Many a person has found a true love through the friends of a blind date.

• You can be taken to wonderful new places by blind dates—places your other friends wouldn't or couldn't take you. When I was in India, I was driven from New Delhi to see the Taj Mahal on a blind date. I might never have seen it otherwise. I don't remember the man who drove me, but I certainly remember the Taj Mahal these decades later!

• You might very possibly need that blind date in the future to round out your table at your next dinner party. Extra men, in particular, are hard to come by. One of your other dinner guests may find something redeemable, even lovable, in that person, despite the fact that you don't.

• Don't always trust your first negative impression. You might be very wrong.

SEX—GOOD, BAD, AND INDIFFERENT

The word "sex" has many connotations, shadings, and interpretations in our society, which often lead to misunderstandings. As a leading speaker at the Aspen Institute said, "Sexual discrimination is bad for people's careers and aspirations, it is bad for the progress of humanity, and"—speaking now much more forcefully—"it is extremely bad for business!"

Everyone has his or her own definition of sex, a most constantly discussed phenomenon. A four-year-old gravely explained to me that sex "is what Mummy and Daddy are doing when they won't let me into their bedroom." A nine-year-old boy defined it as "the magazines my older brother hides under his bed and pays me for not telling our parents about it."

Personal Views (Mine, at Least) of Sexual Relationships

Every relationship requires sensitivity, understanding, and compassion—from me to you, from us to them, and them to us—so that we can get along with one another, move ahead, and witness the flourishing, rather than the deterioration, of this society of ours. Thank goodness people are different from one another. But there is a complex map of relationships with responsibilities we need to follow as we experience life. It should not be a question of our changing someone else's way of living. It should be a question of accepting someone else's way of living, minding our own business, and avoiding acting with intolerance and prejudice.

There are so many major relationships with which to contend:
- Siblings and parents, for example.
- Husbands and wives, their children and their relatives.
- Bosses, supervisors, and subordinates.
- A married person with another person outside of marriage, and the shipwrecks this can cause.
- An unmarried man and unmarried woman (simplicity by comparison).
- People of the same sex.
- People who have relationships with both sexes.

When you come to think of it, all of the above is some pot of stew!

The fortunate results of the activity called sex:
- Joy, pleasure, exhilaration—and the endless terms to describe it.
- The birth of babies—the continuation of mankind.

The unfortunate results of the activity called sex:
- When nonconsensual sex is forced on another person—i.e., rape and sodomy.
- When an unfaithful partner causes great emotional harm to the other partner.
- When unwanted babies are born to unmarried couples.
- When there's a forced marriage because of pregnancy.
- When the unwed father refuses to accept responsibility for the child or children, or when the wedded father refuses to accept responsibility for the child or children.
- When sexual harassment occurs, either by men against women or by women against men.
- When the criminal act of pedophilia occurs.

- When sexual diseases are transmitted from a promiscuous partner to an innocent one.

What Do Manners, Compassion, and Character Have to Do with It?

Answer: Only everything.

1. None of us should be the news bearer to the world of a sexual relationship, including our own. Sex is a completely private matter. Discussing details of it at random is tasteless, undignified, and a great way to lose the respect of others. Whether someone's quality of sex life is discussed joyfully, jokingly, or with braggadocio, it is not a subject for public discussion but for *discretion*. According to the *Oxford Dictionary*, "Discretion is the quality of behaving or speaking in such a way as to avoid causing offense or revealing private information."
2. Instead of passing on gossip about others' sexual relationships, each one of us has the power to shut off potentially harmful gossip before it hurts anyone. We should use that power.
3. Children's questions about sex are better left answered by their parents.
4. Who uses protection and who does not is a personal matter. But I happened to overhear a father of three boys and two girls talking to his kids on the subject of protection and birth control:

I know a lot of guys say they don't like to wear it, that it lessens their pleasure in sex, so the girl gives in, and they have sex without it. Well, isn't that just too bad that the guys don't like using it. I know a solution for this problem. I'll spell it out for you. A-b-s-t-i-n-e-n-c-e. I know you girls always get the raw end of the sex deal—like a baby, for example, or worse, a baby born with the same disease her partner was infected with before he impregnated her.

His words brought back the talks my father used to give my brothers and me, except we didn't have the fear of sexually transmitted diseases in those days. We really did not know what STDs were. As far as my mother was concerned, she left all matters of sexual enlightenment to my father, but she let me know where she stood on the subject. If I were to have sex with a boy, I would go straight to a fully stoked hell, would be unemployable, our family's reputation in the city would be ruined, and my friends would shun me forever.

My friend's husband, talking to his five kids in the kitchen, continued:

When you're on your way to making out with someone of the opposite sex, I'm asking you to visualize a traffic light. When it's green, you hug and kiss and it's all very romantic, sweet and tender. But then the light very suddenly starts flashing yellow, the signal that you're going too far, and I don't want anyone telling me you don't realize when *that* is. Your conscience tells you, and I presume all five of you still have one. So what do you do now? You stop doing whatever it is you were doing, right then and there. Just get out of that place you were in, no matter how sweet it seemed. The traffic light is turning red.

One of his daughters spoke up: "But what if I'm in a car with a guy out in the country, and leaving would mean walking down a lonely road on a dark night?"

Everyone laughed at that thought. One of the brothers piped up. "You could make mincemeat of any guy you know. You're in better shape than anyone on the wrestling team." More laughter all around.

It was time for a father's solution. "Use your cell phone and call nine-one-one." This closed the discussion. "I would hope that with all you've been taught through the years, you would not be stupid enough to be out in the country, alone in a car, with that kind of a man."

One of the brothers would not let his father have the last word. "Only go out with perfect gentlemen, like your perfect brothers."

It was all so déjà vu. It reminded me so much of the self-confidence a young woman needs to help get through her life happy and safe. That conversation between a parent and his children resonated so completely with me. How lucky one is to have parents like that! And brothers, too.

WHEN THE ANSWER IS YES

My own feeling is that sex is much better when there is romance lurking around somewhere. Otherwise, it can become as matter-of-fact as a computer printout.

If you think your date tonight is going to "sleep over" and you welcome that thought, prepare for it. Have some treats waiting in your fridge. Have your bedroom straightened, with clean sheets on the bed, fresh flowers on your bureau, and fresh towels, an extra water glass, and a new toothbrush in the bathroom. A sparkling clean bedroom is enticing.

A Romantic but Polite Point of View

When two people have been intimate, and the sexual encounter was a pleasant experience for both, it should be considered a common courtesy the next day for one to get in touch with the other, if for no other reason than to say "thank you." Neither person should take a thank-you call as a profession of love or as an indication of desire on the caller's part to deepen the relationship. When you make a short thank-you call, it's nothing more and nothing less than a gesture of appreciation for a very enjoyable shared experience.

A friend of mine, now in her early fifties and legendary for her beauty and her great success with men, once showed me the collection of little notes and cards she had received from men when she was young—notes that had accompanied flowers and gifts sent "always the day after a romantic interlude," she explained. One man had written, "Even if our paths never cross again, I will never forget you—or last night." ("He was anything but a poet," she laughed, "but he expressed himself rather well with that short sentence.") Another wrote on a florist's card, "It was the nicest, most unexpected, totally incredible evening." Still another wrote, "The main course at your dinner was excellent, but the dessert was *unforgettable!*"

You are not making a commitment or proposing matrimony with a short note or telephone call. You are merely instilling a welcomed note of romance into both your lives.

Of course, if a sexual encounter was an unpleasant experience from your point of view, there is certainly no need for a thank-you gesture on your part! If you're forever "busy" when the other person calls you, he should get the message that you don't want a repeat experience. It's easier if you're honest right away and say in your own words, "I think you're wasting your time calling me. We're not right as a couple, and in fairness to you, you should devote your energy to finding someone new."

WHEN THE ANSWER IS NO

In any consideration of sexual manners, there obviously is no place for the unforgivable act of sex by force, so that is not included in this discussion. Manners come into play only in terms of sex as an act of free will.

Many people play games all the time, but sex should not be considered one of them. It is the better part of wisdom to tell the truth when you feel no attraction for a person who is pressuring you to engage in sex. It's also a kindness to that person to do so, rather than to fabricate a hundred excuses as to why there won't be any sex tonight ("I'd really like to, I really want to, but I'm just not feeling all that great tonight . . .").

There was a miserable period that began about twenty years ago when men tended to feel that paying the price of a good dinner gave them a license to sleep with their dates—an attitude that really put down the women who acquiesced and that made unpopular (and hungry!) those who didn't. As one young friend of mine expressed it then, "It's kind of an unwritten law. You don't have to do anything for a hamburger—but for something like a good steak, wine, and atmosphere, you're really expected to put out." Today, in spite of the editorial thrust of certain magazines extolling sex as a regular necessity (and their warning that decreased regularity is "hazardous to your health, not to mention your complexion"), no one is compelled to sleep with anyone else.

It's unfortunate that it took a plague of sexually transmitted diseases to change the climate from one in which unmarried people felt a constant social pressure to engage in sex to one in which many unmarried people feel wary of engaging in sex at all.

Personally, I feel that even if kindness dictates considering the other person's ego when you reject a sexual invitation, it's equally important to be honest. In your own words, you might somehow communicate the message that:

• You think the other person is *very* attractive (showing your sensitivity to his or her ego).

• But you are not physically attracted to that person (showing your honesty). Explain that if there's a lack of chemistry on your part, it's no one's fault, just the luck of the draw.

• You enjoy the other person's company very much, but if more is demanded than just your company during the time you spend together, it's time to end the relationship.

Don't sell the other person short. You may find she treasures your friendship and enjoys being with you, too, even without the sex. Or perhaps she thinks that in time you will begin to feel a sexual attraction, too (which is not an impossibility).

Friendships between people of both sexes are very strong and powerful, but diplomacy, tact, and imagination are required to turn a would-be lover into a friend. Often the person you have spurned sexually will disappear from your life, hurt and confused. Then with time, that person may seek you out again, just wanting to spend time with you. When sexual tension decreases (it doesn't have to disappear completely), that's when friendship can strengthen and begin to fill a void. Men and women can—and should—enjoy being with each other without the necessity for sexual overtones to everything they say or do.

WHEN A WOMAN IS AFRAID TO BE ALONE
AT HOME WITH A MAN

If you are a woman who has invited a man to have dinner with you alone in your home and then you begin to have an uneasy feeling about it, don't go through with the evening as originally planned—alone with him. Invite another couple to join you, or have a sudden change of plans and take him out to dinner in a restaurant. You may have a good basis for your fears. You may have seen him in action and witnessed him drink too much or come on to you too fast; you may have heard another woman describe him as too rough. A majority of the rapes that occur take place behind a closed door when the woman is with a man she knows.

The man you don't really know but have invited to come alone to your house may be the most innocent kind of man there is, but if you have a strange feeling about him, trust your intuition and be careful.

If, for security reasons, you have invited another couple for dinner along with your male guest, you can always address the gathering when the couple makes a move to leave—something like, "Well, I think it's a good time for the evening to end for us all. Jim, I hope you won't mind if I call it a day, too." He might reply that he will only stay for "just another ten minutes—just a quick drink," to which you might announce that you need your sleep and have a tough, important week ahead of you. If you keep laughing and joking about it, your male guest won't take offense. The important thing is not to appear frightened.

It also helps if you have told the other couple beforehand that you would appreciate their making sure your male guest leaves when they do.

Women should not put themselves into vulnerable situations with men they do not know well, either personally or by reputation. When you don't know anything about someone to whom you find yourself attracted, have lunch with him and go to events in public with him. You'll get to know and trust him. Then it's time for the cozy evenings "at home" to begin.

BRINGING UP THE SUBJECT OF CONDOMS

We have all seen some pretty tasteless condom promotions, including ads and public relations gimmicks. I recently saw a dispenser that looked as if it contained transit tokens; another condom-holder was a child's cartoon character wristwatch with a secret compartment in the back. These gimmicks may manufacture a quick laugh for some people, but for most they constitute a "cheap shot" kind of humor.

In this confused world of ours, people need to be forthright, frank, and honest with each other. The fear of sexually transmitted diseases, particularly AIDS, is not something to treat in a cute or amusing way. If you're a woman, how do you know that incredibly good-looking man you've just begun to date hasn't been infected with the HIV virus that causes AIDS? If you're a man, how do you know that attractive woman you just met isn't a carrier, having become infected because of a drug injection with a dirty needle?

You no longer have to hem and haw about whether or not to say yes to sex with anyone. You don't have to worry about your manners in turning someone down. Saying no is very polite these days! And if you want to say yes, make it on *your* terms—safe sex only. Use a condom. Make him wear a proper-fitting tear-free, less than three-year-old (see the expiration date on the package) condom.

Anyone who writes about sexual mores writes from a personal philosophy that is impossible to disguise. Mine is very openly pro chastity as the only acceptable lifestyle for the young. Such a philosophy used to elicit derisive laughter during the sixties. It is no longer an old-fashioned joke. Parents can once again impress this on their children. Whereas morality used to be the reason for sexual abstinence, today protecting your life is a new reason. Few people would disagree with the philosophy that love and sex ideally are at their best in marriage.

Many women are much too embarrassed even to ask a male sex partner if he has a condom, much less be ready to supply him with one, but at a certain moment a woman should realize it is far better to suffer embarrassment than to contract a sexually transmitted disease. No pleasure or moment of passion is worth that! If it is difficult for a woman to find the words to ask about her partner's preparedness prior to having sex with him, she had better learn to overcome such reticence. It is no time to be shy when her own life or that of her future child might be affected—by this act of passion this very night. There are several ways for her to handle the situation including:

• Supplying the condoms herself. ("Look, if you don't have any, you'll find some on the first shelf of the medicine closet.")

• Asking him to go out to buy them. ("Since you say you're not prepared, I think you'd better become prepared. There's an all-night drugstore a short distance away.")

• Announcing (the best idea of all) that, "Since you're not prepared, we'll just have to wait until you are. Let's skip sex tonight."

If a woman shows her partner that she is responsible for her own behavior, she will teach any man who really is attracted to her to be responsible about his behavior, too.

Safe Sex and Multiple Partners

The best of all worlds is the romantic attachment of two people who wait until they are married for sex. Since we aren't living in the best of all worlds, let's step down one level of reality and say that the best of what many adults can make of today's world is safe sex—the use of condoms for those who do not abstain. And let's really step down another great number of levels and say that having multiple sex partners is the worst of all worlds. Having more than one partner is reportedly increasing in alarming numbers. My sense of sisterhood is showing when I say that it is totally reprehensible for a man to have an affair with or marry a woman while he is also having sex with others on the side. He is putting her life and that of her future children in danger because of the possibility of transmitting sexual diseases to her. There are no manners that can relate to this kind of deceit.

A Homosexual Relationship

When two people of the same sex openly live with one another in a monogamous relationship they should be treated as a couple in every social sense of the word. In the evening and on weekends, they should be invited together to any kind of event. The men should not be recruited by their hosts as dates or as escorts for single women, except in the sense of friends helping out by providing transportation to and from a party.

When a gay man or lesbian loses his or her partner, the nice thing to do is to write a letter of condolence, send flowers to the funeral, or make a gift in memoriam to the deceased. The homosexual who loses a mate suffers a loss equal to a married person's loss.

If you are not certain of someone's sexual preference, do not ask that person what it is. Respect his or her privacy. And remember that the most hurtful thing of all is to gossip about your homosexual friends or acquaintances. It only adds fuel to the fire of abuse that they already suffer at the hands of many people, and contributes to discriminatory behavior that goes against the very ideals of democracy and freedom that the United States symbolizes.

What to Tell the Mate
of Someone Who's Playing Around

It's incredible the number of times I am asked in telephone calls on radio or TV talk shows, or in written questions (always anonymous) sent up at the conclusion of a lecture, "If you know your friend's husband or wife is committing adultery, do you let your friend know the bad news?"

I always answer, "In the first place, you have to be sure of that accusation, and that is difficult enough in itself. In the second place, let your friend find out some other way—not through you." That is the kind of accusation that you don't talk about to other people, either.

PLEASURES AND PITFALLS
OF THE OFFICE ROMANCE

For many who work long hours and are dedicated to their careers, the opportunities to meet people of the opposite sex outside the office are few. In addition, working in proximity to someone of the opposite sex is a situation that makes the job environment fertile for romantic possibilities.

I have worked in government and for corporations for forty years, and during all those years I have witnessed the following:

• Office romances that ended in marriage, as everyone knew that they would. These marriages helped, rather than hindered, the careers of the couple—even if company policy decreed they could no longer work together in the same division, and even if one person, because of company policy, was forced to find a job with another company.

• Office romances between a married boss or senior executive and a single woman executive. These usually result in the woman's being exploited, made miserable, and eventually fired.

• Long-lasting office romances that resulted in the woman's being exploited, made miserable, and eventually fired. (Of course, in today's world, the predator can also be a female boss with a lot of power.)

• We have all seen the office romance that could end in marriage but drags on interminably without a wedding. This is injurious to the careers of both parties, because everyone in the office is speculating, gossiping, fantasizing, and spreading rumors about them every time one of them comes into sight. That cuts down on total office productivity. Suddenly the two protagonists are viewed only in terms of the status of their romance, not in terms of the work they may be producing. When this continues for months on end, the two find themselves no longer being considered for big promotions or pushed into new creative directions. A senior executive will think to herself, "If those two can't make up their minds about their relationship after all this time, they won't be able to make up their minds about anything."

• When two people do fall in love, become engaged, and marry, it's important to their careers not to let the romance take over their work. Touching, writing love notes, hanging on the telephone interminably, meeting by the copy machine, holding hands, gazing starry-eyed at each other, and entering love messages in each other's computers do not help the productivity of the company. As one executive phrased it in dressing down a pair who were being slightly nauseating in public about their romance, "Do love on your own time. Do work in this office!"

• As for the office affair with someone who is married, it is so stupid of the woman to permit it to happen to her that I simply have no sympathy for her. She is always the one who loses out, who gets left behind. The man keeps his job. She doesn't, and this is not what the new status of women is all about!

The work environment provides a great hunting ground for a marriage partner—in fact, the only "hunting ground" for many people today. Marriage, not an affair, should be the goal.

SEX AND SEXISM IN THE OFFICE

It may be what some call an equal world; still, there is no question but that the woman receives the bad end of a failed interoffice love affair. (She's usually the one to be let go.) As with drunkenness, she is judged far more harshly than a man on moral questions. Unfair, but it's always been like that and probably always will be.

Therefore, a woman must decide: which means more to her, a romantic fling, or success in her career? When a married man with children is caught in an interoffice love affair (forget the "love" part, and change it to "passionate") his peers and bosses chuckle and make jokes about it for months on end. When a woman executive with children is caught in such a liaison, she is, figuratively speaking, at the stake. (Equal world? No way!)

It's a tragedy when a career is stymied because of sexual innuendo or open indiscretions committed by an executive who is intelligent, well liked, a diligent worker, and a great contributor to the company.

Watch Your Language

• Avoid sexist language. Use "women," not "gals" when you refer to female employees. Use "ladies" instead of "girls" when you are also using "gentlemen." Use "men and women" instead of "men and ladies" or "the guys and the women." As one of my totally chauvinistic male friends said, fortunately laughing as he did, "Letitia, just call them 'the men and the broads.'" (He lived to regret that remark.)

• Again, my personal opinion on the following, since I have spent too many years in corporate meetings: Don't change titles just because they sound sexist. They aren't. You call a woman judge a judge, not a "judgess." You call an ambassador an ambassador. "Ambassadress" refers to his wife, so a woman ambassador is an ambassador. Her husband is simply a "spouse." You call a writer a writer, an author an author, not a writeress and an authoress.

Our language is, of course, inconsistent. There is a sculptress, poetess, and actress, but every woman I have ever talked to in my whole life prefers to be called a sculptor, an actor, a poet.

I think we should banish such words as "chairlady." Leave it as "chairman," standing for both sexes, just like "president," "artist," "postman," and "doctor."

But along with all of those titles, we should get rid of others that belong anywhere but at work: Baby, Sweetie, Darling, Honey, Angel-face, and any baby talk whatsoever. It should remain a long trip from the bedroom or nursery to the office.

WHEN SEX CAN CREATE PROBLEMS
FOR A WOMAN TRAVELING ALONE ON BUSINESS

• When you are the recipient of one little pass from a male colleague, don't make a big issue out of it—with him or anyone else. It will be forgotten, and you don't want to get a colleague into serious trouble because of his minor transgression.

• But if you feel a man is seriously coming on to you in the wrong way during business travel, be on guard. The first thing to do is resolve not to drink yourself. You want to stay cool and calm if it looks like there is going to be a problem. You also don't want to unnecessarily antagonize a male colleague who is important to your career. A person who drinks at a party makes unwise judgment calls.

Sharpen your sense of humor. It's your best weapon to discourage someone without angering him.

• If you smell liquor on his breath and he is getting physical with you, slither away from his physical hold and go quickly into another room. No conversation. Leave the party, if necessary.

• If you have a premonition a certain man is bad news, trust your intuition. Never leave yourself totally vulnerable, such as agreeing to meet a man in his or your hotel room to "discuss business." If he arranges to have no one else in the room, it should be a sign of concern to you. Just get away, out of his room, or if he is in your room, open your door, get out into the hall, and motion him out. "Sorry, Dan, but I'm afraid this isn't what I thought it was going to be—a business meeting. I'll see you tomorrow at the strategy meeting." If he is drunk enough to chase after you, tell anyone you see in the hall to call security, that you're "in trouble." That should discourage him sufficiently.

If he keeps protesting, "But we have these business issues to discuss, don't you remember?" give him an answer: "Fine, we'll discuss them in the lobby or the coffee shop." You might even beg a colleague to join you when you are forced to see him, but keep the whole sordid tale quiet. Let someone else broadcast the truth about this guy.

SEXUAL HARASSMENT IS NOT JUST AGAINST WOMEN

There is no question but that more and more men are being sexually harassed in the workplace by aggressive women who run the company or who supervise them, and who demand sexual favors. These are equally as serious as the cases of female harassment, and must be addressed by senior management quickly and firmly. If the woman is the big boss, then the male employee has a very good solution to his problem: leave that company and that job. Then he will be able to heal his wounds and look for another job where the work environment is nothing like his previous one. There is always legal redress, of course, but that can take a long time and perhaps harm his future employment possibilities.

It's always a delicate path to tread. He should have a good lawyer advising him and a strong sense of his own worth. Before he leaves, he should line up some good pals who will go to bat for him and announce to senior management that he has indeed suffered sexual harassment from a certain woman manager.

COHABITATION MANNERS

People who are living together, even if unmarried, have made a serious commitment to one another. Mutual consideration should be their mantra, which means good manners not only toward one another but also toward one another's family, friends, boss, and colleagues. At times a person must work particularly hard to keep from blurting out what he thinks are injustices against his partner or criticizing the company for which his partner works. (Frankness should not be the motto of the partner, but rather "keep a lid on it!")

• As one of a couple, don't accept invitations without first having consulted your partner. Don't slip out to attend social events to which your partner is not invited, unless you have made him or her understand why you are doing it. If you were to go solo to a friend's party, you would be sending them a signal (and your partner, too) that your relationship is unstable.

Sometimes it's a question of educating your friends that you are always to be invited as a couple, and that you will not go out in mixed company without your partner. Many couples have an understanding that if desired, either will spend a night out every so often with just "the boys" or just "the girls," as many married couples do.

• When the person of your choice moves into your home, make room. Give away some of the clothes that take up too much space, i.e., extra blazers that don't fit any longer, heavy ski sweaters, and old parkas. Clean out those bureau drawers and half the medicine cabinet. Don't expect another person to be happy sharing your space if you have hogged most of it. Sharing means just that—splitting, dividing in two, making things equal.

• A person who moves into your home often has completely different taste from yours. When you buy a new sofa, choose paint colors for the walls, or select upholstery fabric, make it a joint selection, even if you are paying for most of it. If your partner has an aversion to the colors olive green and gold, steer clear of that combination in your household purchases. It's little enough to do in order to *make things work*.

• The household budget, cleaning and marketing chores, and cooking schedules should be formulated in unison, according to the talents, amount of free time, entertaining plans, and financial resources of the two individuals.

• Each member of the household should speak well of the other. There will always be times when you feel justifiably critical of your partner, but "put a lid on it." You can always try to work things out when both heads are cool, and if you cannot, make a polite and fair split. When you put down your partner in front of others, it casts aspersions not only on your relationship but on you personally for not knowing how to make it work.

• Some live-togethers hold a "Non-Wedding Shower" or a "First Anniversary Live-Together Party." People might think it's just a cheap trick to get some wedding present loot, which it probably is. Don't mock sacred traditions—start new ones of your own, but if you want them to be successful, make them based on something other than materialism and greed.

• Advise your friends to introduce you as partners, or if in the presence of older, more conservative people, as "Jack Mooney and his friend George Levinas." If a woman introduces another woman as "my partner, Carolyn" it means one thing: They are in a sexual relationship. If she introduces her as "my roommate, Carolyn," they are probably just living together as they did in college, and sharing expenses.

• When family members or close friends ask what kinds of holiday or birthday presents they can give you, suggest things that you need for your household (a toaster, coffee maker, set of dinner or dessert plates, magazine subscriptions, bath towels, and the like). Any family member who disapproves of your cohabiting practices should not withhold love, support, and generosity toward you.

• Be sensitive to how your mutual parents and family members regard you. You should strive for everyone to be as accepting as possible. This may require you to give much more than your family members do. In any case, keep the waters smooth. I remember hearing a mother who did not approve of her daughter's living arrangement sounding off to her one day. "Look, just think of your father and me as the china closet, and you're the bull, charging around in it, doing damage. You're always on the defensive, you're sarcastic, you don't give us a chance to be nice to the two of you. Why don't you stop being the bull? Why don't you talk to us gently, tiptoe around us, and then we'll all get along just fine, and the china closet won't be rattling all the time?"

The mother had a point, but so did the daughter when she answered, "Okay, Mother, but if you and Daddy would greet us with a smile—instead of those embarrassed frowns—you would find a lot of warmth radiating back to you. You are the ones who turn us into people who are always on the defensive." (With a few more frank discussions, they worked it out and are now a close family again.) A question of family manners!

• Welcome your partner's friends into your life, just as he or she should welcome yours. If you're slow to make snap judgments, and if you sit on your criticisms of people your partner happens to like, you'll probably end up liking them, too.

• Don't open each other's mail or listen in on one another's telephone calls.

• Each person should have a certain space—perhaps a desk drawer or a section of a closed cabinet—that is his or hers alone, and into which personal papers can be filed with the knowledge that no one will pry into that area. It's a question of mutual trust.

• If one person is going to be kept late at work or on the golf course, or delayed for whatever reason, it is only considerate to forewarn the other partner. You should keep each other informed, well in advance, of each other's schedules and business travel requirements. Again, we're talking about consideration.

• And whatever you do—again, with my own voice ringing through—get yourself to that church or temple or mosque to get married as soon as possible. Hanging out together within the state of matrimony is much greater than without, for a multitude of reasons.

MAKING A COMMITMENT
EVEN THOUGH YOU DECIDE NOT TO MARRY

Many older couples who have been married and respectively widowed or divorced and have grandchildren, make the decision to live together as permanent companions. But because of the financial and legal complications that a marriage would necessitate, they decide to forgo the legal ceremony and simply express their deep commitment to one another privately.

THE ROMANCE IS OVER

The only comfort to derive from the shattering of a romance is that the breakup of a marriage is ten thousand times more difficult than a breakup between two unmarried people.

When two people involved in a romance tire of each other and feel it is useless to continue the relationship, they simply part company, usually with more than a tinge of sadness. But more often, one person walks out on the other, and that can cause an emotional upheaval that makes the impact of a volcanic eruption seem minor. And where do manners come into this situation, you might ask? Manners come into *every* situation. Manners are simply being sensitive to and concerned about other people's welfare and feelings. From the point of view of fairness, if one person has walked out on the other, the person doing the walking has a responsibility to show as much compassion as possible.

• The person who initiates the break should quietly state to all outsiders that the breakup was a mutually-agreed-upon development and not boast about dumping the other (although if he has a new romance, the reason for departure will be quite evident). Wait before you sympathize with a friend over her lover's departure. Wait until you know it is a true break. Twice in my life I have rushed to a friend, dramatically commiserating with her over the end of the romance, chastising the man in question, only to see the two reconciled like two white doves a week later. That was the end of two great friendships!

• No one should ever criticize a former lover in public, or even reply to nosy people who want to know why the romance is over. ("The reason we broke up? We have nothing to say about that, really," which translated means, "It's really none of your business!")

• Whoever leaves the relationship should neatly tie up all the financial arrangements. (I always advise the man or woman being left behind to get a good lawyer immediately, even if they had no legalized marriage.) One hears horror stories every day. One couple, both executives, had just embarked upon an extremely expensive redesign of the interior of their apartment. The woman abruptly decided to leave her partner for another man, so she left him with already committed expenses to pay on the renovation. When he succeeded in hauling her into court to make her pay her share, there was much cheering among mutual friends. Romance usually gives way very quickly to the reality of economics.

• The person who is leaving should put in writing a list of the wonderful qualities that made the other person so lovable. That kind of a letter can be a great source of comfort in the future to the person left behind. It helps the healing process. There is certainly a way of writing such a letter to salve the ego of the person left behind without indicating grounds for a "palimony" or breach of promise lawsuit. (You might consult your legal adviser. It's unfortunate but necessary in our litigious time.) It constitutes solace if the person who has left eventually goes on record with something laudatory—in any event a laudatory letter left behind to say how much he (or she) appreciated the attention and the love that was given to him (or her). Someone who had just walked out on his girlfriend asked my advice on what his next step should be. My reply was, "Duck!"

PART 3

THE RITES OF PASSAGE

Protocol and tradition begin at the moment of birth and continue all the way through your life to the end. These are the rites of passage that mark your stages of maturation. Your parents, grandparents, and great-grandparents all went through the same ceremonies, which should give even the youngest of us a sense of history and the oldest a sense of the marks we leave in our lives.

You may chafe at some of the rituals that surround you, but you must also admit, when it's your turn it's nice to be the center of attention. It's flattering to have people fussing over you, praying for you, wishing you well, congratulating you, or even sharing your grief. And it is important to be thoughtful and considerate of others when it's their turn.

CHAPTER 11

You're Engaged!

Let the world in on the happy, wonderful news that you are engaged by writing or telephoning the people you care about, by suddenly appearing (or having your fiancée appear) with a ring on the third finger of the left hand, and by having your engagement announcement published in the local newspaper.

Today the engagement process (the official "social notice" of a couple's intention to marry) is a much less important event in the stream of social rituals of a person's life than it used to be. Although in past generations a man formally asked a woman's father for her hand in marriage, many people now decide on their own to get married, without asking anyone. The young man who asks a father for the hand of his daughter in marriage is a rare and endangered species. However, it is still a wise move for the couple, once they have decided to marry, to inform both sets of parents immediately how they plan to make it financially—particularly if parental subsidies will be involved.

The engagement period traditionally lasted from six months to a year. Today the engagement is often announced from a month to three months prior to the wedding, and in the case of people who have been living together, it simply is not announced at all. The wedding date is announced instead.

TELLING THE WORLD YOUR GOOD NEWS

The first people with whom you, the engaged couple, should share the wonderful news are, of course, your parents and other members of the family. (You do not, by the way, send out engraved or printed engagement announcement cards.) If either set of parents has never met your intended, you should quickly make a visit to those parents (unless they live in another country, in which case, plan to visit them as soon as possible). For the sake of future family harmony, it is important to establish good relations immediately with your fiancé's or fiancée's parents.

• Get on the telephone. It doesn't matter if the bride-to-be's parents call the groom-to-be's parents first—or vice versa. What does matter is that they (divorced and remarried parents included) get in touch with each other right away to offer joint congratulations, regardless of how many telephone calls are required to track them down. These are moments of joy that manage to cheer up many people.

If one of the parents is disenchanted with the news, he should keep the disapproval hidden—at least during the first conversation with the other set of parents. In other words, if the bride's mother doesn't like the prospect of having so-and-so for a son-in-law, she should not relay this fact to his parents during the engagement announcement telephone call! It is a matter to be discussed privately with her daughter, and hopefully her daughter will be able to win her over without too much difficulty. Often a good open-ended discussion will influence people to change their opinions.

An engagement is important enough news to warrant making long distance calls to all family members, particularly those far away, who might not hear about it via the grapevine. The word should also be conveyed in writing—not e-mail—to any family members or really close friends not reached by telephone. Anyone who feels close to either of the pair wants to hear such important news directly, because it brings such a joyful reaction to whoever hears it.

If the wedding will be a small one, both the bride's and the groom's sides would be wise to emphasize this fact clearly while conveying the happy news to family and friends. This will help avoid hurt feelings later when invitations don't appear in everyone's mailbox.

WHEN ANNOUNCING YOUR ENGAGEMENT IS NOT NECESSARY

If the bride has been married before, it is not necessary to announce her next engagement. It is more tasteful to announce her wedding instead. Engagements are really for first-time brides.

The engagement process doesn't make much sense either for couples who have been living together for a number of years. Longtime live-togethers, in the opinion of many, should simply tell their friends the happiness of their plans to marry and then get married, without going through all of the engagement rituals. Usually family and friends are genuinely delighted when the couple finally makes the commitment to marry. There's no need for them suddenly to act like a starry-eyed engaged couple (which was the way young people, many of whom had never slept with each other, used to behave before they were married).

Newspaper Announcement
of the Engagement

If one of the engaged couple has a high social, civic, or business position in the community, or has distinguished parents or grandparents, there is a good chance the engagement announcement will make the newspapers. It's a more democratic world today. *One often pays* to have the announcement published.

Many people don't get their act together in time to have their announcement included—newspapers often require engagement and wedding information weeks in advance.

Photographs

If you, the bride-to-be, satisfy the newspapers' social standing requirements and submit your portrait far enough in advance, you have a good chance of its being published. A good head shot (eight by ten inches, black-and-white glossy) is what is needed, or something that is easy to take off the internet. Have your photograph taken by a professional (a snapshot or an amateur's efforts just won't make it). Be sure to have the information firmly attached to the photograph (the names of both bride and groom, the wedding date, and other particulars).

For the photograph, refrain from wearing something fussy or ornate around your face; wear button or simple hoop earrings, not dangling ones. Simplicity should be the guiding factor in the neckline of your dress or blouse, your hairstyle, and your jewelry.

More and more newspapers are now publishing photographs of the engaged couple together. A man may look better in a dark suit and simple tie, but the preferred photo today seems to be of the upper bodies of the fiancée in a sporty top, and the fiancé, tieless, in an open-neck white business shirt.

The Announcement Text

The efficiency with which you handle getting the information to the local newspaper will help get your announcement into their pages. Follow the form of the regular engagement announcements in your paper. It differs in each city. For example, a hypothetical bride (or her parents) would send in to her local suburban paper an engagement announcement such as the following (you will note that the bride's parents are divorced):

ABIGAIL L. TENDERCROFT PLANS MARRIAGE
TO DR. HILARY J. WOLDEN IN FEBRUARY

The engagement of Abigail L. Tendercroft to Dr. Hilary J. Wolden, a son of Mr. and Mrs. Joseph Wolden of Poughkeepsie, New York, has been announced by Mr. Hugh Tendercroft of New York and Mrs. Peter Bordon of Beverly Hills, California, parents of the bride-to-be.

Ms. Tendercroft, an account executive at McComb Advertising Agency in New York, and her fiancé, a resident in anesthesiology at the New York Hospital-Cornell Medical Center, plan to marry in February.

The future bride, a graduate of Miss Porter's School, graduated from Vassar College. She was a member of the Junior Assembly in 2003. Her father is a real-estate developer. Her mother, Marian Boyd, is a syndicated newspaper columnist and author. Ms. Tendercroft is the granddaughter of the late Cameron H. Boyd, a U.S. senator from Michigan.

Dr. Wolden graduated from Kenyon College and the Baylor College of Medicine in Houston. His father is an executive with IBM in Poughkeepsie, and his mother is a teacher in the Pawling, New York, school system.

There are cases in which the parents are divorced and either the mother or father of the bride-to-be is detached from the family and lives far away. In this case, the parent with whom the bride lives or who is closest to her would announce the engagement in the newspapers, but the other parent must be mentioned. For example:

Mrs. Martha Wetkin of San Francisco has announced the engagement of her daughter Sarah Frances Wetkin to Jonathan Wilfrid Schoen, the son of Mr. and Mrs. Heinrich Schoen of Hartford, Connecticut. Ms. Wetkin is also the daughter of Mr. Henry Weeks of New York. An autumn wedding is planned.

Where Engagement Announcements Are Sent

The engagement announcement is always sent, of course, to the papers in the cities where the engaged couple live. If a bride's- or groom-to-be's family is prominent in more than one city, the engagement announcement and photograph should be sent to the papers in the appropriate other cities also. The announcement should be sent to the alumnae magazines of the couple's colleges.

THE ENGAGEMENT RING

Since the custom of a man giving an engagement ring to his betrothed first began, this one piece of jewelry has brought more joy (and on rare occasions, more disappointment) than any other symbol of marriage. In this age of attention to materialism, sometimes the satisfaction or disappointment is based too heavily on the degree of the razzle dazzle and the opulence of the stones. I remember a young friend of mine being teased about the small size of her diamond ring. One of her friends (obviously jealous of her engagement) said that she had better bring along a magnifying glass so that people could find the diamond. The future bride looked crestfallen. Then her older sister whispered in her ear just the right words: "You have a terrific guy; he is so much more important than any ring. Besides, your stone is flawless and of a beautiful color. It's a quality stone."

Here is some old-fashioned advice for the soon-to-be recipient of an engagement ring:

• A diamond solitaire is the traditional engagement ring, set in yellow gold, white gold, or platinum. However, you can choose any stone—ruby, sapphire, or the most expensive, emerald. If you prefer a larger pearl or semiprecious stone such as a green peridot, aquamarine, golden topaz, or pink tourmaline, all less expensive but exciting in color, that's fine, too. Any one of these stones or a combination of these stones makes a beautiful engagement ring, particularly when set off by a couple of tiny diamonds in the setting.

• If your fiancé asks you to accompany him to pick out your engagement ring, tell him yes, yes, yes! If he is an intelligent young man, he will already have visited the jewelry store and discussed his allowable price range with a salesperson. Then when the two of you come in together, that salesperson will show you trays of rings that are in the price range your fiancé can afford. A good reason for helping him select the ring is that you can select the kinds of stones you want. You may greatly prefer an emerald-cut diamond over a round one (but remember, the emerald-cut diamond is more expensive, so be prepared to choose a smaller stone). You can select your preference of design and yellow or white gold or platinum for the mounting. While you are at the store, you can have your exact ring size determined, too, so there are no embarrassing moments in trying to show it off and not being able to get it over your knuckle.

• If your fiancé surprises you with a ring, tell him you love it—even if you don't love it. If he picked it out, he has probably put his heart and soul into the purchase, and it would be too mean, not to mention discourteous, to tell him you don't like his taste. You can make yourself love that ring. Women have been doing that for centuries! However, I have known women who successfully exchanged rings at the store by telling their fiancés that the ring was too loose or tight or some such story. (They had already visited the jewelry store, found their fiancé's salesperson, explained their predicament, and selected another ring in the same price range.) When the woman returned to the store with her fiancé, there were no other rings of the right size exactly like the one her fiancé had purchased, so she looked around and suddenly found a ring to her liking in a totally different style. The fact that the salesperson was in collusion with her remained a secret.

• If he is (or perhaps you are) embarrassed about the small size of the stone but it's all he can afford, tell him you love it as it is—but that you will enjoy adding stones to it someday, or exchanging it for a larger stone, when finances permit.

• If his finances won't permit buying you a handsome ring, but your finances will, offer to contribute toward the ring. You can even pay for all of it (no one will know), if you desperately want a certain ring—in any case, leave his ego intact. If he adamantly refuses to accept any money toward the ring, wear his small one with enthusiasm. (You can always buy yourself a big rock later to go on your other hand.)

• If purchasing your ring would be too great a financial strain for him when you become engaged, tell him you don't need a ring now. I have known many young men putting themselves through law school or medical school, for example, trying to repay government loans and unable to afford an engagement ring when they marry. If their fiancées are right-minded they have made these men feel they were far more important than any rings.

• If you are a woman with large fingers and big hands and your fiancé can afford only a small stone, you may prefer to go without an engagement ring until the day comes when your husband can buy you one suitably large enough for your hands. A single gold wedding ring should suffice at first.

• Some women prefer to forgo a small engagement stone and to wear instead a jeweled wedding band—in place of a small engagement ring and an undistinguished wedding ring.

• If he gives you his mother's or grandmother's engagement ring, learn to love it, no matter how you feel about it. It's not worth the risk of upsetting his entire family by refusing to wear the family ring. Years hence, you can always put it away "to save as a precious family memento for one of the children" and buy a new one for yourself. (If your future children don't want the family ring either, one of them can keep it in the vault for her children. Eventually, one of the descendants somewhere will want it!)

• Unlike a wedding ring, the inside of an engagement ring is not engraved.

• Should you break your engagement, the correct thing to do is to return the ring to your fiancé, as well as any other gifts of jewelry or family keepsakes he may have given you. (If he breaks the engagement, keep your ring!)

CELEBRATING THE ENGAGEMENT

The Engagement Party

The conventional engagement party, usually a cocktail party hosted by godparents or grandparents, an uncle or aunt—or even a close friend—was often a surprise announcement of a young couple's intention to wed. It also marked the first time the young woman was seen wearing her engagement ring. This kind of reception was usually held when the engaged pair had a long time to wait—such as a year—between the announcement of their engagement and the actual wedding.

In this era of short engagements, the traditional engagement party has been supplanted for the most part by showers. If you are engaged, with a long period ahead of you before the wedding, you can always hint to a favorite friend or relative that you would appreciate a party. Make it a surprise for your guests, so that only the engaged couple and the hosts know the real reason for the party.

I remember one engagement party at which none of us knew that two of our best friends had become engaged until the actual end of the evening, when we were leaving the house. Our hostess handed each of us a prettily wrapped gift. We opened our individual boxes to discover a small silver pencil inside. Then we noticed two sets of initials engraved on each. It took a few seconds to realize that these were the initials of two people attending the party. Since none of us had known these two were even seeing each other, it was a secret beautifully kept—and in celebration we started the party all over again. Another engagement announcement I will never forget was a cocktail party at which our host suddenly announced that he had a secret, and that the person who first discovered the nature of the secret would receive a bottle of champagne. We went scurrying all over his house, searching out clues written in poetry on scraps of paper. It was an amusing and cleverly executed puzzle, finally solved by a guest who surmised that two of our friends present were engaged because of a stack of thank-you notes tucked inside a desk blotter.

Engagement Presents

The presentation to the bride-to-be of engagement presents by relatives and best friends is no longer a common custom. These gifts used to make sense when the engagement period lasted about a year. Some older relatives still do like to give these presents, however, as a gesture to start the bride on her marital way. The gift is usually something personal, such as a piece of jewelry, a silver compact, a handbag, a silver dressing table mirror.

The friends of the young couple seldom give engagement presents today.

They are digging deep enough in their pockets as it is, paying for shower and wedding gifts.

SHOWERS: FETING THE BRIDE-TO-BE

Showers are given by close friends in honor of the bride, but the loot collected (with the very strong exception of a lingerie shower!) is appropriate for both the bride and groom. A female relative may host the shower (not the bride's mother or sister). It is important for a bride not to let her enthusiasm for being the honoree carry her away. One shower is sufficient, two should be maximum, and three becomes a travesty. Family and friends do not have enough money to be shelling out constantly for gifts. There is still the wedding gift to come!

Coed showers—held in the evening at the cocktail hour, for the benefit of the bride's and groom's friends of both sexes who work—are the most popular kind of shower given today. These usually have the theme of gifts for the bar (bar glasses, wine bottle opener, bottles of wine, and the like) or gifts for the kitchen (whisks, cheese graters, carving knives, mixing bowls, and so forth). Female friends of the bride often give her a separate girls-only lingerie shower.

A guest does not have to spend a lot of money on a shower gift. It makes a good deal of sense for two or more of the guests to band together to buy a more important shower present.

There are many charming customs involving the old-fashioned all-female shower, where the ribbons are saved and tied to make a ribbon rope to encircle the group of guests. (The girl with the most knots in her hand will be the next to be married.) Then there's the custom of making a bridal bouquet from the various bows on the packages. The bows are pulled through holes made in a round piece of cardboard, so that eventually the cardboard is covered with bright blossom-colored ribbons. (The bride is supposed to use this fake bouquet at the rehearsal of the wedding ceremony the afternoon or evening before the wedding.)

At a coed cocktail party shower, hors d'oeuvres and drinks are served; at an all-girl shower, a light lunch or tea is served in conjunction with opening the gifts.

ASKING SOMEONE TO MARRY YOU

I'm an acknowledged, nonapologetic romantic, so if you do not believe in romance, skip over this advice on how to ask someone to marry you. My first piece of advice, of course, is to be pretty sure that the other person feels the same way you do before you propose spending the rest of your lives together. My second piece of advice is, whether you are male or female, make the proposal scene a memorable one. For example, choose a first-class, glamorous setting with a touch of the Hollywood of the 1930s, or devise a scenario with a touch of David Letterman's sense of humor. Do *something* to make the occasion unusual, so the memory can be recalled as something special for years to come. Every time I see one of the old *Thin Man* movies from the 1930s, I wish I could have been Myrna Loy and had William Powell propose to me in a sophisticated New York nightclub setting. My own marriage proposal, received decades ago in Chicago, was so "unforgettable" that neither my husband nor I can remember it. (I think the dialogue went something like this: *Bob:* "Let's do it." *Letitia:* "Okay, let's.") So it is with no small amount of envy that I recount what has happened to other couples when they became engaged. In each case, one of the couple showed enormous imagination or wit:

• A woman in love stuck a note on top of the tennis balls in the can. When her opponent removed the lid from the can to put the three balls into play, he saw her note: "This is the 58th time we've played singles together. Don't you think it's time we played doubles instead?" Her opponent, who had been thinking along the same lines but had been too shy to do anything about it, vaulted over the net, kissed her, and said, "Will you *please* marry me?" (I never found out if they finished the match, but they did get married.)

• A middle-aged widower went to a recording studio and recorded "People," the song that was playing when he met the new love of his life. His voice was not very good, but when his lady friend listened to the tape and heard him say at the conclusion of the song, "We are two people who are meant to be together for the rest of our lives," she got the message.

• Two graduate music students spent every Saturday together, always at something musical, followed by dinner. One Saturday she was very blue because he was away. However, he had lent her his libretto to follow the opera performance, and when she came to a certain passage, halfway through the opera, she found a tiny diamond ring tied inside the binding of the book with a ribbon. At the bottom of the page, he had scribbled, "I love you. Marry me." (She did.)

• Men have surprised the women in their lives by proposing in extraordinary ways:

  • Having the proposal skywritten by a plane overhead.
  • Putting the proposal on a giant rented sign in Times Square in New York.
  • Putting a diamond engagement ring at the bottom of her champagne glass and then bringing her the filled glass to drink. (To my knowledge, no one has yet swallowed it.)
  • Sending a mime to perform by her desk in her office, making the entire office aware that her boyfriend was too shy to propose directly.

- Proposing to her while the two of them were ballooning, or water-skiing, or ice-boating, or taking tango lessons.

- One crafty young woman baked a note in her beau's birthday cake at a large party she had organized for him. She made sure he was served the piece that had the note in it, which read, "If you want to have birthdays like this forever, you had better marry me." He read her note, looked at her and smiled, and then arose from the table to toast the hostess. In his toast he announced to the group, "Janie and I are going to be married. How could I ever be apart from a woman who bakes birthday cakes like this?"

Now, I'm all for romance and, Lord knows, we need it in this cold, mechanical, technological era in which we live. But if you can't get the perfect romantic occasion together, at least get the marriage together. In other words, if you're short on imagination or wit, just summon up the courage to make one statement and follow it with a question. The statement is, "I love you." The question is, "Will you marry me?"

WHEN A WOMAN DOES THE PROPOSING

Woman have long proposed to men, in spite of the ancient canard that in order for them to live happily ever after, it is the man who presses the suit until his blushing love object finally acquiesces. Now, in the twenty-first century, women are unabashedly open and aboveboard about proposing. (As one young man told me recently, "Without mentioning the word 'marriage,' she made it impossible for us *not* to get married.")

Before the women's movement of the sixties, it would have been considered shocking for a woman to take the lead in marching her man to the altar, but she often did it anyway, playing a deft game of psychological warfare. She would say things such as, "You always say it's such a joy to see me. Wouldn't it make things easier for you to have that joy around all the time, without having to make elaborate plans to meet?" Or if a woman had regularly been cooking a fantastic dinner several nights a week for the love of her life, she might say, "Can you imagine your life without these great feasts prepared for you all the time? Would you like to go back to your cans of tuna fish and delivered pizzas?" While she didn't say, "Will you marry me?" she certainly was forcing the issue.

Some women still use tactics like that. Others use sex as their wedge. ("You know how great we are together, you and I. Can you imagine what life would be like without me around—available, eager, and loving?")

But today's woman really doesn't have to play those games—although she can if she wants to. If she is more honest and direct, she can put her cards right on the table in front of the recalcitrant male: "Look, we've been seeing each other for a long time now. We're very compatible. I love you and I think you love me—at least you act like it. If we get married, our two salaries will make a neat lifestyle for us, and we could produce such beautiful children!" (There's not much romance in a marriage proposal of this nature, but, reworded to each woman's personal style, it seems to work.)

If two people have been living together a long time, it becomes harder to make the one person who has been stalling all along commit—and it usually is the man. The woman in this kind of relationship should perhaps revert to the old style of romance, intrigue, and games to influence the man into thinking that it is in both their interests to formalize their union.

It doesn't really matter who says what and who asks whom, as long as it happens—namely, that marriage license and those wedding rings!

WHEN YOUR ANSWER IS NO

For every proposal of marriage that is accepted, there is another that is refused. To hear you decline an offer of marriage has to be the greatest emotional rejection there is for an adult. Your kindheartedness has kept you from deflating the other person's hopes. Or is it that it's easier to be a coward and simply avoid telling the other person that there is no chance of the relationship moving to a commitment to marriage? That cowardice, however, is a big mistake, because the longer the relationship is allowed to continue, the more the rejection hurts. It's much better for everyone if it is made quite clear early on that marriage is not possible—long before the other person gets to the stage of proposing.

But if the relationship has gone too far, and the other person is full of hope and excitement, turn down the idea of marriage with a sharp, clean, and swift reply. The other person's heart will be broken—there is no more apt term for it—but it should be done as nicely as possible. Find words to soothe the injured party. Here are some of the things that might be said:

• Establish that there is no way you will entertain the idea of marriage, and no hope whatsoever that you will change your mind. (Make this clear, but say it gently.)

• It is not the other person's fault, it's yours for not feeling the same emotions he (or she) does for you; you admit that you should have told him (or her) sooner.

• You probably will never again in your whole life find anyone as sensitive, attractive, smart. (Use every complimentary adjective that could possibly apply to the other person.)

• You will never forget him (or her), or the terrific experiences you shared together. (Explain how much you gained from your relationship, how you will always keep those memories in your heart.)

• He (or she) deserves the finest person in the world as a spouse, and you're certain that person will soon appear in his (or her) life.

The spurned one will probably question you closely as to why you can't say yes—what's wrong, what is the missing element in the relationship, and so on. Be prepared, and be truthful if there is no spark on your part. Simply mention that you are not a match.

If there are other reasons—for example, he can't keep a job and is always broke—explain your reservation diplomatically. "You don't have the job stability I have always wanted in a husband" sounds a lot kinder than "You're a loser and you'd be on my payroll all my life."

If you feel you are simply not on the same wavelength, explain that your interests are so divergent that you would not have the foundation necessary for a marriage to work. Praise the other person's interests, and make him (or her) see that it is not those interests that are at fault. It's the fact that the two of you are too different in your enthusiasms and directions.

If you have a *serious* moral objection to the other person, you owe it to him to come out with it. For example, if the other person is a drug abuser, you should say that you're sorry but you could never marry a person who uses drugs, even occasionally. If he promises to get off drugs or alcohol, be ready to question that fine resolution. Say, "I'd have to wait too long to see if you really do get and stay off. You haven't conquered it during the years we've been seeing each other, and you knew how I felt about it. You and I aren't going to make it." Your frankness may result in the other person's finally seeking the help needed to conquer his problem.

If the person you turn down thinks you did it because of his less than sensational looks, reassure that person immediately that you have enjoyed his company all this time because of other, far more important factors than looks. Maybe the other person won't believe you, but say it often. Keep reminding him of all the great personality assets that have pleased and attracted you. At the same time make the person who proposed understand that you need to be deeply in love with the man you marry, and you are not in love with him.

Think of every possible great thing about the person who has just proposed to you. After you have said no, pelt him with compliments and memories of past wonderful, shared experiences to help coat the bitter pill you have just given him to swallow. Write a letter in which you reaffirm how much the friendship you have shared has meant to you, but now you feel it is best not to see each other anymore. He should be looking for someone else.

It is a difficult, even cruel time for the person who is spurned. But it is a much, much easier blow than the one a divorce delivers!

CHAPTER 12

Weddings

The great decision has been made. The wedding date has been decided. It will be the happiest day of your life for you—the bride—as well as for the groom, your parents, and his parents. And for your friends this is a major moment, too.

The main goal for any wedding should be happiness. Regardless of the size, simplicity, or elaborateness of the ceremony, a wedding should be carefully and lovingly planned. The bride should feel it is her wedding, not her parents'. The groom should feel he is essential to the planning, too. The weeks before the wedding should be marked by great diplomacy and tact, with everyone checking first with everyone else before making major decisions, and with account taken of the hurt feelings that might result from any exclusion.

I am a traditionalist in my attitude toward weddings. To me, the one sacred ritual that remains in this sociologically shaken world is the first wedding. The ceremony and reception are couched in such beautiful traditions that following and respecting them results in an orderly, dignified, and memorable event.

Weddings of the seventies were often chaotic, even weird to many, taking place in farm fields dotted with manure, with guests never knowing exactly what they were witnessing, because the unintelligible vows were homespun. Instead of traditional sacred music, there were zithers, mandolins, and drums. Sometimes a harp would be hauled into the fields, and a beautiful young friend of the bride's, with flowing blond hair and a long white flowing dress to match, would play Bach, followed up by a group of Beatles-era songs.

The bride would wear white petticoats, with garlands of wildflowers woven into her hair. The groom often resembled a white-garbed, white legginged Nehru, Prime Minister of India. If reception guests stepped into poison ivy in the fields by accident, everyone took it in stride.

Today, there is a growing tendency to return to many of the old traditions. Some weddings today even look very old-fashioned. They are so lovely, they just might stick around awhile!

My book reflects the old traditions updated. You are free to follow or change them. It's *your wedding*. It's time to resolve all the infighting, the injured feelings, even if just for a while. It's time to give the bride and groom the greatest moments of their lives!

THE ARCHITECTURE
OF A BEAUTIFUL FIRST WEDDING

There will always be publicity seekers—usually people who have a hard time being noticed in life—who decide to get married while bungee jumping, sports car racing, swimming with singing whales, or trying to emulate Sir Edmund Hillary while climbing some peak or other. A truly beautiful, dignified wedding is *not* a celebrity media event, ruined by photographers and TV lights, bulky cameras, and sweating, angry people pushing one another.

Sometimes the wedding is orchestrated by an experienced wedding planner, or an interior designer or a floral designer, all of whom seem to be assisted by a cast of thousands. Some are directed like a big movie production, but some are small, intimate, and planned by the bride's mother! The older the bride and groom, the more the groom is allowed to enter the planning, but from what I have observed through the years, the groom is delighted to step back and leave it all to the ladies, even if his interventions and ideas are, at least, tolerated.

Weddings come in all signs and flavors:
  • A Victorian wedding. At this lavish wedding the bride wore a nineteenth-century lace and silk dress handed down through her family. The bridesmaids' dresses matched the bride's in feeling, and the bridesmaids carried white paper lace Victorian bouquets. Even the white lace tablecloths (overlying garnet velvet cloths) reinforced the nineteenth-century English feeling.
  • A 1920s-look wedding. At this one the bride wore her grandmother's flapper wedding dress. The bridesmaids wore dresses similar in cut and satin pumps that could have come from a 1925 shoe store. The bride's short dark hair was dressed in the smart bob of that period. The fabric of the circular tablecloths was printed in an Art Deco design. The music was all 1920s Charleston type, and a pair of dance instructors helped the guests learn the steps.
  • A flowered chintz wedding. At this wedding the bride had selected a chintz fabric pattern of pink and blush peonies as the central theme. The bride's and bridesmaids' bouquets repeated the flowers in the fabric. The cushions in the church pews were slipcovered in this fabric, the bridesmaids' white dresses were sashed in this fabric, and the tablecloths at the reception were made of the same chintz. The floral centerpieces were, of course, peonies. It was all fresh, flowery, and fragrant. The only jarring moment came when two guests suffered stings from bees who were as entranced with the peonies as the guests were.
  • A country wedding. At this charming summer wedding, held on a farm,

everything was done in white mixed with pale yellow and blue gingham. The bride wore a white voile dress printed in a white-on-white gingham pattern, and a large straw picture hat with pale yellow and blue streamers down the back. The bridesmaids, carrying baskets of yellow and blue flowers, wore long yellow- or blue-checked dresses with two-toned satin streamers around the waist to match those on the bride's hat. The same gingham fabric was used for the tablecloths at the reception. A straw picture hat filled with blue and yellow flowers formed the centerpiece on each table. The white napkins were tied in yellow- or blue-checked ribbons, and each guest carried home a piece of wedding cake wrapped in a little bandanna made of the checked gingham used throughout the wedding. The bride and groom left for their honeymoon on a two-seated tractor to the railroad station.

• An operatic wedding. When two people involved in the opera world were married, their twenty attendants were dressed in borrowed costumes from *Lohengrin,* and the attendants sang opera selections throughout the wedding ceremony, as did the bride and groom at designated moments. The music played at the reception was all operatic recordings, and parts of opera sets had been borrowed to decorate the plain parish hall in which the wedding reception was held. The reception was a low-budget affair—we ate cheese and drank wine—but I have never heard such beautiful voices raised in song. The entire wedding was unforgettable.

• A silver wedding. One extremely sentimental wedding contained a surprise element for the guests. The bride's dress and her flowers were all in white, but with a silver satin bow on each puffed sleeve. The bridesmaids wore silver taffeta and carried silver-painted roses. After the wedding ceremony, the bride and groom sat down on either side of the altar. The bride's parents rose from their pew and came to the foot of the altar, where the minister awaited them, and renewed their marriage vows in an extremely touching ceremony tied into their daughter's own vows. That was the surprise—it was their silver wedding anniversary! The bride's mother wore a pale gray silk dress. There were a lot of tears in that church when the wedding procession of the young bride and groom followed by her parents went down the long church aisle.

• A skiing wedding. This unique wedding was held up in the Swiss Alps, with the wedding party and some good skiing friends flying from Chicago to Gstaad for a long weekend. The wedding party took their skis up in the lift one morning to one of the highest slopes, where the minister had arranged a simple altar in the snow. It was a brilliant day, with the sun blazing against an azure sky. As one of the participants said, "You felt you were really in God's cathedral." The bride wore a white snowsuit, white ski boots, and a short veil; she held a bouquet of white roses during the ceremony. After the service, the entire wedding party took off on a long downhill run, yelling out their exclamations of joy. A reception lunch awaited them at the Palace Hotel down in the village of Gstaad.

• A beach wedding. Many people who live by the sea stage perfectly beautiful informal ceremonies on the beach, with the bride perhaps wearing a satin-sashed white cotton Mexican wedding dress for the service. These informal weddings are often followed by an informal reception—for example, a clambake. There's frequently volleyball and other games played enthusiastically even if rather badly in the sand.

• A wedding on the water. Some couples charter a small cruise boat, complete with a band, for their wedding and reception, sailing around a river, lake, or other body of water as they celebrate the happy union. Some couples book themselves on a ten-day cruise and are married by the ship's captain. As one bride described it, "We got married, had our reception with all the passengers on the cruise present, and we had time to write all our thank-you notes before we disembarked. It was the perfect one-stop operation. Our parents were along, but as pre-agreed, we hardly saw them after the wedding ceremony!"

It does not matter what theme or color scheme you choose at your wedding. It doesn't matter whether you serve your reception guests roast beef or snails, pasta or stuffed grape leaves. What does matter is that you plan the event in a cohesive fashion and in good taste, that you "produce" something that none of your guests will ever forget, and that everyone involved in the wedding keeps their cool! During this period of your lives you will be the recipients of a great deal of love. A well-planned wedding gives back a lot of that love to the participants.

Most important, your wedding should be something that pleases you, the bride and the groom, but please don't go into hock over your wedding!

THE HOMOSEXUAL COMMUNITY'S
WEDDING AND COMMITMENT CEREMONIES

Formal engraved or printed invitations are sent by couples who celebrate their commitment to one another with a religious ceremony and a reception afterward. The couple often dress alike—gay men in formal dark suits or black tie tuxedos, wearing boutonnieres, and lesbians often wearing long white dresses and carrying wedding bouquets.

Invited guests who do not believe in homosexual marriage rites may attend out of friendship, but they would refer to such a ceremony as a "commitment," not a wedding. The straight guest would send the couple not a wedding gift but a gift of friendship. The enclosure card with the gift would contain wishes for a long, happy, joyous life together, without using the terminology "as man and wife."

In other words, friendship transcends personal feelings of any existing disapproval. There are many things that our friends do that we may not like or accept, but there are probably just as many things that we do that they may not like or accept. We should not allow these negatives to stand in the way of our affection and love for one another.

Sample wording on a formal invitation to a Gay or Lesbian Commitment Ceremony:

> *John Ellison Calteron*
>
> *and*
>
> *Seth Sanchez Faucher*
>
> *request the honor of your presence*
>
> *at their commitment ceremony*
>
> *and to the reception following*
>
> *Saturday the Twenty-sixth of June*
>
> *Two thousand and five*
>
> *at five o'clock*
>
> *The Algonquin Club*
>
> *4000 Connecticut Avenue*
>
> *Washington, D.C.*
>
> *The favor of a reply is requested*   *Valet Parking*

The names of the two hosts are listed in alphabetical order. The example above is for a formal invitation, requiring the recipient to reply by note (think of that!). An informal invitation would contain a telephone number or e-mail address listed by the letters "RSVP." And, of course, there is the cop-out of all cop-outs: an RSVP card, enclosed in the commitment invitation, with a self-addressed, stamped envelope, upon which the recipient has only to put a checkmark in the box titled "Accepts" or "Regrets." (Even with this incredibly simple way of replying to an invitation, thousands, perhaps millions of invitation reply cards go unmailed every year.)

ACKNOWLEDGMENTS FOR COMMITMENT GIFTS OR BABY PRESENTS IF THE COUPLE ADOPTS A BABY

There are two ways of doing this:
1. One person writes and signs the note but says that he (or she) is

"writing on behalf of Robert and me (or Robert Hilary and John Vilar, if you do not know the other people well), to thank you for the wonderful present you sent us," etc.

2. One person writes the thank-you note, and both partners sign it.

YOUR WEDDING INVITATIONS

Next to a White House invitation, a wedding invitation is the most important one on the social scale. Its language and content have remained pretty much the same down through the years. From the sixties to the eighties, many young couples gave vent to their anti-establishment feelings by sending out wedding invitations that were far different from the traditional ones used by their parents, grandparents, and great-grandparents. During this period, wedding guests received curious-looking communications in the mail—everything from rough-textured rice papers to exotic parchments. Often handwritten or printed in nontraditional inks, such as red and ochre, the text was sometimes so esoteric (ancient Japanese poetry or the sayings of Buddha, for example) that many who received these invitations had no idea they were being invited to a wedding!

Fortunately for the bridal business, conventional invitations in this century are once again the favored kind. Anyone who receives one of these knows that she has been invited to a wedding and, further, knows where to be and when.

WHO RECEIVES YOUR INVITATIONS?

Your wedding invitation will be much coveted, so prepare the list of recipients with great care. Hurt feelings can easily result if you overlook some people in a group while inviting many of the others.

• It helps sometimes to organize your list into "Absolute Necessity" names and "Would Like to Invite If Possible" names. For example, your "Absolute Necessity" column would include:

  • Both immediate families.
  • Your attendants.
  • The spouses, fiancé(e)s, or special escorts of the attendants.
  • Both sets of godparents, if they are close to you.
  • Your clergyman or clergywoman.

• On your "Would Like to Invite If Possible" list, you might include:

  • Distant relatives and family friends.
  • Your bosses.
  • Your best friends and your fiancé(e)'s best friends.

- Your parents' best friends, because it would mean so much to them!
- Close workplace associates.
- A particularly significant teacher.
- Lead figures in your extracurricular activities (for example: golf or tennis partner; certain members of your choir, music group, or art class; certain members of your garden club or softball team; fellow volunteers in your nonprofit work).
- People such as your doctor and lawyer and their spouses.

The bride's and groom's families should be allowed to extend an equal number of invitations, but often it does not work out that way. Sometimes the groom's family lives far away, and not many of his family and their friends will be able to travel to the wedding. At other times, either the groom's or bride's family will be very prominent in town and will have more "necessity" invitations to extend. The balance should be worked out between the two families—with peace and harmony in mind—before the invitations are ordered.

Although traditionally the bride's family paid all the related expenses, today such matters are worked out between the two sets of parents or between the couple on an ad hoc basis—particularly when either the bride's or the groom's family sends by far the greater number of invitations.

Invitations are expensive—they can add up to $10 apiece by the time they are engraved on good stock, hand-addressed by a calligrapher, and mailed with their postage. However, rather than looking on it as a matter of "How much is this person worth to me?" look upon sending a wedding invitation to a family member or good friend as a sign of affection and respect, with a desire to make that person feel good about participating in your joy.

THE VARIOUS WAYS
OF INVITING GUESTS TO THE WEDDING

Extending Formal Invitations

The most expensive and traditional way is by *engraved invitations*, which are so handsome and luxurious that they are often kept by the recipients as prized mementos of the wedding. Many brides feel that their wedding is the one time in their lives when everything must be first class, starting with their invitations.

Appropriate Informal Ways
of Extending Wedding Invitations

• In the case of a small, intimate wedding, you may appropriately send notes *written by hand with black ink on fine-quality white or cream-colored notepaper.* Sometimes the bride writes these herself to her and the groom's contemporaries, but her mother often writes most of them, including to family members. An example is the following note from the bride's mother to a family friend:

> George and I would love to have you both present at the wedding of our daughter, Marianne, and Jonathan Mayberry, on Saturday, May fifteenth, at Saint Cecilia's Church on Harney Street at four o'clock. A champagne reception follows at the Wayfarer's Inn on Montgomery Street.
>
> Our whole family hopes you will be with us on the fifteenth to share in this joyful occasion.

Many parents of brides who issue informal invitations for their daughters' small weddings also send out *formal engraved announcements* to a large group of friends after the wedding, including the small group who actually attended the wedding. After all, even if the wedding is for fifty guests, there may be three hundred other people who would love to know about it. That's why announcements are very useful.

• To cut costs, *you may print instead of engrave the formal wedding text on good-quality single sheets of stationery.* Traditionally, you would choose either cream or white stock, but today you may also use color in this kind of informal printed invitation—for example, pale blue letter sheets bordered in dark blue, with black printing. It is perfectly appropriate to send out thermographed invitations (a raised printing process that emulates engraving), but I personally find invitations more honest and attractive when they are either engraved, printed, or handwritten, not replicated in a process that tries to look like engraving.

• If you do not have enough time to order invitations made, *send them by Mailgram.* Recipients will logically deduce when they read the date of the wedding that you did not have time even to write a note of invitation. You may use a formal text in your Mailgram (the same wording that you would have put on a formal invitation).

• Sending an invitation by *e-mail or fax* is easy but ugly and robs the wedding of its feeling of importance.

• A wedding invitation is extended by *telephone* only as a last resort, such as when the couple decides to marry within a few days. A reminder card is always mailed (or hand-delivered) immediately after.

THE FORMAL TRADITIONAL WEDDING INVITATION

Stock, Ink, and Lettering Style

This type of invitation is engraved via a copper plate in black (or sometimes dark gray) ink. A print or script lettering style is used on an ecru (cream-colored) or white stock.

Engraved Styles

Dr. and Mrs. Thomas Allen Greene　　　TCO-1
　　　　　　　　　　　　　　　　　　　BELGRAVE SCRIPT

Mr. and Mrs. Richard Arthur Hyman　　　TCO-2
　　　　　　　　　　　　　　　　　　　HAMILTON

Mr. and Mrs. Richard Murray Barton　　　TCO-3
　　　　　　　　　　　　　　　　　　　LIGHT SCRIPT

Mr. and Mrs. Percival Harold Clayton　　　TCO-4
　　　　　　　　　　　　　　　　　　　MAYFAIR

Mr. and Mrs. John Low Venable　　　TCO-6
　　　　　　　　　　　　　　　　　　　LONDON SCRIPT

Mr. and Mrs. Hugh Robert Scott　　　TCO-7
　　　　　　　　　　　　　　　　　　　PARSIFAL

Mr. and Mrs. Anthony Ross Hagen　　　TCO-8
　　　　　　　　　　　　　　　　　　　SAINT JAMES

Dr. and Mrs. Jay Barclay Woods　　　TCO-11
　　　　　　　　　　　　　　　　　　　TALLEYRAND

Reverend and Mrs. William Carlsen　　　TCO-14
　　　　　　　　　　　　　　　　　　　WINDSOR

MR. AND MRS. SPENCER WOODS MILLER　　　TCO-16
　　　　　　　　　　　　　　　　　　　LEHMAN ROMAN

Mr. and Mrs. Robert William Sloane　　　TCO-17
　　　　　　　　　　　　　　　　　　　SPAULDING CLASSIC

Mr. and Mrs. Daniel Montgomery, Jr.　　　TCO-18
　　　　　　　　　　　　　　　　　　　SHADED ANTIQUE ROMAN

The paper is often a heavy forty-pound weight and is sometimes embellished with a blind-embossed, paneled border. The stationer will show you a sample card of engraved styles of lettering from which to choose. Tiffany and Company, for example, offers the engraved styles shown on page 267, all of which are appropriate and attractive.

You know something is engraved if:

- You rub your finger over it and feel the raised lettering.
- You find a stationer's name in raised, blind-embossed small letters underneath the envelope flap.
- You see an indentation in the paper on the reverse side.

Points to Remember
About Sending Formal Wedding Invitations

- Order them three months before the wedding, or even earlier.
- Make sure you order all the parts you will need (such as a reply card, reception card, and map card, if necessary, to show people how to find the church or reception).
- Be sure to include all of the necessary information in the text. Check the proof for errors *before* it is engraved, even if that entails an additional cost.
- You may certainly have the family crest blind-embossed at the top of the invitation. However, many Americans consider the use of a coat of arms on wedding invitations quite pretentious, all the more so because many people today have had fake family crests designed!
- Tissues are no longer relevant, since the new inks used in printing dry fast and do not smudge.

Composition of a Traditional,
Formal Engraved Wedding Invitation

- The text is engraved on the first page of a *double-fold* invitation.
- The *outside envelope* is hand-addressed in black ink and hand-stamped.
- If the reception will be held in a place separate from where the ceremony will be held, you will need a separate *reception invitation card*. A reception card is also useful if you are going to invite a large number of people to the ceremony but just a few to the reception held afterward in the same place (as, for example, a small reception held in the church parlors after the church ceremony).
- If you are inviting most people to the reception but only a few to the marriage ceremony, you will need a separate *"ceremony card"* for those who should be present at the exchange of vows.

• If you do not have "RSVP" or "The favour of a reply is requested" on the lower left of your invitation, a *reply card* and self-addressed envelope must be supplied. (See illustration on page 288.) Today, these envelopes should even be stamped. (It's a pity the guest will have to lick his own envelope!)

• A separate *at home* card, giving the couple's new address and telephone number, is useful. (This is where wedding gifts should be sent.)

• A *map card* may be necessary, showing guests how to find the church and the reception.

• Other cards, such as an *admittance card* or a *pew card,* may be advisable for security purposes for a very large, prominent wedding with celebrities and VIPs on the guest list.

ADDRESSING AND MAILING THE INVITATIONS

• Arrange for a friend of the bride to volunteer (or pay for a professional) to hand-address (never type) the envelopes in black ink (with a wide pen point).

In large cities there are professional calligraphers who will address your envelopes for a price, generally ranging from $2 to $6 per envelope (including hand-stamping, stuffing, and sealing them). You can find them by asking the people who are professional party givers (look in the Yellow Pages), or the special events coordinators of businesses like large banks that use calligraphy for important parties. Or ask your church or temple, because they probably know of good calligraphers who have done other weddings. There are also computer graphics services that will address the envelopes in mechanized calligraphy. This is relatively inexpensive.

Since hand-addressing a large number of envelopes is a time-consuming process, ask your stationer to supply you at once with envelopes in stock while the invitations are being made up. This allows you time to begin addressing the outside and inside envelopes well in advance of the arrival of the invitations. It's very wise to have your envelopes addressed, stamped, and ready to stuff and mail well ahead of the date you intend to mail them.

• *Hand-stamp* the envelopes with attractive, appropriate postage stamps (for example, flowers or birds). Be sure to weigh an invitation with all its parts in advance of buying the stamps so that you affix the proper amount of postage.

• Handwrite the *return address,* or have it engraved or blind-embossed in the upper left-hand corner on the front of the envelope, or on the back flap. Putting it on the front upper-left allows a much better chance for a misaddressed envelope to be returned to the sender. The name is not necessary on the return address, but an apartment number should be included. The address normally should be that of the bride's parents, although it is sometimes preferable to use another address, including the bride's own address, rather than her mother's (as, for example, when the bride's parents are older and not involved in the mechanics of the wedding). If a grandparent or another relative or a friend is giving the wedding, that person may be the recipient of the RSVPs.

If the couple themselves are issuing the invitations, the bride's own address or the couple's mutual address should be provided in the return address. It is a certainty that unless an "at home" card is included, many wedding gifts will be mailed to the return address on the invitations, so you should decide whether or not the bride's parents or the bride or someone else is to receive all the acceptances and regrets.

- When addressing the outer envelopes, either center the name and address of the invitation recipient, or write it on a slant.
- If possible, mail the invitations six weeks before the wedding.

Protocol on Addressing Wedding Invitation Envelopes

- The *inside envelope* is ungummed and therefore not to be sealed. It is addressed to a person with his or her or their family name and title only—"Mr. and Mrs. Grant" (not "Mr. and Mrs. Jason Grant"). If children are to be invited, their given names are included on the inside envelope under their parents' names. For example:

Mr. and Mrs. Grant
Mary, Beth, and James

A family member over the age of eighteen should receive her own invitation.

- The *outside mailing envelope* is addressed either to a couple or a single person. It is proper to use "Ms." with a woman's given and family names in addressing her, rather than "Miss" or "Mrs.," if she is single or if she is married but has kept her maiden name.
- When addressing a married or unmarried couple, address a husband and a wife who has kept her own name on one line:

Mr. Charles Edward Prentice and Ms. Amy Sturgis Kendl

If their combined names are too long to go on one line, address them as

Mr. Andrew Wigglesworth Throckmorton
and Ms. Patricia Fordyce Kendleton

The use of the "and" joining their names means they are married.

In addressing an invitation to a couple who live together but are not married, you would put their names on separate lines, and place on the top line the name that comes first in the alphabet:

Ms. Caroline Breckinridge Murray
Mr. David Adam Thornton
1345 First Street Northwest, etc.

Stuffing the Contents into Their Envelopes

The "old-fashioned" way of stuffing invitations into their envelopes (still occasionally used today) was to fold the double-fold invitation in half, include the other pieces of the mailing, and then insert it straight up into an envelope that was just a bit large than the folded invitation. This envelope was then inserted into a matching outer envelope that was again a bit larger—just enough to be able to slide in the inner envelope with ease.

Today the more commonly ordered invitation is a larger double-fold style, in a size from 4½ inches by 6¾ inches to 5½ inches by 7½ inches. Today's double-fold invitation is generally folded along the left-hand side, rather than across the middle. This kind of invitation is inserted lying flat (instead of being folded in half) into a larger envelope, which then slides into the larger outer envelope.

• This is the order of precedence of the various parts within the envelope: Hold the envelope so that you are facing the back of it, with the flap open. The largest part of the contents—the double-fold invitation itself—goes in first, faceup.

A double-fold wedding invitation is generally folded along the left-hand side and is inserted lying flat into an envelope, which then slides into a larger one that will be addressed and stamped.

A single card invitation of any kind is inserted in its envelope faceup in this manner.

If there is a smaller card inviting the guest to the reception, it is inserted next, on top of the larger invitation, and if there is an RSVP card, it comes next, lying faceup within the flap of its own envelope (which is, of course, at this point turned facedown). A map or parking instructions or pew number card—whatever is needed—would come next.

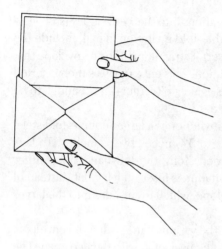

A double-fold invitation may be folded in half and inserted in its envelope in this fashion. A smaller piece, such as a reception card or RSVP card and envelope, would be tucked inside the double-fold piece.

When you stuff an unfolded wedding invitation (or any invitation of two or more parts) into its first envelope, put the smaller piece of stationery (which might be a reception card, an "at home" card, or an RSVP card with matching envelope) in front of the invitation, as shown here.

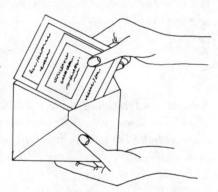

THE CORRECT WORDING
ON WEDDING INVITATIONS

• Names are given in full on invitations, which means no nicknames and no initials. If, however, either the bride or groom dislikes his or her middle name, it may be omitted on the invitation.

• The English spelling of "honour" and "favour" is often used in wedding invitation language, simply as a matter of tradition. If you prefer, use the American spelling and drop the "u."

• Spell out the date and the year. Spell out all words like "avenue" and "street," so that there are no abbreviations, except perhaps "Dr." or "Jr."—and you may even prefer to use "Doctor" or "Junior."

• The hour of the wedding (and reception, when necessary) is written out, following the word "at" on the invitation—for example, "at one o'clock," "at quarter after five o'clock," or "at three-quarters after four o'clock." "At eight o'clock in the evening" is used to make sure no one thinks it's an early morning service!

• Roman numerals, such as in "George Douglas Berkhardt III," are properly used on the invitation.

• When a wedding takes place in a house of worship, then the inviters use the phrase "request the honour of your presence"—a mark of respect for a church or temple. When a wedding takes place in a home, club, banquet hall, or hotel, the inviters "request the pleasure of your company." When a separate reception card is included in the invitation, the hosts also use "request the pleasure of your company."

Invitational Text

A sample formal wedding invitation:

> *Mr. and Mrs. Farnsworth Lee Maguire*
> *request the honour of your presence*
> *at the marriage of their daughter*
> *Elizabeth Anne*
> *to Mr. Tracy McLaughlin*
> *on Saturday, the eighth of May*
> *two thousand and ten*
> *at four o'clock*
> *Saint Cecilia's Cathedral*
> *426 Mission Street*
> *San Antonio*

A separate reception invitation card and a reply card and envelope are provided with the invitation above. In the case of a formal wedding invitation, both ceremony and reception are combined on one only when both take place in the same location:

> *Mr. and Mrs. Robert Agee Sundworth*
> *request the pleasure of your company*
> *at the marriage of their daughter*
> *Gretchen Anne*
> *to*
> *Doctor [or Dr.] Cameron Aimes Johnson*
> *on Saturday, the fifth of December*
> *two thousand and eleven*
> *at half after six o'clock*
> *and at dinner*
> *immediately following the ceremony*
> *The Charles Hotel*
> *Charles Square*
> *Cambridge*
>
> *R.s.v.p.*   *Black Tie*
> *Fourteen Linnaen Avenue*
> *Cambridge, Massachusetts 00000*

THE ETIQUETTE OF NAMES
ON WEDDING INVITATIONS

• The names of those who do the inviting are always given. In a traditional wedding invitation, the parents of the bride do the inviting. If she is a divorcée who is marrying again, the parents usually do not issue the invitations—the couple does. If she is widowed and remarrying in her early twenties, they properly may issue the invitations for her.

• When the two different names of the parents are too long to go on one line in the invitation, put their names on separate lines, joined by "and" (which means they are husband and wife).

• Generally, neither the bride's title nor surname is given on the invitation. The groom's always are. Unless the bride's last name is different from her parents', the last name is not repeated in the invitation text. (She is simply "Elizabeth Anne," not "Elizabeth Anne Maguire" on the invitation.) The groom's full name—e.g., "Mr. Tracy McLaughlin"—does need to be communicated, since his parents' names may not be on the invitation. If his parents are on the invitations as cohosts with the bride's parents, then his honorific is not mentioned.

• If the bride's parents do not have the same last names, as in the case of divorced or widowed and remarried parents, or as in the case of the mother of the bride who has kept her own name in marriage, the bride's surname is given on the invitation to clear up any possible confusion. The following examples illustrate this point:

If the mother of the bride has retained her maiden name in her marriage, both names go on the same line, her name following her husband's. In this case, "Ms." is more appropriate to use than "Miss," because the mother of the bride obviously is married and is not a "Miss."

> *Mr. George Ames Lincoln and Ms. Serena Cooper*
> *request the honour of your presence*
> *at the marriage of their daughter*
> *Leslie Anne Lincoln*
>
> *etc.*

• If the mother of the bride is a widow who has remarried:

> *Mr. and Mrs. George Fillmore Breckport*
> *request the honour of your presence at*
> *the marriage of Mrs. Breckport's daughter*
> *Sarah Anne Simpson*
>
> *etc.*

- If the father of the bride is a widower who has remarried:

> *Mr. and Mrs. Anthony Delgas Stanton*
> *request the honour of your presence at*
> *the marriage of Mr. Stanton's daughter*
> *Marianne Lee*
>
> *etc.*

- When the bride's parents are divorced but her mother has not remarried, the mother uses her given, maiden, and married names on the first line, separate from her husband's:

> *Mrs. Marian McPherson Ormsby*
> *Mr. Robert Sims Ormsby*
> *request the honour of your presence at*
> *the marriage of their daughter*
> *Samantha*
>
> *etc.*

The days are past when a divorced woman had to go formally by her family name and her husband's name, as in "Mrs. McPherson Ormsby." Today she is "Mrs. Marian Ormsby" in most situations.

When both parents have divorced and remarried, the mother's name always comes first, and her ex-husband's name is on the next line:

> *Mrs. Amos Templeton Schulz*
> *Mr. Edmund Holton Draper*
> *request the honour of your presence*
> *at the marriage of their daughter*
> *Louise Marie Draper*
>
> *etc.*

- If the bride has lived with her father and stepmother for most of her life, and her stepmother really raised her, the stepmother would be listed with her husband as issuers of the invitations, and the natural mother would attend the wedding only as a guest.

> *Mr. and Mrs. William Agyropoulos*
> *request the honour of your presence at*
> *the marriage of Mr. Agyropoulos's daughter*
> *Olympia*
>
> *etc.*

- When grandparents or another relative (or even a godparent) give the wedding, their relationship to the bride is always made clear:

> *Mr. and Mrs. Stephen Miller Blaine*
> *request the honour of your presence at*
> *the marriage of their granddaughter*
> *Stephany Lee Blaine*
>
> *etc.*

- The question of who is paying for the wedding is not relevant to the invitations. It is petty for one of the divorced parents to say, "Since I'm paying for everything, I don't want the other parent's name on the wedding invitations." Both parents of the bride should be the issuers of the invitations in one way or another, and the mother of the bride should have her name at the top of the invitation to the wedding ceremony regardless of what bad feelings there may be or who is picking up the bills.

There is an exception to this rule, of course, just as there is to everything. If a woman abandons her child and suddenly shows up just at the time of the wedding, she should not expect to assume her role as mother of the bride—either on the invitations or at the reception—but must defer to the bride's stepmother, who raised her. The natural mother in this case would be present at the wedding as a guest only and would not stand in the receiving line at the reception. (The same holds true for the natural mother or father of an adopted child or for the surrogate mother of the bride if she is invited to the wedding.

- If the bride's first marriage was annulled, she uses her maiden name on her new wedding invitations, just as before.
- Adult children of a widow or divorcée who is remarrying may issue the wedding invitation, as in this example:

> James H. Gibson
> David B. Gibson
> Elizabeth H. Gibson
> request
> the honor of your presence
> at the marriage of their mother
> Evangeline
> to
> Stephen McPherson
> on Saturday, July the fifteenth
> two thousand and ten
> at four o'clock
> Our Lady of Mercy Church,
> St. Louis

The Use of Titles on Invitations

- Using "Esq." on an invitation. If either or both parents of the bride are lawyers who normally use "Esq." after their names, *do not* use it on a wedding invitation.
- When the mother of the bride has a title, her name with title follows her husband's name on the same line:

> *Mr. Andrew Ellison Tate and Dr. Susan Peters Tate*
> *request the honour of your presence*
> *at the marriage of their daughter*
> *Linda Sue*
> *etc.*

• When both husband and wife are doctors, they may issue the invitations in one of two ways:

> *The Doctors Shannon*
> *request the honour of your presence*
> *at the marriage of their daughter*
> *Marilyn Edna*
> *etc.*

or:

> *Dr. Ralph Wolcott Shannon*
> *and Dr. Eve Gaines Shannon*
> *request the honour of your presence*

The above use of "Doctor" refers to medical doctors, not people who hold Ph.D.s. However, it is appropriate for people in academia who hold Ph.D.s to call themselves "Dr." when issuing invitations.

• When the bride herself has a title such as "Doctor" or "Judge" or military rank, she should use it with her full name on the wedding invitation:

> *Mr. and Mrs. Cornelius Robert Jones*
> *request the honour of your presence*
> *at the marriage of their daughter*
> *Grace Ellen Jones*
> *Major, United States Air Force*
>
> *to*
>
> *Mr. Alan Greenberg*
> *etc.*

• The appropriate honorific precedes a very important public dignitary's name on the invitation. In the following example, the mother of the bride is a congresswoman at present who merits the title "The Honourable" before her name on any formal invitation, and who, because of her important official rank, precedes her husband on the invitation:

> *The Honourable Cynthia Wyciekiwiski*
> *and Mr. Stefen Anthony Wyciekiwiski*
> *request the pleasure of your company*
> *at the marriage of their daughter*
> *Annemarie*
> *etc.*

When the Couple Give Their Own Formal Wedding and Reception in a Place of Worship

More and more people are marrying for the first time—as well as for the second and third times—at an older age today, and therefore issue their own wedding invitations, as well as pay for the wedding themselves. Their parents may be retired and living on reduced incomes, while the couple are able to afford the cost of the wedding far better than their parents.

• The woman's name is always placed first on the invitation regardless of whether it is she or he (or the two equally) who is paying the bills for the wedding:

> *Cristina Falchi Bonvento*
> *and*
> *Peter Mark Norgren*
> *request the honour of your presence*
> *at their marriage*
> *etc.*

Neither Cristina Bonvento (whether she is a Miss, Ms., or a Mrs.) nor Peter Norgren needs a title on their own wedding invitations. An optional way of issuing these invitations is as follows:

> *The honour of your presence*
> *is requested at the marriage of*
> *Cristina Falchi Bonvento*
>
> *to*
>
> *Peter Mark Norgren*
>
> *etc.*

• A widow has an option on the wording of the wedding invitation she issues with her husband-to-be:

> *Mary Belle Smith*
>
> *and*
>
> *Gregory Concord Dee*
> *request the honour of your presence*
>
> *etc.*

Or, an older widow, used to using only her former husband's name, might prefer to do this way:

> *Mrs. Peter Philip Smith*
>
> *and*
>
> *Mr. Gregory Concord Dee*
> *request the honour of your presence*
>
> *etc.*

Invitation to a Double Wedding

A sample invitation for two sisters would be:

> *Mr. and Mrs. Anthony Longo Gucci*
> *request the honour of your presence*
> *at the marriage of their daughters*
> *Grace Anne*
>
> *to*
>
> *Mr. Donald White Burton*
>
> *and*
>
> *Jennifer Tod*
>
> *to*
>
> *Mr. George Holland Tree*
> *on Saturday, the tenth of May*
>
> *etc.*

The older daughter is listed first on the invitation.

A sample invitation from two sets of parents to the double wedding of their daughters, who are cousins, would be:

> *Mr. and Mrs. John Wilson Kramer*
> *request the honour of your presence*
> *at the marriage of their daughter*
> *Felicia*
>
> *to*
>
> *Mr. Hans Franz Schmidt*
> *Mr. and Mrs. Gregory Theodore Juergen*
> *request the pleasure of your company*

at the marriage of their daughter

Denise Louise

to

Mr. James O'Neil

Saturday, the twentieth of December

etc.

THE SEPARATE RECEPTION INVITATION CARD

Separate reception invitation cards are often issued when the religious ceremony is held in one place and the reception in another.

An invitation to a "reception immediately following the ceremony" can indicate any of several possibilities. Catholic and Protestant morning weddings are usually followed by a "wedding breakfast," which is really a brunch or a lunch. After a four or five o'clock Christian wedding, a cocktail and hors d'oeuvres reception is usually hosted, while at Jewish Saturday evening weddings, almost always an elaborate meal is served. After a Christian or Jewish six o'clock black tie wedding or a very formal eight o'clock service (before 1960 men used to wear white tie and tails for this), a seated dinner is usually held, with the guests attired in evening clothes.

The reception card inserted in front of the wedding ceremony invitation in the envelope may read as follows:

Reception

immediately following the ceremony

The Waldorf Astoria

The Empire Room

The favour of a reply is requested

Black Tie

• If you plan to serve your guests a meal instead of just a cocktail buffet, say so on the invitation:

> *Lunch Reception [or Luncheon]*
> *immediately following the ceremony*
> *Omaha Country Club*
> *R.S.V.P.*
>
> *139 East Farnam Street*
> *Omaha, Nebraska 00000*

• If you want both the ceremony and the reception (held in different places) to be on the same invitation, it is certainly all right to do so. It makes the invitation less formal. You wouldn't have to include the year, spelled out, for example. Since the invitation is for the wedding in a church and for the reception in another place, you would not use "request the honour of . . ."

> *Mr. and Mrs. Gregory Anthony Jenkins*
> *request the pleasure of your company*
> *at the marriage of their daughter*
> *Evangeline Lee*
> *to*
> *Mr. Stephen Patrick Smyth*
> *on Saturday, the first of June*
> *at five o'clock*
> *Saint Patrick's Church*
> *Seaway Avenue*
> *and at the dinner reception immediately following*
> *The Pavilion Restaurant*
> *1320 Jones Street*
> *Annapolis*
> *R.S.V.P. card enclosed*

When the Reception Is Held Much Later
Than the Ceremony

Sometimes there are too many weddings booked in the desired church on a certain day, and the bride can not obtain the hour she prefers for the ceremony. In this case, she accepts what is given her, everyone comes to the wedding ceremony at the hour stipulated, goes home (or wherever they may be staying) afterward, and then returns to another place for the reception at the specified hour. The invitations for the religious service and for the later reception may be mailed together.

In the case of a daytime service and an evening dinner reception, guests would be dressed in daytime apparel at church and return for the reception in evening clothes. (The wedding party would remain dressed in their special attire for both ceremony and reception.) The card for a later reception following a wedding held at "twelve noon" in a church might read as follows:

Reception Dinner

at eight o'clock

The Mansion

Dallas

R.S.V.P. card enclosed   *Black Tie*

When the Father of the Bride Hosts the Reception
with His Wife, the Bride's Stepmother

When a man remarries and his daughter has a wedding, his present wife, the bride's stepmother, often feels left out. If he is paying for the entire reception, he and his present wife should list their names as hosts of the reception party, and she would act as the proper hostess of the party. However, she should not stand in the receiving line with the bride—the bride's mother should do that—except that if this causes a major battle, the stepfather may stand in the line, too, at the end of the line with the attendants, conveniently away from the bride's mother.

Mr. and Mrs. Jonathan Arnold Miller

request the pleasure of your company

at the marriage reception

of his daughter, Sally Anne

immediately following the ceremony

The Standard Club

Chicago

Reply card enclosed

To Whom Are the Replies Sent When the Bride's Parents Are Divorced?

When the father of the bride and his present wife give the reception, it is silly to demand that the guests reply separately to the bride's mother for the wedding ceremony, and then to the bride's father and present wife for the reception. One reply card is enough, and it should be for the reception.

The reply card for this reception invitation should go to the name and address of whichever divorced parent agrees to be the one most efficient in handling it. This is a time for the mother of the bride and the father of the bride's present wife to bury any animosities (at least for the moment), and to cooperate on the arrangements for the better functioning of the wedding and a happier bride and groom.

If the bride's stepmother and father will be receiving the RSVPs, it is incumbent on the stepmother to make sure the bride's mother knows of every acceptance or regret as it arrives in the mail. If it is decided that the bride's mother will receive all the replies, then it is incumbent on her to inform the bride's father or his wife of the status of the acceptances. No one should feel left out or ignored. It is too important a time in the life of the bride to have infighting over who receives the replies—or handles the wedding gifts. Everything should be worked out in the most efficient manner.

THE CEREMONY CARD

When the major invitation piece will be to the wedding reception and very few people are invited to the religious service, a "ceremony card" should be included in certain invitations. This card is to invite those who are family or are particularly close to the bride and groom to be present at the exchange of vows. (This is particularly appropriate when the bride has been married before.)

A ceremony card enclosed in an invitation simply gives the name, time of ceremony, and address of the place where it will take place:

Ceremony
Saturday, the fifteenth of April
at half after five o'clock
United Methodist Church
3400 Baylor Boulevard
Syracuse

SOLICITING A REPLY TO AN INVITATION

In order to solicit a reply to your invitation, put "R.s.v.p." or "R.S.V.P." or "The favour of a reply is requested" in the lower left-hand corner, with the address beneath. Telephone numbers are not really part of a formal engraved invitation, but sometimes the telephone number and e-mail address are necessary. In the case of a prominent bride and groom for whose wedding several hundred invitations are being extended, it is appropriate to list the bride's mother's telephone, the office of one of the bride's parents, or, in the case of the couple extending the invitations themselves, one of their own office telephone numbers.

The Reply Card

Many (myself certainly included) decry the apparent need for a reply card on which recipients simply check with a pencil in the box to notify their hosts of their acceptance or regret and then mail it back in its preaddressed, sometimes prestamped envelope. However, the "RSVP" card seems obligatory in today's fast-track world. If a reply card and self-addressed envelope are to be included in the invitation, you may engrave in the lower left corner of the wedding invitation: "Reply card enclosed." This removes from the invitation recipient the responsibility to write a formal acceptance or regret note by hand.

The text of a reply card is typically simple and to the point:

> *M/M* _____
>
> *Accept* _____ *Regret* _____
>
> *for the eighth of July*

Some people put "The favour of a reply is requested before the thirtieth of June" (two weeks to ten days before the wedding) on their reply cards, but I feel that is unnecessary. It is simply a testimonial to the fact that the parents of the bride think their guests are so lazy that they have to be jostled into replying before the wedding is upon them.

As for prestamping the return envelope, many of us are at odds with those who feel the return envelope must be stamped before the proposed guest will consider mailing back the reply card. A wedding invitation should not require the hosts to coddle the guests. The guests should feel so privileged to be invited to the wedding that they can at least come up with a stamp for the envelope.

The Formal Acceptance or Regret

The formal acceptance or regret, handwritten and carefully centered on nice stationery, may be disappearing from the social scene, but it is still the really correct way to reply to a wedding invitation. For example:

> Mr. and Mrs. Gregory Samuel Pontius
>
> accept with pleasure
>
> Mr. and Mrs. William Andrew Touletas's
>
> kind invitation
>
> for Saturday, the sixth of May

or

> Mr. and Mrs. Gregory Samuel Pontius
>
> sincerely regret that
>
> their absence from the city
>
> prevents them from accepting
>
> the kind invitation of
>
> Mr. and Mrs. Andrew Touletas
>
> for Saturday, the sixth of May

In the case of extra-busy people, formal acceptances and regrets may be typed by a secretary, rather than handwritten.

When Portions of the Invitation
Are Accepted and Portions Regretted

On occasion, one member of a couple will be able to attend, but not the other. On occasion, a guest will be able to attend the reception but not the ceremony. On a reply card, these variances should be stated by writing a note at the bottom of the card: "Julius Rose accepts with pleasure for the wedding and reception, but because of illness, Mrs. Rose is unable to accept."

In a proper, formally written reply, the wording would be as follows:

> *Mrs. Gregory Samuel Pontius*
>
> *accepts with pleasure*
>
> *Mr. and Mrs. William Andrew Touletas's*
>
> *kind invitation*
>
> *for Saturday, the sixth of May*
>
> *Absence from the city*
>
> *[or illness or whatever]*
>
> *prevents Mr. Pontius from accepting*

"AT HOME" CARDS

When these are sent with the wedding invitations, they simply state the address of the couple and, if they are not already living together, the date after which they will be in joint residence. For example, an "at home" card of a couple who do not live together already might read:

At home

after the fifteenth of January

335 Amory Road

Apartment Fourteen A

Des Moines, Iowa 00000

If you wish, include the telephone number, if it is known at the time. Some people will wait to send their wedding presents to the couple after they are in residence at their new home, so the "at home" address is very useful.

A PEW CARD

Pew cards are a nice touch to include in an engraved invitation to a large church wedding at which a certain number of pews are reserved for special guests down front, on both sides of the church. A pew card would be included in invitations to family members, parents and spouses of the wedding party, and VIPs. The small card would read something like this:

Cathedral of Saint John the Divine

Saturday, the fourth of December

Pew number _____

Present this card to an usher

The number of each family's or guest's pew is written in by hand. These reserved pews will also be recognizable by virtue of special floral decorations or ribbons marking them. The ushers' job is to get the right people into them, according to the list of "special guests" with which each usher is armed.

ADMISSION CARDS

Admission cards are necessary only for the wedding of a supercelebrity, such as a star of the entertainment world or a famous government official, when some kind of control at the church or synagogue doors becomes necessary. Otherwise, the guests might find all their seats taken by curious fans.

> *Please present this card*
> *Unitarian Church*
> *Saturday, the twentieth of May*
> *[Name of guest or couple written here]*

OTHER ENCLOSURES, SUCH AS MAPS AND SPECIAL PARKING INSTRUCTIONS

• A separate card may be included to communicate alternate plans in case of bad weather. For example, if you are planning an outdoor wedding and worry that it may rain, you might enclose an engraved card in the formal wedding invitation that reads:

> *In case of rain*
> *the wedding will be held*
> *in Old Saint Mary's Church*
> *1300 Rosewood Avenue*

• A separate map card may be included if either the church or the wedding reception address is difficult to find. You might think it would be unnecessary to provide separate directions to the reception if the plan is that everyone will be going from the ceremony straight to the reception. You would expect those who don't know the way to follow those who do. However, sometimes people are unable to attend the wedding ceremony, for one reason or another, and go directly to the reception. This is the reason for providing the map.

• An engraved or printed "directions card" is a good idea when a map is not necessary, but exits off freeways and express highways are involved. For example:

From Main Street to Easton:

Take Route 14 to the Southern Beltway.

Go 1¾ miles to Exit 37. Turn right onto Jones Boulevard.

Go 2½ miles to Hathaway Avenue.

Turn left, and enter Grace Church parking lot

immediately on the right.

WEDDING ANNOUNCEMENTS

Wedding announcements, often engraved on the same high-quality ecru stock as wedding invitations, and similar in size, are sent to people who were not invited to the wedding but with whom you want to share your good news. For example, you would send announcements to people who live far away and could not possibly come to your wedding. If you are married with only your family and a very few friends present, you would send announcements to your entire list of friends who ordinarily would have been invited to your wedding. The parents of both bride and groom would also send them to all of their friends, past and present, who were not sent invitations.

You might send an announcement to your former teachers and baby-sitters, your doctor, classmates, business associates, and alumni magazines of any school you attended.

Second-time-around brides find the announcements particularly important as a way of communicating the great news in their lives.

• Recipients of wedding announcements are not expected to send a gift (as those who attend the wedding are). However, many people who feel close to the bride or groom do send gifts—even a small token—to show their pleasure over the news.

• "At home" cards are often included in formal invitations, a separate card giving the couple's address (and telephone number, if desired). The "at home" cards are a perfect way of showing that the bride has kept her own name after marriage, if that is the case. For example:

At home

Martha Renwick Ashton

George Ralston Leigh

1435 Second Avenue

Atlanta, Georgia 00000

000-000-0000

[E-mail, fax number, and cell phone number

may also be included]

Anyone receiving this announcement in the mail will know that the bride has retained her own name.

• For formal engraved announcements, an inner envelope as well as the outer one used for mailing is customary, just as with a wedding invitation.

• For an informal printed announcement, the bride and groom's return address on the envelope removes the necessity for a separate card giving their address.

• It is important to remember that *wedding announcements should not be mailed until immediately after the wedding ceremony.* Many brides ask a friend to be responsible for them and to take them to the wedding in a tote bag—stamped, sealed, addressed, and ready to mail. The friend then goes to the post office to mail them on the way to the wedding reception. Friends who receive the announcements postmarked the day of or the day after the wedding know that the bride and groom had them in their thoughts, and that is what matters.

THE ANNOUNCEMENT TEXT

The announcement text for formal engraved or for printed announcements would be as follows:

Mr. and Mrs. Remigio Grant Ashton
have the honour of announcing
[or have the honour to announce]
the marriage of their daughter
Martha Renwick
to
Mr. George Ralston Leigh
on Sunday, the first of June
two thousand and three
[on informal invitations, the year is given in numbers]
Saint George's Church
Des Moines, Iowa

If the couple are announcing their own marriage, which is often the case with divorced, widowed, or older couples, the text would read:

Mary Simpson Bartlett
Henry Thatcher Jones
have the honour to announce
their marriage
on Saturday, the tenth of January
etc.

Some people send flowery announcements with borders of angels, flowers, musical notes, and the like, and texts such as "We have the joy of announcing happy news we wish to share with you, that we are joined in matrimony," and so on. People are free to do what they please, but you will not find help on sending that kind of announcement in this book!

HOW MUCH WILL IT COST AND WHO WILL PAY?

FIRST, THE BUDGET

In the past, after a couple decided to marry, the groom nervously went to the bride's father to seek her hand in matrimony. Later the wedding would be planned, and a budget would be set by the bride's father, who would be responsible for paying for almost everything.

Today, once both have agreed to wed, the bride's father is consulted only in terms of how much he will pay toward the wedding—certainly not in terms of the young man's asking permission to marry his daughter. Today the rules are no longer strict about the protocol of payment for the wedding. Often the bride's and groom's parents sit around a table and talk about who will (and is able to) pay for what expenses for the upcoming wedding. There is a give and take, which is common sense. There are still some brides whose parents incur tremendous debt by hosting lavish weddings—to give the appearance of being rich and successful—but the majority of weddings today are the result of shared expenses, even including costs borne by the marrying couple.

The budget is important to establish—and adhere to—at the very beginning of the planning activities, because otherwise expenses can get completely out of hand. A wedding can easily cost $100 per guest, $300 per guest, or $1,000 per guest by the time all the expenses are factored into the total amount. If you have three hundred guests, that can add up to a great deal of money!

In drawing up your budget, remember these expenses—some of which occur in any wedding, and some of which occur only in very lavish ones:

The Invitations

Cost of paper, engraving or printing (stationers).
Cost of hand-addressing the envelopes, perhaps by calligraphers.
Cost of postage.

Possible Expenses Involving the Attendants

Paying for their lodging (if they aren't staying with friends).
Paying for the dress and for the airfare of a much-loved bridesmaid or the rental of the usher's suit and the airfare of a much-loved groomsman (who could not afford to be in the wedding otherwise).

Church or Temple Services

Payment to the religious leader who conducted the ceremony.
Payment to the church organist, choir, sexton, and regular staff of the
  house of worship.

The Reception

Rental of room or banquet hall or whatever kind of area.
Preparation and service of food and liquor.
Rental of equipment needed, including tabletop accessories, tables,
  and chairs.
Optional services of party designer or coordinator.
Special linens made for the tables (optional).
Construction of tents for outdoor receptions (including heaters or air-
  conditioners if necessary).

Flowers

For the bride's bouquet.
For the bridesmaids' bouquets and perhaps flower girls' baskets.
Boutonnieres for the groom and male members of the wedding party.
For the church or temple.
For the receiving line area at the reception.
For the tables at the reception.
For decoration of the tent for an outdoor reception.
For the handle of the wedding cake knife.
Corsages for the mothers of the bride and groom (done rarely now, for-
  tunately, since they can ruin the design of a dress).

Photography

Bride's formal portrait made in studio.
Candids of the wedding.
Video recording of the wedding (optional).

Transportation

Limousines to take the bride and groom to and from the ceremony and
  the reception.
Limousines for their families and the bridal party.

Music

In the church or synagogue (organ, choir, chamber music, or other).
At the reception (trio, dance band, or other).

Gifts

From the bride and groom to each other.
Their individual wedding rings.
For their wedding attendants.

Groom's Special Expenses

The cost of the rehearsal dinner the night before the wedding (usually
    given by the groom's parents).
The purchase of the marriage license.
Clergy's fee (often paid for by bride's parents).
Traditionally, the groom paid for the bride's bouquet and his ushers'
    boutonnieres, but it has been proven easier and more efficient to let
    the bride's florist also handle these flowers.
Wedding trip.

PAYING FOR IT

Traditionally, the bride's family bore the brunt of almost all of the wedding
expenses. Today, so many people are getting married at a later age, and so many
people are divorcing and remarrying that these customs are changing. The following are today's options for paying:

• If the groom's family is rich and the bride's is not, the groom's family
pays all or almost all of the expenses, even though the invitations are still sent
out in the bride's parents' names.

• If the bride's family is rich and the groom's is not, the bride's family pays
for everything, including the rehearsal dinner that is customarily the groom's
family's responsibility.

• If the bride's and groom's families both have modest incomes, the
groom's family may offer to pay as big a portion as possible of the wedding
expenses to help out.

• If the bride and groom are both working and in their thirties or older,
their parents may be retired and living on limited incomes. The bride and
groom would pay for their own wedding in this case.

• If the young bride has been divorced and her parents are not in comfortable circumstances, she and her new groom might divide the costs between them.

The important thing to remember is that all details of who pays for what must be ironed out before the wedding is planned! If expenses are to be split between the two families or between the bride and groom themselves (as is often the case in second marriages), it should be recorded in black and white (with a copy for each) as to who is going to be responsible for what.

Another option for a couple splitting the costs of their wedding is to have one person pay all of the bills, with the other member of the couple reimbursing the "treasurer" for half the expenses.

PLANNING FOR A PERFECT WEDDING DAY

CHOOSING THE TIME FOR THE RELIGIOUS CEREMONY

There are special days that are traditional wedding days, such as Saturday for Christians and Saturday evenings or Sundays for people of the Jewish faith. In some Catholic churches, it is considered in questionable taste to be married at a large wedding during Lent. In most religions it is perfectly proper to be married in a religious ceremony on weekdays, but it is difficult for guests who work to be able to attend.

CHOOSING THE PLACE FOR THE WEDDING SERVICE

People get married at home, at city hall, on board ship, and in a judge's chambers. They get married in the bride's family's living room, in a garden, in a hotel parlor, in a public park, or in front of a famous monument. I've even been to a wedding on a grass tennis court. But most often, people marry in a house of worship.

Traditionally, the wedding is held in the bride's or the bride's family's place of worship. Today, with the tremendous mobility of Americans, a bride often finds herself being married in a new city or in a house of worship where neither she nor her family is known. An early discussion with the minister, priest, or rabbi is of paramount importance, because the church or temple may already be booked for the time you'd like for your own wedding. You may have to choose another time of day or even another week for your ceremony. Sometimes there is a great deal of red tape to unravel, so allow plenty of time to accumulate records and perhaps provide copies of everything needed—from birth to baptismal certificates. You both may be required to attend an obligatory marital counseling course—sometimes an all-day session, sometimes classes taking place over a period of several weeks.

Once you have found your house of worship, establish a good pattern of communication with the clergyman or woman. He will be able to give you the rules of his parish regarding certain areas—such as what kind of music you may or may not have and what restrictions there might be on photographers, video cameras, and special lights. He will discuss the kind of service you want to have—and what you may and may not do to alter or add to the official rites of marriage. He will arrange to show the facilities to your wedding co-ordinator or florist, and communicate with them when they should gain access to begin their decoration of the church. He will facilitate on your wedding day the optional laying down of the red carpet ("canopy") from the church door to the curb, and the optional installation of a white "runner." (Just before the bride makes her appearance, two ushers or church employees roll the runner down the aisle on which the bride will walk, each helping guide the huge carpet.

OPTIONS THAT MAKE FOR A HAPPY DAY

You want to make your wedding beautiful, sentimental, and, above all, fun for everyone. And you want your families to be happy, too. All of this can be realized—if everyone gives a little, makes an effort not to voice dissatisfaction with arrangements, and compromises here and there to accede to the bride's and groom's wishes.

As the couple make plans they should realize there are various preferences to take into account that make for a happy day:

• Take into account the strong feelings of both the bride's and groom's parents, because, even though it is *not* their wedding, they may feel it is.

• Take care to invite as guests all those who love you and who would feel deeply hurt not to be included.

• When your parents buck you on your decisions, gently bring them around to your way of thinking, rather than dismiss their suggestions or criticisms out of hand as having no value whatsoever.

• Use your wedding as a great family healer. Tell those members of the family who are estranged that you expect them to be present as full-fledged members of the family circle, with everyone in communication with one another, and with family feuds put to rest.

All too often in weddings one family feels the other family does not have the proper background and educational advantages. The family that feels superior should, to use the vernacular, "sit on it" and keep those feelings in control. The bride and the groom are what matter, not the social prestige and wealth—or lack of it—on one or other side. I remember one mother of the bride who was worried sick that the rehearsal dinner, given by the parents of the groom, would be improperly hosted and embarrassing to the bride's family friends. A sister of the bride cornered her mother and told her to stop being so overwrought: "Mom, let the rehearsal dinner be reflective of the groom's family, and let the wedding be reflective of our family, and then the bride and groom can reflect on one another and forget about all of us!" (A wise philosophy!)

• Become a planning expert in the *human* aspects of your wedding, not just the straight logistics. For example:

   • Arrange to have Aunt Mathilda, who is fragile, picked up at the airport and given VIP treatment during the wedding celebration. Don't expect her to fend for herself.

   • Assign a good friend to introduce your clergy around at the wedding reception and make him or her feel comfortable.

   • Tell a good friend sitting at each table to take home the beautiful centerpiece at that table when the reception is over.

   • Call both sets of parents late, on your wedding night, to tell them how much you appreciate the wedding, how much you love them, and how happy you are.

• Remember that the best way to avoid hurt feelings when you extend your invitations is to establish a firm policy, publicize it, and then stick to it—for example, "It's a very small wedding, only families and a small group of the bridal couple's closest friends."

• A wedding consultant is very helpful for those who would like to turn the entire coordination over to a professional. A wedding consultant or planner knows who the best vendors are and can get the best prices. A wedding consultant does not forget important details, and on the actual wedding day he is supervising everything with a practiced eye—unlike the mother of the bride, who will be busy with her guests. This person may charge a flat fee or may take a percentage of the gross cost of the wedding.

KEEP TRACK OF IMPORTANT DETAILS WITH A WEDDING PLANNER

Devise your own wedding planner to help you get organized. You might buy yourself an ordinary notebook with subdividers, and make yourself entries such as these:

INVITATION LIST

• Include under this heading an *alphabetical list of names and addresses of all recipients of invitations,* with each title correct, and with each word written out (example: "Street" instead of "St.") exactly as the envelope is to be addressed. Give a copy of this list to:

- Yourself, to keep.
- Whoever is addressing the invitations.
- Your parents.
- The groom.
- His parents.

Include this additional information:

- Name of printer or engraver.
- Address of printer or engraver.
- Telephone number.
- Name of your contact with the company.
- Date when you can okay the proof.
- Date when invitations have been promised to be delivered.
- Names of addressers or calligraphers to address envelopes.
- Date when finished envelopes are to be delivered to you.
- Type of stamps purchased, how many purchased.
- Date of mailing of invitations.

Set up two sets of RSVP pages—one to record names of those who accept, one to record those who regret.

The Wedding Party

Put first in this section an *alphabetized list* of members of the wedding party.

Give each attendant his or her own page, and include the following information:

Name _____

Name of spouse or date attending _____

Address and home and office telephone numbers _____

_____

_____

E-mail address _____

Wedding costume

    (1) Size information:

      For bride's attendants:

        Dress size _____ Shoe size _____

      For groom's attendants:

        Pants: Waist _____ Inseam measurement _____

        Coat size _____

        Shirt: Neck _____ Sleeve _____

    (2) Date and hour of fittings _____

Arrival and departure information

Arriving how _____ What day _____ Hour _____

Departing how _____ What day _____ Hour _____

Address and telephone number during wedding festivities _____

_____

Name of parents (if to receive wedding invitation) _____

Address _____

THE WEDDING CEREMONY

Place _____

Clergyman or woman _____

Assistant clergy or secretary _____

Address _____

Telephone number _____

Time and date of rehearsal _____

Time of ceremony _____

    Time for groom and best man to arrive _____

    For ushers _____

    Time for bride's mother to arrive _____

    Bride, attendants, and bride's father _____

Music:

    Soloists or group _____

    Telephone number _____

    Organist's name _____ Telephone _____

Program _____

_____

Flowers:

    Where _____ Type _____

_____

_____

Fees:

    Sexton's _____Clergyman's _____

    Organist's _____ Other musicians' _____

Instructions for photographer(s) during service:

_____

RECEPTION PLANNER FOR A LARGE WEDDING

If you have a wedding consultant, you don't need to make a reception planner. You can take a look at your consultant's planning notebook whenever you wish.

If you are doing your own, you might follow these lists, to work with in conjunction with your caterer.

Protocol Checklist

Staff needed to check in at door _____
No. of tables needed _____
Table cards? _____ In stock _____ To order _____
    No. needed _____ Person in charge _____
Seating charts to be made? _____ Blown up to what size? _____
    By whom? _____
Place cards: No. needed _____ In stock or to be ordered _____
    Names to be: Handwritten _____ Typed _____
    Done in calligraphy _____
    Person responsible _____
Menu cards: No. needed _____ Handwritten _____
    Typed _____ Calligraphy and offset _____
    Person responsible _____
Person in charge of seating _____ Tel. _____
Receiving Line: Where? _____ Names (in order of standing in line)

    _____
    _____
    _____

Will there be an introducer at the reception? _____
Name _____ Tel. _____
Names and tel. of "party workers"

    _____   _____
    _____   _____

No. of copies of guest list required _____

Caterer's Checklist

Name _____ Address _____
Contact _____ Tel. No. _____

	Food to be served	Liquor, wines, nonalcoholic drinks to be served
Cocktail	_____	_____
Hour	_____	_____
	_____	_____
	_____	_____

Dinner _____   _____
         _____   _____
         _____   _____
         _____   _____
         _____   _____

After
Dinner _____   _____
(in the _____   _____
tent) _____   _____

Help hired:

    No. in kitchen _____ No. of waiters and waitresses _____

    Coat checkers _____ Valet parkers _____

    Rest room attendants _____

Rest rooms:

    Suitable for guests? _____

Need guest soaps, guest towels? _____

Are portable facilities necessary? _____

Extra security:

    Necessary? _____ Will caterer provide? _____

    No. needed _____

Name of outside company handling _____

    Contact _____ Tel: _____

Flowers:

    Room decor plans _____

    Table centerpieces _____ No. _____

    Style of container _____

TRANSPORTATION ARRANGEMENTS

Name of car service: _____ Contact _____ Tel.: _____

Buses needed:_____

    For which date and hours? _____

Rehearsal		
Dinner	Pickup Points:	Riders' Names
Date: 1. _____		_____
_____ 2. _____		_____
Address: 3. _____		_____
_____ 4. _____		_____

Hour: _____ _____

Wedding Day   Date:

To the

Church   Pickup Points   Car No.   Riders

Address: 1. _____ _____ _____

_____ 2. _____ _____ _____

Hour: 3. _____ _____ _____

____ 4. _____ _____ _____

5. _____ _____ _____

6. _____ _____ _____

To Reception Riders   Riders

Address: Car 1: _____   _____

_____ Car 2: _____   _____

_____ Car 3: _____   _____

Car 4: _____   _____

_____   _____

_____   _____

WORKING WITH THE CATERER

When you hear that a caterer's meal costs $150 per person, remember that the sum represents not only her profit and the cost of the food and its preparation, but also the service of it and the rental of equipment involved in the serving of it. It never ceases to amaze me how one can eat the same delicious menu at two separate wedding receptions and find one caterer has charged the bride's parents $250 per person, while the other has charged the bride's parents $75 per person. The expense of doing business in a particular location, the cachet of the name of the more expensive caterer, plus perhaps an extra measure of style in service all add to the price of the food.

Remember to add service charges and tax onto the prices you are quoted by the caterer so that you will understand what your true charges will be. Generally a service charge of up to 20 percent is added to your bill (as well as sales tax). If you were *very* well pleased with the reception, arrange to have the director of operations and the captains receive an extra tip of $20 to $50.

The caterer will provide coat checking facilities, if you request those. Some caterers even handle such details as the music, the entire floral and table design of the party, including the lighting, and the organization of valet parking.

The best way to find a great caterer is by word of mouth. When you are ready to settle on the firm, look carefully at the samples of their rented equipment, including the kinds of chairs they will provide for your guests at the table, the style of their serving platters, the color and condition of their table linens, and the quality of their glassware, china, and flatware. Sample what they suggest for your menu, so that you know exactly what will be served and how it will be presented. Most caterers will prepare free tastings for you at their establishment. It's preferable not to hand them recipes of dishes you would like served, because without the caterer's having practiced those dishes several times before, the results could be unsatisfactory, if not disastrous. Have your caterer prepare the kind of food he knows how to serve with a flourish.

- Be sure you understand everything written down in the contract before you sign it. Know what all the costs of equipment rental will be. Read the fine print about the cancellation charges. (Sadly enough, some weddings are called off at the last minute, for one reason or another.)
- Since the cost of drinks and wines is a major part of the contract, make sure the contract stipulates that *quality brands* are to be served. Otherwise, you might find Uncle Freddie's Homestyle Bourbon and Platinum Star Plus scotch being served at your open bars instead of the recognizably good brands.
- Be sure there will be enough waiters or waitresses to serve your guests. New York's Glorious Foods, one of the top catering firms in the world, believes that the food cannot be served properly and at the right temperature if there are not at least one and a half to two waiters per table of eight or ten people. For a cocktail buffet for a hundred people, they feel five waiter/bartenders plus a working captain are needed to handle the crowd. The number of people serving is of paramount importance, because if guests have to struggle to get a drink and if the meal service is interminably slow, the wedding reception will be considered a flop.

THE FOOD AT THE RECEPTION

Whether you hire a caterer or make other arrangements, the food you serve your guests should be:
- Delicious
- Plentiful
- Unusual—or at least not exactly like every other reception in town
- Beautifully presented
- Hot when it should be hot, cold when it should be cold

Wonderful wedding reception food is not stereotyped; there is no traditional wedding fare today. Instead, there is as much variety in the choices as there is in the bride's family's tastes. You can be as imaginative as you wish—within the limits of your budget and the capabilities of the team preparing the food. I have enjoyed an extraordinary clambake wedding reception at the beach (steamed clams and clam broth, roast corn, boiled lobsters), and a delicious roast goose with cornbread pudding at a wedding lunch in snow-blanketed mountains. I have delighted in the taste of perfectly prepared couscous and lamb at an Arab reception; I have savored vegetarian sandwiches served with pink lemonade at a reception in Ohio on a hot summer's day. It was all *wonderful*.

Planning the Menu

The menu for your reception should suit:
- The budget of whoever is paying for it.
- The time of day when the food is served. (A breakfast requires a very different menu from a dinner.)
- The region of the country. (The menu might feature fresh fish at a Cape Cod wedding, Creole dishes in New Orleans, a barbecue in Texas, on a special ham dish in Georgia.)
- The degree of formality of the wedding. (You might serve paella for a reception on an outdoor patio in Arizona, but you would not serve it at a formal dinner in a large city hotel.)
- The ethnic preferences, if any, of the couple to be married.

There are simple nonalcoholic receptions held in the parish hall of a small church after the wedding ceremony; there are celebration picnics set up on a grassy knoll after an outdoor service; there are Chinese, Indian, Italian, Greek, and Mexican banquets served in restaurants; and there are five-course dinners served in hotel and club ballrooms after services in large cathedrals or temples. All of them owe part of their success to careful planning of the menu.

Breakfast

If your wedding reception will be a breakfast following an early morning service, while you are greeting your guests (and before anyone sits down to eat) have your guests offered a tray with their choice of plain fruit juices including cranberry juice, sparkling water, Mimosas (champagne in orange juice), and Bloody Marys (vodka in tomato juice). You might serve a menu like the following:

Creamed chicken crepes
Broiled tomatoes stuffed with pâté, crushed bacon, or grilled mushrooms with herbs

Hot brioches, croissants, bran muffins, and biscuits with a choice of but-
ter, honey, jam, and cream cheese
Hot baked fruit with optional whipped cream
Wedding cake (with which coffee and tea are always served)

By the time the bride and groom cut the cake, it will probably be close to noon. Have champagne served to each guest who wishes it, for toasting purposes and for consumption along with the wedding cake.

An Informal Reception in the Parish Hall or Rectory

Fruit punch (with or without alcohol)
Sandwiches, including cream cheese on orange bread, smoked salmon
and dill in puff pastry, pesto tartlets, and sliced turkey on tiny hot
biscuits with cranberry chutney
Ice cream and wedding cake

A Three-Course Lunch

Cold potage St. Germain (cream of pea soup)
Chicken breasts Véronique (with mushrooms, white wine, and seedless
grapes)
Puree of spinach in avocado halves
Endive and arugula salad vinaigrette
Frozen mocha mousse and wedding cake
White wine until dessert; champagne served with dessert

A Four-Course Dinner

Stracciatella soup (chicken broth with beaten egg)
Salmon timbales (small molds of salmon mousse with hollandaise sauce)
Roast loin of pork with hot prune sauce
Green beans
Baby carrots
Banana sherbet and wedding cake
Champagne served throughout the meal

Of course, if you are among the very rich, you can have a "simple" wedding lunch of only three courses, like that of Mercedes Kellogg and Texas billionaire Sid Bass when they were married at the Plaza Hotel in New York in

December 1988. Their menu cards read at the top, "Celebrating the marriage of Mercedes and Sid Bass." The menu consisted of:

*Caviar de Beluga aux Blini (accompanied by vodka and a Pouilly Fumé
    La Doucette 1985 white wine)*
Carré d'Agneau Rôti au Romarin
Gratin de Pommes de Terre Dauphinois
Flageolets (served with Château Latour 1982)
Soufflé Glacé aux Pralines
Coulis de Poires
Gâteau de Mariage (served with Krug Rosé champagne)
Café

This menu translates to lots of fresh caviar, lamb chops with potatoes au gratin and white beans, and an ice-cream praline soufflé with wedding cake.

At the opposite end of the financial scale, at a wedding lunch held the same day in another part of New York, the menu read:

Cream of asparagus soup with croutons
Spinach-filled ravioli
Salad vinaigrette
Ice cream with chocolate sauce
Wedding cake and coffee
One red wine served throughout

No one could say which lunch was the more delicious.

"Grazing"

During this kind of reception, some small tables with chairs are set up at random, but the majority of guests dance or stand and talk, eating off little plates with food selected from the buffet. In most cases, guests consider the ample choice of hors d'oeuvres their evening meal.

It's very important to instruct the waiters to keep the buffet table replenished and to keep picking up used glasses, plates, and silverware from around the entire party area as guests come and go. The kinds of grazing foods that might be found at this kind of reception:

*Small open-face rye bread sandwiches with rare roast beef, topped with
    a thin layer of horseradish sauce*
*Crudités (fresh vegetables, mostly raw, but some of which—like broccoli
    and cauliflower florets—are lightly steamed) with a dip of choice*

*Small sandwiches (crusts removed) with any kind of filling (for example,
    mushroom paste; shrimp mashed with mayonnaise, shallots, capers,
    and seasoning; red caviar and sour cream)*
Shrimp and crab claws
Poached salmon with a dill sauce
Platter of assorted cheeses and crackers
*Broiled water chestnuts wrapped in bacon on toothpicks (must be
    served piping hot)*
Curried crabmeat tarts
Turkey bouchées (turkey salad in tiny pastry shells)
A pâté of choice
Sliced baked ham
Prosciutto and fresh figs on toothpicks
A cold pasta or rice salad
Bowlfuls of balls of different flavors of sherbet
Wedding cake
Coffee
Champagne served throughout

THE PRESENTATION IS IMPORTANT

Often, all you have to do is explain to the caterer or the hotel banquet manager that you care very much how the food is presented, whether it is individually served by waiters or whether it is presented on the buffet table on platters. For example, it looks pleasing to the eye when:

• A large cold fish, its skin removed, is embellished on its side with a flowering branch (made with fresh dill and vegetable flowers).

• A container of pâté is beautified with geometric designs or even the bridal couple's monogram, made from scallions and sweet red peppers.

• A fresh green sprig of an herb lies across the face of half a hard-boiled egg.

• A bunch of marinated beans is tied like a bunch of logs with a strip of pimiento.

• A hollowed-out cucumber boat carries a cargo of Salade Niçoise.

• A baked half acorn squash is filled with anything from paprika-sprinkled hot creamed chicken to pasta al pesto.

• A grilled skewer is made colorful with cubes of lamb or chicken alternating with slices of red pepper, yellow squash, and green zucchini.

• A mound of yellow molded rice is decorated with a garland of Chinese pea pods, mushroom halves, and cherry tomatoes.

• A large roast on a platter is framed in clusters of fresh (not overcooked) decorative vegetables and watercress.

• Poached pears swim in a creamy custard sauce, each pear topped by a sugar violet or other candied flower.

• A mound of butter pecan ice cream, sprinkled with powdered cocoa, sits on a plate covered half in caramel, half in chocolate sauce (the two sauces meeting in the middle).

THE WEDDING CAKE

Fresh flowers are often used on today's wedding cakes. New York's famous wedding cake baker Sylvia Weinstock finds that most brides ask for a chocolate layer cake with chocolate filling, a chocolate hazelnut torte cake with mocha praline filling, or a yellow cake filled with apricots and Grand Marnier liqueur. Brides are getting away from the more traditional—and boring—white cake with white frosting.

It is a nice tradition, however, to have the decoration of a first-time bride's cake all in white. (Second- and third-time-around brides should properly have cakes decorated with touches of color.)

The wedding cake deserves its own skirted table, which can be wheeled into the center of the room when the bride and groom cut the cake. This multitiered carrot cake with marzipan frosting, decorated with fresh flowers, was made by Cheryl Kleinman for our daughter Clare's wedding.

Be sure, when ordering your wedding cake specially made, to have good references from other satisfied clients of the cake maker and to have seen color photographs of her work. It is preferable to order the exact design you liked in a photograph.

FLOWERS

Sometimes a floral designer rather than a wedding consultant is the mainstay of the wedding organization. Sometimes a floral designer is hired by the wedding consultant as part of her coordinating duties.

A good florist is one thing; a good floral designer is another. He will first survey the premises for every single place that will need flowers or greenery (including the wedding cake), then work with the bride and her parents in drawing up a proposal and budget. After that the bride's family can relax.

Some of these professionals design the entire wedding, not just the flowers. Sometimes they buy their flowers in the wholesale market; sometimes they stock and retail flowers themselves. If you choose a floral designer to do your wedding in conjunction with your own planning endeavors, be sure to find one of excellent reputation. Word of mouth is very important or, as with a caterer whose food you may have enjoyed at someone's big party or wedding, a floral designer may have done a very impressive party that you or a friend of yours attended recently.

Be sure that the floral designer employs a sufficient number of staff.

Flowers are an important item—not only for the church, but in the bride's and her attendants' bouquets, tucked into the men's lapels, decorating the place of the religious service, centering the tables at the reception, and embellishing the tent or the room where the reception is held. They are a major factor in the wedding budget.

• It is possible to hold down the budget for the flowers at the reception by using few flowers and a lot of greenery in the centerpiece and in the arrangement on the serving table. Tall plants or even trees in tubs can be rented to flank the receiving line and to disguise ugly parts of the room. I was once helping a bride by putting the place cards on the tables for her dinner reception in a hotel ballroom when I noticed the distress of the floral designer, who had just seen the bandstand put in place. "This is the ugliest bandstand I have *ever* seen," he said. He disappeared for half an hour, returned with tall flowering quince branches in glass vases, put these on the floor in front of the bandstand, and suddenly you couldn't see it anymore.

• It is a nice touch, of course, if the flowers are integrated into the design scheme of the whole wedding, so that the colors repeat those of the bridesmaids' dresses, the linens used at the reception, and other color-coordinated items. I remember a reception lunch at which people sitting at the round tables noticed suddenly that the flowered tablecloths repeated the design theme of the wedding. There were large white flowers printed on the fabric (the same flowers carried by the bride in her bouquet), and there were small yellow, pale blue, and peach-colored flowers in the rest of the fabric design—the same flowers and colors as in the bridesmaids' dresses and in their bouquets, and in the flowers of our table centerpieces. There were peach napkins and peach linen seats on our chairs. It was all beautifully thought out and executed.

•   The bride should have as large or as small a bouquet as she wishes. She can carry a white prayer book with streamers or an armful of calla lilies. This is the time for her to have the loveliest flowers in the world—her own fantasy fulfilled.

The bride's bouquet, symbolic of all that is beautiful in a wedding, may be all white or touched with pastel colors. It should be beribboned so that its effect, sailing through the air at the end of the wedding when the bride tosses her bouquet to the next young lady to be married, looks all the more sensational. This is our daughter Clare's wedding bouquet, by floral designer Ann McIlvaine.

BRIDESMAIDS' BOUQUETS

The bridesmaids' bouquets, of course, are an integral part of the design of the wedding. They are usually less costly if chosen to reflect the season of the year, such as peonies in May, mums and autumn leaves in the fall, and white, pink, or red poinsettias at Christmas. In today's shipping-by-jet world, you can have any out-of-season flowers you want from anywhere—so long as someone can pay for it!

BOUTONNIERES

The men in the wedding party wear boutonnieres in their left lapels. The bridegroom's and the best man's might be based on the flowers in the bride's bouquet, such as a pink rose with a sprig of stephanotis. The boutonnieres of the ushers and the fathers of the bride and groom might be different, such as carnations, roses of a different color, or lilies of the valley.

PHOTOGRAPHY REQUIREMENTS

THE BRIDE'S PORTRAIT

It is nice to have a formal full-length portrait made for posterity. It should be shot in a photo studio, showing the bride in all her regalia (in color or in black and white). This photograph (eight by eleven inches or eleven by fourteen inches) might be given by the bride as a present, framed, to her husband to grace their own home, as well as to both sets of parents and grandparents for their homes. The maid of honor will want a smaller one (five by six inches) of her best friend or her relative, in a double frame, with a photograph of the entire wedding party on the other side of the frame. The groom may well want an additional smaller one of the bride for his office.

The bride's actual bouquet of flowers will not be shown in this formal photograph, because she's holding a photogenic fake one supplied by the photographer's studios. It doesn't matter, but what does matter is that her hair and veil be shown in the photograph exactly as they will be on her wedding day.

This is usually the photograph the society section of the local newspaper requests for their Sunday or Wednesday bridal section (in an eight by eleven-inch black-and-white glossy form) although many newspapers now request an informal photo of the bride and groom taken together on their wedding day.

THE CANDID PHOTOGRAPHER

The candid photographer handles the most important part of your wedding—the official record. Whatever you do, use a professional to take your candid pictures. If a well-meaning friend or relative volunteers to assume the role of official wedding photographer, she might make disastrous amateur mistakes. Also, when the volunteer is socializing with family and friends and enjoying the reception, pictures of the really important people are forgotten.

In the Church

Many houses of worship will not allow cameras flashing during the services. Some will allow the photographer to come up the aisle only twice—once to photograph the bride and groom at the altar, and once to catch them on their way out, walking joyfully to the back of the church as man and wife. Sometimes the photographer can perch in the choir loft and capture important parts of the ceremony noiselessly and inconspicuously with a long lens. If you intend to have a video camera recording everything, be sure to get permission of the clergy before it is used at your wedding ceremony. And please, only one video camera!

Group Photos

Usually the wedding party is photographed at the place where the reception is to be held, just before all the guests arrive from the church services. The members of the wedding party and the parents should be well warned ahead of time that this is a priority project and that nothing must interrupt it once everyone has arrived at the reception area.

- The entire group should be photographed together (no glasses in hands, please).
- The bride and groom should be photographed with each set of parents.
- The bride should be shown with all her bridal attendants.
- The groom should be shown with his attendants.

Covering the Festivities

Instruct your photographer well before the wedding. Give him a list of the members of the wedding party and all relatives and out-of-town guests. Assign a friend who knows everyone to help scout the important people for pictures at the wedding reception, and to stay at the photographer's side. Go over the wedding schedule with the photographer in advance, so that he knows what must be covered. Here are some suggestions:

- The bride getting dressed.
- Hugging her mother before her mother or a beloved relative leaves for the church.
- Talking to her little sister.
- Chatting with her father in the limousine on their way to the church.
- Any pictures of the groom and best man behind the scenes at the church before the ceremony begins.
- Photos of the ushers in action.
- Guests going through the receiving line.
- The first dances.
- Bride and groom in first dance.
- Bride and groom kissing wherever and whenever.

- Father dancing with bride; groom dancing with bride's mother.
- Bride tossing bouquet.
- Groom tossing garter (Many think this custom needs to be dropped).
- Couple pelted with rice or flower petals as they leave.
- Kissing parents and friends good-bye as luggage is loaded into their car.
- Waving good-bye from back window of getaway car.

Of course, if the couple has been living together for the past five years, some of the above photos are unnecessary.

Logistics and Payment for Candids

Usually the photographer presents you with a book of proofs of all the photographs, and you order desired prints by number. The bride's parents are supposed to make a gift of eight to ten photographs to the groom's family, but usually the latter will want many more than that. The best way to handle it is to let the bride's parents and the groom's parents handle their own orders for everyone in their families, and then let each side pay the photographer directly for their prints. It is a gracious gesture to send each member of the wedding party an eight by ten-inch photograph of the group—but then it is also gracious to allow each member of the wedding party or close family members to view the book of proofs and to order (and incidentally pay for) additional photographs.

A Wedding Pictures Album

It is a very nice gesture if a family member purchases three attractive photo albums to hold the various wedding photographs and presents one to the bride and groom; one to the parents of the bride; and one to the parents of the groom. Each album should be lettered with the couple's name or initials and the date of their wedding. It becomes a treasured keepsake to be handed down to future generations.

MUSIC

If there is going to be dancing at the reception, the music will be as important as the food—maybe even more so. The music sets the ambience and motivates people to mix and dance with each other. People suddenly feel good. Romances start at weddings. Music makes the party come alive. Music that people only listen to while they dine is background for real conversation.

The choice of your music for the religious service is one thing. (See page 325.) Your choice of music for the reception is quite another. First, you must decide: Do you want to have music to listen to rather than dance to at your reception? This is often the case for a morning wedding followed by breakfast or lunch.

For your listening music, do you want a chamber music group? A pretty young harpist? A pianist singing sophisticated, low-key love songs? A jazz combo of guitarist, bass, and pianist playing Cole Porter, Steven Sondheim, and George Gershwin softly in the background?

If you have retained one of the orchestras of the great bandleaders, you know what kind of music they are going to play. If you hire a band that plays South American music, you know what you're going to get. What matters is your own choice. I went to a June wedding where the bride and groom, who had recently taken lessons to learn how to waltz, hired a waltz orchestra, and that was a tremendous hit with the guests. The older guests waltzed the night away, while the younger guests—those who hadn't taken lessons—improvised.

The following week I attended the outdoor wedding of my niece Megan Baldrige to Craig Murray, at my brother Mac's and sister-in-law Midge's farm in Woodbury, Connecticut. Mac was the Secretary of Commerce in the Reagan administration in those days, but his heart was always in the ranchlands, not in the protocol caverns of our nation's capital. There was nonstop dance music provided by Bob Mobilio and his Waterbury band, alternating with a bunch of cowboys who drove up in their old bus all the way from Coleman County, Texas. The latter group was headed by Red Steagall and his country and western band, well-known musicians on the rodeo circuit but totally unknown on the formal wedding circuit. The wedding guests danced sedately and happily to Mobilio's great beat, then lost every inhibition while stomping to the cowboys' music.

• If you want music for dancing, before hiring the group, either listen to it live or listen to its recordings. Look at the outfits the musicians plan to wear (and make them rent alternative clothing if the look is not right). Make sure the orchestra leader knows the kind of music you want played. Perhaps you could strike a deal with your daughter (or, if you are the bride, with your mother) to have a rock band play softly during the seated meal, and then let the amplifiers on the sound system be turned up several decibel points while the young really take to the floor after dinner.

• If you want a conga line at your wedding reception, have a conga line. But make sure the band you hire plays conga music and that there's someone who knows what he is doing to organize the line. Conga lines are out of fashion at the moment, but they can pop back into popularity in an instant.

TRANSPORTATION

If you are planning a high-budget wedding and will transport the wedding party in limousines to and from the rehearsal dinner, as well as to the church and to the reception on the wedding day, or if you are planning a small wedding and will ask friends to help out by transporting the wedding party in their private cars, make the plans well ahead. Put a transportation sheet in your wedding planner and keep it current.

Today many families hold down costs by ordering one limousine to transport the bride and her father from home to the church or temple, and then to transport the bride and groom from the ceremony to the reception. The rest of the wedding party travels by sedans provided by the limousine service or by cars driven by friends, or by a combination of both.

• If you are dealing with a limousine company, send them a typed list of the names of all the people who are supposed to be in any one car at any one time, going to each location. Give them specific times. Make sure the best man has a copy of this sheet, as well as the bride's parents, because among them, they should see that everything goes smoothly. Each member of the wedding party should know the number of the car in which she is supposed to ride every time there is a movement of people from one place to another.

• It is very nice if, at the conclusion of the religious services, there is a bottle of champagne well chilled in an ice bucket in the back of the limo—plus two champagne glasses—for the bride and groom on their ride from the church to the reception. (The limo service will handle that, or the best man or the father of the bride can make it happen.)

WEDDING ATTENDANTS

THE BRIDE'S ATTENDANTS

You need only one attendant for your wedding, but if you are having a big wedding, several more are certainly appropriate. Since a first wedding is such an exciting event in your life—and in the lives of your friends, too—you might wish a scenario like this:

• Ten bridesmaids (we are talking about a wedding for 350 guests or more), including:
• Matron of honor.
• Maid of honor.
• Junior bridesmaid (a sister or a little cousin from age nine to thirteen).
• A ring bearer (a nephew aged three to five) or little boy pages or both.
• One or two flower girls (nieces or children of good friends perhaps, ages

three to five). Some couples are now imitating European weddings and having five or six small children (all related in some way) as junior attendants. They are adorable scene-stealers.

An easily manageable number of bridesmaids for a normal-sized wedding (up to 150 guests) is anything up to six. Don't forget that each out-of-town attendant requires a complicated logistical support system (such as having her met when she arrives in town, and transporting, housing, feeding, and entertaining her for three or four days). When a bride has an overly large number of bridesmaids, they begin to look like a line of Rockettes from New York's Radio City Music Hall. (One wedding I attended recently included fifteen bridesmaids, and the guests, I noticed, spent all their time comparing the height, physiques, and hairstyles of the bridesmaids—completely forgetting to look at the bride!)

If you have only one attendant, she may be single or married. Normally you invite a sister close in age or your best single friend to be your maid of honor, and a sister or a close married friend to be your matron of honor. (Your matron of honor, by the way, today may be a widow or a divorcée, a departure from the previous era.)

In deciding on your other attendants, you might choose a sister of the groom and some of your close friends. There is often a dilemma in trying to pick from among your old chums from childhood in your hometown versus your close friends at work. Your attendants' ages should be close to your own, so if you are in your early twenties, don't feel you have to invite someone in her thirties or older to be in your wedding. If you have to leave out good friends who you know feel they should have been asked to be attendants, talk to them about it. Tell them how much their friendship means to you. Give them important tasks to do in your wedding; make sure they're invited to the wedding parties, if possible. Brief your parents on what to say to make your friends feel they are part of your wedding, even if not actually attendants.

The Pregnant Bridesmaid

A very pregnant bridesmaid can't find a dress to fit, in the first place; in the second place, guests will be distracted from the bride—wondering when the baby is due, whether it's a boy or a girl, if the baby is kicking inside right now, and so forth. A good friend of the bride who will be very far along in her pregnancy on the wedding date should, in my opinion, take it upon herself not to accept the bridesmaid role. The bride in turn can include her friend in all of her wedding events, consider the friend a member of the wedding party even if she doesn't march down the aisle with the others, and have her stand with the bridal party in the group wedding picture. In this way, anyone looking at the picture will realize that the "pregnant one" is an honorary attendant who would have been dressed as a member of the wedding party if her blessed event had not been so imminent.

Bridesmaids' Duties

Between them, the matron and maid of honor should organize with the other attendants the bridesmaids' party that is optionally given for the bride on the same night the bachelor dinner is held for the groom. The lead attendants also organize the joint gift for the bride (which entails the selection of the gift, the solicitation of the money, the possible engraving of the object). They also run errands to assist the bride before her wedding and help her get dressed on the wedding day. They make sure her "going-away" costume and honeymoon luggage are safely ensconced in the room at the reception place where she will dress after she and her groom leave the party. And they see to it that her white dress and veil are taken safely back to her home when she and her husband have left. In general, the bridesmaids help make the wedding a success by assisting the mother of the bride with whatever needs doing and by being gracious to all the guests, particularly the couple's relatives. Of course, today so many of these bridal couples have been living together for some time before the wedding, the attendants have little to do and are important only for ceremonial purposes in the wedding procession.

THE GROOM'S ATTENDANTS

The groom has only one honor attendant—his best man—who is often his brother or best friend, sometimes even his father. (The father acting for his son is part of tradition, but recently, in an overreaction to the women's movement, there have been examples of mothers serving as their daughters' only attendant, too.) The groom should try to match the number of bridesmaids with ushers, but if he has fewer attendants than his bride, it really does not make any difference.

The Best Man

To be asked to be someone's best man is an honor that is not to be refused, if possible. The job carries responsibilities, too, for helping bring off a smoothly run wedding. The groom should pick as his best man not only a brother or a close friend, but someone who is gregarious, aware, and a good manager. He should be an expert, briefing the ushers and making sure they know what to do and when to do it. He should have eyes in the back of his head so as to be aware when anyone from the mother of the bride to the maid of honor might need assistance. If someone becomes drunk and abusive at the wedding reception, if the groom loses his suitcase, if the bride's family runs out of champagne and needs someone to make a quick trip to the liquor store, the best man should see that it's taken care of.

The main job of the ushers consists of escorting lady guests up the aisle to their seats for the ceremony—and in general overseeing the seating of all the guests for the services. They should have been thoroughly instructed about special seating arrangements. They should have been briefed on the guest list by the best man, who has been briefed by the couple's parents. They should be clear on who sits where, who's important, and who needs special attention. ("Great-Grandma Mullens is ninety-four years old and totally deaf. She'll keep shouting 'What?' at you, but don't try to answer. Just take her up the aisle and put her in the second row, right-hand side.")

• The best man communicates with the ushers and makes sure they show up for the fittings on their wedding suits. The best man organizes the groom's attendants' joint present to the groom. During one of the days prior to the wedding, he helps the groom organize the optional bachelor dinner (at which the groom's gifts to his ushers and the ushers' gift to the groom are exchanged). He should also make sure the groom emerges from any mayhem that may occur at this party unscathed and in good physical shape.

• On the wedding day, the best man helps the groom get dressed. He makes sure he has the bride's wedding ring in his pocket in order to be able to give it to the groom at the proper moment in the service. If the groom, not the bride's family, is paying the clergy and church fees, the best man makes sure the money is in envelopes in his possession, ready for the groom to present just prior to or after the ceremony. He makes certain the wedding license has been brought to the church. If the wedding has a ring bearer, he brings a penknife to cut the threads to release the ring. (A less *risky* solution to making sure the rings are taken care of can be found on page 331.)

• He helps the mother of the bride coordinate all the limousines and family cars that may be put to use to carry people to the church, to the reception, and away from the reception.

• The best man also sees to it that the ushers have their wedding ties and boutonnieres in place, have their gloves (if gloves are to be worn), and have their seating lists in hand, and he ensures that they get to the church an hour before the ceremony. He also makes sure he and the groom reach the church twenty minutes to a half hour before the ceremony is to begin.

• The best man leads off with the first toast to the bride at the rehearsal dinner and at the reception. He not only starts the toasting but regulates the order of toasting that follows. He already has in his pocket a list of those who have agreed to be called on to give a toast. The groom and the family members give their toasts first. The best man gives everyone in the wedding party their cues. I have seen best men send scribbled messages to toasters, telling them to sit down when, as a result of having drunk too much, they rambled on boringly and aimlessly. The best man usually succeeds in his mission. I remember one night when a college roommate of the groom was giving a stupid, drunken, and endless toast. He didn't have his glasses and couldn't read the best man's note to him when it was given to him. Thereupon the best man rose and took over the microphone. He read as follows: "This note says 'Finish and sit down—now.'" (The toaster did just that amid great laughter.)

• The best man helps get everyone in the wedding party into a group for an official posed photograph. These photos are usually taken either immediately after the ceremony or at the place of the reception before the other guests start arriving from the church. When the wedding party has arrived ahead of everyone else, it is usually the *only* time the entire group is available for the photograph.

• Besides organizing the toasting at the reception, the best man makes sure the ushers perform their duty dances (with the bride, mother of the bride, grandmother of the bride, little sister of the bride, and all the bridesmaids).

• He oversees the transfer of the luggage to the getaway car, makes sure the groom has the airplane tickets, and that everything goes according to plan for the departure of the couple from the wedding reception to begin their honeymoon.

The Role of the Ushers

If there is an equal number of men and women attendants in the wedding, the ushers escort the bridesmaids back down the aisle at the conclusion of the ceremony. If there are fewer ushers than bridesmaids, the unescorted bridal attendants walk down the aisle in pairs behind the attendant couples

The ushers are usually the age of the groom and comprise his own brothers, perhaps a brother of the bride, and his best friends. Since their main duty is to seat guests for the religious ceremony (and give the bridesmaids a good time during the parties), a family member who is to be an usher should be at least a mature seventeen- or eighteen-year-old.

At a very small wedding, it is nice to include a young usher of ten or older—especially if it is the bride's or bridegroom's child by a previous marriage.

THE REHEARSAL

One or two nights before the actual ceremony in the church or temple, a rehearsal should be scheduled with the officiating clergy. Everyone practices walking up the aisle, and the service is briefly described, so that the wedding party knows what to do, and so that the pageantry is unified and dignified. The organist or at least one member of the musical group to play during the service should be present for the rehearsal to learn the music cues, too. When the rehearsal takes place on the night before the wedding, generally it is scheduled at a time like 5 P.M. before the wedding party attends the rehearsal dinner.

THE REHEARSAL DINNER

This party, usually hosted by the groom's parents, but also optionally hosted by a relative or even a good friend of either the groom or bride, or by the couple themselves if they are paying for their wedding, may be as formal or as informal as the couple wishes it. Separate invitations are mailed for this dinner to members of the wedding party, the relatives of the bride and groom, and to close friends who are coming from out of town for the festivities. The rehearsal dinner may be anything from a black tie dinner in a hotel or restaurant to a barn dance or a picnic in the park. It can be a hamburger dinner at the ice-skating rink or a cookout on the beach. It is meant to be fun, and usually the best toasting of the bridal pair occurs on this evening.

A sample invitation for an informal rehearsal dinner and an evening of lake sailing follows:

Peter Parkinson

cordially invites you

to the Rehearsal Dinner

for Mary Beth Brown

and his godson Peter Wentworth, Jr.

Friday, June twenty-third

at four o'clock

"Gull Lodge"

23 North Lake Road

Lake Minnetonka

R.s.v.p.   *Sailing before and after dinner*

000-000-0000   *Dress: Shorts, slacks, sweaters, boat shoes*

THE WEDDING DAY ARRIVES!

GETTING TO THE CHURCH

Just before the ceremony is to start, the bride's mother is driven in a limousine (or a friend's car, if several limos are not in the budget) from her home to the church. She may be accompanied by other immediate members of her family. Immediately following are the bridesmaids in their limo or series of cars. Then the bride and her father leave for the church in a limousine (the same one that after the ceremony will transport the bride and groom alone to the reception).

MEANWHILE, INSIDE THE CHURCH

By now the ushers, of course, have already been at the church for an hour, seating guests, and the guests are listening to the organ music or any other type of music that has been provided. The groom and best man are waiting backstage, so to speak, in the church parlor or rectory, for the signal to walk from the side into the front of the church for the start of the wedding procession from the back down the center aisle.

At important weddings with pew cards, guests hand the pew card to the usher when they arrive. People often forget to bring their pew cards, so the usher should be able to consult his alphabetized seating list and find the proper pew number with ease. The front pews for the family and special guests are usually marked off from the others with flowers and ribbon—an important decorative detail in the church.

Each usher escorts as many ladies up the aisle as is possible in the time period. The protocol works more or less like this:

• The usher greets the guest. If there is special seating and if he does not know this person, he asks for the name and checks his list to see where the guest should be seated.

• He offers his inside arm to the lady; a male companion or child would follow behind.

• An unaccompanied male guest should be pointed to, or it should be suggested to him, which side of the aisle he should find a seat.

• If several women arrive at once, he offers his arm to the more senior one or the one he knows personally. (If a whole group of women arrive at once, they have their choice of staying in the back to await an escort or of walking down by themselves. Needless to say, young women choose the latter option.)

• The front pews (the ushers know how many are to be saved) are kept for family members (bride's on the left, groom's on the right).

• If there is no special seating, the usher guides guests to pews up in front on a first-come, first-served basis, but again, bride's friends on the left and groom's on the right. He might ask, "Are you a friend of the bride or of the groom?"

If there are few of the groom's friends attending the wedding (as is often the case for a groom who lives far away), the ushers should split up the guests so that there looks to be an equal number of guests on each side of the church.

SEATING IN THE FRONT PEW ON THE BRIDE'S SIDE

In the easiest of situations, the bride's mother and father occupy the front pew on the left. However, with so many deceased, divorced, and remarried parents, it is often not that simple. If the bride's parents have been divorced, regardless of what hard feelings may exist between them and their present spouses, it is very considerate of everyone to put aside their personal animosities in favor of the bride's happiness and allow tradition to be served during the ceremony. In other words, it makes the nicest of weddings if the bride's own mother and father sit side by side in the front pew, with the bride's stepfather and step-mother in the pew behind. If that is too much to ask, it is nice if both the bride's parents (or the groom's parents, if there has been a remarriage), and their present spouses occupy the front pews together. If that is impossible because of animosities, then the bride's mother and stepfather should occupy the first pew, and the bride's father and stepmother would occupy the second pew. Their various other children, siblings, and grandparents should also occupy the front pews on the bride's (or groom's) side of the church.

THE WEDDING SERVICE

MUSIC FOR THE CEREMONY

In some churches the liturgical music is rigorously prescribed, and in many churches or synagogues you must pay the organist, even if you don't use him. In other churches you are allowed a free hand in your musical preferences—anything from a chorus of guitars or a harp or a group of trumpets to Aunt Hortense singing "I Love You Truly." You must find out from your clergy how to plan for the music of your service.

If you do have an Aunt Hortense who wants to sing at your wedding, diplomatically lay obstacles in her path—unless she's a professional. Many a wedding ceremony has been ruined because a relative or close family friend insisted on providing the music and, in doing so, left the guests either flinching or laughing outright. Following are suggestions for each portion of the ceremony.

Prelude

The Four Seasons ("Spring" or "Autumn") by Vivaldi
Concerto Grosso in D, Op. 3, no. 6 (Vivace) by Handel
Serenade from String Quartet, Op. 3, no. 5 by Haydn
Orchestral Suite no. 3 in D (Air) by Bach

Processional

Canon in D by Pachelbel
Water Music, Suite no. 1 in F (Air) by Handel
The Four Seasons ("Winter") by Vivaldi
"Jesu, Joy of Man's Desiring" by Bach
Guitar Concerto in D, RV93 (Largo) by Vivaldi
Sinfonia, from Cantata no. 156 by Bach

Bride's Music

"Bridal Chorus" from *Lohengrin* by Wagner
Trumpet Voluntary by Jeremiah Clarke
"Wedding March" from *The Marriage of Figaro* by Mozart
"Ave Maria" by Schubert
Trumpet Tune and Air in D by Purcell

Interlude

Arioso by Bach
Minuet from *Berenice* by Handel
"Let the Bright Seraphim" by Handel
"Clair de Lune" by Debussy

Recessional

"Wedding March" from *A Midsummer Night's Dream*
  by Mendelssohn
Minuet in F from *Music for the Royal Fireworks* by Handel
"Ode to Joy" from Symphony no. 9 by Beethoven
Allegro movements from the trio sonatas of Telemann, Mozart,
  or Handel
Brandenburg Concerto no. 1 (Allegro) by Bach

THE SERVICE IS ABOUT TO BEGIN

The Mothers Are Seated

About five minutes before a Christian wedding procession is about to start, an usher escorts the mother of the groom to the front right pew. Her family and husband should follow her into the front pews, her husband sitting on her left in the pew. Then, a few minutes later, the head usher escorts the mother of the bride into the front left pew. There is an anticipatory stillness in the church. The music has now ceased, so that when it starts again to announce the procession, there will be a greater dramatic impact.

The place in the pew next to the bride's mother on the aisle has been left vacant, for the bride's father will occupy this seat after escorting his daughter to the altar. The bride's mother is the last person to be seated in the church before the doors are closed and the pageant unfolds.

The Runner Is Laid

If the bride has a long train, an optional white runner (sometimes supplied by the church, but usually by the florist) is rolled up from the front of the aisle to the back, to protect her dress when she walks up to the altar. It is rolled by two ushers or a church employee on the right-hand side of the aisle, because that is the side the bride will use as she walks in on the right arm of her father. (Going out of the church, she should walk down on the left arm of her husband, so that her dress will once again sweep along the runner.)

The White Satin Ribbons
Are Pulled Across the Aisle Posts

Next, another option: Two ushers, one on either side of the aisle, pick up the folded pieces of white satin streamers behind the front pews where the families are seated. Working at the same speed on either side of the aisle, they pull back the ribbons, weaving them in and out of the aisle posts in a straight line, placing the last loop of their ribbon over the last aisle post on their side of the aisle. This "seals in" the wedding guests, so to speak, and the ribbons remain in place until the end of the ceremony, and until the wedding party and the bride's and groom's families have left the church. (After the ceremony, the same ushers carefully roll up the ribbons as they remove them from the aisle posts. When they have completed this job, the wedding guests may rise, depart from the church, and head for the reception.)

The bride comes up the aisle on her father's right arm, preceded by the flower girl (and ring bearer, if there is one), the bridesmaids, the maid of honor and matron of honor, and the ushers. The bridegroom, best man, and the minister, in the meantime, have come in from the side of the altar and await the procession.

THE PROCESSIONAL BEGINS

Out walk the clergyman (or woman), the groom, and the best man from the side of the church. They proceed to the altar and turn to face the rear of the church, where the procession will begin.

The first people to come up the aisle as the processional music is played are the ushers, who march briskly, hopefully smiling, two by two, and then take their place on the right-hand side of the altar as you face it—next to the groom and the best man. Next come the bridesmaids, two by two. Then comes the ring bearer, if there is one; the pages, if there are any; the flower girl, if there is one; the junior bridesmaid, if there is one; then the maid of honor, and the matron of honor. They group themselves on the left-hand side of the altar in a row—or curve or whatever formation the clergyman (or woman) has decreed is the most efficient and attractive way to do it. They all remain standing. (In a Catholic ceremony, there may be kneelers for the entire wedding party to use later.)

Now comes the great moment everyone has been waiting for: the appearance of the bride on her father's right arm. Hopefully, she will be smiling

The wedding principals, once they have marched to the altar, usually form a semicircle, facing the minister and the altar. Their backs are now to the congregation and remain this way throughout the ceremony. The best man (in this case the groom's father) stands to the right of the groom, and the other ushers stand in order of height (tallest to shortest) to the best man's right. The maid or matron of honor stands to the left of the bride, and the other bridesmaids follow to the maid or matron of honor's left.

broadly, looking directly at her husband-to-be, who probably will be looking back at her with a dazed and extremely happy, proud expression on his face. (He should not try to practice this in the mirror at home beforehand.) I myself was not a smiling bride, since I was crying with the emotion of the beauty of the church, the music, and what was happening. I probably looked as though I had lost my best friend. My husband was no help. He was too nervous to smile. Some brides are nervous coming up the aisle and look almost angry with tension. (All brides are smiling and relaxed on the way out after the service.)

Note: If the bride's father is in a wheelchair, he may be in place at the foot of the altar when the processional begins, and she may be escorted up the aisle by another male member of her family before joining him. Or she may walk up the aisle alone. I once saw a very touching wedding processional in which the father of the bride pushed his own wheelchair as the bride walked proudly beside him. There was not a dry eye in the congregation on that day, nor was there the day another bride went up the aisle with her father, who was blind, accompanied by his faithful Seeing Eye dog.

THE ROLE OF THE BRIDE'S ATTENDANTS

• The *matron of honor* "outranks" *the maid of honor* in that she walks closer to the bride in the procession up the aisle. (In other words, the maid of honor walks first, then the matron of honor, and finally the bride on her father's arm.) Either the matron or maid of honor holds the bride's bouquet during the ceremony; they both straighten out the bride's train when she turns around at the altar. If one of these attendants is the bride's sister, it is she who lifts the bride's veil for the husband's kiss (if the kiss is part of the religious service). At the conclusion of the ceremony, when the wedding party starts to walk back down the aisle, the best man escorts the matron of honor, followed by the head usher escorting the maid of honor.

• A *junior bridesmaid* precedes the maid of honor in the procession. She also walks by herself back down the aisle in the recessional—unless there is an extra usher, in which case she has an escort, too.

• The *flower girls* (or one of them) wear dresses either in the same color and fabric as the bridesmaids, or they are attired in pretty white organdy or cotton dresses in the summer or velvet dresses in the winter. They often wear wreaths of flowers and carry little baskets of flowers. When coming back down the aisle in the recessional, they may scatter some wildflowers or rose petals in the aisle from their baskets (that is, if they didn't scatter them all going up the aisle in the procession). If in the excitement they forget to do it at all, it is not important!

• The *ring bearer*, often dressed in satin or velvet shorts (or even knickers with white knee socks) and a silk shirt with a Peter Pan collar, precedes the flower girl or the junior bridesmaid. An option to having a ring bearer is having one or two little boy *pages.* (If possible, all the children wear black patent leather or white Mary Jane shoes and white socks.) The wedding ring(s) borne by the ring bearer on a ceremonial satin pillow are sewn firmly into it, because a little boy could certainly not be responsible otherwise for delivering them safely to the best man and matron (or maid) of honor. Another wise solution is to sew fake rings onto the pillow, while the real rings are safely in the best man's pocket.

If there is a junior bridesmaid behind the ring bearer, she will usually keep him from running off in all directions and make him do his job properly. I will never forget one nine-year-old junior bridesmaid who suddenly departed from her dignified walk, darted off, and caught her three-year-old brother by the arm after he had run off into a pew on the far side of the vast church. She gave him a scolding and a hard slap on the seat of his pants. Immediately he became obedient and followed her back across the church and into the procession. The bridal party, of course, had come to a halt during this drama. The entire congregation, the bride included, were laughing, but it did not at all detract from the beauty of the wedding. It added to it.

VARIATIONS ON WHO ACTS AS THE FATHER OF THE BRIDE

The man who customarily walks the bride up the aisle on his right arm is her father. However:

• If her father is ill or deceased, the bride's teenage or older brother, an uncle, her grandfather, her godfather, a male cousin, or a close family male friend may properly do the honors. If the father is dead and the bride's mother has remarried, her stepfather acts in her father's place. (However, if the bride's relationship with her stepfather is strained, she may ask another male relative to take her up the aisle.)

• If the bride's parents were divorced when she was young and she was raised from early childhood by a loving stepfather, it may be a last act of kindness to her natural father if she consents to be given away by him—unless there is very bad feeling between them. If there is bad feeling, then she should ask her stepfather to take her up the aisle.

GIVING THE BRIDE AWAY

In a Catholic ceremony, once the father has taken his daughter to the foot of the altar, he gives her to her husband in a symbolic gesture of taking her left arm out of his as she reaches out her right hand to her groom. He then returns to his outside seat in the front pew, next to his wife.

In Protestant ceremonies, the minister asks almost at once, as the bride and her father stand together with the groom, some form of the question, "Who gives this woman in matrimony?" The father of the bride answers "I do" or "Her mother and I do" and puts the bride's right hand in the clergy's. Then, after sometimes giving her a kiss on the forehead, for which he or the maid of honor must first lift her veil, he steps back and rejoins his wife in the front right pew. His place at the bride's side is now taken by her husband-to-be.

Today there are variations on this part of the ceremony. The bride's mother may join the bride and her father when they reach the altar, and may reply "We do," with her husband, in answer to the minister's question. Then both parents go to the front pew to sit down. I have also seen a wedding in which the bride was "given away" at the foot of the altar by her remarried birth mother and remarried birth father, and by her adoptive father as well, who had really raised her. The "giving away" answer was a resounding "We do" by three people.

Once given away in a bridal ceremony, that's it for the bride. If she remarries later, she is not given away again. She's been there and done that!

THE WEDDING RING IS PLACED ON THE FINGER

An important part of the ceremony is when the groom places a wedding ring on the bride's finger, or when both exchange wedding rings. (The bride should not be wearing her engagement ring.) Normally, the best man guards the ring that will go on the bride's finger in one of his pockets until it is needed, while the matron or maid of honor either wears the ring for the bride to give her groom on one of her fingers, keeps it stowed in her dress pocket, or has it tied to her sash on a small, thin ribbon.

If a ring bearer brings the rings up to the altar on a pillow, the best man should produce a penknife from his pocket to cut the threads that have sewn the ring or rings to the pillow. The best man then puts the bride's wedding ring in his own pocket for safekeeping, and gives the wedding ring that will go on the groom's finger either to the maid or matron of honor standing nearby.

I wonder how many times, while nervously handing the little ring to the groom or to the bride, someone, either the giver or the receiver, has dropped the ring on the floor of the church. The nice thing is that it is always found again!

RECITATION OF THE VOWS

The vows, the choice of prayers, the music playing during the ceremony, and any creative ideas for special words to be spoken during the service should all be discussed well in advance with the clergyman (or woman) performing the service. Some religions allow great freedom in what is said and not said; others are dogmatically strict. Different parishes have different interpretations of the wedding service, and the bride and groom must fit their own wishes into the rules of the church.

THE KISS

When the groom and bride are supposed to kiss near the end of the wedding service, the matron or maid of honor should lift the bride's veil. Sometimes she forgets and the groom lifts it. Sometimes he forgets and the bride lifts it. It really doesn't matter, does it.

At a Catholic Mass, when it is time for the Kiss of Peace, the bride and groom often give each other a kiss and then go down to both front pews to kiss their parents. This is also done in some Protestant ceremonies.

The bride and groom leave the church in a joyous (and usually brisk) recessional. They are followed by the flower girl (and the ring bearer or junior bridesmaids, if any), and maid or matron of honor and the best man. Then the bridesmaids and the ushers marching in pairs follow.

A nice tender kiss at the altar when the clergyman or woman says to the groom, "You may now kiss the bride," is enjoyed by everyone present. However, he does not enjoy standing there while the bride and groom, still at the altar, engage in a long, passionate kiss worthy of an X-rated movie.

THE RECESSIONAL

For the recessional, at the conclusion of the services, the positions in line are reversed. The bride and groom walk first as slowly as possible, not in a racing mode, smiling at the guests as they go, followed by the ring bearer (who may have gone to sit with his parents by now), the junior bridesmaid, and the flower girl. Then the matron of honor with the best man, or the maid of honor with the head usher, and the bridesmaids—each paired off with an usher. (As noted, if there aren't enough ushers, the bridesmaids walk out two by two.) If there is no runner, the bride may go down the aisle on her husband's right arm; as mentioned earlier, if there is a runner, she would take his left arm in order to walk on the runner.

A DOUBLE WEDDING CEREMONY

When two couples marry in the same ceremony, they are usually sister brides or brother grooms, cousins, or two very close friends marrying two very close friends.

A sister bride may act as her sister's attendant, and vice versa; a brother groom may act as his brother's best man, and vice versa. Or each may have his or her own set of attendants. I remember one beautiful wedding of twin sisters who had the same six bridesmaids act for both their weddings.

Twin brides may dress in identical dresses, if they wish, or in different styles (but these should harmonize with each other).

The two sets of bridesmaids' dresses do not have to match, but it looks much more harmonious if they do—not necessarily in color, but in style. The two grooms and the ushers should wear identical wedding apparel.

In a double wedding of sisters, each with her own attendants, the ushers would march in first in the processional; then would come the bridesmaids followed by the maid and matron of honor—all of the older sister's attendants would march up the aisle, then the bride on her father's arm, followed by the younger sister's attendants, then the younger sister on the arm of a brother, uncle, grandfather, or cousin.

If both girls wish their father to take them up the aisle, the father takes the older one up first, walks briskly back, and then comes up slowly again with his

younger daughter. (In the case of twins, one baby was born first and is therefore older.)

If the church has two side aisles, rather than a center aisle, both wedding
parties may proceed slowly up the side aisles in unison.

The wedding service of the older daughter takes place first. In the case of
two unrelated girls marrying two brothers, the older girl's wedding ceremony
takes place first.

The mothers of two brides who are close friends would sit with their husbands together in the first row. The mothers of two grooms marrying sisters
would sit in the first row together with their husbands. The mother of the older
bride would walk up the aisle and be seated first—since her daughter will walk
up the aisle first and will be married first.

• A double wedding calls for two sets of limousines and two wedding
cakes. Friends of one bride who do not know the other one or the other's husband well do not have to give a wedding present to both couples. Only family
and friends who are close to both couples should give two presents.

A difficult task is that of the best man or of the two best men, to make sure
that neither couple receives short shrift in all of the toasting at the rehearsal
dinner and at the wedding reception.

THE PREGNANT BRIDE

A bride who is in her early pregnancy can wear a simple, loose-fitting, long
white dress that does not shout her happy, blessed state to the guests at her
wedding. A bride who is nine months pregnant but nevertheless marries in
a large ceremony, dressed in a long dress with a train, looks—in the opinion
of many—ludicrous. It is in better taste for this bride to wear a long white
maternity dress with a short veil, but without the fuss of a full-length veil
and cathedral train. Restraint and good taste are important in any religious
service.

A SMALL OR BIG WEDDING AT HOME

How nice to be able to have your wedding at home or in the house of a relative
or special friend! A home wedding is usually small, and the bride's and groom's
parents are wise to keep the guest list smaller than they would ordinarily think
is required, because the available space is quickly utilized by:

• The clergy's requirements for the ceremony.

• The need for a place for the members of the wedding party to assemble
before the procession.

• Racks for coats and umbrellas, perhaps even for boots.

• Chairs for older, frail guests, even if the rest of the guests are standing or sitting informally around the room.

• A place to stash wedding presents (even though they should *not* have been brought to the house on the wedding day).

• The need for changing rooms for the bride, groom, and attendants.

• Space to set up the reception food and drink before the service (assuming the reception will be at home, too).

In the best of situations, the guests are seated on portable chairs set up auditorium style in the living room (or the largest room in the house). If the ceremony is going to last longer than ten minutes, those chairs will really be needed.

The altar can be improvised in front of the fireplace or a picture window or any focal point in the living room. It is better to clear out most of the furniture before the ceremony. One lovely floral bouquet on or at the foot of the altar is all that is needed. When there is seating auditorium style, the chairs should be placed on two sides, with an aisle in the middle. White satin ribbons can mark off the first row or two on each side for the bride's and groom's families to occupy.

The music may be supplied by a pianist (with or without a solo singer), a trio or quartet, a trio of guitars, or an electric organ—anything dignified and appropriate for a religious service. At the sound of the processional music, if there is a large staircase, the bride's attendant descends it, followed by the bride. Her father waits for her at the bottom of the staircase, and they follow her attendant on the short walk into the living room, up the center aisle to join the groom, clergy, and best man at the altar. The bride may wear a long white dress and veil or a street-length white dress or suit. She may wear a late afternoon dress or a dinner gown. (If the wedding is a *very* small one in the home, she would be dressed in white, but not necessarily in a long formal gown; at this kind of wedding, music is not absolutely necessary if the budget will not permit.)

After the ceremony, the bride and groom walk back down the aisle to appropriate recessional music and proceed immediately to the area where the reception will be held. When there is a tent nearby, the receiving line is stationed in the house or near the tent entrance. (There is no need for a receiving line if the wedding and reception are very small.)

On occasion, the bride has a ceremony in the presence of just family and a handful of close friends in the house, followed by a large reception in a tent on the grounds. Her parents would invite guests to the wedding reception only—for example, "at five o'clock." Then family and a few very close friends would be invited by handwritten note to the ten-minute ceremony at a quarter to five. The first reception guests would probably not arrive until ten or fifteen minutes after five, which would give the bride and groom the chance to be photographed, and to sit down and relax for fifteen minutes with or without their families before the receiving line begins.

Tenting Your Yard or Garden

If you plan to hold your reception in your own house and have invited a large number of guests, you would be smart to plan on having a professional tenting company erect a tent off to the side of the house, or in the backyard or garden. Tents can be heated in winter and air-conditioned in summer. The kind with side flaps that can be raised or lowered is essential in case of inclement weather. The see-through plastic kind allows people to enjoy the grounds around them to a certain degree. (It's a nice touch to have rented lights illuminating the trees and shrubs outside the plastic tent for an evening wedding.)

Any kind of tent looks much prettier when at least the interior posts are decorated with greenery and flowers. The florist can make a harmonious decorative plan to include items such as decorated tent poles, table centerpieces, colorful tablecloths, flowers on the serving tables, flower-decorated chandeliers, and a boxwood or flowered hedge around the dance floor. (I remember a Christmas wedding reception in which fresh holly ropes cordoned off the small dance floor in the tent. There was only one drawback: Anytime we women went near the ropes, we caught our dresses on the sharp-leafed holly. It was beautiful.)

THE RECEPTION

The order of events at the reception goes like this:
- The wedding party's group photographs are taken.
- Arriving guests check coats and sign the guest book.
- Arriving guests go through the receiving line while music plays for guests, and libations are passed.
- The receiving line breaks up after most of the guests have arrived.
- The bride and groom dance the first dance; everyone dances from then on.
- Everyone eats and drinks.
- Toasts begin and follow through the eating period (a microphone is necessary).
- The bride and groom cut the cake.
- The bride and groom depart the reception to change into "going-away" clothes.

- On their way out, the bride tosses her bouquet to an unmarried brides maid; the groom tosses her garter to an unmarried usher (if he insists.)
- Bride and groom say good-bye to their parents and best friends and depart for their honeymoon in a car containing their luggage.
- Everyone else goes home. (If the bridal couple has been living together, some of these customs do not apply, particularly regarding the couple's departure.)

When the Wedding and Reception Place Are Combined

If you plan to hold both your wedding and reception at home, there are no problems of scheduling. If you plan to hold both or just the reception in a hotel, restaurant, or club, you must fit into their schedule of already booked events. If you plan to hold your wedding and reception in an informal park or garden, a museum, a historic home, or any revered and protected site that is open to the public, you must adhere to a list of rules and regulations laid down by those entrusted with the administration of the place. However, the visual riches of the gardens or the sweep of the fields in the distance, or the awesome history and the beauty of the interiors of an old house or mansion dating from the eighteenth or nineteenth century are well worth all the restrictions, including some of these:

- Your event must not conflict with any other one scheduled for that day (and some weddings are booked a year or more in advance). Your event must be scheduled after the public hours are over (which is often 5 P.M.)—or perhaps you may rent the facility only on the one day of the week it is closed to the public.
- Some properties, because they are not properly heated, rent only from April through November.
- Some historic sites require that you be prepared for rain, and therefore you must tent the gardens—because the house is too fragile to hold a large number of guests coming inside from the rain.
- There is often a fairly rigid maximum number of guests you are allowed to invite for either a standing or seated event. For example, at a historic Greek Revival mansion with formal gardens and terraces where only 75 guests may be accommodated indoors (12 seated), but 450 may be accommodated in the gardens outside, tenting is required for more than 75 guests.
- There is a wide range of rental fees for these properties. For example, a corporation pays New York's Metropolitan Museum an annual Corporate Patron fee of more than $30,000, which includes, among other pluses, per-

mission to use the museum premises for a party. The bride's parents pay in excess of $2,000 for five hours rental of the lovely house and gardens at Woodlawn Plantation at Mount Vernon, Virginia, overlooking the Potomac. Some other historic places charge $3,000 for six hours. Other smaller gardens or historic places around the country charge $100 plus an hour to rent their facilities.

• Many properties and gardens request an extra fee to cover the security requirements and cleanup of the grounds.

• Some institutions allow alcoholic beverages to be served only in the house, others only in the gardens. Some prohibit the serving of alcohol at any time.

• Some institutions allow you to choose only from their select list of caterers; others oblige you to use their own restaurant facilities on the place.

• Some institutions will not allow amplified music in the gardens but only indoors (because of neighbors complaining about noise); others will allow it only outdoors; others will not allow band music and dancing anywhere.

GUEST BOOK

A nice custom is the signing of names in a handsome leather book at the reception. Guests sign the book with their formal names ("Mr. and Mrs. John A. Howe, Jr."—not "Jack and Joanie Howe"). The book should be placed on a table (of a reasonable height) near where guests check their coats at the reception (or at the wedding itself, if it is held in a home). The book should ask for the guests' addresses, too—so it becomes a useful resource of updated addresses for the future. A young member of either the bride's or groom's family (twelve years or older) might be stationed by the book to invite people to sign. It's very difficult to hurry past a twelve-year-old whose "job" is to request you to sign her book.

THE RECEIVING LINE

The fathers of the bride and groom may cut in and out of the receiving line. Even the bridesmaids may cut in and out of it after the first half hour. But the bride and groom and their mothers should certainly stand through all of it. Their friends can keep everyone supplied with glasses of champagne on the table behind them, and they can turn around occasionally and discreetly sip from their glasses—but members of the receiving line should not be photographed drinking for dignity's sake.

Likewise, guests going through the receiving line should not have glasses in their hands. If the line is long, a guest can always take a glass from a passing tray; then, as he approaches the bride's mother, the glass should be disposed of or hidden somewhere. It should not be in the guest's hand.

The Order of the Receiving Line

If both fathers stand in line at a very large formal wedding:
- Bride's mother.
- Bride's father.
- Groom's mother.
- Groom's father.
- Bride.
- Groom.
- Matron of honor.
- Maid of honor.
- Junior bridesmaid (if there was one).
- The other bridesmaids, oldest ones first.

Flower girls, pages, and ring bearers do not stand in the receiving line—they wouldn't have the patience. Nor do the ushers. (The fathers of the couple often don't, either!)

- Usually only the father of the bride stands in the line—and he sometimes for only the first forty-five minutes. The father of the groom, if he is not in line, goes around the reception making sure everyone is happy.

- If the reception is held at the home of the bride's stepmother, the latter should stand first in the receiving line *in her own house,* to help introduce the guests. The presence of the stepmother would change the lineup, since the

In a receiving line without fathers, the mother of the bride is first, then the mother of the groom, then the bride and groom and the bride's attendants.

With both fathers in the receiving line, the mother of the bride is the first to receive guests; then the father of the bride; then the mother and father of the groom, the bridal couple, and the bride's attendants.

stepmother and the mother of the bride probably would not wish to stand next to each other. In this case the order would be:

- Bride's stepmother.
- Groom's mother.
- Bride's mother.
- Bride's father.
- Bride.
- Groom.
- Matron of honor, etc.
- If the bride's father is newly remarried and the reception is held in his home, his new wife does not stand in the receiving line but plays the role of hostess, greeting everyone as they arrive. The bride's mother stands first in line in this case.
- If the bride's mother is dead and her father has not remarried, her father would stand first in line to greet the guests, with the groom's mother next to him, and the bride and groom next to her.

Going Through the Receiving Line

Generally, the conversation going through the receiving line should be short and sweet. It's important for women guests in greeting the bride and her attendants not to get lipstick on them. It's important for men not to kiss the bride on the mouth, for several reasons. The cheek will do. Women guests, because of their lipstick, should hug the bride, rather than kiss her on the cheek. People who are not close friends of the bride should clasp her hand warmly and not attempt to kiss her at all. Sample receiving line conversations, very pedestrian, but one should not tie up the receiving line with chapter and verse:

Guest to bride's mother: "Mrs. Gaines, I'm Holly Reynolds, a college friend of Abigail's. What a lovely wedding it was—perfectly beautiful. And Abigail is so radiant!"

Bride's mother to guest: "Thank you so much, Holly. I've heard Abigail speak of you often. We're so glad you could come. I know how much it means to Abigail to have you here."

Holly to bride: "You look absolutely gorgeous, old friend! Your dress—your veil—Abigail, you're so beautiful. And George is such a handsome groom. I'm so happy for you both!"

Bride to her friend: "Thanks, Holly. It really went well, didn't it? And we're going to be so happy. I'm so glad you're here! I want you to have a good time, too. There are lots of great single guys here. I'll see to it that you meet some."

Holly to groom: "Congratulations. I'm Holly Reynolds, Abigail's friend from Vassar. We saw each other when you used to come up to Poughkeepsie to visit her. No wonder Abigail married you. And you have the most beautiful bride in the world, you lucky guy."

Groom to Holly: "She is beautiful, isn't she? Yes, I am a lucky guy—and I remember you from those college weekends, too. Great to have you here, Holly."

Holly to father of the bride: "I'm Holly Reynolds, Mr. Gaines, a friend of Abigail's from college days. You have the loveliest daughter in the world, and I can see where she gets those great looks—from her parents. You must be so proud of her."

Father of the bride to Holly: "Thank you for that, Holly. Yes, her mother and I are very proud of Abigail. This is a great day for her, but it's both a sad and wonderful day for us. We're losing our little girl. The house will be so different."

Holly to father of the bride: "But you're gaining a wonderful son-in-law. He's quite a guy."

Father of the bride: "I know he is. Abigail has great taste, and he's a fine young man. We're glad you could be here today, Holly."

Holly to bridesmaid: "You look perfectly lovely. I'm Holly Reynolds, a college friend of Abigail's. What a beautiful wedding this has been!"

Bridesmaid to Holly: "I'm Suzanne Smith. Abigail and I went to school together, and we've been friends a long time. It's so nice you could make it to the wedding. I know Abigail is really glad you're here."

And so it goes. Pleasantries, niceties, and compliments. No dilly-dallying—the line must keep moving quickly. It makes it much more interesting to those standing in the receiving line if the guests passing through give their names and mention how they are connected to the bridal couple. Otherwise, it becomes boring listening to a chorus of "Wasn't it lovely!" "Don't you look pretty!" "Isn't this a happy occasion!"

SEATING THE TABLES AT THE RECEPTION

The Bride's Table

After their receiving line duties are over, the bridal party enjoys the chance to be seated and to eat, drink, and dance. Even if the reception food consists only of hot and cold hors d'oeuvres with ice cream and wedding cake, the wedding party should have a *bride's table* to give them the opportunity to sit, relax over their food and champagne, and dance when they wish. There are place cards for them at even this kind of informal reception. For the rest of the guests there should be small tables scattered around for those who wish to sit when they're not dancing or socializing. (Some of the older people will wish to sit and observe all the time, instead of dancing.)

For a formal seated lunch or dinner, there are place cards and table numbers for *all* the guests, as well as for the bridal tables.

The bride and groom would, of course, be seated side by side at their table. The groom would have the matron of honor on his other side; the bride would have the best man on her other side and next to him the maid of honor. The ushers and bridesmaids would sit in a male-female alternating pattern. If there is room, it is nice to invite the spouses and dates of the ushers and bridesmaids to join this table. If the wedding party is large, there would probably not be room at the table for spouses and dates, so they could have their own separate table nearby.

At most wedding receptions there is a bride's table, at which only the bride and groom and their attendants are seated. For example, the bride and groom are in the center of this rectangular one-sided table, which allows all of the reception guests to have a good view of the newly marrieds. (Frequently, when there is a bride's table and a parents' table, both are round.)

The Parents' Table

There is also usually a *parents' table* at any type of large reception. The mother of the bride would have the father of the groom on her right; her husband (or if she is without a husband, her brother, uncle, cousin, family friend, or boyfriend) would sit opposite with the mother of the groom on his right. The bride's mother might have the clergyman or woman who performed the service on her left; the mother of the groom might have the bride's grandfather on her other side, and so on—alternating family members and any distinguished guests or very close friends.

It is also appropriate to have one very long rectangular bride's table, at which the entire wedding party would be seated.

Sometimes there is a parents' table at the wedding reception. The mother of the bride (facing us) is in the center, with the father of the groom on her right and the clergy on her left. Across from her is the father of the bride, with the mother of the groom on his right and the matron of honor on his left.

WEDDING TOASTS

At a certain moment in the process of eating and drinking, the best man begins the toasts, which continue on and off, under his control, for as long as there are people who wish to offer their good wishes publicly. At large weddings it is important that there be a microphone for everyone's use—either a portable mike passed around from guest to guest, or a standing mike that each person goes to in order to give a toast. It is also an excellent idea to have the toasts at your wedding taped—which provides a fabulous souvenir of a terribly important event in your lives to enjoy in future years.

Toasts are really an important and integral part of the rehearsal dinner and of the wedding reception. Like everything else in the field of ancient rituals, there is an etiquette to be followed. For example:

• The person being toasted never drinks at the end of the toast but simply remains seated and smiles at the person making the toast.

• When you are the one who is toasting, rise to your feet if there are ten or more people at the table. Otherwise, at a small intimate dinner, you can make your toast while seated. If people still talk after you've asked for quiet, don't bang on crystal! You can get the others' attention by standing and saying something like, "Ladies and gentlemen, I have a toast to make," or more informally, "I have" (in a louder tone than usual) "something to say tonight." It is only polite to stop talking. Don't rap too hard on the rim of a good crystal glass to get people's attention, because you will break the glass! Use your voice to get attention, and if you must rap on a glass, make sure it's a cheap one!

• A wedding toast should be *no longer than three minutes,* so don't get carried away. You may appropriately be loving, amusing, sentimental, or teasing in your remarks. You may be serious or clever and lightly poking fun. Above all, you should be self-rehearsed and practiced. (Practice giving it to yourself in a mirror.)

• The order of toasting either at the rehearsal dinner or at the wedding reception is as follows:

  • The best man toasts the bride.
  • The groom toasts the bride.
  • The bride toasts her groom.
  • The father of the bride toasts the couple.
  • The bride toasts her groom's parents.
  • The groom toasts his bride's parents.
  • The matron or maid of honor toasts the couple.
  • The father of the groom toasts the bride.
  • The mother of the bride toasts the couple.
  • The mother of the groom toasts the couple.
  • Other bridal attendants, relatives, and close friends of the couple continue toasting.

The reason for a list of the order of toasts is that it brings order out of chaos, makes the performance work smoothly, and gives courage to people who are shy—and who desperately want to make a toast but are afraid. (When the shy person knows he is on the list, he usually manages to summon his courage when the moment comes, rise to his feet, and get out the words.)

This list is in the hands of the best man. It is he who commands the toasts. Once it starts—once he has made the first toast—he signals each person in the wedding party who wants to make a toast. (He has, of course, asked the individuals beforehand if they wish to make a toast, and if the answer is yes, he explains that they should wait until he calls on them.) Then, at the completion of a toast, he looks over to the next person and nods a signal that means "You're next." That person should then rise and do her stuff.

A successful rehearsal dinner or wedding depends on following a list of the order of toasts, because unless the family and really close friends are allowed to toast the bride and groom first, wedding guests who are not at all close to the family are likely to jump in ahead and upset the members of the wedding party. *Note:* The toasts for the rehearsal dinner may be a bit longer than those at the wedding reception. The ones on the day of the wedding, if there are many guests present, should be kept short, snappy, and focused.

THE BRIDE'S FIRST DANCE

It doesn't matter whether there's a piano or a full band at the reception. There may have been music playing during the entire reception, but people should not be dancing until the receiving line has been terminated and the first dance can be performed by the bride and groom. When the receiving line is broken and the wedding party is now free to take seats at their tables and to dance and eat, that's the moment for the bride and groom to begin the dancing. The orchestra strikes up the tune the bride and groom have asked the orchestra leader to play (perhaps a sentimental song for the couple, played to a beat to which they can comfortably dance). If they are good dancers, they should hold the floor alone for at least five minutes. If they are not, then after about one minute, the bride's father and mother should join them on the dance floor, and the bride's father can cut in on them and dance with the bride while the groom dances with the bride's mother. Then everyone gets out on the floor, and anyone can cut in on anyone else. The more informal and the more changing of partners there is, the better time everyone has.

WEDDINGS IN THE JEWISH TRADITION

Note: Holly Pearl Pressman contributed much of this information.
Marriage is one of the most important institutions in Jewish tradition. A strong, loving family unit continues to be of paramount importance to those of Jewish faith everywhere, so weddings are regarded as solemn occasions, worthy of careful planning. They do not take place on the Sabbath or major Jewish holidays (with the exception of Hanukkah). The ceremony often takes place in a temple or in a hotel or hall where the wedding feast will also be given.

INVITATIONS

Invitations to Jewish weddings are most often issued in the names of both sets of parents, with the bride's parents listed first. The preferred form is the following:

> Mr. and Mrs. Jacob Feldman
> request the honour of your presence
> at the marriage of their daughter
> Rebecca Anne
> to
> Mr. Roger Nathan Greller
> son of
> Mr. and Mrs. Warren John Greller
> on Sunday, the sixth of June
> etc.

Another form is the following:

> Mr. and Mrs. Jacob Feldman
> and
> Mr. and Mrs. Warren John Greller
> request the honour of your presence
> at the marriage of their children
> Rebecca Anne Feldman
> and
> Roger Nathan Greller
> on Sunday, the sixth of June
> etc.

PREPARATION FOR THE WEDDING DAY

In preparation for the wedding day, traditionally for strict religious Jews, usually orthodox, the bride and groom fast and repent, just as they do on the Day of Atonement. After serious reflection and purification, the couple is ready to enter a new stage of life together. If the ceremony is to be held in the evening, the bride and groom may eat a light snack before the ceremony at sunset, the beginning of the next Hebrew day.

THE *CHUPPA*

Traditional Jewish wedding ceremonies are conducted under a cloth wedding canopy, called the *chuppa,* which is often embroidered or decorated with flowers. A handmade, temporary structure, it is reminiscent of the tents of the Jews' nomadic ancestors. The *chuppa* represents the room in the groom's home where the marriage will be consummated. When the groom receives his bride under the *chuppa,* it is religiously symbolic of God's (the groom's) acceptance of Israel (the bride).

THE PROCESSIONAL

The Jewish processional at the beginning of the marriage ceremony is similar to those in Christian churches. It is common practice for each wedding participant of the processional to start walking up the aisle on the right foot.

I have spoken to many Jewish religious leaders about the rites described here. In the United States, Jewish tradition is interpreted by Orthodox Jews with strict adherence to the legal standards of the Bible, but it is interpreted more liberally by Conservative Jews and progressively by Reform Jews. Traditionally, the bride and groom do not see each other before the ceremony on their wedding day, and there are many other customs strictly followed by Orthodox Jews that are not necessarily followed by liberal Conservative or Reform Jews. In very Orthodox weddings, the groom is escorted by the two fathers and the bride by the two mothers—in keeping with the separation of men and women in public. Alternatively, Conservative and Reform Jews often use the following order of the procession:

The rabbi and cantor enter first, followed by the ushers, best man, and ring bearer(s). The groom follows, unless he has chosen to enter with the rabbi and the best man from a side entrance and to forgo a more public entrance up the aisle. The bridesmaids and maid or matron of honor are followed by the flower girl(s) and finally by the bride. In non-Orthodox weddings, traditionally the groom was escorted up the aisle by his parents and the bride by her parents, but today in Reform ceremonies it is acceptable for the bride's mother and the groom's parents to take their seats just before the bride, escorted by her father, comes up the aisle, preceded by her attendants. She steps beneath the *chuppa* to stand at the right of her groom.

The Ceremony

In some very religious ceremonies, the flute is played during the religious ceremony. The music is meant to be joyous yet dignified—and livelier for the recessional.

The cantor begins the ceremony with a short hymn. The rabbi then recites a blessing over the wine and blesses the betrothal. The groom sips some of the wine, hands the cup to the bride, and her attendant lifts her veil so that she can drink, too. By drinking from the same glass, the bride and groom are signifying the beginning of their life of sharing.

The ring ceremony takes place next. The groom places the wedding ring on the bride's index finger, so that it may be seen easily by the two appointed witnesses and by the guests. There is another reason for placing it on her index finger: There is an old belief that a vein in the forefinger runs directly to the heart. (There may be a double ring ceremony, with the bride placing her groom's ring on his index finger.) The ring ceremony is followed by the reading of the marriage contract, then a short talk by the rabbi on the importance of this occasion, and perhaps he makes some brief personal remarks about the couple. Often he incorporates a modern English translation of the seven marriage blessings into his remarks. Then the couple shares the wine again, and with his foot the groom breaks a small glass wrapped in a napkin. It symbolizes that a broken marriage cannot easily be repaired, but it also serves as a reminder of the sorrows of the Jewish people. The glass may require several "stamps" before it breaks. At the sound of the broken glass, the bride and groom kiss, and the family and friends turn to each other to express their happiness and good wishes for the couple.

The Recessional

At the conclusion of the ceremony, the bride and groom lead the recessional, followed by their parents, the maid or matron of honor and the best man (walking together), then the ushers and bridesmaids walking in mixed pairs, the flower girl(s), ring bearer(s), the rabbi, and the cantor.

The Reception

The Jewish wedding celebration is almost always a seated meal, with music and sumptuous food. After the wedding party photographs have been taken, the receiving line is formed. Guests go to their assigned tables and dance until there is a pause in the music. This is the signal for the beginning of the meal.

The rabbi offers a brief blessing over the challah, and everyone eats without dancing (if there's music, it's for background only). Then the bride and groom cut the wedding cake and share the first piece, and the best man begins the toasting. People dance through the rest of the party.

The festivities come to a leisurely end when the bride throws her bouquet to the unmarried women present, the groom tosses her garter to the unmarried men, and they leave to change their clothes and go on their honeymoon.

INTERFAITH MARRIAGES

Twenty-five years ago, no one could have predicted that in the twenty-first century there would be such a rash of interfaith marriages, particularly between Jews and Christians. When either set of parents makes a big fuss over this fact, it can ruin the joy that should predominate on this day of days for the two people who really matter—the bride and groom.

An interfaith marriage can be a very complex situation, because people are dealing with any one of these combinations:

- Bride and groom and both sets of parents with no religious faith.
- Bride and groom with no religious faith but with parents who are fervent in their respective faiths.
- Bride who is very religious and groom who is not.
- Groom who is very religious and bride who is not.

Only the first category is easy. The other categories may present problems, but as with anything, it works when people are up-front with each other and make an extra effort—not only compromising but keeping the promises they have made. If the bride or the groom is a very religious person, it obviously makes sense for the spouse who is not to make concessions to the one who is. The spouse who has made the concessions can then ask for another compromise in return. For example, a friend of mine who won out on the religious question and raised the children in her faith, every year thereafter spent her family's summer vacations on a farm, a concession to her husband's ardent preferences in this area and not her preferred choice at all.

For the sake of the people to be married, who will get married in spite of what anyone says—with or without the backing of their parents—it is common sense for the bridal couple and their parents to sit down together coolly and rationally and *compromise.* I have witnessed beautiful, peaceful interfaith weddings, with very touching ecumenical services. I have also observed parents before and during the wedding itself fighting a war with each other, using their children as guided attack missiles, with relatives on both sides tugging, crying, threatening, throwing up their hands, and in general being divisive. (Fortunately, I have also seen some of the latter realize that histrionics get them nowhere and that pulling together for the sake of their children is the fair and moral thing to do.) I have also known the bride and the groom to sit down with their upset parents in private to reassure them of a personal devotion to their own religions, customs, and values. For example, the promise of a Christian daughter to her parents that "we will be with you for every Christmas and Easter that we can, you know that," and the promise of a Jewish son to parents that "we will be with you for every Yom Kippur and Passover that we can, you know that," helps to soothe a touchy situation.

All of the feelings and worries of the parents, who have been accustomed to a certain religious control of their children, should be aired before the wedding. It is not too much to ask of a bride and groom to relay to their future in-laws their sincere determination to keep relationships pleasant and to acknowledge the religious concerns of a parent.

The raising of the children born of an interfaith marriage should not be an issue at the time of the wedding. No one can predict what will happen—just as we can't predict most things.

The Ecumenical Wedding Service

The bride's family usually is in charge of the wedding arrangements. In an interfaith wedding, the bride's parents are called upon to express kindness, consideration, and tolerance for the groom's faith in the planning for the religious service. The bride's pastor or rabbi should be consulted first, then the groom's clergyman or woman if he or she is of another faith. In this manner a service can be designed that will be balanced, appropriate, holy, and memorable. More than once, however, I have seen ecumenical services in which one representative of a religious faith was not allowed to do anything but just stand there and might as well have not been present. In each case, it made the guests uncomfortable and became the talk of the wedding afterward. (The talk of the wedding should be the bride and groom!)

How much better it is if the couple, their parents, and their clergy swallow pride, prejudice, and every other negative feeling for the sake of a happy, beautiful wedding! There are many ways in which the clergy of two faiths can co-celebrate the ceremony—one officiating for half the service and the other officiating for the second half, one doing the homily and the other saying the blessing, or both giving joint blessings.

Both members of the clergy should be invited to the rehearsal dinner the night before the wedding; they should be seated with equal rank at any bridal tables. At one very lovely interfaith wedding I attended fourteen years ago, at the wedding lunch the Jewish groom's rabbi sat on the Catholic bride's mother's right, and the bride's priest sat on the Jewish groom's mother's right. They all had a wonderful time at the wedding, and now, years later, the bride attends Catholic Mass every Sunday and the groom goes to temple every Friday night. The children alternate services with their parents, and when they go away to college, they will decide what faith to take as their own.

In another very happy marriage, the groom, who cares very much about his Jewish religion, is raising the children as Jews. His wife, of Christian background but not raised to be a devout observer of any faith, agreed to have their children raised as Jews. "I am the recipient of his compromises on many other issues," she said with a smile in talking about her acquiescence on this point. "We've worked it out." (If only all interfaith couples and their parents showed similar wisdom!)

ANOTHER OPTION: TWO CEREMONIES

On rare occasions couples of different religious beliefs choose to have two separate religious ceremonies on the same or even different days. For example, if the bride is Jewish, the ceremony might be held on Sunday afternoon, followed by a large reception for the wedding party, families, and friends. On the preceding day, Saturday, in the late afternoon (after sunset, at the end of the Jewish Sabbath), the couple would have been married by the groom's family's minister in a Christian service, with just toasts in champagne for the wedding party and the immediate families afterward. If the bride is Christian, the large reception would be held after the late afternoon Saturday services, and the small family champagne gathering would take place after the Jewish Sunday service. The wedding party would wear their bridal finery on both occasions and keep their bouquets in water to keep them fresh for both days; there would be only one cake cut (at the larger reception) and only one bouquet and garter tossed (at the larger reception), but the processionals, recessionals, and the other rituals would remain the same at both services.

If the couple wish both services on the same day, the Jewish service would take place after sundown on Saturday, and the Christian service could follow at seven o'clock (depending on season), followed by the large reception. In this case, the Jewish parents would invite their friends to the Jewish ceremony, and the Christian parents would invite their friends to the Christian ceremony. Everyone would be invited to the same reception.

It is *much* simpler (less expensive, too) to have one ecumenical service. Having two services on different days or even the same day is costly and exhausting, but there are times when it is the only way out of a parental confrontation. Everything should be done to get the two married and to make the families happy. Nothing is too much trouble or too costly to accomplish this.

WEDDING APPAREL

THE BRIDAL ATTENDANTS' DRESSES

The bride has a responsibility to select dresses for her attendants that they will really like and that are affordable. Rarely does a bridesmaid's dress emerge from the owner's closet to be worn again after the wedding. (If it looks pretty in the pageantry of the wedding, it serves its purpose.)

The color scheme of the dresses is the bride's decision, and the flowers are usually coordinated with her color decisions. The maid and matron of honor can be dressed in separate colors, while the bridesmaids wear dresses of yet another color. Or everyone's dress can be in a different shade or hue of one color. Or everyone can wear the exact same color. The wedding may even be entirely in white.

If some of the attendants don't fit the standard sizes in which the dress comes, the bride can give a sample dress to a dressmaker and have it copied to the measurements of any extra tall or heavy bridesmaid.

The bride should take the season as well as color preferences and price into account in selecting her dresses. Velvet and satin dresses look heavy in the heat; cotton dresses look unsuitable in winter cold. The dresses can be any style—long or short, with hats or without, with flowers in the hair or not, with shoes that match or contrast. The bridesmaids' dresses should not be overly sexy, with deep cleavages and low-cut backs, out of respect for the house of worship.

Some recent brides have chosen to dress attendants in black—a flouting of tradition, in that black is the symbolic color of mourning. I personally feel this is unfortunate, first because wedding guests might feel the bridesmaids are in mourning over their friend's choice of a groom, but also because black dresses look gloomy at a wedding—they are very appropriate for funerals and jazz bars.

• If a bridesmaid is having a tough time financially and cannot afford to buy her dress and shoes—much less pay for the airfare to the wedding—the bride might approach someone in her family (who can afford it) to help pay for these expenses quietly and make it possible for the bridesmaid to serve.

THE APPAREL OF THE GROOMSMEN

The groom's best man and ushers are dressed in rented finery, and the men should be fast and efficient in sending their measurements to the rental place (as instructed by the best man) and in showing up for a fitting when they are supposed to. Call me conservative, but I feel strongly about how great the groom and his attendants look in dark classic styles, and how inappropriate they look in colored suits or suits with colored piping and frilly shirts. (The latter styles look fine when worn by members of a dance band but not by members of the wedding party.)

The groom may be dressed slightly differently from his attendants (in terms of fabric weight and the kind of stripe in his trousers, for example), but the rest of the group should be identically dressed. It is a good idea if the groom buys new ties for the best man and ushers so that they are the right kind.

For a Daytime Wedding

• Informal for summer or resort only. Appropriate wear would be all-white suits with white shirts, shoes, and socks; or dark blazers with either gray flannels or white trousers, worn with white shirts (French cuffs), conservative four-in-hand ties, and black shoes and socks.

• Informal. For an informal morning or early afternoon wedding, particularly if the bride wears a street-length dress or suit, the groom and his attendants would wear business suits in black, dark blue, or dark gray, with white shirts (French cuffs) and four-in-hand gray or gray-striped ties.

• More formal. Appropriate wear would be single-breasted gray or black strollers, gray vests, and striped trousers. The men should also wear gray or striped gray ties.

• Most formal. The men wear dark gray or black cutaways, gray vests, gray striped trousers, and a wing-collar shirt with gray ascot or a starched fold collar and a striped or checked four-in-hand gray tie.

For an Evening Wedding

• Informal. For an informal evening wedding (after six o'clock), grooms-men wear a black dinner jacket and trousers (a white jacket is correct for hot weather, but black is always better). A single- or double-breasted black vest or black cummerbund may be worn with this. A black bow tie and white pleated dinner shirt, ideally with pearl, gold, or onyx studs and cuff links, are proper.

• Formal. For an eight o'clock wedding, men would appear in a full-dress black tailcoat with white piqué or waffle-weave waistcoat and bow tie, starched white shirt with wing collar, and white pearl studs and cuff links.

Gloves

The groom at a formal wedding may decide to have his men wear gloves (gray for cutaways, white for tailcoats). The men should remove the glove on the right hand, of course, when shaking hands, and both gloves must be removed for eating and drinking. The groom and the best man would also remove their right gloves at the point in the wedding service when the best man hands the groom the wedding ring to place on the bride's finger.

The glove should be tucked in a pocket when not in use. The groom can always hand his right glove to his best man when he is placing the ring on the bride's finger. (Otherwise the ring might be dropped in the transfer.)

Shoes and Socks

Except when wearing all-white summer suits, the men in the wedding party should wear plain undecorated black shoes and black dress socks. For a black tie or white tie evening wedding, they should wear black patent leather shoes and black dress socks.

How the Guests Should Dress

The Men

• For a winter daytime wedding, male guests should wear a dark suit (navy, black, or dark gray) with a daytime dress shirt, a four-in-hand (or bow tie if they normally wear a bow tie), and dark shoes and socks, including patterned socks.

• For a summer daytime wedding in the city, male guests should wear lightweight dark suits, with the same accessories that would be worn for a winter daytime wedding.

• For a summer resort daytime wedding, which is more casual than a city wedding, a dark blazer and contrasting trousers of a "quiet" color are appropriate. A white, beige, or cream-colored summer suit (of linen, poplin, or other lightweight fabric) is also appropriate. Khaki trousers or jeans with a blazer are just too informal for a wedding. Jeans are "out" for any wedding that is not held in a boat or a snowdrift.

• At a very informal summer wedding, a man may wear a summer sports coat (of a bright color or a plaid) with white or contrasting color trousers.

• For a wedding at six o'clock or later, when the invitation reads "Black Tie," a man should wear a winter-weight black dinner suit with a white or cream dress shirt (pleats are nice, but no ruffles, please), cuff links, black hose, and black patent leather pumps or laced black patent leather shoes. He may wear a colored bow tie and matching cummerbund, if he wishes, but black is always right.

In the summer, a white dinner jacket with black trousers is correct for a black tie wedding, but a lightweight black dinner suit still looks best.

• For that very rare invitation to a "White Tie Wedding"—held only in wintertime in the city—a male guest would rent from a formal evening wear shop a suit of tails, complete with white piqué vest and white tie. Black silk hose and black patent leather shoes are de rigueur for this kind of outfit, as are tiny jeweled, onyx, or mother-of-pearl studs with large cuff links. White gloves are optional. In the old days, the guest would have worn a top hat with this outfit, but today it might look silly—alas.

The men in the wedding party, including the fathers of the bride and groom, often wear white tie and tails at a wedding held after eight o'clock in the evening, but usually the invitation to that kind of wedding reads "Black Tie." This means that the men guests wear black dinner suits. The days are past when all "gentlemen" knew that anything after 8 P.M. meant that they wear the full white tie regalia gathering dust in their closets.

The Women

• For a winter daytime wedding, a woman would wear a dress or a dress suit (a soft, not a man-tailored suit). She should not wear something as informal as a blouse and skirt or sweater and skirt, and, in my opinion, pants are not a good idea. A micro-mini on a woman guest, even if she has great legs, is inappropriate—too flashy and sexy. (It's not a guest's but the bride's day to shine and be the cynosure of all eyes.)

• It's advisable for a woman guest to refrain from wearing an all-white costume. If she does, it may seem to others that she's trying to compete with the bride, even though she may be totally unconscious of this impression.

• For a late afternoon winter wedding (after four o'clock), the woman guest's dress length would still be short, unless the invitation reads "Black Tie." By 5 P.M. it is appropriate to wear a "little black dress," in the old vernacular referred to as a "cocktail dress." (Black prints are fine for a wedding at any hour—it's the solid black dress that looks too much like mourning when the sun shines brightly.) From late afternoon on, the woman guest can wear a dress or suit of any dressy fabric (for example, brocades, lamés, velvets). Wait until after six o'clock before wearing sequins and paillettes, however.

• For a six o'clock (or later) "Black Tie" wedding, she could wear a theater suit or a short, three-quarter or floor-length evening dress appropriate to the season, whether winter, summer, or resort. Her shoes would be dressy sandals or pumps, and her handbag a small evening purse. This formal attire can be anything from a clinging crepe sheath to a full satin ballgown. If the invitation says "Black Tie," she can wear her favorite evening dress. (This is the time for her to wear her real or costume jewelry, too.)

• A "White Tie Wedding," seldom seen these days, calls for everyone to be dressed in their most formal attire. A woman would wear a décolleté ballgown, not a covered-up sheath. She would properly wear long white gloves.

THE WEDDING RING

The bride may opt not to have an engagement ring but instead to have an impressive band of diamonds or colored stones with diamonds as her wedding ring. Or she may want to have the traditional wedding band to wear in conjunction with an engagement stone ring. (The wedding ring should be made of the same metal as her engagement ring—yellow gold, white gold, or platinum.)

The bride does not wear her engagement ring to the ceremony on her wedding day—the groom places the wedding ring on her bare finger. Later, she will place her engagement ring on the outside of her wedding ring.

Perhaps the bride will be given one or two guard rings (slim bands of small diamonds or colored stones) for future anniversary or birthday presents. The guard rings would be worn outside and inside the engagement ring.

If the groom will wear a wedding ring, it does not have to exactly match the bride's, but it should be of the same color metal. The bride orders it in his proper ring size and has it engraved on the inside—as hers will be—with both sets of initials and the wedding date.

ANNOUNCEMENT IN THE NEWSPAPER

If you wish to have your wedding announcement published in the local newspapers (preferably the day after the wedding), you will have greater success if you organize yourself accordingly far enough in advance of the wedding date. In large cities, the space for featuring brides and grooms and engaged girls is so small in comparison to the numbers being married that newspapers have become selective in publishing the announcements. Sometimes they will consider only a bride or groom who comes from an illustrious or socially prominent family, or who is a personal success story. Sometimes a wedding will make it into the newspaper of a major city if the groom's grandfather was a famous general or author, or if the bride's great-grandfather founded a well-known company. If the bride or groom is personally successful in the health, education, business, sports, or entertainment world, the wedding announcement will probably be published. (A celebrity bride or groom, of course, means that the news desk will cover the wedding, whether the couple wishes it or not.) More and more papers today publish engagements and wedding announcements only if they are paid!

Sometimes there will be room for the announcement but not for the bride's picture. Sometimes an announcement makes it only because a bride whose photograph was sent in with her announcement is so beautiful that the editors couldn't resist using it. You never know. What can help your chances, however, is to send in a perfectly typed, properly spelled announcement, written in the style of the paper, giving the information the paper generally prints in its wedding section. If the newspaper is going to publish the announcement, an editor will call the bride, her mother, and often the groom to double-check the information. (Always put your home and office telephone numbers on anything you send in to the paper.)

Some small-town local newspapers give a full account of the wedding, including the names of the entire wedding party, a description of the bride's dress, and a description of what kind of reception was held and where. For a newspaper like the *New York Times,* only the "bare bones" information is published. For that coverage the bride's family should send in a glossy photograph (head shot only, whereas most other papers publish anything from a half-shot to a full-length portrait of the bride in her dress and headdress) with the following kind of information:

THE MARRIAGE OF CAMERON EDSON DELANEY
AND EDWARD LEE GRANT, 3/19/04

Cameron Edson Delaney, a daughter of Mr. and Mrs. David Edson Delaney of New Canaan, Connecticut, was married yesterday to Edward Lee Grant, a son of Mrs. Jonathan Wright and Frederick Grant of this city. The Reverend Andrew C. Smith performed the ceremony at Saint James Episcopal Church in New York.

Mrs. Grant, a graduate of the Spence School in New York and Kenyon College in Gambier, Ohio, is a credit analyst in the private banking and securities industries division of the Manufacturers Hanover Trust Company in New York. Her father is the chairman of the Delaney Manufacturing Company in Bridgeport, Connecticut.

The bridegroom, a graduate of the Collegiate School in New York and Princeton University, expects to receive a J.D. degree in May from Harvard Law School. His father is on the editorial staff of *New York* magazine, and his mother is with the real estate firm of Stribling Associates. The bridegroom is the grandson of the late George H. Lewis, Jr., the founder of the Lewis Advertising Agency in Chicago.

LAST-MINUTE WEDDING DISASTERS

Almost every bride—and her parents, too—experiences feelings of panic and attacks of nerves as the big day approaches. It is common for a bride to have certain crises of feelings (fortunately, very temporary ones) about the man she is about to marry. She may begin to feel something akin to stage fright, feelings of inadequacy, and a dread that she simply can't go through with all of the mechanics of a wedding. She may find she no longer wishes to be the center of everyone's attention during the endless rituals and long schedule of events. She finds she can't accept the requirement that she look fabulously put together and dewey-eyed, too, when her feet hurt. And she may find that being unremittingly nice to everyone when she doesn't feel like it is too heavy a task.

These feelings are something of a natural defense mechanism to steel the bride against disappointing anyone during the wedding festivities. Fortunately, they usually disappear as the beautiful and romantic drama of her wedding unfolds. She is the center of attention, and discovers she loves it. And almost everyone agrees that she is more beautiful on this day than on any other day in her life.

The bride's mother has other anxieties: Will the "horrible" new wife of her ex-husband, the father of the bride, try to steal center stage? Will Uncle Louie forget to fetch Grandma from the train station? Will it rain and ruin the garden wedding? Might the caterer have prepared inadequately for the crowds expected? This is not a tranquil time around the house, but in the vast majority of weddings, regardless of the minor slip-ups or even major disasters that loom on the horizon, the bride's and groom's happiness manages to cast light on everything and everyone around them. Problems find their solutions. Disasters become minor nuisances. The show goes on—and it's a fine show indeed.

If you are feeling panicky about your wedding, put your mind at ease by considering some of the things that have gone wrong at other people's weddings—weddings that turned out successful and happy nevertheless, like these:

- Two hours before the wedding, just after the florists had completely decorated the interior, lightning struck the church and burned it down. Without blinking an eye, the bride's parents and the minister shifted the services to the school gymnasium next door, with improvised floral arrangements using flowers gathered from the peony and lilac bushes in sympathetic neighbors' yards. The fragrance from these flowers was far more remarkable than the original flowers had been. And the service in temporary quarters seemed far more touching than it would have been in the church.

- The groom broke both legs in an accident on his way home from the rehearsal dinner the night before the wedding, but he managed to make it to the wedding by ambulance with his legs in casts. He was wheeled by ambulance attendants into the church and to the reception on a gurney, wearing at least the top part of his wedding suit, with its boutonniere in place. The couple's skiing honeymoon was postponed until a year later, on their first wedding anniversary, at which time the groom won the downhill slalom race, and the hotel management gave the couple a totally free vacation.

- The groom got into a fight at his bachelor party, broke his arm, and was married with his cutaway coat cut open to allow his cast-encased arm to be carried in a sling. The bride attached a gardenia to his sling.

• At the end of the wedding ceremony, the bride was left at the church by the excited groom as he took off for the reception with other members of his family filling the limo. The bride's absence was noticed about half an hour later. Someone went back to the church to fetch her and found her sitting alone in a pew, wondering if she had made a terrible mistake in her choice of husband. Later, relaxed and forgiving, she made a wedding toast to her groom, claiming that although she had perfect grounds for annulment of the marriage, she would give him one more chance.

• The bride at the reception following a Conservative Jewish wedding, while joyously borne aloft in a chair by male members of the wedding party—along with her groom in another chair—was tilted so badly that she fell out. She went to the hospital, where she was treated for a slight contusion and a sprained wrist, but made it back to the reception anyway in time for dessert.

• The caterer made a mistake and sent the wedding reception food to a bank's golf-outing picnic. The picnic food went to the wedding reception. The hosts were so busy receiving guests that they did not realize the mistake until the guests were all serving themselves egg salad, hot dogs, kosher pickles, and potato chips. The golfers in the meantime greatly enjoyed the reception food, particularly the wedding cake, though thinking it a little odd as the choice for their dessert. They had demolished three quarters of it by the time the caterer's truck pulled up to rescue it. The remaining piece was brought to the wedding reception, and the bride and groom laughingly cut into the small piece with their beautifully decorated cake knife. Everyone at the party had a tiny piece of it, and the entire crowd really had a good laugh when, following a drum roll, the bride announced at the microphone that the golfing group had placed a wedding present for them inside the remaining piece of cake. She held it up—a shiny new golf ball!

• The father of the bride slugged the mother of the bride's newest husband at the reception after a few glasses of champagne. Everyone witnessed it. The bride's father helped revive his victim and then took over the microphone to say, "I apologize, Don, for that uncalled-for show of aggression. You happen to be a great guy. I want you all to join me in a special toast to a very fine person, someone who has finally made the bride's mother a very happy woman. I drink to Don!" (His toast fixed things up, believe it or not.)

• As the procession was about to start in the back of the church, the bride noticed her athletic three-year-old nephew ring bearer was without his pillow (which had her wedding ring sewn onto it). It had been given to him fifteen minutes before, and he had managed to lose it somewhere between the house, the car, and the church.

The bride lost none of her composure. "Geoffrey will still walk up the aisle in his proper place without the pillow," she said, noting his face was a thunderstorm about to break. "It doesn't matter, Geoffrey." Then she commanded one of her bridesmaids to take off her own wedding ring at the altar and to give it at once to the best man to use in the ceremony. The groom looked nonplussed when he tried to get the ring on the bride's finger and found it was too small to pass her knuckle. "It's okay," the bride whispered, "I'll tell you later." Afterward, at the reception, she asked her nephew what he thought had happened to the ring pillow. His older sister, aged eight, answered for him. "Oh, he threw it out the window of the car." It was the only hitch in an otherwise perfect wedding, and as the jeweler later made a new engraved wedding ring for the bride—gratis.

• The outdoor tent, laden with the weight of too much rain, collapsed early on in the reception. No one was hurt, but everyone was covered with water and plastic. A group started laughing, the laughter spread, and soon the entire wedding party was convulsed as they extricated themselves. The guests didn't seem to mind their ruined clothes and hairdos, and the band resumed playing. The reception lasted four hours beyond its planned length. The caterer brought new food (frozen dishes that they warmed in microwave ovens) and an endless supply of champagne. The latter was the caterer's gift, since it was his tent that had collapsed. The guests, including the entire wedding party, remained completely wet and disheveled. Yet they all stated afterward that it was one of the greatest weddings they had ever attended.

• The father of the bride spent a great deal of money having a thousand balloons blown up to festoon the guide ropes and the tent supports for the reception tent. It was an extremely hot day, and the balloons, scraping against the ropes, began to explode with loud bangs. The thousand balloons popping off over a period of two hours made it sound like war inside the tent. Although that made things difficult for the musicians, it added to the general excitement of the reception.

• A limousine full of bridesmaids bound for the church was hijacked by an escaping thief and his accomplice. The concert of screams from the back seats drove him to desperation, so he chauffeured them to the church—they made it to the service only slightly late. After they got out of the stolen limo, the thieves drove off at high speed, only too glad to have the screaming damsels out of their lives and back to their wedding duties.

• The father of one bride announced on the microphone to the happy, dancing throngs at the reception, "The cars of everyone here who parked on State Street have been towed away by the Police Department and have been impounded across town." Then he put all the couples and families whose cars were involved into the chartered bus that had carried wedding attendants and family from the church to the reception. The bus driver took them to the car pound with the flamenco band from the reception on board, too, playing merrily away throughout the trip. The driver had also been given a large check to be turned over to the police to pay for the release of all the impounded cars.

It was an unexpected, unbudgeted expense for the wedding, but it was one the father of the bride felt was important.

Hundreds of receptions regularly run out of food, drink, and ice. Hundreds of neighbors' freezers then contribute to the ice supply. Hundreds of best men, ushers, or bridesmaids have scurried in cars to replenish the food. The merriment at a reception always seems to continue unabated for the guests, most of whom don't know about the behind-the-scenes drama.

Hundreds of best men or grooms have forgotten or lost the bride's wedding ring. (One groom's little brother "lost" the ring right before the ceremony in the family's oversized aquarium—where it was swallowed by one of twenty huge fish.) In each case, a friend in the wedding party or in the congregation lent her wedding ring for the ceremony. . . . Hundreds of brides or bridegrooms faint during the religious ceremony, and all are rehabilitated quickly, in time for the service to proceed. . . . Hundreds of best men or grooms have forgotten to bring to the reception the bridal couple's passports or air tickets, with the result that the couple misses their flight overseas. It is never the end of the world, and often the adventures they have on their alternative wedding night turn out to be far more exciting than flying off on a plane on schedule. . . . Hundreds of stepparents or stepchildren or stepsiblings have let loose with some kind of animosity at some point during the wedding festivities, but these transgressions are quickly forgotten by the protagonist and have no effect on the majority of the guests' enjoyment of the wedding.

In other words, things can go wrong—but nothing should be magnified. Seeing the humor in a situation will get you through anything, and almost nothing is so important that it should ruin the day. Solving the dilemmas that present themselves during a wedding requires creativity, kindness, fast action, and humor—always humor!

GIFTS

Wᴇᴅᴅɪɴɢ Gɪғᴛ Rᴇᴄᴏʀᴅ Booᴋ

Every bride should keep careful records of the wedding gifts received in a Wedding Gift Register. You can purchase a handsome notebook and make your own headings, such as these:

WEDDING GIFTS

Who Sent	Address	What Sent	Store	Arrival	Date of Thank-You

(If the groom writes some of the thank-you notes, which he should, his initials would be written in the "Date of Thank-You" column.

The Exchange of Gifts Within the Wedding Party

There is a delightful, well-established tradition of gifts involving members of the wedding party. There is, for example:
- The engagement ring given to the woman by her fiancé.
- Her engagement present to him—usually a personal gift such as a new photograph of herself in a handsome frame, or a pair of cuff links.
- The groom's wedding ring for his bride.
- Her wedding ring (optional) for her husband. (Advice to the bride: Don't make your husband wear a wedding ring if he really doesn't wish to.) The bride's and groom's rings should be the same color of metal, but they do not have to be the exact same design.
- His or his family's gift of jewelry to his bride for their wedding—for example, a watch, string of pearls, gold pin, bracelet, heirloom locket on a chain.
- Her gift to her husband for their wedding—for example, a watch, set of studs for his black tie, a gold tie clip, a leather desk set.
- The bridesmaids' gift to the bride—often a joint gift, such as a charm bracelet, an engraved piece of silver, or an etched piece of crystal, such as a box with each bridesmaid's initials, plus those of the bride and groom, and the wedding date.
- The bride's gift to her attendants—perhaps a silver picture frame that will eventually hold a photograph of the wedding party, engraved with the wedding date, or a leather one, embossed in gold; a charm for a bracelet; an engraved silver pen, mirror, or compact; or something in crystal, such as a water pitcher, etched with the wedding date and the bride's and groom's initials.
- The attendants' gift to the groom—such as a small silver tray engraved with their signatures and the wedding date, something for his car (like a tape deck or a television for the backseat if he has small children), a briefcase, a set of bar glasses etched with the initial of his last name.
- The groom's gift to his attendants—a silver or leather frame, like the one the bride gives her attendants; a leather stud box with his initials, the wedding date, and the usher's initials; a silver pen engraved with the initials of the recipient; an engraved silver jigger for measuring liquor for drinks; a wallet with the recipient's initials embossed in gold.

GIFTS FROM FAMILY AND FRIENDS
TO THE BRIDE AND GROOM

Family members and friends who send wedding gifts most often use these points as their guides:

- How close they are to the bride or groom.
- How much they have to spend.
- How much the bride and groom need help in furnishing their household.

No one should overspend on a wedding present, no matter how much affection there is for the couple. The note accompanying the wedding present is often as important as the gift itself—a note carefully written by hand, in which the donor expresses love for the couple and very special wishes for their future.

BRIDAL REGISTRY

It is very useful for everyone if the bride registers—not in many stores, but in one or two that are easy to reach, either in person or on-line. Bridal registries have become so sophisticated today that if you call some large chain and ask if a certain bride is registered there, the operator will look up the bride's name and may say, "Yes. Would you like to be connected to the department where she is registered in crystal, silver, china, appliances, or kitchenware?" In smaller stores, there is only one registry in which the bride has listed everything she would like in that store.

A bride can register for certain useful items that are expensive in the hopes that a group of her relatives or friends may join together to buy one of them. But she would be wise to list items she really needs and that are not out of the ballpark, costwise. If she registers for her silver pattern and expensive plates or something like a new digital sound system, she, her family, and her friends should be briefed to inform anyone who asks that she has registered for certain things that would have to be the gift of several people, or that she would appreciate the gift of just one fork or one spoon or plate in her pattern. A bride who registers at ten places, with elaborate gifts listed, deserves the instant reputation of being labeled mercenary and spoiled.

THE GIFT OF MONEY

Money from a relative or close friend is always an acceptable gift. At many weddings, particularly ethnic ones, it is traditional to give money as the wedding present—and to slip it in an envelope to the bride or groom (most often the groom) at the reception. The money may pay for the honeymoon or be used for a car, household furnishings, or other needs.

It is best not to give cash—it is too easily lost or stolen. Before the couple leaves on the honeymoon, they should both endorse the checks, assuming they have a new joint account, and a member of the family or wedding party should deposit the checks, with a properly filled-out deposit slip, at the next available banking hour.

In sending notes thanking for money, the bride and groom should express their thanks for "the generous check," without stipulating the amount. It is much more tasteful if neither the donor, the bridal couple, nor the couple's families publicly state how much any one person gave the couple.

RETURNING AND EXCHANGING GIFTS

It can really hurt feelings if the donor discovers you have exchanged his present for something else. (Duplicates, of course, can be returned; so can items of which you have been given more than one, such as a water pitcher or a salad bowl.) Often a family member will have a prized family possession that she gives the couple as a very sentimental gesture, such as Great-Aunt Mary's silver cake knife. If it is a "hideousity," as one recent bride described her grandmother's Victorian lamp, it must be kept and displayed when that family member comes to their home. I kept certain of my own "hideousity" wedding presents (from 1963) in the back of a closet; they have since become rather chic again, so I now sometimes use or display them.

Couples should keep in mind the disappointment someone they truly love may feel when he comes into their home and finds that his wedding present is nowhere in sight. Out of respect and affection for the donor, the couple can always keep "Aunt Mabel's bowl" for a year or two, and then the bowl can quietly be put away or "retired" to a thrift shop.

THANK-YOU NOTES

In the past, it was the bride's chore to write all the thank-you notes, not only because most of the guests and most of the presents came from her side of the family, but also because she was at home. Today, when the bride and groom often work equally hard, the groom should write thank-you notes, too—if not half the load, at least those to his relatives and his parents' friends.

• Thank-you notes to people who gave parties for your wedding should be written *the day after.* You should also send flowers to your hosts, but what you say in your letter is what counts most of all. A sample note:

Dear Aunt Midge, Uncle Bob, and Aunt Nancy,

You will never know how grateful Jim and I are for the incredible rehearsal dinner you gave us last night. Everyone in the wedding party had the best time—and you should have heard them all extolling the virtues of the great cuisine, the lovely flowers in the center of the tables, and not only the quality of the champagne, but the endless amounts of it!

You are the most generous aunts and uncle in this world. Jim and I will never forget your toasts to us, either, and I only hope that someday we can become the great uncle and aunt to our nieces and nephews that you have been to us.

It is the morning of our wedding day, and I must hurry to get dressed, but I wanted you to know that as far as I'm concerned, you've already made this wedding a success! Am I not lucky to be getting a man like this in my life?

Affectionately,

• Thank-you notes for wedding gifts should be written within two weeks preferably—at the outside maximum, within two months. I know of couples who have taken six months to write their thank-you notes, which leaves many people wondering if their presents ever arrived, and others wondering why they spent so much time and money selecting that wedding gift! I remember a spunky great-aunt of the bride's who rang the doorbell of the bride and groom's home one day and announced that, since she had heard nothing for nine months from the day she'd sent her gift, it obviously was not appreciated. And since the gift had cost her an infinite amount of trouble and a great amount of money to buy, she proceeded to ask where it was and took it back home with her! (I am sure a lot of other wedding present donors would like to do the same thing but don't have the nerve.)

• Thank-you notes should be written on good-quality stationery, by hand. If the bride can afford it, she uses notepaper engraved with her new monogram (not to be used, however, until *after* the wedding ceremony). If she writes her thank-you notes for the presents as they arrive, weeks before the wedding, she sends thanks for them on her about-to-be-abandoned social stationery (paper engraved with her maiden name or monogram). If engraved stationery is not within the bride's budget, she should purchase good-quality plain notepaper (single sheets or folded notes) with matching envelopes—in any color and with any color border.

The groom should use for his stationery either plain notepaper or, after the wedding, he may use jointly with the bride social stationery engraved only with their home address (and perhaps home telephone number) at the top of the sheets.

If the bride or groom has unintelligible handwriting, he or she may type the thank-you note on a computer, printed out on good social stationery.

What is unacceptable is a printed studio card that says "Thank you" on it, to which the bride simply signs her name and her groom's with no written message. I've seen that several times lately. Help!

• An unacceptable thank-you note from the bride leaves out any mention of the gift that was sent:

Dear Mrs. Castro,

George and I really like your wedding present. Thank you so much, and I hope we'll see you soon.

> Sincerely,
> Susan

For all anyone knows with this kind of letter, Mrs. Castro could have sent George and Susan a lawnmower or champagne glasses for their wedding present. Such a note is better than sending nothing at all, but only slightly better!

• An acceptable thank-you note from the bride:

Dear Mrs. Castro,

George and I are absolutely delighted with the beautiful place mats and napkins from you and Mr. Castro. The pale blue is such a perfect color, we have decided to repaint the walls of our dining area a pale blue, too. [What a compliment to match the wall color to your wedding gift! You would say this only if you were really painting the walls blue.]

We have already used them at dinner for my parents, and we will use them again when my boss comes to dinner next week. We really appreciate this useful, wonderful present, and I hope the Castros will be coming to Topeka some day soon, so we can have you to dinner. We will be using blue place mats on the table.

> Sincerely,
> Susan

P.S. Married life is terrific!

• An acceptable thank-you note if it's the groom who writes it:

Dear Mrs. Castro,

Susan and I really appreciate the Castros' gift. We have already used those blue place mats for a special dinner for my in-laws, and somehow they even made our food look better! They are really great.

Susan is at her night class in business school as I write this. We are both very happy and very busy—and your place mats and napkins are making our lives easier, too, when we entertain. You gave us a perfect present.

Sincerely,
George

POSTPONING THE WEDDING

It happens. Sometimes the wedding must be postponed. There may be a death in the immediate family. The groom may be quarantined. The bride may be in a body cast from an auto accident. There may have been a fire in the bride's home, where the wedding was to take place. The groom may have been called up by the National Guard.

If the invitations have already gone out but there is plenty of time to get postponement announcements printed and into the mail, then the parents of the bride would send a printed announcement like this, in the same typeface as the original invitation:

Mr. and Mrs. Duncan Forsythe Teston

announce that the marriage of their daughter

Suzanne MacDonald

to

Mr. Henry Foscue Cavalchini

has been postponed from

Saturday, the ninth of May

until

Saturday, the sixth of September

at five o'clock

Saint Barnabas Church

Boston

If the postponement decision is because of the death of a member of the family, that may certainly be included in the announcement:

> *Mr. and Mrs. Duncan Forsythe Teston*
> *announce that because of the death*
> *of their son Geoffrey*
> *the marriage of their daughter*
> *Suzanne MacDonald*
> *to Mr. Henry Foscue Cavalchini*
> *has been postponed*
> *etc.*

If the postponement decision does not leave enough time to have these cards printed and mailed, fax or e-mail the same message to each of your guests, and be prepared for a host of worried telephone calls from all your friends wondering why the postponement, if you did not mention the reason in the mailing. In fact, instruct whoever answers the telephone at your office and at your home to explain quickly the reason for the postponement. Human curiosity knows no bounds.

CALLING OFF THE WEDDING

Sadly, it also happens that a decision is made not to go on with the wedding. It is a very difficult time for everyone. Again, a formal printed announcement may be mailed—if there is time to give people enough advance warning to change their plans with ease.

> *Mr. and Mrs. Thatcher William Gray*
> *announce the marriage of their daughter*
> *Ruth Leigh*
> *to*
> *Mr. Saxton William Baines*
> *by mutual agreement*
> *will not take place.*

This is a time for face-saving and compassion. Anyone connected with the wedding should say whenever the cancellation is discussed, "Both decided it was the best thing to do . . . Both equally agreed that the wedding should be called off." Of course, it is almost never a mutually agreed-upon decision, but for the sake of saving the injured person's pride, everyone should play his part. With time, the sadness and perhaps even the humiliation suffered by the woman or the man will subside.

The woman should return her fiancé's engagement ring, unless he called off the wedding, and in this case he should return any of her gifts to him. If he is the one to call off the wedding, she would probably not wish to wear the ring again anyway. If it were me, I'd welcome the ring but would have it reset so as to be unrecognizable. (I know of some cases in which the spurned fiancée has managed to exchange her engagement ring successfully at the jeweler for a totally different kind of jewelry.)

All wedding presents should be carefully wrapped and returned at once to the donor with a short note announcing the wedding is off and expressing the couple's thanks "for your beautiful, generous present." That's all that has to be said.

PRENUPTIAL AGREEMENTS

Thanks to the proliferation of divorce in this country, the prenuptial agreement has become common. It has also sadly become a common topic of conversation among friends, like hanging out the family's dirty laundry on the line for anyone to see. Prenuptial agreements used to be considered relevant only for billionaires, movie stars, and highly paid athletes. Today they are prevalent enough to inspire many states to adopt the "Uniform Premarital Agreement Act"—the benchmark legislation for marital contracts. This act greatly assists someone with an agreement who moves to another state and then worries about the validity of the agreement under the new state's laws.

Prenuptial agreements make the most sense for people who will remarry and wish to protect the assets of their children in the future. They make sense, too, for a very rich person marrying for the first time. However, for a young couple with limited assets marrying for the first time, a prenuptial agreement puts a sour note into what should be an exhilarating, optimistic experience. It is almost asking for trouble in the marriage. A great deal of misunderstanding and hurt feelings can result from the premise upon which these agreements are based—that one person will try to cheat the other in case of a breakup. Some people talk about their agreements the way others talk about what their psychiatrists told them this week. It suddenly all becomes very distasteful!

From the point of view of etiquette, it's important to keep the following in mind:

- Don't discuss the financial and legal ramifications of your marriage contract.
- If anyone asks if you have a prenuptial agreement, mention that the subject is a private matter, which it definitely is.
- Never discuss the details of it with anyone except your spouse and your lawyer.

A good agreement strikes a happy medium between preserving your marital relationship and protecting your property.

WHEN YOU MARRY MORE THAN ONCE

Second and third marriages have become so common, that by the time they reach the age of forty-five, many people are attending more of their friends' remarriages than they are of their friends' children's marriages.

When you marry for the second time, the protocol is fairly rigid, but you can choose not to follow it, and many brides do not follow it! In this section I will lay on the table what is proper and in good taste in the conventional sense, guaranteed to ward off any criticism behind your back. Of course, you are free to accept it or not.

The religious ceremony, whether you have it in a church, temple, your home, a club, or a hotel, should be small and include only family and the very closest friends. The participation of your more extended circle of friends should be centered on the wedding reception, which can be anything you wish—with no limitations as to number of guests invited or lavishness of food and entertainment.

WHO DOES THE INVITING?

Usually the small number of people who are to attend the ceremony itself are invited by the bride or groom by personal note or telephone call. As for the reception, if the bride is very young, her parents once again invite the guests to the reception. If the bride and groom are in their mid-thirties or older, usually they extend the invitation to their reception and pay for it as well:

> *Agatha [or optionally, Mrs. Agatha] Henley Freeman*
> *and*
> *Chapman [or Mr. Chapman] Delano Blaine*
> *request the pleasure of your company*
> *at dinner*
> *following their wedding*
> *on Thursday, March third*
> *at seven o'clock*
> *The Colony Club*
> *New York City*
>
> *R.S.V.P.*   *Black Tie*
>
> *000-000-0000*

It is important, in the case of a second or third marriage, to disseminate as many postwedding announcements as possible to all friends of the bride and groom, because they will want to be aware of the good news. Recipients of these announcements are not obliged to send a present, but close friends always do.

CHANGES IN THE RITUAL

When a woman remarries, tradition decrees a change in her attire and in certain symbolic aspects of the wedding ritual. Of course, you are free to go against tradition and repeat the whole ceremony once again—long white dress and cathedral veil, being "given away" by your father, and tossing your bridal bouquet to an unmarried bridesmaid. Some women who eloped or who didn't have the money to be married with all the fuss the first time, long to "do it up right" the second time. That's a woman's right. But if you wish to remarry according to traditional etiquette, and not to attract criticism, there are certain things to remember:

• *You would avoid having an official announcement party.* Instead, you and your fiancé call and write all family members and friends with your very happy news. If someone wants to give you a party, great—but call it "a party for us," not an "engagement party." A woman who is remarrying does not go through an "engagement period." She just gets married.

- You would avoid wearing a long white bridal dress with a train and a veil.
- You would avoid having a galaxy of bridesmaids. Instead, you and your groom have one attendant each. Yours may be a married or unmarried friend or relative. You and the groom may wish as your attendants one of your own children—hopefully thirteen or older and mature enough to understand the solemn significance of the marriage vows.

HOW THE BRIDE DRESSES

A man always dresses to match his bride. If you are in a long, flowing white dress and veil as a first-time bride at a large formal afternoon wedding, your groom would wear a cutaway. Or after six o'clock, he would wear a black tie. There is no symbolism in *his* clothes, as there is in the bride's.

The Bride

Your second wedding may be a daytime (informal or formal) affair, or a black tie evening affair. If you wish to get married after six in a floor-length gown with your groom in a black dinner suit, then the invitations should spell it out to the guests by including the words "Black Tie"—meaning the guests are to come attired in evening dresses and tuxedos. (This is no time for that odious phrase "Black Tie Optional," which should be relegated to its graveyard!)

When a bride is being married for the second time, a full-fledged formal white tie wedding, held at eight o'clock or later, is simply inappropriate.

For a very informal daytime wedding, you would wear a street-length silk dress or dressy suit (a strictly man-tailored style of suit is not appropriate) in an off-white or pastel color (not red or black). You could wear a hat, a flower in your hair, a short veil, or nothing.

For a more formal, larger afternoon wedding, you might wear a dress of a rather formal fabric (silk, crepe, chiffon, organza, velvet, brocade, or whatever, according to the season) and in any length you desire, including floor length. For a six-o'clock-or-after wedding, you could wear a long evening dress.

You may carry a bouquet of the flowers of your choice—or a white prayer book with flowered ribbon streamers. You may wear a hat, bandeau, bow, or flowers in your hair, but forget the veil. It is a nice touch if your shoes match your dress. What is inappropriate is to be married in a house of worship wearing a backless dress that is cut extremely low in front, even if you have a great shape and the dress bears the label of the number-one dress designer.

Although the wardrobe departments of Hollywood and TV land often don't seem to realize it, a woman marrying even for the fourth time should exude a sense of dignity appropriate to the occasion.

The Groom

His wedding attire matches his bride's, according to the time of day. He would wear a dark business suit for an informal daytime wedding, perhaps a stroller and gray-striped trousers for a more formal daytime wedding, and a black tuxedo for an evening wedding. For a daytime wedding in hot weather, the groom would be dressed in a dark blazer and gray flannel or white trousers.

Their Attendants

The groom's attendant would be dressed similar to the groom, with an identical or slightly different boutonniere. If the bride's and groom's children from previous marriages attend their parents, they should be dressed in their best clothes. (I attended one wedding recently in which the groom's attendant was his nine-year-old son, dressed up in a tuxedo. It looked ludicrous.)

The bride's attendant would be dressed in a style to echo the bride's. If the bride is wearing a long chiffon gown, for example, the bridesmaid might wear a chiffon dress of an identical or different color but in a harmonious design. For a daytime wedding, the bride might wear a long dress and her attendant a short one of the same kind of fabric. For a very informal wedding, the single attendant may wear any dressy daytime dress (not a suit) as long as it is not white, red, or black, and as long as any pattern in the fabric is not a strong one. She could wear a hat, flowers or a bow in her hair, or nothing. She should not be dressed more elaborately than the bride.

THE CEREMONY

There is no processional or recessional in your second wedding. There may be organ music (or any kind of church music), but preferably not the traditional "Here Comes the Bride" or the wedding march from *Lohengrin*. You are not "given away" by your father, since you were already given away at your first wedding. There are no ushers seating people. There is no runner and no satin ribbons to pull through the posts of the pews. Your two families simply sit down in the front rows, with your closest friends behind them.

At the musical signal that the wedding is to begin, your attendant precedes you as you walk unescorted from the vestry door at the side of the front of the church to join your groom and his attendant at the foot of the altar. (A very young bride the second time around may wish her father or another male relative to escort her to the groom's side, and that is perfectly fine, but she is not "given away" a second time.) The ceremony should be brief; almost always, in this kind of intimate and personal environment, it is very touching and sentimental.

Parties and the Second Wedding

Showers for a second-time bride are simply not appropriate. You had that kind of festivity the first time and supposedly became equipped with what you and your husband needed for your household. If your husband absconded with all of the household possessions at the time of the divorce, then your friends might give a shower kind of party to help out, but it wouldn't be labeled a "kitchen shower." It would just be referred to as a "party to fix up Mamie's kitchen."

There would not be a rehearsal dinner as such, given by the groom's family the night before the wedding, but the latter might give a dinner "in honor of" the bride and groom to fete the occasion. (There doesn't usually have to be a rehearsal of the simple wedding ceremony—just a talk with the clergyman or woman during the week before the ceremony.)

Gifts the Second Time Around

Do you give a wedding gift the second time around? Yes! When you love, or even like, a person, no matter how many times he or she is married, you want to bless the union with your good wishes. You do not have to give a friend to whom you gave an expensive present the first time an equally lavish gift the second or third time around. If you attend the wedding, you should send a modest gift. Even if you were not invited to the small wedding, if one of the pair is a good friend of yours, hearing about the wedding or receiving their wedding announcement should move you to send a little something to show you are delighted with the news.

The note that accompanies your gift is as important as the gift. You wouldn't write a note like this one, recently received by a friend of mine who was being married for the third time:

Dear Nancy, I hope this time it will finally work! Love,

Instead, you might write a warm word like this on the gift card enclosure:

Nancy, along with this small present goes a multitude of good wishes for you and Hank. You deserve great happiness, and you make a wonderful pair. This is going to be a terrific year for you both!

STEPCHILDREN, STEPPARENTS,
AND GRANDPARENTS

When a man or woman with children from a former marriage remarries, a sizable emotional problem presents itself, one that requires every bit of tact, compassion, and self-sacrifice humanly possible for its solution.

The following scenarios, for example, are repeated all over the world when a divorced parent plans another wedding:

• The wife has been deserted by her husband for another woman, and he wants his children to attend the wedding to his new young wife. Or the husband has been deserted by his wife for another man, and she wants the children to participate in her wedding to a new husband. In both cases, the wronged partner is ready to declare war.

• The children of a parent about to be remarried are upset by the advent of a new stepparent and stepbrothers and sisters coming to live in their household. They fear they will no longer dominate the scene in their own house and feel they must now fight for their turf.

• The grandparents of the children whose mother has been divorced by their son feel that now that their son has abandoned his home, their grandchildren will no longer be available to them. They feel that their ex-daughter-in-law will keep the children away from them for spite.

• The children who will accompany the parent who has remarried and move after the wedding into his or her spouse's home have a new stepparent to contend with. In addition they feel inordinately threatened by their stepsiblings, who already call that house home.

• The new stepfather or stepmother worries about how to gain the acceptance of the new stepchildren, plus worries about how his or her own children are going to accept this disruption.

In short, *everyone* is under great emotional pressure as the wedding day approaches. When the wedding of people who have children from prior marriages takes place, it's wise for all persons involved—adult and child alike—to take a deep breath, and to say to themselves, "This is happening. It won't go away. I will do my best to make it happen with the least amount of pain to the people I love. I will do my part to make it a good day for everyone involved."

If ever strong character and self-sacrifice were needed, it is now. The generations of family involved with one another should talk it out calmly, be frank in expressing how they feel, and discuss the emotional ramifications of the wedding for the sake of protecting the feelings of the children, who are always the ones who suffer most. It's a question of each person's calling upon his personal strength—an extra measure of emotional adrenaline—to help get through the wedding period with flying colors, behaving in such a kind and gracious manner that he will be a pacesetter. One person's brave behavior alone might help smooth the path of harmony for many months to come. A wedding involving upset ex-husbands and ex-wives, widowed parents, and new stepparents and stepchildren is an opportunity for any individual to become a leader and a star in the complicated family firmament. For example:

- The deserted wife swallows hard and tells her children that of course she wants them to attend their father's wedding; or the deserted husband tells his children that of course they should attend their mother's wedding—with his blessing. It helps if the deserted one has planned a lovely treat for herself, like a wonderful trip to take place at her ex-husband's wedding time. (It would also be nice if the ex-husband pays for this trip.)

- The children on both sides of the family are taught to approach their new stepsiblings with enthusiasm, because after the petty little problems are ironed out (mostly questions of turf and seniority, not questions of who is the most or the least loved), they will have *much to gain* from each other. They will have fun together.

- The new spouse writes a letter from the heart, telling the deserted one how much it means to him to have the stepchildren present at the wedding. The new spouse expresses his love and admiration for the children, compliments the deserted spouse on the way the children were brought up, and pledges to do everything possible to keep peace and harmony in the family.

- The deserted spouse refrains from talking against the new spouse who has taken her place—either to the children or to friends. The deserted one knows that expressed criticism and bitterness solve nothing but make matters worse for everyone.

- The deserted spouse makes sure that the newly married spouse has constant access to the children, and that the grandparents do, too.

- The newly married spouse takes very seriously the times of visitation to the divorced spouse's household, being careful never to cancel an appointment with the children. He never talks against the former spouse in front of their children or in public. Instead he tries to speak well of this person.

- The widow who remarries invites her late husband's parents to her wedding. She is careful to explain that no one will take the place of their son in her heart, but that she is now walking down a new path. She is careful to maintain their relationships with their grandchildren.

The above scenarios are a reflection of an ideal world, which, of course, this world is not. But everyone should make a supreme effort for the children's sake at the time of the emotional shock of a parent's wedding to someone else. The one who gives the most ultimately gains the most.

Of all the rites of passage, a wedding is certainly the biggest production of them all—it is the most expensive and the most emotional, and offers the greatest potential for frayed tempers and possible disagreements. If all those involved will only keep telling themselves to act in a concerted manner to stay calm, think of the happiness of the bride and groom, not pursue their own agendas, and think positively about all the arrangements, the wedding will be a monumental success. And if the prepared script isn't quite followed here and there during the proceedings, what does it matter? A year later, the rough spots will have been forgotten; only the rosy memories will remain. If you personally had a hand in helping someone else at the wedding forget the rough spots, you can take personal satisfaction in the strength of the new marriage.

CHAPTER 13

Pregnancy, Birth, and Other Rites of Passage That Welcome a Child into the World

When we attend a rite of passage of a good friend or of a child, we feel blessed to be present at this kind of celebration—except, of course, for the ultimate rite, a funeral. Until that last rite is performed, there is a sense of joy when a family comes together, when there's a reunion of good friends, and when everyone present partakes of each great step forward in the maturation and development of a beloved person's life.

THE HAPPIEST EVENT OF ALL: THE BIRTH OF A BABY

POLITE PREGNANCY AT WORK

If she can manage it—and this requires a lot of willpower—it's very wise for a woman not to tell anyone at work until she actually shows, even in loose-fitting dresses or suits (this could be as late as the fourth or even fifth month). Once the fact is known, there will be much conversation about her condition, with many questions asked (including overly personal, prying ones) and many stares. That is why it is much better to put off the inevitable holding of center stage in her workplace as long as she can.

The pregnant woman should be productive—as the others around her should be, too. She should be courteous in her answers but cut off any pregnancy conversation amiably and turn it back to her work:

Q. "Are you having that nausea that most women have in the early months?"

A. "Oh, I feel just fine—none of that. What worries me is where is that statistical report from the Budget Division that we need for Monday's meeting? Has anyone seen it?"

Q. "Has the baby begun to kick and move around yet? Is that a twitch I just saw?"

A. "This is a good baby—it never moves when I'm at work. Tell me, Agnes, how are we doing with the new Antco account? Are they happy with our work?"

Q. "Have you looked into that new kind of life insurance for the baby, which dates from the hour of its birth?"

A. "Maybe you could tell me about it when we take the bus home tonight. I'd be interested in getting information on it when I have the time to think about it."

The less complaining any woman who works during her pregnancy does about fatigue and the fewer comments made about the baby's progress within her, the better. (Such subjects as gas pains, swollen ankles, and frequent urination should not become part of the daily office agenda.)

In other words, in deference to the people who are paying her salary, she should show everyone that she is absolutely delighted about the baby but is not going to let baby conversation overtake her productivity at work. This is one of the workplace problems every career woman must overcome.

Returning to Work After the Baby Is Born

If she plans on returning to work after a hiatus of several weeks or months, the prospective mother should inform her office and stick to her promise of when she is to return. During those weeks at home, she should read all the informative material circulated at work that she can get her hands on. (Maybe a friend will bring her a packet once a week.) She should make some calls to her colleagues in the office from time to time, asking them how this or that is proceeding, so they know she is interested in her work. Perhaps she should keep in touch with her regular clients or customers. She should drop in to the office once every three or four weeks (without the baby), looking well dressed, as she would for an important meeting. These occasional drop-ins to say hello to everyone (members of senior management, too) and to be informally briefed on what is happening are very helpful moves to exude an aura of professionalism. Her appearances remind her colleagues that she is keeping up and will soon be back in their midst.

The new mother should be able to sneak the time at least to skim the trade journals she normally would see if she were in the office. She should keep informed not only on the work of the office but on the gossip, too. (Short office visits are well worth the cost of paying for a baby-sitter's services at home.)

A company that holds a woman's job for her and that grants her a decent maternity leave has the right to ask that she keep in touch with her work. It is paramount in earning the respect of colleagues and superiors.

NURSING THE BABY

There are some young women who not only feel it is a woman's right to nurse her baby anywhere at any time, but they take it as their moral obligation to do so "in your face" in public whenever they can. That is one school of thought, but the other school feels that nursing a baby is a private, beautiful act that should be done away from the public eye. Many people feel that nursing a baby in a public place, such as in a restaurant, is intrusive, but this is a dilemma that will probably never be solved. Any sensitive company will arrange for a private place for a nursing mother to be alone with her baby.

THE BIRTH ANNOUNCEMENT

There are many ways to announce the birth of a baby. One happy father had a skywriter announce it in puffs of white in a bright blue sky over his town's busiest section at noon. Another one hired an actor, dressed him up as an early eighteenth-century colonial town crier, handed him a proclamation written on a piece of parchment, and had him ring his bell all over town, shouting "Hear Ye, Hear Ye" followed by the name, weight, and hour of birth of a baby girl. (Some observers thought he was an escaped lunatic.) New York parents have advertised their babies' arrivals on giant billboards in Times Square on more than one occasion. But there are more conservative ways of doing it!

For example: Mail announcements. You can buy pretty pink or blue ones at gift card shops, with lines on which to fill in the information. Or you can have announcement cards printed or even engraved. Quality stationers usually provide pricey engraved cards, bordered in pink or pale blue, for those who can afford them. The information on these cards is engraved in black in a classic typeface; the baby's own tiny calling card is attached to the larger announcement card by means of a pale pink or pale blue satin ribbon bow.

Many parents announce the birth of their baby by e-mail, including a photo. Some proud parents enclose a snapshot of the baby in their Christmas card by way of announcing the birth; others have the baby's photo printed on a card that becomes their Christmas card. Many use their baby's footprint made for the hospital's records for the birth announcement. One rather over-enthusiastic but well-heeled couple had their three-week-old baby's portrait painted in oils by a well-known artist; the colored photograph of the oil painting was then mailed as an announcement card to all their friends.

The cleverest announcement I've ever seen (or rather heard) was a cassette tape that arrived one day in the mail, with absolutely no information on it and no return address. I naturally played it out of curiosity, thinking it was probably going to be something cheap and tawdry. Instead I heard ten seconds of a baby's cry. Then the father's voice was heard saying, "The lusty squall you just heard came from the seven-day-old lungs of a future tight end for the Chicago Bears. His name is Matt." Not only did I love it, but that cassette was played for everyone who came into the office that day; everyone smiled, then laughed, and felt good about the state of the world.

The information that should be imparted on a birth announcement is:
- Full name of the baby
- Birth date
- Parents' name
- Parents' address

Optional additional information:
- Hour of birth
- Name of hospital
- Birth weight

(A birth announcement printing the number of hours the mother was in labor is too much!)

It's much nicer, of course, when one of the parents personalizes a printed announcement with a little sentence or two written by hand, anything from "He's so sweet, we can't believe he's here" to "She's the longest baby! She'll be an Olympic basketball player, there's no doubt." When the father pens a note on a birth announcement, he inevitably says, "The baby, of course, looks just like me," and the mother inevitably agrees and writes, "She looks just like her father." I have a feeling this is a concerted campaign to make the father feel he had more to do with the baby's birth than just help with the breathing exercises. (The truth, of course, is that a newborn doesn't look like anyone!)

HOW TO REACT
TO A BIRTH ANNOUNCEMENT

When a good friend mails you a birth announcement, or you hear via the grapevine that the baby was born, react right away—with a letter, telephone call, e-mail, or gift with a note. Such happy news should not go unacknowledged—particularly if it's a couple's first baby. (By the time the sixth child arrives in that family, you can be a little more blasé about it!)

EXTENDING CONGRATULATIONS
FOR THE NEW BABY

PRESENTS FOR THE PARENTS

The baby receives so much attention that the parents often rate hardly a glance. Therefore, if you are close to the parents of a newborn, it's amusing, gracious, and appreciated to give *them* a gift rather than give one to the baby. One of the things my husband and I most appreciated when our first was born was a case of wine, with a card from friends that read, "You are *really* going to need this within a short time, so enjoy!" I also will never forget receiving a gift certificate in the mail from a friend to avail myself of a "Miracle Morning" at Elizabeth Arden. It arrived a week after Clare was born and presented a glorious opportunity to get my tired, misshapen body out of the house and into a salon to have my hair done and take advantage of other options, including a massage, facial, pedicure, manicure, sauna, paraffin wax bath, and general pampering. The baby received nothing from the donor, but I loved my friend for thinking of me, the one who needed it most! My husband will always treasure the present he received from actor Vincent Price when our first was born, because "the father never receives anything, and he deserves everything."

PRESENTS FOR THE BABY

The firstborn inevitably receives a raft of presents, the second child a token amount, and the third almost nothing. So one of the nicest things to do is to be sure to give presents to the subsequent children when they are born. Even an inexpensive little book (the baby's first book for his library) is a symbolic and important note of welcome.

When a second child comes along, it is very thoughtful to give a small present to the first child, too, because the first one, having lost center stage, usually feels threatened by the newcomer and wishes it would go away. (Our daughter tried to make her little brother go away by standing over his crib when he was ten days old and grinding fresh pepper into his face with the pepper mill.) When the siblings receive a little gift, too, somehow that gesture makes having the baby in the house not quite so hard for them to take.

STUDIO CARDS

Even if you are not particularly close to a new mother who works with you or whom you know through your church or synagogue, your tennis group, your volunteer team, or other connection, the arrival of a baby is important enough to commemorate with a studio card or a note. If you decide on a greeting card, remember that the little message you write by hand is as important as the card. Something as short and innocuous as the following, penned on the bottom of the card, will sufficiently personalize it: "We were all so thrilled to hear about Bobby, and can hardly wait to view your new creation. Congratulations! When will he be able to play tennis with us?"

LETTERS OF CONGRATULATION

A well-written letter congratulating the parents—or the baby itself—is usually reread several times by the entire family and often is placed in a scrapbook, where it will be saved for the baby's own family to enjoy someday. A good letter is really appreciated by the family receiving it. When Maurice and Joan Tobin of Washington had a little girl, Alexis, after several years of marriage, many of their friends wrote them, including my late brother, Mac Baldrige, who at that time was Secretary of Commerce in the Reagan administration. This is the kind of letter that gets saved:

> Dear Alexis,
>
> While presently you are probably shorter than your name of Alexis Dorette Bouffleur Tobin, you will soon outgrow that and enter a fascinating life with your mother and father. They are two special people, and it will be a lot of fun for you to grow up and help educate them.
>
> Of course, they will give you a lot of advice—I'll let them do that. But I have some of my own, also. My advice would be: Don't study too hard if it interferes with your playtime; be sure to play in the mud whenever you can or you will miss a lot of enjoyment, no matter what your mother says about your new dress; and learn to hit back if a boy hits you first.
>
> Best regards from your special friend,
> /s/ Mac Baldrige

Don't forget to make a scrapbook of the letters and congratulatory messages sent to you or your baby at the time of the birth. That book will mean a lot to him or her thirty years later.

TRADITIONAL CHRISTIAN CEREMONIES
MARKING THE CHILD'S ARRIVAL AND MATURATION

THE CHRISTENING

The first invitation you could ever receive involving another person is to a child's christening. Catholic children are usually baptized within the first six weeks of life, in fact, often by two weeks of age. Protestants (except Baptists) are usually baptized by six months of age, but it is not unusual to have the ceremony later. When unbaptized adults convert to the Christian faith, they go through the same religious ritual the baby does, except that they can do what a baby cannot—select their own godparents and stand up through the ceremony.

In most Protestant faiths, the pastor prefers that the godparents of the baby be of the same religion as the parents, but it is not obligatory; in the Catholic faith, the godfather and godmother must be Catholics, although co-godparents do not have to be.

It is a great honor to be chosen a godparent, but it isn't just an amusing gesture. It is a serious responsibility. The godparents should be very close friends or relatives (like an aunt or uncle or an older cousin). The main duty of godparents is to oversee the spiritual education of the child, particularly if the parents are deceased. Sometimes godparents are made legal guardians of the child by its parents in case the parents die prematurely. If that happens, the godparent then takes over the raising and education of a godchild.

A godparent who is unable to attend the baptismal ceremony may have a proxy stand in for her. The godparents separately or jointly give the baby a present. If there are financial problems in the family, they would give the baby something practical, like a complete layette, a stroller, or a freshly opened savings account in the baby's name. If there are no financial problems, they might give a piece of sterling silver engraved with the child's name and birth date (like a frame, small cup, baby spoon, or silver teething ring). If possible, a godparent should send the child a present every Christmas or birthday until the godchild becomes an adult.

I have attended several weddings at which, because the father of the bride was deceased, the bride walked up the aisle on her godfather's arm. Godparents and godchildren can have a very strong, meaningful relationship throughout their lives. They can become surrogate parents and children for one another.

The Christening Party

Generally, only the godparents, family, and perhaps a couple of very close friends attend the actual christening service in the church. (Protestants sometimes have their christening services at home; ask the minister what will be needed other than a silver bowl to use as a font.) Afterward, there is often a reception—which may be an informal, light buffet lunch after a morning christening, an afternoon tea following a two or three o'clock ceremony, or champagne and cocktails taking place after a christening at four or five in the afternoon.

Invitations are usually extended by note or by telephone call, although it is certainly proper to use a fill-in kind of invitation purchased from a store selling stationery and studio cards. It's wonderful to make the christening party a family affair, so that the young members of the family and close friends can help celebrate the happy event.

The baby should be dressed in the prettiest long white lace and ribbon-trimmed dress that can be borrowed from a relative or friend. Except for occasional passes through the party group to be shown off in the arms of a parent or older sibling, the baby should be kept in peace in her crib. She has already been through a lot on this day—including having a shock of cold water on the head—and has the right to be cranky and fussy in a house full of people, strange lights, and noises.

• The highlight of the party is when the baby is toasted. There should be a christening cake (a white cake with white icing, with perhaps the baby's initials and birth date carved in frosting). The first piece is cut by the baby's parents together (shades of cutting their wedding cake!). Then the godfather or godmother should raise a toast to the baby. (The baby should be present at this moment in the proceedings, unless she is crying lustily.) There should be wine, punch, or champagne in each guest's glass at this point (soda, of course, for any children or nondrinkers present). After the godparents have had their say, anyone else who has a clever or sentimental thought should make a toast. I'll never forget when a friend toasted our six-week-old son Malcolm at his christening. She made a very sentimental toast as I was holding him. Everyone raised their glasses to him, and his godfather said, "Well, now what do you say to that?" There was a stillness in the room, then Malcolm replied by letting out a huge burp that resonated throughout the room—right on cue. Perfect timing.

Everyone has his favorite christening stories. The parents should write down all these happenings in the child's baby book, so that he or she can laugh over them many years later. The presents given to the baby should also be recorded in this book. It's also a great idea to have a tape recording made of the toasts so that they can be saved for posterity.

FIRST COMMUNION

When a Catholic child in a Catholic school reaches seven (the "age of reason"), he takes a course in Catholic doctrine, and the class makes its First Commu-

nion together, usually at a regular Sunday morning Mass. The priest gives a special sermon to the children and gives them the Sacrament of the Eucharist
before the others in the congregation receive it. (Non-Catholic guests invited
by the family are not supposed to join the others in receiving Holy Communion
or in taking the wine—nor do they have to "bob and kneel up and down," as my
Protestant father used to describe our Catholic Mass. If they want to follow the
Catholics' "bobbing," they certainly may; if they prefer just sitting in the pew,
that is okay, too.)

When a boy or girl is not a student in a Catholic school, he or she takes religious instruction outside—usually once a week for a few months. The child may
then be the only one to make a First Communion at a particular Mass. The girls
dress in white dresses with white veils for this occasion, the boys in dark blue
or gray suits (or white, in summer resort weather), with either long pants or
shorts (white knee socks with the latter).

Family members and close friends who are invited to attend the First
Communion Mass would go on afterward to a breakfast or a brunch, usually
in a public place close by.

As a gift for the occasion, a godparent would give the child something religious—for example, a book on the lives of the saints or a rosary that was blessed
by the Pope in Rome. Others would give the child a present like an amusing
book or a game.

Confirmation in the Protestant and Catholic Faiths

The confirmation ceremony signifies that the child has officially become a
member of the congregation. Children in the seventh or eighth grades are
given instruction in their faith to prepare them for this important day in their
lives (they must be able to answer a detailed quiz). It is usually a quiet family
occasion, with only the godparents and relatives present. Some very simple gifts
are presented, sometimes religious in nature, but usually not. There is almost
always a festive lunch held afterward, often hosted by a godparent. The boys
and girls are dressed in their festive best.

Traditional Jewish Ceremonies Marking the Child's Arrival and Maturation

Brith Milah

Eight days after a Jewish baby boy is born, he is circumcised, given his name,
and given godparents. This ceremony can take place in his parents' home or

in a special room in the hospital. Only a few family members and close relatives attend the ceremony. Gifts for the baby are sometimes presented on this occasion.

A girl is given her name on the first Sabbath after she is born (in a service in the temple). Her father is called up to the Torah, where he recites a short prayer and states his daughter's name. The rabbi then recites a special blessing. Afterward, there is a small reception hosted by the baby's mother.

In the Reform congregation, the child's name is given and a prayer is said at the earliest religious service that both parents can attend after the baby's birth.

BAR AND BAT MITZVAH

The celebration of the Bar Mitzvah takes place when a thirteen-year-old boy student of the Talmud traditionally comes of age and hears the thrilling message from the rabbi during the service, "You are now entering the Congregation of Israel." It is one of the most important events in a Jewish man's life.

In the conservative and Reform congregations there is a similar ceremony for girls, called a Bas or Bat Mitzvah. This ceremony also takes place when the girl is thirteen, though she can be as young as twelve. It is not permitted in Orthodox congregations. (Before the 1970s, girls were usually confirmed at the age of sixteen, when they graduated from religious school, and some families still prefer to have their daughters confirmed only.)

The Bar or Bat Mitzvah is a most touching and impressive ceremony, lasting three hours in an Orthodox temple, one and a half to two hours in the Conservative temple, and just about an hour in the Reform temple. The young person has studied, practiced, and rehearsed long and hard for this great day in his or her life. After the indoctrination into the Congregation of Israel on the Sabbath, the immediate family may gather in a private room at the temple to talk with any members of the congregation who wish to offer their congratulations. This is often followed by a seated luncheon or dinner in a temple reception room, hotel, restaurant, or banquet hall. There is often dancing, beautiful flowers, and decorated tables. Sometimes the child will change from his conservative temple clothing to more dressy clothes for the party following the ceremony. Guests often attend in formal dress.

It is not appreciated when friends who were invited to a Bar or Bat Mitzvah attend the usually lavish party following the service, but not the service itself. In the family's eyes, to miss the child's reading of the lesson, which has been practiced for months and months, is to miss everything.

Gifts for the Jewish Child

Gifts for the boy or girl should not be brought to the temple. In fact, it is better to send them to the child's home, rather than bring them to the reception. Presents are very important to young people on the occasion of their Bar or Bat Mitzvah. For many years, it was traditional to give a young man a fountain pen, so there is an old Jewish joke that the boy says, "Today I am a fountain pen" (instead of "Today I am a man"). The children naturally like gifts but also appreciate checks, and the latter often range around $500. My old friend from my Kennedy White House days, lawyer Mike Feldman, a devout Jew, does not believe in giving money. He gives every young person a year's subscription to the Jewish Publication Society in Philadelphia. The young person then receives for one year one or two excellent books every month on Jewish life and traditions—a very appropriate gift for this solemn religious occasion, to reinforce his faith. But today's Bat or Bar Mitzvahed child also receives gifts such as computers, cell phones, and the latest entertainment systems.

Confirmation

Confirmation in a temple, for a boy or girl, usually takes place at the age of sixteen, seven weeks after the second day of Passover (on "The Feast of Weeks"). Children attending Hebrew school are confirmed as a group.

In Conservative congregations, some rabbis confirm both boys and girls, while others will Bar Mitzvah the boys only at age thirteen, and confirm the girls only at age sixteen.

SPECIAL BIRTHDAYS FOR GIRLS

The Quinceañera

Sometimes called simply a *quince* (for fifteen), this birthday celebration is the biggest thing in a young Latina's life. It is constantly talked about in the family. The young girl starts dreaming about it early in life, and when the moment arrives it is a glorious celebration of her coming of age. There is often a religious ceremony before the party. She is dressed in a beautiful (usually white) evening gown, with a fancy hairdo, sometimes white lacy gloves, and a diamond or pearl necklace and bracelet borrowed from a relative.

The party is often a mini-ball, with guests in formal evening wear, an orchestra, and buffet supper. The honoree's father dances the first waltz with his daughter on an empty dance floor, and then the others begin dancing.

(Fathers often say that they are far more nervous dancing with their daughters at this party than they are at their daughters' wedding receptions.)

Guests should send presents to the young woman's home, rather than bring them to the Quinceañera party. Checks are always more than welcome, too. And for every gift and every check, a polite fifteen-year-old gets her thank-you notes written and mailed quickly. (Try to discourage your child from saying thanks by e-mail.)

Sweet Sixteen Parties

These are still held in some regions of the country, although not as often as in the last century. The honorees are girls, not boys, although boys are invited to the big party.

The party is hosted by the young lady's parents, aunts and uncles, or godparents. If a girl is planning on making her debut two or three years later, the Sweet Sixteen party is omitted from her social schedule. The family may present her with a modest piece of jewelry or a gift certificate to a major department store, music store, or even, heavens above, a bookstore! The party may be coed or all female. It can be very informal, such as one held at a local ice-skating rink, or in summer at a swimming pool. It can consist of taking a group of twelve girls to a Saturday afternoon movie, followed by a fancy dinner in a restaurant. It can be an all-night slumber party, complete with a movie and an all-night orgy of hamburgers, scrambled eggs, and pizza. The girls are usually ready for a bacon and pancakes breakfast, too, the following morning. The birthday cake can be served at any moment in the festivities, including at breakfast!

The Sweet Sixteener who fires off an instant thank-you note for every present received is setting a great example to her friends.

DEBUTANTES

Today's "deb," who "comes out" after graduating from high school or after completing her first year of college, is a far cry from the glamour girls who preceded her before 1965. The youth rebellion and the women's movement of the mid-sixties all but sabotaged the tradition of the debutante year for young women of social standing who traditionally, by virtue of making their debuts, were now ready to be married off.

The days of the lavish single parties—dinner dances and private balls given for one young debutante alone—are over. Most young women come out in a group at one or two large, beautifully produced benefit dances. Their parents make a donation to the charity sponsoring the party.

Today's deb usually goes to three or four large parties, besides the ball at which she officially comes out. She wears a white dress to her own ball, and perhaps dresses of different colors to her friends' balls. She may have two or three escorts. She may use her brothers as her escorts. No one is looking at her escorts as possible husband material, which they used to, in the good old deb days, when all a young woman had on her mind was going to the next party and getting engaged. Now it's all about having a good time without getting married. Now, at eighteen or nineteen, their minds are on jobs.

There are many churches today, particularly in the African-American community, that sponsor debutante balls as fund-raisers. They are "very big deals" in a young black woman's life, and in her family's.

If you are a relative or a very close friend of the debutante's family, it is nice to give her a personal gift (like real or costume jewelry, makeup, or a handbag).

Manners come into play from the time a child is born until that child is released into adulthood and independence. They are important in all the rites of passage that mark the stages of a child's development into that special adult that parents hope their children will become. Hopefully, we teach kindness, grace, and manners from the heart all the way.

CHAPTER 14

The Last Rite of Passage: Funerals

It is a custom, in some forthright families where good relations abound, to discuss death and funeral plans frankly and honestly—but not ghoulishly—with elderly or ailing relatives while they are still living and able to make decisions. Usually, it is that person who wants such a discussion, to make sure that his wishes are carried out. The tenor of all such discussions should be loving, with deference demonstrated to those wishes.

No matter whether a family is prepared ahead of time or death catches them by surprise, the procedures described in this chapter will help anyone go through this last rite of passage more easily and in the proper manner.

TAKING CHARGE OF THE ARRANGEMENTS

When a relative or a close friend dies, someone should immediately shoulder the responsibility of ensuring that the bereaved family members are being helped and that immediate steps are taken to plan the funeral. There is much to be done—quite apart from trying to console the family affected by the death. A relative or close friend of the deceased (such as a brother-in-law, a business partner, or an adult sister of the deceased) should offer to serve as "director of funeral events." As such he will be responsible for the overall smooth coordination of the funeral and interment, and also for helping the surviving family in every possible way. The person acting as director of the funeral events would be there most of the day with the family for two or three days, or until the funeral events are finished.

She should first make a checklist of what has to be done and appoint the logical volunteers to get these various chores done responsibly. She should also make sure that everyone is doing what they promised to do and that every action represents the wishes of the deceased's spouse, parent, sibling, or child—whoever is the prime adult survivor.

The person in charge should:

- Find someone to take charge of the small children of the deceased, if there are any—to feed them, play with them, and keep them occupied. This may necessitate taking the very little ones home to the friend's house to stay with the friend's own children.
- Find a person to be in charge of the telephone at the home of the deceased, to make sure that there is a capable adult (or several working in shifts, if necessary) handling the constantly ringing telephone. That person should also make sure that:
  - All family members and close friends of the deceased are notified by telephone of the death and the funeral arrangements.
  - The deceased's boss and place of employment are notified of the death and, if necessary, that the grieving survivor's boss is notified.
  - All queries as to when the services will be held are answered correctly. •
- Immediately notify the lawyer of the deceased.
- Notify the funeral home and deal with its director in terms of
  - Possibly arranging a viewing or wake to be held there prior to the funeral services.
  - Selecting the casket and arranging for it to be open or closed during the viewing.
  - Deciding on the burial clothing and getting it into the hands of the undertaker.
  - Coordinating burial plans with the church and the cemetery (or crematorium).
- See that someone is put in charge of getting food on the table for everyone staying in the house during the funeral period.
- See that someone is in charge of the logistics and invitations for the lunch, tea, cocktails, or supper to be served immediately following the interment. This gathering is held either at the home of the bereaved, at the house of a close friend or relative of the bereaved, or in a hotel private dining room or a private club. The mourners invited to this gathering after the burial would include:
  - Members of the family.
  - The minister or priest in charge of the service.
  - Ushers and honorary pallbearers, if there were any.
  - Close social and business friends.
  - Family retainers (the housekeeper, baby-sitter, gardener, or cook).
  - Anyone who came from out of town for the services.
- See that someone at the house is in charge of listing all incoming messages, with carefully noted names and addresses, so that thank-you messages will be sent later. These might include:
  - E-mails and faxes.
  - Telephoned messages of sympathy.

- Hand-delivered letters of condolence.
- Mass cards—for a deceased Catholic only. A person of any religion may arrange with a Catholic priest anywhere to have a Mass said for the soul of the deceased. When this is arranged, a card to this effect is mailed to the family, giving the priest's name and parish, and sometimes giving the date of the special Mass. The person who ordered the Mass said—or the "novena of prayers," another option—usually makes a gift of approximately $25 to the priest or the church, according to what she wishes to pay. A payment, however, is not obligatory.
- Condolence cards, which may be purchased from a stationer or greeting card shop. (Don't just sign a name; write a sentence or two by hand at the bottom of the message printed on the card.)
- Flowers. (In my opinion, the best time to send them is a few weeks *after* the funeral to cheer up the household, when the surviving family is really feeling depressed.)
- Gifts of food for the family—frozen meals, fruit baskets, pastries.

- Make sure that someone is at the house to assume charge of all out-of-towners coming for the funeral:
  - Getting them hotel reservations, if necessary.
  - Meeting their planes, trains, or buses.
  - Providing visitors with transportation during the one or two days they are in town.
  - Making sure their meals are taken care of.
- Appoint someone to call the local newspapers and have a paid death notice put in the earliest possible edition of the local newspapers.

PREPARING THE OBITUARY

Here is a sample death notice for a newspaper:

Rutherford, Alana. On July 17. Age 38. Beloved wife of Hamilton, devoted mother of Geoffrey, James, and Alana. Sister of Marian Berquist and Geoffrey Teaman. Friends may call at Frank E. Campbell, 1076 Madison Ave. at 81st St., Sunday 2–5 P.M. Mass of Christian burial at St. Thomas More Church, 65 E. 89th St., Monday 10 A.M. Interment at St. Mary's Cemetery, Yonkers, N.Y.

- If the deceased was a prominent person, appoint someone from the family or the company to write the obituary and supply a suitable photo. Be sure to check the facts in the obituary with the spouse, parent, or sibling of the deceased. The obituary should be hand-delivered or e-mailed as soon as it is ready to the Metropolitan Desk of the local newspapers (as well as sent later to the alumni magazines of the deceased's schools or to the journal or newsletter of any organization to which the person belonged). An obituary for a prominent person would contain the following information:

- Name and address of person.
- Date and place where he or she died.
- Cause of death.
- Name of spouse.
- City of birth.
- Name of his or her company or place of work and title.
- Education, including both earned and honorary degrees.
- Military service, if any.
- Corporate directorships.
- Any major awards received.
- Titles of published works, films, or plays and names of museums where the individual's art is exhibited or major theaters where that person may have sung or danced.
- Names of survivors and their relationship to the deceased.
- Details of the funeral services and interment.
- Name and telephone number of the person to be called in case further information is needed by the newspaper.

• It is not necessary to include the age of the deceased in the death notice—only if it is a personal preference—but it is of interest to most.

• If the family do not wish people to go to the cemetery, they omit the inter-ment notice. If the family do not wish anyone at either the service or the interment, they state "Funeral private" in the paid death notice.

• If the family wishes to designate where contributions may be sent in the name of the deceased, the information is included at the end of the paid notice. For example: "Contributions may be made to the Arthritis Foundation" or whatever the charity may be. Some families put in the death notice, "Contributions to be made to the donor's favorite charity."

THE PROPRIETIES IN CONNECTION WITH A FUNERAL

WHAT DO YOU SAY?

People are usually at a loss for words when it comes time to talk to the family of someone who has just died.

All you have to do is tell the survivor in just a few words:
- How sorry you were to learn of this sad news.
- How much the deceased will be missed by friends and colleagues.

- How much you loved this person and what a personal loss you feel.
- How much you grieve for those left behind.
- What a wonderful person the deceased was. (Recount warm, loving anecdotes about your late friend, and laud her accomplishments.)

SENDING FLOWERS

There are options on where to send flowers:
- To the home of the bereaved.
- To the funeral home.
- To the church.
- To the gravesite.

The family will state its preference or choice of the last three categories.

Flowers sent to the funeral home are usually transferred to the gravesite on the day of the interment.

Flowers are never sent for any Jewish funeral. Often the family will make known in the announcement of death or some other way a charity donation may be made in the deceased's name.

In a Catholic church, only a spray of flowers for the top of the casket (from the family) and perhaps one other bouquet of flowers for the altar are permitted. (People will never forget the simple white cross of gardenias atop Jacqueline Kennedy Onassis's casket.) In Protestant churches, flowers are permitted on and near the altar.

The Card for Funeral Flowers

The white envelope, containing the card, would be addressed as follows:

> The Funeral of Anthony Stedwell Creighton
> [Address of the funeral home or gravesite]

The envelope should also contain the name and mailing address of the donor of the flowers.

The white card, on which the message is written in black ink, should state simply something like this: "With deepest sympathy from the Reynolds Family"; or, if sent by colleagues from the office: "With deepest sympathy from the Granger Insurance Company."

ATTIRE FOR FUNERALS

• The widow should be dressed discreetly in a dark dress or suit. The days are past when she had to wear a black dress, hat, and veil to the services. (The widows of high officials still do observe the black mourning attire.)

• The young daughters of the deceased should wear their best dresses and party shoes, out of respect for their late parent. *Little boys* should be in gray shorts with gray or white knee socks, or gray slacks, with a navy blazer, white shirt, and tie and well-polished shoes.

• Teenagers and grown children should wear appropriately quiet clothing. Young men and grown sons should dress as the ushers and pallbearers do, in dark suits, white shirt, dark tie, and dark shoes.

• Honorary pallbearers and ushers would wear dark suits, white shirts, black four-in-hand ties, and black shoes and socks.

• Friends and colleagues attending the services would be dressed in quiet clothing—the women in modest dresses or suits of a solid color (or at least, a print that is not too colorful and flashy), and the men in dark suits. Forget about revealing décolleté outfits and micro-minis. Pantsuits are fine, not sporty tops and slacks.

CEREMONIES FOR OR HONORING THE DECEASED

A VIEWING OR WAKE

A viewing or a wake is often held at the funeral home the day before the funeral or, if the person was prominent, on two successive days before the funeral. Usually it lasts about two hours, and it is often held late in the afternoon or early evening, so that people who work will be able to come. Everyone who comes signs the book that is at the entrance to the main rooms. The casket is present (open or closed), often all of the flowers sent to the home are on display, and the family stands together in a kind of receiving line if there are large numbers of people coming. Otherwise, it is informal, without a receiving line. Everyone greets—and perhaps hugs or kisses—the grieving family members, whispering words of comfort.

THE CHRISTIAN FUNERAL SERVICE

At a large funeral of an important and prominent person, there may be honorary pallbearers and ushers, all of whom are chosen by the family of the deceased. It is a great honor to be asked to serve in this capacity, and although traditionally pallbearers have been men, today a woman may also be asked to serve.

• Ushers help seat the attendees. They are young men and women friends or relatives of the deceased—perhaps office colleagues, nephews and nieces, or godchildren. They direct people to their seats, filling the front of the church first. (The very front pews, however, are reserved and marked for the family on the right side, and for the honorary pallbearers and the ushers on the left side.)

• The pallbearers, employees of the funeral home, actually handle and carry the casket in and out of the church.

• Honorary pallbearers, usually from four to ten in number—the men in dark suits, the women in dark dresses—precede the casket in and out of the church, walking two by two in a procession. It is easier if the casket is already in place at the altar at the start of the services (in Protestant churches, it is often covered with a blanket of flowers). The honorary pallbearers march in just before the service begins and take the front left pews, opposite the family. (The ushers have already seated themselves to the left, behind where the honorary pallbearers will sit.)

An honorary pallbearer is a distinguished person, someone who is known and respected in the community but also a good friend of the deceased. He or she may have been a business associate or someone like the deceased's doctor or lawyer. This person may have been active with the deceased in some civic or political activity or may just have been an old golfing buddy.

• The family of the deceased enters from the vestry, and family members take their seats in the front right-hand pews. The service is now ready to begin.

The Music

The music for a Christian funeral is usually organ music. The church music director confers in advance with the family of the deceased to see if they have any special wishes; if not, there is almost always a repertoire of appropriate organ music ready for this sad occasion. Other music groups, such as chamber music groups, a harpist, or brass quintets may also be asked to provide the music.

There is often a soloist—hopefully, a professional singer who freelances for church funerals. It is better to dissuade an amateur, whether a relative or friend of the deceased, from singing. (I remember the sister-in-law of the deceased at one funeral I attended who insisted on singing; she was so flat the entire time that the congregation had all they could do to keep from laughing, despite their sorrow. Her performance flawed an otherwise dignified and moving service.)

The Eulogy

For the funeral service (or for a later memorial service), this is usually given by the minister and by a relative or close friend of the deceased. The family decides who may speak other than the clergyman or woman; if three or more will speak, a sheet showing the order is given to each person, so that he or she will approach the pulpit or podium at the right moment. Sometimes a teenage (or older) son and daughter will speak about the late parent. A brother or sister of the deceased might say something. There are no rules about who speaks from the pulpit or how many do it, but if you are going to give a eulogy, there are rules to help keep the service from dragging:

• Get in and out of the pulpit quickly. If you go slowly from your pew up to the pulpit when it's your turn to speak, the interval between speakers may take several minutes, and the service will seem to drag interminably.

• Speak for no longer than seven minutes. Three minutes is all right, too, and five minutes is just about perfect.

• If you should completely choke up while you're talking, don't try to continue. (Perhaps the toughest time of all to speak is when it concerns the death of a child.) If you're sobbing and out of control, just say, "I'm sorry," and step down. Everyone will understand.

• Be respectful and affectionate; tell a nice, sweet, humorous story that will make those present smile with fond remembrance. If you worked in the same office as the deceased, mention how much he was loved and respected by everyone in the company. If you sailed or played tennis with the deceased, mention some humorous incidents involving his skills in the sport. Always end on a note of high praise—for example, mentioning how much he loved his family and what a great legacy he has left them.

A Funeral Service Program

A funeral service program to distribute to each person who attends the services is a nice touch. This is often a double-fold pamphlet, printed in black on heavy white paper. It sometimes includes a headshot photo of the deceased, banded in black (so that it looks like a black frame), with a special prayer printed beneath the picture. The order of events, the names of the clergy and the speakers, and the order of the hymns (as well as the words, so that all can join in) are included in the program. Often special prayers are printed in the leaflet, too. It is a very nice memento of the service and helps people follow the clergy in saying the prayers and singing the hymns.

A CREMATION

A cremation is preceded by a funeral service in a church. Afterward only a few relatives and close friends go to the crematorium, where another brief service is held. The ashes are then given to the family and dispersed by them in a place the deceased stipulated in her will. Sometimes they are placed in a container, often an urn, which is then placed in the family burial plot. (The care and disposal of the ashes is regulated in some states by law.)

JEWISH SERVICES

Orthodox, Conservative, and Reform Jews have different customs for funeral services. Attention is given to the bereaved family, the members of which stay home in mourning for a set period of days. In the Orthodox congregation, for example, following the burial of the deceased (within twenty-four hours after his death), the family remains in the home for seven days, "sitting shivah." Neighbors bring them food, but they do not have any social contact with the outside world, nor do they conduct business, take telephone calls, or do any kind of work. Every evening, close friends may come to the home to sit with the family and bear witness to their grief.

Reform Jews often have one brief religious service with a rabbi in their home right after the burial. They spend from one to three days at home, refraining from social and business contacts following the death of a loved one. In the evening, they light one or two Sabbath candles, and an adult in the family says the blessing. All Jews try to visit the graves of their parents once a year—between Rosh Hashanah and Yom Kippur. Devout Jews do not miss a year, even though the graves may be far away from where they live.

MEMORIAL SERVICE

A memorial service is held to honor a much loved or famous person after the deceased has already been interred. It can be held in a funeral home, a church, a community auditorium, a school auditorium, or other similar setting. A memorial service is best held within two months of a person's death, but it may be held later than that. If the person was prominent, there might be two or three memorial services held in the different cities in which she was well known.

A religious leader may lead the service, but often it is a layperson with close connections to the deceased who presides, if the ceremony is held outside a church setting.

The person in charge of organizing the service arranges ahead of time for people close to the deceased—as few as two, but often many more—to give eulogies at the ceremony (and asks that they be kept brief). At the time of the service these people are called upon to come forward and speak.

There may be prayers and hymns or other appropriate music before, during, and after the service.

I remember one memorial service for a beloved patriarch of an entire town, held on the great lawn of his estate with most of the town in attendance. He was of Scottish descent and had many Scottish connections, so in honor of this a bagpiper stepped forward after the eulogies. Silence fell as he began piping his way toward the water at the lawn's end, playing "The Flowers of the Forest." The volume of the music lowered with each step the piper took, until it faded away altogether at the water's edge and the ceremony was over.

Following the service, the family may receive in a nearby room in the church or auditorium, and coffee and cakes may be served. Or the family may simply stand outside on the steps or sidewalk afterward, to talk to those who came and thank them for their support.

There may be lunch or cocktails served in a nearby house, including the deceased's, or in a nearby public place after the service.

Often, there is a book on a table in the vestibule of the place where the service is held, in which you sign, so that the family will know you attended the service.

AFTER THE FUNERAL OR MEMORIAL

THE SURVIVOR WRITES A THANK-YOU

After the sadness of the funeral period is over, when the main surviving members of the family feel strong enough to tackle the job, one of them should write a personal note of thanks to:

- The relative or friend who served as director of all the proceedings.
- The clergy person who handled the services.
- The honorary pallbearers and ushers.
- The people who gave eulogies. (It is not necessary to write family members, but it is a nice touch to do so.)
- Everyone who sent a telegram, condolence card, Mass card, condolence letter, or flowers.
- Everyone who gave a charitable contribution in memory of the deceased.

The family of a prominent person whose death created a large outpouring of sympathy (and on whose behalf hundreds of acknowledgments must be sent) should order from a good stationer white cards edged in black, engraved with a message of thanks from the family. The wording is simple, something like this:

> The family of Gregory Johnson Caldwell
> greatly appreciates your kind expression of sympathy.

However, it is nice to personalize these cards. A handwritten word by a family member at the bottom makes the card a strong personal statement of appreciation from the family.

The task of writing and addressing thank-you notes and acknowledgments should be apportioned out to all family members. (In other words, one person should not be saddled with the entire job.)

If you plan to acknowledge expressions of sympathy toward a deceased member of your family on notepaper, buy boxes of good white stationery—either single sheet or fold-over notes or correspondence cards. After you express your thanks in your note, write something like, "Dad always loved you, I hope you know that," or "We will miss her terribly, and we particularly appreciated your sending those lovely roses—because they were her favorite flowers."

SHOWING CONTINUING SUPPORT

When someone has died, there is a lot of rallying around his family at the time of the funeral. Everyone seems to be calling, writing, offering sympathy. But this support *really* matters when a surviving spouse or child is left alone afterward. Two, four, eight months later—that is when your presence is most needed. Call your friend. Invite him for dinner; include him in your leisure activities. That's when friends really stand up and are counted! Remember your late friend each year by getting in touch with the family of the deceased on her birthday—a happy memory—rather than on the anniversary of the death.

There is nothing more difficult to accept nor more absolute than death. It's the time when heart counts more than anything else in this world. It's not the cost of the huge bouquet someone sent to the funeral that matters to the grieving family; it's the warmth of your words that counts and your promise to "be around to help—always."

PART 4

THE ART OF ENTERTAINING

CHAPTER 15

Entertaining Today's Way

This section contains my point of view about entertaining—its human side—and is based on the theory that if your heart's in the right place, *your event will always be a success*. Never mind whatever goes wrong.

Americans are entertaining less and less in their homes these days. There are repetitive excuses given for this sad state of affairs, none of which, in my opinion, hold up:

- "I'm so busy and pressured; I work too hard." Rebuttal: *Everyone* is busy and pressured. Entertaining fits into your life simply by making it one of your priorities—like the two Chicago ad agency executives, a married couple who each work a sixty-hour week, have two children who help with their parties, and give a buffet supper for friends mixed with clients the first Sunday evening of every month in the year, August included!

- "We can't entertain until the children are grown." Rebuttal: Again, if you want to, you can arrange to give time and thought to "having people over" several times a year. You just fit it into your schedule and arrange for baby-sitting help. You work on getting your party ready a little at a time, several nights before or the weekend before, when small members of the household are asleep.

- "My apartment is too small." Rebuttal: No apartment is too small for staging a dinner party for four or six. People do miraculous things in small spaces by borrowing folding bridge tables and collapsible chairs, keeping the ice in the bathtub and putting a board over it to use as a bar, and sliding trays of dirty dishes temporarily under the bed because there's no room in the sink!

- "We can't get any proper help." Rebuttal: Yes you can, with a little effort. There's always someone who needs extra cash who will come to help make your party a success—like that teenager in the neighborhood or in the apartment house who is always asking if he can wash your car or mow your lawn or baby-sit.

- "I don't have a clue to how to make up a guest list." Rebuttal: Composing a guest list is a stimulating exercise, totally creative. Who but you would have thought of seating your children's lovely-looking young gym teacher next to your overweight bank executive friend who's trying to slim down, and who becomes so inspired by his dinner partner that he resolves to start an exercise program the next morning? Who but you would have thought to seat your recently widowed best friend as a surprise next to your old friend from college days (himself also recently widowed), who you heard was visiting in your city? The best guest list of all is a mixture of people you know, and bringing together unexpected combinations is the key to success.

• "I really am not a cook." Rebuttal: You don't have to be. There are frozen foods in the supermarket that can be enhanced by adding fresh vegetables. There are gourmet food takeout places that will do the major part of the work for you, such as preparing your chicken pot pie and dessert, so all you have to do is rustle up a green salad. (Or, if you can afford it, the caterer will do an entire gourmet dinner for you. No apologies necessary to your guests.)

• "I don't have the proper table accoutrements." Rebuttal: A poor excuse. That's what friends are for—to borrow from!

• "I can't cope when things go wrong—like the guest of honor doesn't show up, or something's wrong with my food, or people don't seem to be having a good time." Rebuttal: Those things don't always happen, and when they do, you can turn it into a plus (like my fancy roast turkey dinner, at which I discovered, just before the guests arrived, that I had never turned on the oven to cook the turkey; we ate delivered cheeseburgers and it was one of the best parties I've ever given).

The rewards of personal satisfaction you receive for entertaining will far outweigh any efforts you make to psych yourself into becoming a host. "Entertaining" is a general term covering all kinds of efforts, small and big, that you make for other people. You're entertaining when you invite a lonely elderly neighbor for a cup of tea, as well as when you invite twenty-four people important to you in business for a seated dinner. You're entertaining if you're a woman serving three other ladies a cold chicken salad lunch on a hot summer's day or if you're a man serving "a bunch of the guys" hot corned beef and cabbage after a poker game on a cold winter's night. In all these cases, you have taken the time and trouble to invite people to your home—or perhaps out to a restaurant for a meal.

When you host people just for the sake of pleasing them—to give them a good time and make them feel happy and glad—you're reaching out to them and thinking outside, not inside, the box. All the pleasure and contentment you give them will come back to you, multiplied.

So just do it. Call people and ask them to come be your guests. And while you're at it, go on the record—send them a reminder by mail, so that they won't forget the logistical details communicated in the telephone conversation!

I'm not going to tell you very much in this book about what to serve or how to cook it. That's up to you—and there are many books and TV shows out there on the subject. I'm going to give you all the *reasons why* you should want to have people over, why you should make an effort, why entertaining is a worthy priority on your list of activities. I'm going to tell you what makes a good host and guest, which today is a far cry from all the ludicrous, anachronistic formalities of yesteryear's entertaining. There are, however, some traditional tried and true ways of doing things, everything from knowing where you place forks on the table, to being aware that one serves from the left and picks up empty plates from the right of the guest. I'm going to teach you how a dinner should properly be served, so that if you have someone serving who doesn't know how to do it, you can do a little training on the spot. (That person serving may be your own teenager.) These rules are not capricious or foppish; they have evolved from experience through the years; they represent the most efficient way to do something.

I'm not going to tell you what wines to buy, but rather how to serve them. I'm not going to advise you what flowers to put in the center of the table, because you may want to put beach pebbles and shells there instead. My job is just to give you a few ideas that will stimulate your own imagination. I won't agonize over how many courses you will serve at your meal, because that's your choice, but I will advise you to serve very few—two or three for economic and health reasons—and to use your energy for making what is simple and easy taste good and be easy to serve. I won't sympathize with you over your fear of breaking someone's wineglass in his house or spilling food on his table. Instead, I'll tell you how to clean up whatever mess you may have made, and how to apologize so nicely that your host won't give a second thought to what you consider a disaster.

The important thing to remember is that whatever position you are in, that of a host or of a guest, you have responsibilities and creative possibilities. As one individual you have the capacity to make or break a party. That sober thought should instill in you a feeling of power!

This chapter is all about making a party successful. And to me, two people make a party as well as two thousand. What a wonderful feeling it is to serve a meal or to host an event the guests will talk about with admiration for months to come. And what fun it is to be a guest at someone else's party that is worthy of your remembering for months to come.

It's all up to you. No one else turns you into a consummate host or a consummate guest. You do. And remember, too, that in order to break the rules of entertaining with verve and panache, you have to know what they are in the first place!

HOW ENTERTAINING BRINGS FRIENDS
INTO YOUR LIFE

People's motives for entertaining—or, let me correct that, the reasons people *should* be motivated to entertain—encompass a variety of considerations. The most important one, of course, is that people need to be with people. Loneliness is a common ailment; humans need to get out of their homes and to interact with other humans once in a while. The most effective way to answer the need for human companionship is through entertaining. If you really don't have the proper home in which to entertain, take your guests out—to a restaurant, hotel, club, or even a fast food place. The truth is, however, that many people who think their homes aren't worthy to use as a backdrop for receiving guests are "copping out." I have a young friend who entertains all the time in a small, ugly apartment (his description) in New York (it's all he can afford). He says, "My friends are the decoration around here. I have wonderful friends who make my apartment beautiful." Another friend who also hates her apartment (it's all she can afford) lights her dinner parties only with candlelight, so that no one can see what the surroundings look like! Too many people use the excuse of an insufficiently grand home as justification for never entertaining.

If you're entertaining on business or at charity events, which is the nature of most entertaining these days, the gathering usually takes place in hotels and restaurants and is often cold, without a vestige of warmth from a personal touch. But you can change all that—you can make it warm, personal, and individually exciting. I'll tell you how.

Perhaps you will find yourself in one of these categories:

• You owe someone who has entertained you. Bachelors of the world, this means you, too. Just because you're single men and in demand does not mean that you can continue to be constantly feted, without ever repaying your social obligations!

• You meet someone who interests you, and you'd like to get to know that person better.

• You feel a great need to enlarge your social circle; you're stuck in the circle you are part of now, and it's not getting any better.

• You're new in town and are starting from scratch socially.

• You want to rekindle an old romance.

• You want to ignite a new one.

• You feel compassion for someone who's lonely.

• You want to help a friend or relative of a good friend who asked you for help in making social contacts.

• You realize that your hosting expertise will help expand your business success.

- You want to show your gratitude to a person or a group for what they did for you personally, or for what they did for one of your favorite causes.
- You want to go to work on someone in a sympathetic environment, so that she will offer you a job, lend you money, help you run for office, write you an important letter of reference, get you on a board, invest in your company, maybe even want to marry you!
- You feel invitationless and friendless, too, so you conclude that maybe if you start to entertain, others will entertain you back.
- You want to honor a special person, to make him feel very good, either because that person has done something extraordinary and deserves the honor, or because he is sad and depressed.
- You want to mark a special occasion—an anniversary, the opening of something, the honoring of someone, the awarding of something to a person or an institution.
- You just want to please someone.
- You have a sudden desire to shake yourself up and do something totally out of character. It's like turning on the ignition and getting the motor started.

THE KINDS OF ENTERTAINING
PEOPLE LOVE

If you're wondering about the kinds of occasions on which people love to be included, have a conversation with those whom you'd like to invite along any of the following lines:

- "Come on over after church next Sunday to join us for a big family breakfast."
- "I'm giving a breakfast for the organizing committee of our big benefit a week from Monday, the seventh, at eight A.M. at our home. It should be a productive meeting, and I'm also a very good omelet and waffle maker!"
- "Come for lunch on Saturday, the twentieth. It will be a surprise birthday party for Leslie, so don't say a word to her."
- "We'd like to invite you to an open house to inaugurate our newly redecorated house on Sunday the second, from noon to five o'clock. This time it's for adults only."
- "We're new in the neighborhood, so we're having an open house for all our neighbors, children included, the Saturday before Thanksgiving, from four P.M. to seven-thirty P.M. It would be nice to get to know your family, so please drop by."
- "Why don't you come by for a cup of tea Saturday at four o'clock? I haven't seen you in such a long time, and I want to catch up. By the way, you can have something other than tea."

- "We'd like to invite you two for dinner Friday, the twenty-fifth, at seven o'clock. We'll sit down at the table at seven forty-five." (There are no rules about where your dinner must be served. It can be in the house or in the garden, in the kitchen, on the patio, by the pool, on the back porch, in the gazebo, out in the yard, up in the treehouse, on the dock, or at the beach. Don't forget the bedroom, either.)
- "Do stop by for 'a drink and a bite'" (before or after the concert, play, art exhibition, movie, or your children's piano recital).
- "Come for supper at eight-thirty, before the club's big Leap Year Dance."
- "Join us for one of our Sunday evening chili suppers on the thirtieth at six o'clock. If chili is too hot for you, there will be less incendiary food also included on the menu."
- "I'd like to invite you to my 'Singles Only' party—with after-dinner drinks and dessert ('Bubbles and Sweets'), on Wednesday, April fifteenth, at nine o'clock."
- "Remember the date—a week from Saturday, for a cocktail-buffet at our apartment. We'll have lots of food, so you won't need dinner afterward!"
- "We're organizing a big family picnic for the first Sunday in July. We'll supply the games and athletic equipment. I'm counting on each family to bring one dish—enough to feed the entire gang. Would you, for example, be able to bring the salad?"
- "Join us after the theater—we have some of the other benefit attendees coming by our house to collapse, talk about the play, and have a glass of champagne."
- "We'll have some hot food and beer waiting to warm you up after Sunday afternoon's football game at the stadium."
- "Our gourmet club is meeting at my house this month. It's Spanish Night. Hope you can join us on the thirtieth for a little *Olé*-ing, and I have some nifty classical guitar CDs to put us in the mood."
- "We're starting a book club, because we all feel we could use some intellectual stimulation. Two weeks before we meet we'll all start reading the same book, and then we'll discuss it at dinner. This first session is at our apartment. I hope you both can join us, Friday the first, at seven."
- "It will be your choice, whether you want hot chocolate or soup at four after ice-skating Sunday afternoon. Come to our house, and we'll warm up watching the Winter Olympics skating finals on television."
- "Yes, we'd like your whole family to join us for a pool party on July Fourth, from four P.M. to ten P.M. Just bring your own bathing suits and towels. We'll supply the rest and the city will supply the fireworks at nine."
- "I'm *finally* having a dinner party, so would you both be able to come for dinner at the Palm Restaurant on Thursday the fifth, at seven-thirty? I thought it would be fun to dress up for a change, so I'm making it black tie. I'm

inviting ten close pals to say thanks for being so nice to me since Jeffrey died, and you are at the top of my list."

• "Yes, come see me tomorrow morning at ten-thirty with the baby. We can put her in Jennifer's old pen, and she can play with Jennifer's old toys. You and I can have some coffee and some sinful Danish that is waiting for us in the freezer. We'll have a long, much-needed chat."

Any kind of invitation can be very meaningful to the person who receives it. And by extending such an invitation, the host gives the recipient much more pleasure than he probably realizes.

Every kind of invitation—formal or informal, to a big event or to one with only one guest—requires thought, planning, and, to be really successful, a caring and kind heart.

EXTENDING INVITATIONS

The invitation is what makes people come to your party. If you are anxious to have people come to whatever you're planning, concentrate on extending the best possible invitation for that event, and use the most effective method for extending it. Perhaps it's the warmth of your own voice and the excitement and enthusiasm you convey over the telephone that will make a potential guest eager to come to your party. Or perhaps it's your handwritten note or the look of the distinguished or amusing printed piece that you mail that will entice your guests to come.

There is a wealth of creativity in the field of invitations today, and your options are numerous. (As the late Elsa Maxwell, a legendary party giver, once said in an interview, "Make them *die* with anticipation to come to your party because of the invitation, and once you get them there, don't let them down!")

How Far Ahead Do You Extend an Invitation?

An invitation extended well in advance is more appreciated than one extended casually a week or less before the date. If someone calls you on the telephone and invites you for dinner at their house in three weeks' time, you feel very differently about that evening than if your host invites you two days before.

Most people seem to computer-generate invitations, but if you plan to have invitations printed for a large party, remember it can take from two to four weeks. (Count on at least four weeks to have them engraved.) Then you must also address the envelopes and hand-stamp them. Add five days between the day you mail them and the day they reach their destinations.

Naturally, there are many invitations for get-togethers that are last-minute and spur-of-the-moment that turn out to be great fun. However, most successful social planning involves mailing invitations that arrive well in advance of your event.

- If you have a choice on your entertaining timetable, follow this rule of thumb for mailing or telephoning your invitations. *Put your invitations in the mailbox:*
    - Two to three weeks before a business or social lunch.
    - Three weeks before a cocktail party.
    - Four weeks before an important business or social dinner.
    - Three weeks before an informal dinner.
    - Six to eight weeks before a wedding.
    - Four to six weeks before a dance.
    - Two to three months before a weekend in your home.

- Don't be insulted if you receive a last-minute invitation. Some people organize all their dinners at the last minute. Don't feel slighted if you're invited only a couple of days before or even on the morning of the party. And don't be miffed if you know you weren't on the host's original guest list but are part of the last-minute fill-ins for dropouts. When I'm asked if someone will lose face in accepting an invitation when she is obviously a last-minute substitute for a guest who dropped out, I say no. The invitee should readily accept this kind of invitation—because she will probably have a great time (which turns out to be true more often than not). It is also a golden opportunity for the last-minute guest to prove so attractive and such good company that she will land on the host's first list the next time a party is given in that house.

SAVE-THE-DATE CARDS

A "save the date" card is sent usually three or four months in advance for a very large and important event, which could be anything from a corporate centennial celebration to a large fund-raising event such as a charity auction or a benefit ball.

The save-the-date card, which may be a simple printed postcard or a specially designed printed card with matching envelope, is the first news a potential guest has of the event. Therefore, it should be well designed and well executed—a hastily scrawled postcard is not going to make much of an impression.

A sample text follows for a card announcing a forthcoming private function. The hosts' names in this case are at the bottom:

> *Please Save This Date*
> *Thursday, September 28*
> *for a black tie dinner dance*
> *in honor of our parents' fiftieth anniversary*
> *at the David Browns' farm*
> *corner of Spring Lake and Ransome Roads*
> *Invitations will be forthcoming*
> *The David Browns; Susan Brown; the Richard Tysons*

A sample hold-the-date card for a fund-raising benefit:

> *Hold This Date*
> *A Benefit for the Institute of International Education*
> *Saturday, June 15*
> *Black Tie Gala*
> *8 o'clock to midnight*
> *in celebration of the opening of*
> *Il Mondo Chic store*
> *The World Mall*
> *Newport, California*
> *Invitations to follow*
> *(For information, call 000-000-0000)*

PARTS OF A FORMAL INVITATION

A formal invitation should follow the traditional form simply because over the decades it has proven to communicate the information most efficiently.

For example, the following invitation, in nine parts, is a good form to use for your own social functions—adapted, of course, to your own needs. You might wish to substitute your dress instructions ("Black tie") in the lower right-hand corner for "Valet parking." You might wish to change what is written in the lower left of this invitation, where the RSVP information is given, according to whether you wish to furnish only a telephone number or an e-mail or a street address, or whether you wish to say "RSVP card enclosed" or whether you wish to put nothing in that corner (an enclosed, self-addressed RSVP card is, after all, self-explanatory).

Standard Form for a Formal Invitation

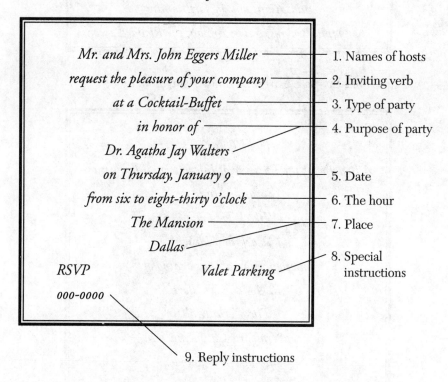

Mr. and Mrs. John Eggers Miller —— 1. Names of hosts

request the pleasure of your company —— 2. Inviting verb

at a Cocktail-Buffet —— 3. Type of party

in honor of —— 4. Purpose of party

Dr. Agatha Jay Walters

on Thursday, January 9 —— 5. Date

from six to eight-thirty o'clock —— 6. The hour

The Mansion —— 7. Place

Dallas

RSVP   *Valet Parking* —— 8. Special instructions

000-0000

9. Reply instructions

WHO DOES THE INVITING?

It's important always to have a host on your invitation, not just to use a corporate name. In other words, an invitation that reads "The Corner Stores, Inc., invites you to . . ." or "Miggs National Bank cordially invites you to . . ." does not sound right. A human being or a group of human beings should always do the inviting, and proper names are best. At least a person's title should be present on the invitation, if for some reason you don't wish to list names—for example: "The Chairman of the Corner Stores, Inc., cordially invites you to . . ." or "The Board of Directors of the Miggs National Bank requests the pleasure of your company . . ."

When there is more than one host:

• You may list their names vertically or horizontally on the invitation; your graphic artist may wish to list the names as part of a special design scheme of the invitation.

• List the names alphabetically if the hosts are on a par in age and importance; otherwise, list the titled and senior people first on a social invitation, or the company's officers first on a business invitation.

• If the party is being given in someone's home, list that couple's name first, the other cohosts after.

• Use a uniform system of listing names if there are many, such as on a benefit committee. In this case, it is preferable to list people by their given and surnames, without titles, as shown in the column on the left, and not with a hodgepodge of titles, as shown in the column on the right:

Correct Listing	Incorrect Listing
Marilyn Acorn	Mrs. John Acorn
John Agnew	Mr. John Agnew
Evelyn Andrew	Mrs. Evelyn Andrew
Victoria Arthur	Mrs. Tazewell Arthur
Benjamin Barnwell	Benjamin Barnwell, Esq.
Barbara Berson	Ms. Barbara Berson
Jennifer Bierwirth	Miss Jennifer Bierwirth

There are exceptions, of course. In an alphabetical listing, a medical doctor and an officer in the military service should be given their titles after their surnames, and others, too:

Barnwell, Benjamin O., Esq.
Galeazzi, The Reverend Anthony
Gallagher, Robert A., M.D.
Johnson, Marianne C. (Lt. Col., U.S. Army)

THE LANGUAGE OF INVITATIONS ("INVITATIONESE")

For a large, formal party, a calligrapher or someone with a fine hand should write all the invitations. There are engraved and printed invitations that can be purchased at stationers' with blank spaces to be filled in for a specific party. Invitations have a language all their own.

Informal:

> *Mr. and Mrs. Seamus O'Brien*
> *cordially invite you to*
> *dinner, etc.*

Or, formally:

> *Mr. and Mrs. Seamus O'Brien*
> *request the pleasure of your company*
> *at dinner, etc.*

Or, even more formally:

> *Mr. and Mrs. Seamus O'Brien*
> *request the pleasure of*
> *Mr. and Mrs. Robert Hoguet III's*
> *company at dinner, etc.*

Options for Stating the Purpose

Much the same phrasing is used for either a formal or informal invitation, except that for a formal invitation the British version of "honor" ("honour") and "favor" ("favour") is often used.

The honored guests' names or the reason the party is being given is placed either:

• In the upper left-hand corner of the invitation, where it may be written by hand, or

• On the line below the description of the kind of party being given

More formal:

> *George A. Stephenson*
> *President of Markton, Inc.*
> *requests the pleasure of your company*
> *at a luncheon*
> *in honour of Samuel R. Magill*
> *Monday, the eighth of February*
> *etc.*

Less formal:

> *In honor of Samuel R. Magill*
> *George A. Stephenson*
> *President of Markton, Inc.*
> *cordially invites you to*
> *a lunch*
> *Monday, February 8*
> *etc.*

How the Date Is Written

- On a formal invitation, the date is written out:
on Sunday, the eighteenth of September
- On an informal invitation, figures may be used:
on Sunday, September 18

How the Time Is Written

- On a formal invitation, the hours are spelled out and "o'clock" is used: at seven-thirty o'clock
- On an informal invitation, figures and "A.M." and "P.M." may be used, such as on this cocktail party invitation:
      . . . Cocktails
          from 5 to 7 P.M.

How the Address Is Written

On a formal invitation, there are no abbreviations. For example, "Washington, D.C." and "2000 Mason St. NW" would be incorrect. "Washington, District of Columbia" and "2000 Mason Street, Northwest" would be correct.

However, there is an exception to this rule. For the sake of space considerations, the address *under your* RSVP in the lower left-hand corner of the invitation may have words like "Street," "Northwest," and "District of Columbia" abbreviated. Also, ZIP codes are listed with the two-letter abbreviations for the states.

REMINDER CARDS

These cards are used for two purposes:
- For people who have accepted your invitation by telephone but have nothing on the record to help remind them of the what, when, and where of your party.
- For people who were sent invitations four or five months ago for your very special occasion and need to have their memories jogged.

These are the kinds of reminders you can send:
- You might write a simple postcard reminding your guest:

Dear Sally and Mark,
    We're delighted you can come! Dinner is Thursday, November 2, 7:30 P.M. at our house (132 Ridgewood Terrace).
                                                    The Griersons

- You might send that same message in a fax, if you have invited people only a few days before the event and a mailed reminder might not get there in time.

• You might have reminder cards printed for a large party and mailed to your already accepted guests ten days before—with a text like this:

> *This is to remind you that*
> *Mr. and Mrs. Winthrop Bates*
> *expect you for dinner*
> *on Wednesday, the sixth of October*
> *at eight o'clock*
> *The Hunters Club*
> *1900 Georgetown Street*
> *Washington, D.C. 00000*

• If you entertain regularly and need reminder cards on a continuing basis, it is easier and less expensive to buy them by the box from a stationer. These are engraved fill-in reminder cards (you fill in the blank spaces by hand *in black ink*). The text already engraved on the cards reads as follows:

> *To remind you that*
> [write in host's name here]
> *is expecting you*
> *for* [write in lunch, dinner, or cocktails]
> *on* [the date is written here]
> *at* [give hour] *o'clock*
>
> *RSVP*   *Your name*
> 000-000-0000   *Street address*
>   *City, State ZIP*

KINDS OF INVITATIONS

When you decide to have a party, you have many options for how you will invite your guests. In the hypothetical case of Betty Knowlton, for example, who is giving a dinner party in honor of her husband's fortieth birthday, the hostess might do any of the following:

- Write notes on her good personal stationery:

Dear Rose and Gregg,

I'm asking a few friends for Sunday dinner, July 23, at 7 P.M., at our house (1420 First Avenue), to celebrate Bob's fortieth birthday. It's a surprise. You just have to come. You're essential to the party. Please call me at home (000-0000) or at the office (000-0000). And please arrive *without* a gift!

Cordially,
/s/ Betty Knowlton

- Send faxes to all invitees, if the hostess does not have time to call or write them regular letters:

Please come to our house (1420 First Avenue) for dinner Sunday July 23 at 7 P.M. for a surprise celebration of Bob's 40th birthday. RSVP home (000-0000) or my office (000-0000).

Betty Knowlton

- Design her own invitations: She has fifty copies made of a five by seven-inch black-and-white photo print of Bob Knowlton when he was a baby, and on the back of each she hand-writes the invitation to the fortieth birthday party for her husband.
- Purchase fill-in invitations at a card shop or stationery store; either the formal kind, or an amusing greeting card type.
- Buy engraved fill-in cards from a stationer (as shown opposite).
- Order from a stationer her invitation text printed, thermographed, or engraved on cards (as shown opposite).
- Telephone the recipients: This is the least expensive method of all. She must remember to send everyone who accepts an informal reminder card.

An engraved fill-in invitation:

> Betty Knowlton
>
> *requests the pleasure of the company of*
>
> Tom and Susan Wheeling
>
> *at* Robert Knowlton's Surprise Fortieth Birthday Dinner
>
> *on* Sunday, the twenty-third of July
>
> *at* Seven o'clock
>
> *R.S.V.P.*
>
> 000-0000   1420 First Avenue
>
> Fort Worth, TX 00000

An invitation with the full text printed:

> *Betty Knowlton*
> *hopes you will join her*
> *for dinner*
> *to celebrate with gusto Bob's 40th*
> *and to make him feel 20 again*
> *Sunday, July 23, at 7 P.M.*
> *1420 First Avenue*
> *Fort Worth*
> *RSVP Card enclosed*

Creative Possibilities

If you want to be creative, look at what other people do. People love receiving invitations that reflect the host's own poetic spirit. If there's some small different touch about your invitation, it will jump right out at the recipient and impress itself on her memory.

- A wedding anniversary—for example:

Jamie and Bill Hartman
Cordially invite you
To a cocktail dance
In celebration of their 10th wedding anniversary
Saturday, May 7
5 to 8 P.M.
The Octagon Club (where they were married)
1st and Pierce Streets
and with the same receiving line
and with the same band, the Fortnighters,
that played on their wedding day.
RSVP

000-000-0000

When the George Graebers of Washington, D.C., celebrated their twentieth anniversary, they sent out a little poem, printed in red script, on a vertical white invitation card. (Betty Beale was a leading society columnist in Washington for many decades.)

George and Betty Beale Graeber
It would give us the greatest of pleasure
if you would take time off for leisure
and join us on the nineteenth of May
for cavorting at a dance buffet
to celebrate our twenty years of bliss
at the Chevy Chase Club edifice.
Come when it pleases you anytime
between the hours six-thirty to nine.
But for heaven's sake don't bring a gift
your very selves will give us a lift.
RSVP—000-0000

Another couple sent out as an invitation for their thirty-fifth wedding anniversary a card on which was printed a photograph of the bridal pair cutting their cake at their wedding reception. The text did not give the hosts' names—just the date of the anniversary dinner dance, the address of the club, the hour of the party, and the telephone number for the person at the club handling the replies. Some guests who had not known the couple in their youth had trouble identifying them, but eventually everyone figured out who their hosts were. The invitation made the anniversary party just that much more fun.

• A christening. One couple handwrote their baby's christening invitations on pieces of pale pink rice paper with matching envelopes, which they had purchased on a visit to Japan but had never before had occasion to use. They wrote:

Nothing would give us greater pleasure
than to have you join with us
in the celebration of the beginning of life
of the sweetest, dearest little girl
ever born
Amanda Gilchrist
Born March 12 at St. Joseph's Hospital
Come drink a glass of champagne with us
after her baptism
Sunday, April 3 at five o'clock
0000 Lake Shore Drive
Chicago, Illinois 00000
And if you cannot be with us that day
please say a prayer for her
to wish her a long, happy, and blessed life.
Ruth and Jeremy Farrell   000-000-0000

• A Valentine's Day thought. The hostess for the Valentine's Day dinner party for eight, with budget a consideration, cut out a heart for each guest from red file folders purchased at an office supply company. On the back of each heart she wrote her invitation to a "romantic dinner" on February 14, and mailed them in bright red office envelopes, also from the stationery store—just a little extra work that resulted in a major effect.

REQUESTING A REPLY

• You may request a reply in the lower left-hand corner of your invitation: "R.S.V.P." (or "RSVP" or "R.s.v.p.") with an address or a telephone number on the line below.

• You may enclose an RSVP card with a self-addressed envelope. (Many hosts timidly stamp these envelopes, thinking that this will cause more people to accept the invitation; I feel that the least a guest can do is pay for a stamp and stick it on the envelope!)

The text for an RSVP card (which is engraved if the invitation is engraved, or printed if the invitation is printed) looks like this:

M/M _____

_____ *will attend*

_____ *will not attend*

Dinner at Mr. and Mrs. Anson Mooney's on

Saturday, June eighth at eight o'clock

Regrets Only

It is correct to put in the lower left of your invitation "Regrets Only" with a telephone number. However, in my opinion this is a cop-out to help lazy people become even lazier in replying. It is a negative on the invitation and sticks out like a sore thumb. Of course, a guest should let the host know if it is not possible to attend the party, but the guest also should let the host know if it *is* possible to attend the party. Use "Regrets Only" if you wish. I would never use it. I expect my friends to be nice enough to reply to my invitations, regardless of whether they accept or regret.

A Reply Requested by a Certain Date

Many people add at the bottom of their RSVP cards, "Please respond by [day, month, and year]."

You are certainly at liberty to add that phrase or more formally: "The favour of a reply is requested by such-and-such a date." This is yet another reinforcement of social laziness, because people should deem it an honor to be invited to your party and should reply quickly, with pleasure, rather than be threatened with a deadline for the arrival of the reply. However, some people believe the phrase goads recalcitrant guests into making up their minds sooner about attending the party. (My response to that is, "Who needs guests like that?")

"No Gifts" on Invitations

Many people, when they host birthday and anniversary celebrations, are serious about not wanting guests to bring gifts, so they include that fact on their invitations. I think phrases such as "No gifts" or "Please, no gifts" join a phrase like "Regrets Only" in the negative category on an invitation. Instead, pass the word around among your friends when you talk to them that you are serious about the policy of no presents. A guest can always send a present to their home before or after their party. (If guests disobey the order concerning gifts, don't open the packages in front of the guests.)

An Invitation from the White House

Perhaps the most thrilling invitation that could ever arrive in your mailbox is one from the White House to a state dinner. (The sight of that raised gold presidential seal on the top of each piece of White House stationery makes anyone's pulse beat a little faster!) The President's house on Pennsylvania Avenue is, after all, the scene of the most important social functions held in the world. An invitation from the White House is an invitation to regret only in the most exceptional circumstances.

White House entertaining follows the highest standards of international protocol in the state dinners for foreign leaders. This is evident in:

- Its stationery.
- The pomp involved in the welcome accorded to a visiting head of state and spouse by the president and his wife at the North Portico.
- The playing by the Marine Band of the president's arrival music ("Hail to the Chief") as the hosts and guests of honor proceed into the East Room to join their guests.
- The manner in which the guests are organized into a receiving line according to their rank.
- The carefully thought-out protocol of seating at the tables in the State Dining Room.
- The order of toasts at the beginning or at dessert time of the dinner.

The aesthetics of the dinner—the food and wines, flowers, design of the table decorations, and the nature of the entertainment—set the nation's standards of style and talent. Although we cannot duplicate the White House and the scenario for presidential entertaining, we can certainly derive inspiration from it. We can learn from how they do things in the White House and adapt it to the best of our capabilities. For us, it's a matter of simplifying and adapting presidential ways according to our own wishes and resources.

White House social stationery contains the raised, embossed presidential seal in gold at the top. The envelopes and the engraved invitations are lettered with the guests' names in calligraphy performed by experts on staff and supervised by the Social Secretary. We can follow the form of this in our own printed or fill-in invitations, reply cards, table cards, place cards, and menus—without, of course, that gold-embossed presidential seal! As for the invitation text, "Mr. and Mrs. John Tadwell Smith request the pleasure of your company . . ." sounds *almost* as good as "The President of the United States and Mrs. Reagan request the pleasure of your company . . ."

The President and Mrs. Reagan
request the pleasure of the company of
Mr. and Mrs. Hollensteiner
at dinner
on Thursday, October 6, 1988
at 7:30 o'clock
Black Tie

A separate card (3½ by 4½ inches) announces the purpose of the dinner:

On the occasion of the visit of
His Excellency
The President of the Republic of Mali
and Mrs. Traore

The white invitation card (4½ by 6½ inches) bears the raised, embossed presidential seal in gold.

The invitation also includes a reply card and instructions on security clearance at the gates.

A matching menu card (4½ by 7 inches) is at each place. The menu is given in a combination of English and French:

DINNER
Honoring His Excellency
The President of the Republic of Mali
and Mrs. Traore

Vegetable Terrine
and Lobster Medallions
Curry Mousseline
Fennel Leaves

Roast Loin of Veal with Wild Mushrooms
Semolina Gnocchi
Sautéed Zucchini

Radicchio and Endive Salad
Bel Paese Cheese

Cold Pumpkin Soufflé
with Candied Ginger
Petits Fours Sec

CHÂTEAU ST. JEAN *Chardonnay 1986*
STERLING WINERY LAKE *Pinot Noir 1986*
SCHRAMSBERG *Crémant Demi Sec 1984*

THE WHITE HOUSE
Thursday, October 6, 1988.

This example of White House "social literature" was used for a dinner in honor of the president of Mali, hosted in 1988 by one of our most popular presidential couples, Ronald and Nancy Reagan. Not shown but also part of a White House state dinner invitation are:

- A reply card
- The security clearance card for the gate
- A table card to inform each guest of his or her table number
- A place card

The guest will also be given a card when he arrives, giving the guest's table number information, and, of course, another piece of calligraphy is a place card at his seat at the table.

WHEN YOU REPLY TO AN INVITATION

Every invitation should be replied to within a week. A host deserves to know possible problems with the invited guests' schedules—she should not just find out about it at the last minute, when the guest doesn't show up! Use any manner possible to reply—telephone, e-mail, fax—just get it done!

SENDING A FORMAL WRITTEN REPLY

The best possible form, of course, is to send a written reply to a formal invitation. It is written by hand (or typed, if your handwriting is as impossible as mine) on a piece of good stationery—personal letter paper, a correspondence card with matching envelope, or folded notepaper. The reply is written and centered on the page in the exact form as the invitation itself.

The Long Form of Acceptance

Mr. and Mrs. Walter Lodge
accept with pleasure
the kind invitation of
Mr. and Mrs. Donald Allen Rice
for dinner
Saturday, the eighth of August
at seven-thirty o'clock

. . . or, optionally:

Mr. and Mrs. Walter Lodge
accept with pleasure
Mr. and Mrs. Rice's
kind invitation for dinner
(or whatever the occasion)

The Short Form of an Acceptance

Mr. and Mrs. Walter Lodge
accept with pleasure
the kind invitation of
Mr. and Mrs. Donald Allen Rice
for Saturday, the eighth of August

The Long Form of a Regret

I am of the philosophy that if you are regretting an invitation, even formally by letter, you should explain why. That's why I recommend including a phrase explaining the reason for regretting the invitation, even if it makes the reply less formal. For example:

Mr. and Mrs. Walter Lodge
regret that
because of absence from the city
they will be unable to accept
Mr. and Mrs. Rice's
kind invitation for dinner
Saturday, the eighth of August
at seven-thirty o'clock

Or the reason given could be "because of illness" or "owing to a prior engagement" or "because of Mr. Lodge's speaking engagement on the same evening"—whatever the reason for being unable to attend.

The Short Form of a Regret

Mr. and Mrs. Walter Lodge
regret that
they will be unable to accept
Mr. and Mrs. Rice's
kind invitation
for Saturday, the eighth of August

When One Spouse Accepts and the Other Regrets

Let us say hypothetically that Mr. Lodge will be out of town the night of the dinner, but Mrs. Lodge really wants to go to that party. Their reply would look like this:

> Mrs. Walter Lodge
> accepts with pleasure
> the kind invitation of
> Mr. and Mrs. Donald Allen Rice
> for Saturday, the eighth of August
> Mr. Lodge regrets
> that owing to absence from the city
> he will be unable to attend

GET YOURSELF ORGANIZED

It's no secret that entertaining is hard work. Those stories of famous hostesses who manage to organize fabulous parties on the spur of the moment and can throw together a little dinner for twenty on a few hours' notice are all myths. Either they have been working hard for a couple of weeks on their parties and won't admit it, or they have well-trained staffs who are paid high salaries to move fast without advance notice.

The great thing about entertaining often is that you become practiced, skilled, and fine-tuned. In my twenties in New York, by the time I had produced within three months my sixth buffet supper of coq au vin with noodles, French string beans, salad, rolls, and store-bought coffee ice cream with hot butterscotch sauce, I could do it in my sleep. Since it was so easy to do, I kept on doing it year after year. Then I realized that some friends had been served this same menu so often that they had no trouble predicting it. So I apologized—only to be told that they would gladly have the same menu once a week, if I would just invite them!

The tough part of entertaining—remembering how to get organized and overseeing all of the details and logistics—really does become easier each time. One friend who does all her own work for her parties proudly states, "I have become the best-trained chef and the most experienced butler anyone has ever known." Another friend always does her buffet dinners back to back on consecutive nights, so she can use the same wines and liquors; the same flowers, and even the same food. (It's an easier job marketing—buying only once and in a large quantity—for two dinners.)

Another great plus about gaining experience in the entertaining field is that you become immune to the problems that may develop. You realize that in spite of the crises that may be occurring, the party does continue. I once saw one of the waiters in a caterer's retinue become so sloshed that he had to be noisily evicted from the party by two strong male guests, but the hosts nonetheless kept their cool and consoled the headwaiter, not themselves. On another occasion, the orchestra's bus broke down en route to a friend's dance. You learn to compensate, substitute, change directions—or just laugh a lot, so that your guests follow suit. At the dance, our host got on the microphone and told everyone what had happened to the band and then added with great enthusiasm, as though she were organizing a cheerleading squad, "What was to have been 'the dance of the year' will become as of now 'the cocktail party of the year!'" Everyone cheered and applauded, resolved to have a good time for the host's sake—and they did. Never has a "non-dance-dance" been a greater success.

Basics of Good Entertaining Planning

• Set up a *"party notebook"*—your *manual*—into which every pertinent item will be entered, from the budget to the invitation list, and from the kind of room scent to be purchased for the bathrooms to the number of lemons and limes needed for the bar. *Everything* should be in this notebook—all items pending, all names, addresses, telephone numbers—every bit of information. This should be your constant companion during party-preparation time, the ultimate checklist of checklists. Make a habit of recording any kind of party in your party notebook. Each one will make you better prepared for the next.

• Make a *budget*—always the next step—and if your means are limited, resolve to stick to it. (See page 437 for a sample budget.) Keep referring to it as your bills mount. You may have to cut back on some items if expenses prove to be higher than you estimated. That's all right. You can always find ways to do your party for less. For example, cut back on the number of fresh flowers ordered from the florist and have him substitute more greenery in your arrangements. Drop one course from your menu—perhaps something that should not have been in your budget in the first place, like smoked salmon. (Your guests won't know the difference.) Don't buy less wine than you originally planned; simply buy a less expensive but nonetheless good wine.

• Set your party date—one that will not conflict with any of your town's biggest social events or a night when everyone wants to be home watching television (for example, Academy Awards night).

• Decide on the type of party you want to give. Buffet dinner? Small lunch? Family-style beach picnic? Cocktail reception mixing business and social friends? Pizza and beer party for engaged friends before going to the circus? A party for singles only? For people who have been divorced? A Saturday afternoon old-fashioned tea party?

• Decide on the place and the hours for your party. The place may be anywhere you choose, as long as it is comfortable and accessible for your guests, and if it is logistically possible to serve food there.

The classic party hours are these:

- Breakfast: 8 A.M. or 9 A.M., according to what business or social activity will follow. Usually lasts about an hour.
- Brunch: 11 A.M. Lasts an hour to an hour and a half—held on Saturday or Sunday.
- Lunch: 12 noon or 12:30 or 1 P.M. Lasts usually one and a half to two hours.
- Tea: Anywhere from 3:30 to 5:30. Lasts an hour.
- Cocktails: 5 to 7, 5:30 to 7 or 7:30, or 6 to 8 P.M. Some guests tend to stay much later than they should—unless the host shuts off the bar a half hour after the supposed end of the party. (For a cocktail party from 6 to 8, if the host shuts the bar after 8:30, he is acting in an appropriate manner.) Nothing brings a cocktail party to a speedier conclusion than closing the bar!
- Cocktail buffet: 6 to 9 P.M. Again, shut the bar down by 9:30 or your hangers-on will never leave.
- Dinner: 7, 7:30, or 8 P.M. Lasts usually three to three and a half hours, unless there is dancing or other entertainment, in which case it could last until midnight or later. Remember, for any kind of evening party, the cocktail hour preceding the meal should not last longer than forty-five minutes to an hour.
- After-dinner reception: 9, 10, or 11 P.M., depending on whether it follows a theater performance, museum opening, or the like. Usually lasts no more than one to one and a half hours. Most people are exhausted after an evening affair followed by an hour-long reception; therefore, this kind of function should consist of the fast service of champagne or wine and whatever light food (usually desserts) is to be served.
- A private dance (a rarity today): 10 P.M. Since guests usually eat dinner beforehand, they tend not to arrive until 10:30 or 11. The dance music usually continues until 2 A.M. (A dance can last beyond 2 A.M., provided the host is willing to pay musicians overtime.) A light supper of something like hot pasta or omelets or chicken hash, with a salad, rolls, and dessert may be served at midnight, along with beer, wine, and champagne.

• Enter in the book what you would consider the best possible guest list. First make a long list of possible names and put them in different categories, so that when you pare it down to a final list, it will be a varied, interesting mix (always the best recipe for any kind of a party, large or small).

Some possible categories:

- People you owe.
- Newcomers to the city who would appreciate the chance to meet people.
- Friends you haven't really seen in the past couple of years but would like to touch base with again.
- People who have become important to you in the last year—for example, possibly your congressman, the new pastor, the children's school superintendent.
- One marvelous conversationalist per twelve other guests (insurance against embarrassing, heavy conversational lulls).
- An important business contact and her spouse.
- A friend from your extracurricular life: classmate at your art, cooking, or exercise class; a tennis partner; fellow bird-watcher; fellow volunteer at the hospital; fellow karate student.
- A couple from an older age group, if you're young; a couple from a younger age group if you're middle-aged or older.
- A celebrity in town whom you happen to know well—anyone from a news anchor to a college football star.
- A foreign business colleague or student (always adds interest to a gathering of Americans).
- A friend who has been having a tough time (has been ill, has just been separated or divorced, lost a job, or in whose family there has been a death). If you have a mix of people, whether it's a huge cocktail party or a small dinner, and if you introduce everybody warmly to one another, your party will be a *success*!
- Put a copy of your invitation in the book, if you had it handwritten, printed, engraved, or e-mailed. If you telephoned your invitations, put a copy of the reminder card sent (to those who accepted) in the book. Or if you just telephoned the invitations, mark that fact down, too, with the date you telephoned and the replies.
- Keep a beautifully documented guest list in your party book, with the latest tally of acceptances and regrets so that you'll know exactly where you stand with your quota of guests. If you have many regrets, start telephoning the invitations to your "B" list of desired guests at once.

WORKING WITH THE CATERER

At least two months ahead, *sign up your caterer and/or the extra help needed for a large event*, whether the extra help consists of a cook, bartender, baby-sitter, clean-up squad, or someone to mow the lawn before the guests have to wade through your ankle-deep grass. List all names, addresses, and telephone numbers, plus their advance price quotes, and note how they are to be paid. Some caterers, for example, need a percentage, even half of the total bill a week before the party; others might expect to be paid all costs at the end of the party itself.

- There are several ways to find a caterer:
  - You see one in action firsthand at a party and are impressed by her teamwork, service, food, and style.
  - Someone you know recommends a caterer he has used.
  - You read about a caterer's success at a party in the lifestyle section of the newspaper.
  - You find a list of caterers in the Yellow Pages of the telephone book, and you call several or all of them to compare prices. You also check their references.
- Decide on your menu—all the courses, including the hors d'oeuvres, cocktails, and wines. If you use a new recipe for this party, include it in your party notebook, so you can find it again if you want to repeat it for another party, but don't give the caterer an overly complicated task, whatever you do.
- Make a list of everything needed for this party. Write down all items that you must purchase or have on hand, from toothpicks to dishwashing detergent, cocktail napkins to jars of olives, miniature pieces of rye bread to diet sodas, sugar cubes to guest bathroom soaps, decaffeinated coffee to arugula, and place cards to cherries for the Cherries Jubilee dessert. Don't forget to list even the most standard items that must be on hand that night—like salt, pepper, paper towels, soft drinks, tonic water, and sparkling soda.
- Order in advance everything you can, well ahead of time, including wine, liquor, spices for cooking, tomato paste, butter, and so forth. The more you do ahead, the less onerous the entertaining chores will seem.
- Enter detailed descriptions of your table decorations for that particular event, including the kinds of flowers, the colors of the table linens, and the like. Take snapshots or Polaroids of your decor, so you'll be able to call it to mind easily later—and perhaps repeat it at some party in the future.
- If you have entertainment at your party, make an entry for it in your book. Write down the name, address, and telephone number of any entertainer (and later how you felt about his, her, or their performance). Include how much the entertainment costs, the agent's name and telephone number, and what is

required logistically for the entertainer (platform, sound system, lectern, special lighting, and the like).

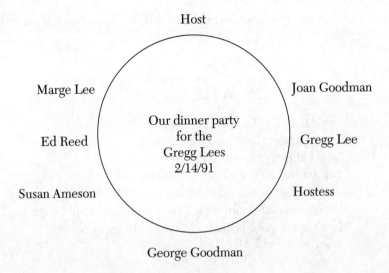

If your party is a seated dinner, it's good to have a record in your party planner of who sat where around the tables. Even for a dinner for eight, an informal sketch is a nice reminder of the evening.

If you are planning to use only your own musical tapes for entertainment, or if you or a guest will play the piano, include that, too. Write down what selection of tapes are to be played (interesting to look back on).

SAMPLE PARTY PLANS—A POTLUCK MEAL

A very pleasant custom is that of a host organizing an informal dinner at home, inviting each guest (or guest couple) to supply part of the meal. It is an American way of entertaining, and a good one at that—easy on everyone's budget and easy on busy people's time schedules.

The host usually supplies the cocktails, wine, main course, and coffee. In asking people what they would prefer to bring, the host also helps decide what dish in that particular category would be appropriate, so that the menu works. For example, to a guest who wants to bring a fruit salad, she might say, "We are having fruit for dessert, so would you mind bringing a mixed green salad instead?"

Each guest or couple should bring the course in a nice-looking container that can go from refrigerator or stove straight onto the buffet table. (In the best of all situations, the hosts wash the containers and return them within a week to their owners, rather than making the guests troop out to the kitchen to wash their own containers and carry them home.)

An entry in a party notebook would be a simple one page, such as this one, showing who is responsible for bringing what:

Potluck Supper
March 12th at 6:30 P.M.

Hors d'oeuvres: Lucy and Jim McGrath
Wine and beer: Gordon Matson
Grilled lemon chicken: Us
Corn soufflé: Joan and Pete Schultz
Baked tomatoes and onions: Gerry and Phil Miller
Mixed green salad and rolls: Ginny and Hans Mittendorf
Mom's apple pie à la mode: Mike and Jessica Feldman
Coffee and decaf: Us

SAMPLE PLANS FOR A SMALL DINNER

Everyone's concept of what makes a party big or small is a personal judgment. To me, dinner for six or eight is a small one; a cocktail party for twelve to fifteen people is a small one. However, for those rarities—people with huge houses and domestic staffs—even a dinner for twenty-four is small. (Let's use my numbers—not those of the person with the big house and staff—in this book.)

Preparing a party checklist or a party plan for any size gathering makes sense, and helps you get organized. For example, here are the entries in the party notebook of a couple who have small groups for dinner once a month, and who keep good records:

Dinner for Eight

Date: Wed., Feb. 14   Time: 7:30
     Valentine's Day
Guest List: Gregg and Marge Lee, Ed Reed, Susan Ameson, George and
     Joan Goodman, Us
Invitations: Homemade red paper hearts, mailed Jan. 20
Menu:
     Cocktails
     Hors d'oeuvres: Crudités with yogurt dip, hot bacon-cheese puffs.

First course:	Cup of hot shrimp bisque (canned) with slice of lemon and a sprig of fresh dill
Second course:	Roast chicken stuffed with herbed rice
	Steamed broccoli
	Mixed green salad
Dessert:	Peppermint ice cream in heart mold with chocolate sauce

Espresso

| Wines: | Choice of red or white |

Decor:

Flowers:	Tall arrangement of laurel leaves in foyer
	Low bowl of multicolored anemones on coffee table
Dining table:	A small glass of water at each place, containing red and white carnations. Red and white votive candles in ring in center.
Table favors:	Red satin heart box containing chocolate-covered caramels at each place
	Valentine place card at each place

Music: Frank Sinatra love songs throughout evening (on CD or tape)

Budget:

Buy and plan according to budget, which in the case of this dinner
for eight is $800.00

Purchases include:

Hors d'oeuvres
soup; chicken
vegetables and salad
ice cream and cookies
7 bottles of modestly priced wine for cocktails and dinner
bottle of gin, vodka, and Scotch
cocktail napkins
ice from supermarket
sodas, regular and diet
lemons, olives
8 heart boxes containing chocolates
flowers in living room and table center
8 Valentine place cards
services of baby-sitter and high-school neighbor cleaner-upper

THE LOGISTICS
OF PLANNING A LARGE DINNER

In organizing a large party, you go through an exercise much like a painter does in facing his canvas: first the rough, broad outlines, and then the minute details are filled in. The party notebook becomes even more crucial. You will want every dollar you spend on such an expensive undertaking to be used to best advantage, to make certain the event accomplishes your goals. It's very easy to throw money away when you're stepping into elaborate entertaining. Therefore, keep your wits about you, write everything down in your notebook, and *stay in control.*

One very accomplished hostess I know, who recently gave a dinner for fifty—the big blast of the season for everyone present—around an Easter spring theme, kept careful notes as she went along. She entertained at five round tables of ten (rented from the caterer), using two in her dining room, two in her living room, and one in the library. Her entries in her notebook were organized in the following manner:

Big Budget (Five round tables of Ten) Dinner for 50

<u>Date:</u> Easter Saturday night   <u>Time:</u> 8 P.M.   <u>Dress:</u> Black tie
<u>Caterer:</u> Harris Caterers   <u>In charge:</u> Alexandre
<u>Tel:</u> 000-0000
<u>Invitation:</u>

An entire page in her notebook was dedicated to this. She had taped an example of her engraved "fill-in" invitation to the page. A calligrapher had written in the necessary information.

<u>Guest List:</u>

She listed on this page guests who had accepted by the names that would be written on their place cards in computer-generated calligraphy—for example, "Mrs. Abernathy, Ambassador Abernathy, Ms. Nelson, Mr. Wyeth." She had a telephone number by each name, in case she had to reach anyone quickly. She also made a running list of everyone who had regretted, just for her files.

<u>Table Placement:</u>

This page contained five circles, representing her five round tables. She gave each table a number from 1 to 5, and penciled in each guest at his or her proper place at one of the tables. (She explained that the names were penciled in because she had to keep changing the seating as guests canceled and new ones took their places.)

<u>Menu:</u>

On this page, she wrote what was to be served at the cocktail hour and for dinner, and what was to be passed after dinner. For example, she had written:

Drinks:
    Peach Bellinis
    Scotch, gin, and vodka
    White wine
    Tonic water and club soda

Passed Hors d'Oeuvres:
    Mushroom caps stuffed with pâté
    Figs wrapped in prosciutto
    Tiny grilled cheese sandwiches (Swiss on dark rye)

Dinner:
    First course: Fresh asparagus with lemon sauce and capers
    Second course: Roast lamb
                  Fresh mint sauce
                  New potatoes with butter-herb sauce
                  Carrots in a chopped walnut–butter sauce
                  Endive and arugula salad
    Third course: Chocolate soufflé
                  Vanilla sauce
                  "Dentelles" lace cookies
                  Chocolates
                  Demitasses
    Wines: Pouilly Fumé (French)
                  Cabernet Sauvignon (American)
                  Schramsberg Blanc de Blancs (American)
    After dinner: Remy Martin Cognac
                  Framboises and Eau de poire liqueurs
                  Glasses of club soda and ice

Decorations:
    On this page the details of how she decorated the house were listed for the record.

    <u>Front hall table:</u>
    Large crystal bowl with gardenias and white votive candles in crystal
        holders floating in water
    <u>Living room and library:</u>
    Vases of white lilacs, lilies, and very pale pastel tulips
    Tall vases of branches of forsythia and apple blossoms
    <u>Centerpieces for the five tables:</u>
    Lavender and mauve tulips with peach roses in crystal bowls
    Mauve and peach tie-died Easter eggs to ring each bowl of flowers
    Tall white candles in crystal candlesticks
    <u>Linens:</u>

Five round tables of 10: mauve and peach plaid cotton cloths to the floor

Mauve napkins (tied with peach satin ribbons)

Entertainment:

On this page she wrote all of the information on the three Spanish guitarists who serenaded the guests after dinner—their names and telephone numbers, their price, and how long she wanted them to play. She made a note that she had instructed them to "come bursting into the living room, strumming quickly and dramatically, as a surprise—as soon as the guests assembled there for after-dinner coffee."

THE COCKTAIL PARTY

A cocktail party is a wonderful way to entertain a large number of people informally and relatively easily. This kind of social event is supposed to have a duration of from one and a half to two hours (although it is expected that some people will stay unfortunately much longer than that). Since alcohol traditionally is not served until after five, a cocktail party's beginning hour is five, five-thirty, or six. In Europe most cocktail parties begin at seven P.M. and supposedly end at nine P.M. (Before five, a get-together would be called a "tea"—see page 449.)

• Since the only way to have a successful cocktail party come to an end is to shut off the bar, everything works more smoothly if this is understood by the bartender(s) ahead of time. Let the bar stay open until a half hour after the party was supposed to end. If, for example, your cocktail party hours are from five-thirty to seven-thirty, instruct your caterer or bartender to shut off the bar at eight, and hopefully the hangers-on will get the message.

THE SOCIAL ASPECTS OF ALCOHOL

With the exception of a child's party, it's impossible to discuss entertaining without a section on alcohol. A business host's responsibility today, sadly enough, is not only to entertain his guests well but to control alcoholic excess in his party place. If you are the host, remember the following:

• Your legal responsibility for a guest leaving drunk and causing an accident.

• Your responsibility never to allow an alcoholic, a recovering alcoholic, or a potential alcoholic to go over the edge because of your social function. It is obvious when someone has had too much to drink: clumsy movements, slurred speech, glazed eyes, loud and out-of-control speech, a liquor smell on the breath, bellicose behavior, withdrawal from the group, unreasonable fits of rage or joy, and perhaps even passing out.

There are people who normally are not part of the problem, because they abstain from alcohol:

- Pregnant women and children who have been taught at home what "No" means.
- Those who do not indulge for religious reasons (members of the religious right, Mormons, Muslims, etc.).
- Those who don't like the taste (the very fortunate people!).
- Those who are recovering alcoholics and face the fact that they must battle with a serious addiction for the rest of their lives.

Definition of a "Social Drinker"

Someone who brags about drinking only on occasion, who claims to be expert at handling alcohol, but who is often so very wrong about that and when he or she wakes up with the hangover bragged about not getting ever, he or she knows not to drink for a while—and doesn't think about it anymore—until the next New Year's Eve party.

A Social Responsibility:
A Sensitive Treatment of a Recovering Alcoholic

A person who is "in recovery" has been through treatment and knows that for the duration of his or her lifetime, alcohol is an addiction and a drug that is poisonous to the system.

A recovering alcoholic is someone who "wants a life." Since he will never be "recovered" from the disease but will be "recovering" (present tense) *for life,* he deserves to be supported and encouraged by family, friends, and colleagues *for life.* That's what friends are for. Each one of us should be sensitive to the serving of alcohol on our watch at parties—our responsibility, therefore. Some points to remember:

1. Don't grill someone by asking if he is a recovering alcoholic. It's an NOYB question (none of your business). Don't point her out at a party as though she were an exhibit in the zoo—"That's Cynthia over there. She has just been through a tough treatment program, and is a recovering alcoholic. Isn't that great?" Yes, it is great, but congratulate her in private. Don't put a spotlight on her.

2. If your guest refuses a drink, don't ask why. Never cajole him into accepting it. Never make anyone feel you will be displeased if he doesn't drink at your party. When I was a young woman, if you didn't take a drink at someone's party, you were practically ostracized. I didn't like the taste of liquor, so I learned to take a ginger ale in a tall

glass with ice; it looked like a Scotch and soda. Today it is common to see people drinking fizzy water all night.

3. Give this guest his drink of choice (which could be fruit juice, mineral water, soda water, hot coffee, iced tea, or cranberry juice), but don't single him out, make him very noticeable. Don't suggest to his face that he "of course will want a soft drink." Treat him like everyone else. If you're pushing your mint juleps at the party, ask him if he'll have one. (He will decline, politely.)

4. Serve non-alcoholic drinks in your prettiest glasses, not your cheapest. (I have seen them served at parties in things like empty, even if well-washed, peanut butter jars that are used as glasses!)

5. The fact that a recovering alcoholic is coming for a meal does not imply that cocktails and wine should not be served to anyone. A recovering alcoholic is accustomed to being the only one at the table without an alcoholic beverage. After all, as time goes on, she becomes stronger in her recovery.

6. If you wish to avoid serving any alcohol at your dinner party, take my advice and give a luncheon instead.

7. Don't set the recovering alcoholic's place at your table without a wineglass, nor set the wineglass turned upside down. It's unnecessarily conspicuous. *As a signal of refusal,* the guest may say to the server, "No thank you" when the wine is about to be poured into his glass, or he may place his fingertips on the rim of his glass as a sign of no thank you. Or he may allow wine to be poured into the glass but will not touch it.

8. There is danger in cooking with alcohol. A majority of the alcohol used in cooking burns off in the process, but steer clear of serving a recovering alcoholic any of the following:

   • A dish you have heavily laced with wine: Beef Burgundy, for example, or crème brûlée, a dessert prepared with a major dose of cognac in the custard that is also poured on top of the burnt brown sugar crust.

   • Pastries soaked in rum and brandied fruitcakes are popular and hazardous to the drinker as well. Check your guest list and your menu before accidentally placing a known recovering alcoholic in danger because of a menu with a hidden but strong alcohol content.

   • A very strong liqueur like framboise (raspberry) or slivovitz may be poured over your fruit for dessert. If the host passes it separately, and announces what it is, guests can stay away from it. A popular summer dessert is a fresh fruit compote or sherbet splashed with undiluted vodka over it. Again, any host should pass the vodka separately—in a small pitcher, for example—and state what it is. Recovering alcoholics will not touch it.

(Again, if he or she should take the vodka, say nothing. Anyone who is going to fall off the wagon will do it at any time, anywhere, regardless of your dinner menu.)

What Do You, a Recovering Alcoholic, Do at Toasting Time?

1. First of all, you can raise a glass to your lips and pretend to join in the toast even if you're not even sipping the wine.
2. Second, it's an old wives' tale that one must make a toast in alcohol, never in water. A recovering alcoholic, or anyone else, for that matter, should not be embarrassed to hoist aloft a glass of water, ginger ale, or fruit juice while joining in a toast. There will be people on diets joining you, too.
3. If you don't have a wineglass before you, you can make a symbolic toast by raising an empty hand aloft, as if holding a glass in salute to the person being toasted.

How Many Bars, How Much Help, and What Supplies Are Needed

Bars Needed

Two bars are best for a party of fifty guests, but one efficiently run bar can handle up to sixty guests, particularly if guests will help themselves if the bartender is busy and if the liquor, ice, and glasses are all accessible on the table. For a party of sixty to a hundred, two bars are needed. (The hosts usually help out, too, at an informal party, making sure the guests' glasses are filled and that the hors d'oeuvres are being passed around.)

Help Needed

These specified numbers of help needed are based on the premise that a host, or a husband and wife host team, will be working, too, if necessary at the peak hour, to make sure the service goes smoothly.

- If you have a party for fifty, a bartender and an assistant waiter or waitress can handle the crowd, particularly since the fifty people arrive at different times during the two-hour period, and the host couple is working, too.
- A group of sixty to eighty will be immersed in a logjam if you have only

one bar and one table full of food. It is better to have drinks served by bartenders at two stations, and to have the hors d'oeuvres passed by a waiter or waitress, rather than make people crowd up against one table to get food. (What happens is that the people in front of the food table begin to socialize and chat with each other, instead of serving themselves and stepping away to allow others to approach.)

• For a crowd of ninety to one hundred twenty, three bartenders and two waitresses will be needed. The serving help have more to do than just pass hors d'oeuvres or make drinks; they must carry out glasses, bring in fresh glasses, keep the hors d'oeuvres replenished, pick up, clean up, carry ice, and the like.

• When you're going to have a very crowded party, and you don't have the space for two bars, you would be wise to have a second bartender making drinks in an out-of-the-way area, such as the kitchen, and then passing through the crowd with guests' orders for drinks on a tray. If the crush gets worse, have this second bartender make tray after tray of assorted drinks, and send them out with a waiter into the crowd, so the guests can simply help themselves from the tray.

• For a champagne reception, a special celebration with champagne being served, such as at an "opening," christening, or an engagement party, you would need two waiters and an additional person to keep passing hors d'oeuvres. There is no need for a bar. Two waiters with trays of champagne can pass constantly through a crowd of up to seventy or eighty; there should always be a few glasses of soda or fruit juice mixed in with the champagne on the tray. You would also need small bowls of nuts, cheese straws, and other munchies left around within everyone's easy reach, as well as having a few hors d'oeuvres passed. (Never leave expensive shrimp or crab legs lying on platters on a table. Party "vultures" will take them all in one fell swoop, leaving nothing for the other guests. This is why you must have them passed.)

Checklist of Things Needed for a Cocktail Party at Home

You will need the following items:
• Table(s) and cloth(s) for the bar(s).
• Ice (keep any overly large bags of ice ordered in containers, like a roasting pan, so they don't leak all over the floor).
• Ice bucket.
• Ice crusher.
• Cutting board.
• Bar knife.
• Lemon and lime wedges (also thinly cut lemon peel "zests" for martinis or glasses of soda water).
• Olives and/or cocktail onions.

- Maraschino cherries (if you are serving a fruit drink with rum or vodka).
- Pitcher with long-handled stirrer for making martinis.
- Large water pitcher.
- One-and-a-half-ounce jigger or shot glass.
- Bar towels.
- Corkscrew.
- Paper cocktail napkins—buy pretty ones, don't use the boring all-white ones.
- Trays and platters (for carrying glasses and passing hors d'oeuvres).
- Your selection of liquor, wines, beer, mixers, sodas, fruit juices. (If you're serving a drink like Bloody Marys, you would be smart to have them premixed, ready for the bartender simply to add vodka and ice. Otherwise, have at the bar the tomato juice and all its paraphernalia, including: lemons, Worcestershire sauce, horseradish, salt and pepper, lemon squeezer, and strainer.)
- Glasses (any combination of the following):
  - Tall highball glasses for long drinks, including Scotch, bourbon, or whiskey and soda or water; gin or vodka and tonic; rum and soda or tonic; sodas; beer; and bottled water.
  - "Old-fashioned" glasses for serving wine or wine on the rocks, sherry, aperitifs, martinis on the rocks. (All-purpose wineglasses may substitute for old-fashioneds.)
  - Delicate crystal, stemmed martini glasses, and other specialty glasses are not used for large cocktail parties, simply because of logistical problems. (They break and can't be safely put in dishwashers.) They are better used when a couple of friends come by your house for a drink.
  - Don't use plastic glasses indoors either, if you can possibly help it. Borrow or rent your glasses. (Plastic ones are fine for a party held on your deck, patio, or front yard.)

How Much Wine and Liquor to Order

The advantage in ordering wines and liquors for a cocktail party is that, unlike food, they don't spoil. You can always use what is left over, or you can give the leftover bottles of liquor through the year for holiday and hostess gifts. Most liquor stores where you are known will take back unopened bottles of liquor if you have overordered.

I think it's wise always to stock more for a cocktail party than you think you'll need, because you never know what will be the big drink of the hour. The latter changes according to the age of the guests, region of the country, and the time of the year. For example, ten years ago my husband and I gave two business-related cocktail parties for fifty each, back to back. We prepared by laying in a large supply of vodka and tonic, since everyone that hot summer seemed to be drinking it; we decided to purchase only one large (1.75-liter) bottle each of Scotch and bourbon. The guests at our first party surprised us by ordering large amounts of Scotch and bourbon and almost no vodka and tonic. The next day I rushed to the liquor store to return most of the vodka and to lay in a supply of Scotch and bourbon for the second party. Our guests surprised us again. Almost everyone ordered white wine, of which we had only two bottles on hand. For the next summer's first cocktail party, we filled our fridge with beautifully chilled bottles of white wine. Only two people asked for it; the majority of drinkers asked for rum. The moral of the story is, don't be surprised. (I might also add that we no longer give cocktail parties!)

If you're watching your budget and want a limited instead of an open bar, decide beforehand on what you are going to offer your guests. If you decide, for example, to have soft drinks, white wine, and only Scotch as your hard liquor, offer guests their choice of those, saying, "What would you like? A soda, or perhaps some white wine, or a Scotch and soda?"

It's comforting to realize that today you don't have to offer guests faddish cocktails like Bellinis, Cosmopolitans—the latest *cocktail du jour*— or even old standbys like Whiskey Sours and Manhattans. Nor is any host today obliged to have a blender whirring away with all the latest exotic drinks!

• Always have on hand a good supply of nonalcoholic drinks, like a variety of sodas, diet sodas, bottled waters, and fruit juices.

Some Suggestions on How to Stock Your Bar

In noting the following suggestions, keep in mind they will be tempered by region and age, and by seasonal differences in drinking habits.

• If you have the twenty-one- to twenty-seven-year-old set coming to your party, you might have on hand:
> Cold beer (half of it light)
> Nonalcoholic beer
> White wine
> Red wine
> Soda (half of it the diet variety)

• For a party for people in their thirties and older:
> White wine
> Martinis
> Scotch
> Vodka or rum in the summer, gin in the winter (again, according to your own preference)

Mixers of club soda, tonic water, and ginger ale (which, along with your diet sodas, may also serve as your inventory of nonalcoholic drinks).

- For a full open-bar party, you might have on hand:

White wine
Vodka
Gin
Scotch
Rum (dark or light)
Whiskey
Dry vermouth for martinis
Sherry
Mixers, sodas, bottled waters, and a fruit juice
Cold beer (light)
Nonalcoholic beer

- To determine quantities needed, use 1.5 ounces as an average serving of liquor per drink. (Use or have your bartender use a jigger or shot glass as the standard measure for the drink that is poured into the glass.) There are about twenty-two drinks in a liter bottle of liquor, that is if you're not exaggerating the amount you put in each drink.

How to Buy Your Beverages

- Particularly for a party for the young, watch the wine sale ads, and buy a modest-priced wine by the magnum (1.5-liter size, sold six to a case) or by the 4-liter bottle (sold four to a case).
- Buy your mixers, sodas, and bottled waters by the case at a special price when they are advertised in your local stores.
- Buy liquor by the large 1.75-liter bottle (you can save money). Do not buy cheap brands—people can taste the difference.
- If your cocktail party is in a hotel or some public place, you may have an unlimited consumption arrangement with the establishment, whereby it charges you a flat fee per guest, regardless of how much a guest does or does not drink. (For example, if the first-class hotel charges $10 per drink, not including tax and gratuities, and counts on each guest having three drinks, you would be charged around $35 per guest for the liquor, including tax and gratuities.) Or you may pay for your liquor by the bottle. In that case, you yourself should keep count of the bottles actually used for your party, and return any unopened bottles to the hotel's inventory for reimbursement.

Hors d'Oeuvres

Serve what you can handle easily. In other words, if you don't have much help, have a menu of at least three cold hors d'oeuvres made ahead of time and only one or two hot ones, so that you are not always dashing into the kitchen to check on what's in the oven.

• If guests are coming to have an informal drink with you at home, you only need to have two cold hors d'oeuvres, which might be something as simple as crudités with a dip and cheese and crackers.

• If you are having a full-fledged cocktail party, in addition to small bowls of nuts and munchies throughout the entertaining area, you might consider serving:

Three of these	*Plus two of these*
Open-faced canapés made with pâté, egg salad,smoked salmon, or the like	Toasted rounds with peanut butter topped with crumbled bacon
Tiny open-faced sandwiches of smoked turkey or rare beef on rye with mayonnaise	Miniature pizzas or quiches Grilled sausages on toothpicks
Crackers spread with crabmeat and a dash of Worcestershire	Miniature hamburgers Grilled water chestnuts in bacon on toothpicks
Endives stuffed with pâté	Hot cheese or salmon puffs
Crudités with salt and pepper or a creamy dip	
Raw oysters, fresh shrimp, crab claws (very expensive)	

A COCKTAIL BUFFET

A cocktail-buffet signifies a cocktail party that usually lasts from two to three hours (five-thirty to eight-thirty, for example). More food is served here than at a cocktail party. There is a buffet table and at least one hot dish is served. Most guests eat their dinner at this kind of an informal buffet.

There should be a few small tables with chairs, each table covered with a cloth and perhaps decorated with a small bouquet of flowers in the center, near the food service area for guests who do not like to eat standing up.

As each group of guests finishes using one of these tables, a waiter should clear it off again for use by the next set of guests, who may want to sit down to eat and chat with friends for a short period.

Cocktail Party Manners

As a guest, you should not:
- Smoke, even if you find a hiding place.
- Arrive even one minute before the start of the party, or arrive fifteen minutes before it is supposed to end and then expect to stick around for an hour or so talking to the exhausted hosts and whoever is left.
- Shake hands with a cold wet right hand. (Hold your drink in your left hand.)
- Shake hands with a mayonnaised hand after holding hors d'oeuvres in it. (Either hold hors d'oeuvres in your left hand, or carefully use a cocktail napkin after every drippy bite.)
- Talk to someone while looking over and around that person to see if someone more important has arrived (a common rudeness at cocktail parties).
- Monopolize celebrity guests, so that others cannot even get near them.
- Tie up the host in extended serious conversation, as the host has a lot more to do than talk to you all night!
- Monopolize either celebrity guests or the table of food, so that others are kept away.
- Break something and not tell the host.

As a guest, you should:
- RSVP if that is called for on the invitation.
- Bring a guest only if you call first and get your host's permission.
- Drink only as much as you can hold well.
- Drink your beverages from a glass, not from a bottle. (Women look particularly unattractive walking around guzzling beer from a bottle that they hold by the neck with two fingers.)
- Introduce yourself to newcomers, and carefully introduce newcomers to your friends.
- Write a short thank-you note to your host afterward.

AN INVITATION TO TEA

The tea hour (anytime from 3:30 to 5:30 P.M.) is becoming more and more popular as a business meeting time—presenting the opportunity to get away from the office for a much-needed break in the afternoon. You meet a person or a small group in a hotel that specializes in the tea service, and you return to your office, if you care to, greatly refreshed and ready for some more work.

Traditionally, tea was served by the female head of the house for her female friends. It was the highlight of the afternoon visiting hours, when the lady of the house was "at home" to her friends on a specific date. The table was invariably spread with a beautiful white lace or damask cloth, tall sterling candelabra, and a bowl of fresh flowers in the center.

Also on the tea table were:
- A large silver tray on which sat a sterling tea service comprising:
  Teapot, perhaps on an alcohol lamp
  Hot water pot, perhaps on an alcohol lamp
  Sugar bowl with tongs or teaspoon
  Container for artificial sweetener
  Strainer and bowl for used tea leaves
  Small plate of thin slices of lemon, with a small fork
- Porcelain teacups and saucers, each with a sterling silver teaspoon.
- Porcelain plates for food.
- Dessert forks (for pastry).
- Sterling teaspoons for sherbet or strawberries.
- Cups of sherbet or bowls of fresh strawberries.
- Sterling silver container of cream.
- Plates of delicious little sandwiches, cookies, hot buttered scones, fruit tartlets, or brownies.
- Dainty white tea napkins (usually embroidered or trimmed in lace).

Today more people are enjoying tea but, except for certain debutante teas still held in the South, the formal tea table has disappeared. When we ask people to come by "for a cup of tea," we give them just that—hot tea in a mug or iced tea in a glass, and perhaps one little sandwich and one dessert item. It is no longer considered a sacrilege to serve tea bags instead of brewed tea.

Having someone over for tea is a wonderful way to give pleasure to friends. It is a warm, friendly custom, and businesspeople find that absenting themselves from the office to take tea in a nearby hotel is not only a happy break, but also an excellent opportunity to carry on an important confidential meeting, face to face.

MAKING AN EFFORT: SET AN ATTRACTIVE TABLE

There are several reasons why we set our tables much more informally today than in past generations. Very few people have domestic help; it's a generally more informal world in which easy-care synthetics have been accepted; and everyone seems too busy to give much attention to the formal rituals of life. Easy-care table coverings and paper napkins are here to stay for family meals.

I firmly believe, however, that when you have guests, it's time to make an effort. They deserve better in your home, after all, than paper napkins, paper plates, and plastic glasses. (The latter belong out-of-doors.)

When you go to an obvious effort to make things attractive and pleasant for those you have invited to your home, the event almost always succeeds. People feel festive and pampered—and you become *appreciated.* Wine served in a pretty glass, for example, has a totally different taste from wine served in a paper cup. A piece of meat loaf tastes very different when it's served on a pretty piece of china than when presented on a plastic plate.

Set a standard in your entertaining, even if it's an old pal of your mother-in-law coming for dinner:

• Serve your food to any guest on a handsome plate with a sense of pride, whether it's spaghetti or roast pheasant with truffles.

• If you don't have any nice stemware and flatware to use when you entertain, borrow them from a friend, or, more probably, from the mother of a friend.

THE ROLE OF LINENS IN TABLE SETTINGS

The table linens you use—whether tablecloths or place mats and napkins—play a starring role in any table setting. They give a certain zip to the entire surroundings.

• Mix patterns and colors without fear, but it helps to know what you're doing! It's great fun to mix things, but there has to be a logic or a color bond in there somewhere. A plaid mixed with a polka dot fabric makes sense if there is a common color scheme. So does a silky fabric used for a tablecloth, combined with rough-textured napkins.

• Easy-care fabric napkins are not expensive. Make your own if you have a special color or pattern in mind to give your table decor a particularly eye-appealing look. And don't be afraid to give yourself a pat on the back when you do make a special effort for your guests. ("How do you like these napkins? I made them myself last week!") It's not difficult to pamper your guests and simultaneously show off your hosting imagination, ingenuity, and organizational abilities. What an asset!

Handsome Tables

• One of the best-looking tables I ever saw was one that combined over-sized navy place mats, thinly striped with white, with crisp white napkins patterned in large navy polka dots. (They were made by our hosts from dish towels!) The hosts also used white china on their table, navy crystal water glasses and wineglasses, and a centerpiece of navy and white porcelain flowers.

• A romantic table setting I once photographed was a "white on white" scheme used by a famous French hostess. Her dining room carpet was white; the Louis XV dining room chairs were upholstered in white satin. She covered her round table to the floor with a cloth made from a heavy white embroidered fabric, and used another shade of white oversized dinner napkins. Her china was of yet another tone of white. White tapers in white porcelain candlesticks flanked the centerpiece. But then came the color! In the center, in a large white *blanc de Chine* porcelain bowl was a mass of bright-red and purple anemones. Unforgettable!

• Another artfully conceived table setting was made for a Maryland wedding reception. The round tables were covered in pale green moiré, with overskirts of sheer pink organdy. Pale pink roses and dark green leaves in baskets formed the centerpieces. The little ballroom chairs at the tables had cushions of pale green moiré, tied at the corners with pink tassels. There were pale green napkins, each one festively tied with a pink sash ribbon. There were little baskets of pink and green mints as table favors at each place. The china was pale pink, green, and white. The bride's mother told me that the table linens provided the theme for the entire table. Working on a budget, she made the tablecloths and napkins herself, and put the bridesmaids to work in making the seat cushion covers. I asked her how she could possibly get all this designed and executed so beautifully when she was already so busy in other projects. She explained, "I just flick the creativity switch in my brain and it takes off. Then I get to the moment of truth—making the creativity conform to a strict budget. That's when the work ethic must really take over!"

Creativity does not depend on spending a great deal of money. I remember what the CEO of a major corporation once told me about the few really successful managers on his team. "There are those who go by the book and are excellent robots," he explained, "and then there are those who take the time to think how something can be done better, faster, and cheaper—whether it's a question pertaining to paper clips or important documents. They find creative solutions to their everyday job problems to help all of us work better. They are the ones who really contribute to our profits, and they are the pool from whom my successor will be chosen."

Creativity plays a very big role—in corporate planning or in entertaining. It's that same old philosophy again—caring, thinking of others, making an effort for someone or something else.

DECORATING THE TABLES

Setting a party table or a group of tables is the moment to let your imagination soar to new heights. Just plunking down a florist's arrangement of flowers in the center of the table, flanked by four candlesticks, is what our mothers and grandmothers used to do—on an all-white tablecloth at that. But the scope of our imaginations and the age in which we live have carried us far beyond that pedestrian kind of decor, and we expect the centerpieces we face during a meal at our host's home to amuse, delight, or challenge our aesthetic eye.

The way you learn to use your imagination in such matters as table decor is first to inspire it, which is accomplished by an exercise such as one of these:

• Carefully peruse the photographs of table settings in the decorating and home publications. (Even the china, silver, and glassware in manufacturers' ads can give you inspiration.)

• Attend table setting demonstrations given in your local department or fine jewelry store.

• Listen to descriptions of beautifully decorated tables at parties given around town.

• Check through the photographs in books on entertaining.

• Make notes of particularly striking table decorations at private parties and benefits you have attended or heard described by your local newspaper's "Lifestyle" reporter.

• Experiment yourself with flowers and fruits of the season, mixing them in different containers and judging them with your table linens for maximum visual effect.

Ways to Experiment

The more you experiment, the easier it becomes to be creative with table settings. You never have to use the same table setting twice, because linens mix and match with different pieces of china, different growing things go on the table according to the season, and you can look at your possessions from a different perspective each time. For example, one day you might want to use your favorite crystal bowl to serve ice cream for dessert; for the next party you might want to fill it with silver Christmas tree ornaments for the centerpiece; and for a Sunday lunch, you might want to use it as a centerpiece filled with colorful lettuces and chopped vegetables to be consumed by the guests during the latter part of the meal. Perhaps you are given a large amount of fresh asparagus as a present. You either serve it for a dinner party, or you tie it in bundles with pretty ribbons and stack it as a centerpiece for your table for that party.

- When you remember something beautiful that pleases you, replicate it on your table. I remember my mother saying that her favorite flower combination was lilies-of-the-valley with small pale pink roses. It gives me such pleasure to repeat her favorite combination on my own table—and its fragrances evoke very special memories.

I will also never forget a friend on Nantucket who remembered my having said that the most romantically beautiful thing about Nantucket for me was the sight of the incredible blues of the hydrangea bushes blooming against the weathered gray shingled houses. When I next came to spend a summer weekend with her, she gave a dinner party with a rough-textured shingle-gray cloth on the table. The centerpiece was a large gray stone container holding a mass of different shades of blue hydrangeas. That's called using the imagination, but it's also called "going outside the box," in that she paid homage to my treasured memories of Nantucket colors and textures.

- Use whatever it is you collect on your table—like putting your collection of toy soldiers in battle positions (or your collection of porcelain figurines) in and around a cluster of small plants and votive candles in the center of the table. I have a friend who has a collection of antique porcelain carnations. She often uses them in the center of her table, combined with different combinations of fragrant leaves or smaller fresh flowers.

- Make an enchanted burning white forest with white candles in a variety of candleholders down the center of your table. Keep your dining area dark to make the light from the candles really dramatic. The candleholders (single ones will do, as well as pairs) may be of crystal, silver, pewter, tole, porcelain, wood—anything. (Borrow your friends' candlesticks, if you don't have a collection of your own.) It's even more effective if they are of varying heights. Some hosts prefer to make "enchanted burning forests of flowers" in the center of their tables, interweaving crystal candlestick holders with tall, slender crystal champagne flutes, each holding one beautiful flower.

- Take items in the same color family and mix them with contrasting shades of green leaves, such as green pears and matching green grapes with contrasting dark green leaves tucked into the centerpiece bowl arrangement, or eggplant and black grapes with dark red geraniums held in little glass orchid vials that you get from a florist, tucked in securely.

- Go against traditional color taboos and put clashing flower colors together in the center of your table—such as a bowlful of red carnations, orange lilies, and purple violets, perhaps on a smashing background of a black linen tablecloth.

- Surprise your guests with unusual combinations in a porcelain or silver cup, mug, or glass at each place. For example:
    - Place a mass of snow-white carnations around a center cluster of fresh green parsley in a silver cup (something the late American Ambassadress Evangeline Bruce liked to do).

- Mix sprigs of pussy willow branches with delicate little cymbidia orchids, which the late Clare Boothe Luce used to do.
- Put a small, beautiful crystal perfume bottle containing a few little sprigs of fragrant lily-of-the-valley on the table close to your guest of honor's place.
- Build a pyramid of lemons for a centerpiece and tuck an occasional white gardenia into the sides.

One of my favorite hostesses will do anything to please her guests—such as when she was giving a dinner party in March in Camden, South Carolina. The morning of her party, she was still visiting a friend outside Hartford, Connecticut. The air was cool on this early spring day, so she picked several beautiful brilliant yellow forsythia branches from her host's bushes, wrapped them in wet paper, and flew home with them. She entertained again in May (it was now hot and muggy in South Carolina), she picked fresh white peonies from her own bushes. Then she combined the peonies with the forsythias in tall, graceful arrangements around her house for the dinner party. The fragrance was magical. We were aware of the season the moment we walked into her house.

- Make table favors out of your centerpiece. You might make an eye-catching arrangement of small flowering plants in the center of the table, for example, and then ask each guest at the end of dinner to select his own plant to take home (in a paper tote bag supplied by you).

Table favors, in fact, always make a tremendous impact on guests. Men and women become equally enthusiastic to find an amusingly wrapped "goodie" at their place at table (just as they become equally bored by the same old loot bags of commercial product samples handed out at benefit balls).

During the Christmas holidays your table favor might be:
- Chocolate snowflakes.
- Miniature gingerbread houses.
- Mini-fruitcakes.
- Christmas tree ornaments wrapped in colorful tissue.
- A miniature frame containing a snapped head shot of a member of that guest's family.

At Easter, it might be:
- A candy Easter egg inside an egg-shaped box encircled with ribbon.
- Six freshly baked cookies shaped like bunnies or lambs and charmingly gift-wrapped.

On Valentine's Day, it might be a:
- Chocolate heart.

- Giant chocolate Hershey's Kiss.
- Small book of love poetry.

Even when it's not a special holiday, you as host can always celebrate something with a table favor. One host announced to us that "this dinner is in celebration of "Don't-Be-Late Day,'" which none of us particularly understood—until we opened the festive little boxes at our places and found travel alarm clocks inside.

PLACE CARDS

Place cards make sense when you have eight or more people coming to lunch or dinner. When dinner is ready and guests go to the table, the host or hostess may be occupied picking up the cocktail glasses and ashtrays in the living room and tidying up, or they may be putting finishing touches on the first course about to be served to the guests. The hostess may not be near the table at the moment some of the guests take their place. That is why the place cards are efficient. People can see where they are supposed to sit at the table. Here are some guidelines concerning place cards:

- The fanciest kind of place cards are made of thick white stock, thinly bordered in silver, gold, or a color, and measure approximately 2 by 3¼ inches. (They may be any variation of that size.) These are sold in packages (usually of fifty or one hundred) at stationers or in the stationery section of large department stores.
- Place cards may be single cards meant to lie flat on the table, or they may be folded "tent" cards, which stand up on the table.
- For informal dinners in your home, you can make your own cards out of letter-writing paper. (Many is the time I have made last-minute place cards cut out of manila file folders!)
- If you're really trying to "put on the dog," you can order from the stationer place cards engraved with your monogram in gold or in a color. A rarefied few have their cards engraved with a legitimate family crest at the top; some social climbers go to the extreme of fabricating a family crest that too many guests know is fake, so it really doesn't serve its purpose!
- The place card is set on the table in any one of several places: on top of a napkin set in the middle of the plate; on the table above the forks at the upper left of the place setting; leaning against the stem of a water or wineglass; or just above the middle of the plate on the tablecloth.
- The cards are handwritten in black ink (hopefully by someone with a good hand), or they may be typed (jumbo type, please) for a business meal. The most posh way is to have them written by a calligrapher or computer-generated in calligraphy.

What You Write on a Place Card

• For an informal party of friends who know each other, all you need on the place cards are first names ("Pat," "Joanie," and so on). However, if you have two Bobs or two Nancys, put both first and last names of the people with duplicate given names.

• For an informal party when the guests don't know each other, use both names on the place card, so each guest can glance at her dinner partner's card and be reminded exactly of who this person is ("Jim Grierson," "Annie Keogh," or whoever). The person's title (Mr., Mrs., etc.), is omitted.

• For a formal dinner party, such as a business dinner or a corporate function for a foreign guest—or any meal at which there will be people of rank—you use only the surnames on the cards ("Mr. Carruthers," "Ms. Smyth," "Colonel Anderson," "Dr. Anson"). If you have two "Mrs. Joneses" or two "Mr. Martins," you must use their full names on their cards—for example, "Mrs. Keith Jones," "Mrs. Ronald Jones"; "Mr. Henry Martin," "Mr. George Martin." It is proper to use only a title and the person's surname, but since guests often need to know both names, more and more often the proper way gives way to the more efficient way, and each person's first and last name is given on the place card.

• A person who has held political office, or a military officer of rank, or someone who holds a high appointed office is called by that rank or title on his place card, regardless of whether he still holds that office or rank. For example, your mayor at present would be "The Mayor" on his place card, which can last forever, as a courtesy token. When he is no longer mayor, as a courtesy he is called "Mayor Johnson" on his place card. The present governor of your state is called simply "The Governor" on his card. When he is no longer governor, he is still called "Governor Stuyvesant" on his card.

Once an ambassador, one holds that rank always. "Ambassador Reynolds" is "Ambassador Reynolds" all through her life, just as a retired military officer is still called by his rank forever—again, as a courtesy.

Menu Cards

Menu cards are a nifty extra touch—a detail that immediately transforms what may be a very simple meal into a special event. Menu cards may be handwritten in black ink, typed (very suitable for a business meal), or, nicest of all, written in calligraphy or by anyone with a beautiful hand. The menu card may lean against a glass or rest flat on the table to the left of the forks. You can provide one for each plate or one for every two guests.

It's fun for guests to know in advance what they're eating. It also helps them judge how much they will eat. A vegetarian, for example, will know he can serve himself two helpings of the salad or vegetable courses, to compensate for the meat course he will not eat. Someone on a diet will decide to skip the Yorkshire pudding when it is passed and go heavy on the fresh fruit compote.

It is proper to use a mixture of English, French, Italian, German, and other foreign terms for specialties on your menus. If you are familiar with the proper foreign term for a particular dish you are having served, use it without fear of being called pretentious. For example, *Pasta Primavera* sounds a lot more exciting written on the menu than "Noodles with Vegetables." I learned many of my French words as a child during the Depression years of the 1930s, when my parents would bring home the dinner party menus (which was common practice in those days). I understood *Glace vanille* (what child wouldn't be able to translate "vanilla ice cream"?), but the *Sauce Fraises* written on the menu beneath the *Glace* would throw me. "*Glace* means ice cream, and *Fraises* means strawberries," Mother would explain, and I would brag to my friends, "I know how to say 'strawberry sundae' in French!"

The two menus illustrated here are examples of a very formal dinner with two wines and a champagne, and a very informal meal with one simple wine. Both show a mixture of foreign and English dish titles, and both show the reason for the party (written at the top). Guests often like to take their menu cards home with them as a souvenir of a very special occasion. At a White House state dinner, for example, you will often see an entire table of ten people signing the backs of each other's menus, so that when they take theirs home, they will have a record not only of what was served at the White House but of who sat at their table.

A White House menu card:

Déjeuner du Vendredi Juin 2010

Menu

Tartare de Saumon

Mignons de Veau aux Truffes

Salade

Assorted cheeses

Ile Flottante

Auxey Duresses 1983

Château Batailley 1983

Mumm Cordon Rouge

Farewell Lunch Party for Anne and Hans

Saturday, April 10th

Menu

Asparagus with lemon sauce

Mignons de veau with rice

French green beans

Floating Island

Ginger snaps

Demitasses

A NOTE ABOUT TODAY'S MENUS

It seems as though every rich woman with a rich husband is constantly dieting herself to death. A member of the jet set featured in *Women's Wear* and *Vogue* is not supposed to weigh over 125 pounds, even after Christmas dinner. Every person is worried about health in general, heart and cholesterol in particular, and acid reflux across the board. It is the duty of a host to supply plenty of good food for those who want it and may need it at that very dinner. It is a party, after all. The hostess may wear a size 2 dress, but her guests do not have to follow suit. They should not be given a sermon about heart health before sitting down to a meager dinner with fresh pansies bordering the plate. The guests should be fed excellent food, and they can pick at it, not eat certain parts of it, eat all of it, eat nothing, or ask for seconds. The great food should be there. Otherwise, it's not a "dinner party," it's sadism on the hostess's part.

• It's okay to be creative for informal affairs. I really admire a friend who lives in the country, is a great cook, and gives informal Sunday night suppers for six or eight right in her kitchen. We sit down around an old refectory table, on old French chairs with rough straw seats (our legs are protected by red-and-white-checked cushions that match the tablecloth), and eat wonderful things like stew, bouillabaisse, couscous, or Indian curried chicken. She has a blackboard on an artist's standing easel, which she pulls up to the table. The menu of food and wine is written on the blackboard in white chalk. As she knows full well, people sit by their telephones, waiting for an invitation from her.

A Birthday Menu Card

In Honor of Ellen's 26th Birthday

Dinner

June 14, 2008

Hearts of Palm Salad

———

Chicken Pot Pie with Truffles

———

Butter Pecan Sundaes

Birthday Cake

Demitasses

Brolio Chianti Classico 2004

Moët et Chandon

KNOWING THE RULES
FOR CONTEMPORARY TABLE SETTINGS

WHAT'S ON THE TABLE AT THE START OF THE MEAL?

The rules of table settings hinge upon what is logical and efficient. If you are going to hold your fork in your left hand and your knife in your right for cutting food, then it's logical that the fork be placed on the left side of the plate and the knife on the right side. Since most of us are right-handed and reach for our glasses with our right hands, then it's logical to place all glasses in the upper right portion of the place setting.

As you approach it, a table set for guests should contain:
   • Centerpiece decoration, including candles *if* your party is an evening one (however, candles are not appropriate for lunch)
   • Either a bare place or a plate ready to receive food or your first course already served on a plate
   • Butter plate and butter knife (optional)
   • Napkin

The table is set for soup, a main course of meat, and dessert— for a family meal. A little extra effort in making the table look pretty makes the food taste better. The glassware is simple— just a water glass.

- Flatware
- Glasses
- Salts and peppers in place

Although in their ads and sales promotion pieces china companies inevitably show an empty teacup and saucer on the right-hand side of the place setting, that is incorrect. They place it there just to show the item to the customer,

Some hostesses like to place the napkin in an empty water or wineglass, making a pretty fan shape or even a flower motif.

The napkin may also be folded and placed in the center of the plate. Or it may be folded imaginatively, as shown here, and tied with a bit of ribbon. Some hostesses use decorative napkin rings.

which confuses many people into thinking it is supposed to be there from the very beginning. It is not on the table until the end of the meal.

Where the Napkin Goes in the Place Setting

Napkins may be folded in many ways and placed in a variety of positions on the table. If you are a fan of fancy napkin folding, there are many excellent books and magazine articles on the subject, telling you exactly how to do it. (Look it up on the Net.)

Napkin rings are coming back into popularity again as decorative table accents, not because they hold your napkin for a week at a time, which is why they were invented, but because they come in such pretty materials. When they were invented, so to speak, each person in the family had a personal napkin ring, often monogrammed silver, and by rolling up the napkin after each meal, it lasted a week and saved greatly on the house laundry. Today, with bright colored napkins, including paper ones, the napkin rings are part of a unified decoration, but the custom of reusing them to save on laundry is a remnant of the past.

Butter Plates

These small plates seem to be disappearing from our tables, except in grand houses and in first-class restaurants. Set the butter plates on the upper left of

Some hostesses prefer to set the table with the napkin in its traditional place to the left of the forks. It looks best with its outside folds facing left.

the table setting, above the forks. Place the butter knife horizontally on the top of the plate. The butter plate should be preset with two small pats of butter or margarine and a roll or breadstick. The guest may also want to add her choices from the relish dish that is passed around the table, containing raw carrot and celery slices, pickles, radishes, and olives. The olive pits end up on this plate, too!

If you don't own butter plates, you can always pass around the table a pretty porcelain dish with pats of butter, or a pretty round container holding a tub of margarine.

Salts and Peppers

If you have enough small salt and pepper sets, place a pair of them above the plate at each table setting. If you don't have enough, place a pair between each pair of plates. If you don't have even that many, place a pair at each end of the table. Most people don't even use them these days, and it's a great compliment to the cook if no one needs them. It means that the food is properly seasoned. If you are a guest and see that your host has some antique "salt cellars" on the table (often of silver, vermeil, or crystal, with tiny silver salt spoons to match) it's polite to mention them to your host. Bringing the family heirlooms (or the results of their antique hunting) to the other guests' attention, is a very nice thing to do.

Candlesticks Are Only for Evening Parties

Glowing candles are magical at nighttime, but for a lunch, they serve no purpose except to make guests feel the host doesn't know what he's doing.

For evening parties, you can mix and match candlesticks with total abandonment. Crystal with porcelain, pewter with wood. Votive candles of every color. Little candlesticks, towering ones, no matter. The beauty of the glorious light of candles is undeniable.

Candy at the Table

It's nice to have a candy dish at each end of the table. A small bowl of silver, crystal, or porcelain makes a nice container. So does a tall-stemmed wineglass. A footed compote is perhaps the nicest of all, but far more important than the quality of the serving container is the quality of the candy. Chocolates, mints, caramels, even sour balls will do the trick. Guests are supposed to eat this at the end of the meal, but few people wait!

Candy looks pretty in a footed compote—or even in a small bowl. Put a pair of them on your table. I always make a bet with my husband as to how many chocolates will be left by the time dessert is served—because our guests invariably eat them during the soup and meat courses, too!

SALAD PLATES
AND THE SERVICE OF SALAD

The ubiquitous plate that ranges in size from about seven and a half to eight and a half inches in diameter has many uses. It can serve as a:

- Salad plate
- Dessert plate
- Underplate for a footed compote or for a soup cup and saucer
- Server for small cookies, brownies, chocolate truffles, and the like

When you serve a separate salad course between the main course and dessert, it should be more than just a lettuce leaf! Shown here is a guest plate with an endive and Boston lettuce salad, cheese, and crackers.

People eating informally today usually serve their salad right onto their dinner plate and thus have no need of a separate salad plate.

If you have guests, however, it's nice to give them separate plates for salad that is served with the main course. (Give them a separate salad fork, too, in this case, although it's not the end of the world if the guests have to eat their salad with their dinner forks.)

If you are serving a separate salad and cheese course (on individual salad plates) in between the entrée and dessert courses, supply your guests:

- First with a salad plate in the center of the place setting.
- Then pass the salad bowl.
- Then pass a cheese tray with a cheese knife.
- Follow with an assortment of crackers (preferably warmed).

(Guests will require a salad fork and a small knife among the implements in their place setting for a course like this.)

A Favorite Complaint

I have long been an ardent opponent of what is common at restaurants and at hotel banquets: A plain, boring green salad is served as a separate course, giving it an importance equal to the entrée. That's a waste of time and slows up the service for nothing. It's far better to make the salad part of the entrée service and thus permit the guests in the ballroom or restaurant to go home almost an hour earlier!

USING THE RIGHT FLATWARE

When You're a Bewildered Guest

It is not uncommon for a person to sit down at a formal dinner table and confront an inexplicable array of eating utensils, all terrifyingly lined up in battle formation. Panic may ensue, with the guest wondering which to use for what.

It's easy for something to go wrong. The waiter may not have set the table properly. Or one can make a classic error, such as I did at a black tie dinner party when I used a spoon to eat the stuffed avocado first course instead of using the tiny fork on the far left that was specified for that course—with the result that when the creamy dessert was served, I had only a tiny shrimp fork left with which to eat it. To make matters far worse, everyone at my table had followed my lead, thinking I, given my profession, of course, knew what I was doing. I had to ask the waiter to bring spoons for the entire table. It was a humiliating moment.

The table is set so that *you eat from the outside in*—in other words, you take the outside utensil or utensils for the first course, and then proceed, course by course, selecting the next utensils toward the plate until finally you have used them all up.

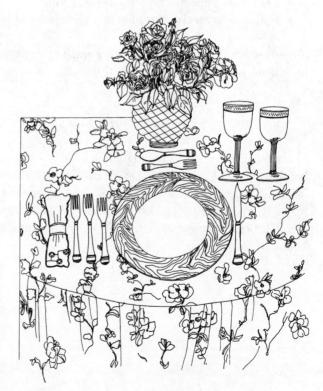

Even one guest for dinner (in this case, a fish dinner) merits an extra effort to make the table look pretty. A white wineglass joins the water glass on the table.

Dessert Implements

Dessert utensils may either be left at the top of the place setting, as shown in the illustration below, or the dessert spoon may be placed on the inside right of the place setting. Or at a formally served dinner the waiter will bring you an empty plate with the proper utensils on it when dessert is about to be served.

If you set your table with the dessert implements lying horizontally at the top of your plate, put the spoon on top (its bowl pointing left) and the fork beneath (its tines pointing right). By the way, it's not absolutely necessary to use two implements for the dessert course. It just makes eating a little easier for the guests if they have something to help push the dessert onto their fork or spoon. If you can't supply both a fork and spoon for dessert but only one of them, don't worry. If you're eating pie or cake, you would use a dessert fork and spoon. As long as the implements with which you set the table convey the food to the guests' mouths, you have done very well as a host!

Most of us don't possess a great variety of flatware. You can always improvise. For example:

- A salad fork may be used for fish, salad, or dessert.
- A luncheon fork, smaller than a dinner fork, may be used for the same varied purposes as a salad fork.
- A fruit knife may also be used as a cheese or dessert knife.
- A steak knife may also be used as a dessert knife.
- A teaspoon may be used for dessert if you don't have large dessert spoons.

When special guests—your boss, for example—come for dinner, the table setting becomes more complex, because the menu is, too. There is crabmeat cocktail as a first course, roast beef and Yorkshire pudding for the second, salad and cheese for the next course, and strawberry shortcake for dessert. Both white and red wineglasses join the water glass for this kind of meal.

THE TABLE ACCOUTREMENTS YOU SHOULD HAVE
FOR ENTERTAINING TODAY

Some people who can't afford top-of-the-line accessories for the table use that as an excuse for not entertaining.

It is *not* a legitimate excuse to avoid entertaining. You can buy nice things slowly, and use what you have in the meantime. You don't have to set a table with lavish objects. Instead, set your table imaginatively, without apology, and make an excellent meal for your guests. The spirit of hospitality you display is far more important than the cost of the table accoutrements you display.

You don't have to buy an entire set of anything. You can mix and match. As a single woman into my mid-thirties, I did not have any of the "loot" brides receive, but I entertained all the time anyway. I bought things slowly on the installment plan, and borrowed things I really needed from married friends who had an excess of wedding gifts. It's fun to grow with your possessions as you grow in your entertaining skills.

• Learn to use your possessions for more than just one purpose. Your individual wooden salad bowls can make fine dessert bowls. Your porcelain teapot can serve as a nice flower container for the table centerpiece. Your extra wineglasses can be used to serve cold soup or dessert—or to hold the mixed nuts you offer guests during the cocktail hour before the meal.

If you don't have demitasse cups, use teacups to serve after-dinner coffee; if you don't have teacups, serve after-dinner coffee in the mugs that you undoubtedly have in your cupboard.

In entertaining, where there's a will, there's a way. Don't be ashamed of what you have. Go ahead, use it all, without apologizing. Have people over for a meal or a party! It's the idea and the effort to please that matter.

BUYING YOUR CHINA

A place setting of china consists of:
  • Dinner plate
  • Dessert or salad plate
  • Butter plate
  • Cup and saucer

You don't need to buy complete place settings. What if you would like dinner plates in one pattern and dessert plates in another? Buy only the items you need. (Merchants will kill me for saying this!) If you are going to have dinners for six, purchase six dinner plates and six dessert plates and six demitasse cups and saucers from open stock. (You can always drink everyday coffee or tea from everyday mugs.) The dessert plates and demitasses do not have to match the dinner plates. If, when you start out entertaining, you find yourself with an assortment of dinner plates of different patterns, it doesn't matter—show off the variety of design and color as a plus. One young friend of mine has twenty-four dinner and twenty-four dessert plates—all different—which she has picked up during her forays in thrift shops. Instead of looking poor, the plates are beautiful—and an enhancement to her frequently held buffet dinners for twenty-four people.

BUYING TABLE LINENS

Buy what appeals to your eye. You should like what you buy—don't buy colors or patterns because they are the current fad and considered chic. (One year, it seemed everyone had to buy mirrored place mats; the next year it was flowered chintz tablecloths; the year after that it was bold geometrics.)

Coordinate the colors and patterns of your china and linen, so there's an intelligent approach to your table decor. You may use multicolored napkins or napkins of different patterns, as long as they color coordinate with your tablecloth or place mats. If you have a tabletop that is scarred or not in good condition, use a tablecloth to cover it instead of place mats. If you can't find or afford nice linens, buy inexpensive fabric and run them up yourself, or pay a friend who uses a sewing machine to hem them for you.

Now the full galaxy of the hostess's table accoutrements is in use for an elaborate dinner of soup, fish, veal, and a chocolate ice-cream praline bombe for dessert. The white wineglass is properly lined up on the far right, then the red, then the water glass, and last, but certainly not least, the champagne goblet in the rear.

BUYING FLATWARE

You do not have to be a bride to buy flatware. Many men and women marry late in life, as I did, and you most assuredly don't have to wait until you're married to have nice things on your table.

It's *very satisfying* to own sterling silver flatware, but in today's era of informality, you can certainly make do with silverplate or stainless steel. If you don't have sterling silver candelabra, you can make do with porcelain, glass, brass, or wooden candlesticks.

If you approach a store like Tiffany's to buy sterling silver, the salesperson will ask if you want to buy place settings of luncheon- or dinner-sized flatware. (The only real difference between the two is that the dinner knives and forks are about an inch longer than the luncheon-sized and are more expensive.) A *place setting* consists of: fork, knife, teaspoon, dessert spoon, salad fork, and butter spreader.

If you're on a strict budget, as I was as a young single working woman, buy what you will need on the installment plan (or time account). Don't buy by the place setting, because that is not the thrifty thing to do. What are you going to do with all those butter spreaders? And you can buy your dessert spoons later— for example, when you get your next promotion.

As with china, buy pieces of flatware according to the number of dinner guests you usually have. If, for example, the maximum number of people you can entertain in your small apartment is six, you will need:

- Six soup spoons
- Six dinner forks
- Six dinner knives
- Six teaspoons
- Six salad forks

Purchase items like serving pieces, dessert spoons, and luncheon forks and knives when you have the money and as you need them. You can always ask family members to give them to you as Christmas and birthday presents. You can pick up little demitasse spoons reasonably in thrift shops or old silver shops. As with your china, the coffee spoons do not have to match one another.

BUYING GLASSWARE

When you first start to entertain, you need only six all-purpose wineglasses, six old-fashioned, and six water glasses for the table. (Make that eight, to allow for the broken ones.) As your income expands and you entertain more lavishly, you can start to buy the champagne flutes, white wineglasses, liqueur glasses, and brandy snifters. Matching stemware is wonderful, but your glasses do not have to match. Water glasses of one pattern and wineglasses of another pattern look great together on the table. Your guests will care much more about the flow of wine and the quality of the conversation than they will about matching stemware.

THE SERVICE OF THE SEATED MEAL— WITH OR WITHOUT HELP

One of the most important aspects of entertaining gracefully is knowing how to serve the meal—or knowing how to direct whoever is serving it to do so properly. (In today's society, there are all too many untrained waiters and waitresses working at their profession.) If you are using raw recruits for serving your party (your children included), it helps to stage-manage a quick run-through of how things are to be done. If you are paying a lot of money for a catering staff and you fear they are not up to snuff in the art of serving, it helps to give them a quick rehearsal run-through, too. The ritual of proper serving is totally functional—how to get the food on and off the table gracefully and efficiently. Knowledge of the ritual of service helps avoid accidents, collisions, awkwardness, and sloppiness in the service of your meals.

WHO IS SERVED FIRST?

When there is no help, the person serving the meal—or the host couple, as the case may be—first serves the woman on the host's right (or the man on

The waiter, when offering a platter of food, serves from the guest's left. One hand is behind his back, the other hand, with his palm up (protected from the heat of the platter by a napkin) offers the platter close to the guest. The serving implements should be in position to make it easy for the guest to pick them up and use them.

the hostess's right), who is the guest of honor, and then continues on around the table counterclockwise. The guest of honor is the most important person present at the table by virtue of age, senior family relationship, or prominence in the community. Or it may be someone who is being honored for another reason—such as a person visiting from another city, someone celebrating a birthday, or a friend who is moving away.

When an important couple are present, the woman sitting next to the male host is served first, rather than her husband sitting to the right of the hostess. After serving the guest of honor, the waiter then passes the bowl or platter around the table counterclockwise. If the wife of the important couple is served first, then the host beside her would be the last to be served at that table.

How Does the Waiter or Waitress Serve?

One person can handle a table of eight, but with ten or twelve guests to a table, it is more efficient to have two people serving. If two servers for your large table are not in the budget, go with one, but be content with having the service very slow.

The person serving passes the food from the left side of the guest, and removes each finished plate from the right side of the guest. If a serving dish is hot, the waiter places a folded napkin under it to protect the palm of his hand. The wine, of course, is served from the guest's right side, where the wineglasses are in place. (To serve the wine from the guest's left side would require reaching across the guest's face to get to the glass.)

A trained waiter is capable of removing a used plate with the right hand while simultaneously putting down a clean plate with a flourish of his left hand. If you are serving your guests yourself, you may not be that dexterous, in which case it is easier first to remove finished plates, one in each hand, and then bring in the empty plates for the next course, one in each hand, on the way back to the dining table. (In my first apartment while I was earning a pittance, I had one set of plates, which I quickly washed in my kitchenette between courses and reused them!) Even a caterer's so-called trained waiters often must be reminded to take out plates, one in each hand, instead of scraping the remnants of food from several plates onto one plate (in front of everyone) and then carrying out the stack of used plates (and the garbage!) into the kitchen. It may be a lot speedier to scrape several plates at the table before taking a stack into the kitchen, but it is also a lot noisier and slightly disgusting.

Waiter #1 serves in this order, below:

7. Host

1. Woman guest of honor		Woman guest 6.
2. Man guest		Man guest 5.
3. Woman guest		Woman guest 4.
4. Man guest		Man guest 3.
5. Woman guest		Woman guest 2.
6. Man guest		Man guest of honor 1.

7. Host's wife

Waiter #2 serves in this order, above:

When there are more than eight or ten guests, two waiters are needed, as for this dinner for fourteen. Waiter number one begins serving the woman guest of honor; waiter number two begins serving the man guest of honor at the other end of the table. Each waiter ends up serving the host or hostess last.

The proper way to remove a guest's finished plate is to remove it from the person's right with the right hand and to clamp down on the fork and knife (or whatever implements are being used) with the right-hand thumb. In this way, the trip is made to the kitchen safely and gracefully. (No clattering of fallen plates and flying knives!)

Watch out! If the waiter at your party (or a son or daughter who is helping you out) removes the plates from the table in this fashion in order to bring on the next course, there will inevitably be some unexpected sound effects—and some new bills to pay in a china and glassware store.

SERVING A DINNER PARTY
OF SIX WITHOUT HELP

It is much more efficient for a small group of six or eight if either the host or the hostess acts as the server for the group. Then one of them will be in the dining room at all times to keep the conversation going. If both keep getting up and going in and out of the kitchen, the guests are distracted, to put it mildly. If you are single and doing the serving, appoint a friend to act as host when you have to be absent in the process of serving.

A smart host keeps firm control of the service of the meal so that there is a minimum of noise and confusion as it is served. Couples who are skilled at giving dinner parties keep aprons handy in the kitchen—and don them only in the kitchen. As the designated server carries two used plates out into the kitchen, behind a closed door the food is quickly scraped and the plates are rinsed and then stacked into the dishwasher. In this way the kitchen is always tidy and there is enough room to cope with the next tide of dirty dishes.

Should the Guests Help?

If you are like me, you don't particularly want the guests, however well intentioned, meddling in your kitchen. Not only could they ruin your efficient system and create havoc, but they could also spill food and splash water on their party clothes at the same time. The place for guests is in your party area, not in your kitchen. An exception to this rule is, of course, if you have one of those handsome large kitchens where everything, including the dining table is in one vast room. (But even here there is no reason for guests to help.) I could never operate in one of those party kitchens, nor can anyone else like me who needs total concentration and generally makes a terrible mess of the entire kitchen environment while cooking.

TRAINING YOUNG PEOPLE TO WAIT ON TABLE

In our world today, with help so difficult to find and expensive to hire, a little imagination and footwork can ease the burden. If you have teenaged children or if there are teenagers in your neighborhood or apartment house, you are all set.

Train these young people in the art of serving a meal. Teach them what to do and have them practice first at a couple of family meals or make-believe dinner parties. Pay them nicely for the services they perform in serving, dishwashing, and cleaning up after your party. What a teenager receives depends upon the part of the country and what the local market will bear, like baby-sitting rates; some parents pay their children $8 an hour, others more. Have the boys dress in dark pants, white shirts, and black bow ties; the girls can wear black skirts and white blouses and perhaps black ties too. Your guests will be delighted to have the meal served by attractive young people with smiling faces. Moreover, the training you have given them will help them earn money in college. There are many functions on college and university campuses in need of trained waitstaff—particularly parties given by the president, faculty members, and administrators, for whom entertaining is an important part of the job.

Advice to Waitstaff
on Serving a Typical Three-Course Meal

- Fill the water glasses three-quarters full. Check the table to make sure that no guest's place is missing anything, such as a fork or a napkin.
- Wait until the guests are seated. Then, if the first course is not served on a plate and already at each place on the table, pass this course to the guests. It should be passed first to the woman on the host's right, or to the man on the hostess's right; it should then be passed counterclockwise around the table, with the host and hostess served last. Remember to always serve from the left.
- Pass the rolls, crackers, relish tray, or anything that goes with that first course.
- Pour wine into each glass, moving around the table counterclockwise after first filling the female guest of honor's glass. If a guest puts her fingers over the rim of the glass, it is a signal that she does not wish to have wine poured in the glass.
- When you notice that all of the guests have finished eating, or when you receive a signal from the host, it's time to remove the plates containing the first course and bring them to the kitchen area. Standing to the right of the guest, remove his plate with your right hand and transfer it to your left; then go to the next person on the right and remove that plate with your right hand—so that you can bring two plates into the kitchen at once. If there is a fork and knife or spoon on each plate, hold onto the utensils with your thumb so they don't fall off the plate while you are en route to the kitchen.
- Now that the table is empty of used plates, bring in the clean plates for the next course, one in each hand, and lay each in front of the guest, again from the left side. (By the way, clean hands and nails are necessary!)
- Pass the next course, serving from the left. Then pass anything accompanying the entrée (sauces, vegetables), again from the left. Always readjust the serving utensils if they have been put back on the platter the wrong way, so that the next guest to be served can get at the food easily. If one of the guests has

managed to get sauce all over the handle of a serving utensil, wipe the handle with a napkin before putting it back on the platter. (Of course, this is French service. It's much easier, but less elegant, to plate the food in the kitchen, and set the full plate down in front of each guest, so many hosts prefer this.)

- Pour the next wine on the menu, or refill glasses with the first wine.
- Pass the rolls again (if there are any).
- Pass again anything your host previously instructed you to pass twice—provided, of course, there is a sufficient amount left. If there is very little left of any one item, don't pass it again.
- When it's time for dessert, remove the entrée or salad course plates, being careful to hold onto the eating utensils with your thumbs, so they don't fall from the plate. Remove the salts and peppers and any sauceboats or condiments from the table. The table should be devoid of anything having to do with previous courses, including butter plates and knives.
- Crumb the table, using a folded white napkin to push the crumbs from around each place setting onto a plate held just beneath the tabletop, or use

If you don't have a special "crumber," fold a napkin and use the smooth end to push the crumbs from the table onto a small plate, held below the table edge.

the "crumber" (perhaps a Silent Butler) provided by the host (which you use with a decorative little brush).

- The dessert plates are brought in next. Optionally, there might be finger bowls, which you set down before each guest on a doily that has been placed in the middle of the dessert plate. The finger bowl is three-quarters filled with water.
- Now pass the dessert, which may be served in two parts—for example, ice cream with a sauce passed afterward, or a soufflé with cookies passed afterward.
- Refill the wineglasses, or pour the champagne into its special glasses.
- If the guests have not already served themselves from the candy dish (and if there's any candy left!), the waiter or host should pass it now.

Serving Coffee After Dinner

After dinner, coffee should be served in little demitasse cups and saucers, with small accompanying spoons. The host will have instructed you (assuming you're the waiter for the night) before dinner whether coffee is to be served at the table or in another room.

• If coffee is to be served at the table, put down a three-quarter-filled demitasse cup and saucer (the coffee spoon balancing on the right side of the saucer) to the right of each guest's place setting. (Naturally, as with wine or other beverages, this is served from the right instead of from the usual left.) Then pass to each guest the tray containing the cream, sugar, and artificial sweetener.

An alternative to serving coffee at the table is to put in front of the host, seated in the living room, a large tray on the coffee table containing the coffee cups and saucers, a group of coffee spoons, the coffeepot, a sugar bowl, and creamer. The host serves each guest separately, pouring the coffee and passing the guest her cup, saucer, and spoon with whatever the guest asked for in the coffee. (*Note:* The spoon is a bother and is often dropped, so it should not even be given to a coffee drinker who drinks her coffee black.)

Often the only coffee served these days after dinner is decaf, but a truly considerate host makes available to the guest a pot of regular coffee as well as decaf for those of us who drink the real thing even at night.

• When coffee is served in another room, the waiter may pass among the guests with a large tray containing already poured cups of coffee, allowing each

In most houses, after-dinner coffee is served from a tray brought to a room other than the one where dinner was served. This permits guests to get up from the table to mix with each other. This tray holds a pot for regular brewed coffee, a pot for decaf, a bowl of sugar cubes with tongs, a creamer, and a small bowl for packets of a sugar substitute.

At the end of the meal, after the demitasses have been served, bring in (or have your server bring in) your prettiest tray set with bottles and decanters of port and liqueurs, plus small liqueur glasses and brandy snifters.

guest to serve himself from the creamer and sugar bowl. Another option: The host may serve the coffee herself while seated on the sofa, with a tray containing the coffeepots, cups, saucers, spoons, sugar bowl, and creamer in front of her on the coffee table. As guests approach her, she asks how they would like their coffee, and then she hands each a properly prepared demitasse.

After-Dinner Liqueurs, Drinks, and Glasses of Water

During the after-dinner coffee hour, when everyone has been sipping their coffee, the waiter reappears with a tray bearing a bottle of cognac and one or two sweet liqueurs, plus several brandy snifters and small liqueur glasses. Guests either serve themselves, or the waiter serves them. The tray is too heavy to hold and serve from at the same time, so when the waiter "gets a customer," so to speak, he should put down the tray before attempting to fill the guest's order. For more on after-dinner drinks, see page 484.

Then the waiter might reappear with a tray of tall glasses of ice water and pass them around the entire group. He should first approach the host with the tray of glasses of ice water, so the host knows what is going on. At this point the waiter would also ask a guest who has not taken a brandy, liqueur, or glass of water, "May I bring you something else to drink?" That guest may be longing for a highball (Scotch, ice, and water or soda in a tall glass), but if it's not offered, it's politer to suffer in silence.

THE ART OF THE SERVICE OF WINE

The service of wine is an art and a mealtime ritual replete with history and romance—and one that is taken seriously by a caring host.

Your water glass is filled about two-thirds and a red wineglass only about halfway, as shown here.

It is wise—and entertaining as well—to educate yourself about wine by:

• Reading good books on the subject (there are many).

• Attending wine tastings (and really *listening* to the lecturer, as well as enjoying the sipping).

• Conversing as often as possible with a knowledgeable salesperson at the liquor store (obviously when he or she is not busy).

• Having a chat with the restaurant wine steward (sommelier).

• Going through a well-established winery in America or Europe to learn how wine is made.

TIPS ON THE SERVICE OF WINE

• To be correct, fill the red wineglass halfway, and the white wine glass three-fourths full.

• Whether at home or in a restaurant, show the label to your guests if you are particularly proud of the wine. (A nice guest, sensing that a good wine is about to be served, will ask you, "What is the wine?" thus giving you a good excuse for naming and praising it—just a bit.)

• If you are not particularly proud of the wine, first decant it into a good-looking crystal decanter. (Unlike a wine bottle, a decanter will not mark the table, so it does not need to be put on a coaster.)

• Many connoisseurs feel that fortified wine (such as port and sherry to which brandy is added) should properly be decanted. There is an old French saying that a fine red wine *merits* being decanted to allow its real flavor to develop, whereas a humble red wine *needs* to be decanted, to help it along.

• Most red wines should be served at a cool room temperature. If you serve your guests a good red wine that for some reason is too cool, suggest that they hold the bowls of their glasses in their hands to quickly warm the wine the necessary few degrees. It makes the wine seem extra-special when it really isn't.

• Chill your white wine in the refrigerator at least two hours before the meal, or if you have a wine cooler, chill the white wine in it for twenty-five min-

A bottle of white wine is kept cold either in a wine cooler with ice and water, shown here, or in a cold thermos holder.

utes in a bath of ice cubes and ice water. (The finer the white wine, the less chilling it requires.) If you're really in a jam timewise because you forgot to prechill the wine, stick the bottle in your freezer for fifteen minutes. (But whatever you do, don't forget and leave it there!)

• Some people today prefer to drink one wine of their choice all evening. Therefore, a caring host places both a bottle of red and a bottle of white on coasters on his table. A cold thermos holder for a bottle of white wine doesn't look very pretty on the table, but it's a practical assist on a hot summer's night.

• As host, you should stand up to serve your guests around the table the first time, going counterclockwise, starting with the person seated at your right and finishing with yourself. Then you might ask someone at the other end of the table to assume the responsibility for keeping the glasses refilled at that end of the table, using the bottle or carafe at that end. If you offer your guests red

Put a wine bottle coaster at each end of your dinner table—with a bottle of red on one and white on the other. The host should keep an eye on the bottles and replace them during the meal when they are empty. In this kind of informal service, guests help themselves, or a few are "assigned" to the task of keeping the wine flowing.

and white wines at a dinner for eight or more, you should provide two bottles of wine, one white and one red (each on a coaster), at each end of the table.

• Never allow a guest to pour a new wine into a glass he used previously for another kind of wine. It's a principle of good hospitality involved here, not that the taste of a new wine would be altered greatly by having it poured into a used glass.

• Unless you are a true expert, you will probably need a napkin held under the neck of the bottle as you pour wine into guests' glasses. The napkin catches errant drops of wine. The more you twirl the opening of the bottle in an upward motion as you pour, the less wine you will spill, and the less you will need that napkin!

• Occasionally you will see a bottle cradled in (and served from) a basket in almost a horizontal position. This keeps the sediment from mixing into the wine in the bottle.

THE MAJOR CATEGORIES OF WINE
AND THEIR PROPER SERVING TEMPERATURES

Several states in the United States produce very good wines today, but excellent wines come also from France, Italy, Germany, Spain, Portugal, Australia, Chile, and several other countries.

Red Table Wines

The Bordeaux, Burgundy, Beaujolais, Chianti, Barolo, and Rioja wines (from France, Italy, and Spain, respectively) are in this group. So are the varietal wines, such as Cabernet Sauvignon, Pinot Noir, and Zinfandel from America, Australia, and other countries.

These wines should be served at a cool temperature (no higher than 70°F). Traditionally, they are served with meat, fowl, and cheese (although today the rules regarding what kind of wine one drinks with any particular food seem to be broken fearlessly).

Rosé wines are known for their lovely pink color and refreshing taste when served well chilled in hot weather. They are not, however, great wines (see also Sparkling Wines on page 482).

White Table Wines

These include Burgundy, Chablis, Meursault, Chassagne-Montrachet, Muscadet, and Sancerre (all from France); Gavi and Pinot Grigio from Italy;

Chardonnay, Sauvignon Blanc, Chenin Blanc, and Chablis from France, the United States, Chile, Australia, and New Zealand; and the sweet Rieslings from Germany.

Dry white table wines should be served chilled, but not to the extent that the flavor and bouquet are altered. Traditionally, white wines were served with light foods such as fish, fruit, veal, and chicken. Today some people use white wine as their preferred predinner cocktail choice, and some prefer to drink it all through the meal (instead of switching to red during the meat entrée).

Appetizer Wines (Aperitifs)

Aperitifs such as dry or sweet vermouth, red or white Dubonnet, Campari, Cinzano, and Lillet are served as a before-meal drink, usually in a small portion. They are served according to your preference—at room temperature in a small glass, or chilled, or in a small old-fashioned glass with ice.

Dry sherry, an important member of the aperitif family, is usually served at room temperature—and in a sherry glass, if possible. (Use a liqueur glass, if you don't have a sherry glass, and if you don't have a liqueur glass either, use any small wineglass or bar glass.) Appetizer wines taste best when there is an accompanying plate of almonds, cheese straws, or anything in the dry, salty munching category.

Dessert Wines

For several decades sweet dessert wines like Sauternes (which are served chilled in white wineglasses) went into a decline in popularity, but now they have come back into vogue. A glass is put down at your place at the table, and the wine is poured from a decanter after dessert is served. Germany has some fine examples of sweet white wines. Sweet sherry, port, and Madeira are normally consumed after dinner at room temperature.

Sparkling Wines

The fifth category comprises sparkling rosé wines, such as Italy's Asti Spumante, and the really excellent sparkling wines from California. (Several prominent houses in the Champagne region of France have started wineries in California, too.) Italy, other parts of France, and Spain also produce large quantities of good sparkling wines at reasonable prices. The queen of this category is, of course, champagne from the region of Champagne, France.

Champagne Etiquette

Glasses

Coupe-shaped champagne glasses are no longer in vogue, for practical reasons. They are difficult to clean, and the champagne grows warm inside any hollow-stemmed glass—because of the warm fingers clasping the stem. A flute or tulip-shaped champagne glass, usually about seven ounces in capacity, is therefore more desirable. (Pour four ounces into such a glass.)

Opening the Bottle

First, you must remove the wire enclosure ("bonnet") around the cork. Once you begin this operation, don't stop and change your mind about opening the bottle. (Pressure begins to build up inside and could explode the cork right out of an unattended bottle.) Brace the bottom of the bottle into your abdomen and begin twisting the cork with your fingers. Some people prefer optionally to hold on to the cork while rotating the bottle with their fingers. Whatever you do, take care to aim away from the faces of your friends, as well as nearby crystal pieces, porcelain, or anything fragile. (I will always remember the story told about an English art collector who acquired at auction an "Old Masters" painting of his life's dreams. That evening he invited two close friends to celebrate. One of them opened his gift—a bottle of champagne—carelessly, and the cork put a hole right through the painting.)

Rather than anticipating with joy the sound of a big pop as the champagne cork finally exits the mouth of the bottle, it is better to strive for only a gentle hissing sound as it emerges. A noisy pop encourages the escape of air and disperses the much-desired bubbles.

Of course, wines today are sold in screw-capped bottles, which used to be considered a major crime, but screw-caps are now acceptable, except for champagne and sparkling white wines.

• It's important to remember that champagne should be served very cold to be enjoyed to its fullest. Once you have removed the cork, keep the bottle in a wine bucket half full of ice and ice water, or put it back into the fridge until it's time to refill the glasses.

Champagne is the symbol of happiness, celebration, and a special moment in life. That's why it's important to buy a good-quality champagne, to serve it ice cold, and to use beautiful flutes. It's all part of the mystique—the romance and the ritual.

AFTER-DINNER DRINKS

When people are enjoying their demitasses after dinner at the table—or when the host moves the guests from the dining area into another room for their after-dinner coffee—it is time to pass after-dinner drinks. Two kinds of glasses are useful here—brandy snifters for serving Cognac or Armagnac, and small stemmed glasses to use for sweet liqueurs. Port may also be served in a regular wineglass.

The most popular of the after-dinner drinks are these:
- Port.
- Cognac and Armagnac, which come in several price levels, according to the quality and grade. VSOP, for example, is less expensive than a Napoleon Cognac, and vintage-dated Armagnacs are more costly than nonvintage-dated ones.
- Eaux-de-vie—clear brandies made from distilled fruits. Poire (pear) and framboise (raspberry) are the most popular ones.
- Green or white crème de menthe (often served over cracked ice).
- Cointreau.
- Cream-finished liqueurs—for example, Irish cream and crème de cacao.
- Peach-based cordials (and also peach-champagne cocktails).

If you have serving help at your dinner party, the server should pass a tray to each guest (and the host last), containing from two to four bottles of the various after-dinner drinks being offered (brandy should be one of them) and an assortment of empty glasses appropriate for those drinks. The tray may also be placed in a central location in the party area (such as on the coffee table in front of the sofa), where guests will help themselves (at the host's urging) to the drink of their choice.

If you don't have serving help, you might place a bottle of brandy plus an optional sweet liqueur on the table as you are finishing coffee, and serve your guests. You don't have to be hosting a fancy black tie dinner with waiters in attendance to enjoy an after-dinner drink.

For after-dinner drinks: Brandy snifters (for brandy or Cognac), liqueur glasses (for liqueurs or dessert wine), highball glasses (for Scotch and water or soft drinks)

HOW TO OPEN A WINE BOTTLE

One of the easiest-to-use wine bottle openers is the "Screwpull" variety. You plunge a Teflon-coated screw into the center of the cork and then squeeze the two arms together around the neck of the bottle; as you turn the top lever, the screw easily extracts the cork from the bottle. There are all kinds of new inventions of bottle openers appearing on the market. They all eventually break down!

Once you have the cork out, pour a very small amount of wine into the kitchen sink, to remove any bits of floating cork. Also take a clean damp cloth and wipe around the outside and inside of the neck to remove any grime.

A Bad Cork

If you have a bad cork that disintegrates as you try to extract it, you might end up using everything from a screwdriver to a letter opener to try to get it out. If, as my bad corks always do, your lacerated cork gets pushed down into the bottle of wine, don't despair. Hold a small strainer over a water pitcher and then pour the bottle of wine through it. Now you can transfer the wine from the water pitcher to a decanter that will look attractive on the table.

I have learned by experience from my own dinner parties always to have an extra bottle or two on hand, in case disaster strikes while opening the wine.

The easiest way to open a bottle of wine is to use a Screwpull.

I would much prefer to give our guests good wine from the bottle, rather than "strained wine" from an embattled bottle. (We drink the latter ourselves the next night.)

Always open your wines gently, well in advance of the guests' arrival. Then if there is any cork difficulty, it will have occurred in private and will have been coped with successfully before your guests arrive.

TASTING THE WINE AT HOME

As the host, after you have opened the wine in the kitchen in advance of the guests' arrival, you should taste it immediately to make sure that it is in good condition. The wine sampling should not be done in front of your guests at home—only in a restaurant.

TASTING THE WINE IN A GOOD RESTAURANT

In a good restaurant, it is quite a different story. After you have selected your bottle of wine, the wine steward or captain or waiter will present it to you. (Never, by the way, be embarrassed to solicit his help and advice in making your selection.) When the bottle is brought to your table, you, the host, should then taste it on behalf of your guests. (If you know absolutely nothing about wine or do not drink alcohol, ask one of your guests who you know is familiar with wine to taste it for you.) The sommelier, maître d'hotel, or waiter (once he has opened the good bottle of wine you ordered) will present it to you, so that you can tell by the label the wine is exactly what you ordered. (The custom of the diner then squeezing and smelling the cork is passé.) The sommelier (a wine steward who appears only in the poshest, most expensive restaurants) now pours a small amount in the glass of the person who ordered the wine, usually the host, for that person's tasting and hoped-for approval. The taster should swirl it around a bit in his mouth, sniff it to appreciate the bouquet, and pronounce the wine to be "very good" or something equally simple. The wine is then poured into every glass around the table.

Returning a Bad Bottle

Do not grimace and tell the wine server to "take this bottle back" unless you are on firm grounds and know what you are doing. On a rare occasion, the wine will have turned and will taste bitter, in which case the wine server will take a taste of it himself in his own glass. If he agrees that this particular bottle has gone bad, he will bring you another one at once. (In really fine restaurants, the sommelier will be the first to taste from your bottle, to avoid ever serving a wine that has gone bad.)

It's embarrassing if, when acting from lack of knowledge, you request the wine to be replaced and no one except you finds anything wrong with the bottle. I remember as a young woman being very embarrassed when my date returned an expensive bottle, calling it defective. He was showing off, and everyone in the restaurant was watching us. Then the maître d' noted the clean scent of mouthwash on his breath. My date had just returned from the men's room, where he'd rinsed his mouth with Listerine, which meant that the wine would not taste good under any circumstances. After the maître d' gently pointed out this fact, my date apologized and drank from the same bottle fifteen minutes later, now greatly enjoying the taste of the wine and resolving never again to use a mouthwash before tasting wine.

WINEGLASSES

A wineglass should be a clear, sparkling stemmed goblet—the thinner the better and the more enjoyable to hold and to drink from.

The bowl of the glass should be larger than the rim, so that the bouquet of the wine can waft up to your nostrils as you drink.

When you need an array of wineglasses on your table to go with the different wines being served, group them on the table chronologically, starting from the outside right as the first wineglass, and going into the center of each person's place setting for the champagne and water goblets. These glasses do not need to be set up in a straight row. They can be informally grouped, but in a manner so that you know which is the next one to use.

Of course, if you are having only a red or only a white wine all through the meal, the best glass to use is an "all-purpose wineglass," suitable for red or white.

For a very formal, classic dinner, use these glasses: sherry glass, white wineglass, red wineglass, water glass and champagne glass (never place liqueur glasses on the table; pass them on a tray after dinner).

Champagne deserves its own special container. If you don't have champagne glasses and you are going to have a special celebration, borrow some glasses from a friend. (And never serve champagne—or wine either—in a plastic or a paper cup inside your house. It's a crime!)

HOW MUCH WINE TO BUY

If you are having a dinner party, buy your wine by the case (it's usually less expensive that way, and you can always enjoy the rest of the case at a future time or use leftover bottles as gifts.) It's better to have too much on hand than too little, and if you arrange it ahead of time, most liquor stores will take back any unopened and unchilled bottles you have ordered and don't wish to keep.

Never bring a half-gallon or gallon bottle of wine to the table. Instead, decant the wine into a pretty decanter.

Normally, you can pour six glasses of wine from a bottle. I always count on two-thirds of a bottle per person for a dinner party. (Some people drink much less than that, some people more, so it averages out.) If some of your guests drink white wine for cocktails, as well as preferring to drink it straight through the meal, you must order more white than red.

For a dinner party of eight:
• Order three bottles of white wine for the cocktail hour regardless of what other wines are served for the meal.

• If you will serve only red wine for the meal, order five bottles of red; if you will serve only white, then five more bottles of white.

• If you will serve both white and red during the meal, order five of each. (Even though your guests will not consume this much, have it on hand—in case they drink more red or more white than you expect.)

WINE STAINS

If you spill white wine, be grateful that it's white you have spilled, not red. Just make sure the moisture does not go through the linens to the wooden table-top, because it will hurt the wood surface. Fortunately, white wine rarely stains linens and will come out in the laundering process. Mop it up with your napkin, or ask the hostess if you can go to her kitchen to get some paper towels (to put between the wet tablecloth and the wood surface).

Spilling red wine is much more serious, and everyone has a favorite method of fighting a possible permanent stain on the table linens. If you are the guest who has spilled red wine, or if you are the host at a party where a guest has spilled it, it is worth a momentary interruption of your conversation to cope with the situation. If, as the guest, you hear your host saying, "Stay put, please, I mean it. I will tend to it," then do just that. If there is a waiter serving, that person will tend to it. Of course, you should apologize abjectly, and if there is no serving help, and if your host does not object, rush to the kitchen for some paper towels, clean dish towels, salt, or club soda.

First mop up the wine underneath, blot the stain from on top, and put paper towels underneath the cloth to protect the table surface. You have options on the next step. Some people prefer to energetically rub a great deal of salt on the fresh red wine stain on the tablecloth. Others prefer to pour club soda over the spot and then blot it a few times with a clean dish towel. Others prefer to pour white wine over it and then blot. All of these work to a greater or lesser degree. If anyone has spilled red wine on a fabric place mat, soak the mat in cold water immediately (and use a large napkin in its place at the place setting for the rest of the meal). Soak your large wine-stained table-cloth overnight in cold water—after the guests have left.

The main thing to remember, if you are the host, is to make the guest who spilled feel that you are not at all upset, indeed that you have already forgotten the incident. If you are the guest who spilled, the main thing to remember is to blot it as best you can, and if the stain is a serious one, offer to pick up the linens the next day to take to your city's best dry cleaner.

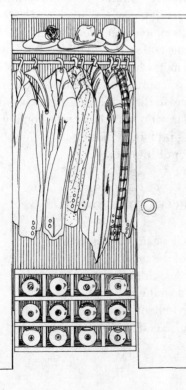

There are any number of ways to make room for storing wine in a small house or apartment. One way is to put your bottles in a wine rack on the floor of a closet. When I was in my first apartment, I stored my wine bottles under my bed, because there was no other place to store them. When people sat on my bed to use the only available phone, their heels always clanked against the bottles, causing them great merriment.

WINE AND CHAMPAGNE SAVERS

For people who wish to save and use again their partially consumed bottles of wine, there is a device on the market (available in fine houseware stores) that pumps out nearly 95 percent of the oxygen, which, if left in an opened bottle, would spoil the wine. This invention consists of a special stopper you place in the unfinished wine bottle, with a pumping device over it with which you pump out the air. The device allows you to conserve the wine for two or three days before oxidation begins. (A new stopper must be used for each bottle; the pumper may be used again.) The device for champagne consists of a reusable stopper and a pumper that puts the sparkle back in the bottle by creating an equilibrium of pressure inside.

STORING YOUR WINE

There are lavish prebuilt or custom-built wine cellars on the market for wine lovers with a high income. There are also modestly priced racks that hold anywhere from ten to fifty-six bottles. You can buy fancy cellar thermometers and cooling units that keep temperatures in your wine closet or storage area between 53°F and 57°F and the humidity between 60 and 70 percent.

If you're just starting to develop a love for and an understanding of wine, begin slowly in amassing the paraphernalia and storage facilities. Buy a wine cellar book and keep a careful inventory in it, whenever you buy wine, of the name, the winery, the number of bottles you purchased and on what date, the price, and the dates on which you consumed the bottles. Also note how you and your guests felt about that particular wine. Put your bottles on a wine rack in the coolest part of your home—preferably not close to throbbing machines such as the washing machine or dishwasher.

SERVING MEMORABLE FOOD

The success of the food you serve at your parties depends on:
- What you serve—the constitution of the menu.
- Having the right quantities of food and drink.
- The skill and imagination of the preparation.
- The quality and freshness of the ingredients.
- The appropriateness of the menu selections for the season and the occasion.

- The presentation of the food on the plate.
- The attractiveness of the serving containers.

A good entertainer is a good planner, someone who thinks far ahead and gives great thought to the food being served—even if little of it will be prepared in his kitchen but instead will be picked up at a gourmet shop, made in a hotel kitchen, or prepared by a catering staff.

A noble Italian friend of mine, noted for her inestimable *cucina*, once told me that the secret to her being a good cook—and, she intimated, to *my* one day becoming a good cook—were these four "assets": time, love, a good cookbook, and a good nose.

"There must be enough *time*," she explained, "to spend experimenting in the kitchen. Think of it as being in love, in *love!*" As she talked, she embraced the concept of her entire kitchen with graceful arms moving in a circle in the air. "A love of cooking," she said with sparkling eyes, "grows more passionate, rather than cools with the passage of time."

She told me I would need an affection for and a trust in one or two cookbooks—to have with me always, to know every page, so that it would cover my failings and idiosyncracies ("like that comfy feeling you have for your favorite worn bedroom slippers, Letizia," the contessa added). Above all, she counseled, "Letizia, you need *a nose for food*. A nose for food," she continued, "is the nose of a lover. It draws you into the marketplace. It makes you aware of the sensuousness of fresh foodstuffs. The nose seeks them out—the freshest, the most exquisite tastes and aromas.

"You must have a nose that makes you long for the dry salty taste of prosciutto," she continued, rolling her eyes heavenward, "a taste that curls up the tip of your tongue, but then soothes it with the sweetness of the luscious ripe fig wrapped within its folds. You must have a nose that makes you dream—as you pass by a mountain of fragrant, plump strawberries—of having them in a bowl with crème fraîche caressing them like an airy chiffon stole."

The contessa explained that her nose gave her fantasies about such things as a sauce she would prepare simply because the aroma of different exotic mushrooms in the market stalls had suddenly wafted into her nostrils and reminded her of "past great meals shared with past great loves."

"Remember, it takes you the same amount of time, *cara*," the contessa assured me, "to prepare your mind to serve roast chicken for your forthcoming party, as it does to prepare your mind for chicken with a lemon glaze on a serving platter garnished with artichoke hearts, stuffed with puree of spinach, and topped with minced egg yolk. Don't forget the small bunches of snow peas, tied with strands of fresh dillweed and tidily piled into tiny potato baskets."

If you really care about cooking for guests, follow the contessa's advice and you'll see what wonders you create!

WAYS TO INTEREST YOURSELF IN COOKING FOR GUESTS

• Try different cookbooks, until you discover the one that suits you perfectly. The perfect cookbook is something you must seek, like the proverbial treasure-hunter, and once you have found it, as the contessa advises, "never let it out of your sight."

• Experiment with the recipes that appeal to you in the gourmet cuisine specialty magazines, as well as the much easier ones published in the newspapers. Make a notebook of great recipes. Paste the cut-out recipes (or duplicated copies of same) on blank notebook pages. Separate the material in the notebook with dividers into any categories you wish—such as hors d'oeuvres, soups, pastas, meat dishes, fish, desserts, and vegetable dishes. Take my advice: Put only recipes you have actually made with great success into this notebook. (Don't clutter it up with recipes you would like someday to make, because soon you won't be able to find any you can safely make.)

Remember, too, it's wise to practice a dish successfully three times on your family or close pals before you try it on dinner party guests. They will give you more criticism than you want, but that's all right. Return to the original roast chicken recipe.

• Strive for balance. When it comes time to settle on your menu, ask yourself:
  • Is there too much starch in this menu?
  • Is there more than one fried item?
  • Is there a green vegetable? (It's also a comfort food!)
  • Is the food oversauced?
  • Are there too many fruity elements? (One dinner I made had fruit in the soup, a fruit sauce with the duck, fruit jam with biscuits, and fresh fruit for dessert. My husband asked, "When do you bring out the fruitcake?")
  • Is there good color content? (Don't do as I did at the American embassy in Rome in planning the menu for an important state dinner, when as social secretary I exasperated my boss, Ambassador Clare Boothe Luce, with an all-white dinner—white creamed soup, white fish in white wine sauce, *blanquette de veau* in white sauce, a white endive salad, and an all-white dessert!) The ambassador's husband, famed publisher Henry R. Luce, asked me if I was perhaps color-blind?

How Many Courses Should You Serve?

You don't have to have a galaxy of courses when you entertain. Have a sufficient amount of what you do serve, but suppress the number of courses and side dishes you consider. Some menus are given here as examples, to serve only as a guideline to the number and kinds of dishes you might prepare for a specific kind of event. Although coffee and decaf are not listed, they should be offered at the end of every meal (or tea, if that is your preference).

The following courses are listed only to jog your imagination into devising your own creative food planning!

• For a small seated dinner without help, you can get away with a bountiful main course (meat, vegetable, rice, and salad) plus dessert, with a choice of red or white wine.

• For a more formal dinner, you would have a first course in addition (such as hearts of palm, or half an avocado stuffed with baby shrimp, or soup, or a fruit cup), and a choice of red or white wine.

• For a pull-out-all-the-stops dinner, you might serve:
  • A light soup first.
  • A light fish course.
  • A main course of meat or fowl.
  • Two accompanying vegetables (or one vegetable and potatoes).
  • Salad and cheese served as a separate course.
  • A light dessert.
  • A white *and* a red wine with the first and the main course.
  • Champagne served with dessert.

• For an informal supper, such as one given on a Sunday night, you might serve:
  • One large dish (like a beef Burgundy with noodles or a hot pasta or a poached salmon).
  • Salad.
  • Dessert.
  • Beer or one kind of wine.

• For a summer lunch, you need only a cold main course (poached salmon with green sauce, for example, served with small cucumber sandwiches on dark brown bread) and dessert. Serve white wine or iced tea.

• For a winter lunch, you need only something like a hot cheese soufflé or a hot pasta dish with a salad and dessert, plus red wine or beer.

• For a large buffet breakfast party, you might offer:
  • A hot egg dish (shirred eggs, creamed eggs) or an omelet.
  • Baked apples.
  • Hominy grits (if you're down South) or pancakes.
  • Hot biscuits and muffins or sweet rolls.

- Bacon or sausage.
- Fruit juice.
- Cantaloupe or grapefruit.
- For a weekend brunch, you might offer, again, buffet style:
  - A hot dish such as creamed turkey, Hungarian goulash, or seafood Newburg.
  - Piping hot grilled cheese sandwiches (made on freshly baked dark bread).
  - Broiled tomatoes with bread crumbs and spices on top.
  - A mixed green salad.
  - Hot baked fruit (with an ice cream such as rum raisin).
  - Wine, or any one of these drinks might be offered to your guests: Bloody Marys (basis of tomato juice).
    Bullshots (basis of bouillon).
    Screwdrivers (basis of orange juice).
- For a cocktail party, you might serve:
  - Two hot hors d'oeuvres.
  - Three cold hors d'oeuvres (including crudités with a dip).
  - Small bowls of nibbles and nuts strategically placed all around.
  - An open bar including sodas, bottled water, and fruit juices.
- For a cocktail buffet, you might offer:
  - A hot pasta dish.
  - A platter of sliced roast meats (such as chicken, roast beef, or turkey) with several different sauces.
  - A large basket of assorted breads (rolls, pumpernickel bread, and focaccia) and butter or margarine.
  - A platter of assorted cheeses.
  - Crudités with a dip.
  - Fresh fruit compote.
  - A gooey dessert like chocolate mousse cake.

Note: "Cocktail party" connotes assorted hors d'oeuvres and canapés. A "cocktail buffet" offers a demi-dinner with hot casseroles, pastas, salads, and desserts. Guests eat light hors d'oeuvres with their cocktails before the buffet.

- For an evening reception (such as after the theater or a museum exhibition opening or a lecture), you might serve:
  - Champagne, wine, and fruit juices.
  - Small crustless sandwiches, such as watercress and creamed cheese, chicken salad on whole wheat, rare roast beef and mustard on small pieces of rye bread.
  - Sweet things, such as cookies, petits fours, small fruit tarts, and chocolates.
- For a postdance supper (midnight or later), along with champagne or wine, serve:

- A hot pep-em-up dish like spaghetti *alla Carbonara*.
- Or piping hot, thin-crusted quiche.
- A green salad.
- Ice cream and sherbet.
- Small cakes or frosted cookies.
- For a picnic, there should be a big choice. That's what makes a picnic fun.
  - If the budget can stand it, pack cold cooked shrimp and slices of smoked salmon and pâté into small separate self-sealing plastic sandwich bags, put them all on the picnic table, and let people take the bag (or bags) of choice to put on their plates.
  - Serve a variety of small sandwiches, crusts removed, cut into four pieces—for example: chopped mushrooms, egg salad, and minced shallots; chicken salad and bacon wrapped in spinach leaves; chopped vegetables with basil on bread brushed with olive oil.
  - A salad like coleslaw or a dish like ratatouille.
  - Cold pasta *primavera* (pasta with vegetables).
  - Slices of roast beef, duck, or any fowl.
  - Dessert: brownies, a fruit pie, cookies, apples, oranges, and bananas.

ADVICE FOR MAKING ENTERTAINING EASY, ATTRACTIVE—AND MEMORABLE

- When people call to ask if they can "bring our houseguests to your cocktail party" or "bring along my old college roommate who's in town," if you have enough room, be gracious about it. Your guests will be coming and going at different times—some early, some late—so your empty space will appear to open and close like an accordion. Therefore you can probably accommodate a few more bodies. You can also always count on some people who have accepted not to arrive, just as you can count on some who didn't respond at all to show up!
- If you're having a seated dinner party and have a full complement of guests, be firm about not accommodating a friend's friends. Explain that you have just enough food, chairs, and room at the table for the people already coming, and really can't fit in any more. (It is rude of a guest to try to palm off his friends on you for a seated dinner.) If the person who has called you reacts to this news by saying, "Well, then I won't come either," respond with, "Fine. I'm sorry, but that's the way it has to be." Too many hosts are intimidated by their guests into inviting strangers they shouldn't have to entertain and whom they can't afford to entertain.
- If you end up with an extra woman or two or three at your dinner party, don't worry about it. I've noticed that when someone drops out of a dinner party at the last minute, it is invariably a male. It is not the end of the world to

have too many women around the table. A woman would rather talk to other attractive, intelligent women than be seated between hopelessly unattractive, boring men—so don't scrape the bottom of the barrel trying to balance the sexes at your table.

• If you're having a large party to which most guests will be driving their own cars, make things easy for them: Arrange for valet parking. Unless your own college-aged children and their friends can handle it, call on a professional car-parking organization.

In some parts of the country, although the host is paying for the gratuities, guests give the young men or women a $1 tip when they get into their car to leave the party, in more expensive areas, $2 or $3.

• If you're giving a large party in an apartment house and have coat checking in the lobby or hallway, be sure to have a guard for the fur coats. A combination security–coat checking service is a practical idea.

• If your party is going to run late and you are going to have music and your neighbors live very close, either invite them to your party or apologize in advance and send them a gift, so they won't hate you as much.

• Remember the joy of mixing scents at your party, so that people are aware of more than just the smell of your wonderful food. Add to the ambience of your party: a scented candle burning in the corner of your living room . . . a small cluster of paperwhites next to a guest's chair during cocktails (if you don't know about these small aromatic flowers, ask your florist) . . . tiny pots of potpourri tucked into the table's floral centerpiece, and into which you add some fresh drops of your favorite perfume before the guests sit down . . .

• Go easy on the hors d'oeuvres you offer your guests. People don't want to eat a lot before dinner, and if you have all kinds of tantalizing canapés and things to immerse in rich dips, your guests will probably overindulge and regret it later. Your dinner should be the climax of your guests' anticipation of the evening. If they're no longer hungry, dinner will be a gastronomic let-down—after all your hard work, too! I've become lazy about hors d'oeuvres. I just don't serve them anymore—just some nuts and "munchies."

• Don't bring people to the table until either the first course is already in place on the table or it is ready to be served the minute the last guest has taken a seat. People are hungry when they sit down at the table. Too often the hosts get their guests seated and the first course doesn't appear for fifteen minutes, particularly at hotel dinners. By the time the guests have devoured their rolls, played with their butter, stolen some of the chocolates from the candy dish that are supposed to be eaten at the end of dessert, they are ready to eat their napkins from hunger, and the party atmosphere has sagged.

• If you've noticed that an aggressive guest has changed the place cards on you to give himself more exciting or well-known people to talk to during dinner, don't let that person get away with it. Simply change the cards back again. (I assure you that guest won't ever change place cards again, he will be so ashamed.) It helps, too, if you say something like, "I just can't believe you did that, but I'll forgive you—this one time!"

• If you are having a large party, don't seat husbands and wives, sisters and brothers, or best friends next to one another. If you are using several tables, put husbands and wives at different ones. Give them a chance to make new friends, to give pleasure to other people, or at least to have a stimulating conversation with someone they don't see all the time. (It makes for much better pillow talk!)

• If you're secretly trying to match two single people who are die-hard "not interested, thanks" types, it's more subtle to seat them opposite rather than next to each other at the table. Then they don't feel under any pressure. They can glance at each other through the meal and perhaps long to be seated next to each other, but they will be grateful their hosts haven't tried to force them on one another. (After the meal, watch them get together in a corner!)

• If you have several sauces to pass around, put them all on one small tray, and then pass it around. For example, if you have mint jelly and mint sauce for the lamb, or if you are offering a choice of chocolate, strawberry, and butterscotch sauce with the ice cream dessert, put them in little milk jugs or creamers on one tray. And don't be surprised if you occasionally see someone pouring all of the sauces on the dessert.

• Since the host is in charge of the conversational flow at his party, here are some "conversation management" ideas:

A shy guest needs special attention. A host should point out that person to a gregarious guest during the cocktail hour or after dinner—"Jane, I'd *really* appreciate it if you'd go over in the corner and do something about Dick Creedon, sitting over there alone. He's very shy and he needs someone like you to make him join in the conversation and be glad he's here tonight."

• If the dinner table conversation has descended to depths that are really low—dirty talk—it's the host's responsibility to pull it up again.

• If there's a nasty argument, the host must intervene to diffuse it. War is perhaps the most combustible subject. Politics is another subject about which people can feel personally antagonistic. Abortion is another. Foreigners can become very emotional about events in their countries. Another reason dinner parties disintegrate on rare occasions is that one person begins to character-assassinate a friend of someone who is present.

In any of these instances, it's time for the host to say something like this: "Look, arguing and getting mad is very bad for the digestive system. Suzy spent hours preparing this lovely dinner for us, and I think that in her honor we should change this down discussion to an up one!" Most likely another guest will pick up her wineglass at this moment and say something like, "I'll second that!" and everyone will drink a toast to the ending of the confrontation. Then someone else will gamely start talking about another subject, and within a few minutes, things will be calm and easy again.

- If the meal is a culinary disaster, which mine have been on more than a few occasions, a sense of humor will save the day. Laugh about your mistakes. Don't try to hide the fact that the roast is burned. Say something like, "You all get a certificate of good behavior at the end of this meal for eating this meat!" If you have too small an amount of something, joke about it—"I decided you're all so stylishly slim, you weren't going to eat any dessert tonight, so I just made a little." (When children are teased, it's usually terribly difficult for them. When adults are teased, it means that their friends love them, enjoy them, and that they are secure people to be able to take the teasing. When you can tease yourself in front of others, it means you're a secure person.)
  - If a guest has had too much to drink, either:
    - Take his car keys away and send him home in a taxi.
    - Have a guest drive her home.
    - Let him sleep at your house.

ALTERNATIVE PARTY IDEAS

There is a lot of creativity in the air. Young Americans have broken out of the mold of doing the tried and true and are trying out new ideas. For example:

THE GARAGE PARTY

Some people who live in small homes do not have sufficient space in which to entertain. A garage can solve this problem for a summer party. The hosts park their cars elsewhere, clean out the garage, put tables and chairs in it, decorate it ingeniously (often according to the musical theme of the evening), lay down a rented dance floor (often vinyl) in the driveway or on some flat ground near the garage, set up a sound system with a disc jockey inside the garage, and put card tables and folding chairs around at random. Each table is covered with a pretty cloth, some flowers, and a candle in a hurricane lamp, or perhaps votive candles in glass cups with flowers around them. The garage party in mild weather solves a big space problem for the owner of a small house. It also means the inside of the house doesn't get all messed up (and the garage gets a much needed cleaning!). If it rains, everyone can continue partying inside the decorated garage. (This requires the guest list to be confined to the pre-arthritic set!)

PARTIES AROUND GAMES
THAT REQUIRE USING YOUR WITS

Young careerists in particular seem to love games that require mental agility—perhaps a reaction to this era of television and VCRs. There are parties given today that focus completely on games, puzzles, and treasure hunts.

• One host invited twenty-four guests for a literary treasure hunt and dinner and gave them six weeks' warning that they had to do a lot of homework. By party night, they were required to have at least a surface familiarity with all of the books on that week's *New York Times* fiction best-seller list. As the guests arrived, the host gave each one a copy of a typed list of two hundred clues, based on characters or themes within the books (no names given, of course). There were two hundred objects in open view around the first floor of her house (none in the kitchen or baths) that matched these clues. People were given notepads to write down the book each clue represented, and the character, if they remembered it, or the place. The game was difficult and challenging, and everyone raced against the clock. Prizes were awarded to those who finished first and had the most details correct.

When guests first arrived that evening, they spent a half hour drinking and meeting each other, then spent a half hour walking around with drinks in hand, clue searching. The hunt continued for another hour after dinner. The guests kept meeting one another at various points in the house or in the garden, each trying to divine what the other was looking at. Strangers soon became friends. During dinner no one mentioned the game, because people didn't want to drop hints to competitors as to what they had personally uncovered as clue objects.

The prizes, of course, were wonderful editions of books. One guest, upon saying good night to her host, admitted that she had not been as mentally exhausted since the days when she had studied for her bar exam.

• Two brothers gave a fund-raising dinner for their affluent friends, at which guests arrived with checkbook in hand, knowing they would make a donation for $2,000 that evening. There were thirty guests, and thirty different charities were to be the recipients of those checks, chosen by each person in advance. The host had devised a treasure hunt, and the first one to find the clue that represented his chosen charity received a prize of an additional donation of $2,000 for that charity from the host. (There was a donation of $1,000 to the second fastest person to find the clue.) After a wonderful dinner, the brothers turned their guests loose in the dark in the yard—first arming each one with a flashlight—to search for their charity's clue. The first winner came rushing into the house with a small doll that had been hidden in a tree trunk—which she felt represented her pet institution, Children's Hospital. The second prizewinner came in with a choco-late heart wrapped in foil, which he found decorating a blooming on a bush, and which he knew represented his charity, the American Heart Association. The evening began and ended with champagne and a compar-ing of notes. It was a great success, and a wonderful way to raise such a grand sum.

• Another couple held a museum party on a Sunday. The guests were served a buffet lunch at the couple's home, then everyone went off to the local museum with a long set of clues printed on paper to compete with one another in a contest. Their task was to work through a series of twenty-five clues in order to find the painting, statue, or artifact in the museum that most perfectly fit each clue. (Examples: A reference to gold treasures in a page reprinted from an edition of Homer's *Odyssey* turned out to be some Greco-Roman bracelets; a sonnet about a fisherman at sea turned out to be a Winslow Homer painting of a man at sea.) The hosts recorded the exact time the guests handed them their finished (and in many cases, unfinished) clue sheets. After an hour and a half in the museum, the party regrouped at the couple's house for tea, petits fours, and the awarding of prizes to those who had finished first and most accurately. The prizes were, appropriately, art books from the museum's bookstore and annual memberships to the museum.

It was a very successful party, and as a result, every guest present became a proud and knowledgeable supporter of the museum, which previously most of them had known sketchily, if at all.

AN EXERCISE PARTY

It is possible, considering America's obsession with health and fitness, to give an imaginative party dedicated to the theme of exercise.

• One young West Coast woman banker invited forty "in shape" guests to "A Spa Party" from "six-thirty to ten o'clock" at her house. Her invitations were made with the silhouettes of weights on the outer fold. She ordered guests to come in their "sharpest exercise outfits" and to bring their own towels to use after showering. The invitation also noted that guests would be served their choice of a "500-Calorie Supper" or an "800-Calorie Supper."

When guests arrived, they were offered their choice of a half-hour aerobic dancing class with a beautiful young instructor in the hostess's mirror-lined master suite, or running in a professionally timed five-mile race. (The partic-ipants in the latter were given maps to follow; cars were stationed here and there along the route, with flags on their aerials for identification. The occu-pants of the cars offered cups of water and helped check on the condition of the runners—and also, as the hostess explained it, "made sure no one cheated by riding in a taxi for part of the race.")

After their various exploits, the guests were awarded their prizes (which were gift certificates to fitness and sporting goods stores). There were consolation prizes for the last racer to arrive and the most hopeless of the aerobic dancers. Guests then had a "cocktail" hour consisting of soft drinks, water, and health drinks (fruit shakes, vegetable juice concoctions, and the like). Guests lined up to use the two showers, although not everyone bothered. They ate dinner outdoors at little tables—delicious low-calorie meals that had been prepared by a new young caterer and the recipes for which were supplied on each table. There was, however, an enormous four-layer chocolate cake, too, for the weak of heart—which was totally consumed, of course. At ten o'clock the hostess rang a big school bell and told her guests that everyone had to go home and have a healthy night's sleep.

The event was unforgettable.

ENTERTAINING OUT AND ABOUT
(SEE ALSO TIPPING, PAGE 150)

YOUR PERSONAL TOUCH

When you decide to give a lunch or dinner in a club or public place like a restaurant or hotel dining room, you may either put your party in the hands of the banquet manager and decide with him on your menu and then let the establishment do the rest, or you can keep firm control over the party and put your own strong personal stamp on the proceedings. This personalization is achieved through a combination of some of the following actions:

• Working hard with the chef to make a very special menu.

• Choosing special linens . . . or having them made . . . or bringing them from home, particularly your own beautiful lace-trimmed napkins.

• Having your own florist do the table decorations.

• Bringing some of your beautiful centerpiece decorations from home, such as your candelabra, silver pieces, porcelain candy dishes, porcelain birds, and the like.

• Supplying chocolates or nuts on the table in pretty containers.

• Having a favor at each place at the table.

• Using place cards with matching menu cards.

• Arranging for a trio of musicians to serenade during the cocktail hour or during dinner.

THINGS TO REMEMBER

- Get there early, so you can oversee the placement of your place cards and check on all the last-minute details that inevitably require correcting.
- Hopefully you have already solved the problem of how your guests will park, and have given instructions on your invitations (in the lower right-hand corner).
- How clean are the rest rooms for your guests? Check them out in the planning stages, and insist that they be freshly cleaned on party day. Bring in your own guest soaps, paper guest towels, and room freshener from home to put there on the night of your party.
- Call the day before the party and request that the linens, if being supplied by the hotel or restaurant, be freshly pressed for your party.
- Make certain there is a comfortable place for your guests to mingle during cocktails, preferably not in the room where you will have dinner. Have nuts and little things for guests to nibble on during the cocktail hour.
- Sit down to dinner right on time, when the food is at its height of preparedness—even if some guests have not yet arrived.
- Bring along some extra cash to tip at the end of the evening the maître d', the chef ($30 to $50 each), and the main waiters ($25 each), if you were pleased with their performance the night of your party. They will bask in the warmth of your praise and appreciation.
- Arrange to bring your beautiful, expensive flowers home after your party—or arrange to have them picked up and taken the next day to a hospital, hospice, or home for the elderly.

RESTAURANT MANNERS

It's very offputting to someone if you continually finish your conversations with "We *must* lunch sometime" or "I'll call you for lunch" but then you never get around to it. Observing the philosophy that one should "put up or shut up," you should either make a lunch date with that person or stop saying that you intend to.

Having lunch or dinner in a restaurant is a most pleasant way for friends to get together. But the restaurant is also the main place of business outside the office, and an executive's manners, or lack thereof, are under merciless public scrutiny here.

The following are a few etiquette tips to be observed by people eating in a restaurant for social or business purposes:

When You Are the Host

• If you must cancel this date, call your guest yourself to apologize—don't have your secretary do it. Reschedule the lunch right then and there, before you forget about it and lose a friend or potential customer.

• If you have to cancel again, reschedule the date at once, and send a note of apology. If you have to cancel a third time—which does happen in this crazy business world—reschedule the lunch, but also send that person a gift (like a basket of fruit), with a note of apology, so your guest will really believe that you are as upset as you say you are over the inconvenience you have caused her.

• Be very specific about date, time, and place when you extend your invitation.

• Select a restaurant close to your guest's office or home, featuring food he or she likes. Ask about food preferences before booking a table at a place featuring fish or Far Eastern, Spanish, Scandinavian, African, Indian, Mexican, or Ethiopian food.

• You, by virtue of having called the other person first and having reserved a table, are the one who pays. There should be no confusion about that. In fact, don't ever go to a restaurant with anyone without the matter of who pays being clearly understood beforehand.

• Reconfirm with your guest (or that person's assistant) on the morning of the lunch appointment.

• Reconfirm also with the restaurant, and reiterate your desire for a good table. (My definition of a good table is one that is not in front of the kitchen's swinging door, does not face the rest rooms or telephones, is not in front of the main door on a cold winter's day, and is not directly beneath the main air-conditioning duct on a hot summer's day.)

• Arrive five minutes before the meeting time in the restaurant. Go directly to your table, after checking your coat. It is most embarrassing—even infuriating—to the guest if the host is late. The host should be awaiting any guests at an untouched, pristine-looking table (which means that you don't touch your napkin, order a drink, use your bread and butter plate, or crumble breadsticks all over the table).

• As host you should rise when the guest approaches the table, or in very crowded conditions at least make half an attempt to do so.

• The guest(s) should always be given the best seats (against the wall on banquette seats, for example, or in the seats facing the main part of the room). If there is a chair facing a blank wall or the rest room, take it yourself instead of allowing a guest to sit there. If there is a seat in the direct path of the waiters rushing in and out of the kitchen, it should be occupied by the host, not a guest.

- If you have several guests, know ahead of time where people will be seated around the table. Make a penciled drawing of your table plan and put it in your pocket (or handbag) before going to the restaurant. Then your guests can take their proper seats quickly, without confusion and without clogging the aisles.

- Allow your guests to choose their menu selections themselves. For a large group, you would pre-order the meal, giving them only a choice of a meat or fish entrée.

- Even though you may not drink yourself, offer a premeal drink to the guest. If she orders something, wine or nonalcoholic, you should join her. If you want a glass of wine with lunch but your guest does not, feel free to order one for yourself.

- Help your guests with their menu selections. If the restaurant is noted for certain specialties, mention what they are. Be able to translate the foreign names for dishes (because you have briefed yourself on the menu beforehand). If your budget is limitless, mention to the guests, "The lobster here is fabulous." (If you're on a tight budget, you shouldn't be in an expensive restaurant in the first place.) If you suggest items in the low or middle price range to your guests, they will probably follow suit and order in that price range, too.

- When a guest's order arrives, urge him to begin eating at once, while it's hot. If your order arrives before your guest's, however, wait until his food has arrived before you begin eating.

- If you see your guest not touching the food on his plate, inquire once casually, "Is it all right?" If it is not, you can take action with the waiter. (Your guest may wish his meat cooked more, or he may have ordered the main course without sauce and they brought it with sauce.)

If, however, your guest dismisses your question with a shrug, saying, "No, I guess I'm just not hungry, that's all," don't press him further. Let it be. There is something he does not wish to say publicly, so don't make him. (He may think the fish is tainted, or the meat may be too rare for him to eat but he doesn't wish to send it back, and the like.) Some people love to be conspicuous in restaurants, but most would rather eat nothing than raise a fuss. So play it by ear.

- As host it is your responsibility to cut the banter short, and get down to the business discussion. Usually about ten minutes of small talk is sufficient.

- Never give the waiter or captain a hard time in front of your guests. Save the sermons and criticisms of the terrible service for after the departure of your guests. (Go back to your office or home and write a letter to the management—they should know what went wrong.) To criticize the waiter in front of your guests will only upset them.

When You Are the Guest

• If you must cancel the date, call your host yourself; don't have an assistant do it. Ask your host if you can reschedule the lunch date right then and there, but with you as host this time.

• Be absolutely punctual. If you are going to be even ten minutes late, have someone call the restaurant to pass this message on to your host.

• If you arrive before your host, go directly to the table, but don't order a drink or eat bread. *Leave your napkin undisturbed.*

• If you are late, don't slow up the meal service for the rest of the people at the table. Simply order the next course being served, so that you eat in unison with the others rather than forcing them to wait for you.

• If your host does not drink but offers you a drink before the meal and you want one, order one. The polite thing to do is to say, "Look, I don't want to hold you up if you have a time problem today. "I'll take a glass of wine with lunch instead of now."

• Either one cocktail or two glasses of wine at a meal are enough. If you order more, your host will surmise (probably justifiably) that you have a drinking problem. When you order that glass of wine, do it carefully. You don't want to order (innocently) a terribly expensive one which could conceivably cost more than your entire meal.

• If nothing is said by your host about ordering wine, don't bring up the subject. You can always live through a meal without wine.

• Don't order the most expensive items on the menu. Take your lead from your host as to the price range in which to order. If he gives you no helpful suggestions, order in the middle price range, not in the lowest nor the highest.

• As a guest, never deal directly with the waiter; that's the host's job. If you want something, softly mention it to your host, and he will call over the waiter.

• If you are at a business lunch, don't try to force your host into discussing business before he is ready. Continue to make small talk at the beginning of the meal. It is the host's prerogative to give the signal when it's time to get down to business.

• If you are someone's guest, don't even try to pay the check.

• Write a thank-you to your host within three days' time. An e-mail is enough, but a letter is more appreciated. It doesn't have to be longer than three sentences, taking five minutes to write, address, and stamp, as for example:

Dear Joe,
    It was wonderful seeing you today, and to see you looking in good form, as always. And how I enjoyed those soft-shell crabs! Thank you for a memorable lunch . . .

When you write a thank-you note, even for something as pedestrian as a restaurant lunch, it gives pleasure to your host. It also signifies that you are a person of refinement and good manners—a good reputation to have.

Behavior to Avoid in a Restaurant

- Table hopping (an obvious attempt to draw attention to oneself; also a hazard for passing waiters).
- Talking on a cell phone—a cardinal sin—illustrating the desire to draw attention to oneself.
- Strewing the table with papers and documents, so the poor waiter can't even find a landing place for the plates for your meal.
- Putting a handbag or a tote bag or briefcase on the table.
- Talking loud and boisterously.
- Eating so slowly that you hold up everyone else and make them fidgety.
- Remaining at the table when you have a long choking or sneezing fit, instead of quickly departing for the rest room.
- Using your napkin as a handkerchief (instead of quickly departing for the rest room).
- Using a toothpick or a fork to dislodge food in your teeth (instead of rinsing your mouth out with water in the rest room).
- Putting on makeup, if you are a woman (except for a quick, inconspicuous swipe of powder from your compact at the end of the meal).

MUSIC MAKES THE WORLD GO ROUND

Nothing gives more zip to a party than music. Talented hosts use it to create a mood, to "decorate the air of my party place," as one woman described it, and to make people feel relaxed and comfortable—or alternatively, to wake them up and get them going on the dance floor.

BACKGROUND MUSIC

Background music is strictly that—pleasant sounds in the background against which people greet each other, chat, stroll around, or sit conversing at the dinner table. Your guests are not supposed to be straining to listen to the lyrics in background music. Singers should not perform as background musicians, nor solo instrumentalists either. A cocktail party, for example, is not the moment to stop the action, grab everyone's attention, and have them listen attentively to someone give a solo performance. It can't be done.

Background music is very attractive during the cocktail hour. (If you're using CDs, have someone turn up the volume bit by bit as more people arrive, so that a snatch of music can be heard along with the babble of voices in the air.) The music should be turned off during the meal, so that no one with even a slight hearing problem will have trouble hearing and talking. After dinner, it makes sense to change the music from the cocktail hour selection, to introduce a new part of the evening.

If you are lucky enough to have live musicians, during the cocktail hour you might have a piano player, or even better, a combo (piano, guitar or sax, and drums, for example). You might have a harpist or chamber music quartet play throughout a large dinner. (Before the musicians leave the dining area at the conclusion of dinner, as host you should go up to the group, thank and praise them, turn to your dinner guests, and invite your guests to applaud them, too.)

Classical Music

There are good classical musicians in every region, and usually they are eager—and need—to make money by playing or singing at your parties. The lesser-known ones (we're not talking about having Byron Janis come by to give a Chopin concert on an excellent rented piano after dinner for you) might charge you anywhere from $300 to $500 per performer for playing at your party. (In smaller towns, the charge may be less.) Check into the music teachers in your community, as well as the faculty and advanced students in the music departments of the local schools and universities. Others will have heard them play, and you can go on their recommendations. But first listen to them *yourself.*

If you are hiring musicians, be sure to:
- Sign a contract with them or their agent.
- Have them understand exactly what you want them to do.
- Go over the content and length of their program with them.
- Settle on when they should arrive.
- Check on what they will be wearing. (To be on the safe side, tell the men to come in black tie, the women in long black dresses—they can't be conspicuous fashion disasters if they conform to that!)
- Be firm about the exact length of time they are to perform.

An after-dinner concert of any kind of classical music should last no longer than thirty to forty-five minutes. People are relaxed, full of good food and wine, and want to have some conversation time before they go home. An interlude of concert music provides a perfect polish to a dinner party, but it should not drag on, no matter how excellent the musicians may be.

A friend once hired a chamber music orchestra and told them to play for thirty minutes after dinner. They wouldn't stop. They went on and on for an hour, while the host kept jumping up to applaud them after each "final" piece. Without giving him a chance to intervene, they segued into the next piece. The situation became comical. Finally the host told the conductor of the quartet that the piece they were playing was *absolutely* the last one. (Embarrassingly enough, some mild applause was then heard coming from the guests!)

DANCE MUSIC

How nice if you can afford an orchestra for a dance! In a big city, there are usually two or three musical organizations headed by well-known band leaders that supply orchestras, pianists, trios, quartets, and bands of any size for any kind of party. If you're holding to a tight budget, there might be a school or college dance band in your town that is terrific. Perhaps you can persuade a rock or jazz group in one of the local spots in your town to play—provided you hold your party on the group's night off. You might have heard that someone in town had a great little dance band at their daughter's wedding reception. Call and find out who it was. Often the orchestra or group will have its own agent, so you would deal with that person, not the musical leader.

HIRING A MUSICIAN OR ANY KIND OF PERFORMER

Some performers have horror stories of how badly they have been treated when performing in a private home. One told me how a well-known woman kept him waiting to perform four hours after the agreed-upon time. He was made to stay in the pantry and stood, leaning against the wall, because there wasn't a chair and he wasn't allowed to find one. He was not given anything to eat or drink; he was not given a hanger or a place to change his clothes—he had to do that in a utility closet. Fortunately, that kind of story is the exception.

You are a considerate host, as far as the performer is concerned, if the performer:
- Is paid in full exactly on time.
- Is given an opportunity to rehearse, try out the piano, or look over the sound system or whatever else needs checking.
- Is given a bathroom to use to check makeup and appearance and a room in which to change and rest, with a comfortable chair.

• Is provided with an iron and ironing board, if that is needed for any costume.

• Is given something to eat and drink, either before or after the performance, as requested.

• Is properly introduced to the audience by the host before performing. (If a group is involved, the name of each person in the group should be stated.)

• Is properly thanked for a good performance by the host—if it *was* a good performance!

• Is sent a letter soon after the party, praising the group's performance. (It is very valuable for a performer to have written recommendations in order to obtain new bookings.)

To Tip or Not to Tip

You do not have to give a performer anything beyond the amount specified in the signed contract for the performance. However, if a fantastic performance was given—if your guests were immensely pleased, and you were, too—it is nice to give the performer(s) a gift of money to show how pleased you were. You would never tip a Pavarotti who sang at your fancy New York benefit, but you could certainly give $20 to $50 over and above his performance fee to a singer-pianist in Toledo who absolutely made your party. Musicians like to be thanked, and since most have to scratch hard for a living, they enjoy seeing a host's appreciation backstopped with a little cash.

USING RECORDED MUSIC

If you want to have a dance at home to the accompaniment of your own carefully selected CDs, hire a good disc jockey. It is worth the money. He supplies the sound system, knows when and how to change the tempo and kind of music—and when to adjust the volume. The perfect disc jockey for your party is a college or postcollege friend of your children's (preferably one who does this professionally) who loves all music, who is up on all the latest musical crazes of the young but appreciates the Frank Sinatra–George Gershwin appetite of the older generation, too. I remember asking one disc jockey how he handled the musical choices at his jam-packed nightclub, and he replied, "I look over the crowd and divide it into three categories: the 'AARP set,' who want the music of the forties and fifties; the 'yup-heads,' who want pop rock and music like the flamenco beat from Spain; and the 'kids in their twenties,' who want to hear anything their parents wouldn't want to listen to."

PROTOCOL FOR YOU, NOT JUST FOR ROYALTY

A knowledge of the basic tenets of protocol in entertaining helps you entertain graciously and efficiently. It helps to know how to receive people, where to seat them at the table, and how to toast them as guests of honor. It also places you a cut above everyone else on the list of great hosts.

HOW TO RECEIVE YOUR GUESTS

If you are a couple and entertaining at home or a club, one of you should be stationed with an eye on the front door, so you can immediately greet every person who steps through it and direct individuals to where they should put their coats. The other half of the couple should be in the living room or wherever cocktails are being served, to make sure the guests are meeting one another. If you are giving the party by yourself, you should station yourself between the cocktail serving area and the door, so that you can do both jobs at once.

Should There Be a Receiving Line?

If you are having a cocktail party for more than thirty people, you and/or your spouse and guest of honor should be in an informal receiving line as close to the entrance of the room as possible. ("Informal receiving line" means the hosts stand around talking to guests in small groups, keeping an eye on the door and staying ready to regroup quickly to greet any new guest who arrives.)

If you are having a party of a hundred or more, you should have a receiving line of yourself and your spouse (who can cut in and out of the line), and any guests of honor. There should never be more than five people greeting the guests. The number-one guest (either gender) should stand next to the number-one host (either gender) of the party. At purely social parties, spouses always stand in line together. At business parties, the spouses may or may not have to stand in line—rarely at a large lunch, but often at a large dinner. There are different formulas for receiving lines. For example:

• The company's chief executive officer is giving a party for a very important Japanese businessman. The formation of the line might be as follows:

1. The chairman and CEO of the host company.
2. The Japanese guest.
3. The president of the host company.

• If the Japanese businessman's wife accompanies him, the receiving line would look like this:

1. The chairman and CEO.
2. The Japanese businessman (honored guest).
3. The chairman's wife.
4. The Japanese businessman's wife.

• Mr. and Mrs. John Mowinckel, Jr., are hosting a big wedding anniversary cocktail buffet for his parents. The receiving line would look like this:

1. Mrs. Mowinckel, Jr.
2. Mrs. Mowinckel, Sr.
3. Mr. Mowinckel, Jr.
4. Mr. Mowinckel, Sr.

Advice on Handling Your Receiving Line

• Never have more than four or five people in the line at any one time, if you can help it. It becomes ponderous and too much like a wedding reception to have so many people standing together. Also, the longer the line, the more interminably long it takes to get through. The guests should restrain themselves. A receiving line is no place for a conversation. It should move quickly, without hesitations along the row.

• Spouses can cut in and out of the line, subbing for their mates. At a large corporate party, senior management can take turns standing in the receiving line with the guest of honor.

• When the receiving line becomes a veritable logjam, with people stretching out into the street, the following steps should be taken:

• Someone representing the host should urge people to come inside, get a drink, and go back into the receiving line later.

• The guests should decide for themselves to go get a drink—and pass through the line later when it isn't so congested.

• On the subject of drinking in a receiving line:

• Hosts should not have drinks in their hands—there should be a small table behind them, to hold whatever it is they are drinking. They can turn around and take a discreet sip every now and then, without anyone really noticing they have a mixed drink, champagne, or anything else on that table behind them.

• Guests should not go through the receiving line with drinks in their hands. They can sip their drinks until shortly before passing through the line. Then they should put down their drinks somewhere and retrieve them after meeting their hosts.

• If almost everyone has arrived, the receiving line may be disbanded, but sometimes guests continue to arrive virtually throughout a two-hour period. If your large cocktail party (for hundreds) is from five-thirty to seven-thirty, the host or hosts and guest of honor should stay in the receiving line from five-thirty to seven.

- Many times at large parties the guests and hosts do not know one another. In the receiving line, either the guest introduces himself to the host, or the host gives his name to the guest; the host then turns to the person on the right and introduces the guest to that person, who then introduces the guest to the person standing next on her right, and so on. (At a really fancy party, an "introducer" brings each guest up to the head of the line and gives that person's name in a strong, firm voice. It's pretentious but also helpful.)

- If a couple is giving a large party involving mainly the husband's business associates, he stands first in line, so he can introduce people to his wife standing next to him. If they are giving a party for *her* business associates, *she* stands first in line, so she can introduce people to her husband.

NAME BADGES

Don't use them unless you absolutely have to! They look terrible on anyone's suit or dress—particularly on a dress. They are much too commercial to look decent at a party in someone's home or club. If there is no name badge, people have to be more alert and do their own detective work to find the identity of the person to whom they're talking. That helps make the party go, rather than deterring it.

If you are required to have name badges at an evening party (no one really minds them at lunch or in a hotel ballroom or convention center), wear yours high up on your upper right shoulder. Your name is most easily read in that spot by right-handed people. (If you're at a convention of all left-handed people, wear your name badge on your upper left shoulder!)

A name badge should contain the person's first and last name, and company name, if it is pertinent. For a host corporation, if the company name is already printed on the name badge, the person's title should be included under her name, if she is part of senior management. People like to know the positions (in other words the importance) of the people they are talking to.

SIGNING THE GUEST BOOK

If you plan to have a guest book at your party (a handsome leather or fabric-covered one), put it on a table away from the congestion created by arriving guests. In other words, don't make guests sign, check their coats, and wait in a receiving line all at the same time. Put the person overseeing the guest book signing in a chair at a table in a corner of the cocktail area.

The best way of handling a guest book, in my opinion, is not to have one, because it creates one more traffic problem—and there is, after all, a guest list. The second best way to handle a guest book is to have someone carry it up and down the receiving line, letting people sign as they wait to go through the line.

One more caution: *Have a supply of good black pens for people to use for signing the book.* (Forget emerald green and shocking pink pens.)

SEATING ARRANGEMENTS

People have friends over for dinner all the time, and no one worries about who sits where. However, it's more efficient and more stimulating to seat guests, even old pals, with thought.

Family Meals

Within your own family, it certainly does not matter who sits where at the table (unless you have to separate certain young siblings who tend to fight all the time). Even so, it is helpful for young people to learn that their father and mother—the figures of authority—sit opposite each other at the ends of the table or in the center of a rectangular table, and that grandparents are seated comfortably and in "places of honor." (If the family dining table is round, the parents take seats opposite each other at some point in the circle, as in the illustration on page 514.) It is all part of teaching children *deference* and *respect* for their elders, which includes passing the food to them before taking it themselves, and waiting to eat until their elders have begun.

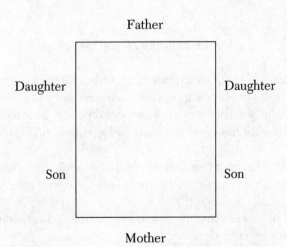

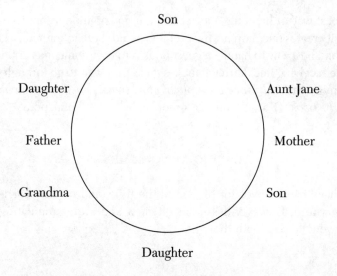

| | | Eldest | | Youngest |
| Son | Grandma | Father | Daughter | Son | Daughter |

| Daughter | Son | Mother | Grandpa | Oldest | Aunt |
| | | | | Son | Cynthia |

Who Sits in the Hosts' Seats?

There is always a host for every gathering. Often there is a cohost who sits opposite the host—such as a spouse or a business associate close in rank or importance to the host. In the case of a widowed person, a brother or sister, an in-law, or other adult family member may act as cohost, taking the seat opposite the host.

A word of caution here to someone who has recently lost a spouse: Do not put someone you have been dating in the cohost's seat soon after your spouse's death. Others feel a little squeamish seeing the late spouse's seat at the table occupied by a newcomer who unconsciously (or consciously) assumes the role of a person only recently departed.

When there are several tables, for a large private business party, a member of senior management acts as a host of each of the round tables. There are duties attached to this honor—for example, making sure everyone is fully introduced and ensuring that the conversation flows around the table, without leaving anyone sitting with no one to talk to. This is why you should choose people who are competent, not just important (or rich!) as the hosts of your or your company's party tables.

At a corporate-sponsored affair in a hotel ballroom, for example, you might have the chairman, president, senior vice presidents, and board directors hosting separate tables. At your wedding anniversary dinner dance, you might have your sister Anne, brother-in-law Bill, your aunt Louise, and your college-aged son Harry hosting four of your tables. It does not matter whether the host is a man or a woman. What does matter is that it should be a person who will represent the family or your company in an attractive, well-mannered way.

Seating People According to Rank

• It is a mark of graciousness to give any prominent guest in your home a seat of honor. The number-one seat for a man is at the hostess's right; the seat for the second most important man is on her left. The number-one seat for a woman is at the right of the male host; the second most important woman sits to his left.

• A person who has rank deserves a place of honor (see also "The Official Ranking for U.S. Officials," page 658, and "Addressing People Properly," page 650). If you have invited a person of rank to dinner at your house, or if that person will be your guest in a restaurant, seat the individual to the right of the host of the opposite sex.

> • A present (or past) elected official—governor, mayor, senator, congressman, police chief, alderman.
> • A present or past appointed official (an ambassador, head of a commission).
> • A high-ranking military officer.
> • A White House appointee (member of the president's cabinet or sub-cabinet, head of a government agency).

Even when a guest is no longer in office (or on active duty), that person should have a seat of honor.

• A person holding a high religious office deserves a place of honor at your table. However, a clergyperson should not have to be as high as an archbishop to deserve a seat of honor. Your own rabbi, parish priest, or minister deserves a good seat at your table out of respect for his ministry.

- There are people of no rank who are given "top" seats nonetheless at business or social affairs out of courtesy:
  - An greatly respected elderly person.
  - An international guest.
  - An adult houseguest.
  - The honoree(s) of the party—someone with a birthday, wedding anniversary; someone who is retiring, being promoted, going away, has gotten engaged, had a baby, earned an honor, won a competition.
  - A distinguished musician or artist.
  - A senior professor.
  - A community leader.
  - A respected, older business leader.
- The spouse of a person of rank enjoys equal rank at the table. In other words, if a man is the number-one ranked person at the party, he is seated on the hostess's right and his wife is seated on the host's right as the number-one ranked woman present, unless there is a woman guest of rank on her own (for example: a woman senator or ambassador). If he is the second ranked person, he sits on his hostess's left and his wife sits on her host's left. For example, at this dinner party at which a congresswoman is present, she is seated on the host's right, and her spouse sits on the hostess's right (unless, of course, the President of the United States is coming to dinner).
- Anyone who entertains a lot and has guests with city, state, or national rank, should know where to go for help in seating that meal.
  - For questions on the rank of city officials, call the mayor's secretary and ask who handles protocol matters for city hall.
  - For questions on the rank of state officials, call the governor's secretary and ask who handles protocol matters for the state capital.

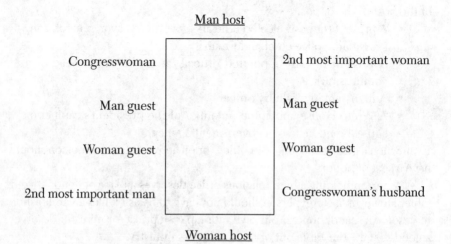

Man host

Congresswoman   2nd most important woman

Man guest   Man guest

Woman guest   Woman guest

2nd most important man   Congresswoman's husband

Woman host

- For questions on the rank of congressional figures, consult the Congressional Directory (Government Printing Office, Washington, DC 20401).
- For questions on the rank of White House staff, Cabinet members, and Washington diplomatic corps officials, consult The Green Book, which lists the precedence of the major officials (The Social List of Washington, D.C., 10335 Kensington Parkway, Kensington, MD 20895). For questions of military rank, any local military office will give you the order of rank of the officers of any of the branches of the military.

"Givens" in Seating Any of Your Guests

- Seat people in alternating sexes around the table—man-woman—unless you are short one or two of either gender, in which case, you would be obliged to seat two of the same sex next to each other (which is no great problem). You might put one of those same gender guests on your left, so she will feel honored instead of feeling a mere "extra" at the party.
- Make sure that you don't seat two bores next to one another, two overly shy people or two overly talkative people next to one another. The success of a table conversation stems from variety and balance, not from the overkill of people in conversational competition.
- When friends come to dinner, seat them next to people with whom they would most enjoy themselves. There are logical reasons for who should sit next to whom at your parties. Think it out ahead of time, like this hostess, who pondered her dinner party and decided to:
  - Put saucy Abigail next to cranky old Mr. Hamilton, because he loves pretty young things. In recompense, Abigail will have an attractive young man on her other side, so she won't mind putting up with Mr. Hamilton half the time.
  - Put Louise next to the exchange student from France, because Louise speaks French, and the exchange student is newly arrived and hasn't learned enough English yet.
  - Seat George next to Jim Jones's wife, because George is job hunting and has revealed that he has an appointment with Jim Jones next week to see about a job. George might be able to impress her and do himself some good.
  - Put Alfonso and Jennifer next to one another, so they can talk about wildlife conservation all night. Both are hipped on the subject, they have never met each other, and it is a stroke of genius to seat them together.

- Seat Grace next to Bill. He has been so despondent since his wife's death, and if anyone can bring him out of his funk with sparkling, funny, wonderful conversation, it's Grace.
- Put Mark on my left, because he drinks too much and has become impossible lately, but he and his wife are dear old friends and I know I am the only one, other than his poor wife, who will take it.

You, as host, know better than anyone else how the synergism of talents of your party guests will work, according to how you seat them. People should enjoy or learn from the people they talk to at dinner. If they are brimming with personality, they achieve happiness in giving to the others, in leading the conversation, in making people laugh. If they are quiet and good listeners, they counterbalance the talkers while enjoying the flow of conversation around them. The host should put all of the guests on his chess board, figure out the moves, and do the best seating possible to aid the party chemistry.

Problems of Seating a Table of a Multiple of Four

At tables of eight (or four couples), and all multiples of four thereafter, you should seat the cohost down one to the right, instead of opposite the host in her rightful place. To illustrate, at a dinner of twelve, with six men and six women, if you put the cohost opposite the host, there will be people of the same sex sitting next to each other around the table:

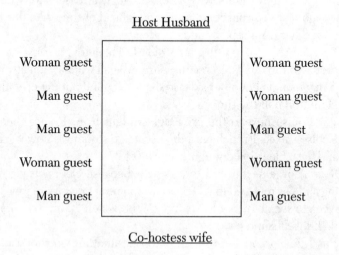

Host Husband

Woman guest		Woman guest
Man guest		Woman guest
Man guest		Man guest
Woman guest		Woman guest
Man guest		Man guest

Co-hostess wife

However, if you seat the woman cohost "down one" instead of at the end of the table, the sexes will be able to alternate around the table:

Host husband

Woman guest		Woman guest
Man guest		Man guest
Woman guest		Woman guest
Man guest		Man guest
Woman guest		Co-hostess wife

Man guest

If you have one person too many of one sex at a table of a multiple of four (such as seven women and five men), there is no problem in having the cohost sit opposite the host. Two people of the same sex will be sitting next to each other on either side of the table, allowing the cohost to sit opposite the host, as illustrated in this luncheon for twelve:

Woman host

Man guest		Man guest
Woman guest		Woman guest
Woman guest		Woman guest
Man guest		Man guest
Woman guest		Woman guest

Man co-host

Logistical Details of Seating a Large Party

If you're in charge of a large function, whether a business dinner or a social event like a wedding anniversary dinner dance, the procedures used to seat the dinner are the same. Here are steps to follow:

1. Decide on what kind of round tables you will use—those that seat eight, ten, or twelve people. (Tables for eight or ten are better for conversation.) Let's say you are giving a dinner for fifty and will use five round tables that seat ten each.

2. Take five large sheets of plain paper. Draw a circle four inches in diameter on each. Number each table 1 to 5. Put ten little nicks around the circumference of each table, to designate a guest's place.

3. Make a seating chart name card for each of the fifty guests on a piece of paper. Do this by typing separate lists of male guests and female guests, leaving enough space around each name so that you can cut them out and use them to put around the table charts, as in the following example:

Georgia Ames	Roderick Ames
Marianne Andrews	Joseph Andrews
Fabienne Arthur	Dr. Lee Arthur
Susan Barker	William Baskin
Georgia Berrigan	Charles Berrigan

4. Decide who will be the host (and cohost, if there will be one) for each of the five tables. Take their names (from the guest list you have just cut up into name tabs) and with tape attach them to the designated table in the host's place.

5. Put the guests of honor in their proper places to the right of the hosts of each table.

6. Seat all the other guests by attaching their name tabs by tape to the various tables, making sure to seat husbands and wives at different tables and to alternate men and women guests—unless you have too many of one sex.

7. When the seating has been decided for your party, wait until just about two hours before the party starts to have the final flat list of guests' names with their table numbers revised and printed out. The reason is that there are often last-minute dropouts in large parties, necessitating changes in seating . . . and in the flat list numbers . . . and in the table card numbers . . . and in the placement of the place cards on the tables.

Once you feel there will be no more last-minute changes, have the list of names and table numbers printed out in duplicate copies. Give one to everyone involved in running your party, so that there will be several people helping guests find their tables in the small ballroom when the cocktail period is over and people come in to dinner.

8. Little table cards with each person's name and table number should be placed alphabetically on a table in the entrance area. The guests can be directed to that table to find their cards after checking their coats and before greeting you, the host. (A man usually sticks his table card in his jacket pocket, a woman in her handbag. I inevitably manage to lose mine before going in to dinner. Thank God for party assistants with their guest lists to assist careless guests like me!)

9. Inside the ballroom, there should be a stanchion on each table, holding a large white card upon which the table number is printed. (The headwaiter should be instructed to have the stanchions removed once the guests have found their proper seats and have sat down, because they obstruct guests' view of the room.)

The Script for an Official Social Function

1. Dais guests march into the small ballroom (to an optional drum roll). Guests stand by their designated seats and listen quietly.

2. Colors are posted by the military. Guests stand for this, at respectful attention.

3. Guests sing "The Star Spangled Banner" (optional), remaining standing.

4. A member of the clergy gives the invocation while guests remain standing.

Flag Protocol

• The flag of the United States of America is always accorded the place of honor, with flags of other countries positioned to its own right (to the left, from the perspective of people sitting in the audience and gazing at it on the stage).

• When there is a row of domestic flags on poles of equal heights, the United States flag should be in the center, raised on some sort of platform, so that it is slightly higher than all the other flags.

• When the flag is displayed vertically or horizontally against the wall, the flag's stars should always be on the top, to the flag's own right (to the audience observer's left).

- The American flag always flies at the top of the pole when more than one flag is flying from the same pole.
  - The flag may *not* be used:
    - To cover a car or any vehicle (except when firmly attached to a staff).
    - To cover a ceiling.
    - To cover a lectern.
    - To drape a platform. (Use striped red, white, and blue bunting instead, with a dark blue stripe at the top.)

(For more information on the display of the flag, contact the National Flag Foundation, Flag Plaza, Pittsburgh, PA 15219.)

TOASTING IS AN ART AND AN IMPORTANT PART OF PROTOCOL

The ancient ritual of toasting with wine is a special skill anyone should learn—that is, anyone who expects to have guests for a meal on occasion. Knowing how to toast is an act of kindness, because it makes people feel good; it is an art, because its success depends on timing, intuition, and a smooth articulation of a message. It is a skill replete with nuances. It doesn't matter what kind of drink you have in your hand—a glass of water will do if you are merely making a symbolic gesture. When you raise a toast to a person for some reason, suddenly the place where you are and the people present take on a special cachet. You might suddenly raise a glass of soda to the person standing next to you at the beach hot dog stand—"Geoff, the news you just told me is *great!* Congratulations! Here's to you!" Suddenly, your hot dog and soda lunch becomes a celebration, and you have made the object of your toast feel very happy.

It doesn't matter if a foursome is having lunch in a cafeteria or eating dinner at a five-star restaurant, at least one toast is always appropriate. (As a friend of mine expressed it, "There's always something to celebrate—like being alive, for example.")

SHORT TOASTS

It is a nice gesture, when you have ordered drinks in a restaurant or in a bar and the drinks arrive, to make a toast to the person or people in your group. You simply raise your glass quickly to the person present and say:

- "Here's looking at you."
- "Here's to you."
- *"Kampai"* (Japanese).

- *"Kampei"* (Chinese).
- "Here's mud in your eye" (World War I vintage).
- "All the best."
- "Cheers."
- "Skoal" (the Scandinavian toast used throughout the meal).
- *"Salut"* (international).
- *"Cin-cin"* (Italian).
- *"À vôtre santé"* (French).

You immediately take a small sip from your glass, and the other person (or people) then repeat what you said and take a sip, too. It is the person buying the drinks who ordinarily makes this short toast, but it does not necessarily have to be that person.

WHAT PROMPTS A TOAST?

- Someone is starting a new venture: "Good luck with the new company."
- Congratulations are in order (for getting married, having a baby, being promoted, winning the lottery, losing the desired twenty-five pounds, and the like): "We're very proud of you, Giovanna. This is sensational news. Congratulations!"
- Thanks are in order: "We owe you a big vote of thanks, Jim. You really rallied around. Here's to a great friend of this family."
- A foreign business colleague is your guest: "Henri, it's good to have you here with us—and in such good form, even after having just made the long flight from Paris. I raise a toast to you, to your dear wife, Madeleine, back in France, and to the success of our project!"
- A friend's good news deserves special mention: "Hey, Pete, I just heard your daughter Melanie graduated from law school at the head of her class. She's a real credit to her old man. I raise my glass to Melanie!"
- A guest decides to praise his or her host: "I don't know about the rest of you, but I've just had the best dinner I've had in years. I suggest we toast the person responsible for this culinary splendor. Here's to Mary—thank you, and what night will you invite us again?"
- A great friend raises a joking, teasing toast to the groom-to-be at an engagement party: "Well, Harry, you've finally come into your own. At college you were always a hundred yards behind me. I was always making better grades ["Not true!" jovially interrupts the groom], and I was always much more adept at sports ["Not true!" laughs the groom again], and I was always better liked and much handsomer than you ["Not true!" shouts one of the ushers], but somehow," the toaster continues, "you captured the loveliest, smartest, sexiest, and most sought-after woman in this city. ["True! True!" interrupts the bride.]

Harry," continues the toaster, "I would like to say, old buddy, that you are one lucky guy, but also a very smart one. I drink to my friend, and congratulate you on getting Sally before any of the rest of us did. A toast to the fortunate Harry!"

WHEN DO YOU TOAST?

- When you sit down at the table, don't grab your glass of wine and start drinking it right away—because your hosts may be planning on making an immediate welcoming toast, and you wouldn't want to begin drinking before that. However, if none is forthcoming and you see your host and hostess drinking from their wineglasses, follow suit, because they are obviously not planning on giving an opening salute to their guests.

- In many European countries and often in this country, it is the custom at the beginning of the meal for the host to give a welcoming toast to the guests, usually from a standing position. A formal kind of person might say, "My dear friends, welcome to our house. We are happy to have you around this table, and let us all enjoy each other and this food." An informal kind of person might say, "Georgia, Ruth, Sam, Aggie, and Walter, it's good to see your smiling faces around this table. Welcome, and let's enjoy our dinner!" The sequence is as follows:

  - Host toasts his guests, takes a sip, then sits down.
  - Guests mutter low-voice thanks for the welcome (a phrase such as "Nice to be here") and then raise their glasses seated, in a return gesture of thanks to the host.
  - All present may now drink from their glasses.
  - More toasts may be raised at dessert time, when the host may wish to toast the guest(s) of honor.
  - After the guest of honor has gratefully returned his host's toast, other guests who wish to toast, may now do so. Allow the principals to make the first toasts. It's important not to upstage the host—or a member of his or her family, or a businessperson who wishes to make the first toast to his important business visitor. If the end of the meal is in sight, and no one has done any toasting, you may certainly whisper to your host, "Is it all right if I make a toast now?" Nine times out of ten, your host will be eternally grateful, because he may be frozen when it comes to toasting. On that tenth occasion, your host may whisper back frostily, "I intend to toast her at dessert." (In other words, don't you dare make a toast in front of mine.)

- One of my more celebrated gaffes occurred at the famous New York nightclub El Morocco, on the occasion of Jackie Kennedy and Aristotle Onassis's black tie fifth wedding anniversary dinner. All of the Kennedy clan were there, and they treated it as their own homecoming evening, jovially telling family stories and toasting one another constantly, but never once mentioning the Onassis wedding nor the groom by name. Dinner was almost over, no one had said anything personal about our hosts, and I felt this omission deeply, so I rose to the occasion by signaling the band leader that I wanted to make a toast. The music stopped. I was going to talk about romance and roses, all the stuff that was missing from this evening. The spotlight was on me in the totally darkened room. I could see nothing, but I did hear a voice calling out my name. I stopped talking and turned around, only to find a friend of Jackie's signaling me to say that neither Jackie nor Ari were in the room. Ari was out settling the bill, obviously glad to see this night end, and Jackie was in the ladies' room. I said "Sorry" and went back to my seat. A few of the guests applauded me, feeling for my embarrassment! Moral: Always make sure the object of your toast is present.

- When you are making a toast, say the words with a good volume, well enunciated, so people will stop talking and listen to you. Look straight into the eyes of the object of the toast while you are speaking, and at the end, raise your glass to him or her, nod in a salute, and sip from your glass. The others will now follow suit.

- If you are on the receiving end of the toast, do not raise a glass to yourself when the others have all raised theirs to you. Don't even pick up your glass. Just sit there, smiling appreciatively. If you wish to return the toast to the person who made it or the gathering in general, you can stand up and do it then or later in the meal.

- Practice your toast many times beforehand, if you are subject to attacks of nerves. Don't use notes. Memorize the remarks, and the more you practice (particularly in front of a mirror), the more confident and successful you will be. When you see all those smiling faces gazing up at you, you will actually find yourself having a lot of fun, and perhaps be on your way to becoming a bit of a ham.

- Stand up when you give your toast (unless you are even slightly inebriated, in which case, stay seated). If you remain seated, the other people in the room can't see you, and your voice tends to collapse down into your diaphragm. Besides, it pays more honor to the person you're toasting if you are standing.

- Remember to take small sips. There is a long evening ahead.

- Brevity is key. I have seen more toasts absolutely ruined when the toaster, who knew he had a good thing going, went on and on and on. Two minutes is a perfect toast length. Five minutes is all right if you're witty and well prepared. Most of us can't hold people's attention for that long. When everyone is full of wine, they don't want to have to concentrate listening to someone's long toast; they just want to be entertained.

- Stand up if you're at a big table, even if your toast is only a minute or two in length. People who are seated can't see you when you talk down the table from a sitting position. Besides, it does more honor to the person you're toasting if you stand for him.

- If you're sitting at a table for ten or twelve, and your remarks are very informal, remain seated, but get everyone's attention, you might announce in a voice slightly louder than usual, "I'd like to say something!"

- Be careful of protocol—don't give a toast to the guest of honor before the host does! If there is a champagne glass on the table along with a wineglass, it means that champagne will be served with dessert. It is most likely that the host will rise just after the last glass at the table has been poured and give a toast to the guest of honor or to the special occasion for which the meal has been organized. If you feel like giving a toast to your hosts and it is obvious as dessert draws to a close that your host is not going to raise a toast (nor is anyone else), rise and thank your host for the good dinner with a short toast. It will be appreciated by everyone around the table, I assure you, because they've all been too shy to do it themselves.

- Leave bathroom humor out of your remarks. It does not work in mixed company—and often does not work in company with just your own sex.

- If you know you have a good sense of timing and people laugh easily at your sense of humor, tell one quick joke (or two at the most.)

- Always end on an up note, even if you've been teasing the honoree during your entire toast. People want to be left with a nice feeling, not a possible joke at someone's expense.

- Know when to stop the toasting at your party. This is a responsibility of the host or whoever is in charge (like the master of ceremonies at a banquet or the best man at wedding festivities). This person should be intuitive enough to know when the evening should come to an end. At a certain moment, enough is enough. Long, awkward pauses between toasts are the signal, and instead of waiting for yet another person to jump to her feet, glass in hand, ready to make another toast, the person in charge should say, "All good things must come to an end, such as this dinner [or lunch]. Thank you all very much for coming." This signals the evening is over.

LOVING CARE OF THE WEEKEND HOUSEGUEST

WHOM TO INVITE

- Invite the proper number of guests—not just one person if that person is heavy going, and never too many people for the available space. Houseguests deserve to be comfortable! Experienced hosts know this rule, usually learned through experience.

- Invite only the people you really crave as guests. If you are forced to entertain for business or some other reason, invite any "tough to take" people for lunch on Saturday or Sunday. You can always put up with someone for one meal, but businesspeople you don't know well can be misery-creating houseguests!

- Invite those you really want far ahead of the date. The recipient of your invitation will be flattered and will probably arrange to have a free schedule, too. If you're inviting friends to ski in the mountains, invite them in September for February. If you're inviting them to visit you in Washington during the Cherry Blossom Festival in April, ask them in November.

- Think kindness. You might have a friend who has suffered a blow recently and needs cheering up. You might know someone who has recently moved into your town and really hasn't had the chance to meet people. Introducing that person to congenial company at a weekend house party could be the best thing that will ever happen to him (or them). You might be able to introduce an unmarried friend to another single person she has never met, and be responsible for the start of a new romance—or a lifetime friendship, which is even better.

- Become a master at designing the perfect weekend group. You don't have to have people all of the same ilk and interests. Insert a little spice into the group—perhaps a friend from another country, a stranger in town, a person of entirely different interests from those of your own friends. People are basically nice, want to meet new people, want to be nice to them, and want to get along with them.

On the other hand, if you invite a professional tennis star, there should be someone present who knows about tennis; if you invite someone who loves to dance, there should be others in the group who like to dance also. If your guest of honor only likes to play bridge—constantly—you had better make sure there are three other adamant bridge players around somewhere!

In all my years of spending weekends in many countries, time and time again I have been part of a completely diversified group of strangers who shared no background or interests with one another. In a letter to my mother, written when I was a single woman in my early thirties, I raved about a house party in a big Schloss outside Salzburg. The party consisted of our hosts and their guests: an Austrian ski instructor with the "brain of a pea," as I described him; a very leftish French journalist, who kept baiting me with his anti-Americanism; an incredibly intellectual couple of music professors from the University of Geneva, who gave us all an inferiority complex (he played the cello, she the flute); a painfully shy Indian student from the University of Salzburg; and myself. Yet we had an absolutely splendid time and formed lasting friendships. It was all thanks to our host, the group designer, so to speak, who had assembled a very unlikely combination and *made it work*.

WHEN NOT TO INVITE HOUSEGUESTS

If you are exhausted from the wear and tear of having houseguests every single weekend at your resort place, resolve this year to save at least every other weekend for yourself or you and your family alone. Next year you might plan on having houseguests only once every three weeks. This will immeasurably reduce your exhaustion. A summer or weekend place should, after all, provide you with some rest and relaxation. To anyone who asks to visit you on one of your "private weekends," just say, "Unfortunately, we're busy that weekend." (They don't have to know that you'll be busy with yourselves that weekend!)

GETTING YOURSELF ORGANIZED

To host people with great success—whether it's for a week, weekend, or just overnight—requires deft planning, executed with a talented manager's skill.

One couple who entertain every weekend during the summer months make two plans, one for themselves, to remind them what to do before the guests come, and a second schedule that is drawn up and sent to the guests to help them get organized.

The schedule you make for organizing yourself for the weekend might include:
- Arrival and departure times for each guest, including information on flights, trains, buses, or car services.
- Which room will be assigned to each guest.
- List of guests' known food allergies (such as shellfish—important to know at a seaside place!).
- Full menus for Friday, Saturday, and Sunday.
- Hours for food to be served in-house.
- Logistics on all party activities outside the house, including transportation arrangements.
- Golf course tee-off times and tennis court reservations.
- List of extra athletic equipment on hand to lend guests.
- Church service information for Sunday morning.
- Alternative activities planned in case of rain.
- Number of cars needed to borrow or rent.

The schedule you send to the guests might include:
- The approximate hour at which they are expected on Friday evening and the hour at which they are expected to leave at the end of the weekend.
- A map of how to get to your house.

- A list of—and a brief, amusing description of—the others who have been invited (even if it's just one person).
- A list of the times and places for all athletic and social events, meals, and free-time periods for shopping and sightseeing opportunities.
- The athletic equipment required ("Better bring your own clubs"; "Bring some tennis balls"; "Don't forget your boat shoes").
- A list of the clothes they will need ("You'll need whites for our tennis club"; "Men will need sports jackets but no ties"; "Bring a raincoat or a light topcoat"; "It's cool up here in the mountains, so bring sweaters").

PREPARING THE HOUSE

I once asked the late Gloria Guinness, renowned for her beauty and her considerable talents as a hostess, what she considered the rule of success for having houseguests. "Very simple," she replied. "Sleep in your guest room before any guest does who is too polite to tell you what's wrong."

I've always remembered that—and remembered all the times I've been someone's houseguest and there was no trash basket anywhere, or the bed table light didn't work, or there were holes in the screens and the mosquitoes sailed in at night to hold a regatta over my bed.

You will hear other houseguests complain—out of earshot of their hosts, of course—about there being no vestige of even a corner of a bureau drawer in which to put clothes, or a free hanger in the closet on which to hang a dress or suit. The litany of hosting mistakes includes forgetting to leave soap in the bathroom, insufficient towels and face cloths, lack of a warm blanket or a quilt for the bed when it's cold, and a mattress so full of lumps it's guaranteed to make its occupant unable to sleep.

Welcome Additions to the Guest Room

A good host not only checks out the comfort of the bed and bedding but also makes sure there is:
- A meticulously clean and sweet-smelling room.
- An electric fan or air conditioner available in the guest room on an incredibly hot night, or an electric heater on an incredibly cold night.
- Something interesting to read—books and magazines—on the bedside table.
- Something delicious to munch on in the room (cookies, candies, fresh fruit) in case the guest becomes hungry.
- Strong lightbulbs in the reading lamps.
- A clock that works.

- A radio or television.
- Pencil, pen, and a writing tablet—even stationery for a last-minute letter that needs to be written (plus a few stamps!).
  - A thermos of water and a glass.
  - A small vase of fresh flowers.

Welcome Additions to the Guest Bathroom

- An extra roll of toilet paper.
- A box of paper tissues.
- A shower cap.
- A sponge and detergent so the thoughtful guest can clean the tub after use.
- Insect repellent for summertime use.
- Air freshener.

These items would also be gratefully acknowledged by guests:

- A fresh razor and blades, in case these were forgotten.
- New toothbrush and toothpaste, in case either was forgotten.
- Shampoo and hair conditioner.
- Clean comb and brush (often forgotten).
- Hair dryer.
- Hair spray.
- Deodorant.
- Adhesive bandages.
- Aspirin or analgesic.
- Mouthwash.
- Hand lotion.
- Sun block.

How to Organize the Sleeping Quarters

- Usually the oldest person in the group gets the best room or bed. (Or, if you have a guest who is frail, he merits the most comfortable quarters.)
- High school students or younger can make do with individual sleeping bags, if necessary, for a weekend.
- If you have parents or a parent with a young child, put them the farthest away from the other guests because of the inevitable noise. Borrow a cot for a young child who's out of a crib; don't make her sleep in a parent's bed. (If you have an infant accompanying a parent, borrow a crib and linens from a friend or neighbor.)
- Don't expect two tall or husky people to fit into a twin bed, no matter

how much passion the two may generate together. In fact, two large people can't even fit comfortably into a regular double bed. If you don't have enough single or queen-sized beds, invite fewer houseguests (or else invite only very small people!).

• Before the weekend, ask your two houseguests who have been dating each other if they want to share a room or not. If one of them shows any hesitation, put them in separate rooms!

If you feel it is morally wrong to have two unmarried people sharing the same room in your house, put them in separate rooms but tell them beforehand—"We are putting you in separate rooms." The unmarried couple should understand. Your house is your house, and guests should conform to *your* standards and rules, not theirs.

HOW TO PLAN THE FOOD

Give your guests the kind of food that you like yourself, and they'll be happy. As a host, you should not have to spend all your time preparing complicated dishes to feed everyone. In this world of takeout food and frozen gourmet meals, there is no need to spend long hours toiling over the kitchen stove.

If you have planned and prepared your menus and then a houseguest arrives with food and wine, expecting to see you serve it that very evening or at some point during the weekend, don't be ashamed to say no. Explain to the guest that you are absolutely delighted with such a delicious present, but, because all of the food (or wine) has been planned for this weekend, you will freeze (or save) his wonderful gift for a very special occasion in the future.

Here are the menus prepared by a talented cook for her six houseguests during a weekend on Cape Cod. She prepared most of the food before her guests walked in the door, so she was able to be with them, not in the kitchen, most of the time.

• Friday night dinner: boiled lobster, coleslaw, garlic brown bread, lemon sherbet and brownies, white wine and coffee.

• Saturday breakfast: choice of three cereals, fresh fruit, bacon, eggs, English or bran muffins, coffee, tea, or milk.

• Saturday lunch: hamburgers or hot dogs at the beach concession stand.

• Saturday dinner: Barbecued marinated steaks, mixed green salad, a casserole of chopped spinach, artichoke hearts, and sour cream, fresh fruit compote, macaroons, red wine and coffee.

• Sunday breakfast: Melon, fruit juices, the hostess's renowned waffles with strawberry jam or maple syrup, coffee or milk.

• Sunday lunch: Beach picnic (or, if it is raining, a living room floor picnic) of roast tarragon chicken, a cold pasta with vegetables, whole wheat rolls, fresh raspberries with crème fraîche, wine, beer, and coffee.

This hostess always plans her food a week ahead and markets, cooks, and freezes in bits and snatches during the week before her guests arrive so that she does not have to spend long periods of time preparing the meals. No gourmet restaurant could do it better.

I know other hosts with weekend retreats who bring everything with them from the city in hampers and cold storage bags. They don't spend much time in the kitchen either. One such host remarked, "I have everything so organized ahead of time that my major job in getting a meal on the table is opening the bottle of salad dressing and pouring it on the prewashed salad ingredients."

NECESSARY ATTRIBUTES
IN AN ACCOMPLISHED WEEKEND HOST

• A love of one's fellow men and women. Let's face it, you really have to love people to put up with them as houseguests. Seeing friends for lunch or an occasional dinner party is nothing like having them totally dependent upon you for room, board, and emotional sustenance hour in and hour out. This is when the mirror cracks. But if you love people—if you are a caring, wonderful host— this is your moment to shine. Nothing gives your friends greater pleasure and nothing relaxes them or cheers them up more than a wonderful weekend at your home. They will remember your many kindnesses forever, and you will go to the top of their list of "people we love."

• An intuitive expertise in the science of group mixing, which includes dealing with infighting, as when one houseguest accuses another of cheating on the tennis court . . . another guest tries to bed down someone else's spouse . . . or a guest drinks too much and becomes verbally abusive. Developments of this kind call for a weekend host sometimes to serve as a counselor, referee, discipliner, or grown-up nursery school teacher!

• Patience. The host needs an unlimited supply to deal with moments such as when a guest borrows the host's desperately needed car and disappears for hours . . . or uses up the whole household's supply of hot water with an endlessly long bath . . . or breaks the host's favorite $400 Steuben highball glass by letting it fall off the porch railing . . . or announces, as the group is leaving for the dinner dance, that he is so badly sunburned that he wants to go to the hospital's emergency room instead of the country club.

• Creative talent, so that when things go awry, a substitute plan as good as, if not better than, the original one can be put into execution. (For example, the snow's not good enough for skiing, so the host arranges a hike to a nearby aviary and wildlife center with a forest ranger scientist guide.)

• A large supply of elbow grease. Guests require a lot of work, if you count the number of sheets and towels you have to wash; the number of salad greens you have to buy, wash, and chop (perhaps from your garden); the cases of beer, wine, and soda you have to lug from the store to your kitchen; and the energy (and false smiles) you have to summon when your sixth houseguest finally gets up and wants breakfast at the sixth separate time that morning.

THE HOUSEGUEST WHO IS ALWAYS INVITED BACK

Here are some basic tips on how to be the kind of houseguest who receives repeat invitations:

• Have a positive attitude from start to finish. Be determined that nothing—the poor quality of the weather, the other houseguests, your host's children, the discomfort of the bed assigned you, or planned activities that go amiss—will affect your cheerfulness and enthusiastic participation. I have seen more than one "up" houseguest who laughed at everything that went wrong and made the others laugh, too, and who was invariably enthusiastic about anything the host suggested.

• If you're not feeling well, cancel out beforehand. If you should arrive, for example, with a strep throat, half the household will be miserable worrying over you, and the other half will be worrying, quite logically, that they will catch your germs. If you come down with a bug during your stay, don't say anything about it, but stay away from close contact with anyone else. Suffer through the weekend gamely and courageously. Like everything else, there are exceptions. If you think you have come down with something very contagious, like chicken pox or measles, do say something about it and go home at once.

• Don't ask to bring your children or your pet—and certainly don't show up with them as a surprise! Children should be expressly invited by the host (not subtly suggested by the guest), and about the only kind of unannounced pet you can bring that won't upset your host is a goldfish in its own small bowl.

• Arrive when you say you will—not before, not after—and leave when you're supposed to. This rule of good conduct means that, even if your flight home is canceled or your car breaks down as you leave the driveway, you do not burden your hosts with it. You simply find a solution by yourself.

• If you don't have presentable luggage, borrow some for the weekend. It's a real downer for your hosts to see you arrive with all your possessions in plastic shopping bags. They won't want their neighbors to see you!

• Bring the proper clothing. If you don't know what to bring, if you don't know what's scheduled, or if you're not familiar with the climate in the place where your host lives, ask some detailed questions before you pack. Don't expect your hosts to provide extra sweaters or rain gear. Provide your own. Bring your own athletic gear, too, whether it's ice skates and skis or tennis racket and balls. If there is a Saturday night party somewhere, find out how to dress for it. And if you have to share a bathroom "down the hall" with other guests, pack a bathrobe.

• Have your own agenda, in case your hosts are busy with chores and don't want you helping them. In other words, bring a good book! Do not bring your cell phone or portable computer. You are supposed to be having a relaxing or athletic couple of days.

• Offer to pitch in and help with everything, whether it's fetching someone at the station or picking up extra ice for the cocktail party, arranging flowers or making hors d'oeuvres, taking great-grandmother for a drive or watering the parched lawn. The dishwasher might need emptying and the table might require setting for the next meal. Your host's child might need an hour of baby-sitting so your host can run some errands. Just offer to do anything. But if told a firm "No," take your hostess at her word. Many host couples prefer to do all the chores themselves, so that things are done properly and on time. A guest offering to help is sometimes more of a hindrance than a help. (However, guests who offer to do nothing will usually head that host's "Do not Invite" list for the future.)

• Accept your host's schedule with a smile. Be a joiner and a good team member for the weekend. At the same time, if your hosts are the kind who like their guests to organize their own activities, be a creative self-starter. Don't keep asking, "What should we do now?" Beat yourself at solitaire, or try your hand at a jigsaw or crossword puzzle. Bring some good books with you, or take long walks by yourself and commune with nature. (If it's a book-reading weekend, here's a tip: Bring along your own 100-watt lightbulb for your room, because guest rooms are famous dangerously low-wattage places!)

• Be neat in your room. Keep it tidy and picked up all the time, so that your hosts will enjoy walking past it instead of feeling the need to hire a professional cleaning squad after your departure. Make your bed first thing (yes, that includes the bedspread). Keep your towels on the bathroom racks, not on the floor, and your toothpaste in the tube instead of all over the basin. Keep your makeup or shaving paraphernalia in a neat pile, so that other guests or family members using the bathroom will have room to stow their things, too.

• Be on time. The entire group appreciates any member who is punctual and mindful of the schedule to be followed. It's important not to sabotage the logistics of moving people from one place to another, which is the task with which your house party hosts must cope.

• Don't do business during the weekend even if it was a business associate and his spouse who invited you. Show that you have a sense of humor and that you're not a business bore but an imaginative, "up" person to have around.

• Don't try to discipline your host's children, even if such action is warranted. Grin and bear it. You will soon return home to a childless household again, or to your own home with your relatively well-behaved children.

• Don't complain, even when there's just cause. If the ski lifts are so crowded that you can't get on them . . . if the motorboat has no gasoline, so you can't use it . . . if the tennis courts are so soggy that all tennis for the weekend is canceled . . . if the ice never arrives for your host's cocktail party, speak not— just help out. Keep smiling and joking, and say it doesn't matter. You'll be able to talk yourself and everyone else around you into believing that it really doesn't matter.

A HOUSEGUEST WITH A PRESENT IS MORE WELCOME THAN ONE WITHOUT

The better you know your host, the more sensitive you probably are to his desires and needs in relation to household presents. I know houseguests who:

• Brought an inexpensive camera and several rolls of film to grateful hosts who didn't have a camera but could really use one.

• Brought homemade frozen casseroles to their grateful hosts, parents of children whose mouths were constantly open, like baby birds waiting in the nest for food.

• Brought bottles of wine to grateful hosts who drink wine with every dinner. The wine was a better quality than their hosts could afford, and it was given with the admonition, "This is only to be enjoyed by you two, not consumed by your houseguests!"

• Stocked the lakeside cabin of their grateful hosts with a new set of family games every time they visited, because it inevitably rains and they knew how often those new games would be used.

• Always brought some new outdoor sports equipment—a badminton set, a croquet set, or a volleyball and volleyball net—enabling the family and guests to play games together all weekend.

• Could be counted on each year to bring a bagful of movie tapes (with accompanying boxes of popcorn) to keep everyone happy if it rains.

• Brought all the latest magazines to leave behind for their hosts' enjoyment.

• Stocked their hosts' pantry with difficult-to-find gourmet goodies to enjoy in the future—such as a basket of fresh fruit, gourmet pâtés and crackers, ice-cream sauces in jars, and tins of special puddings, cookies, and cakes.

The host makes the weekend by having the kindness to invite and prepare for the guest—but the guest really makes the weekend by showing her enjoyment of it. It's a mutually pleasant operation!

NOT TO FORGET: THE THANK-YOU LETTER

As a houseguest, you may have brought a present with you, or you may have sent it afterward, but neither the generosity of your gift nor the enthusiasm of your thank-you telephone call nor your e-mail lets you off the hook. *A written thank-you on good stationery is obligatory* in the world of manners.

When you stop to think of all the trouble, caring, and expense your host went to, to go on record with your thanks seems a small enough labor. A well-written letter of thanks brings a smile to your host's face, is passed around to his family, is read and reread, and if it's a really beautiful letter, it's saved. Who knows, it may turn up someday in a collection of twenty-first-century letters if a publisher could ever find enough good letters from our era to fill a book (which is doubtful at this point in time).

The structure of a nice thank-you letter from a houseguest to the host is as follows:

• The guest writes on behalf of herself and her spouse (or accompanying children) and addresses it to the wife of the family but makes it clear the letter is meant for both husband and wife. ("Dear Joan, George and I had the most magical time with you and Allen this past weekend . . .")

• The first paragraph should elaborate on what a great time the visitors had. ("We were both work-weary and you managed to give us a wonderful rest, but also a tremendous amount of fun. It was the best kind of therapy for your bedraggled stressed out city friends . . .")

• The second paragraph would discuss how nice the house is—or the lake or mountain or farm vista, or whatever the place has to offer. ("Each morning I looked from my bed out across that luxurious rolling green lawn to the flower beds and concluded that my hosts are living in a paradise, not just the country . . .")

• The third paragraph should mention what fun you had participating in the various activities. ("I will never forget our doubles game. Even though George and I almost got a divorce in the middle of the first set, we finally had to agree on something—that you two are far superior players, and that you were charitable even to play with the likes of us . . . The Sunday picnic was memorable. I'm going to spread blue cheese salad dressing on my sandwiches from now on. You managed to feed us a feast with such seeming effortlessness! We are in total admiration . . .")

• The fourth paragraph might comment on the other guests, if there were any, or on the host's children. ("We really enjoyed meeting the Abells—

stimulating, amusing, and nice at the same time. And of course, the biggest treat was seeing how Jessie has grown into such a lovely young lady. You must be very proud of your daughter. She interacts with the adults with such ease.")

• Then restate your appreciation and sign off. Be sure to thank both hosts equally. (A friend of mine recounted how often her new husband's friends would visit them in Gulfstream, Florida, and write him a thank-you note without even mentioning her name—after she had done all the work!)

REMEMBER THIS ABOUT THE ENTIRE SUBJECT OF ENTERTAINING

If it is a lot of work to have someone over—whether it's for a sixty-hour weekend, a three-hour dinner party, or a sixty-minute drink—it is also one of the most rewarding of activities. The amount of pleasure you give by extending the warmth of your hospitality to others is immeasurable. But it's also an investment. You get back all that pleasure you gave, with interest, by realizing what you have contributed to other people. Entertaining is the way to make friendships grow deeper, the route to newly acquired friendships, and the most effective way of adding to your own personal growth.

Have you ever noticed how a good host is basically a very happy person?

THE MOST PRESTIGIOUS INVITATION OF THEM ALL: DINNER AT THE WHITE HOUSE

You may never receive one, but it's certainly fun to dream about. What if you were to receive an invitation to a state dinner at the White House? Just what happens at an affair like that?

If you are lucky enough to receive one of those beautiful engraved invitations, handwritten in calligraphy, with the presidential seal embossed in gold at the top, be prepared to do your company—and yourself—proud with your self-confidence and knowledge of how to proceed.

1. Reply at once and, of course, affirmatively. It's a command invitation. The only reason for regretting is if you are ill or getting married that day.
2. If it's for lunch or a cocktail reception, dress in your very best business attire. If it's a black tie event, gentlemen wear tuxedos (rent the full regalia if you don't own one) and ladies wear an evening dress (a full-length, a ¾ length, or a very dressy one to the knee). No micro-minis. (If your legs are great, everyone will realize it during the course of the

evening without your having to hike up your skirt!) It's also the one time in your life when you'd feel more comfortable in an evening gown than in a dressy pant suit. Be sure your accessories for a dinner are evening ones. No big leather handbags for ladies, nor chunky shoes. (Think "restrained" rather than gaudy!) Men should realize that their black tie should be just that—a conservative black tie—and not a wild red plaid one with matching cummerbund. They should also take note that their regular black business dress shoes, the kind they wear to the office, are not White House–appropriate. (You need black patent oxfords with laces or slip-ons, worn with black silk hosiery. These also can be rented.)

3. You will be told in the invitation what to do on party night with your car (it's much easier to come by taxi, unless you're limo-spoiled). In order to get through the gate at 1600 Pennsylvania Avenue, you will also have to present more than one official piece of documentation, such as your driver's license and passport, for security and identification purposes.

4. When you arrive *on time* at the appropriate gate (East, North, or South), you will be ushered into the mansion to the coat check area (by the way, don't tip *anyone* during the evening). Then you will be ushered by the military social aides up a large marble staircase to the main floor. Women with sweeping skirts should practice beforehand picking up their skirts so as not to trip when ascending the stairway. If you are disabled, a footman will take you upstairs in the President's private elevator, which is always a treat. (Since I have divulged this piece of information, do not pretend to be disabled just to get a peek!)

5. You will be offered a glass of wine or champagne in the East Room where all the guests mill around, waiting for the President and First Lady to arrive. The beautiful music made by the scarlet-coated Marine musicians out in the hall will inspire you. If you or your spouse have rank (a cabinet officer, ambassador, member of Congress, a member of the official party from the country of the guest of honor, a high-ranking military officer), you will be lined up according to rank and then pass through the receiving line after the President, First Lady, and their official guests have entered the room and gathered in line to the sound of "Ruffles and Flourishes," the President's own song. There may be a flash of military parading, with the "posting of the colors" by four men representing the armed services as the flag is raised in the state dining room ahead. (If this is a dinner in honor of a head of state, that nation's flag will be posted as well.)

The guests go through the receiving line *quickly* (no time for idle chatter), and then through the awe-inspiring Green, Blue, and Red Rooms and on into the State Dining Room.

6. You will have been given your table number when you checked in earlier, so you look at the numbers on the stanchions to find yourself at the proper round table for eight or ten, with little gold painted ballroom chairs. The tablecloth might be anything from a heavy, jewel-toned damask to a light white organdy, embroidered with field flowers. Your name place card will tell you where to sit. You'll find a menu at your place as well, also done in calligraphy, with the gold-embossed presidential seal on top, listing the different courses and accompanying wines. (No photo-taking is allowed inside the White House, of course, so take your place card and menu home with you after dinner—they are the best possible souvenirs of an evening of history.) There will be a beautiful arrangement of flowers in the center of the table, never so large as to obstruct your views of the dining room and the people in it. There will probably be many candles lit, and the fragrance of perfume and flowers will be noticeable everywhere. The climax of the dinner is not only the marvelous food but also the toasts given by the President to the visiting head of state, and the latter's response toast to the President. This is always very stirring, often greeted by a few emotional tears among the guests.

7. After dinner, the guests mingle with their demitasses in the great hall and all of the public reception rooms, while the Marine Orchestra plays superbly once again. Then follows a special half hour performance in the East Room of anything from poetry readings to jazz, from comedy routines to ballet, and from opera to an excerpt from a Broadway hit show. You are sitting once again on the little gold ballroom chairs.

Most likely you will not be able to say good night personally to the President and First Lady when everything breaks up at about eleven or shortly thereafter. They slip upstairs unnoticed, after saying good-bye to their heads of state visitors. Everyone will have had a long, long day of meetings, negotiations, and pomp and circumstance. You will be able to return home, boasting that you had a magical meal, "Dining with the President of the United States and the First Lady in their own home!" *Lucky you.*

CHAPTER 16

Gifts That Show You Care

Gift giving requires thought, sensitivity, and a sense of humor.

There's a little bit of the child in all of us that makes us love receiving presents all through our lives. It's a delight when someone puts a gaily wrapped box into our hands. There's the anticipation of untying the bow, then removing the ribbon, and finally opening each end of the festive paper to take a peek. Even the very rich who claim to be blasé about gifts, who will yawn and say, "There's nothing, after all, I really need, and there's nothing I really want," confess to feeling at least a twinge of excitement when they see a box they know is for them lying on the table or under the tree.

In a way, it's too bad that gift giving for holidays, special occasions, and joyful celebration has become such a big business. We have become so materialistic, particularly the children, that "the spirit of giving" is often eclipsed by the philosophy of greed.

Gifts for business reasons are very important, but sensitive too. They must be appropriate and without a tinge of bribery.

WHEN YOU SEND FLOWERS

Flowers are a joy to receive at any time of the year. Some people prefer florists' arrangements already firmly anchored in a bowl, to which the recipient need add only a little water. Others much prefer receiving a gift of cut flowers—even six long-stemmed roses will do—that they then arrange in their own handsome container.

• You send flowers or a plant—preferably a plant—to someone who is ill in the hospital, but it is preferable to send them later to the patient's home, when he has returned and is recuperating.

• Flowers or a plant are a nice way to say thank you for a meal. It is preferable to send them the afternoon before the dinner, so they can be used for the festivities; otherwise, send them the day after to say "thank you for the dinner." While it is an international custom for guests to show up at the door the night of the dinner with a gift of cut flowers, this frequently throws the host into a panic of unwelcome extra work—trying to find a vase for them and putting them in just the right place while greeting guests and getting the dinner into shape.

- Flowers are a great way to say congratulations—for graduating, getting engaged, having a baby, being promoted, winning a tournament, doing well in a TV game show, sticking to a diet, successfully stopping smoking, and being elected to do a tough job for a nonprofit organization. I heard of a charming person—a man who won a state lottery and then sent enormous floral bouquets to all of his friends, with a card saying "I won, so I can now afford to send you these much more than you can to send them to me."

- They are a traditional way to recognize a pertinent holiday—such as Mother's Day, Valentine's Day, a birthday or wedding anniversary, and Christmas, Hanukkah, Easter, and Passover.

- They say "Cheer up!" when someone has been having a tough time and could use a little sunshine in her life.

- They are an ideal way to say "I'm sorry" (don't forget the note) after you have offended someone, intentionally or not.

- They are a wonderful way to welcome someone into a new house or apartment.

- They say a warm "Welcome home" to someone who has been away on a trip or otherwise absent for a prolonged period of time.

WHEN A WEDDING IS IN THE OFFING

How Many Showers Are Too Many?

Weddings can be prohibitively expensive for young friends of the couple, particularly when they are just starting their careers and are suddenly confronted with presents to buy for several friends who are marrying all at the same time. The wedding attendants feel particularly hard hit by the financial obligations. Therefore, two showers are *enough*, one a lingerie or kitchen shower for the bride, for example, and the other a coed evening cocktail party "bar shower." If the bride's mother's friends want to give her a shower, just among themselves, that is fine, because they can afford it!

Brides should remember that the more shower gifts are demanded from their friends, the more "watered down" the main gift becomes. (See the suggestions in that category for wedding presents, page 362.)

BAR SHOWER

Glasses make great gifts. Friends can band together and give a joint gift of a dozen of one kind or another. Individuals can buy two glasses of any kind and give them as a bar shower gift. Bar glasses don't have to match anymore:

- All-purpose wineglasses.
- Beer mugs or pilsner glasses.
- Aperitif glasses.
- Highball glasses.
- Stemmed martini glasses, martini pitcher, long stirring spoon.
- Old-fashioned glasses.

Other bar shower gifts:

- Cocktail shaker.
- Wine bottle opener.
- Bar knife.
- Can opener–bottle cap remover.
- Small cutting board and sharp knife.
- Peeler for lemons, oranges, and limes (to make "zests").
- Wine bottle storage rack.
- Bar towels.
- Small electric blender.
- Wine bottle decorative corks.
- Ice bucket and tongs.

Lingerie Showers for the Bride

The most important thing to remember about this kind of shower, usually given in a home by one of the bride's women friends for women only, is that the hostess must know the bride's exact size for the various kinds of lingerie and communicate that to the guests while organizing the shower. (After all, some women are bigger on the top than on the bottom, and vice versa, so knowing that the bride takes a "Medium" slip will not help you when you are buying bras or panties for her.)

Many of the items in the list of suggestions below are very expensive. It is logical for two or more friends to band together to give a joint gift if the item is expensive.

- Nightgown and matching peignoir.
- Flannel nightgown.
- Bras.
- Pantyhose.

- Silk camisole top and pants set.
- Lacy garter belt.
- Winter or summer bathrobe.
- Panties.
- Lingerie cases.
- Full-length slips.
- Half-slips.
- Winter or summer bedroom slippers.
- "Racy" patterned stockings.
- Summer bathrobe.
- Teddies.

At the end of a lingerie shower the groom often makes an appearance, goes over the presents to accompanying laughter, and is even surprised with a boudoir gift of his own, like a playboy kind of pajamas (usually arranged for by the hostess of the shower.)

WEDDING PRESENTS

The bride and groom are really fortunate if they:
- Have registered in the bridal registry at either a local store or a store with branches all over the country that is listed on the Internet. In this way, they will receive something they need and in their taste.
- Inherit wonderful antiques and bibelots from relatives (one-of-a-kind objects, either valuable or valued for their sentiment and family history).
- Are given checks (for which there are many uses!).

Someone on a tight budget who is giving a wedding gift should:
- Band together with two, three, or more people who are in the same bind, so that the joint present will be a nice one.
- Haunt everything from an auction house to a tag sale, to pick up some small memento that is attractive, unique, and inexpensive.

A first-time bride and her groom need:
- Furniture.
- Bedding—mattress pads, sheets and pillowcases, blankets, electric blanket or quilt, blanket covers, bedspread, dust ruffles, pillow shams.
- Bathroom paraphernalia—towels, washcloths, bath mats, bath rugs, wastebaskets, towel racks, storage cabinets, matching accessories.
- China, glassware, and flatware for dining and entertaining.
- Table linens—place mats or cloths to fit the table, and napkins.
- Barware (see Bar Shower, page 542).

- Lamps (she can never receive too many of these as gifts).
- Wastebaskets for living room, den, and bedrooms.
- Decorative accessories.
- Vases, cachepots, and other flower containers.
- Storage containers.
- Cleaning equipment—vacuum cleaner, carpet sweeper, mop, broom, pail, or whatever.
- For their kitchen (to give as shower or wedding presents), almost anything you can think of—from a really substantial gift like a microwave oven or food processor to small accessories that every cook needs, and that you can find in profusion in the kitchenwares section of all good department stores. If you buy assorted small accessories you can tie them together with ribbon, plunge them into a small pitcher or pot, shape wrapping paper or foil around the pitcher or pot, allowing the utensils to stick out of the top, and tie ribbon streamers around the container.
- For their china, silver, and glass gifts, you may follow their dictates in the various bridal registries, or if they have not registered, review the china, silver, and glassware needed for an average meal and purchase what you can afford in any of the categories. It is wise to ask their parents—or the bridal couple themselves—what they really want and need. Today, young couples are not shy about letting you know!

Other things that newlyweds might need or appreciate include:
- Delivery of the morning or evening newspaper for a year.
- Their choice of a subscription to a decorating or a travel magazine to start as of their wedding date.
- A monogram die from a stationer's for the bride to order her new stationery. (The gift of the monogram die and a box or two of engraved or printed stationery is very welcome.)
- Gift certificates to everything from a gourmet food shop to a sporting goods store.
- A clock for their mantel or bookshelf.
- A gift certificate to a good print shop (rather than selecting a print itself, as your taste probably won't be theirs).
- Gift certificate to a lamp store.

Gifts for a Couple Who Marry
After Living Together a Long Time

A couple who have lived together for a year or more will often already possess many of the basics, such as common cooking equipment. However, they often do not have a full complement of pretty, nonutilitarian possessions. Ask them what would please them most (if they are not already registered in a store). They may, for example, have all the frying pans they need but no beautiful sheets and pillowcases. They probably have a trash pail, but no good-looking wastebaskets. They probably have an odd assortment of wine-glasses, but not one full set of good ones. If you've been in their home before the wedding date, all you have to do is look around to discover something that they need.

Gifts for the Second-, Third-,
or Fourth-Time Bride or Groom

It doesn't matter how many times a family member or a good friend marries. It doesn't matter how much money you figure you have expended on someone's wedding gifts over the years. It doesn't matter whether or not you are invited to the latest wedding. What does matter is that you show you are a friend and supporter and that you wish this person all the happiness in the world. Instead of being cynical, take a positive attitude. *This* marriage is going to work!

The oft-married bride is going to have the basics in her household, so you don't have to worry about buying her sheets or knives and forks. In all probability, she is well supplied (though a divorced man is probably in poor shape in regards to practical accessories). Give a new bride a little bibelot or a small gift you find in your general wanderings through stores. For example, you might come across:

- An attractive pair of bookends.
- A pretty telephone book slipcover.
- A pair of unique-looking salad servers.
- A picture frame (for their new wedding photo).
- A pillow with the saying: "Someone absolutely *adores* you."
- A set of bar glasses (as these items are always broken over the years and a new bride needs some matched sets).
- A set of dessert plates (because the same applies as above).
- A pair of giant coffee mugs for their breakfasts.
- A new coffeemaker (because the old one is probably battered).
- A music box that plays "That's What Friends Are For."

THE BRIDE'S DILEMMA:
TO RETURN OR NOT TO RETURN GIFTS

• A bridal couple who receive an ugly eyesore of a gift from a family member or a very close friend should not return it. A family member's gift should be received with enthusiasm and delight—even if you find it grotesque. It is far better to put up with a monstrosity than to hurt someone's feelings, especially when that someone means a lot to you. Put the monstrosity in the closet or garage, and take it out for display every time the donor comes for drinks or dinner. After a year, you won't even have to do that anymore.

Also, remember that decorative objects go in and out of fashion. How I would love now to have so many of the things my grandmother tried to give me. I felt they were hideous and fended them off, but pieces of Victoriana and *la Belle Epoque* would now be considered so chic—and are worth so much! So save the inherited eyesore. It might come back into vogue.

• A bride who has received three identical presents (water pitchers, for example) should return two of them and get something else she likes in return. Her friends do not have to know about the duplicates.

PRESENTS FOR THE HOLIDAYS

ORGANIZING THE LIST

It is a very good idea to list all of the gifts you have given—and received—each year (on your computer) so that you can update the list annually and review the record to remind you how to organize this year's gift list. Purge the list of names and addresses of people to whom it is not necessary to give a gift this year. Update all the addresses, name changes, and marital status of your married or now divorced friends, as well as remarried and deceased ones! Many people organize their holiday gift lists into these categories:

• Family.
• Close friends.
• Business associates (including assistants).
• Apartment building staff.
• People who make life worth living (including any of these: physician, housekeeper, baby-sitter, hairdresser, masseur, gym instructor, building superintendent, newspaper delivery person, and the like).

Just because you gave a gift to someone last year does not mean that you must do the same thing this year. Gift giving should never become a meaningless habit; it should be a sign of special remembrance or a way of saying thank you for something very special done for you. Perhaps you want to cheer up someone who has had a tough year. Next year, if things are better for that person, you won't have to send a gift.

Just because someone gives you a present does *not* mean that you must give one in return. Someone may give you a present to say thank you for any number of reasons, and you do not have to return that gesture. Simply write a warm thank-you note.

Baking and Making Your Own Gifts

If you don't have the money to buy gifts this year, don't borrow money or go into debt. Your family and friends will understand. For years one of our favorite Christmas presents in New York came from a friend who was eternally broke and in financial difficulties. Each Christmas morning at eight she would arrive on her bicycle to drop off one of her warm, freshly baked loaves of bread, wrapped in silver foil and tied with ribbon. She did this for all her friends in our area. It was a wonderful present, and now that we have moved away from New York, our family still misses it very much at the Christmas morning breakfast table.

I know other people who are creative and have written poems or done original sketches on a blank card as their Christmas presents for their friends. One friend, an unpublished writer who is always without funds, gives a long, brisk walk to the dogs of her friends who live in the neighborhood during the busy two-week Christmas season. It is considered a first-rate gift by the dog owners.

Never be ashamed not to be able to afford a gift. Buy a Christmas card or write a letter to friends in which you say you wish you could send them a gift, but this year it is not possible—but send them the gift of love and admiration and warm wishes for their good health and happiness. Isn't that what Christmas is all about anyway?

Organizing Your Own Family's Christmas Day

Here are some tips on bringing order out of chaos on Christmas Day (or on Christmas Eve), when the presents will be opened:

• If you were really forward looking, you would have bought a large quantity of Christmas wrap the preceding January, when stores dramatically slashed the prices of this normally expensive item.

• Gather the gifts you have bought, the gifts from family members to one another, and presents that have arrived from the outside, and place the items for each member of the family in a large, fresh plastic bag (did anyone say "garbage"?), with a name tag attached to the enclosure. Then the bag can be emptied by each person in a special spot for that person by the tree—or wherever the gift-opening will take place. As each gift is opened, the wrapping can be stashed back into the plastic bag. (Don't throw out these garbage bags for a couple of days, in case a gift card or an address or even a gift is missing.)

• Give each person a little notebook and pencil, to write down who gave him what as each package is opened. This will facilitate written thank-you's later. The lists of gifts for the little ones, of course, must be handled by an adult, or even better, by an older sibling who writes well; it's good practice for his social education, to realize the importance of the *thank you.*

Presents to and from One Another in a Very Large Family

Large families (five children or more) usually find that, as children grow well into their teens, the business of buying gifts for one another becomes a giant logistical as well as financial puzzle. The problem is compounded when the children of that family marry and have children of their own but still gather for the family Christmas.

One solution that many have found viable is having the children—in the summer, when they are all together for some occasion—draw the name of a sibling or a cousin from a hat. That person will give a handsome present to the person whose name he drew, and if that sibling is married, he takes care of the spouse's and their children's presents, too. He is not expected to give anyone else in the family a holiday gift.

THANK-YOU'S FOR HOLIDAY GIFTS

Yes, every gift definitely should be acknowledged in writing—not just an e-mail, a telephone call or thanks said in a chance meeting on the street, but a bona fide note, written in your own hand, or typed on a word processor of same kind. *Gifts should be acknowledged on the record,* not just casually mentioned in a telephone call. The thank-you note should be written no later than two weeks after receipt of the gift. If parents spent more time helping their young children write their thank-you notes to Grandma and Aunt Sally for their Christmas presents, the children would grow up into adulthood writing these letters automatically. There would also be many happier Grandmas and Aunt Sallys than there are today. (So many today become apoplectic with anger at nieces, nephews, and grandchildren who never say thank you for the Christmas and birthday presents their relatives labored long to select, wrap, and mail!)

Here's a Christmas thank-you a friend of mine received from her wonderfully polite little grandson:

Dear Gramma,
    You are rely nice to sen me the red truk. It goes fast and krashes rely wham. I lov you Gramma. You sur no yur truks.

That grandmother has showed that thank-you letter to everyone from the postman to the manicurist, and it became dog-eared from being read and reread. She will save it among her treasures forever.

You don't have to write a thank-you note to a member of your immediate family, but it's a lovely gesture if you do. It bonds you strongly together, even if this person lives in the bedroom next to yours. The written word lasts forever.

BUSINESS HOLIDAY GIFTS

Some heads of corporations and large professional firms don't care about the gifts they give—and it really shows. On the other hand, there are many chiefs of industry, finance, and the professions who care a great deal about showing their appreciation at the holidays to all their associates and hardworking employees.

The way in which a business gift is given is as important as the gift itself. When an executive has his executive assistant pick out a gift and mail it, with just a business card attached to identify the donor, the present is cold and impersonal. When the executive selects a gift he *knows* will hit the spot with the recipient, and then has it wrapped beautifully and writes a charming note to go with it, *that* becomes a great holiday gift!

When a person spends time on the selection of—and really researches—her gifts, they have tremendous effect. An executive who realized that the head of his ad agency was crazier about his dog than anything else in life gave the man a new doggy food bowl and a mat to put under it, both inscribed with the dog's name, as his holiday present. (It cost very little, but it was a major success.) An executive who realized that the president of her company was an ardent bird watcher gave her a really fine new pair of binoculars. An executive whose doctor lived in a Japanese-style house and was a fan of anything Japanese gave him an antique shoji screen picked up at a junkyard sale.

An Executive's Holiday Gifts

The executive first establishes her budget for that year. Then she chooses any of the following people to be the "gift manager" and to handle all the gift chores:

- An executive assistant.
- A very smart spouse with plenty of time.
- A personnel office executive who knows he has to do a good job.
- A gift consultant who is paid to be smart about the subject.

This gift manager should have:

- Good taste (right down to the wrapping on the gift).
- An ability to bargain for the best prices.
- A thorough knowledge of the market—what's new and great, what's "in" and "out" in consumer tastes.
- A knowledge of certain businesses' rules of ethics. (For example, some media people are allowed to accept gifts only up to $50 in value; others may accept only what they can eat.) In this era of problems with corporate ethics, management must be careful with any gifts.
- A talent for selecting an item that reinforces the company's desired image.

Something extravagant, gaudy, or tasteless should never be chosen as a gift, because it would affect the way in which the recipient thinks of the company. A gift that has absolutely nothing to do with what the company makes, would also do nothing to help the corporate image. For example, a paper products company would send customers a great box of fine stationery, not a silk umbrella; a steel manufacturer would send customers a handsome stainless steel picture frame, not one made of wood or velvet. A pasta manufacturer would send customers a smartly designed pasta serving bowl, not a basket of oranges.

The gift manager works through the following avenues:

- By buying from the leading mail order catalogs in the country.
- By working with the personal shoppers or the corporate gift departments of the leading stores in that city.
- By dealing with the outside gift consultant's resources for custom-ordered items.

In almost all cases, a person buying a large number of items or making a costly order can get a "corporate discount" to make the total bill less onerous. It's up to the bargaining powers of the company's head of business gifts.

The people who receive the senior executive's gifts are:

• Close friends and peers in the business community. This gift might be anything from a $250 case of wine to a $2,000 new sound system for the friend's boat.

• The board of directors. These are the people standing by the CEO in times of great travail and spending long hours coping with crises. The CEO might send a handsome clock to each director, with just his card enclosed. But then again, he might pen a handwritten note that says, "This clock will never be able to mark all the supportive, helpful hours of your time that you have given me this past year. I appreciate your help more than I could ever express in words." (Now that is a real present!)

• Senior staff members. If bonuses are given, then a small gift—with a personal touch—is all that is necessary for the three or four very top people. A new recording from the city symphony or an art book from a city museum would be appropriate. If it is the kind of business where bonuses are not given, then each top lieutenant of the CEO might receive something nice for his home, such as a new entertainment center, a piece of equipment for his favorite sport, or some excellent additions to a connoisseur's wine cellar.

• Customers or clients. A gift for a customer, if it bears the company logo, should bear it modestly. Only someone who works for the company may not be embarrassed to wear a necktie with the corporate logo or use a key chain with the logo emblazoned on it. Smart executives manage to downplay the advertising aspect in their holiday gifts, so that the recipients will really use them. For example:

> An ice bucket will have the logo incised inconspicuously on the inside of its lid. Fine.

> A set of four bar glasses will have the logo etched in a minuscule fashion, so that you would have to look hard to see what it is. Fine.

> A wine bottle opener would have the logo incised almost invisibly on one of the arms. Fine.

> A leather diary for the coming year would have the company logo stamped on the inside back page, requiring a magnifying glass to read it! Fine.

• A senior executive's personal assistant:

> If she has been with him a year, something not too personal, like a handsome plant.

> If she has been with him five years, a $300 gift certificate to a leading handbag store.

> If she been with him ten years, stock in the company and an impersonal gift, such as a handsome porcelain bowl.

> If she has been with him twenty years or more, she should be on the company bonus list; also she should receive a gift of stock in that

corporation and a check big enough to take her and her husband or, mother, or child to Europe for two weeks.

What Employees Give to Superiors and One Another for the Holidays

- You do not give your boss a gift. It would embarrass him or her, and think how expensive it would be if every boss felt that she had to give a present in return to every employee who gave her one! Besides, to give the boss a gift (other than a nice holiday greeting card, something you have baked at home, a book, or something else that is just a gesture of friendship) looks like apple-polishing.
- Employees should not make a big thing out of exchanging presents in the office. An office that is awash in gift wrap spread all over the desks and cabinets is a nonproductive office. Give your gifts to friends in tote bags that they can take home, rather than open gifts in the office. Better yet, send each gift to the person's home, so she won't have to lug it home on public transportation. (If your friend has a car, then there is no problem.) Exchanging gifts in the office is also very tough on those who don't receive gifts, because it looks as if they have no friends. Of course, if you are the kind person who brings into the office a Christmas tree ornament or a chocolate Santa for everyone in the office (not exceeding $5 each), that is really nice. (Find a non-Christmas chocolate gift item for Jewish or Muslim friends or for anyone who does not celebrate Christmas.)

Gifts for Office Messengers and Other Service Personnel

There is a whole category of employees who serve the corporation who should be remembered either by the boss, the boss and the senior executives, or by everyone in the office. When a gigantic box of cookies goes into the mailroom for the mail people and messengers, with some small plastic bags and ties (so that each person can take home his or her fair share of them), it is really appreciated by those who are so often overlooked. So is an enormous basket of fruit, or a box of individually wrapped cheeses. This kind of gift is also appreciated by:

- Employees in the nurse's office.
- The company garage staff, including drivers and mechanics.
- The men and women in the mailroom or copy machine area.
- The maintenance people, including the night cleaners.

All of these people do their share to make it a very pleasant place to work, and they should be remembered during a holiday gift season.

Give thought to the appropriateness of a gift for a coworker, especially a coworker of the opposite sex.

Nice gifts for women to give other women:
A frame with the recipient's child's picture in it.
Travel makeup kit.
Gloves.
Handbag.
Nightgown (be sure of the proper size, of course).
Hosiery (in the right size).
Fragrance.
Lipstick (in the color the recipient wears) or other cosmetic items.
Potpourri or sachets for bureau drawers.
Lingerie or stocking case for traveling.
Bureau drawer organizers.
Desk accessories.

Nice gifts for men to give other men:
Tennis or golf sweater.
Colored socks for a natty dresser.
Silk tie.
Men's fragrance.
Large bar of shower soap.

Gifts (not overly personal) for either sex to give either sex, married or unmarried:
Items for a desk—inkstand, family picture frame, letter opener, clock, leather-covered dictionary, bookends.
Books relating to the person's business or interests.
Music tapes or CDs for the car.
Golf balls or tennis balls (whatever the preferred sport).
A beautiful plant for the office or home.
A gourmet food basket.
Chocolates.
Wine or the person's liquor preference.
Membership in a local museum.
Fruit or Pastry of the Month subscription.
Clever new calculator, pocket radio, or gadget of the year.
A pen and pencil set, or just a good new pen.
Leather agenda for the upcoming year.

Year's subscription to a new art magazine (if the recipient is interested in art), any special interest publication.

Chef's apron and cooking tools.

The newest-style sunglasses.

Two theater, ballet, concert, or opera tickets or tickets to a sporting
event.

Set of bar glasses.

Set of wineglasses.

Gift certificate to a leading restaurant.

HANUKKAH PRESENTS

Hanukkah (also spelled "Chanukah") is an eight-day celebration revered in
Jewish history. It marks the rededication of the Temple in 165 B.C. by the Mac-
cabees after it had been desecrated by the Syrians. The menorah, an eight-
branched candelabrum, is often seen in the window of Jewish households
during this time, and also shares the lobby space of office and public buildings
along with the Christian Christmas tree. Hanukkah, the dates of which change
on the calendar each year, is usually close to Christmas week.

An additional candle of the menorah is lit each day during the celebration,
until all eight are lit.

Jewish people give their family members and friends gifts at this time. Gen-
tiles and members of other religions should also give their Jewish friends their
gifts during this period rather than at Christmas. There are special Hanukkah
cards that a person who is not Jewish may appropriately send to Jewish
friends in place of Christmas cards.

GIFT SUGGESTIONS FOR OTHER PEOPLE
AND OTHER OCCASIONS

BABY PRESENTS AND CHRISTENING PRESENTS

Many of the presents you might give a baby will be suitable only when he is
older—the first book for his library, for example, or a gift of stock, or a silver
porringer to be used as a bowl for nuts or chips in his first apartment.

When you're buying an article of clothing, buy something for an infant a
year old or two years old, because the parents and grandparents will have
outfitted the baby for the first months of his life. Also, babies grow very fast.
Look at the baby's parents. Are they big people? Buy sizes way ahead in this
case. (My husband and I are both big people, and our children were already

in six-months-size clothes when they came home from being born at the hospital, and were wearing two-year sizes when they were eleven months old! Of course, a gift certificate to a store specializing in baby clothes solves the size problem.

Suggestions for Baby

A parent or godparent (or a group of office associates who know that money is tight for this couple) might band together to buy the nursery furniture and the stroller for the infant. Among the possibilities:
- Stroller.
- Bureau.
- Changing table.
- Child's wardrobe (armoire) and children's closet hangers.
- Nursery lamps.
- Crib bedding and bumpers (blanket, sheets, baby pillow, and pillowcase).
- High chair.
- Nursery mirror.
- Play yard (for the future).

Other Gifts from Relatives and Friends

Find out from the parents if they need a practical item such as those listed below:
- Set of practical terrycloth bibs (for feeding).
- Nightgowns.
- Cotton carrying blankets.
- Crib mobile.
- Decorative box for diaper pins.
- Two-part electric feeding tray.
- Electric bottle warmer.
- Nursery wall clock.
- Birthday candle (to celebrate 1 through 18 years).
- Music box.
- Clothing (or even better, a gift certificate to a store).
- Nursery night-light.
- Picture frame.
- Baby book.
- Baby's first books to start a library (good edition of classics).

- A check.
- Shares of stock.
- Money market fund opened in child's name.

Welcome Gifts in Silver

- Rattle.
- Teething ring.
- Mug (engraved with baby's initials and birth date).
- Pusher.
- Long feeding spoon.
- Short-handled fork and spoon (engraved with baby's initials).
- Frame (with birth date engraved).
- Silver or pewter porringer (with engraved initials and birth date).

SUGGESTIONS FOR GIFTS TO GIVE TEENAGE CHILDREN ON ANY OCCASION

The occasion could be Hanukkah, eighth grade graduation, confirmation, Bar or Bat Mitzvah, birthday, or whatever. These gifts can run the gamut from $10 to $1,000.

- Pet of one's own—if the parents agree.
- Private telephone line at home or cell phone.
- A book (ask a good librarian what to get, according to the age and sophistication of the teen).
- The best new dictionary on the market (again, ask a librarian).
- A globe of the world (since geography is so dismally taught!).
- A gadget for the child's bicycle, if that is the favored mode of transport.
- Physical fitness and exercise aids (for boys anxious to develop their muscles or girls anxious to be slim).
- Gift certificates to a video rental shop, music store, electronics store, clothing store, or costume jewelry store and cosmetics department (for girls).
- Camera and related equipment.
- Items related to the sport of choice (a new basketball or volleyball, tennis racket, skis, baseball bat, golf clubs, hockey stick, tennis or golf balls, or ice skates).
- Clothing related to the sport of choice.
- Heavy sports sweaters for any age, any size.
- Newest kind of skateboard (for the expert in the art).
- Goggles and snorkeling equipment.

- Hours of riding with an instructor at a riding academy.
- Diary (with an excellent lock on it).
- Suitcase or backpack (whichever is needed more).
- Portable tent with sleeping paraphernalia.
- Latest calculator.
- Shortwave radio.
- Sewing machine and set of lessons for using it.
- Pair of tickets (for teenager and friend) to a much-prized sporting event, rock concert, Broadway show, or classical music event (if the teenager is musical).
- Series of lessons of choice in computers, piano, guitar, other instrument of choice, a foreign language, karate, any sport, ballroom dancing.
- Trips (for teenager and family member–chaperone) to:

    Any American city filled with history, such as Washington (with visits to Mount Vernon, the FBI building, the National Gallery, Smithsonian Institution, the Air and Space Museum, and the Library of Congress, for starters).

    Europe (with a parent or teacher along on this one).

    The city where tickets to a major event are waiting (such as the last game of the World Series, the Rose Bowl, or a great historic celebration).

    New York for a great concert or opera (for a musical teen).

    Tickets for Disneyland or Disney World.

- Money.
- Bond.
- Gift of stock.

GIFTS FOR THE ELDERLY

The elderly deserve special thought in the gift you present at holiday time, on their birthdays, or when you go to visit them in a retirement or nursing home.

Do some research before you buy that gift. Don't waste your money buying something you guess will be appropriate. Do some homework on the project. Talk to the person who either lives with them or sees them regularly (a relative, nurse, or home care specialist).

- In a cold climate, there might be a need for flannel pajamas, a warm robe, bed socks, a wool scarf, gloves, or a throw.
- What kind of reading material do they most enjoy *now*? Would a magazine subscription be more appropriate? Is there someone to read to them?
- If she uses a cane, how about a new cane in a special color or design? (Have someone measure the person's cane, so that you buy one of the proper height.)

- If the elderly person's living space is gloomy-looking, how about something to cheer it up? Maybe a new lamp with a white transparent shade to give maximum light, a pretty plant in a porcelain container (requiring little care but with a long life), a saucy new pillow to put at the person's back when she is sitting, some room fragrance to make the area have a lovely scent.
- The newest photographs of the grandchildren, attractively framed.
- Books in large print for people who have trouble with their eyes; books on tape for the visually handicapped.
- Food to please the palate—perhaps a mailing from Fruit of the Month or Pastry of the Month.
- A lively new hobby to espouse—for example, an aquarium, complete with gravel, decorative rocks, and plastic plants for the bottom, air filter, heater, lots of tropical fish, fish food, and a booklet that teaches the owner how to care for these lively creatures!

For Someone Who Is Seriously Ill or Injured

Here are just a few ideas:
- Bring your tape recorder to the office and have all of the patient's close friends record a short message to give her the office news.
- Bring your camera into the office, and take a group photo of your sick or injured friend's office colleagues, all grinning and holding a big sign that says "Get Well!" Blow it up; have it framed and placed by the patient's bed.
- Construct a free-standing "tree" on a table in the ill person's room, on which the get-well cards can be hung.
- Make sure that the patient has a light, delightful book to read.
- When the person is feeling much better and the doctor permits it, see that he has plenty of allowable edible treats and plenty of friends who come for short, non-noisy visits.
- Bring the patient (whether in a hospital or at home) something that smells delicious, like bath soap, body lotion, or room fragrance.
- Arrive with a box of notepaper and an attractive pen, and the patient will love you, because there are always so many thank-you notes and "I'm okay" letters to write. If you have a stamp already affixed to each envelope, the patient will love you even more.
- Remember, for a child, no matter how many stuffed animals she might have, there is always room to love one more.

A Houseguest's Present for the Host

A first-time houseguest would bring something like:
- A baked ham, for everyone's enjoyment (and the gourmet mustard and rye bread slices to go with it).
- Fresh berries the host may not be able to buy in that town.
- A large cheese, like Bel Paese, Brie, or Edam (with assorted gourmet crackers, too).
- The newest, hottest book that everyone is talking about (complete with a bookbag mailer, addressed to the bookstore, to allow for the exchange of the book for another choice, if the host has already read this one).
- Paper cocktail and dinner napkins, printed with the hosts' initials or the name of the house.

An old-hand houseguest, knowing the foibles of the house, would bring something like:
- A new blue shower curtain to replace the ratty old blue one in the guest bath.
- A new set of badly needed towels—or beach towels—for the household.
- A new ice bucket to replace the one with the broken handle.
- A matching set of bar glasses, because none of the host's glasses match anymore.
- An oversized tin of the hostess's secret, unmitigated passion: a special kind of butter brickle.
- New set of mugs, since the hosts' mugs are all mismatched, even chipped.

Gifts for a Housewarming

When you attend a party in someone's new house (or newly decorated apartment), it is customary to bring some small gift to mark the event. You are, in effect, congratulating your hosts on their good taste and their luck in finding such a great new home.

There are certain gifts that are always useful. (If your hosts have one of these, it may be old and dilapidated and they would enjoy a fresh new one.)
- Telephone book cover.
- Wastebasket.
- Bedside lamp.
- Decorated tissue box cover and matching toothbrush caddy for a bathroom.
- Hanging board to hold a host of keys on a wall.
- Bulletin board for family telephone messages.

- Message pads with the family name printed on them.
- Marvelous framed color photograph of the exterior of the new house.
- Year's subscription to a leading decorating magazine.
- Monogrammed doormat.
- Large box filled with lightbulbs of different wattages (very useful!).

A LITTLE ADVICE

- Perishable gifts (flowers and certain foods) should be delivered only when the recipient is home. This requires someone to call ahead to find out when the family or person will be in residence.

- Put your full name and address on the card or on the enclosure envelope. Make it easy for the recipient to identify who sent the gift (a card scrawled "Pat," "Betty," or "Joe" might be any one of five people). The address on the gift enclosure makes it easy for the recipient to send you a thank-you note.

- Don't put your gift in a box from a fancy store like Tiffany's, hoping the recipient will think it came from there. (The recipient may try to exchange it and discover the deception, and your gift will be a loser.)

- Take care in the presentation of the gift. If you have beautifully wrapped it, drop it off in a handsome tote or shopping bag, so that excitement and anticipation is immediately created by the outside wrapping.

People love to receive a gift with something tied to the ribbon. At the holiday season, you can find everything from little snowmen and miniature Christmas tree balls to small angels, miniature ice skates, and little skis. You can tuck fresh holly into the ribbon at Christmas, tie on a sprig of violets in February. One young man I know, in pursuit of a young lady, sent her a gift beautifully wrapped with many ribbons, and from the bow dangled a shiny new key (the key to his apartment, which to her was the best gift of all!).

The Japanese, the greatest gift presentation experts in the world, wrap very special gifts in beautiful kimono fabric on the outside with paper wrap inside. Leftover remnants of fabrics used in making clothes can be used for gift wrap; so can leftover unused wallpaper. One young impecunious artist friend of mine wraps up his home-baked cookies each year in brown butcher paper, and then paints an enchanting Christmas scene for each person.

Taking a few pains with the look of your gifts means simply that you have made an extra effort, which will be appreciated.

- People love imaginative gifts that include an element of personalization or a surprise. Here are some examples of "thoroughly merchandised gifts" that really please the recipients:
    - Anything engraved, incised, stamped, or embossed with their name or initials. (Be sure the initials are correct!)
    - A stamp box filled with stamps from the post office.

- A camera with a roll of film ready to go for indoor photos.
- A picture frame with a photo of the recipient's spouse, child, dog, house, or boat inside.
- A tie case for him for traveling, with three new ties inside it.
- A hosiery case for her for travels, with three pairs of pantyhose in high fashion colors inside (and in the correct size).
- A suitcase with the person's name printed on the attached luggage tag.
- A gym bag containing a towel and two pairs of athletic socks.
- A pretty plant in a pretty porcelain cachepot.
- A decorative tin box filled with cookies or chocolates.
- A book on fishing, with two new flies attached to its cover.
- A French dictionary that, when opened, reveals two round-trip air tickets to Paris.

- The gift you give as a surprise—when there is no reason for it—is the best kind of all. For example, it is an act of love:
  - When you bring home from a trip abroad an item that a friend collects, indicating that you really had that friend on your mind.
  - When you surprise a friend who married recently with a tape cassette you had secretly recorded of all of the toasts made to the bridal couple at their reception.
  - When you cut up a tree that fell in your yard and deliver a neatly tied bundle of wood to your friends who have fireplaces.
  - When you deliver vegetables or flowers from your garden with a note saying, "Hope you will enjoy these!"
  - When, after your friend tells you she is giving a big party and doesn't know how to cope, you leave a list under her front door the next day of all the equipment you will lend her for the party (such as card tables, trays, glasses, plates, flatware, and tablecloths).

Next in value to the gift of life—the one gift we all have but rarely appreciate sufficiently—are gifts from the heart. They have absolutely nothing to do with money and everything to do with timing, presentation, and what is written on the gift enclosure.

The successful gift is an act of love. It makes the recipient feel pampered and loved or admired. The price or the purpose of the object does not matter—whether it's a vacuum cleaner, a gold ring, a fishing rod, or a thermos jug. It's the way in which it is given that matters. Many of us would rather receive a little sketch a friend made of our little beach house than an emerald necklace, simply because the sketch comes from the heart. When you show someone that she is worthy of your thoughts and "research," you have made that person feel very special.

PART 5

DIFFICULT TIMES:
HEALING YOURSELF AND OTHERS
WHEN TROUBLE STRIKES

The resilience of the human soul and body is truly incredible. People can have bad things happen to them repeatedly and yet overcome every disastrous development with courage, determination, and even humor.

Of course, there are always those who take something like the advent of a hangnail as a disaster and spend most of their time griping about one thing or other, however minor, all day long.

This section is not for those other people and their hangnails. This section is about serious difficulties, and hopefully it will offer at least a few ideas for helping and healing those wrestling with real problems. There is a solution to almost everything in life if you look hard enough, if you have people around to help, and if you have a little thing called faith—faith in God, country, or just yourself.

When you have been dealt a blow in life, it's a call to arms in defense of yourself. If you call up the determination and adrenaline needed in striving to overcome—and mix it well with the energy derived from others who care about you—you'll possess a very powerful strength. And as you learn to cope with the little things that go wrong, you will find yourself able to face bigger challenges with aplomb.

You may rightfully say to yourself that there's a large chasm between recovering from the loss of your spouse and recovering from making a social gaffe, but the act of recovery is the same. It means you are in charge, you are in command, you are going to settle accounts—do what you have to do (always with others' feelings in mind) and get on with life. Healing yourself, apologizing, making amends, assuming new responsibilities—each requires drawing on that precious energy we all have but sometimes deny having. When facing a giant personal setback, you should look at that proverbial glass and tell yourself it's still three-quarters full, not one-quarter empty!

How to Help Someone Deal with the Loss of a Spouse

It is shattering to lose a spouse, whatever the circumstances. I remember what a friend said who had gone through a terrible divorce. "Everyone always feels so sorry for someone whose loved one has died. I don't want to sound self-pitying, but I'm bitter about the public perception of a widowed versus a divorced person. At least the widowed person may have had a happy married life—at least he or she had that. And everyone gives a widowed person so much sympathy, love, and support. Not divorced people. When a husband or wife cheats and walks out the door to marry someone else, no one feels noble sorrow for the one left behind. Patronizing sympathy, perhaps. Real sorrow, no. The general attitude is, 'Well, she obviously did something to deserve that kind of treatment!'"

DEALING WITH A DIVORCE

The best way for a good friend to help a divorced person is to rebuild his pride and sense of self. It is, of course, much tougher to be the person who was left behind in a divorce. Not only is there the sense of personal loss, but there is also the gossip in the community to confront. There is the pitying that begins for the jilted person, and the constant irritant of the former spouse who has found a new lover and now circulates among old friends wearing a happy face.

How Should You Behave When You Have Divorced?

- It's wise not to divulge every gory detail of the marriage breakup to whoever will listen. "Less is better" at a time like this. Let it all out to a couple of close friends, ask them to remain discreet, and keep the personal details out of your general conversation. If you wear a Mona Lisa smile and remain aloof from the gossip, everyone will know you are going to be fine and recover quickly. (People like to be around winners, not eternal losers.)

- Leave out of your conversation any financial details or legal matters, including custody rights pending in the court.
- It's better not to date someone or even be seen in public with a single person of the opposite sex until after the decree is signed. Not only is circumspect behavior important in regard to your reputation in the community, but it is an important factor in the legal proceedings.
- The people who matter the most are, of course, your children. Make a conscious effort to spend much more time with them than usual. They are suffering as much as you, perhaps more.
- Refrain from criticizing your former mate to your children at any time—now or in the future. No matter how responsible your former mate was for the breakup of the marriage, making recriminations against her to your children is wrong. It is cruel and unnecessary to break down any trust a child has for his divorced parent. Do everything you can to maintain that trust.
- If your former mate has a new love, avoid spreading gossip about the relationship. You will only look jealous and spiteful to others. Attempting to sully the reputation of your former spouse in your community will have the worst possible effect on your children and reflect badly on you.
- Don't imitate those who mail printed "divorce announcements" to their friends, as though there was some happy news to impart. (Some people even send out engraved divorce announcements, which cost the same as wedding announcements!) Call your family and intimate friends in the city with the news, and notify your out-of-town relatives and close friends with short personal notes, giving your new address and telephone number if they are to change. A sample note:

Dear Denise and Bob,

I thought you should know that Greg and I have decided to begin divorce proceedings. It is really very sad, but it has been a long time in coming. Greg is living temporarily at his mother's (telephone: 000-0000). The children are holding up well, and they and I will be staying in this house for now. We're going to hang tough and get through this, so don't worry about us.

There should be happier news the next time we communicate. Love to you both.

HOW SHOULD PEOPLE BEHAVE
WHEN THEIR FRIENDS DIVORCE?

- If you love both people, don't take sides. Don't criticize one to the other, even if one person has obviously wronged the other. Your job, as a friend, is to try to get each member of the couple into an affirmative, cheerful mood once again—to turn away from the hatred, disappointment, and embarrassment he or she may be feeling. It takes time, but a friend with a positive attitude who keeps talking about interesting things to do and see, great books to read, wonderful trips to take, will probably gradually break through the emotional paralysis of a thoroughly upset friend.

• Don't keep probing for the reasons for the split. If your divorced friends want you to know the reasons, you'll be told. When a friend tells you she is being divorced don't automatically ask, "Is there someone else?" You'd be justly accused of being a "gossip-digger."

• If there *is* someone else, don't serve as the gossip conduit, supplying information to the one left behind regarding all the activities of the other spouse and the newfound love.

• If you are friends of both divorcing spouses, extend an equal number of invitations to them the first year of their separation, so that one won't suffer the added crisis of feeling that the other has taken away her good friends. If you invite one to dinner, invite the other to dinner a couple of weeks later, and let each know that's the way you're playing it. If you give a party with eighty or more people—like a Christmas open house—you can successfully invite them both. Make sure they know that they are both invited, so there will be no unpleasant surprises. They can "operate" at different ends of the room with no interaction.

After that first year, if you are much more friendly with one than the other, you can forget about inviting them an equal number of times. Hopefully, by then the other person will be able to fend for himself socially.

Of course, if one member of the divorced couple behaved very badly in the marriage, there is no reason to keep your friendship flourishing with that person.

• A divorce is a time to really help out your friends—by doing things for their children. These real victims of divorce need all the attention they can get at this point. If you get them out of the house, take them to amusing events, help them laugh and enjoy themselves, allow them to talk about their sense of loss in the divorce, you are performing a generous act of kindness for everyone involved. Don't forget the children in the months to come; they will need your continuing kindness. Never make a critical remark about the parent who left the marriage.

WHEN YOU ARE WIDOWED

In today's world we observe far fewer rigid symbols of mourning than in years past. It is not necessary for a widow to wear black and a heavy veil at a spouse's funeral, nor are guests any longer required to wear black; nongarish, modest clothing is acceptable. The obliteration of starchy rules about mourning attire is one more step toward helping the bereaved get on with a normal life. (This doesn't mean that it is acceptable for anyone to show up at the funeral dressed as though headed for the golf course or doing the gardening or going out to a party after the service.)

In the weeks following a funeral, others may feel uncomfortable around someone who has been widowed. Most people don't know what to say. They don't know whether to ask how you feel, wordlessly hug you and pat you on the back, inquire about how they may help, or else ignore the entire unpleasant subject and talk about happy things.

Many of your friends and acquaintances simply can't handle seeing you, someone they love, immersed in grief or depression. Everyone wants you to snap back to your usual good self; they feel helpless when confronted by your display of grief. Even if it doesn't matter how many times in private you open that door of grief and let it emerge, as time goes by you should close it in public and put a lock on it.

A sense of humor, of course, is the greatest saving grace of all. A widowed friend of mine, who had had a great marriage and lost his wife to cancer, was complimented by a group of his friends on his incredible spirit and snap-back ability. He laughed and said, "It's all of you who helped me put her death behind me. You were impossible—so embarrassed, unnatural, and ill at ease when trying to comfort me. I finally couldn't stand it any longer. I had to return to my old self in self-defense!"

Having young children, of course, is a real blessing. They need your attention and you need theirs; suddenly you'll notice there is a marvelous in-house support group already in place and functioning. The dependence of a child of any age upon you is the best therapy in the world. Again, willing a positive attitude is key. If you conclude that your spouse certainly would have wanted you to get on with your life, you *will*.

• Seek the help of bereavement support groups and/or therapists. (See the next section of this chapter, page 571, When You're on Your Own Again, for more detailed advice.)

• Use your closest friends or relatives as volunteer punching bags for your emotional outbursts.

Sometimes you really need to let it all hang out, particularly during those early, terrible sinking spells. There are times when it's a good idea to express in words how bad you feel, so *talk*—to the right person. An occasional emotional explosion in front of one or two really close friends allows you to hold your emotions in check in public. This is a period in life through which you should not delay your passage or procrastinate. Rather, see yourself passing through it quickly. Since we're all different, some manage faster than others. But remember that your "punching bag" friends cannot serve you endlessly in this capacity. It is not fair to them, nor productive for you. Look upon your passage through a state of grief as a learning experience from which you will graduate and go on to an obviously different but satisfying, productive life.

When you reach the point where you can talk about your loss in a normal way with friends and business associates, and when you can once again discuss other subjects with enthusiasm, you will have attained a major victory. When others look at you without immediately thinking of a crippling sadness in your life, you really are on the road to recovery. People who recover from a terrible sadness are stronger, better people.

• It's very normal to have mementos and framed photographs of your late husband or wife around the house. Hopefully, you won't try to paper the walls with them. That can make others feel very uncomfortable. One widowed friend reported that her suitor told her one night that if she reduced the number of framed photographs of her late husband from twenty to three in her house, he would ask her to marry him. The next morning she wrapped up nineteen of the photographs and put them away to distribute later among her grown children. That night, when there was only one photograph of her late husband left on display, her suitor put a ring on her finger, and they were married a month later.

Another friend, a divorced man, had two photographs of his very beautiful ex-wife in his rather active bedroom. When he told me he wasn't having any real, lasting success with women, I suggested that he get rid of those photographs. He did, and now the only photographs of females in his house are those of his new wife and baby daughter.

DATING AGAIN AND REMARRIAGE

Advice on when a widowed person should resume a social life should be tailored to each person—because some are ready sooner than others. A widowed person who starts dating within a week of the funeral is asking for public disapproval. (Some don't care if there is public disapproval; my remarks are targeted at those who do.) It is appropriate for a widowed person to have dinner quietly with a person of the opposite sex within a couple of weeks, particularly if the dinner takes place in the widowed person's home. It is also appropriate for a widowed person to go out for dinner in a group as soon as he feels like it, but it's wise to wait from three to six months before regularly dating another person *alone in public*. Even if it is the most harmless of get-togethers, your dating may be perceived by the local gossips as a relationship.

It is just better taste to wait a while before anyone can float the rumor of your having an affair or even looking for another marriage partner. I remember one friend's description of how she felt when she learned her daughter-in-law was seen dining and dancing with a man ten days after the woman's husband, my friend's son, was buried following a plane crash. "It was exactly as though she had whacked my face with an ice-cold washcloth," she described it, "and then whacked my heart with several more."

• The parents of a mourning spouse are very important. After all, they are suffering from an intense grief, too, and your sensitivity will help them. Spend time with them following the funeral. Don't shut them out in your own grief. Talk about their child—your spouse. Share funny, wonderful anecdotes and memories of the great times with them. Give them photographs and mementos of your late spouse that will give them great comfort in the years to come.

• If you remarry, tell the family of your late spouse before anyone else. Bring your fiancé(e) to meet them for a brief moment, and try to make the transition of your new marriage smooth for them. Make them understand that you and their son (or daughter) had a special relationship and love that should not be compared to your love for anyone else. You are only embarking on a new and different life. Invite them to your wedding but understand their reasons if they regret.

• The most important responsibility in your remarriage is to keep the relationship strong between your children and those grandparents. Some of the ways in which you can do this:

  • Invite them to all the children's birthdays and special days like Christmas and Valentine's Day.
  • Allow, even urge, the grandparents to take them out for an occasional Saturday lunch and the rest of the afternoon.
  • Invite the grandparents for special observances, like Mother's Day and Father's Day.
  • Make sure your children remember their grandparents' birthdays with a card and a telephone call, and the holidays with a small gift—perhaps something they make at school.
  • Invite the grandparents to those special times when the children are performing (such as a ballet recital, class play, team sports game, and the like), and of course, to activities like school graduations.

It is quite normal for your ex-in-laws to fear your new mate will keep their grandchildren from them, or that you will lose interest in keeping their emotional bonds strong with your children. Quickly address those fears, and never forget your promises to them.

WHEN YOU'RE ON YOUR OWN AGAIN

THE TASK OF HEALING YOURSELF

Regardless of the circumstances surrounding the loss of your mate, there's some very good advice contained in an old Chinese symbol for crisis: Half of it signifies danger, the other half signifies opportunity. A newly single person should fixate on the *opportunity* half. If you have lost your husband or wife, your life is undergoing great changes. Look upon those changes as a positive force for the future, not something to be feared.

Utilize the energy of the forces that catapulted you against your will into a newly single life. Channel that energy into shaping a frame of mind that will help you automatically to respond to opportunities as they arise. Use that energy for sharpening your senses, expanding your horizons, making new friends, and remaining open to fresh ideas. If you have children, look upon your crisis as an opportunity to grow much closer to them and to help them become much happier, even stronger human beings as a result. In other words, grow with them.

Remember, too, that *the more energy you will yourself to have, the more you will have, the more you will get done, and the happier you will become.* There is always a reservoir of energy inside you waiting to be tapped. Don't waste it. Harness it to get you through this period of hostility against a divorced mate or departed lover—or grief, guilt, and perhaps even anger against a loved one who died. There's a new life to be led, with personal accomplishments most definitely part of it!

Help is available right under your nose—perhaps in a caring, imaginative friend or in a member of the clergy at your house of worship. You usually receive this encouragement passively; it's almost handed to you. But much of the most effective assistance available to you must be actively sought, not passively received. It needs to be researched and discovered through your own ingenuity. To put it in the vulgar vernacular, "Get off your butt!"

- For those with the right mind-set, help equals opportunity. The first step in the process of self-evaluation is *not to be ashamed to seek all the help you can get.* Many widowed and divorced people or people who have lost their longtime lovers are walking a very rocky path because they feel it is weak and embarrassing to seek psychological counseling or to enter a support group. If you are such a person, tell yourself that those experts and those services are there to help *you,* not just *everyone else* in the world.
  - Find out about the free counseling services offered by your local social service agencies.

- Your house of worship should be of *great* help. If you don't have one, *get one.*
- Ask your doctor about counseling services she recommends for you.
- Seek out other newly single people who have sought—and found—effective assistance.
- Check the activities of single, divorced, and widowed groups listed in the newspapers, particularly the various church and temple groups. Attend their self-help meetings. If you don't like one group, try another. Try them all!
- Through your children's school faculty or parents' group you may hear of a counselor who will have answers you seek.
- The head of human resources at your office might have some leads.
- Volunteer service in a field you feel passionate about will be fulfilling because *it feels good* to know you are helping others who need you.
- There might be a new hobby that will consume you with enthusiasm and fill your hours with a really enjoyable activity. Anything that gets you going again is good in itself.

One young widow I know, two weeks after her husband's death, forced herself to attend her suburban church altar guild meeting for the first time. When she was introduced by the chairman to the forty-odd women present as someone who "is new in town and who has just lost her husband," and then genuine applause erupted, she couldn't help herself. She burst into sobs and the entire group rallied to comfort her. A women's network went into action. Within two weeks, the young widow was enrolled in a computer school run by the sister of one of the guild members, and she had a new, reliable baby-sitter—found by one of the other members. She also went to see a counselor suggested by another member. A year after that first altar guild meeting, she had a job she loved at an important nonprofit foundation; she later married a man introduced to her by another guild member.

I'm not suggesting you are going to have that kind of incredible luck because of one meeting, but usually you get something out of anything you try to do with an open mind. Have patience. There's no magic wand to be waved. As you gain experience in trying out new solutions, you will find you have become a first-class survivor, not a third-class one. It's the person who stays imprisoned at home endlessly wallowing in self-pity and trying to make everyone else join him who faces a life of depression and never-ending grief. He or she is the one who is *third class.*

A Real Friend

When one of your friends goes through a divorce and is left behind because the former spouse is involved with a new love, it's time for friends to rally around. And that's doubly true when a friend loses a mate through death. You don't have to start racking your brains to find dates for your newly single friend. Keep in mind that he may need some time to adjust to life without the former partner and won't be open to forced gaiety or new involvements immediately. Have him over for dinner with your family, or take your friend out to a restaurant and a movie. Help your friend fight loneliness on the battlefield. Conjuring up interesting or amusing things to do, particularly in the evening or on a weekend. You don't have to serve as a supply source for potential new mates. Of course, if you should be responsible for introducing a new love into your friend's life once he is open to that again, everyone will realize that "that's what friends are for."

There Is a Difference Between Alone and Lonely
(see also You Are Single but Still Part of A Family, page 27)

If you are newly single, it's important to concentrate on the positive side of being by yourself. An affirmative attitude makes it easier to find a mate and get married again—if that's your hope. You're more attractive when you're a happy, positive person. People want to have you around, and invitations follow. And if you don't wish to remarry, concentrating on the up side of life will make you even more content with being alone and determined to get the best out of life. I've noticed that the happiest divorced and widowed people are those who appreciate the gift of life.

It's a good idea every once in a while to stop and think, "I have a will and I control my life."

There are many emoluments to living alone. Just ask some of the people who as adults have always lived by themselves and lead active, involved existences with plenty of fun attached. Don't even think about the sour, selfish hermits you may know, because they are not typical of those who live alone, and remember that there is a great difference between *being alone* and *being lonely*.

• Realize that you have the choice of either sinking into a self-pitying lethargy or of springing into action. You can willfully summon your own supply of adrenaline to provide increased energy. Now is the time to establish new goals. Now is the time to get your life, your home, your children's lives organized. Start by writing down on paper (or making a file in your computer of):

- Your financial assets and how you will seek the best advice on managing them.
- Your liabilities and what steps you are taking to cope with them.
- Desired travel plans and what's out there available to you (charter groups, cruises, museum-sponsored tours, and more).
- Educational and artistic goals you would like to seek—to play the piano, learn Spanish, take a course in philosophy, join a bridge group, take a music appreciation or art history course, learn how to sew, garden, and cook Chinese food.
- Volunteer work you will undertake—to help feed the homeless; become a docent at the museum; visit the elderly; read to the blind; help your church, temple, or hospital; train to become a literacy volunteer.
- Physical self-improvement activities (after getting your doctor's okay)—start to jog, join an exercise class, work with a trainer, undertake a supervised diet; have a makeover and change your hair, cosmetics, and fashion look

- Read—voraciously, with joy. Not just the junk stuff, but good literature. Discover it for the first time, or rediscover it from your college days. Reading is a great soother and a leveler. It fuels your conversational abilities and makes you more interesting to be around.
- Write letters. Reach out to all your old pals everywhere. Write them catch-up letters, not just e-mails destined for deletion, to tell them where you are, what has happened to you, your new plans, and how you won't waste time on tears. There's too much to do in life. You'll probably hear back from every one of them. Your upbeat letter will cause them to reach out to you again, and you will find all kinds of nice things happening because of renewed friendships—the very best kind.
- Realize you now have a new independence, enabling you to schedule yourself as and when you please. (Now you can go to all the ballgames instead of having to alternate with the concert series because of your mate's decree.)
- Make the interior of your home more attractive, even if you don't spend any money on it. You have more room to display and properly store your possessions. Consider simply rearranging the space to be more comfortable and efficient. Try a more cheerful coat of paint on the walls, and some new lampshades to change the lighting in this environment.

All of the above takes time—and sometimes money. You now probably have more time on your hands (unless you're someone with small children). As for the money it costs to try new things, you can become creative in do-it-yourself mode.

I know a widow who went on a month's expedition to Egypt, first class, fulfilling a lifetime ambition to see the Nile. She paid for the entire trip by spending several hours every week for a year, typing corporate reports on her computer at home. (She made a reputation for being faster and more accurate than any of the in-house typists, and the company, for whom her late husband had worked, kept her busier than she even wished to be.)

The key to a quick recovery if you're newly alone is to establish new personal goals for yourself, so that you become the best person it is possible to become—as well as the most attractive and the most giving. A person like that is never lonely—just alone on occasion, and actually very glad to be alone on occasion!

The Newly Single Woman's Name

The Widow

Traditionally a widow lived out her life using her husband's name—for example, "Mrs. John Brown"—on her checks and printed stationery. However, many women today, after remaining widowed for many years, have begun to use their given names. Mrs. John Brown, for example, after five or ten years begins to use "Cynthia Brown" on everything from her stationery to her charge accounts. It is a natural evolution.

Today's nontraditional widow resumes her given name almost immediately on all correspondence. Instead of Mrs. Anthony Garrett, she becomes Jane Jensen Garrett (her maiden name was Jensen) as soon as her "Mrs. Anthony Garrett" stationery runs out. When she orders new monogrammed towels, for example, she uses "JJG" (Jane Jensen Garrett) instead of "aGj" (her and her husband's former joint monogram).

The Divorced Woman

A divorced woman may no longer call herself by her husband's full name. She is no longer "Mrs. Martin Boucher." She is "Mrs. Mary Louise Boucher." Her old stationery printed or engraved with "Mrs. Martin Boucher" at the top is no longer usable, and she can't really cross out "Martin" and insert her given name with a pen. She can always cut off and throw away the top part of the letterhead (printed with the incorrect name) and then use the rest of the sheet for scratch paper. That can even be therapeutic!

Many women take back their maiden names after divorce, which I think is an excellent idea if there are no young children and if the ex-husband has remarried.

If the divorced woman has custody of the children, it is less confusing when they are growing up if they have the same last name as their father's. But if there are no children, or if they are out of the nest, she should feel at liberty to resume her own name. For example, Gretchen Campbell Marsden marries and becomes Mrs. David O'Connor. When she divorces, she can be either Mrs. Gretchen O'Connor or Ms. Gretchen Campbell Marsden again. (I'm all for the better decision.)

In the "old days," a woman who divorced was known socially by her family name combined with her ex-husband's family name. Thus thirty years ago Gretchen O'Connor after her divorce would have been known only as Mrs. Marsden O'Connor. Fortunately, since that is clumsy—and since it does not impart the woman's first name—it is not used much in the new society. She is more efficiently known as Gretchen Marsden and not Gretchen O'Connor.

CHAPTER 18

When Someone Is Ill or Injured

When a friend has been or is still seriously ill or hurt, facing a long recovery time, a large dose of depression usually goes with it. That's why it's important not just to make a nice gesture when you first hear the bad news, but to keep at it. At least once a week, check in by telephone or e-mail. No matter how busy you are, you can always spare five minutes to do something for that family member or friend who has had tough luck.

There are people who simply can't talk to someone who is ill. They go to pieces, don't know what to say, get depressed if they see someone laid up. Then there are the others—thank God for them—who are always calling up with a cheery voice to ask how the patient is feeling; always sending a little something to make the patient feel good (like his favorite ice cream or her favorite flower); always ready to take a person out shopping, run helpful errands, go to the lending library—always showing that they care. That kind of support goes beyond good manners; it shows an open heart.

MINDING YOUR MANNERS IN THE HOSPITAL

When a good friend or relative is hospitalized, there are things you can do to show you care—and things not to do, too.

• Don't constantly telephone the patient. If the person is feeling very ill, you won't be able to speak to him anyway. If the person is on the mend, constant incoming telephone calls will be so exhausting that they could set back recovery. Also, when from two to four patients are sharing a hospital room, the constant ringing of a telephone is unfair to the others in the room. With a shortage of nurses, even the sickest person sometimes has to pick up the telephone to answer a persistent ring, either because she hasn't had telephone service cut off or doesn't know what to do about it. If the call answered under duress is from you, trying to find out how things are going, she will put your call in the same category as a kiss of death, rather than as an affectionate gesture of greeting.

• Do call the patient's family or office to find out the latest news and to transmit a message of cheer. A few days later, ask a family member when it will be all right to call the patient. Some patients instruct their families to have all calls held until they are home from the hospital.

• Check with the patient's family to see if there is already a supply of fresh flowers in the room. If there is, don't add to the lack of oxygen in the usually overheated hospital room by sending more. (The nurses are too busy to take care of them anyway, and there is nothing worse than a hospital room full of dead flowers!) Instead, have flowers sent to the patient when he has returned home. Nothing cheers up a person more when he is feeling better and is back home recuperating in familiar surroundings than to see them embellished with lovely fresh flowers or a plant.

• Even though hospital food is notoriously bad, your patient friend might not be able to eat certain things you bring him. Therefore, watch what kind of gift of food you send. Ask a relative of the patient if you can bring a dish of hot pasta or if you can put some ice cream with your friend's name on it in the fridge at the nurses' station. The doctor has to give the okay. If the patient is not nauseated, a large box of chocolates is a great idea—to steal from personally on occasion, if the doctor permits it, but basically to offer to visitors, doctors, and nurses when they come into the room. Having a treat to serve visitors warms the atmosphere in the hospital room.

I will never forget one friend who, while lying in traction in her private hospital room, kept a constant supply of ice in a plastic bucket, in which sat one bottle of champagne after another. She wasn't allowed any herself but decided to serve each of the ten bottles she had received as gifts as hospitality to her visitors. (She had suffered a bad accident at the end of a downhill ski race—which she had luckily won.) Everyone who came to see her (hospital staff excepted) was offered cold champagne in the hospital's paper cups, which made her hospital room one of the most popular visiting spots in town.

• Do send reading material that is light, easy to read, and upbeat. A hospital stay is no time to launch into War and Peace or Dante's Inferno, but it is a time to read a collection of popular magazines that were presented as a gift, all tied up with a festive satin ribbon. One or two new paperbacks to appeal to the patient's reading tastes are also nice to bring or send, but remember, someone who is hospitalized probably won't feel like reading too much. When he is recuperating at home, that's when the patient will start to read, enjoy food, and take pleasure in talking on the telephone with friends again.

• Amusing or attractive get-well cards are always welcome in the hospital. You should personalize such a card with two or three sentences, not just sign it. (Example: "The office is like a morgue without you. Everyone keeps asking how you are, and we all command you to get well quickly, so that the company becomes productive again.") If you don't have access to a studio card, send a note. Mail is always a treat for someone who is hospitalized. Fortunately, the patient is not obligated to send a written thank you.

• Of course, the classic present for someone who is in the hospital for a very lengthy stay is a cassette player with a recording of the voices of everyone in the family or in the office, sending special messages to the patient. I know one patient who was hospitalized for three months, during which time he received a weekly tape from his family, which he listened to cheer himself up whenever he was feeling bad. He always knew when he had come to the end of the recording, because the signoff signal was the barking of a dog—the family dog barked on command.

• Visitors in a hospital room should keep their voices low, not only for the patient's sake, but of any other patient in the room or in neighboring rooms. It is not a time for boisterous, raucous humor, just gentle jokes and calm conversation. A patient loves to be cut in on the office gossip, to hear people tell about amusing parties they attended, good games or plays they saw, and amusing or upbeat things that are going on in the world. Sitting by a hospital bed is not the time to go into detail about the latest oil spill and how many animals and fish it will kill. Sitting by a hospital bed is the time to recount the story of the elephant that got loose at the circus and sauntered up a main thoroughfare of town before being captured.

• Don't tell someone who looks terrible that she looks "just great." Instead talk about "how much better you're going to feel soon," and how "next week you'll have the roses back in your cheeks and be flirting with all the really good-looking doctors or nurses." (Since there are male and female doctors and nurses as well, either will do.)

• If you're the one who's the patient, on your departure morning it's nice to leave a big box of candy or basket of fresh fruit at the nursing station to say "thank you" to all the staff who helped take care of you. This includes doctors, nurses, nursing aides, orderlies, and volunteers. If you forget to leave a present behind, you can always drop a note to the head nurse of your floor, expressing your thanks to them all. Hospital staff work so hard, are so short-handed, and bear so much grief these days that any show of appreciation on the part of a patient brings a tremendous ray of sunshine into their lives.

WHEN A GOOD FRIEND DEVELOPS
A LIFE-THREATENING DISEASE

You cannot act too quickly to show your concern when a good friend develops a life-threatening disease, such as cancer. When you hear a bad piece of news like this, speak first with someone close to the person who is knowledgeable about the case, to determine how serious the condition is and whether or not the person involved wishes the nature of the illness known. In this way, you will be able to help dispel rumors, and you will become either an accurate source of information or the instrument of embargo on information concerning the patient—all based on your friend's wishes in the matter.

- When you hear bad news about a person's health and then happen to see that person in public, you certainly don't want to rush up and pour out your sympathy to someone who's valiantly trying to keep his condition secret.

- Your quiet, unpublicized assistance to the family in coping with your friend's serious disease is a great gift. Someone who works silently and efficiently behind the scenes to help with anything that requires attending to becomes a beloved hero in the eyes of everyone. This help may consist of fetching special equipment, coping with legal matters, answering mail, making telephone calls, doing the banking and bill-paying, filling out medical insurance forms, watering the plants, sending over casserole meals, helping with nursing chores, or whatever.

- After sympathizing with how "bloody awful" your friend who has cancer, heart, or lung disease must feel, take an upbeat approach with that person— "Of course, you're going to beat it! Of course, you're going to get well."

- If you know of others who have had the same disease and are now—long afterward—on top of their physical problems and leading productive lives, use them in conversations with your friend as illustrations of successful victories over the disease.

- Do research for your friend, seeking out current major articles on the strides being made in the fight against whatever malady she is suffering from. If a woman friend has had a mastectomy, and you run across articles on exercise tips or on fashions like special swimsuits, save them for her. Your thoughtfulness could make a difference in her life.

- When someone undergoing chemotherapy suffers temporary hair loss and must wear a wig, the polite thing to do is ignore it. I have seen people thrown for a loop by the sight of their friend in a wig, then make a joke of it (inappropriate) or go into phony raptures over how great the wig looks (also inappropriate). It is best to ignore the entire subject unless your friend brings it up.

- If she looks seriously ill, don't gush, "Gee, you look great today!" because your friend will know you are being insincere. But if a cancer patient really does look good in her new wig and has obviously made an effort with her appearance, a compliment is very much in order. "You look terrific today!" Just don't mention the wig. (Some people, of course, have a great sense of humor about their wigs, but it is best to let them initiate the jokes on the subject—not you.) One story I like to tell, whether it's apocryphal or not, is about an entire grade school class shaving their heads so that their cancer-recovering friend won't feel awkward coming back to school with a bald head.

- As the months go by, don't keep confronting your friend with the past illness every time you see him. People get cured, or if not cured, so stabilized that they lead normal lives. In other words, just stop inquiring about the person's health or mentioning the "recent" sickness, which may not be so recent anymore. After I passed through and out of colon cancer, I began to resent the people who for the next ten years clutched my arm anxiously every time they saw me, saying, "How *are* you, *really?*"—as though they expected me to keel over and die right in front of them. It made me uncomfortable that they still perceived me as being sick, when in actual fact I was much healthier than many of them. When you beat something like cancer or a heart attack or a lung operation, you expect others to forget you ever had it.

• When someone is actually dying, of course, any peppy, upbeat approach is inappropriate. Just be there by his side, quietly talking when the person feels like it, and remaining silent when the person is tired or is dozing off. Hold the patient's hand, and don't be afraid to touch or kiss him. And if, for a person who is actually dying, you can offer religious comfort and discuss the joys of the "life hereafter," *do it.* It will be one of the last real favors you can perform for that person. I have a friend who is a proud atheist, who vehemently proclaims there is no God. Yet I will never forget the description of his actions one night when he sat beside the bed of a sick mutual friend. The nurse had just gone out of the house on a short errand. The patient suddenly sat bolt upright and said, "I need to see someone about God." Without hesitation the atheist visitor picked up the telephone by the bed and called the rectory of the Episcopalian church across the street. A priest was there in ten minutes—just in time to ease his friend's passage from this world to the next.

The fact that you are a constant visitor when someone is dying—even if you are not permitted in the room for more than a minute or two at a time—is a great comfort to the person who is sick, and also to the person's family. A grave illness is no time for abandonment but rather a time for patience and solid support. Your friend's family may send you away because there is nothing you can do, but if you have left your name and telephone number and the message, "I'll be waiting; I'll always be there when you need me," you have no idea how much comfort that gives the grieving family. You also have no idea when someone in that house will pick up the telephone and dial your number because you *are* needed.

When You Have a Good Friend with AIDS

• Don't ask her about it. Let the person tell you first. She may not want you to know at first.

• Stop others from broadcasting the news about the illness prematurely, because there is sometimes severe discrimination against a person with AIDS. Ask the rumor-spreader, "Did she tell you herself she has AIDS? Do you know it for a fact? Well, then I think you shouldn't be telling me—or anyone else— that you 'think' she has become infected."

• When the person's condition becomes public knowledge, rally around her (or around the family, in the case of a child who has contracted it). If you are a caring colleague of a person with Acquired Immune Deficiency Syndrome, make sure he has seen an AIDS counselor. When conditions worsen and the person grows weaker, make sure someone is taking charge of his meals and baths and keeping the sickroom clean.

• Urge everyone to visit your friend regularly, to call to find out how he's doing, and to send over treats (which, even if he can't eat them, will be enjoyed by all his visitors!)—a "special flavor" ice cream or a favorite casserole, for example—and to make certain he is receiving the proper care, such as taking medication regularly, seeing the doctor when necessary, being given regular baths, getting clean sheets put on the bed regularly, and so forth.

Some people totally reject an AIDS victim, and some families have been known to be downright cruel when confronting a relative with the disease. I will never forget a friend who suffered from AIDS whose lover had abandoned him and whose family had not spoken to him from the time they learned he was gay. When the parents learned their son was dying of AIDS, they took action only once, and that was to take every stick of furniture out of his apartment, except the bed on which he was lying in a weakened condition. His apartment had been furnished with family antiques, and his parents were afraid these would go to his lover, so they left him to perish in a bare apartment.

We should do everything we can to help anyone die with dignity—whether that person is male or female, homosexual or heterosexual. We are all just human beings, after all.

WHAT YOU SAY TO THE PERSON
WHO HAS JUST SUFFERED A LOSS

I remember talking to a very recent young widow when she was trying to explain how she felt. There was a need for her to put her feelings in words at that particular time. A third friend present, a man, was convinced that our widow friend should not even be allowed to discuss the tragedy. As she tried to eject from herself bits of grief, one at a time, he interrupted constantly, chattering on about what was happening in the Super Bowl contest. She finally turned to him and said in the nicest possible way, "Henry, I know you're trying to cheer me up. And I love you for it. Normally I am incredibly interested in the Super Bowl. Next year I will be again, but not this year. Would you mind?"

• Be sensitive in your comments. A friend should never say, "You're young, you'll be married again right away." That is not the comfort the survivor needs. When a person says to a widow, "Well, thank heavens you don't have any children, for it will be much easier for you to remarry," the insensitivity of the remark cuts right through her. It is also wrong to take away from the seriousness of a widowed person's grief by claiming that the children of the marriage will make everything instantly all right—"Oh well, you have Jennifer and Bobby to think about now. You won't have time to think about yourself anymore." Widowed people like their friends to acknowledge the seriousness of their loss, even if there is the comforting presence of their children.

When Someone Loses a Lover

If a relative or a good friend of yours loses a lover—someone with whom there has been a long-standing relationship—that person feels the same grief as a married person who loses a spouse feels. Don't put down the person by thinking, "It's not as if they were married . . ." Whether the lover died or left your friend, the emotional devastation is the same as if the two had been married. *Even if you have disapproved of their relationship,* remember that the person left behind is suffering and deserves your support and sympathy. It's a time for you to:

• Check in on your friend or relative often, to see how he is doing. A friendly voice on the telephone just asking, "How are you coming along?" can mean so much to someone in distress.

• Invite that person to dinner or for activities over the weekend—the toughest time of all to be alone.

Real friendship means support—in good times and in bad.

When a Parent Loses a Child

There is nothing that bears down so grievously on the lives and hearts of parents as losing a child. Friends are desperately needed to stand by at the time of the death, and to be there in the future when a parent wishes to discuss that death. Understanding friends are needed for years to come, too, if a parent refuses to discuss that death and keeps bottling up the grief tightly inside. Some day all those emotions just might explode.

Be there for your grieving friend at the time of the funeral, but also in future years. Don't be afraid to bring up the child's name in a natural way in your conversation as the years go by. ("How Joey would have loved watching this game with us. I remember how he'd always sit absolutely spellbound in this very chair, with his feet up on the hassock, shouting and cheering in front of the TV during the whole Final Four games of the NCAA.")

Most parents become bitter if they feel their child has been forgotten by the world around them—either because the child's life is a subject that is past and not relevant to the present, or because the subject is considered too painful for friends to mention.

It's important to remember the special pain the family feels at times like holidays. Write down the child's birthday in your diary, and remember it in some little way every year. (Don't observe the anniversary of the child's death. Most parents prefer you to remember happy living memories, like birthdays.)

I know someone who has contributed children's books to the library of his small town on his friends' little girl's birthday every year since her death in a tricycle accident. The books are in a special section of the library, marked with her name "In Memoriam for Terry" and the years of her life. There are now 150 books there, each one reminding its young reader of the girl in whose memory the books were given. It's nice to do something special like that to remember a child. It means the child will not be forgotten as long as the library is open, and the books are there.

WHEN YOUR FRIEND HAS A MISCARRIAGE

Be very careful and sensitive in talking to someone who has suffered a miscarriage. If there is one thing she does *not* want to hear, it's, "Oh, it's nothing. You'll have another one right away again. Cheer up!" That kind of "comfort" downgrades her grief. And if there is one thing the grieving parents don't want to hear it's "You're lucky. There was obviously something wrong with the embryo. Thank heavens he was never born!"

We pour out love and consolation when a friend loses a child. Yet when a woman suffers a miscarriage, we are often insensitive. Let your friend know that you are aware of the terrible shock she and her husband have suffered. Let her know that you know—"This is a very tough time for you. It's a tragedy. I'm here to help in any way."

CHAPTER 19

Making Things Right:
When You've Really Messed Up.
Send Roses

To me, one of the worst feelings in the world is when I've done something to make myself look like a fool or, worse, because I've done something to offend someone else in a major way. Everyone has her own way of reacting to such a negative situation. When I find myself in one, my pulse quickens, I sense my heartbeat accelerating, there's a feeling of panic, and the bottom of my stomach feels as though a boulder rolling down the Grand Canyon had just hit it. Obviously, relief must be sought in a situation like this. In my case, relief comes only when I feel the people I've wronged have forgiven me.

After years of practice in surviving such disastrous events, I have become an expert on what to do. Just to give you a look at a few experiences:

At age nine, I was a "portal page" along with my friend Patsy Garrett at the Ak-Sar-Ben Ball in Omaha, Nebraska. This was the biggest social and civic event of the year, magnificently staged, with the crowning of a prominent king and queen, whose identities were kept secret until that night, and a procession of beautiful debutante "princesses and countesses of the Royal Realm of Quivera" in magnificent designer ballgowns.

Patsy and I were beside ourselves with the honor, prestige, and excitement of being the door openers. Twenty-five thousand people had jammed into the Coliseum to witness the pageant, and we, the portal pages, were to initiate the entire proceedings. Clad in white satin, rhinestone-studded knicker suits, with white plumed satin berets, we were to open the great ceremonial doors when we were given the signal from backstage that the pageant was to begin. Our signal finally came: the blaring of what seemed like a thousand trumpets (but were probably only fifteen). Patsy and I moved across the stage in perfect unison (how often we had rehearsed) and in one graceful motion pulled on the great gold knobs of the giant doors. Nothing happened. Twenty-five thousand pairs of eyes were on us. The trumpets kept blaring. Some workman for some insane reason—most likely revenge against the ball officials—had nailed the portals shut right before the performance. We could hear the pageant director swearing at us from behind the scenes. Finally backstage they realized our problem, and we heard the director's voice through the doors: "Be calm. While the carpenter is summoned, stand together, you two, straight as arrows, your arms akimbo as though you are guarding the gates, and smile. Smile like you have never smiled in your life!" (Those were words of tremendous wisdom. I don't know about Patsy Garrett, but I've used that advice about smiling when in great adversity in public many times in my life.) The trumpets continued trumpeting, we stood there smiling as though this entire humiliation were all part of the show. Finally the hammers arrived, the nails came off, and we could open the big doors.

There was an even worse embarrassment the night I played a Rachmaninoff solo on the piano at a Convent of the Sacred Heart recital in eighth grade, and the top of the grand piano came smashing down because of an improperly placed stick prop. The piano strings resonated with loud dissonance through my entire piece, and I could see my mother with her face buried in her hands (whether in grief or in laughter, I could never decipher), but my father's face read, "Continue—you have to go on." I smiled at the audience as I asked God why He had let this happen to me, but I finished.

It's very intimidating when you embarrass and merit the wrath of the president of the United States as I have. I made President Kennedy furious his first Monday in office, because of the party I'd produced the night before in the White House, a reception for all of the new ranked government officials. Applying my many years of embassy experience, I had open bars strategically placed around the main floor to make a smooth flow for the party guests. The morning papers the next day screamed headlines about the Kennedys shattering several sacred traditions—serving liquor with the press present (never done before); having bars for the first time in the White House; and having a party on a sacred day, Sunday. I had broken every rule in one easy sweep, and a delegation of Baptist belt congressional leaders immediately called on the president to express their horror and disgust. The president summoned me to the Oval Office and gave me a dressing-down for getting him into a well-publicized mess on his first official day in office.

I was mortified for having caused him such embarrassment. I told him I felt like doing myself in. I told him I'd hire a skywriter to write in the sky that it was all my fault, not the Kennedys'. I told him I would march into the muskets of a firing squad, if it would help expiate for my crime. He laughed, put a consoling hand on my shoulder, and congratulated me on a really effective apology. "Never forget how to apologize like that, Tish," he said. "You're very effective, even if you did rob me of the chance to really give you hell." (By the way, there never again have been bars in the White House; drinks are always passed at official functions.)

I have had to apologize many times, not only in my embassy and White House lives, but also in my business career. I have survived some real disasters.

One was in connection with Burlington Industries' national interior design project, the Burlington House Awards. These were the days when Burlington was the largest textile producer in the world. These prestigious annual awards were given to people who had tastefully and creatively designed their home interiors. One year, as usual, I gave our mailing house a list of the thirty-two winners and a separate list of the many losers in the competition. I wrote a sympathetic prototype letter to be sent to the losers over my facsimile signature, thanking them for entering, praising them for their lovely homes, but regretfully informing them they were not winners.

I wrote another prototype letter for the winners, congratulating them, telling them of the awards ceremony to come and the glory of all the publicity they would receive. Unfortunately, there was a small error in the actions of the mailing house: They inadvertently switched the lists of names and mailed the "Congratulations, you have won a Burlington House Award" letter to the enormous list of losers, and to the small list of winners, they mailed the "Sorry, you lost" letter.

After meditating a few minutes on why God had let this happen to me, I concluded that the combination of AT&T's telephone lines around the country plus some acting prowess on the part of my staff could pull us through this impossible situation. I called the staff together as well as some of my friends with acting ability to become volunteers. We took over several of Burlington's telephone lines for the next two days. I gave everyone a detailed rehearsal—an acting lesson, in fact—on what to say and how to sound as if performing in a Greek tragedy. We called hundreds of people, moving from one time zone to the next, calling back repeatedly if necessary until there was an answer. Finally, after two days, we had reached every single family of losers who thought they were winners. We used drama and pathos to explain our "unpardonable mistake." We threw our emotions full force into our voices, sounding truly upset and sincere about our apology. (*"Please* forgive us, Mrs. Snodgrass. *How* could we have done such a thing to you? Will you ever forgive us, Mrs. Snodgrass?") With the exception of one person who was downright nasty about the mistake, the people we called were understanding and nice, and we were forgiven. They kept saying to one of my telephone brigade, "Look, it's all right. I'm not upset. Please don't worry about it!" (This proved once again that my philosophy really works—when you apologize so fervently, and the wronged person ends up consoling you!)

I told the management of Burlington about the mailing errors *after* everyone had been informed and the psychological damage was already healing. The power of an abject apology is unlimited!

MAKING AMENDS

YOUR GUESTS HAVE ARRIVED
BUT YOU HAVE MIXED UP THE DATES AND NOT REALIZED
TONIGHT IS YOUR SIT-DOWN DINNER PARTY

If you forgot a lunch date with a friend who stood miserably on the corner in the rain and wind for forty-five minutes waiting for you, that friend is going to be justifiably angry—to put it mildly. Your feelings of anxiety and embarrassment for having done that to your friend probably will be even stronger than his resentment toward you. When you stand up someone—whether a customer or a friend—you never quite heal from embarrassment over what you put the other person through. You should make not only quick amends but artful ones as well. An out-of-town business colleague of mine who left me waiting for him in an airport for over an hour and never came at all, did the following when he realized his error: (1) sent me a long message of apology; (2) sent me a dozen long-stemmed roses; (3) took me to lunch at the 21 Club the next time he came back into town; and (4) ordered a car to pick me up at my office and take me back again after the lunch. (I call that *expiation in style*.)

A friend of mine who had been stood up on a date was equally impressed when the blind date who had done this terrible deed baked two batches of Toll House cookies for her to prove his sincerity. Another friend, who inadvertently forgot a business meeting with someone she hadn't seen for two years, sent him a large, expensive imported Italian prosciutto, which she knew was his favorite gourmet food. Her note read, "With every stroke of the knife as you slice this ham, think of it as a knifing of me for having forgotten our meeting." He told her later he had only kind thoughts of her when he cut off paper-thin slices of prosciutto, and since she subsequently landed his business, it all goes to prove two concepts: that not all missed appointments bring disastrous results, and that there is a little ham in us all.

I have forgotten more than my proper share of accepted dinner invitations because of being overextended, but also through sheer carelessness in how dates are entered in my agendas. (The keeping of two books, one at the office and one in my briefcase, is often responsible for these mistakes.) My husband and I have also arrived more than once at a dinner party on the wrong night, thanks to my error. (It's a great feeling to arrive at someone's house all dressed up and to have your hosts answer the door in their pajamas and robes.) I have also put down engagements on the wrong date in my diary. Not to excuse myself, but these are all good reasons why a hostess should send reminder cards, containing all of the salient facts, to any guest who accepts her invitation on the telephone and may have forgotten to record the details.

I have even invited people for an informal Sunday night supper at our house and then forgotten about it, forgetting even to mention it to my husband. When this happens, you have options. You can play upon your guests' sympathies, apologize with pathos and drama, and immediately invite them to a later, much better dinner party than you had originally planned for them. Or you can bluff right then and there, pretend you were expecting them, and feed them pot luck that evening. (If you take the latter approach, keep an outward calm when you are in the living room with your guests, even if your mind is moving like a whirling dervish, trying to think what is in the refrigerator to serve.)

The more absentminded you are, the more creatively apologetic you must be in order to heal the wounds. I have taken all of the steps listed below after being an unintentional no-show at a party given by friends—and I have been forgiven, so the same responses will probably work for you:

• Telephone your hosts and make a dramatic, really sincere apology. Admit that they have the right to be furious, and tell them you know how humiliated they must have felt with that empty place (or places) at the table. Ask your host if it would be a good idea if you casually called some of the other guests whom you know well to explain the mixup—why you weren't there when you were supposed to be. (Often there is a legitimate excuse—an assistant may have written down the wrong date on the boss's calendar—and when the other guests know this, they are relieved.) The main problem to alleviate may be the social anxieties you have caused your host, particularly if it is someone you do not know very well.

• Go to your host's house or office to offer an in-person apology. This always makes a big impression.

• Send or leave a note (your apology thus goes on the record), accompanied by flowers or a gift.

Or follow through with with a combination of all three of the above.

WHEN YOU COMMIT A SERIOUS GAFFE
IN MAKING INTRODUCTIONS

Having spent many years in diplomatic circles, when I was required to introduce people properly, I have pulled some giant boners. At the American embassy in Rome, when the border wars between India and Pakistan were at their height, I introduced the new ambassador from Pakistan to the entire diplomatic corps as the new ambassador from India. (He did not immediately understand what I was doing, since I was introducing him in Italian, a language he did not yet know how to speak. When he was apprised of the mistake I had made at his first formal introduction to the diplomatic corps, he left in a terrible huff. I called him at the embassy; he wouldn't take the call. I wrote him two dramatic letters of apology, which he did not acknowledge, and finally I sent him a dozen long-stemmed red roses with yet another apology. He called me immediately, saying he could not resist a young lady who sends him roses, and I was forgiven. (I have been sending red roses to men ever since!)

Most of us make mistakes in introductions all through our lives, although of lesser gravity than my India-Pakistan debacle. If you, for example, introduce an old friend by her former husband's name (knowing full well that she remarried years ago), just apologize and explain that you are "so bad at names, so careless with past and present names. *Please* forgive me for doing that." It's when you don't say anything and leave your mistake hanging in the air that the person you have misintroduced becomes embarrassed, sometimes even infuriated.

I remember Clare Boothe Luce, my boss at the embassy in Rome, telling me how often throughout her life she was publicly misintroduced. As a speaker, she was constantly presented to large audiences as "the celebrated actress, Miss Claire Luce" (an actress with a similar name with whom she detested being confused). The author of *The Women*, a famous play about bitchy women all in the act of getting divorces, Claire Luce doubled over with laughter on the lecture platform in front of two thousand people upon being introduced as "that famous author of *Little Women*" (Louisa May Alcott's famous novel about a nineteenth-century family). Clare Luce told the audience she was delighted to have her book confused with Louisa May Alcott's incredibly successful classic, but added that she doubted Louisa May would feel equal pleasure.

When my father, a well-known Republican, was running for Congress from the state of Nebraska, he was introduced to a national radio audience as "that famous leader of the Democratic Party from the state of Nebraska." He laughed and said that although his party was Republican, he would be very happy to annex the Democratic party into his own and give it the leadership it had been lacking all those years.

I remember how embarrassed a business friend was when he introduced a military officer above his proper rank. The officer spoke to the large throng and thanked his introducer for introducing him two ranks higher instead of two ranks lower. "You're going the right way," he said. "Just remember that anyone in the military will be delighted to be introduced at a higher rank any time— just any time!"

A flash of humor—and not a solemn correction—is what is needed when someone mis-introduces you. If you forget a good friend's name, or someone forgets yours, make light of it. Don't let the other person suffer. "Andy, I, too, forget names all the time. Don't think a thing about it. I'll forget yours next week. There, will that make you feel better?"

In other words, if you embarrass yourself by making a mistake in regard to someone else, you can contain the mistake by the speed and the creativity with which you offer your apology. And if someone else is embarrassed because you have been the victim of his or her error, keep your sense of humor and show everyone that you are a good sport.

When you make a minor social gaffe and apologize promptly and sincerely, instead of losing a growing friendship you often can cement it by showing that you are concerned and really care about the other person's feelings.

CONTROL THAT TEMPER!

One way to make sure that others won't like us is to be unable to control our anger, whether that anger is justified or not. All of us become angry at one time or another—it is almost impossible not to–but there are ways of dealing with it. Some people deal with it by becoming unacceptably hostile. But most of us do not become antisocial. Instead, we kick the desk, put our head in our arms and cry, pound the table with a fist, or look around for a voodoo doll into which to stick a pin or two.

I believe that yanking your sense of humor from your subconscious and sending it up to do battle in the front lines with your temper is the very best way to handle the situation. For example:

• Have a private chat with your dog, pouring out your emotions and reciting all the injustices done to you. There is no being more supportive, no pair of eyes more sympathetic and understanding. Perhaps your cat or your bird would also be a good listener, but a dog—even a borrowed one—is probably your biggest eye-contact sympathizer.

• Write an absolutely furious letter to the person who wronged you. State everything that should be said, and castigate the recipient in the richest prose you can summon. Read the letter aloud—with great dramatic embellishments—at least five times. Then tear it into shreds and destroy it. (*Under no circumstances* should you mail it!)

• Try some yoga. Get a book on yoga if you are not familiar with any of its techniques. You either will relax from the breathing exercises and forget why it is you're so angry, or you will become tired and relaxed from trying to understand how to do the yoga. Either result will be beneficial to anger control.

• Practice any sport in which you have a glimmer of interest. Smash tennis balls against the backboard, bounce the basketball as hard as you can in the driveway, and drive your golf ball as though it were the devil incarnate. You should become spent from all that physical effort—enough to make you stand back from your anger, get a proper perspective on it, and need a shower.

• Clean house as if you've never cleaned it before. Pretend you're vacuuming up your enemy into the dust bag or wiping him away with your polishing cloth.

• Do a physically demanding, much-hated chore—like raking all the leaves in the yard or taking everything off the kitchen shelves, washing them and the shelves, and putting everything back. You will be so proud of yourself afterward that the edge will be off your anger.

• Follow any great physical effort with a nice warm bath, including bath oil or bubbles or a special fragrance. (I'm addressing men as well as women!) It's hard to retain negative feelings lying in such a relaxed, sweet-smelling place.

• Go see a movie, and crunch hard on your popcorn. That munching action is very therapeutic and relaxes an overly tense jaw.

• Better yet, go to a museum. There are so many anguished- or angry-looking people in the famous Old Masters paintings hanging on the walls; you'll conclude that they're far worse off than you ever could be. You will begin to feel calm by comparison.

• Play music—your soothing, beautiful CDs, whether they're Ella Fitzgerald, Schubert, Chopin, or Sting recordings. Listening to music is a wonderful way to calm down.

In other words, defuse your anger with deliberate countermeasures. Then the next day you won't have done or said anything you have to be sorry for. You'll be *in charge of yourself.*

PART 6

THE KEY TO GOOD
COMMUNICATION:
MORE THAN ELECTRONICS

You can spend your life pressing keys, buttons, and whistles to get your thoughts across electronically, but the ability to use language, to communicate with people in times of joy and sorrow, and to persuade, soothe, enchant, or calm another person, is a great gift. It's also an art. We all can become accomplished in this art, if we just make ourselves aware of how important it is to both our success and happiness.

We have a lot of difficulty keeping in touch with one another in today's busy world. Nevertheless, we need the support of our friends, we need the affection of our relatives, and we need to tell people we still think about them, that we hope they are well and happy. It does not take very much time. Whether you are making your second telephone call of the week on your cell phone to your shut-in grandmother, writing an old college friend who has been ill, or telling friends you see at dinner that their children are wonderful, *you are performing a human service, an act of kindness.* You are epitomizing communication at its best.

CHAPTER 20

How to Be an Interesting Conversationalist

It's no secret that our society is not doing too well these days conversationally, despite the multitude of talk shows. Many of us spend all day in front of a monitor, staring at a new kind of Esperanto computerese on a screen. Then we spend our evenings sitting in front of another electronic screen, or else we wear our Walkman earphones like wallpaper over our ears to shut out the sounds of the world. Where is the human element, the sparkle of the spoken word, the harmonious music of the human voice in all of that?

In our stressful times, more than ever it's people, not computers, we need. No one has ever called a computer warm and fuzzy. But no one needs people who are inherently boring, either. It's the good conversationalists who make us feel good, season our days, and serve as insurance that others in our presence will enjoy themselves, too. Stimulating people are magnets around whom we cluster quite happily.

The affirmative aspect of conversation is that anyone of average intelligence can become quite good at it. To be a good conversationalist is to be unselfish—as well as constantly learning. It requires a process of continuous self-education and an attitude of caring about other people—getting away from oneself and thinking of others. A good conversationalist thinks outside and beyond himself; he is neither limited to what is inside him nor constricted by an obsession with himself. He knows that a little digging will always unearth something interesting in the other person.

You don't have to have graduated from a great university to be a good conversationalist. You don't have to be rich or social. You just have to be seized with a passion for life, a curiosity, a *desire to learn* every day of your existence. Even if you're stuck with an unmitigated bore for a long period of time, you can make yourself dig a little into that person, ask some questions, and there is no doubt but that you will find something interesting as a result of this labor. You can talk about it the next day at the office, or at the PTA meeting, or with your children. A lesson you have learned can be a lesson they learn.

THE TWO V'S: VOICE AND VOCABULARY

Your conversation is certainly enlivened and more "listenable to" with a good vocabulary, but it is also transmitted far more effectively if there's a good voice behind it. When you hear someone saying that a person has a great speaking voice, it probably:

- Is well modulated
- Is easy to understand, with good enunciation
- Is not strained but rather has a low, comfortable pitch
- Projects enthusiasm, rather than fatigue or boredom
- Is not strongly accented, never guttural nor unintelligible
- Has good volume control, neither too loud nor too soft
- Is neither too fast nor too slow, but well paced

Most of us don't have a clue what we sound like, and when we finally hear ourselves on a recording, we are often surprised, even disappointed and incredulous. "Do I really sound like *that*?" If you think your voice doesn't muster up, ask a good friend or two. If they agree with you, don't despair, there's plenty of help. Buy a good voice recorder. Recite poems and editorials from the daily newspaper. Try this when you are feeling tired and refreshed. Then listen carefully to all the tapes yourself. Next, ask family members to listen, or colleagues or close friends. If they begrudgingly admit your voice *could stand a little improvement,* go to work. You will find freelance speech therapists in most cities. There are drama coaches at local colleges or repertory groups, public speaking teachers, any of whom need to earn a few extra dollars—yours! You will be given simple daily exercises to improve your breathing, diction, and tone. When you become a confident, persuasive speaker, whether you are sitting with a client at the dinner table or out with old friends at dinner in a fast-food joint, you become suddenly a more likeable person.

THE FORCE OF A DYNAMIC VOCABULARY

Ears turn toward someone speaking with an imaginative vocabulary like planes picking up radar. Our English language is superbly full of nuance and subtlety. We should be proud to use it well. Unfortunately, today there is more abuse than proper use of our language.

My former boss, the late Clare Boothe Luce, said one day, "Good language is contagious." The trouble is, so is bad language. Street talk with its obscenities, including on TV, is used almost like a badge of honor. Many say "No problem" following anything another person says, which has nothing to do with what has just been said. When it's shortened to "No prob," the abyss grows deeper. People who make a word such as "like" follow every verb they utter absolutely destroy the meaning of their sentences. Foul language is now so common, it no longer shocks most people (they may find the language distasteful, but not shocking). When this happens, a society should realize it's in *real trouble.*

TV anchors, earning in the millions of dollars, make one grammatical error after another on air ("That's real nice" . . . "When he gave it to her and I" . . . "How do you feel, Jane? *Real* good.")

A good vocabulary is fostered in a child within a nurturing family life. One family I know devoted five minutes at their dinner table every night to a word game. A new word was learned, and each child then had to make up a sentence using that word properly. Occasionally a dictionary had to be brought to the table. Those parents instilled a love of the language into those four children that has grown and flowered into their very successful adult lives.

When a wordsmith like William F. Buckley, Jr., is on TV, listeners should keep a dictionary and a pad by the set to write down every new word he tosses out so casually. Just throwing a new word into the hopper of your computer is not as effective as actually writing it down and using it in conversation before adding it to the list of words in your computer.

Can We Start a Literacy Crusade in the Workplace?

Just as parents should be the role models for their children in using good English, so managers in the workplace have a great opportunity to work with their employees on good language usage. If supervisors use good English and develop rich vocabularies, even in their written memoranda, the junior staff members might just try to follow suit. Who knows? We might be able to beat street talk back into the streets and out of our homes and businesses.

SMALL TALK

One dictionary defines "small talk" as "casual or trivial conversation," a subject that terrifies many young people when they enter the business or professional world. They are advised by senior colleagues not to talk business the minute they sit down at a business lunch, for example, but to make small talk for ten minutes or so, and then jump feet first into the project at hand. My own definition of small talk is "amiable, unhurried communication." You make small talk with strangers when you're standing in the lengthy post office line during the holidays. You make it when standing on the station platform waiting for the commuter train to pull in. You make it with friends and strangers alike. It's an effective social tool. Traditionally, small talk began with comments about today's weather, but fortunately that subject is now considered hopelessly trite. Discussing the weather does not exactly bring out the creative best in people!

When you're sitting next to someone who would best be described as "a little old lady" at dinner in your vice president's home, you had better speak to her, try to charm her, particularly if she's your boss's mother-in-law. Then she will speak very well of you in subsequent conversations with her son-in-law.

In spite of its diminutive aspects, small talk is important. Knowing how to make it effortlessly is a gift as well as a social tool. It often becomes a combined business and social plus. It is an instrument of communication that renders a person attractive and makes him or her pleasant to sit next to at a dinner party, or across from at a lunch where business is being conducted. It's important to remember that:

At a business lunch

If you're the guest, make small talk until your host signals that it's time for the business discussions to begin.

If you know the other person is married and has a family, ask him a very general question about it. If he drops the subject fast, follow suit. If he continues on the subject, it signals he is flattered by your interest.

Bring up light business subjects such as new companies starting up, stories of human interest, funny happenings. The other person wants to enjoy her meal, not be depressed with your latest statistics of business failures or national emergencies.

If you know a good joke, the best time to tell it is during the soup course, before the serious business discussion begins—or quote an apt proverb, such as business advice from Abraham Lincoln: "When you can't remove an obstacle, plow around it."

At a social function

Give equal time to everyone around you, particularly both dinner partners, even if one person is much more attractive and amusing than the other.

If conversation bogs down, get the other person talking about herself, a guarantee that the conversational ball will keep rolling during the meal.

Launch light topics of conversation, not depressing ones. Your partner is not going to want to hear about the auto accident that befell the man who lives down the street; he would rather hear about the beautification project on your city's waterfront.

If you can quote an appropriate proverb, dazzle your dinner partner with your sense of timing. For example, if he expresses agreement with you, tell him you now feel like the great Disraeli, who said, "My idea of an agreeable person is someone who agrees with me."

The main thing to remember about small talk is to keep it light and upbeat. If you remember to smile while you talk, you'll make the person listening to you smile, too. The same thing happens when you second.

When Not to Make Small Talk

Of course, there are times when it is best to remain silent. When someone is concentrating—working, reading, intensely involved in the task at hand—leave her alone. At a dinner party, people are supposed to make chit-chat during the service of a meal. On an airplane, on a bus, a train, in the doctor's waiting room—wherever—a person concentrating should be left alone. *This includes one's boss when you are accompanying her in a car or waiting to see a client.* If your boss is studying papers in her briefcase, let her open up the conversation if she chooses to. And if she does, but then you see her start to go back to her papers with her eyes, return to your papers and let her work again.

If you are talking to someone sitting beside you on an airplane and he is working, leave that person alone. If you are the one being bothered by a "talker" (I seem to get one of these on almost every long trip), be very pleasant but firm: "I wish I could talk to you. I can see you are a very interesting person. But unfortunately I'm on a deadline and have a great deal of work to do before we land. I hope you don't mind."

SO WHAT *ARE* YOU GOING TO TALK ABOUT?

• A good conversationalist is very aware of the kinds of subjects that please most people, so he, in an act of leadership, pulls out just the right topic for the occasion. Then the give and take among the people present seems to ignite.

• The good conversationalist also knows that a successful "conversational launch" depends not only on the subject but on the occasion and on the kind of group.

• If only one person in the group plays golf, a good conversationalist does not go on about that sport, because she knows only one pair of ears will really be listening.

• If she is at a funeral, she does not discuss the latest gossip she has heard, because it's simply not an appropriate time to discuss such frivolous (albeit fascinating) things.

• One of his funny and only slightly off-color stories may break up a group of men in the locker room, but that same story could fall with the thud of a sack of bricks in mixed company at his office.

• A good conversationalist takes the temperature of the group and the occasion before leading the discussion. She is successful when she is sensitive to others and wants to please them—an unselfish point of view. In general, there are some topics that please more than others.

Good Conversational Moves

- Taking an item from that day's newspaper that's fun to talk about or introduces an unusual topic of interest.
- Asking parents about their new baby.
- Congratulating someone for having recovered from an operation or illness.
- Proposing new ways of raising funds for an illness like AIDS.
- Providing news on sports of major national interest, such as the Olympics or World Series.
- Discussing any heartening news of the economy.
- Starting an informed discussion on local civic problems.
- Describing fascinating new educational experiments you have heard about.
- Providing happy news of mutual friends.
- Talking about the latest cultural performances of excellence.
- Divulging good news on the health and nutrition fronts.
- Telling people to be sure to watch an upcoming TV program that is purported to be excellent.
- Discussing how the local real estate market is doing.
- Talking about ways to help a mutual friend who has lost his job.
- Talking about someone's lucky break.

Bad Conversational Moves

- Taking a grim, depressing item from that day's newspaper, guaranteed to make everyone feel discouraged.
- Asking someone if his marriage is breaking up.
- Asking someone to relate the gory details about an illness or operation.
- Asking a couple if it's true their son has AIDS.
- Giving a discourse on a sport known to few if any of those present.
- Giving seriously depressing news of the economy.
- Becoming enraged and emotional about a community issue.
- Damning the entire local school system as being outdated and hopeless.
- Providing information on everyone's miseries.
- Criticizing every new artistic event in town.
- Telling everyone how they now "can't eat this and can't eat that."
- Warning everyone that the upcoming program is reportedly inferior, not worth watching.
- Asking anyone an overly personal question such as what they paid for their house or apartment.
- Wondering aloud about what a mutual friend did to get fired.
- Discussing how our society is going to hell.

A good conversationalist is upbeat and searches for the provocative topics that most people present care about.

If You Don't Want to Be a Bore

You can test to see if you are a bore by becoming aware of how people are responding to you at any given moment while you hold the floor and are talking. If they are looking around the room at other people or things . . . if their eyes are slightly glazed over . . . if they have sunk deep into their chairs so that they are practically lying down instead of sitting up . . . if they have given up trying to interrupt you . . . if, out of the corner of your eye, you see them glancing at their watches, beware—you are boring them.

It's the conversationalist who overdoes it, who won't get off the subject, who sticks to his topic like a gummed label who is the bore. The three topics most likely to bore are your health, your job, and your children.

If you have had a serious illness and you run into your friend Gregg in the street, he will ask with genuine concern, "How are you, Jennifer?" Give him a simple ten-second answer. He knows you are in the land of the living, and he is really not interested in your medications, the changes in the doctors handling your case, the status of your X rays, and the quality of your digestive system at present. You can answer, "I've been out of the hospital a month now and am doing just fine, thank you. I'm really lucky." Enough!

If on the bus you sit next to someone you haven't seen in a while and, to be polite, that person asks you about your children, mention each child's name (she will probably have forgotten their names) and give a report of only a few seconds' length on each. "Jim graduates from junior high this year, Harvey made the tennis team at Lehigh, and Mary Alice is finishing college this June and is going to Europe with some of her friends. They are all in fine form." Enough!

If you mingle after church in the courtyard with some friends you haven't seen for a while and someone asks you about your job, give a quick report. "I left Eagleton and have a new job in computer programming with Steers and Company. It's a great company and I really like my new job." Enough! The intelligent thing to do after someone has asked you about your children, health, or job and you have politely answered them, is to turn quickly to a new subject—one that veers in their direction, away from yours. "Enough about me. How is Hal? And your mother? Are you going to the lake this summer?"

EXTRICATING YOURSELF
FROM A CONVERSATIONAL DILEMMA

It's a good idea to bring up an entirely new subject of conversation when:

• A nasty argument has erupted. (That's the time for a hero in the group to say something like, "Enough about that subject. What I want to know is who here is willing to make a wager on the outcome of the upcoming elections? Who's savvy enough even to know who all the candidates are?")

• The stories are getting dirty in mixed company, which leaves everyone feeling uncomfortable. ("Would anybody mind if I asked George a question? I'd really like to hear the good news about his promotion.")

• Someone or several people are making mincemeat out of a friend of the group who is not present to defend herself. ("Let's stop attacking Suzanne and go in to dinner and attack the shrimp cocktail instead.")

• The conversation is way over the heads of most of those present. Even though two computer hacks may be enjoying their rapid dialogue on computer technology, a few minutes is long enough for them to hold the floor while cutting out the others in the group who do not understand the jargon. (It is appropriate for someone to then interrupt, "You're too smart for the rest of us—it's time to come down to our planet again.")

• Someone has just committed a gross gaffe (such as making an uncalled-for ethnic joke, in response to which one of the people present says that it impugns his wife, and he does not appreciate the humor). What follows is usually a terrible stillness. It really helps if one person has the courage to break the chilling quiet. ("Well, I'm sure there will be apologies later. For now, I'd like to ask Terry, who has just returned from Russia, and who has been trying all night to tell us about her trip, to take the floor and tell us all.")

It also helps if the person who picks up the conversational ball as a good soldier starts to talk and talk, in order to dissipate the tension. Hopefully, too, the person who made the error will take his offended friend outside and make the most earnest of apologies. (Such an offense also calls for a carefully written letter of apology, not just a verbal one.)

I don't know about you, but it happens to me all the time—I become stuck in a conversational booby trap by remarks I initiate to get a conversation going. As Clare Boothe Luce used to say, "No good deed goes unpunished."

Here is an example:

Me: "I noticed your handsome wedding ring. Do point out your wife to me."

Dinner partner: "She died six months ago."

Me: "Oh, I'm so very sorry."

He: Silence

If your find yourself in a situation like this and there is a long meal ahead yet to be served and eaten, you might face up to the challenge. To the man who lost his wife, real sympathy is in order: "I imagine these last months have been very hard for you. Do you have people—children perhaps—who are helping you cope?" (The usual reaction on his part will be to talk gratefully about the children, the in-laws, the friends who are giving him assistance; this conversation can last throughout an entire meal.)

The safest way to extricate yourself from an awkward situation is to direct the conversation toward the other person. Almost everyone likes to talk about him- or herself—even someone who seems loath to do so. Just keep floating different topics in his or her direction until that person reaches up to grab one of those colorful balloons.

The Conversational Hero

A conversational hero is the person everyone wants to sit beside. I remember sitting near a young man at a Sunday barbecue lunch; he had been asked by his hostess to talk to her tongue-tied, painfully shy young niece. He asked her question after question, with one-word answers coming back. He told her about himself—his job, what he did in his leisure time—with practically no reaction. Finally, he put his elbow on the table, rested his cheek in his hand, looked her gravely in the eyes, and said, "I've told you everything about myself. I've asked you everything about yourself. Would you like to hear about my dog?"

With that she burst out in laughter; the ice was broken. He was and always will be a conversational hero, because he's basically kind and he uses his sense of humor to open up others.

A conversational hero inevitably:

- Listens. The primary asset of any good conversationalist is the ability to listen attentively to others.
- Does not interrupt. No matter how hackneyed or boring, every speaker deserves to be allowed to finish what she is saying.
- Shows a great sense of humor. To laugh at oneself—without putting oneself down too much or too far—creates an alluring ambience.
- Works tirelessly to charm a bored or boring, even bellicose, guest, an individual who may have been important for the host to invite for some reason, but who, left to his own devices, is a real party destroyer.
- Is able to talk on any subject. This means that the person is well read

and knowledgeable. It also means the person knows how to participate, even when the subject being discussed is not in the realm of her information.

• Knows how to defuse someone else's lugubrious conversation.

Before dinner one evening, I overheard the following discussion between two tired women from Wall Street:

"I feel terrible tonight."

"I don't feel so hot either."

"I got bad news about a friend today."

"Join the club. My best friend died last week."

"Well, I bet you don't have the mess at your office that we have. Another ten percent fired this month."

"The very same thing's about to happen to us, only higher than ten percent."

The host, who heard part of this dialogue, moved in with lightning speed, like John Wayne at a fast gallop, to save the conversation. "From the sound of the two of you, you'll never make it into dinner, you're both so depressed! Cheer up. Come over here to this group. They're discussing just what you need—the incredibly funny Wall Street satire last night on Dave Letterman's TV show."

• Knows how to take a topic of conversation to new, interesting depths. For example, people might be discussing all the historical pageantry of various national anniversary celebrations ranging from George Washington's presidency anniversary to Central Park's one hundred fiftieth year (there's always a celebration somewhere), which causes one person in the group to talk about the thrill of bringing his kids to see Mount Vernon, George Washington's home. This causes another person to talk about a little book of our first President's— the amusing *Rules of Civility* (in essence, an etiquette book for young people, written when Washington was fifteen). Someone else then discusses the new American history book that challenges the entire relationship between the American and French revolutions, which prompts someone else to bring the discussion to Hollywood—and a movie being made on an aspect of the two revolutions.

Good conversation is a pleasant—and kind—give and take on a subject of mutual interest. People weave in and out of it, Virginia Reel–style, as spectators, listeners, and participants. There are some people you always love to talk to—because they're upbeat, amusing, or informative. These are the people who make you feel relaxed and part of their orbit. These are the people who, when you run into them or join them in a business or social situation, cause a reflex reaction in your facial muscles—a nice big smile.

Handling Prying Personal
Relationship Questions

People may not have the right to ask prying questions about relationships between people, but they do anyway. When impertinent, even infuriating questions are asked of you, remember to:

• Keep your cool. Control your quite justifiable anger, because if you become upset, it will only make you look guilt-ridden. You can teach others a lesson only when you are in absolute control of your emotions—and your vocabulary.

• Embarrass the interrogator with a deflecting nonanswer. Never answer directly an impertinent, uncalled-for question. This is a time for sarcasm or at the very least a direct hit—almost to shock the person who asked this question into realizing how out of line he or she was in asking it. For example, whether there's truth to the rumor or not, if someone asks you if your marriage is over because your husband is leaving you for another woman, reply with something like "Divorcing my husband? Whoever told you that?" That will put your interrogator on the spot.

Or if someone asks you, a bachelor, if you are going to be, or are, living secretly with a certain woman, as rumored, answer something like, "Why? Are you hunting for a roommate?"

Or if a friend asks you how far you have gone in your relations with a man you've been seeing, answer something like, "Why don't you ask George that question? Why me?"

• It's all right to challenge your interrogator. For example, "I can't believe that *you*, of all people, would ask me a question like that," or "I can't imagine a real friend delving so far into something so private." Or, "How would *you* feel if I asked you a question like that?"

THE ART OF GIVING
AND RECEIVING COMPLIMENTS

When a compliment comes your way, doesn't it sound nice, and doesn't it feel good? Unfortunately, our society is so uptight and sometimes so overly frank that compliments don't exactly flow around us every day. Many people are afraid to give them, because they don't want to let anyone know what they're feeling inside. Others are afraid to receive them, because they're cynical and suspicious of the motives of any person praising them.

What a nicer, happier world it would be if more of us told one another nice things more often! If there was ever a true statement made, it's that as humans we *need* to be complimented. Children learn to be complimenters from their parents. If, for example, a little boy sees his father watch his wife come down-stairs dressed to go out for the evening, and his father exclaims, "Don't you look *beautiful!*" that little boy has a good chance of growing up to say the same kind of thing to please his wife when he is a grown, married man, too. Too many wives never bother to tell their husbands how handsome they look, and too many husbands neglect even the most basic compliments, such as when a wife asks her husband, "Well, what did you think of my dinner tonight?" and he answers, "I ate it, didn't I?" (He may think that is an incredibly amusing answer, but it's not.)

• You don't have to lie when asked if you like something, and you don't. Some people are against paying social compliments just to please someone, unless the statement is totally accurate. I don't believe a person should lie, but a compliment that is said just to make someone feel good is, to me, a good end in itself. Today, many years after my four-year stay in Rome, I remember fondly certain Italian men whispering in my ear that I was "the most beautiful woman in the world." I knew they were saying the same thing to almost every woman they talked to, but it made me feel happy and wonderful; I couldn't have cared less about the insincerity of the remarks. It was a kind of game of pleasant teasing, but it bubbles going down just like good champagne.

For those who must be 100 percent honest all the time, someone might ask you if you like her new dress when you think it's most unbecoming. You would be truthful if you said "No, I don't like it, it's not becoming." But telling her the truth could really hurt her feelings. *Something* must be a positive about her appearance, so find it and mention it. Her dress might have one redeeming feature—its color, a pretty collar, or even nice buttons. Mention that detail, without saying whether or not you like the dress as a whole. "It's a very nice blue color," or, "That's a good neckline on you."

COMPLIMENTS AS ICEBREAKERS
WHEN CONVERSATION HAS BOGGED DOWN

A compliment is the nicest kind of icebreaker when you are having a tough time getting a conversation going with another person. Even if the other person is as shy as you are, when you pay that person a compliment, she will usually react positively, and the compliment just might cause the recipient to start rowing her end of the boat.

I was seated in an airport gate area one weekend, waiting for my plane to depart. On the seats next to me were two people, obviously employees of the same company, who were trying to make conversation and not succeeding very well. There were many awkward pauses. Although I was reading a newspaper, I was aware of the shyness of both men, particularly the younger one.

His colleague finally said, "Skip, I noticed how good you looked when you got here tonight. Great suit!" Immediately, his companion smiled. "Thanks," he said, "I just bought it last week," and unconsciously straightened up in his chair and began to speak in a much more animated tone. From then on, their conversation flowed with ease. (I, of course, checked out the suit when he stood up, and it was very good looking.)

• When you're shy about speaking to someone of the opposite sex, remember the power of a compliment. It really helps your conversational flow. It's as though you turned on a heater in a cold room. Even if the other person is too shy to give you a snappy reply, your saying something nice gets the words started. Think ahead about complimenting an acquaintance you would like to get to know better. Rehearse your compliment-paying before going out on a date—open a new file of compliments in that computer brain of yours. Then, when you're seated speechless next to your date, go into that file, select an appropriate compliment, and come out with it. It doesn't matter whether it pertains to the other person's good looks, personality, ability, or intelligence—say whatever seems appropriate at the moment. For example, it might be difficult for a shy young man to say to his date what he's thinking, "You are so beautiful," but he might be able to say, "You look really good tonight" . . . or, "I watched you at the meeting the other day. You were terrific" . . . or, "You know something, you have very pretty eyes" . . . or, "I like dancing with you. You really know how to dance" . . . or, "I like the way you laugh. It's a nice laugh" . . . "That's a really neat dress you're wearing" . . . or, "You have a great sense of humor!"

Here are some standard occasions on which a compliment should be paid:
- When you know someone is wearing a new dress or suit. ("Hey, George, you look really special" . . . "Mamie, that's a great new coat!")
- After your hosts have served you a delicious meal. ("Joan, that was the best lasagne I've had in years. You're a master pasta chef!")
- After someone has made a public appearance. ("Your speech was *very* effective. If anyone can get that fund drive launched, it's you. Well done!")
- After there has been recognition or an honor bestowed, either on your friend or colleague or on a member of that person's family. ("What wonderful news about Henry! He's a chip off the old block. He's headed for the top.")
- When someone has expended great effort on a project. ("Mary, your entry in the show was sensational. Your plantings were just so perfectly designed and installed; the whole Garden Club must be proud of you.")

- After a person has successfully and intentionally altered his physical appearance. ("You look slim and trim. The weight loss is very becoming" . . . "Your makeover course was a great success. You look terrific.")
- When a person has done something courageous. ("The way you stuck up for Roger and defended him was wonderful. You are the kind of friend everyone should have.")
- When a friend did a good job in competitive sports, whether he won or lost. ("Mark, you played so well today! It's a shame you lost, but you were brilliant out there and next time you'll win.")

KNOW HOW TO ACCEPT A COMPLIMENT

If we Americans are not good compliment-payers, I think it's safe to say that we're even worse compliment-receivers! How often do you tell someone how great she looks and instead of receiving a thank-you, you're given a protest? For example:

"Mary, you look so pretty today."

"Oh no, I don't! I have this awful pimple on the end of my nose, and the hem is coming out of my dress. I look ghastly."

"Albert, you gave an excellent presentation in the Board Room this morning."

"Oh no, it was awful. I choked up several times. I had a feeling no one could hear me, and I forgot the punch line to the entire thing. It was a disaster!"

When someone says something nice to you, say "Why, thank you!" or, "Aren't you nice to say that!" or, "I really appreciate those warm words." Whatever you do, don't deny the compliment or try to refute it. It puts down the other person, who was only trying to please you. The perceptible lack of ability to accept compliments is symptomatic of our national uptightness. Instead of feeling embarrassed and compelled to belittle yourself, be grateful and thank the other person for the nice things said to you. Relish them. Write them down and tuck them in a desk drawer. You can take out that note later and read it when you're feeling down. (If a grandchild finds it thirty years from now, think how proud you'll both be!)

When You Notice a Friend's Physical Change for the Better—or If You Notice It's a Change for the Worse

If a person has done something to greatly enhance his appearance, compliment that person without referring to a specific improvement. For example, to say, "You look absolutely wonderful!" may elicit a response such as, "Oh, so you noticed my weight loss," or "Do you really like my new hair color?" Then there will be further conversation. Or, your compliment may elicit only a curt "Thanks," in which case you should pursue the subject no further, because that person is obviously sensitive about people noticing any change. Some men violently object to being accused of having any plastic surgery done, which is probably a sign they have had *a lot* done!

If a good friend looks ill to you, don't comment. Just continue talking about pleasant, upbeat subjects. If she brings up the subject, then, of course, you can come forth with all your sympathetic, loving support.

To have the reputation of being a great conversationalist will bring magic into your life. You will be sought as a guest at everyone's party; people will lean in your direction to hear what you have to say; people will quote you—the sincerest form of flattery. It's well worth acquiring the self-discipline and the knowledge it takes to become a good conversationalist. And when you become one, think of this: You will even amuse yourself!

CHAPTER 21

Great Telephone Manners at Home

HOW YOU SOUND AFFECTS HOW PEOPLE SEE YOU AND FEEL TOWARD YOU

You undoubtedly know people whose voices on the telephone are so attractive that speaking with them is always a pleasant experience. Theirs are happy voices that give a psychological lift to the atmosphere because the warmth in them is contagious.

If we don't listen to our own voices, find the defects in them, and then try to eradicate those, we will go through life with a serious detraction. Consciously put a smile in your voice when the telephone rings. Say "Hello" as though you were glad to come to the phone (instead of cursing it!). If you had to emerge from the shower, dripping water everywhere, in order to answer it, and if the caller was someone trying to sell you magazine subscriptions, be polite. It is a great exercise in character building.

IT'S IMPORTANT TO TEACH TELEPHONE MANNERS TO THE CHILDREN, WHICH MEANS YOU HAVE GOOD ONES YOURSELF!

• Your voice demonstrates whether you're a cold, detached person ("Hey, Joe, what's up?") or a caring person, interested in others ("Joe, it's *great* to talk to you! How's Debbie? And how's that busted ankle of yours?").

• Say hello with enthusiasm, as though you were greeting the stars on Oscar night.

When the call is for someone else, don't scream out that person's name, if he or she is on another floor or behind a closed door. It upsets everyone within hearing distance to hear:

"Andy, it's for you.

"ANDY, TELEPHONE!

"ANDY YOU CREEP, PICK UP THE PHONE!"

Instead of that unpleasant screaming, go looking for him to tell him he has a call. Then, perhaps when he answers a call for you, he won't go screaming to find you.

- Always apologize when you dial a wrong number. To hang up without saying you're sorry will give that person bad indigestion all day.
- Watch the background noises. Don't have the TV or music on.
- If you call someone and the line is disconnected for some reason or other, *you* are supposed to call that person back, even if you're sure it's the other person's fault.
- Don't eat while you are on the phone. Sounds are greatly magnified. Popcorn can sound like gunfire, eating a pizza can sound like a baby sucking on its bottle, and slurping soda can sound like a waterfall occasionally intruding on your conversation.
- It's rude to leave your home phone unanswered for more than four rings. If you move around a lot in your home, and are often far away from the phone when it rings, put additional extensions in your home. Many people use their cell phone for outgoing calls and keep the family line for incoming calls.
- Keep a notepad and sharpened pencil by every telephone in the house. Then no one will have an excuse for not recording a message.
- We should always return calls, preferably within the same day when we take messages off the answering machine or are given written messages from someone in the house. I received a classic written message from a very polite second grader the other day when attending a meeting in a colleague's house: "Ant Tish call your frend." Her mother was proud of her, but added another lesson: "You should have included the word 'Please.' Aunt Tish, *please* call your friend." (The fact that no one had any idea of the identity of the friend who called was immaterial.)
- It's really helpful when family members take good messages and give good information on behalf of a person who is away. "This is Georgie's husband, Mac, calling you back on her behalf. She's away until Monday. Is there anything I should tell her when she calls me tonight from the West Coast?"
  - Adults and children alike should apologize when they dial a wrong number. "Oh, I am so sorry I misdialed. Please excuse me." When a person has been awakened by someone who apologizes sincerely for disturbing him, his anger is greatly abated by the apology. When the caller simply slams down the receiver in the ear of the person she has just awakened, it is infuriating.
  - Call when it's convenient for the other person, not just for you. Start off the conversation with "Is this a good time for you to talk?" Some people prefer to handle personal matters in the evening at home, others early in the morning before going to work. Still others don't wish to be bothered at home with personal calls, and want to be

called only at their offices. If you call someone at home, that person may be taking a soufflé out of the oven, feeding the baby, or arguing with a spouse over their quarterly income tax filing. A caller should always be sensitive to the time pressures on the one he is trying to reach. I find that by asking an important person's executive assistant when the best time is to call, the result is invaluable information.

- The caller should also be sensitive to the other person's ability to stay on the line for a lengthy period. There are people who live alone and are lonely; there are those who are bored; there are others who like nothing better than to while away the hours talking. Then there are those who always seem to be frantic, overscheduled, and suspended in a continuous state of crisis and emergency. (I know this latter group well, since I am one of them.)

- It is an act of human kindness to remember to call regularly those who are lonely and in need of the human contact of another person's voice. It is also an act of human kindness to call those who are overly busy only when necessary, and always with a minimum of time expended.

- Show concern for the elderly when telephoning. Since many elderly people have difficulty getting to the telephone, allow it to ring much longer. Give your relatives the gift of a telephone sound amplifier.

- Use the telephone as an effective tool of kindness, which it is. Call your aging grandparents and impart some family news. Call anyone in hospital, particularly a classmate. Call your father in his office, simply to leave a message that you love him.

TELEPHONE SECURITY WHEN THE KIDS ARE HOME

Be sure the child knows a telephone number to call, including 911, in case something has happened.

If a stranger asks a child on the telephone, "Is your mother home?" the child should be taught that if he does not recognize the voice as that of a relative or a good family friend, he should answer, "I'm sorry, but she is unable to come to the phone right now. I'll have her call you back as soon as she is free."

If the stranger presses further—"Well, is she having a meeting there?" or "Does she have company?"—the child should respond, "She can't be disturbed."

Your child is not telling a lie; you have trained him to state that mother cannot come to the telephone right now. You can put your child at ease with this if you practice calling, acting as a stranger would, playing the devil's advocate, and rehearsing your child to react in such a way so as not to give a stranger any information. As you practice, there will be a lot of giggling and horsing around at first, but eventually the lesson will stick in the child's mind.

Some mothers, forced by economic circumstances to leave their junior-high children home alone while they are at work, have a system whereby no one answers the phone while the children are alone. If a parent wants to get through to the child, she dials twice in rapid succession—a kind of code—and the child knows then to pick up. ("Usually, however," a mother told me, laughing, "I can never talk to them anyway, because they are on the phone with their outgoing calls in alternating turns, so there is no chance for any bad person—or good person—to get through to my house."

THE OFFICE TELEPHONE

Your office telephone is properly answered informatively. In the case of a woman who works for a large real estate firm, for example, the company might instruct her to answer in this manner:
- "Newstead Properties, Joan Jackson speaking," or
- "Joan Jackson, Sales," or
- "Joan Jackson, Commercial Sales."

If an assistant answers for her, it might be:
- "Joan Jackson's office," or
- "Ms. Jackson's office," or
- "Ms. Jackson's office, Ms. Farnham speaking."

- An executive assistant should never answer with just her first name. She loses dignity for her position and herself with the use of a first name only. It is much too informal—and also not informative enough. If, for example, you have to go through an entire organization, trying to track down a "Betty Sue" instead of "Betty Sue Brown," you will have one tough time finding her.

Note: Some of the information systems businesses have a rule—part of their corporate culture—that only first names are to be used. That may work well inside the company, but it can't work all that well in relationships with the outside world. Many people are upset when on the telephone someone they do not know calls them by their first name. We need some dignity and a modicum of formality in order to make life more graceful and efficient.

- Another cold and information-poor way to answer a telephone is with an extension number only. One man I know automatically responds with a question every time he hears a voice answer his call with just an extension number: "Is this the computer speaking?"

- Work with the assistant of the person you're calling. Some people are so ego-driven they speak only with the boss of the office they have called; they are incapable of dealing with the secretary. Well, the smartest way to deal with an executive who has an intelligent assistant is to go through her, leaving substantive messages, impressing upon her the importance of certain actions you hope will be taken, imbuing her with enthusiasm for an idea that you want to sell to her boss, and making her aware of your timetable. Many times in my business life I have realized that the executive assistant understands the nature of my call far better than the boss does. Therefore, I always explain carefully the purpose of my call. She inevitably responds with good advice for me ("Call him back tomorrow morning"; "Write it in a short letter and I'll put it on his desk so he sees it right away"; "Send it FedEx or UPS to his vacation address"; or whatever).

Educate Your Executive Assistant
in Good Phone Manners

- *Instill in him the priority you place on courtesy* in handling incoming calls.
- *Train him not to overscreen your calls* and make you inaccessible to people. No one should be put through the third degree when they try to reach you, such as:

   "What is the nature of your call?"
   "What is the business of your company?"
   "And your position within the company is?"
   "And when did you last speak to Ms. Thatcher?"
   "Will she know what this is about?"

As his boss, you should furnish him with:
  - A list of everyone—family, friends, doctors, teachers—who should be put through to you immediately. ("Just one minute, Mrs. Ellsworth, I know Mr. Henry will wish to speak to you.")
  - A list of secondarily important people whom you would like to speak to if you have the time. ("I know that Mr. Henry wants to take your call. He is on long distance right now, and there are two calls waiting, but when he finishes these three, we'll call you right back.")
  - A list of people you never wish to speak to. ("I'm sorry, Ms. Rogers, but Mr. Henry is really tied up on several important projects at the present. He simply does not have the time to take any calls, so the only advice I can give you is to put whatever you wanted to say to Mr. Henry in a letter, and to send it to this office.")

- *Teach him not to put someone on hold for longer than fifteen seconds.* If you have to help someone on the other line longer than that, have your assistant tell whoever is on hold that you will call back within minutes. (And then do it!)

- A young executive should place his own calls to upper management and not have an assistant do it. The junior person is supposed to be waiting for him, not making the senior person wait once he picks up.
- When you are not in the office, your assistant should automatically say, before she asks for the caller's name, "No, I'm sorry, Ms. Gates is not here. Who is calling, please?"

If the assistant were to answer, "Who's calling, please?" and then say, "Oh, I'm sorry, Mr. Jones, Ms. Gates is out of town," Mr. Jones may very well think that Ms. Gates is giving him the runaround and that she's actually there.

- Teach her to be a deft transferrer of calls. In other words, teach her about the company and who does what, so that when you are not available, she will know to whom she can intelligently transfer a call—to a person who will be able to get action or solve the problem, as well as to someone who will report back.

TAKING GOOD MESSAGES

People should take efficient, legible messages for each other. Otherwise, they should not answer someone else's telephone.

- The caller should not "overload" when leaving a message. A message should not be more complicated than this:
  - The person's name leaving the message, plus the telephone number (with area code and extension number, when pertinent).
  - The time the person called.
  - The name of the person to whom the message is going.
  - One simple piece of information or instruction to be transmitted.

If you leave a message laden with *if's*, *and's*, and *but's*, you can almost be certain that it will not be transmitted with perfect accuracy or efficiency. (The exception, of course, is a competent assistant, who can take the most complicated of messages perfectly, and who acts with speed to get any job done.)

The Person Who Has an Appointment with You and Is Sitting by Your Desk Has Priority

The visitor who is now sitting by your desk, and who took the trouble to call ahead and choose the most convenient time for you to see her, has priority over everything else (short of a fire in the building or shooting heard in the halls). If you have no assistant to screen your calls, learn to be tough, whether it's Aunt Mathilda calling with family news, or a disgruntled customer calling to let you have it. Turn on the charm. Just say, "I'm terribly sorry, but I'm going to have to call you back. Something has occurred that needs my immediate attention. As soon as I can, I *will* call you back. My word!" There's urgency in your voice. The visitor should understand and gesture, asking if she should leave. You have not said the thing she would despise the most: "Won't you put it in an e-mail?"

• Your next responsibility is to remember you must call back the angry customer or whoever it was, immediately after the meeting. Write down his number and put it in large letters next to your phone extension. You may end up with five notes to yourself, in one afternoon, but no matter. It's better to do that than be rude to the visitor sitting by you.

• If you are the supplicant, the one sitting in someone else's office, trying to raise that company's annual Red Cross contribution, and that person begins to talk on an incoming call, whisper, "Should I step out?"

In most cases, the answer will be No, but don't just sit there staring at the person on the phone. It will make him extremely uncomfortable. Look elsewhere. If the call goes on and on, get a newspaper from a nearby desk to read. Look at the scenery. Write some memos to yourself.

• If you misdial on your office phone, do not just slam down the receiver in the other person's ear. Always apologize. It's not asking too much of you to say, "I'm sorry, I dialed the wrong number. Excuse me." Then hang up. The other person will have a better day because of your politeness, and maybe you don't care whether or not he has a better day, but this world would be a much better place if we all did care.

• If there's a disconnect, the responsibility to call back immediately rests on the shoulders of the person who made the call in the first place.

DEALING WITH A WELL-MANNERED
ANSWERING MACHINE

When answering machines first began to worm their way into our lives, I swore I would never use them. I found them infuriating, inhuman, tacky, and without redeeming features. Now, because really great answering service organizations using real people are fewer in number, I have a different machine attached to each line—at home and at the office. They may still be infuriating, but they're a lot better than a telephone that rings unattended in a void. An answering machine allows you to communicate with someone without endless redialings when you're in a jam, such as when trying to catch a plane, with five angry people in line behind you, all waiting to use your pay phone!

GOOD MANNERS FOR THE ANSWERING MACHINE OWNER
(OR VOICE MAIL USER)

• In your recorded outgoing message, do not inflict your latest flight of humor on the ears of those who call you. If someone is trying to reach you from a department store to arrange delivery on your new mattress, he should not be forced to go through a long recorded joke (which you thought screamingly funny, but which really is not) before being able to tell your answering machine what day your mattress will be delivered.

• Do not assault your caller's eardrum with a high-volume rendition of your favorite new, rather weird music before the beep sounds to take a message. A cool, refreshing silence is what most people want—between the answering machine owner's recorded voice and the beep signal.

• Keep your message brief and to the point. Feeling rotten one day with a fever and a cold, I called a friend on an urgent matter, only to have to listen to the friend's essay on problems between the Kurds and the Turks before I could finally leave a message. Even though I was impressed with her knowledge, my temperature rose several degrees while being held hostage to her spiel. (If you have hopes your answering machine will make you into a professional performer or lecturer, it won't.)

ADVICE TO THE PERSON LEAVING A MESSAGE

• Talk distinctly. Don't mumble. Speak slowly when you come to numbers, difficult names, or addresses. Repeat a telephone number you must supply, so there can be no mistake about it.

• Give your name, the date, and the hour of your message, which, hopefully, the machine's owner already asked you for on her outgoing message tape. If you're calling from out of town, say so.

• Come to the point of your message quickly.

• Say "good-bye" in an up voice. If you sign off without one word, the other person may think you were cut off.

• Say something friendly, too, before you sign off—such as "Hope all goes well with you, Johnnie. Good-bye."

A CAUTION ABOUT ANSWERING MACHINES

The first piece of advice: Be sure to place your answering machine up high, so no small child can reach it. Often we rely too heavily on these machines. They can be inoperable, for example, without our being aware of it. The outgoing message may have been erased, or the machine may have run out of tape, or someone may have accidentally deleted your entire message. Any number of little glitches may have occurred. Don't be angry at someone who "has never called back," because he may never have received the message in the first place. It's up to you to get in touch again with anyone who does not get back to you.

Nine times out of ten the person who listens to his or her voice mail messages doesn't want to hear them, so make yours sound efficient, upbeat, interesting, and cognizant of how busy the other person is. Make the person you're calling actually anxious to talk to you, so erase the boredom or negativism from your voice.

There's a great difference between a bright voice saying:

"Jen, I've got good news on finding the right location for us, so call me at such-and-such number as soon as you can," and a voice saying:

"Jen, I've spent three exhausting days on this project, but I think I may have what we need location-wise, at least I hope I have. There are lots of complications—negatives, I guess you'd say—but I want to go over five or six possibilities with you. It's really not a good time to be doing this with the market in its present condition, but I guess we should forge ahead regardless, and soon."

No one particularly wants to call back after listening to a message like that!

Cell Phone Etiquette

People handle their own phones as they wish, making guttural sounds, letting their voices die to an inaudible whisper, or laughing so hard and loudly into the mike that the other person's ears are injured. Cell phones pass between the worlds of answering dire emergency needs, but also comedy and business. In one corner of the airport are four people standing, all chatting away on their cells. One is a businessman, checking on the day's receipts, and while he's at it, since his plane doesn't leave for another forty-five minutes, he wants all the office news, every bit of it, and so it's given to him. One is a prostitute, checking in with her john about tomorrow's appointments. The cell phone has changed her life for the better. One is a student, who's playing hooky from school and begs his "best bud" to lie for him tomorrow at classes while he's watching the Cubs game in Chicago. One is an eleven-year-old, talking to another eleven-year-old about what makeup they'll each wear for the Halloween Romp at school.

The cell phone is a glorious invention, helping people stay in touch with one another, and relieving the minds of countless parents. So, love it for what it is, realize that it annoys more people than it helps, and resolve to yourself that you will always use it politely, not infuriatingly!

The telephone can be a wonderful human extension of you. It really is an out-of-this-world instrument. There's nothing wrong with the telephone—it's the people who abuse it who are wrong.

If you use a telephone with care and express your personality through its mouthpiece, the person on the other end of the line will *always welcome your calls*.

The telephone is an instrument to be respected, whether utilized for business, cementing relationships, or even as an antidote to loneliness. Respect for it means that you, the user, understand the rights of others in your house to use it, as well as the rights of those who are trying to call in to your house—not to mention the rights of the one person who is paying the monthly bills!

CHAPTER 22

Classic Correspondence: Writing Good Letters and Notes

A good letter not only relays feelings and emotions but leaves them on the record. A letter means that someone has put time and effort into crafting a personal message to you, which does not necessarily hold true with a communication faxed from one person's office to another's, or an e-mail, or with a message relayed on someone's voice mail.

WHEN AN E-MAIL ISN'T APPROPRIATE

Frequently an e-mail is inappropriate or just not as successful as a written communication, i.e., *the letter.* E-mails and instant messaging are a brief, crisp way of communicating. A letter has many more social "ruffles and flourishes" (think of the ceremonial heralding of the arrival of the president of the United States.) A letter requires more effort on the sender's part, and consequently packs more punch.

THE OLD-FASHIONED LETTER
(SEE ALSO BUSINESS LETTERS, PAGE 623)

A letter should be handwritten for a social or personal matter, sometimes even in a business situation, provided the writer's penmanship is neat and legible. If it is not, the letter should be typed and printed out on one's computer. Too many hours of our lives are wasted in trying to decipher our fellow citizens' handwriting!

When it is well written, a letter accomplishes goals that might not be accomplished otherwise. Since letter writing is gradually dying out as a means of human communication, today's younger generation will probably be unable to look back with fond remembrance on special letters received that marked the ritual passages of their lives. In the pre-electronic era, the following kinds of letters traditionally were sent to you during childhood, and also as you grew up and finally took your place in the adult world. You would receive a very special letter:

- From a relative upon your graduation from the eighth grade and high school.
- From a grandparent when you finished college.
- Perhaps from a close friend who could not be there for your wedding.
- Even from a boss who found something exceptional in your work and wanted to praise you.
- Or from your baby's godmother on the occasion of your child's birth.
- Or simply from someone close to you who just felt like "talking to you in a letter" at that particular moment.

A verbal compliment or expression of thanks is heard appreciatively but then disappears like a footprint in the wet sand, whereas a written sentiment may be savored again and again, and be put away to enjoy at future times.

A beautiful letter is a work of art that lasts.

These are the kinds of letters it is helpful to know how to write:

- Business letters (even if they are becoming extinct in the era of new technology).
- Thank-you letters (for nice gestures like gifts, favors, lunches, dinners, and weekends).
- Letters of complaint (about a product, service, or an individual).
- Notes—a short letter used to pass on a piece of information or to serve as a reminder.
- Catch-up letters—newsy epistles sent to family members or close friends.
- Letters of reference, written to:
  Introduce a person.
  Vouch for a person's character or fiscal responsibility.
  Help a person get a job.
  Help someone become a member of a private club or purchase an apartment in a co-op.
- Letters of congratulation for any good news concerning a relative, associate, or close friend.
- Letters to cheer up someone who is ill or feeling depressed.
- Letters of apology to someone you have offended.
- Letters of condolence to the family or a close friend of someone who has just passed away.
- Love letters (lucky you!).

Each kind of letter has a purpose and helps us get along with one another. This is why we should try to keep the art of letter writing alive and well.

HELPFUL HINTS ON LETTER WRITING

WRITING GOOD LETTERS

- Pick a time when you're relaxed and feeling up. Use a comfortable desk, chair, and a good light by which to write.
- Research the address of your recipient, including the person's proper title and postal address.
- Use an excellent pen with just the right point for you. Use black or a dark color ink.
- Use good stationery—good quality stock, and in an appropriate color:
  Pale gray, cream, or white for office stationery for women. Ditto for men's personal stationery
  Any pastel, blue, green, gray, cream, or white for women's personal stationery
- Either write or type a neat letter on a computer or typewriter.
- Think before you write. Make an outline of the points you wish to cover, and you will write cohesively—without forgetting any major point.
- Edit your letter. Read it carefully and make indiscernible corrections of spelling and punctuation mistakes.
- No letter is too brief. One of the best letters I ever received was simply "Dear Tish, that's it!" (meaning I had *finally* learned a lesson I needed to learn).

NEGATIVES TO WATCH OUT FOR

- Don't write letters when you're tired and disgruntled. Your physical state influences the way you write and the message you convey. (You'll be sorry tomorrow if you mail it tonight.)
- Don't use a leaking pen or one running out of ink. Don't use a kooky color; it makes your letter look eccentric.
- Don't dash off a note on a piece of legal paper or a sheet torn from a looseleaf notebook. The quality of your communication takes on the quality of the paper upon which it is written. It can leave behind an unpretty portrait of you.
- Never send a messy, crossed-out, ink-stained letter to anyone, even to someone who "won't mind."
- A rambling discourse—without a beginning, main part of text, or a con-

clusion—leaves the recipient feeling you did not care enough about him or her to do a good job.

- Never send out letters with misspellings and grammatical or punctuation errors.
- An overly lengthy, disorganized letter makes the reader feel lost, wandering about in confusion, searching for the reason behind the communication.
- Never send through the mails a letter that you have not signed, or that your secretary has not signed for you (with her initials after your name or with the words "signed in his absence by xyz."

LETTERS THAT FIT THE OCCASION

BUSINESS LETTERS

Always personalize your business letter, particularly if you know the recipient, even if you have met that person only once. The personal touch usually fits in most easily as a last paragraph before you sign off. Some basic examples include:

- To someone you have just met:

"It was nice to meet you at the sales meeting last week. I'm glad finally to be able to fit the face to the very pleasant telephone voice."

- To someone you know well:

"Best wishes to you, but particularly to Betsy and the boys. I hope they'll come with you the next time."

- To someone you know well, but whom you have been compelled to criticize or against whom you must take some negative action:

"This has been a difficult letter to write, because we have been friends for a long time" (or "because we have always had such a good business relationship" or whatever).

- To a good business customer, you might add a personal touch such as this in your closing:

"Your business means a lot to me personally, so I want to make sure that this transaction is carried out perfectly. I also hope that by now you have shaken off that nasty case of bronchitis and are feeling fit again."

- To a business associate who has had bad news in his or her life. If someone has had news such as a death, divorce, or scandal, you don't have to write a soliloquy on the subject, but it might seem odd to the recipient if you make no reference to it whatsoever. You might put a gentle reference to it in your last paragraph or in a P.S.:

"I know you've been having a tough time lately. I've been thinking about you—and pulling [or praying] for you."

Closing a letter with a trite phrase such as one of the following is better than nothing:

"Hope our paths cross soon again."

"Have a great summer."

"I hope life is treating you well."

"Here's wishing you lots of luck in your new venture."

"Hope things are looking up [or going well] for you."

"See you very soon, I hope."

THANK-YOU LETTERS

You should send a thank-you note—even a very short and informal one—every time you are:

- Given a present.
- Sent flowers.
- Asked to lunch or dinner.
- Invited for a weekend.
- Asked to a concert, the opera, the theater, even a movie.
- The recipient of a favor—such as when a person writes a letter of reference to help your child get into college, or refers a client to you, or finds you an apartment, or serves as a matchmaker for you, or does a lot of research to help you out.

A thank-you letter can be as short as three sentences:

Dear Charlie,

Lunch today was splendid—from the point of view of the restaurant, the food, the company, and the conversation!

Many thanks. It was important and pleasant catching up with you.

When some people receive a present, they write a trite, blah, nothing note, such as:

Dear Mathilda,

Thank you for your nice gift. It was very sweet of you, and I appreciate it.

After reading a note like that, Mathilda probably doesn't even remember what she gave you as a gift!

Others thankfully enthuse a lot and tell the donor how they are using the present:

Dear Mathilda,

You cannot imagine what pleasure your scarf has given me. The pinks and blues of the paisley print are lovely; they pick up my tired old winter dresses and make them look fresh again. I receive many compliments on the scarf every time I wear it, and I seem to be wearing it constantly.

If you had spent weeks trying to find the perfect gift for me, you could not have chosen a better one. (Perhaps you did spend weeks finding it!)

Bless you. I really am delighted with your choice.

• A thank-you note from a man to a woman. Sometimes men feel sheepish when women give them presents—such as when a woman gives a man a tie at Christmas (a common business gift, because it is not personal). Here is a sample thank-you from an executive to the woman account executive in his advertising agency:

Dear Jen,

Your inimitable taste has made my old pin-stripes take on a new lease in life. I feel as though I can once again go to lunch at Le Cirque feeling properly dressed.

My staff thinks I might even develop some taste in ties as a result of being exposed to your excellent choice. I certainly hope so—and I thank you for showing me the way!

Have a great holiday.

• A thank-you note for a dinner party. In this example, one spouse writes to one of the hosts but thanks both on behalf of both:

Dear Marian,

You and Harry gave a beautiful dinner last Thursday. We enjoyed meeting your guests, your table looked lovely (I will never forget those white gardenias floating in the centerpiece crystal bowl), and your dinner was superb. You may have noticed how George and I were not exactly reticent about helping ourselves to that incredible roast veal!

You two are wonderful hosts, and we thank you for including us in your delightful party.

• A thank-you note from the dinner host to a guest who sent flowers the day after the party:

Dear Susan and Bob,

Such beautiful roses! You shouldn't have sent them, but I'm glad you did. We put them on the coffee table, and that delicious coral color has brightened up the living room considerably.

It was a joy having you with us.

• A thank-you for a favor:

Dear Mort,

You really came through for your old friend. It was thanks to your very persuasive letter that our child was accepted for nursery school. I never thought it would be as hard to get a kid into nursery school as it is to get him into the Wharton Business School.

Anyway, your word was obviously the deciding factor. I promise we won't bother you again—at least for another twelve years, when Maria will probably need some help getting into college!

LETTERS OF COMPLAINT

The best way to go on record with a complaint in a situation in which you are justifiably angry and feeling out of control (and I, for one, always feel my complaint is justified) is to write three drafts of the letter but mail only the third one.

When I am emotionally upset, I tend to write an overheated, rambling, sarcastic letter that commands no respect whatsoever on the other end. Also, the recipient usually does not even understand the reason why I am so upset. By the third or fourth try, I have calmed down, can make sense, and am in control of my words once again.

When writing a letter of complaint, it's a good idea to:
• Write in a calm, controlled manner. (Your letter will be much more effective that way.)
• Leave sarcasm out of your writing (a major fault of mine, one that totally clouds the issue and confuses the recipient). Sarcasm, to be understood, requires a human voice, as well as words.
• Write an outline of all the points you wish to make—before writing the letter. Then subtract the weaker, less compelling points. Make certain your final letter addresses all the major points.

For example, if you write to the owner of a restaurant where you had a very bad scene with a waiter, you might write an emotional letter like this:

He could not have cared less about the shambles of my lunch party. I was humiliated in front of my guests. I just couldn't get over how rude and unfeeling he was, when I was so upset. And he knew it. And didn't care. It was just terrible . . .

Or you could write an in-control letter like this:

. . . I relayed to this waiter how important these particular guests were and he feigned complete indifference. He was responsible for the following:

1. Having to be summoned three times before he finally took the order, even after I had warned him twice of our time problem.

2. Making a mistake on the orders of three of my five guests.

3. Throwing up his hands and making faces, as though he were being persecuted, when one guest sent her undercooked meat back to be cooked some more.

4. Purposely laying down the dishes in front of each guest in an overly noisy manner.

5. Sighing with disdain whenever we addressed him.

6. Not bringing the check until fifteen minutes after it was called for.

I felt badly for the reputation of your fine restaurant, knowing how you pride yourself on your fine service. I knew it would be important to you to realize what happened this noon at your restaurant.

Sincerely,

LETTERS OF REFERENCE

If you are asked to give a letter of reference but feel unable to write it enthusiastically, it is far better to make an excuse not to write it. A lukewarm letter smacks of hypocrisy and can harm the person's cause. For example, any person on the membership committee can see through a letter like this one, addressed to a private club's chairman of the membership committee:

Dear Frank:

George Chilton asked me to write a letter on behalf of his application for membership in the club.

I told him I would—even though I have known him only for a short time and only in a business atmosphere. He is well known in his law firm. I have, however, never known him socially.

Sincerely,

There is no way that George Chilton will get past the membership committee with that kind of letter written about him.

A good letter of reference brims with enthusiasm and praise. However, before launching into the hyperbole, state up-front in the letter:

- The reason you're writing it.
- George Chilton's full name, address, telephone number, and e-mail.
- Any other statistics that are important to the recipient, such as:
  The individual's spouse's name and position.
  His university or college class and any clubs or honor societies
  Any children's names, ages, and schools.
  The individual's scholastic record.
  The person's career record.
  Special talents (skilled in foreign languages, or music, for example).
  Involvement in civic activities.
  Any published works.
  Important political activities.
  Any important awards or honors.
  Special skills in sports or hobbies.

A good letter of reference is informative, enthusiastic, and well organized. It should be easy for the recipient to read and find specific bits of information to which to refer when necessary.

If you send a letter of introduction on anyone's behalf, the following actions should take place:

- The recipient should acknowledge receipt of your letter.
- The recipient should contact the person about whom you have written.
- The person you are helping should write to inform you about the meeting with the person to whom you wrote—and should thank you very warmly for the trouble you went to on his or her behalf.
- You should write the recipient of your letter of introduction once again, to thank him or her for having taken action after receipt of your letter.

This is what should happen in the best of all worlds, but unfortunately, it does not always happen. Someone drops the ball, and manners fly out the window!

LETTERS OF CONGRATULATION

It's one thing to pass a friend on the street and say, "Hey, that's great about George's promotion!" or, "I hear your daughter and son-in-law had a son. What wonderful news!" or, "I read in today's sports page that you won the tennis tournament. Congratulations!"

It's quite another to sit down with pen and paper (or word processor) and write a warm letter of congratulations. Such a communication is read, reread, passed around to family members or at the office or at school, perhaps copied and sent to relatives and friends all over the world. It may end up in the subject's scrapbook and be handed down to posterity. The words in a telephone call or the ones spoken in the street are not permanent. The words in a letter are.

It does not have to be long. You may prefer to buy a greeting card and write a message on the back. What matters is that you write it and write it quickly after you hear the news. A letter of congratulations sent three months after an event occurs is like ice cream that has lost its flavor from being left in the freezer too long.

Your congratulatory letter might contain the following:
- How you heard the good news and how thrilled you were.
- The fact that you are spreading the word far and wide.
- A description of the delighted reactions of people you know in common when they, too, heard the news.
- A statement of how personally proud you are.
- Wishes for continued good luck in the future.

To communicate with someone at the time of great good news means so much to that individual. If you know only the spouse, child, or parent of the person to be congratulated, write that person, because anyone close to someone with good news feels part of it—and is part of it.

CATCH-UP LETTERS

These are important letters that communicate your news to a major figure in your life. It could be your grandmother, a friend who is ill, your sister who is a student in the Soviet Union longing for mail, or the person you are hoping to marry. This kind of letter is very important when you are away from home and is almost always answered with welcome news from the other end. It is much more memorable than the easy way of communicating (a telephone call), because the recipient knows you have taken time out to stop and think of her. If you're on a trip to Chicago, for example, you might:

- Tell the recipient of your letter what you're doing, how you're feeling.
- Write your impressions of the city you're visiting and the people you're meeting.
- Give the human side of the news—not just the fact that "we went by bus to the South Side of Chicago on an architectural tour."
- Talk about what you saw—the examples of the different schools of Chicago architecture, for example—and your reactions to walking through one of Frank Lloyd Wright's houses.
- Describe your feelings about the Chicago skyline on the shores of Lake Michigan.
- Don't just write, "And then we had lunch." Talk about what you ate, what the place looked like, how people looked the same or different from people at home.
- Talk about the tempo, the smells, the sounds of the city. All of a sudden, you will find yourself recalling far more than you realized you were collecting as impressions.

We so seldom write letters like this anymore, and yet they give so much pleasure. You will remember to write these letters if you leave a box of stationery on a piece of furniture that is always within range of your vision. When you have already stamped and addressed some envelopes inside the box, you will be drawn to it. *And you will write those letters to the people who will be made very happy to hear from you!*

LETTERS OF APOLOGY

When you have hurt someone's feelings, it is time to act. You may have a tart tongue, you may be very clever and witty in making critical remarks about others while they, unbeknownst to you, are standing listening to your group. Whether you make an unkind remark about someone's new beard and it gets back to him or you inadvertently (or on purpose) take a crack at someone's ideas in the conference room in front of your colleagues, you should apologize—verbally, right on the spot, and then in writing, with a personal note hand-delivered within twenty-four hours of the incident.

Apologies never totally make up for something one did, but at least they are better than nothing. When, for example, the person who has wronged you takes no action, your resentment can fester over time and eat away at you, ruining your productivity. Therefore, knowing how you yourself demand some kind of retribution for a wrong done you, remember to make retribution yourself when you are at fault.

It helps to send flowers (from a man or a woman, to a man or a woman) with your note of apology. There's something serene and soothing about flowers. Your note can be long and detailed, if you are trying to justify just how this unpleasant experience happened, or it can be as short as this:

Gerry,
    It shouldn't have happened, but it did. I am a first-class lout, and there is no excuse for what I said. I just hope that since I am such bad news, you will show your usual big heart and forgive me. There's a lot to forgive, I know, but I want you to know I am truly, truly sorry. If you forgive me, I shall be forever in your debt. Please put me in your debt!

CONDOLENCE LETTERS

If you are close to a family member of someone who dies, you should send a condolence letter by hand the minute you hear the news. (So much more effective than an e-mail!)

If you read or hear about the death of someone who is connected to you somehow—through a friend or an office colleague—mail a letter of condolence to the person you know the best. For example, if you know the son of a woman who dies better than you know her husband, write to the son and express your condolences to both him and his father.

If you hear about someone's death long after it occurred—such as reading about the death of a classmate in your college alumni magazine months later—it is not too late to write that person's spouse, parent, or child.

In fact, in the matter of a death, at no time is it "too late" to express your condolences.

A condolence letter should consist of:
- An opening statement of how terrible the news is, and how you know how much the family is suffering from the loss.
- Any special memories of the deceased person—particularly warm, sunny, and amusing recollections. Make them personal and fun to read. (Recall pranks played back in college days, things that happened at the office, jokes you played on each other on the golf course, or whatever.)
- Words of praise for the deceased and mention of how much the loss means to you personally. ("You cannot imagine how much I am going to miss that wonderful, funny, warm, kind wife of yours. She used to help me whenever I was low. She was always there for me, so I cannot bear to think of her not being around anymore. She was, as you know full well, a bright, blithe spirit, shedding warmth wherever she went.")
- A sincere offer to "be of assistance in any possible way that I can."

Even if you did not know the deceased, it is a nice gesture to write to the bereaved member of the family whom you do know. For example, a young executive would write his much more senior boss this kind of a letter when he learns of the death of the latter's wife:

Dear Mr. Hasker,

I wish to express my condolences to you at this very terrible time. Although I never had the pleasure of meeting Mrs. Hasker, I have heard you mention her with such fondness, and I have also heard from others in the office how close you were, and what a wonderful woman she was.

I am so sorry for you and your family, and hope you will receive the comfort and strength needed to bear this immense loss.

LOVE LETTERS

The main advice to give about love letters is:
- Send them.
- Don't put any promises in them that you can't keep.

Love letters are probably the most cherished letters of all. It's sad to contemplate that in our electronic age millions of people will never receive a love letter in their whole lives!

If you are single and in love with someone else who is single, send love letters whenever you can. A note as short as this can make someone's heart take off on a flight of exultation: "You can't possibly imagine how many times I think about you when I'm away from you. I am *utterly* infatuated."

You can recite love poetry in a love letter. You can write—as I saw one happy young woman read from a letter she received—a litany of the loved one's physical and mental qualities. You can just send a short message like this: "You know I'm no good at writing letters. I just *love you!*"

You can write as long or short a letter as you wish. Just write it, because it makes the recipient so happy. If you're married, a love letter to a spouse is like adding cement to the foundation of whatever you're building in your lives.

NOTES

Notes should be short and to the point, and if they can be amusing, so much the better. They should be efficient, because there is always a purpose to be served.

- You send a note, for example, to remind the recipient of something:

Dear Harry,

Just to remind you to bring the Chase file when we meet at the commuter terminal on Monday at 5 P.M. You told me to put a string around your finger. I can't do that, but try sticking this note in your buttonhole in the interim.

                                                                                    Until "Chase file time" Monday . . .

- You send a note simply to please someone, too:

Dear Abby,

I thought these old snapshots of you, Jack, and me taken in Frankfurt thirty years ago would bring back a few good memories. I don't think we look thirty years older today, do you? I think we look thirty years younger today!

- You send a note to pass on information. It's a gracious gesture that is really appreciated:

Dear Geoff:

Found the attached article in an in-flight magazine on my way to Chicago today. Since it mentions your firm, I knew you'd be interested.

or

Dear Ruth:

I remember your great interest in scrimshaw, so when I saw the enclosed booklet on the subject in a mall bookstore the other day, I thought of you.

- A note or a studio card with a handwritten note on it wishing the person well are communications that mean a great deal to someone who is ill, recovering in the hospital, or depressed and feeling blue. Sometimes a well-written letter can bring the recipient right out of a minor depression—make a person laugh and forget, at least temporarily, some vestige of pain or sorrow.

Of course, if a male friend is dying, you would not send a humorous card about his flirting with the pretty nurses. You would send him instead a letter or a card of a beautiful scene or perhaps of cartoon characters in an amusing situation.

If a female friend is having an operation in the hospital, you would not send her a tasteless card with a sex joke on it, but you would send her a happy, bright, funny card.

To anyone who is ill, written words of good cheer like these will help:

The office has simply ceased to function without you. I always knew you were important, but you don't have to be that important! You had better hurry up, get well, and get back to us—or the office will close down. That's how we all feel!

To someone who's alone and feeling depressed:

I'm waiting to hear when I can take you to a great movie I heard about, and we'll go to that nifty pasta restaurant afterward. You are very much missed around here. I know you're having a tough time, but life is full of great things ahead for all of us. So buck up, give me a call, and we'll make that movie date.

Where there is a monogram, printed or engraved, do not write on this top side. When there is no monogram, you would start writing your letter on the top side as page one.

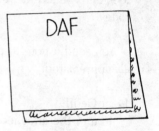

The foldover note, lying open, showing how a letter would be written on the inside. The top and bottom inside portions would be sides one and two if the notepaper had a printed monogram on its top side. If the notepaper had an engraved monogram on the top side, you would start writing on the bottom half of the inside as side one. (The top half would bear an indentation from the engraving on the front, so it would be difficult to write on it.)

The underside of the foldover note is the last page for writing.

GREETING CARDS AND HOLIDAY MESSAGES

Sending a greeting card is a thoughtful gesture that gladdens the heart of the recipient, whether its purpose is:

- To commemorate and reinforce a joyous occasion, such as a birth, First Communion, Bar or Bat Mitzvah, graduation, birthday, engagement, wedding, or anniversary.
- To mark a special holiday, such as Thanksgiving, Easter, Passover, Halloween, Valentine's Day.
- To show you are thinking of someone at a tough time, such as when the recipient is in the hospital.
- To send your condolences at the time of someone's death.
- To say "Thank you," whether for a gift, a dinner party, or whatever.

Know the difference between a tasteless card and an appropriate one. There are studio cards—attractive, witty, beautiful, sometimes roaringly funny—available in every card shop. However, remember that a card you stood and roared over in the shop—for example, one with unexpurgated sexual connotations—may go over like a lead balloon with the recipient. After all, you don't know who is going to see it—perhaps the young woman's mother, or your buddy's wife, or a child.

Send a card that represents you—that is tasteful, that you wouldn't mind anyone's attaching your name to if they picked it up. It does not have to be a syrupy, sentimental one (although there many older people who love those). There are clever, funny ones out there that are in complete good taste. Send *that* kind.

CHRISTMAS CARDS

The most important card season is Christmas and the New Year, and here is some advice:

- Send religious (Nativity scenes, Madonna and Child) or Christmas motif cards (Santa and his sleigh, Christmas trees, wreaths, holly, and bells) to Christian friends only.
- Send "Seasons Greetings," Hanukkah cards, or New Year's cards to Jewish friends at the appropriate season.
- For a Christian-Jewish couple, send a "Seasons Greetings" card.
- To Arabs, Muslims, and followers of the Buddhist religion, send "Seasons Greetings" or "Happy New Year" cards.
- To everyone, write a message by hand with black or dark blue ink, and sign your name. The message is the most important part of the card—it per-

sonalizes it and communicates your love and affection for the recipient in a way no printed message can.

- This is the kind of message you might write on holiday cards:

  "We hope you have a great holiday season," or

  "Lots of love to you and yours from all of us," or

  "Hope you have fun this holiday season!" or

  "Hope your holidays are wonderful—and that the New Year will be the best ever!"

If you have time to write a personal comment about some good news in that family, please do, because it means a lot. ("Isn't Christmas wonderful with a new baby in the family?")

- To a Christian you might write:

  "May you have a holy and happy Christmas—and we're delighted about the news of Andrea's upcoming confirmation!"or

  "May the Star of Bethlehem guide you through the New Year and keep you safe, and may you all come visit us again next summer at the lake!" or

  "A blessed, holy, joyous Christmas season to you all! We'll miss you this Christmas, but we'll be thinking about you."

- Update your list of holiday card recipients. It is wasteful, thoughtless, and even infuriating to send a holiday greeting card full of good cheer to a couple who are now divorced or when one of the couple is now dead. Cull and correct your list carefully. There must be some names you can even drop, and perhaps an equal number of new faces to add. Correct all addresses of people who have moved and the names of women who have changed their names and marital status. Make a fresh, accurate list each year, and you will be running a tight, no-waste operation.

- Always sign your Christmas cards, even if they are printed with your names. As part of the important personalization of Christmas and other holiday greeting cards, sign each card with a dark-colored ink, even if your name is right there in glorious print. Put a diagonal slash through your printed name (or names) and sign beneath it. You can use only your given name on a card to someone you know well—but not if your name is a very common one, like "Betty."

If you, a woman, know the couple to whom you are sending a particular card much better than your husband does, sign it "Barb and Joe Michaels." If you, the husband, know them better, sign it "Joe and Barb Michaels." It does not really matter which name comes first—husband's or wife's—but it makes sense to put the most recognizable name first for a couple who knows only one of you. (A woman in business should sign all her cards with just her own name, sending them to people who know nothing about her personal life; a man in business would do the same.)

- You may hand-address your envelopes or type them. Be sure to put your return address on the upper left-hand corner of the front of the envelope (not on the back flap), because the people in the post office are too busy to flip over envelopes to return improperly addressed ones to the sender. If your return address is on the front of the envelope, all a post office employee has to do is draw an arrow from the addressee's name to your return address, and you'll get the misaddressed card back.

Raised Embossed Cards with a Holiday Motif

Some people eschew greeting cards and purchase instead rather formal thick white or cream-colored stock cards, bordered in red or green, with an engraved text, and a raised embossed motif at the top center—for example, a wreath, a striped stocking, a bunch of holly, or a small decorated tree. These can be ordered from good local stationers. They are either engraved with a message such as "The So-and-so Family sends you warmest greetings of love and good cheer for the holiday season," or they are left blank and the person sending them writes a short note on each card by hand. They are expensive—and very attractive, the opposite of an over-decorated, garish holiday card.

Cards with Family Photos

Recipients usually enjoy the photographic cards sent to them by good friends who either have had a family photo printed on each card or slip a color snapshot into each greeting card. Please don't send an inferior snapshot, like the overexposed one we received last Christmas of what could have been a baby, but then again, could have been a puppy! (Please, no photo of the embryo in your womb!)

The photo may be of any part of the three generations of the family or of all three grouped together at a family reunion. The photo may also be of the sender's new house, dog or cat, horse, or boat.

I have also seen Christmas cards devoted to someone's new car, but perhaps that is going too far! I personally feel it is egocentric to send one's own portrait without children as a Christmas card—or a photograph of oneself traveling in some foreign land or enjoying a summer vacation—but many people do it, and it's popular.

Every year for almost thirty years the Kenyon Bolton family of Cleveland sent a large, wonderful Christmas photo card showing the immensely attractive family of seven all in a row, all dressed alike in a costume, often in a winter scene. There was a warm, handwritten message in red under the family photograph. That was the card that everyone put in the center of the mantel!

HOLIDAY NEWSLETTERS

Many people laboriously prepare a catch-up letter with all the family news in a typed one- or two-page single-spaced letter that has been reproduced in as many copies as there are holiday cards. I find these great fun to read and enjoy them thoroughly—except for those that go into detail on what little Susie's milk formula is and how Fido had worms last spring but is all better now. A friend who gushes a lot called me up recently and said, "Tish, I need help. I have written a four-page letter about the family activities this past year. It took me three weeks of work. What do you advise me to do about reproducing it? Should I have the type shrunk in size to save on paper and postage costs?"

"Give it to an English professor at your university, Carol," I advised her, "someone who doesn't know you. Pay him or her to edit it down mercilessly to one page—or even half a page. Then it will be wonderful!" (I'm waiting to see if she did that or if I have lost her as a friend.)

THE PERSONAL STATIONERY YOU USE

Your personal stationery says a lot about you. If a handsome-looking pale gray envelope arrives in your mail, holding a letter inside that is written on fine gray paper, with the name engraved across the top in royal blue, you cannot help but be curious and delighted to open it. If you receive a letter on lined scraps and sheets from a yellow legal pad, which are then stuffed into an anonymous envelope, that letter says to you, "I don't care much about you." Of course, there are times when you don't have anything else to write on and must get something into the mail quickly, in which case you can apologize in the letter for the "non-stationery on which this note is being written." I wrote one letter on the back of a menu once, and was criticized by my friend for just trying to show off. (It was a well-known restaurant!)

There are many kinds of letter paper and notepaper available for purchase—all sizes and shapes—but if you are looking for a must-have wardrobe of personal stationery, I would advise the following for a man or a woman:

• Quality engraved or plain correspondence cards and matching envelopes. (An alternative to the correspondence card is the foldover note—see below.)

• Quality engraved or plain half sheets (that fold in half) with matching envelopes.

• Lesser-quality letter-paper sheets and matching envelopes printed with the person's name, address, and telephone number for everyday use.

SINGLE STATIONERY HALF SHEETS

Men's and women's good-quality personal letter paper differs in size. The traditional man's size is about seven by ten inches. The traditional woman's size paper is around five by seven inches. However, there are many women today who choose the men's larger-size paper, because there is more room to write on.

Men traditionally used only white, cream, or gray personal stationery; now they are using pale blue, tan, and pale green as well, with black, dark gray, dark blue, maroon, dark brown, and dark green engraving or printing colors. Women use any color stock of their choice, including the palest of pastels, with darker lettering (for example, dark red on pink or dark brown on yellow).

You are supposed to use second plain sheets if your letter is longer than one page (don't use the back of your first sheet unless the stock is very heavy). The letter is folded in half—with the bottom edge of the paper brought up to the top edge and inserted into the envelope, as you face the back flap, with the fold on the bottom and the two edges held together at the top.

You may have your name, address, and telephone number put at the top of your stationery. The return address on the envelope should be on the upper left-hand portion of the front, if possible, *not* on the back flap, to make it easier to return misaddressed envelopes.

CORRESPONDENCE CARDS

These may be four by six inches or slightly smaller. They may be plain with an engraved (or embossed or printed) name or monogram in the top center or on the upper left corner of the card. Options include a colored border to match the lettering, as well as matching tissue-lined envelopes. The cards are usually

A foldover note is inserted into its envelope in this fashion.

made of a heavy stock, in a white, ecru, or gray color. (Women also use pastels in their cards.) You may write on both sides and may use the cards for writing notes, invitations, "reminder" cards, or gift-enclosure cards.

LETTER PAPER FOR EVERYDAY USE

This is a lesser-quality paper, printed with your name, address, and e-mail address (also telephone number, if you wish), to use for writing about things you have ordered, questions about your bills, requests for information, and the like. In other words, use this kind of less expensive stationery to communicate matters of your personal business life. It may be ordered from any stationer, department store, paper goods store, many office supply stores, or through countless mail-order catalogs.

VERY NICE TO HAVE

There are other items in a stationery wardrobe, one or two of which might be useful to you, to keep in stock in your desk at home.

Monogrammed (or Plain) Foldover Notes

These measure approximately three by five inches and are used as a substitute for correspondence cards (mainly by women). They are very handsome, whether plain or edged in color, with a monogram engraved or printed in the center, or with a monogram or address only in the center plus a narrow matching colored border.

When writing on a foldover note:
• Don't write on the top side of a monogrammed note (or on the underside, either, if it's engraved—because of the indentation made by the engraving on the paper). Start writing your letter on the bottom inside half of this kind of note, which would be page one. Page two would be the underside of page one, which you flip up and write on from the top of the edge of the paper, down to the bottom of the sheet.

• If, however, your foldover note is plain, the top side (side one), could be used for the beginning of your note; the underside of the top page would be side two, the bottom inside half would be side three, and the backside of page three would be page four. These notes are used for writing short letters or extending invitations. The written invitation would go on the inside bottom half of the foldover note.

Lined Envelopes

It's rather chic to use lined envelopes, usually in the same color as the engraved monogram. It's nice for the Christmas holidays to use stationery with envelopes lined in red or green for writing your thank-you notes. However, it is an added expense.

Informals

These small foldover notes with a person or a couple's name formally engraved in the front center are not used much anymore; they used to be one of the first things a woman ordered when she was married. ("Formally engraved" means that a woman would have "Mrs. Anthony Leigh Brownstone" as her engraved name—never "Barbara Brownstone," which would have been unthinkable before 1950.)

Postcards

Postcards are a convenient way of communicating. They're suitable for personal business matters and as "reminders" for a social event; some consider them too informal to use as invitations, but others find them efficient.

You can order yours (from a stationer or office supply store, for example) with your name and address printed at the top—and with a colored border to match the printing, if you wish. Remember to be careful of what you write on postcards, since many pairs of eyes read them. (I learned this the hard way when, in my youth, I got a friend in real trouble at her office. She was job hunting in secret, and I referred to this fact in a postcard sent to her office from abroad. The matter came to the attention of her boss, who was, to say the least, displeased, and it took me a year of apologies to make her forgive me.)

Visiting/Business Cards

Before the women's movement, "ladies" had their own small engraved calling or visiting cards, with their married name (or maiden name if they were single) engraved in the center. A lady would use this as a gift enclosure, as a reminder to someone to come to lunch or tea, or as a calling card to leave at someone's house if the person she came to see was not there. Today, women use only their business cards. If a woman is not in business, she should have her own cards made anyway—with her full name, address, and telephone number. These cards have a purpose: to leave with people so they know how to get in touch with her. She may use either her husband's name on her cards ("Mrs. John Templeton Gardner") or her own name ("Mary McAdoo Gardner") or, yet another option, a combination of her own name and her husband's, which is the most informative of all:

Mary McAdoo Gardner
(Mrs. John Templeton Gardner)

Monograms — Single and Married

When you are a single woman (or man), you would use the first letter of your given, middle, and family surname to create a monogram. Or a woman might make her surname initial oversized and use it in the middle, flanked by her given and middle names. (In that case, Virginia Hampton Biddle's monogram would be VBH or, used less often, vBh.)

When a woman marries, she drops her middle name and adds her husband's surname. Therefore, when Virginia marries Gil Thurston, her monogram changes to VBT (or vTb) for linens and silver. If she were to divorce and become known by her maiden name again, she would revert to VHB. If she were to become a widow and then marry a Mr. Smith, she would keep her first husband's surname to use as a middle initial, instead of her own middle name. In other words, the widow would become VTS in her monogram (unless she and Gil had gotten a divorce, in which case she would return to her family initial and not Gil's: VBS).

A man is lucky; he just keeps his same three initials throughout his life—until he marries and adds his wife's given name initials to make the couple's new monogram for certain wedding gifts. For example, as a "married" monogram on engraved silver, etched crystal, or embroidered linens, Virginia and Gil Thurston might use vTg as their joint monogram. Virginia may also use her maiden name only starting with her wedding gifts (some people joke that they know the reason for this!).

THE ELECTRONIC REVOLUTION

TECH MANNERS IN THE MIDST OF NEW SIGNALS, FLASHES, DASHES, SQUEAKS, VIBRATIONS, AND ABOVE ALL, UNIDENTIFIABLE NOISES

It *is* a revolution, with combat teams seemingly at constant war on cybernetic battlefields. The revolution is supposed to be just *all about communication,* but it calls for an added, expensive education of our young, and an adaptation to a new inventory of manners and conduct. Let's admit that our society is markedly changed from a decade ago—the way we think, talk, write, even react to any situation. Even the little ones, who some think should be living in the traditional world of *Winnie the Pooh* and *Alice in Wonderland,* are pressing buttons, watching screens, and skating a mouse around on an ice-rink pad with the ease of an Olympic skating star.

People of all ages are being criticized for their ringing cell phones, which destroy the concentration and peace of those around them. As one multiteched person complained, "I have so many gadgets with which I can communicate, I never know which mobile phone, Palm-top computer, handheld organizer, or instant messaging device to bring with me at any time. I can't remember which one needs a new battery, which one requires only a battery recharge, or which one works well enough with my computer system to allow for printing out anything, much less an entire document or letter!"

THE BEST PART OF THIS NEW SOCIETY

• The fact that we can now communicate with infinite speed anywhere, anytime, in any of several ways gives a natural, healthy impetus to the growth of businesses. From a human point of view, the impact of the e-mail revolution is particularly important for those whose loved ones live in another country.

• The conveyers of these rapid communication systems are numerous, and are becoming less costly with the passage of time and the volume of the business.

• The ease with which family members and friends can now communicate with one another, talking back and forth with instant messaging can help keep the family glued together. Everyone needs to belong somewhere, and even if there are disputes and angry confrontations, the disappearance of an individual's on-line "family" could prove to be one of the most depressing developments in her life.

• Your voice can now be heard in the halls of Congress. You can let your senator and representative, even the president, know your feelings. Find a nonpartisan site like "E the People" to send on-line petitions to people who count—members of the Electoral College.

Perhaps the only thing remiss in this rosy, glowing picture is that a good measure of humanity is lost in the process. The beauty of our language is disappearing in the cyberbabble of careless or nonexistent grammar, misspellings, shortcuts, and *gobble-gobble* (some people use "gobbledygook").

YES, E-MAILS HAVE THEIR OWN ETIQUETTE, TOO

Teach Your Staff How to Write a Grammatically Correct E-Mail (And Lots of Luck, Too, When Trying to Accomplish This!)

There is *always an addressee.* Put the person's real name in a salutation, not just somewhere in the text, and don't use just a bunch of numbers or a code name. If you reread an important message a year from now, you may want to know from whom it came!

E-MAILS: WING-FOOTED MESSENGERS OF SPEED

The intrinsic nature of an e-mail is brevity. For example, a marketing manager answered my request for his opinion on something with an instant reply: "Go for it!"

The Villain in the Process: Lengthy Attachments

A lengthy attachment destroys the reason for the e-mail. If you receive a two-sentence e-mail accompanied by a ten-page attachment, of which half a page is relevant to the subject, you have the right to complain. The author of the e-mail should excerpt sparingly the part of the ten-page attachment that really concerns you, and send it separately.

• Write a salutation. Put the person's name on it, not just a phrase full of letters and numbers. You don't have to put a "Dear" in front of the addressee's name. A colon after the name suffices:

Amelia:
Your absence from the annual meeting today was noted by everyone. It would have been much less boring if you had been there. Hope you're OK. /s/ Stephen

- Always sign your e-mails with your first and last name if you don't know the addressee well.
- Be up-front with the reason for your e-mail:

English source for our best-selling toy soldiers no longer available. Our holiday catalog about to go to press. Any suggestions for replacement source to avoid disaster? We're frankly desperate. Thanks!

- Show gratitude for any assistance offered by another company. "REALLY appreciate what you did. It was so important to the success of the project. We're all grateful to every single person in your group." (You might even follow up this e-mail with a gift of some kind, but first go on the record promptly with thanks.)
- Acknowledge receipt of the e-mails sent to you, with the exception, of course, of ads and promotions. Don't leave your e-mailer in a void. Just hit the Reply key on the e-mail and send a brief word: "Got it!" or "Received" or simply "OK." Further action may be necessary, but the solved problem is instant communication.

What to Avoid in E-Mail

1. An epidemic of junk mail (spam), an unforgivable time-waster, a scourge to every recipient.
2. A barrage of abbreviations and acronyms: BRB (Be Right Back); GG (Gotta Go); IMHO (In My Humble Opinion); TTYL (Talk To You Later). Some people refer to this as "monkey talk." It can be just too cute: (U r 2 nice 2 do it.) It's nauseating to many.

   Our beautiful English language becomes an undigested porridge of grunts, hiccoughs, and belches, instead of a handsome feast of well-constructed sentences, paragraphs, and a properly spelled, punctuated text. I heard a CEO addressing his staff on the subject of e-mail abbreviations one day. After saying several times that he disliked to see the use of one letter or a few letters as a shortcut for words, he announced that the only allowable abbreviation within the company in the future will be: "IYLYJSDT." Smiling, he gave as a translation for this acronym: "If You Like Your Job, Stop Doing This."
3. A plethora of jokes, sent to you and everyone else unsolicited on the sender's endless address list. By the time you have read the fifty-seventh corny joke, you are probably in as upbeat a mood as when you attend a funeral. You have also lost *a lot of time*.
4. E-mail spoofing, the digital equivalent of forgery. If someone sends a

person an e-mail with your name and address as the sender, irreparable harm can result. The recipient of a spoofed e-mail should immediately forward a copy to his Internet service provider. By looking at the header information on the e-mail, the identity of the culprit may be discovered, and legal action may be taken.

5. Writing in the subject line at the top of the e-mail, and then nothing more in the body of the message. If a person feels she does not have anything more to communicate than to fill out the subject line, then that missive deserves to be deep-sixed upon its receipt. It deserves no respect.

6. A profusion of emoticons, those irritating little punctuation marks and smiley faces, which some adults use even in business correspondence, and which render the text indecipherable, and the sender's image less than mature.

7. The use of colorful, handwritten signatures. When one sees a clash of orange and green ink used in an e-mail signature, one might wonder whether that person longs for a return to kindergarten or is just "having a bad day."

8. The time-wasting chain letters. It's bad enough that you've wasted company time reading the one you received. Don't send it on to others to waste their company's time, too. What you do on your home computer, of course, is your business.

9. The danger of misdirected e-mail. You are supposed to redirect any e-mail with its attachment that came to you by mistake. Unfortunately, these are the ones that through fate are often delicate and confidential, with information that is not supposed to be made public. Here is where your personal ethics come into play. When you redirect the entire correspondence to the sender, write reassuringly, "I hope you know that I will keep this matter in total confidence. You do not have to worry."

10. The people who are in offices next to one another who communicate solely by e-mails and never by getting up from their desks. (They should probably be brought to a gym at once, for therapeutic exercise, because they obviously need it.)

11. The people who always conclude their e-mail messages with something along the lines of "A Thought for the Day." Many join me in not wanting to know what that person's thought is for that day, or for any day, for that matter.

12. The person who keeps sending message after message and attachment after attachment for no important reason, thus overflowing the addressee's mailbox and keeping him from receiving messages of importance.

When a Letter or a Faxed Letter Is Better Than an E-Mail

- A condolence message for a death.
- A job resignation.
- A criticism of someone's job performance.
- A strong recommendation of someone for an important job.
- A *lukewarm* recommendation for someone for a job, an enrollment acceptance by an educational institution, or a membership in a private club. (In other words, what to do when you have to do something but don't want to.)
- An enthusiastic letter of thanks for any favor received, from a wonderful wedding present to a loan of money, career advice from the addressee, or help in the preparation of party food.
- A request of management for a raise or a promotion.
- An attempt to mend a personal or business relationship.
- The delivery of an uplifting, encouraging message to someone who is depressed.

BEEPERS AND PAGERS

Their upside—when they are noiseless, left in their vibrating mode:
- These devices have been a godsend for people who are busy and must reach others, but particularly for those engaged in emergency services, like doctors, firemen, policemen, ushers, guards, and security officers.
- They are a tremendous help for parents trying to reach their children or their caretakers, as well as anyone engaged in business transactions.

Their downside:
- Some people (particularly kids) use pagers to impress others.
- It is unpardonably rude when the device goes off:
  - In a meeting.
  - In a restaurant.
  - In a hospital visitor's pocket or tote bag.
  - In a funeral home.
  - At a movie, concert, theatrical performance, etc.
  - In a church, synagogue, or mosque, and at any religious ceremony.
  - In class—particularly during a lecture.
  - In the library.
  - At a game.
  - On any form of public transportation—train, bus, plane, etc.
  - In a place where people are meditating, studying, praying, and concentrating.

- At a meeting or at the dinner table, particularly obnoxious is the person seen checking his pager for sports scores.

The Speakerphone

Surely we cannot forget the speakerphone, one of the noisiest, most aggressive pioneers of the tech world. It has many plus factors, of course, when used properly in a conference call situation, to allow people outside the building, even outside the country, to listen in on an important meeting or briefing at headquarters. Many people have it attached to their regular telephone. Usually, the person on one end of the line can tell when she is on another person's speakerphone. There is an undeniable echo and a change of voice tone.

To many people, it is irritating, aggravating, and dishonest if the person being called is unaware that she has been put on the caller's speakerphone. This is a time when anyone in the world might be listening, while the person speaking is unaware of it. This is also when embarrassing things are said—intimate observations made by one good friend to another in a supposedly private moment that she would never want made public.

There should be a set of ethical rules that govern speakerphone use.

1. In a teleconference, *no one should interrupt the person speaking*, because the resulting jumble of voices will make all sounds unintelligible to everyone.
2. If the system of one sensitive mike in the center of the table is being used, someone sitting close to it should be put in charge of *turning it in the direction of any person speaking, so that everyone in on the call can hear her.*
3. The person on the speakerphone should address the mike head-on, and not turn her head from side to side to notice how others are reacting to her comments. When she does this, her voice fades away like a ghost's. It is extremely annoying to be sitting, straining to hear the speaker, who may be across the world or even one floor away.
4. Don't waste people's time during a conference call with an overdose of joking around. Anyone on this kind of business call, sitting in another place, is just waiting for it to end, not to hear about nonessential subjects in an atmosphere of hilarity to further distract the meeting focus. Most people on the phone want to say, but they're too polite to do so, "For heaven's sake, let's get on with it!"
5. Don't be a Tele-Pig, an unflattering name for people who try to dominate the entire conversation and won't let others contribute their opinions. Tele-pigs usually do not have much of substance to say. Of

course, it takes a good meeting manager to control the participation so that everyone has a chance to contribute.

6. Dress appropriately. You are not onstage. Don't try to rivet anyone with your wardrobe. Soft muted colors are best, or black with accent colors. Do not wear loud ties or flashy scarves. They stick out like a pimple on your nose.

CHAPTER 23

Addressing People Properly

People like—and have the right—to be addressed by their proper names and titles. It jars the psyche to be called by an improper name or to see one's name misspelled. If the person you are addressing has a very unusual name (as, for example, the Hogg sisters of Texas—Ima and Eura), check the spelling before writing. My brother, Bob Baldridge, who many years ago decided to spell his surname with a second "d" (because everyone has always misspelled our family name) does not like it now when the second "d" is left out, whereas the rest of the family bristles when the second "d" is included.

A major in the army does not like being addressed as "Captain"; a bishop does not like being referred to as a priest; a former ambassador does not like receiving mail without the "The Honorable" in front of her name; and a United States senator is justifiably miffed when he receives a piece of mail addressed to just plain "Mr." or "Mrs."

It is difficult to keep up with it all, but it's important to do so. Each of us has a responsibility to care about addressing other people properly.

HOW SHOULD YOU BE ADDRESSED?

Along with your right to be addressed, referred to, and introduced correctly, you also have a responsibility to let other people know how you should be addressed, referred to, and introduced correctly. If you have a difficult name or title, or there's been a change in your name or title, it's your job to educate those with whom you correspond on a regular basis. You should, for example:

• Always put a telephone number on your letterhead, so that someone's secretary, or the person herself, will know how to call you easily to find information that may be lacking in your letter.

• Always keep your biography updated if you are well known and distribute your biography before a personal appearance, or if you are included in one of the *Who's Who* publications. Lecture agencies, for example, often send out very out-of-date bios of their speakers, with the result that the speaker is inaccurately introduced, but it's no one's fault other than the speaker's.

650

- Always send out a *change of address* (or change of e-mail, telephone, fax, and telex numbers) card to everyone with whom you communicate.
- Always send out a card announcing a change of name to your friends and people with whom you do business.

WHEN YOU CHANGE YOUR NAME

- A newly married woman communicates the change of her name in:
  - Her wedding invitations.
  - Her new stationery.
  - A note to her clubs, associations, and school alumni magazines for their class notes.
  - Newly printed checks with her new name and address
  - Newly printed or engraved business cards.

She also obtains a new driver's license, passport, and credit cards with her new name.

- A bride who retains her maiden name after marriage communicates it on the "at home" card in the wedding invitation or announcement (when she puts her maiden name and her husband's together with a joint address), and also when her name stays the same on her stationery after the wedding.

When she is known by her maiden name, she must be careful on social occasions to introduce her husband by his name—something I have had to do always. It means speaking very slowly and deliberately, "This is my husband, Bob Holl-en-stein-er." (Woe unto the man or woman who thereafter calls my husband "Bob Baldrige," which is my brother's name.)

- A divorced woman would send a printed card to her friends, business associates, her lawyer, doctors, her children's school administration office, the alumni office of her former schools, all the stores where she has charge accounts, her clubs and associations, house of worship, and the like, announcing:

> Mrs. Barbara Tucker has resumed her maiden name, and is now known as Ms. Barbara Anderson.

The announcement should include her present address, telephone number, and her e-mail address. She would also apply for new credit cards, driver's license, and passport and order new checks printed once again with her maiden name.

WHEN WRITING LETTERS OR SPEAKING TO SOMEONE

- In letters always use a title with a name. To mail out letters that are addressed simply to "John Jones" or "Mary Williams" instead of to "Mr. John Jones" or "Ms. Mary Williams" is rude. Unfortunately, this bad habit is ingrained in the mail procedures of many companies today. It's a cop-out. It's lazy and sloppy and should be discouraged at all costs.

- If you are writing to someone you don't know and you do not even know the sex of the person—because the name could be either masculine or feminine—call the person's company or home to find out. "Excuse me, I'm calling to find out if it is a 'Mr. Cameron Clark' or a 'Ms. Cameron Clark' to whom this letter is being addressed." The recipient of your letter will be appreciative that you cared enough to do some research. (Most people don't bother—they just send the letter addressed to the wrong sex!)

When you have no way of determining the sex of a person with a name that could belong to a man or woman (for example: "Clair," "Morgan," or a family name such as "Caldwell" or "Berkeley" used for a person's given name), it is better not to guess the sex. In this case, send the letter without a title in front of the name.

If you are a person with such a name, always include a title in your return address or in your signature block when you write to someone who doesn't know you. In this way, the recipient of your letter will know how to address you. For example, Morgan Elliott would sign her letter in this way: "(Ms.) Morgan G. Elliott." If Morgan Elliott were writing a letter to someone who knows her husband but whom she hasn't met, she would end her letter with her husband's given name beneath hers, so that the recipient of the letter can readily identify her:

Sincerely,
Morgan Elliott (signature)

WRITING TO PEOPLE
WITH PROFESSIONAL TITLES

You do not use a "Mr." or "Ms." when you use a person's professional title after his or her surname. For example, it is correct to write:

Duane O'Donaghue, M.D. (not Dr. Duane O'Donaghue, M.D.)
Agnes Toda, R.N. (not Ms. Agnes Toda, R.N.)
Janet Oenslager, Ph.D. (not Dr. Janet Oenslager, Ph.D.)
Timothy Winthrop, Esq. (not Mr. Timothy Winthrop, Esq.)

When a person uses the initials of his professional organization after his surname, once again you do not use a title before his name. For example, if a man identifies himself as "George O'Hara, A.I.A." (which means he is a member of the American Institute of Architects), it is incorrect to write to him as "Mr. George O'Hara, A.I.A."

Using "Ms."

The use of "Ms." is no longer as controversial as it used to be. It's here to stay and is in common usage. Today "Miss" seems old-fashioned and slightly archaic, except when addressing girls up to the age of eighteen. "Miss" is still used in addressing adult single women on formal invitations, but it is no longer necessary even there.

I applaud the increased use of "Ms." for every written communication. Why should a woman's marital status be known by everyone because there's a "Miss" or a "Mrs." in front of her given name? ("Miss" means she's never been married; "Mrs." in front of her husband's name means she is or has been married; "Mrs." in front of her given name means she's divorced.) Men do not have this marital branding with their title of "Mr."

Using "Miss" in Speaking

Let's face it, for some people it's easier to pronounce "Miss Reynolds" than "Ms. Reynolds" when making an introduction, because "Ms." almost sounds like a bee buzzing around. "Ms." is easy to write but difficult to say, so if you find yourself saying "Miss" in conversation, you're like everyone else!

When a Man Is a Jr., Sr., 2nd, 3rd, or 4th

When father and son live in the same city and share the same name, the father uses "Sr." after his surname and the son uses "Jr." after his. When the father dies, the son usually drops the "Jr." within two years' time, since there is no longer a confusion between the two men—unless, of course, the man is the son of a very famous man (like the late Franklin D. Roosevelt, Jr., who, all during his life felt the need to use the "Jr." to distinguish him from his late father).

When a son is named "the 2nd," he is the nephew or grandson of a man of the same name. In other words, he is not named after his father. If he were, he would be "Junior."

When a boy is named "the 3rd," he is named after his great-grandfather or great-uncle of the same name.

A suffix may be given in an arabic numeral or a roman numeral form—that is, either "2nd" or "II" after the surname.

The numbers are supposed to make a distinction among living men of the same name. When Lawrence Baugh II dies, for example, Lawrence Baugh III would do well to drop the "III" and become "II" within a year or two. If there were a Lawrence Baugh IV, he would similarly move up to "III" after the death of Lawrence Baugh II.

USING "MESSRS."

"Messrs." (an abbreviation for the French word *messieurs*) is used as a title for two or more brothers. For example, if you were sending an invitation to George and Edward Wasserberger, two brothers who used to own and manage the Mark Cross leather stores, you would address the envelope to "The Messrs. Wasserberger."

ADDRESSING ENVELOPES FOR INVITATIONS
(SEE ALSO ADDRESSING AND MAILING THE INVITATIONS, PAGE 269)

To a married couple:

> Mr. and Mrs. Philip Geyelin
> Their address

To a married couple, if she has kept her own name:

> Mr. Philip Geyelin and Ms. Sherry Parker
> Their address

To a married couple whose combined two names are too long to put on one line:

> Mr. Richardson Henry Pratt III
>   and Ms. Antonia Dellarosa Quantobella
> Their address

(Indent three spaces for the second line and write "and" followed by the spouse's name.)

To a couple who are living together but are not married:

> Ms. Cynthia K. Talbott
> Mr. Richard Anderburg
> Their address

(Unmarried live-togethers receive one invitation. They are listed on separate lines in alphabetical order, and there is no "and" joining their names. The "and" linking two names is reserved for married couples.)

When both have military rank, the higher ranked person is listed first:

Major Gregory Swanson and Lieutenant Deborah Swanson
Address

When the woman is higher ranked than the man, her name comes first on the envelope:

Judge Diana Renshaw and Mr. Mark Renshaw
Address

When both are doctors:

The Doctors Branton, or
Dr. August C. Branton and Dr. Susan G. Branton

When inviting a young boy (nine or under):

Master William Berkeley

When inviting a young girl (up to the age of eighteen):

Miss Agatha Primton

WHEN YOU DON'T HAVE A CLUE ABOUT THE PERSON TO WHOM YOU ARE WRITING

When you don't have a name and must write a letter to a store, company, or institution, you may do it in any of several ways. My two preferred ways are as follows:

• Use "Ladies and Gentlemen" for a salutation, which makes the recipient of either sex feel good upon opening the letter.

• Use a memo form, much crisper and less friendly, such as this letter of complaint to the Armshaw Plumbing Company:

Writer's address
Writer's telephone number
August 5, 2006

to: Armshaw Plumbing Company
     Company's address
re: Improperly executed repairs of furnace at 311 South Fairmont

The statement of complaint would follow, without a salutation, and would be signed by the writer without a complimentary closing above his name.

THE SOUTHERN USE OF "SIR" OR "MA'AM"

Down South, well-mannered children are trained to say "sir" and "ma'am" repeatedly as a mark of respect to almost anyone older than themselves. When they are out of college and working in another part of the country, they should try to drop the usage of the "sir" and "ma'am," which, although very polite, seem slightly reminiscent of an attitude of servitude to many people who are not from the South. The non-Southerner feels embarrassed. Instead of using "Yes, sir" and "No, ma'am" all the time, a polite young person from the South could substitute the older person's name: "Good morning, Mr. Peters"; "Thank you, Ms. Reynolds"; "Good night, Dr. Jenkins."

CALLING PEOPLE BY THEIR FIRST OR LAST NAMES

We are a very informal country, but many people feel that the informality has gone too far in many respects, resulting in inefficiency, a lack of respect for senior authority, and a total misunderstanding of proper deference. I'm with the protesters, so forgive me if I sound a little starchy about this.

• When you are in your twenties and you meet someone in his or her forties or older, call that person by a last name until told not to.

• When you know a person only slightly, write a letter using the person's surname in the salutation, instead of the given name. If you feel the person is much older and more important than you, sign your own full name; to use your given name only would be too informal.

• If you had a really lengthy chat during your first meeting with this person, but you still feel a bit uneasy about using only the person's first name in the letter salutation, use both names (i.e., Dear Mary Thurston, or Dear Henry Pelham). Or, if you feel you both got on very well the one time you met, you might write as a salutation: "Dear Mary (if I may):" This holds true for personal or business letters.

• When you first meet someone and you write or call him or her, don't use that person's unusual nickname when it is used only by his or her good friends. If you meet a man named Wilson Nollon, for example, and you hear a couple of people who are obviously his good friends call him "Roly," address him or write him as "Wilson." My blood chills when young people I don't know well at all call me by my very familiar name "Tish" instead of "Letitia," and I think most people over the age of forty feel that way. (Of course, what I like best of all is to be called "Ms. Baldrige" until I know the other younger person a little better.)

If you are called by a nickname most of the time, something like "Slim" or "Red," for example, be sure to have your real name included on your stationery letterhead and on your business cards. You may always put your nickname in parentheses after your given name, but it is very uncomfortable for a person who has never even met you to have to address an envelope to "Mr. Shorty McLean" or "Ms. Peaches Cornwall."

HOW TO ADDRESS SPECIFIC GROUPS

The tables that follow, showing how to properly address people in official life, cover many forms of address that you are likely to encounter. Because of limited room on the page in these tables, names and titles are run in columns and hyphenated to fit into the space. For example, please remember that:

• You write a husband's and wife's names on one line on an invitation, unless they are too long. In the latter case, you would write their names on two lines, indenting the spouse's name three spaces:

> The Honorable Scott Kilduff McLean
>   and Mrs. McLean

• If you are writing a letter to a foreign ambassador, you would write:

> His Excellency
> Joseph Hardwick (or, if he is *titled,* Sir Joseph Hardwick)
> Ambassador of Great Britain
> (Embassy address)
> Dear Ambassador Hardwick (or Dear Sir Joseph):

UNITED STATES OFFICIALS

Any executive who deals with government officials should have a copy of the latest United States official ranking in her office, in order to know how to address them properly and how to seat them at a meal. Each president of the United States makes a few changes to suit him in the precedence of the officials he addresses or sees. The table that follows, the precedence of April 2003 in the George W. Bush administration, will obviously undergo small changes in the years to come.

The Official Ranking for United States Officials

The President of the United States
The Vice President of the United States
Governor of a state (when in own state)
The Speaker of the House of Representatives
The Chief Justice of the Supreme Court of the United States
Former Presidents of the United States
American ambassadors when at post
The Secretary of State
The President of the United Nations General Assembly (when in session)
Secretary General of the United Nations
President of the UN General Assembly (when not in session)
President of the International Court of Justice
Ambassadors of foreign powers (accredited and when in the U.S.)
Ministers and envoys extraordinary of foreign powers accredited to the
    U.S. (in order of presentation of their credentials)
Widows of former Presidents of the United States
Associate Justices of the Supreme Court of the United States
Retired Chief Justices of the Supreme Court
Retired Associate Justices of the Supreme Court
Cabinet Members:
    The Secretary of the Treasury
    The Secretary of Defense
    The Attorney General
    The Secretary of the Interior
    The Secretary of Agriculture
    The Secretary of Commerce
    The Secretary of Labor
    The Secretary of Health and Human Services
    The Secretary of Housing and Urban Development
    The Secretary of Transportation
    The Secretary of Energy
    The Secretary of Education
    The Secretary of Veterans Affairs
    Administrator of the Environmental Protection Agency
    Chief of Staff to the President
    Director of the Office of Management and Budget
    The United States Trade Representative
    Director of the National Drug Control Policy
    Director of the Homeland Security Council
    President, Pro Tempore of the Senate

The Senate (ranked by length of continuous service, or if the same, they are listed alphabetically by state)

Governors of states (when outside their states, and when together, they are ranked by earliest date of admission of their states to the Union)

Acting heads of executive departments

Former Vice Presidents of the U.S. or their widows

Members of the House of Representatives (by length of continuous service, and if the same, by date of admission of their state to the Union, or alphabetically by state)

Delegates from the District of Columbia, Guam, Virgin Islands, and American Samoa to the House of Representatives

Residential Commissioner from Puerto Rico to the House of Representatives

Governor of Puerto Rico

Counselor to the President

Senior Advisor to the President

Assistant to the President for National Security Affairs

Assistant to the President and Deputy Chief of Staff for Policy

Assistant to the President and Deputy Chief of Staff for Operations

Deputy Secretary of Treasury

Deputy Secretary of Defense

Deputy Secretary of Attorney General

Deputy Secretary of Interior

Deputy Secretary of Agriculture

Deputy Secretary of Commerce

Deputy Secretary of Labor

Deputy Secretary of Health and Human Services

Deputy Secretary of Housing and Urban Development

Deputy Secretary of Transportation

Deputy Secretary of Energy

Deputy Secretary of Education

Deputy Secretary of Veterans' affairs

Administrator of National Drug Control Policy

Permanent Representative of the U.S. to the United Nations

Administrator of the Small Business Administration

Director of Central Intelligence Agency

Director of Emergency Management Agency

Solicitor General

Administrator of the Agency for International Development

Director of the Arms Control and Disarmament Agency

Assistants to the:
    Chairman of the Council of Economic Advisers

Chairman of the Council on Environmental Quality
Director of the Office of Science and Technology Policy
Chargé d'Affaires of Foreign Powers
Chargé d'Affaires at Interim of Foreign Powers
Former Secretaries of State
Former Cabinet Members
Director of the United States Information Agency
Undersecretaries of State and Counselor of the Department of State
Undersecretaries of Executive Departments when third in rank
Ambassadors at Large
Secretary of the Army
Secretary of the Navy
Secretary of the Air Force
Postmaster General
Chairman, Board of Governors of the Federal Reserve
Chairman, Council on Environmental Quality
Chairman, Export-Import Bank
Chairman of the Joint Chiefs of Staff

Addressing Government Officials: A Sampling

Personage	Introduction and Addressing Envelopes	Letter Salutation	Speaking to	Place Card
The President	The President The White House Address (Abroad he is introduced as "The President of the United States of America.")	Dear Mr. President:	Mr. President	The President
The First Lady	Mrs. Madison (She is the only official woman always addressed out of respect as "Mrs. Madison," without a given name.) A social invitation would be addressed to: The President and Mrs. Madison	Dear Mrs. Madison:	Mrs. Madison	Mrs. Madison

Personage	Introduction and Addressing Envelopes	Letter Salutation	Speaking to	Place Card
The Vice President	The Vice President The White House Address A social invitation would be addressed to: The Vice President and Mrs. Adams	Dear Mr. Vice President:	Mr. Vice President	The Vice President
Vice President's Wife	Mrs. John Adams Address	Dear Mrs. Adams:	Mrs. Adams	Mrs. Adams
Speaker of the House	The Honorable Michael Duncan Speaker of the House or, socially: The Speaker of the House and Mrs. Duncan	Dear Mr. Speaker:	Mr. Speaker	The Speaker of the House
Chief Justice	The Chief Justice The Supreme Court Address or, socially: The Chief Justice and Mrs. Warner	Dear Mr. Chief Justice:	Mr. Chief Justice	The Chief Justice
Associate Justice	Justice Zissu The Supreme Court or, socially: Justice Zissu and Mrs. Zissu	Dear Justice: or Dear Justice Zissu:	Justice or Justice Zissu	Justice Zissu
Cabinet Member	The Honorable Desmond Palmer Secretary of Labor Address or, socially: The Secretary of Labor and Mrs. Palmer	Dear Mr. Secretary:	Mr. Secretary or Secretary Palmer	The Secretary of Labor

Personage	Introduction and Addressing Envelopes	Letter Salutation	Speaking to	Place Card
Under Secretary of Labor	The Honorable Otto Norgren Under Secretary of Labor or, socially: The Undersecretary of Labor and Mrs. Norgren	Dear Mr. Under Secretary:	Mr. Under Secretary (subsequently Sir)	The Under Secretary of Labor
Attorney General	The Honorable Edward R. Warden Attorney General of the United States or, socially: The Attorney General and Mrs. Warden	Dear Mr. Attorney General:	Mr. Attorney General (subsequently Sir)	The Attorney General
Director of Central Intelligence	The Honorable Agnes L. Schmidt Director of Central Intelligence Address or, socially: The Director of Central Intelligence and Mr. Helmut Schmidt	Dear Director:	Madam Director	The Director of Central Intelligence
U.S. Senator	The Honorable Frederick H. Lee United States Senate Address or, socially: Senator and Mrs. Frederick H. Lee	Dear Senator Lee:	Senator or Senator Lee	Senator Lee
U.S. Representative	The Honorable Sarah Thune House of Representatives Address or, socially: The Honorable Sarah Thume and Mr. Christopher Thune	Dear Ms. Thune:	Ms. Thune Sarah	The Honorable Thune or Ms. Thune

Personage	Introduction and Addressing Envelopes	Letter Salutation	Speaking to	Place Card
American Ambassador Abroad	The Honorable David R. Luce American Embassy Address or, socially: The Honorable David R. Luce and Mrs. Luce	Dear Ambassador Luce: or Dear Mr. Ambassador:	Ambassador Luce	Ambassador Luce
Governor	The Honorable Francis L. Fine Governor of Florida Address or, socially: Governor and Mrs. Francis L. Fine	Dear Governor: or Dear Governor Fine:	Governor or Governor Fine	The Governor of Florida
State Senator	The Honorable Jorge Morales or, socially: State Senator Jorge Morales and Mrs. Morales	Dear Senator Morales:	Senator Morales	The Honorable Jorge Morales
Mayor	The Honorable Stanley Breck, Jr. Mayor of Providence or, socially: Mayor and Mrs. Stanley Breck, Jr.	Dear Mr. Mayor: or Dear Mayor Breck:	Mayor Breck	The Mayor of Providence
Judge	The Honorable Robert Quinlan Judge, Appellate Division Supreme Court of the State of New York or, socially: Judge and Mrs. Robert Quinlan	Dear Judge Quinlan:	Judge Quinlan	Judge Quinlan

- When a president is no longer in office, he retains the title as a courtesy, but there are variations in the way in which he is addressed. Instead of writing him simply as "The President, The White House," you would address him as "President Reagan" and use his office address.

Instead of writing simply to "Mrs. Reagan, The White House," as when President Reagan was in office, after the end of the administration, you would write to "Mrs. Ronald Reagan," care of her office address in California.

The salutation in a letter to the president in office is simply "Dear Mr. President." Once he has left the office, the salutation is "Dear President Reagan."

These are small nuances, but they matter in the scheme of things.

• It's important to note that a U.S. senator's and a U.S. representative's place cards are not done identically. For the senator use "Senator Lawson," but if the person is a representative, his card should read "Mr. Lawson" or, preferably, "The Honorable William Lawson."

• A person of rank should either have his place card written according to his position (e.g., "The Secretary of Labor" or "The Ambassador of Great Britain") or the place card should contain his title and surname ("Judge Atkins"; "Major Jones"; "Dr. Clark"). See the tables given in this chapter for the correct forms of address.

• If you are in doubt as to someone's title, or as to whether or not you should put "The Honorable" or the guest's position on the card, use "The Honorable." With the exception of medical doctors, judges, and the military, you can always flatter a person who holds or has held an official job by putting on the place card "The Honorable David Atwater" or "The Honorable Susan Walters." It's a safety valve—like calling a woman from another country "Madam" when you can't remember her name.

Addressing Officials by Their Titles in Conversation

It is customary to address a very important official by title and not by name. For example:

"Mr. President" (or "Madam President") when speaking to him (or her).
"Mr. Secretary" or "Madam Secretary," for a cabinet position.
"Mr. Under Secretary" or "Madam Under Secretary."
"Mr. Ambassador" or "Madam Ambassador."
"Mr. Mayor" or "Madam Mayor."

Note that we say "Governor" when talking to a governor, not "Mr. Governor." We say "Mr. Ambassador," not "Mr. Special Representative to the United Nations." The only definitive statement we can make concerning American protocol is that there is no rule without an exception!

ADDRESSING WOMEN

Addressing the Spouses of Officially Ranked People

	Introduction and Addressing Envelopes	Letter Salutation	Speaking to	Place Card
When an official's wife uses her husband's name	The Secretary of Commerce and Mrs. Roe	Dear Mrs. Roe:	Mrs. Roe	Mrs. Roe
When an official's wife goes by her own name	The Secretary of Commerce Mr. Ralph Baldwin and Ms. Marian Smith	Dear Ms. Smith:	Ms. Smith	Ms. Smith
Spouse of high-ranking woman	Senator Ann Green and Mr. David Green	Dear Mr. Green:	Mr. Green	Mr. Green
When both husband and wife have rank	The Honorable David Green and The Honorable Ann Green	Dear Senator Green:	Senator Green	Senator Green
	Commander Jerome Tate and Lieutenant Tate	Dear Lieutenant Tate:	Lieutenant Tate	Lieutenant Tate

The wife of an official goes by her husband's name in official life—i.e., Mrs. Theodore Wells (rather than Mrs. Elise Wells) in the United States; Signora Antonio Carici in Italy; Madame Henri Blanche in France, Belgium, and the French part of Switzerland (as well as French-speaking African countries); Frau Hans Kauffmann in Germany, Austria, and the German part of Switzerland; Señora Miguel Flores in Spain and Spanish-speaking Latin America.

In the United States, women who work under their own names are addressed by their own names, but rarely does that continue for the American woman who accompanies her official husband abroad. She should not try to use her own name when she is with her husband on a trip involved with his work, not hers. It creates protocol problems for the officials of a host country that does not have many women in top positions.

Of course, if it is the woman official who is the senior ranked person and her husband is accompanying *her* on her mission, she would use her own title and name, not his.

Use "Madame" When Addressing a Woman from a Foreign Country

We call women in this country "Mrs.," "Miss," or "Ms.," followed by a surname. When we meet a woman from another country, we often have trouble catching a complicated name, and we don't know whether to call her "Miss" or "Mrs." The solution is to call her simply "Madame." French is the language of diplomacy throughout the world, and "Madame" is almost as much of a catchall as "Ms." in the American idiom.

Use "Madame" for a woman who is out of her teens or if you know for a fact that she is married. It makes life very simple. You don't have to say "Madame Abdourahmane" when you're talking with her. Just "Madame" will do.

"THE HONORABLE"—A TITLE OF RESPECT IN AMERICA

"The Honorable" in front of a person's name is a title held for life by a person who holds or has held high office at the federal, state, or city levels. However, there is a nuance that must be remembered: A person who is addressed by others as "The Honorable" should not put the title on her own business cards, a personal letterhead, or on the invitations she extends. If, for example, an ex-official is now a partner in a law firm, on the firm's stationery his name would be listed with the other partners with "The Honorable" before it, but if it is his stationery alone, his name should not bear that honorific. In other words, it is a distinction bestowed by someone else on a person, not by the person on himself.

The following are among those who carry "The Honorable" title through their lives:
   The president and the vice president
   Cabinet members, deputy secretaries, under secretaries, and assistant
      secretaries
   Presidential assistants
   American career and appointed ambassadors
   American representatives (including alternates and deputies) to inter-
      national organizations

The Chief Justice of the Supreme Court, associate justices, judges of
   other courts
All members of Congress
The secretary of the Senate; the clerk of the House
The sergeants at arms of the Senate and House
Librarian of Congress
Comptroller General (General Accounting Office)
Heads, assistant heads, and commissioners of U.S. government agen-
   cies
Governor and lieutenant governor of a state
Secretary of State, Chief Justice, and attorney general of a state
State treasurer, comptroller, or auditor
State senator, representative, assemblyman, or delegate
Mayor
Members of the city council, commissioners, etc.

In addressing an invitation to a married woman who is *in office* and whose
husband has no rank, her name precedes his:

> The Honorable Julia Rosen and Mr. Geoffrey Rosen
> Address

When she is no longer in office, she still retains "The Honorable," but her
name returns to its place after her husband's:

> Mr. Geoffrey Rosen and The Honorable Julia Rosen
> Address

THE BRITISH:
OUR FRIENDS WITH MANY TITLES

Since we do much business with Great Britain, it is important for those having a great deal of contact with the country to understand its layers of leadership: the Crown, the government, and the peers of the realm.

Protocol for the Royal Family is carefully prescribed, and even though philo-
sophically we Americans do not adhere to the principles of a monarchy, we
should respect our British friends' admiration for it. It is impossible to please
the British in their own country and to please British businesspeople visiting
here if we are totally unknowledgeable about their country's history or the
Crown.

Some pretty silly, petty storms have raged in past years over such questions
as whether or not an American ambassador's wife should make a formal curtsy

in greeting the Queen. When greeting Her Majesty in the United States, an American woman would make a slight bow while shaking the Queen's hand. On British soil, most American women I know do what every other woman in the place does in meeting the Queen, make a slight curtsy to Her Majesty. When American ambassadresses (the wives of ambassadors) have curtsied in the past, the American press has become apoplectic, shouting "We are not a monarchy!" Some Americans have made such a fuss over this question that it has been now decreed that no American official woman should curtsy to the Queen. That doesn't mean that the rest of us, us American commoners, can't sneak a curtsy to Her Majesty on the sly in Great Britain or over here!

We don't have a peerage in this country, but Americans should understand their formal way of proceeding and adhere to the protocol as much as possible. Many peers drop their titles when they're over here, which disappoints far more Americans than delights them. Members of the British Commonwealth outside of England are not as formal as the English; certainly the Canadians are informal by comparison.

The following tables on English officials and the titled peerage represent what is proper for the American businessperson to do when speaking to, introducing, or writing to them:

The Royal Family

* One does not write directly to a member of the Royal Family; write to "The Private Secretary to . . ."

> Her Majesty the Queen
> His Royal Highness, Prince Philip, The Duke of Edinburgh
> His Royal Highness, The Prince Charles, Prince of Wales
> Her Royal Highness, The Princess Anne (married to Commodore
>   Timothy Lawrence of the Royal Navy)
> His Royal Highness, The Prince William
> His Royal Highness, The Prince Harry
> His Royal Highness, The Duke of York
> Her Royal Highness, The Duchess of York
> His Royal Highness, The Prince Edward (married to Sophie Reese
>   Jones, The Countess of Wessex)

* If you are fortunate enough to be invited to tea by Her Majesty the Queen, your invitation will come from her *Master of the Household,* and it might read as follows:

> The Master of the Household
> is Commanded by Her Majesty to invite
> [your name written on this line]

to an Afternoon Party at Buckingham Palace
on Tuesday, February 4th from four to six o'clock

The British Government

Official	Introduction and Addressing Envelopes	Letter Salutation	Speaking to	Place Card
The Prime Minister	The Rt. Hon. Mary Smith, M.P. The Prime Minister (M.P. means Member of Parliament) or, socially: The Prime Minister and Mr. Ivan Smith	Dear Prime Minister:	Madam Prime Minister	The Prime Minister
The Home Secretary (Equivalent of our Secretary of State)	The Rt. Hon. Ronald Coates, P.C., M.P. Home Secretary or, socially: The Rt. Hon. Roland and Mrs. Coates	Dear Mr. Coates: or, if titled: Dear Sir Ronald: or Dear Lord Coates:	Mr. Coates or, if he is titled, it might be: Sir Ronald or Lord Coates	The Home Secretary
(Other cabinet posts would be addressed in a similar manner.)				
A British Ambassador to the United States	His Excellency David Leeds Ambassador of Great Britain or, if he is titled, it might be: His Excellency Sir David Leeds et cetera	Dear Ambassador Leeds: or, if titled: Dear Sir David:	Mr. Ambassador or Sir David	The Ambassador of Great Britain

Note: The British would close a letter to one of their officials with "Yours sincerely," which an American may use in a letter to a British official; "Sincerely yours" is also proper.

Many British officials and peers have initials after their surnames, standing for orders, honors, and knighthoods. You should always write to such a person in the same manner he writes his name to you—with or without the initials.

For example, a titled knight might be addressed as: Sir George Creighton, G.C.M.G.

The Peerage

Peer	Introduction and Addressing Envelopes	Letter Salutation	Speaking to	Place Card
A nonroyal duke	The Duke of Oakford or The Duke and Duchess of Oakford	Dear Duke: Dear Duchess:	Duke Duchess	The Duke of Oakford The Duchess of Oakford
(The English often address a duke and duchess as "Your Grace" and speak of them as "His Grace the Duke of . . ." but Americans are not expected to follow this procedure.)				
Duke's eldest son and daughter-in-law	Marquess of Chester or, socially: The Marquess and Marchioness of Chester	Dear Lord Chester: Dear Lady Chester:	Lord Chester Lady Chester	Lord Chester Lady Chester
Marquess's eldest son; Earl's wife, a countess	Earl of Meads or, socially: Earl and Countess of Meads	Dear Lord Meads: Dear Lady Meads:	Lord Meads Lady Meads	Lord Meads Lady Meads
Viscount, eldest son of an earl	Viscount Brentwood or, socially: Viscount and Viscountess Brentwood	Dear Viscount Brentwood: Dear Lady Brentwood:	Lord Brentwood Lady Brentwood	Viscount Brentwood Viscountess Brentwood
Baron Baroness	The Lord Lyndhurst or, socially: Lord and Lady Lyndhurst	Dear Lord Lyndhurst: Dear Lady Lyndhurst:	Lord Lyndhurst Lady Lyndhurst	Lord Lyndhurst Lady Lyndhurst
Baronet	Sir Albert Northrop, Bt. or, socially: Sir Albert and Lady Northrop	Dear Sir Albert: Dear Lady Northrop:	Sir Albert Northrop Lady Northrop	Sir Albert Northrop Lady Northrop

Canadian Officials

Official	Introduction and Addressing Envelopes	Letter Salutation	Speaking to	Place Card
Governor General	His Excellency Eric C. Johnson or, socially: Their Excellencies Governor General and Mrs. Johnson	Dear Governor General:	Governor General	The Governor General of Canada
Lieutenant Governor of Canada	His Honour The Honourable Gerald L. Dowd Lieutenant Governor or, socially: Lieutenant Governor and Mrs. Dowd	Dear Lieutenant Governor:	Lieutenant Governor Dowd	The Lieutenant Governor of Canada
Prime Minister of Canada	The Right Honourable Andrew C. Fitch, P.C., M.P. Prime Minister of Canada or, socially: The Prime Minister and Mrs. Fitch	Dear Mr. Prime Minister:	Prime Minister Fitch	The Prime Minister of Canada
Premier of a province of Canada	The Honourable Carolyn Cadré Premier of the Province of Quebec or, socially: The Honourable Carolyn Cadré and Mr. Jacques Cadré	Dear Madame Premier:	Premier Cadré	The Premier of Quebec
Member of Senate	The Honourable Laura Flynn The Senate, Ottawa or, socially: The Honourable Laura Flynn and Mr. Lesley Flynn	Dear Senator Flynn:	Senator	The Honourable Laura Flynn

Official	Introduction and Addressing Envelopes	Letter Salutation	Speaking to	Place Card
Member of House of Commons	Samuel Morris, Esq., M.P. House of Commons or, socially: Mr. and Mrs. Samuel Morris	Dear Mr. Morris:	Mr. Morris	Samuel Morris, Esq., M.P.
Mayor of a city or town	His Worship Mayor Kenneth Woods City Hall or, socially: His Worship Mayor Kenneth Woods and Mrs. Woods	Dear Mr. Mayor:	Mr. Mayor	The Mayor of Toronto
Chief Justice	The Right Honourable Roger C. Bolton, Chief Justice of Canada or, socially: The Right Honourable Roger C. Bolton and Mrs. Bolton	Dear Mr. Chief Justice:	Chief Justice Bolton	The Chief Justice of Canada

Note: Since people in Great Britain and the Commonwealth spell "Honourable" with the "u," it is proper to use their own spelling.

DIPLOMATIC PROTOCOL WITH OTHER NATIONS

Writing to Officials of Foreign Republics

When you write to officials of a foreign republic, follow the style given in this table of the country of France:

Official	Introduction and Addressing Envelopes	Letter Salutation	Speaking to	Place Card
President of the Republic	His Excellency Henri Vaudoyer President of the Republic of France Address	Dear Mr. President:	Mr. President	The President of the Republic of France

Official	Introduction and Addressing Envelopes	Letter Salutation	Speaking to	Place Card
	or, socially: The President of France and Madame Vaudoyer			
Prime Minister of the Republic of France	His Excellency Jean de l'Abeille Prime Minister of the Republic of France or, socially: The Prime Minister of France and Madame de l'Abeille	Dear Mr. Prime Minister:	Mr. Prime Minister	The Prime Minister of the Republic of France
Minister of Foreign Affairs of the Republic of France	Her Excellency Jeanne d'Arcy Minister of Foreign Affairs or, socially: The Minister of Foreign Affairs and Monsieur Pierre d'Arcy	Dear Madame Minister:	Madame Minister	The Minister of Foreign Affairs of the Republic of France

"His Excellency" or "Her Excellency" for Foreign Officials

Americans use "The Honorable" as a title in front of a person's given name and surname to note the importance of the person's present or former position. For the heads of state, ambassadors, cabinet officers, etc., of other countries (as well as for high-ranking members of the clergy), it is proper to use "His Excellency" (or "Her Excellency") before the given name and surname. For example, an envelope is addressed:

> His Excellency
> Giovanni Nanni
> Ambassador of the Republic of Italy

We would introduce the dignitary to an assemblage in the same manner. In most cases, we address the envelope in the way we formally introduce the person. (*Note,* however, that the British Commonwealth nations do not use "His Excellency" but rather "The Right Honourable.")

What is confusing is that what we properly call a foreign official in the United States may not be the way he is properly addressed in his own country. For example, we address a foreign ambassador to this country as "His Excellency" on the envelope and letter address as well as in an introduction, but we call him "Mr. Ambassador" to his face. In many foreign countries, he is called "Your Excellency" to his face. The nuances are subtle but important. It is important to learn how to address foreign officials in this country. If you have business abroad, you should also learn the protocol in whatever country or countries you are doing business.

WESTERN EUROPEAN TITLES

The king or queen of any foreign country is addressed as "Your Majesty" and referred to as "His Majesty" or "Her Majesty" respectively.

The prince consort to the queen is referred to as "His Royal Highness" and is addressed as "Your Royal Highness."

When royal titles still exist in a country that is not a monarchy, even though these titles are meaningless, they are still treated with respect by the people in that country. Western Europe has a long history and a love of tradition, and therefore people who have inherited defunct but legitimate titles may have the royal crest engraved on their stationery, on their silver flatware, etc.

In order of rank, the titles are these:

• Prince and princess. (You call them by their title and surname, not their given names, when introducing them; in conversation call them "Prince" and "Princess.")

• Duke and duchess. (You call them by their title and surname, not their given name, when introducing them; in conversation, call them "Duke" or "Duchess.")

• Marquess and marchioness (*marquis* and *marquise* in France, *marchese* and *marchesa* in Italy, *marques* and *marquesa* in Spain)

• Viscount and viscountess

• Count and countess

• Baron and baroness

You would write an invitation to them in this manner: "Count and Countess Philippe de Beaumont." If one of the couple is titled and the other is not, use the title for the one who holds it: "Signor Emmanuele Capriccio and Contessa Eleanora Capriccio."

Many Western Europeans do not use their titles when doing business in the United States, but when you write to them in their country and when you are visiting in their country, you should use their titles.

THE UNITED NATIONS

Unlike the diplomatic corps accredited to Washington, D.C., the United Nations diplomats change in rank and precedence on a rotating basis (which means that length of service in the job or importance of the country has little to do with who outranks whom).

Official	Introduction and Addressing Envelopes	Letter Salutation	Speaking to	Place Card
The Secretary General	Her Excellency Françoise d'Estain Secretary General of the United Nations	Dear Madame Secretary General:	Madame Secretary General (Madame d'Estain, subsequently)	The Secretary General of the United Nations
A foreign UN ambassador	His Excellency Koto Matsumada Ambassador of Japan Permanent Mission of Japan to the United Nations	Dear Mr. Ambassador:	Mr. Ambassador (Sir, subsequently)	Ambassador Matsumada
The United States Representative to the United Nations	The Honorable Henry Gregory United States Representative to the United Nations	Dear Mr. Ambassador:	Mr. Ambassador (Sir, subsequently)	Ambassador Gregory

Invitations to UN ambassadors and their spouses are addressed to their residences as follows:

His Excellency Koto Matsumada and Madame Matsumada

or

Her Excellency Françoise d'Estain and Monsieur Eric d'Estain

MILITARY RANK

- The Army, Air Force, and Marine Corps have the following commissioned officers according to rank:
  General
  Lieutenant General
  Major General
  Brigadier General
  Colonel
  Lieutenant Colonel
  Major
  Captain
  First Lieutenant
  Second Lieutenant

- The Navy and Coast Guard have the following:
  Admiral
  Vice Admiral
  Rear Admiral
  Captain
  Commander
  Lieutenant Commander
  Lieutenant
  Lieutenant, junior grade
  Ensign

Note: All officers in the Navy and Coast Guard are addressed as "Mr." up through the rank of lieutenant commander. A woman officer is addressed "Ms." or "Miss," never "Mrs."

A captain in the Navy or Coast Guard has a higher rank than a captain in the Army, Air Force, or Marine Corps.

A warrant officer's rank lies between that of a commissioned and a noncommissioned officer.

How to Address a Military Man or Woman

Examples of Military Rank	Introduction and Addressing Envelopes	Letter Salutation	Speaking to	Place Card
First lieutenant	First Lieutenant Richard Dix, USMC or, socially: First Lieutenant and Mrs. Richard Dix	Dear Lieutenant Dix:	Lieutenant Dix, or Lieutenant	Lieutenant Dix
Captain in the Navy	Captain Joseph Piteo, USN or, socially: Captain and Mrs. Joseph Piteo	Dear Captain Piteo:	Captain Piteo, or Captain	Captain Piteo
Lieutenant colonel	Lieutenant Colonel Frank Haig, USMC or, socially: Lieutenant Colonel and Mrs. Frank Haig	Dear Colonel Haig:	Colonel Haig, or Colonel	Colonel Haig
Chief warrant officer	Chief Warrant Officer Jane Turner or, socially: Chief Warrant Officer Jane Turner and Mr. Anthony Turner	Dear Chief Warrant Officer Turner: or, informally: Dear Ms. Turner:	Chief Warrant Officer Turner or, informally: Ms. Turner	Ms. Turner
Noncommissioned officers in Army, Air Force, and Marine Corps	Master Sergeant Tony Tatum or, socially: Master Sergeant and Mrs. Tony Tatum	Dear Sergeant Tatum:	Sergeant Tatum	Mr. Tatum

(Follow same form for any rating, including Sergeant Major, Sergeant First Class, Platoon Sergeant, Corporal, Specialist [classes 4 to 9], Private First Class, etc.)

Examples of Military Rank	*Introduction and Addressing Envelopes*	*Letter Salutation*	*Speaking to*	*Place Card*
Enlisted person in Navy	SN Robert Peltz Address of his command or, socially: Seaman and Mrs. Robert Peltz	Dear Seaman Peltz:	Seaman Peltz	Seaman Peltz
Retired officer in Army or Air Force	Major Robert Orr, USAF Retired Address or, socially: Major and Mrs. Robert Orr	Dear Major Orr:	Major Orr	Major Orr

Retired officer in Navy or Coast Guard°	Rear Admiral Spencer
	Davis, USN
	Retired
	  Address
	or, socially:
	Rear Admiral
	    and Mrs. Spencer
	    Davis
		Dear Admiral Davis:	Admiral Davis	Admiral Davis

Cadet at West Point (same for Air Force Academy, with address change)	Cadet Mark Boland, U.S. Army Company—, Corps of Cadets United States Military Academy West Point, NY 10996	Dear Mr. Boland: or, Dear Cadet Boland:	Mr. Boland	Mr. Boland
Midshipman at U.S. Naval Academy; Cadet at U.S. Coast Guard Academy	Midshipman Joan Doan U.S. Naval Academy or Cadet Stephen Cole United States Coast Guard Academy	Dear Ms. [or Miss] Doan: Dear Mr. Cole:	Ms. or Miss Doan Mr. Cole	Ms. Doan

°Only Navy and Coast Guard officers with rank of commander and above retain their titles after retirement; officers in the Reserve do not.

RELIGIOUS OFFICIALS

In closing a letter to a very high religious official, use "Respectfully yours," or use "Sincerely" or "Sincerely yours."

Protestant Clergy

Official	Introduction and Addressing Envelopes	Letter Salutation	Speaking to/ Place Card
Clergyman with Doctor's degree	The Reverend Dr. Amos E. Long or, socially: The Reverend Dr. Amos E. Long and Mrs. Long	Dear Dr. Long:	Dr. Long
Clergywoman without Doctor's degree	The Reverend Anne Smith or, socially: The Reverend Anne Smith and Mr. Peter Smith	Dear Ms. or Miss Smith:	Ms. or Miss Smith
Presiding Bishop of the Episcopal Church in the United States	The Right Reverend James Gard, Presiding Bishop or, socially: The Right Reverend James Gard and Mrs. Gard	Dear Bishop Gard:	Bishop Gard
Bishop of the Episcopal Church	The Right Reverend David Webb Bishop of Washington or, socially: The Right Reverend David Webb and Mrs. Webb	Dear Bishop Webb:	Bishop Webb
Methodist Bishop	The Reverend Michael Forest Methodist Bishop or, socially: The Reverend Michael Forest and Mrs. Forest	Dear Bishop Forest:	Bishop Forest

Official	Introduction and Addressing Envelopes	Letter Salutation	Speaking to/ Place Card
Dean	The Very Reverend Angus Dunn or, The Very Reverend Angus Dunn, Dean of St. John's or, socially: The Very Reverend Angus Dunn and Mrs. Dunn	Dear Dean Dunn:	Dean Dunn
Archdeacon	The Venerable Stewart G. Dodd Archdeacon of Boston or, socially: The Venerable Stewart G. Dodd and Mrs. Dodd	Dear Archdeacon Dodd:	Archdeacon Dodd
Canon	The Reverend Randolph Tate Canon of St. Andrew's or, socially: The Reverend Randolph Tate and Mrs. Tate	Dear Canon Tate:	Canon Tate

• The highest officials of the Episcopal Church, the Archbishops of Canterbury and York, are Privy Counsellors and have seats in the House of Lords. You would address the envelope to "The Most Reverend and Right Honourable Archbishop of Canterbury [or York]." The salutation would read: "Dear Archbishop."

• Clergy with degrees optionally use their degree initials after their names: "The Right Reverend James Gard" or "The Right Reverend James Gard, D.D., LL.D."

• An Episcopal cleric who is not in a religious order may call himself "Father." In writing him, use his surname, rather than his Christian name—for example, "The Reverend Father Smith."

• A Protestant minister who retires remains "The Reverend So-and-so." If he or she resigns, that person normally becomes "Mr." or "Ms."

Mormon Clergy

Official	Introduction and Addressing Envelopes	Letter Salutation	Speaking to/ Place Card
Mormon Bishop	Mr. Timothy Blake Church of Jesus Christ of Latter-day Saints or, socially: Mr. and Mrs. Timothy Blake	Dear Mr. Blake:	Mr. Blake

Roman Catholic Hierarchy

Official	Introduction and Addressing Envelopes	Letter Salutation	Speaking to/ Place Card
The Pope	His Holiness, the Pope or His Holiness, Pope Augustus III	Your Holiness:	Speaking to: Your Holiness
The Apostolic Delegate in Washington (the Pope's representative)	His Excellency The Most Reverend Bishop of Washington, D.C. The Apostolic Delegate Address	Your Excellency:	Your Excellency/ His Excellency the Apostolic Delegate
Cardinal	His Eminence, Joseph Cardinal Sheehan Archbishop of St. Louis	Your Eminence: or, Dear Cardinal Sheehan:	Your Eminence/ Cardinal Sheehan
Bishop and Archbishop	The Most Reverend Paul Murphy, Bishop [Archbishop] of Chicago	Your Excellency: or, Dear Bishop Murphy:	Excellency/ Bishop Murphy
Monsignor	The Right Reverend Julius Cuneo	Dear Monsignor Cuneo:	Monsignor Cuneo
Priest	The Reverend Father James Orr Church rectory address	Dear Father Orr:	Father Orr

Official	Introduction and Addressing Envelopes	Letter Salutation	Speaking to/ Place Card
Brother	Brother David Maxwell	Dear Brother David: or, Dear Brother Maxwell:	Brother David or Brother Maxwell
Nun	Joan Reynolds, R.S.C.J. or, Sister Mary Annunciata	Dear Sister:	Sister Reynolds or Sister Mary Annunciata

Eastern Orthodox Communion

Official	Introduction and Addressing Envelopes	Salutation	Speaking to
Patriarch	His Holiness, the Ecumenical Patriarch of Constantinople	Your Holiness:	Your Holiness
Bishop and priest	Same as Roman Catholic Church		
Archimandrite	The Very Reverend Gregory Costos	Reverend Sir:	Father Costos

Jewish Faith

Official	Introduction and Addressing Envelopes	Letter Salutation	Speaking to	Place Card
Rabbi	Rabbi Melvin Schwartz Address or, socially: Rabbi and Mrs. Melvin Schwartz	Dear Rabbi Schwartz:	Rabbi or Rabbi Schwartz	Rabbi Schwartz

Official	Introduction and Addressing Envelopes	Letter Salutation	Speaking to	Place Card
Cantor	Cantor Samuel Stein Address or, socially: Cantor and Mrs. Samuel Stein	Dear Cantor Stein:	Cantor Stein	Cantor Stein

Military Chaplains

Introduction and Addressing Envelopes	Letter Salutation	Speaking to	Place Card
Major John Martin, Chaplain Address	Dear Major Martin: or, Dear Chaplain: or, for a Catholic, chaplain: Dear Father Martin: or, for a Jewish chaplain, Dear Rabbi Martin:	Chaplain or Major Martin	Major Martin or, for Catholic, Father Martin or, for Jewish, Rabbi Martin

FOREIGN PROFESSIONALS

We should accord foreign professionals their titles when addressing them. For example, in Italy, if you have finished university and earned your degree, you are called "Dottore" (for a man) or "Dottoressa" (for a woman) as the title before your surname for the rest of your life. In writing a letter, one may abbreviate the title to "Dott." in front of either his or her surname—"Dott. Cavalchini." We Americans should use this title if we have any correspondence on personal or business matters with an Italian who merits this honorific.

In many countries a man or woman who has earned a professional degree is thereafter addressed by the title of that profession (and not necessarily by his or her name) for the rest of that person's life. For example, in France, in speaking to a person, you would address a lawyer formally as "Monsieur l'Avocat" (Mr. Lawyer) or a woman ambassador as "Madame l'Ambassadeur." In Italy you would say "Signor Avvocato," and you would call your architect "Signor

Architetto." In Germany, instead of calling the CEO of the company "Herr Schmidt," you'd call him "Herr Direktor"; an engineer would be addressed as "Herr Ingenieur," and so on. (It makes life very easy for people who can't remember names; all they have to remember is a professional title!)

Once an American becomes involved at length with a foreigner in a country where a professional title is important—whether it's a business or a social matter—the polite thing to do is to use his or her title in addressing that person. Learn the foreign pronunciation, learn how to write the title in the foreign tongue. Your foreign colleague will be pleased and respect you more because you are showing respect for him.

FOR QUESTIONS RELATING TO PROTOCOL

When you're in a protocol quandary, here's where to go for help. (Be sure you have first checked the tables contained in this book.)
- For further information on titles and precedence of U.S. Government officials, and for listings and addresses of the Washington diplomatic corps:
  - Call The Department of State, Office of Protocol, Ceremonial Section (202-647-1735).
  - Consult *The Social List of Washington, D.C., and Social Precedence in Washington* (published by Thomas J. Murray, 10335 Kensington Parkway, Kensington, MD 20895 [301-949-7544]).
- For information on British government officials and the peerage, consult *Debrett's Peerage and Baronetages* (published by Debrett's Peerage, 73–77 Britannia Road, London S.W. 6 2JR, England).
- For information on the United Nations precedence, call the United Nations Office of Protocol in New York (212-963-1234).
- For information on protocol questions in your state government, call the Governor's Office in the State Capital; for city government, call the Mayor's Office. For questions of military rank, call the nearest military establishment.

Note: The captain of a commercial airliner is always addressed by his name and title, such as "Captain John Doe." Although he or she is not in the military armed forces, this person has an enormous responsibility for many lives, and should be given the honor of the title "captain" at all times.

So should a person of rank in the police and fire departments. A commissioner is always referred to with his title—the highest rank in those departments.

AFTERWORD

If you have spent time carefully reading most of this book, you have earned not only my undying gratitude but also a good handle on human behavior—even inhuman behavior! You've also been showered with my own personal philosophy. It's there, on every page. Perhaps I should be paying *you* for having read this book!

No matter how dark the horizon may seem at any given time, such as during a war or an economic downturn, remember that life is a gift—to be enjoyed, not constantly complained about. We've been labeled a species of crybabies by modern-day philosophers. If life is a precious gift, we have a duty to take care of it. This is where manners enter the scene. There's joy in being decent to one another and receiving thanks in return. There's also efficiency, law, and order woven into this behavior. It's quite a package!

It's a great feeling to know we're doing the *right thing,* whether we've learned it or whether it's instinctive, from the heart. In knowing the rules, we have the license to become intelligent mavericks and rebel against them *in a tasteful way, of course.* ("No, Mom, I don't have to write Aunt Tizzy a thank-you note. I thanked her on the telephone, again in person, and that's enough for her thoughtfulness in giving me a small cordial glass for a graduation gift!")

Let's lead our children—and anyone else's—through this early part of the twenty-first century, rejoicing in the technological innovations of our time, but being much more sensitive to those around us. Isn't a warm, sensitive human being far more important than a shiny new gadget that enchants the tech world? To some, maybe not. To most of society, the answer is a great big overwhelming YES.

INDEX

Page numbers in *italics* refer to illustrations.